Genocide and Rescue in Wołyń

ALSO BY TADEUSZ PIOTROWSKI
AND FROM MCFARLAND

*The Polish Deportees of World War II:
Recollections of Removal to the Soviet Union and
Dispersal Throughout the World* (2004; paperback 2008)

*The Indian Heritage of New Hampshire and
Northern New England* (2002; paperback 2008)

*Poland's Holocaust: Ethnic Strife, Collaboration with
Occupying Forces and Genocide in the Second Republic,
1918–1947* (1998; paperback 2006)

*Vengeance of the Swallows: Memoir of a Polish Family's Ordeal Under
Soviet Aggression, Ukrainian Ethnic Cleansing and Nazi
Enslavement, and Their Emigration to America* (1995)

Genocide and Rescue in Wołyń

*Recollections of the Ukrainian Nationalist
Ethnic Cleansing Campaign Against
the Poles During World War II*

Edited by
TADEUSZ PIOTROWSKI

McFarland & Company, Inc., Publishers
Jefferson, North Carolina, and London

The present work is a reprint of the illustrated case bound edition of Genocide and Rescue in Wołyń: Recollections of the Ukrainian Nationalist Ethnic Cleansing Campaign Against the Poles During World War II, *first published in 2000 by McFarland.*

LIBRARY OF CONGRESS CATALOGUING-IN-PUBLICATION DATA

Piotrowski, Tadeusz, 1940–
Genocide and rescue in Wołyń : recollections of the Ukrainian Nationalist ethnic cleansing campaign against the Poles during World War II edited by Tadeusz Piotrowski
p. cm.
Includes bibliographical references and index.

ISBN 978-0-7864-4245-4
softcover : 50# alkaline paper ∞

1. World War, 1939–1945 — Atrocities. 2. World War, 1939–1945 — Ukraine — Volhynia. 3. Poles — Ukraine — Volhynia — History — 20th century. 4. Volhynia (Ukraine) — History, Military. I. Title.

D804.U35W67 2008   940.54'05'094779 — dc21   99-88668

British Library cataloguing data are available

©2000 Thaddeus M. Piotrowski. All rights reserved

No part of this book may be reproduced or transmitted in any form or by any means, electronic or mechanical, including photocopying or recording, or by any information storage and retrieval system, without permission in writing from the publisher.

Front cover: A Polish village set on fire by the Banderowcy (photograph courtesy of Antoni Szcześniak).

Manufactured in the United States of America

*McFarland & Company, Inc., Publishers
Box 611, Jefferson, North Carolina 28640
www.mcfarlandpub.com*

With heartfelt sorrow
to Wołyń's Polish victims

With heartfelt gratitude
to Wołyń's Ukrainian heroes

Contents

List of Tables and Maps	ix
Preface	1
Introduction	7
1 — Dubno County	29
2 — Horochów County	33
3 — Kostopol County	46
4 — Kowel County	56
5 — Krzemieniec County	73
6 — Luboml County	81
7 — Łuck County	92
8 — Równe County	107
9 — Sarny County	116
10 — Włodzimierz County	120
11 — Zdołbunów County	145
Appendix A: Ukrainian Victims by County	148
Appendix B: Three Stories From Eastern Galicia	167
Appendix C: Excerpts from Documents	175
Appendix D: Chronology	222
Appendix E: Mutual Declaration of the Presidents of the Republic of Poland and Ukraine Regarding Understanding and Reconciliation	255
Notes	257
Bibliography	282
Index	295

List of Tables and Maps

Tables
All tables except Table 3 are drawn from official 1931 census figures.

1. Population of Wołyń by Mother Tongue 7
2. Population of Wołyń by Religious Affiliation 7
3. Population of Wołyń According to Jerzy Tomaszewski's Adjusted 1931 Census 7
4. Population of Dubno County by Mother Tongue 29
5. Population of Dubno County by Religious Affiliation 29
6. Population of Horochów County by Mother Tongue 33
7. Population of Horochów County by Religious Affiliation 33
8. Population of Kostopol County by Mother Tongue 46
9. Population of Kostopol County by Religious Affiliation 46
10. Population of Kowel County by Mother Tongue 56
11. Population of Kowel County by Religious Affiliation 73
12. Population of Krzemieniec County by Mother Tongue 73
13. Population of Krzemieniec County by Religious Affiliation 81
14. Population of Luboml County by Mother Tongue 81
15. Population of Luboml County by Religious Affiliation 92
16. Population of Łuck County by Mother Tongue 92
17. Population of Łuck County by Religious Affiliation 107
18. Population of Równe County by Mother Tongue 107
19. Population of Równe County by Religious Affiliation 116
20. Population of Sarny County by Mother Tongue 116
21. Population of Sarny County by Religious Affiliation 116
22. Population of Włodzimierz County by Mother Tongue 120

23. Population of Włodzimierz County by Religious Affiliation 120
24. Population of Zdołbunów County by Mother Tongue 145
25. Population of Zdołbunów County by Religious Affiliation 145

Maps

1. Wołyń—1939 8
2. Dubno County 30
3. Horochów County 33
4. Kostopol County 47
5. Kowel County 57
6. Krzemieniec County 74
7. Luboml County 82
8. Łuck County 93
9. Równe County 108
10. Sarny County 117
11. Włodzimierz County 121
12. Zdołbunów County 146

The Foundling

When they found her on the steppes
an orphan, no older than the war
growing amid the grain
she had an old look about her

It would not take much, they thought
to end her sorrow
reunite her with her family
they knew how it was done

Instead, they took her in
gave her a good home
made her feel safe
renamed her Bohumyla

Bogumiła, the perfect child
she never laughed
she never cried
she never loved

At sixty-one
she is still five
child of war
Kyrie eleison

— *Tadeusz Piotrowski*

Preface

After the Soviet invasion of Eastern Poland on September 17, 1939, after the massive deportations to the Gulag, after numerous executions, after Katyn, Kharkov, and Kalinin, after the last-minute liquidation of Soviet prisons and the murder of tens of thousands of incarcerated inmates; after the German invasion of Eastern Poland on June 22, 1941, after the onset of the German reign of terror, the executions, the pacification of numerous villages, and the massive deportations to forced-labor camps in Nazi Germany; and after the horrors of the Jewish Holocaust ... all hell broke loose in southeastern Poland, where the Polish population was subjected for the third consecutive time during World War II to a policy of systematic genocide. This is the story of that great tragedy.

The memories that fill the pages of this work are no ordinary memories by any stretch of the imagination. They are the memories of old people who survived a terrible ordeal over fifty-five years ago in the Polish province of Wołyń (Volhynia). They represent but a few of the hundreds of similar accounts from Wołyń that did not fall within the purview of this work and therefore were not included. To these hundreds, additional hundreds of equally tragic and compelling accounts could be added from southern Polesie (Polesia), the Lublin region, as well as from the three Polish provinces of Małopolska Wschodnia (Eastern Little Poland), also known as Eastern Galicia. (Three such stories—one from each of the latter provinces—have been included in Appendix B.) Taken as a whole, all of them would still represent but a very small fraction of the entire story involving the brutal slaughter of tens of thousands of men, women and children ... only because they were Poles. The stories of the murdered victims will never be told, except in the third person. They have been silenced forever—not by the Soviets during their 21-month reign of terror in Eastern Poland, nor by the Nazis during their even longer and equally brutal occupation of those territories, but by the Ukrainian Nationalists who were, like their victims, Polish citizens.

Moreover, not all the survivors—even after all these years—have found the strength to set down their own experiences in writing, and who can blame them. One person, whose story appears in this work, wrote:

> I don't remember how much time elapsed before I gathered enough courage to return to my home. There, I saw my father lying in a pool of blood by the entrance to the house. Not too far away lay the butchered remains of my brother, Adam. Two-year-old Basia lay outside by the window. She was also dead, pierced through either with a bayonet or a knife. I found my mother's lifeless body next door in my uncle's yard; her head was cut to shreds. Not far away lay

my Uncle Aleksander, murdered together with his two daughters aged seven and nine. This was my very first confrontation with death, and it was the death of all of my loved ones. Confusion and chaos filled my brain. I was seized by a strange paralysis of mind and body. I don't know how long I remained in that state of shock.

Another person explained:

> I have attempted many times to record this genocide, but believe me, I could not do it. It was beyond my strength. Now that I have reached an advanced age, I am determined to leave some trace of the bloody deeds that took place in my own village. That nightmare, despite the passing of over half a century, still haunts me in my sleep. Although I try not to think about this great tragedy, my thoughts return to it with ever greater intensity. They have been imbedded deeply within my memory. I sympathize with all those from Wołyń who must continue to live with this terrible burden. Whoever did not live through this will not understand, because such things are truly difficult to understand, and more difficult still to live through.

A third echoed the same sentiments:

> It is difficult for someone who has lived through it all and has lost everything and everyone nearest and dearest to him to write about these matters. It's like reopening an old wound that has scabbed over. I carry this sorrow within my breast constantly. It haunts me at every turn. I have to swallow my tears every day.

These three survivors, like so many others, became children on the run — an image that kept welling up in my mind as I read, trembled, and kept on reading these horrifying recollections. That troubling image was not only the product of my reading and my imagination. After the Leonówka massacre in which my relatives were cut down in cold blood by the Ukrainian Nationalists, our own house was burned to the ground in nearby Ryświanka Colony, and my two brothers (Franciszek, 12 years of age; Jan, ten) and I (three) were among those children on the run. Fortunately, we had our mother to comfort us; not all of Wołyń's children were so lucky.

Our homes, villages, colonies and settlements were burned in the middle of the night. Our families, relatives, neighbors and friends — irrespective of gender or age — were shot, beheaded, stabbed, eviscerated, buried alive in ant hills and dung heaps, burned to death in homes and barns and churches, flayed alive, hung, impaled on fence posts, crucified on barns and fences, sawed in half, tortured, mutilated, desecrated and slaughtered in hundreds of unspeakable ways. Their bodies were left to rot, tossed into rivers, dumped into wells, or buried in shallow mass graves. Mothers were forced to watch their children being murdered. Fathers were given choices between saving themselves and their families or killing their relatives. Polish husbands were betrayed and even killed by their Ukrainian wives. Polish wives and their "half-Polish" children were murdered by their Ukrainian husbands and fathers. On rare occasions, crying children were even removed from hideaways or were suffocated therein (either accidentally or on purpose) to prevent them from giving the rest away. People committed suicide. They went insane.

In Karpiłowka, a Catholic priest was tortured and then finished off by having his heart cut out of his battered but still living flesh. According to the Ukrainian residents of Borowe, an adjoining village, the perpetrator had developed a macabre penchant for piercing the excised hearts of his victims, then timing the length of their beating by his watch. A Polish account describes how in Korytnica another Catholic priest was repeatedly stabbed, then placed in a wooden trough and sawed in half.

We children on the run remember the depravity, the devastation. And we remember the running. We ran from exploding grenades tossed into our homes in the middle of the night, and into our churches during holy services, and into our schools where people were forced to gather. We ran from bullets and from knives; from scythes, axes, pitchforks, bayonets, swords, saws, hammers, and clubs. We ran from men on horseback, from men on the march, and sometimes from coldhearted next-door neighbors with whom we had been on friendly terms just a few years ago. We ran from total annihilation. We hid in fields, in underground shelters, in swamps, and in forests. We lived in constant terror. And on our journey out of that playground of Satan, we were pursued and attacked again and again. They hunted us like wild animals, and wild animals both we and they became.

And yet, amazingly, the accounts contained herein — and by and large all the rest that I have perused — are relatively free of rancor, bitterness, and thirst for revenge. Their main purpose, it seems, is simply to document a terrible episode in the history of humankind and thereby perhaps also to ease the pain of memory.

The selections (actually fragments of selections — to have included the accounts in their entirety would have required a considerably larger volume) in this work differ in one important respect from all the rest: They speak not only of cold-blooded murder but also of heroic compassion. These children and some of their relatives survived because, while some Ukrainians were murdering their families, other Ukrainians — at great personal risk to themselves and their own families — lent a helping hand. Unfortunately, being children at that time so long ago, those rescued did not always remember the names of their saviors — usually friends of the family or neighbors. They remembered, however, that they were Ukrainian. As one survivor put it, "There were very noble people among the Ukrainians who were against this criminal action and who more than once risked their own lives to save the Poles."

One such Ukrainian, Pasichnyk by name, lived in Ryświanka Colony. His small act of kindness, at a time when the smallest of such acts required extraordinary heroism, saved my family. For that act of kindness, and for befriending us throughout our ordeal, he and his family paid the ultimate price (or so we heard after the war). We Piotrowski children do not remember his first name.

These Ukrainian heroes warned our parents of impending Ukrainian-Nationalist attacks, bandaged our wounds, healed us with their folk remedies, gave us food and drink, comforted us, provided us with temporary shelter, hid us in their cellars and attics and doghouses and pigsties and chicken coops and barns, protected us from their murderous relatives, adopted us as members of their families, dressed us in their Ukrainian clothes, taught us their Ukrainian prayers, collected and buried our dead, transported us to hospitals and safe havens, told us where to run, and sometimes defended us from the butchers with their own breasts.

This is all the more remarkable because in Eastern Poland there was no Ukrainian organization comparable to the Polish *Żegota* (code name for Council for Aid to Jews in the General Government) to assist them in their heroic efforts. Alas, the hierarchies of the (Eastern) Orthodox Church and the Uniate (Greek or Byzantine Catholic) Church, like the entire Ukrainian leadership in "Western Ukraine," also remained "neutral" until the worst of it was over. Even then, only a few appeals were made, and these fell on deaf ears and nothing more was done. Some radicalized Ukrainian clergymen not only actively supported the Ukrainian Nationalists from their pulpits, they also blessed the instruments of death and themselves participated in the atrocities to the bitter end. The participation of these fanatic clerics and their sons and daughters in the ethnic-cleansing campaign surely ranks among the most scandalous chapters in the history of both the Orthodox and the Uniate churches in Eastern Europe. The rescuers, therefore, had to act entirely on their own and be prepared to reap the consequences for their brotherly concern. A few names of the Ukrainian victims of the Ukrainian Nationalists have been included in Appendix A.

Each chapter in this book represents a county in the province of Wołyń, with the counties presented in alphabetical order. The survivors' accounts are arranged alphabetically *by names of the Ukrainian rescuers*. When names are not known, the accounts are offered in roughly chronological order *under the names of villages or towns*. It is my firm hope that this arrangement will serve two purposes: to honor the rescuers, and to clearly distinguish the Ukrainian *people* from the perpetrators who were also Ukrainian.

Let no one, therefore, accuse the Ukrainian people as a whole of the atrocities herein described so vividly and simply by the survivors. These deeds were primarily the work of the members of the Ukrainian Insurgent Army (Ukrainska Povstanska Armiia, or UPA—the military arm of the Fascist Organization of Ukrainian Nationalists [Orhanizatsiia Ukrainskykh Natsionalistiv, or OUN]) and the so-called Kushch Self-Defense units (Samooboronnyi Kushchovi Viddily, or SKV) subservient to the OUN-UPA. As Polish citizens, these "freedom fighters" embarked upon an ethnic-cleansing campaign in the southeastern territories of Second Republic during World War II as a means of achieving "Western Ukrainian" independence in the postwar years. "Freedom at any price" was their motto; dishonor was their reward. Their leaders are best described as Fascist fanatics, the sort for whom the end justifies the means—any and all means. Let no one confuse the Ukrainian Nationalists with the Ukrainian people.

The accounts included in this work come from the following collections: the archives of the Main Commission for the Investigation of Crimes against the Polish Nation—Institute of National Memory (in Warsaw) and its regional branches (in Białystok, Kraków, Łódź, Lublin, and Rzeszów); the Association of the 27th Wołynian Division of the [Polish] Home Army (in Warsaw); the Karta Center—Eastern Archive (in Warsaw); the Military Historical Institute (in Warsaw); the Society of the Friends of Krzemieniec and the Wołyń-Podole Territory (in Lublin); the Association for the Remembrance of Poles Murdered in Wołyń (in Zamość); and the Association for the Remembrance of the Victims of the Crimes of the Ukrainian Nationalists (in Wrocław). Some of these recollections have been previously published, others have not.

I have also perused various published works which speak of Ukrainian rescue efforts and have included these references in the main body of my work. Several of the accounts enclosed herein are based on my personal interviews.

Except for my own family's account, these narratives have never appeared in the English language before now. All translations are my own. It is my sincere hope that this initial effort, which I have co-dedicated to those Ukrainians who helped the Polish victims, will in time be supplemented by Ukrainian accounts as well. Many of those heroes are no longer among the living, but surely their heroic deeds must be a part of the oral tradition of their own children. It is high time that Poland formally recognize these people in the same special way that it has recognized another group of Polish citizens, the Righteous Among the Nations, for the assistance they rendered to their Jewish brothers during the Holocaust.

But there are two other, more important, reasons why I am publishing these accounts. These reasons are best stated in the words of the survivors themselves.

I survived that frightening nightmare of my youth. My fortune also improved in later life. I have raised children and have grandchildren. The memory of those terrible days in 1943, however, has never left me. I have written this account in the hope that someone may eventually publish it as a warning to those who follow us. May they always be on guard lest the days of blind hatred toward people who are of a different nationality or faith return. Such a threat is present today in the resurgence of those who have inherited the legacy of the UPA.

That is all that I remember of those cruel times. Perhaps my recorded memories will serve as a "memento mori" [a reminder of death]. May they hail a beginning of the return to normal relations between the Poles and those Ukrainians who were and are decent human beings, not murderers. I hope that time will heal our injuries and cleanse our minds.

There are five appendices in this work. Two of them (Appendix C, which contains excerpts from Ukrainian, Polish, Soviet, German, and Jewish documents; and Appendix D, the chronology) would have been greatly enhanced (and lengthened by some 50 pages) had I been able to incorporate the wealth of documentary information and the chronology contained in a recently released work by Władysław Filar, *Eksterminacja ludności polskiej ma Wołyniu w Drugiej Wojnie Swiatowe*; (The Extermination of the Polish People in Wołyń During World War II). Regrettably, Filar's book came out when mine was already being finalized. I was, however, able to sneak his work into my bibliography.

I am particularly indebted to the following two publishers for their kind permission to quote the many passages contained herein: Towarzystwo Przyjaciół Krzemieńca i Ziemi Wołyńsko-Podolskiej (Society of the Friends of Krzemieniec and the Wołyń-Podole Territory) for Jerzy Dębski and Leon Popek, comps., *Okrutna przestroga* (Cruel Warning) and for Leon Popek, Tomasz Trusiuk, Paweł Wira, and Zenon Wira, comps., *Wołyński testament* (Wołynian Testament); and Światowy Związek Żołnierzy Armii Krajowej, Okręg Wołyń (World Association of the Home Army, Wołynian Branch) for Stanisław Biskupski, comp., *Świadkowie mówią* (Witnesses Speak).

I thank my New Hampshire friend, Michael Curran, for the maps of Wołyń Province and its eleven counties — his first venture in the field of cartography. I also thank the Polish Library in London, England, for making available to me the detailed military maps of Wołyń, upon which the maps in this work are based.

To Teresa Radziszewska, president of the Stowarzyszenie Upamiętnienia Polaków Pomordowanych na Wołyniu (Association for the Remembrance of Poles Murdered in Wołyń), my sincere thanks for sharing with me the many as yet unpublished recollections gathered by her association. To Czesława Grygorczyk, who shared with me the accounts she has gathered that deal with her own family history and the village of Skorodyńce in the province of Tarnopol, many thanks.

I am grateful to the University of New Hampshire for the Faculty Scholar Award, which released me from my teaching responsibilities for one semester, and for the university's financial assistance.

To Richard Tyndorf for reading this manuscript and his helpful suggestions, a heartfelt "Thank you."

Finally, I am deeply grateful to all my correspondents, and to Adela Katarzyna Socha, Emilia Krupka, and Helena Wysocka for the privilege of allowing me to conduct in-depth interviews with them.

As always, I thank my wife Terri and my children, Renia, Ala, and Andrzej, for their continued patience with my scholarly endeavors.

Tadeusz Piotrowski
Manchester, New Hampshire
Fall 1999

Introduction

In the post-World War I reconstruction of Europe, Wołyń (the western part of Volhynia, now a part of northwestern Ukraine) became one of the eastern provinces of the Second Republic of Poland. According to the last pre-World War II census, just over two million people lived in that province in 1931. The following tables provide their ethnic background.[1]

Table 1
Population of Wołyń
by Mother Tongue*

Ukrainian	1,418,324
Ruthenian	8,548
Polish	346,640
Jewish	205,545
German	46,883
Czech	30,977
Russian	23,387
Belorussian	2,417
Lithuanian	90
Other	657
Unreported	2,106
Total	2,085,574

Table 2
Population of Wołyń by
Religious Affiliation

Orthodox	1,455,882
Roman Catholic	327,856
Uniate	11,137
Protestant/Evangelical	53,427
Other Christian	27,952
Jewish	207,792
Other Non-Christian	143
Not Specified or Non-Religious	229
Unreported	1,156
Total	2,085,574

Table 3
Population of Wołyń According
to Jerzy Tomaszewski's
Adjusted 1931 Census

Ukrainians	1,445,000
Poles	326,000
Jews	208,000
Germans	47,000
Czechs	31,000
Russians	23,000
Other	5,600
Total	2,085,600

Tomaszewski's adjusted census figures above indicate that 69.3 percent of Wołyń's inhabitants were Ukrainians, 15.6 percent were Polish, 10 percent were Jewish, and the remaining 5.1 percent consisted of Germans, Czechs, Russians, and other minorities. About 97 percent of the Ukrainians lived in villages. They belonged predominantly to the Eastern Orthodox Church. The majority (about 80 percent) of the Roman Catholic Poles, however, also lived in villages. Although there were only 745 exclusively Polish villages in Wołyń in the mid-1930s,

*All tables except Table 3 are drawn from official 1931 census figures.

WOŁYŃ-1939

the Polish people lived in 5,200 settlements out of a total of 6,800.²

Just to the south of Wołyń, the three Polish provinces of Eastern Galicia (Lwów, Tarnopol, and Stanisławów) contained about 3.26 million Ukrainians, 2.3 million Poles, and 616,000 Jews. (The city of Lwów, the historic capital and largest city in Eastern Galicia, had a Polish population of 158,000, a large Jewish minority of 100,000, and a Ukrainian population of 50,000.) The Ukrainians in Eastern Galicia belonged mainly to the Uniate or Eastern-rite Catholic Church; the Poles were Latin-rite Roman Catholics.

Thus, although a total of about 4.7 million Ukrainians inhabited these four provinces in 1931 (collectively called "Western Ukraine" in Soviet and Ukrainian propaganda), the overall character of these ethnically mixed lands was determined to a large extent by the presence of about 2.6 million Poles and 824,000 Jews, whose upper strata gravitated toward the Polish language and culture.

In addition to "Western Ukraine," pockets of Ukrainians were located in the southerly part of Polesie Province (some 219,000) and the westerly part of Lublin Province (some 123,000). Moreover, about 59,000 Lemkos (a Ruthenian population with a strong regional identification) lived in the southern part of Kraków Province.

In Wołyń, the total number of *non*-Ukrainians in 1931 was therefore either 667,250 (official figure) or 640,600 (adjusted figure); in all of "Western Ukraine," it was either 5,200,100 (official figure) or 3,592,700 (adjusted figure).³ The vast majority of these non-Ukrainians were indigenous inhabitants. These figures are worth keeping in mind because, like the millions of Jews to be annihilated on the list prepared by the Nazis at their January 20, 1942, Wannsee (Germany) conference, these millions represent the "occupants" who, according to the political agenda worked out at the January 28 to February 3, 1929, Conference of Ukrainian Nationalists in Vienna, had to be "removed" from "Ukrainian lands." The Nazi Party failed to complete its task; so did the Fascist Organization of Ukrainian Nationalists. In both instances, there were survivors. The terrible story of the Ukrainian-Nationalist ethnic-cleansing campaign (the "removal") is told in the pages of this book by some of the Polish survivors, its primary targets. A few Ukrainian accounts, rare as they are, have also been included. It will take the reader but a few pages to determine whether a distinction should in fact be made between the Jewish case, involving a policy of "annihilation," and the case of the "occupants of Ukrainian lands," involving a policy of "removal."

But this is not all. Since that "removal" was to encompass all "Ukrainian ethnographic territories," some of which have been mentioned above, there were to be many more victims. How did this colossal human tragedy come about? And why did this Ukrainian-Nationalist ethnic-cleansing campaign begin in "peaceful Wołyń"?

Much has been written about the reasons for the age-old animosities between the Poles and the Ukrainians. In former times they were generally attributed to the universally present manorial system which resulted in peasant revolts (for example, the 1490-92 uprising in Red Ruthenia), various brigand and *haydamak* movements and revolutions, including the Khmelnytski rebellion of 1648, and those uprisings of 1734, 1750, and 1768, which writer Taras Shevchenko describes so eloquently in his masterful *Haydamaks*. This onerous economic system weighed heavily on all peasants irrespective of nationality, both in the East and the West. An overlord was an overlord; a peasant, a peasant. In Eastern Poland, the overlords happened to be Polish, or rather, Polonized Ruthenians; the peasants, both Ukrainian (Ruthenian) and Polish.⁴ These economic burdens were further exacerbated by the attempts on the part of the Polish rulers to impose Roman Catholicism on the "schismatic" Orthodox Ukrainians that finally led to the tenuous Union of Breść (October 8, 1596)—the acceptance on the part of a number of Orthodox dioceses of the spiritual hegemony of the Church of Rome.

Then came the partitions, and Wołyń went to Russia while Eastern Galicia fell to Austria.

After World War I, when Poland regained its independence, a war was waged over Eastern Galicia (the 1918-19 Polish-Ukrainian [Galician] war) which Poland won. Eastern Galicia was then placed under the military control and administration of the Second Republic by the Supreme Council of the Four Powers (June 25, 1919). On April 21, 1920, Poland and Ukraine signed a treaty of alliance against the Soviet Union in which the Ukrainian Directorate led by Symon Petliura agreed to abandon its claim to "Western Ukraine." This region was formally incorporated into the Polish state on the basis of the Treaty of Riga (March 18, 1921) between Poland and Russia that delineated the border between Poland and Soviet Ukraine along the Zbrucz River. On March 15, 1923, the League of Nations' Council of Ambassadors formally recognized Poland's sovereign rights over this territory; the United States seconded that decision on April 5. Whether Poland could have or should have created an autonomous Eastern Galicia under its auspices, as it was urged to do by the Council of Ambassadors, is an open question. Given the great instability in that region after World War I, compounded by a series of continuing wars, Soviet expansionist ambitions, and worldwide economic depression, that could have been a costly mistake, and not only for Poland.

Poland was not at all averse to the existence of an independent Ukraine *east of the Zbrucz River*. In fact, it supported the Ukrainian counterrevolutionary movement after World War I and offered military assistance to Ukraine against Bolshevik Russia. The above-mentioned Polish-Ukrainian treaty of alliance attests to this historical fact, and the resulting Piłsudski-Petliura offensive on Kiev during the Polish-Russian war almost ended in a disaster for Poland. Poland wanted that buffer zone between itself and the Soviet Union. That is why it was the first nation to recognize Ukrainian independence in 1991, even though this recognition meant the relinquishing of its "historical" right to its former eastern territories.

After 1923, the legal Ukrainian political parties sought to reconcile themselves with the Polish state and embarked upon a program of accommodation through various political, economic, social, and cultural institutions. In time, it was hoped, some type of peaceful coexistence could be reached with Poland. Unfortunately, the Polish government embarked upon a program of assimilation (Polonization) which was both prejudicial and discriminatory to the native Ukrainian as well as other minority populations.[5] As always, the seriousness of such practices needs to be assessed from a comparative contemporaneous perspective, not from the vantage point of our own times. Suffice it to say, such practices, and much worse, were often the norm throughout Europe of that day.

During the interwar years, in addition to accommodation as well as a rather weak attempt to embrace the Communist solution, there was another response on the part of the Ukrainian people to the Polish rule: Ukrainian integral nationalism.

This movement, also known as "active" nationalism, began in the southeastern provinces of the Second Republic of Poland in 1920 with the founding of the Ukrainian Military Organization (Ukrainska Viiskova Orhanizatsiia, or UVO) in Prague. Eventually, the UVO became the military arm of the Organization of Ukrainian Nationalists (OUN), founded in 1929 in Vienna. During the interwar period, this separatist movement, backed by Germany and other countries hostile to Poland, launched a campaign of terror against the government and people of the Second Republic that resulted in thousands of serious acts of sabotage, assassinations of prominent Polish government officials (for example, Minister of Interior Bronisław Pieracki), and the murder of numerous Ukrainians suspected of "treason," that is to say, siding with Poland.[6] In a widely disseminated but illegal brochure entitled "UVO," put out by UVO's Propaganda Section, we read:

> UVO constitutes a revolutionary organization whose fundamental task is to propagate the idea of a general revolutionary uprising of the Ukrainian people, the ultimate aim of which is the establishment of our own independent and undivided nation. As an organization that conducts its activities on Western Ukrainian lands, it considers as its obligation the carrying out of a planned preparation for this revolutionary uprising, even now, against the Polish occupant.... Decidedly rejecting an orientation toward both Poland and the Bolsheviks, UVO also considers as traitors to the wars of liberation of the Ukrainian people those individuals from among the Ukrainians who propagate an orientation to one or another occupant of Ukraine and attempt to evoke friendly feelings toward Moscow or Poland from the society. The UVO evaluates no differently those Ukrainian politicians who reconcile themselves to the condition of Ukraine's enslavement and, under the guise of "real" or "positive" politics, propagate the development of Ukrainian life within the framework of a foreign nation. The UVO considers the former as "khruni" [blind masses, the herd], and the latter as "appeasers".... We must change the psychology of our society and the psychology of the enemies, and influence world opinion. Terror will be not only our means of self-defense but also of [revolutionary] agitation which will reach everyone: our own people as well as the outsiders, regardless of whether they desire it or not.[7]

Among the contemporary slogans of the Ukrainian Nationalists we find the following, so characteristic of all social revolutionaries: "Blood is needed — we will provide a sea of blood! Terror is needed — we will make it hellish." "We are not ashamed of murders, robbery and burnings. In war there are no ethics."[8] Clearly, the Nationalists were not interested in improving the lot of their people under the Polish rule. On the contrary, they wanted the situation to deteriorate. "The worse it is," they said, "the better."[9] No concessions from the Polish government would have appeased them. It was not reform they were after, but revolution. As one Ukrainian leader told a British correspondent in 1930, "We are fundamentally disloyal. We do not want peace. If our people are allowed to enter into friendly cooperation with the Poles they may cease to cherish the dream of an independent Ukraine, which we hope to realize in 30 or 40 years' time. Whatever is done for us, we must always be discontented."[10]

The self-appointed task of the UVO-OUN during the interwar period was to create a state of "constant revolutionary boiling" which would prepare the masses for the "final reckoning with the enemy" at the "appropriate moment."[11] In 1926 Osyp Dumyn, director of UVO Intelligence Department in behalf of Germany, submitted his report *"Die Warheit über die ukrainische Organisation"* (The Truth About the Ukrainian Organization [UVO]) to the German Ministry of Foreign Affairs. A two-paragraph section entitled "Program and Military Plans of the UVO" reads:

> The mission of the UVO was to conduct an incessant and uncompromising war with Poland. The objectives of the UVO were to destroy Polish rule in all Ukrainian spheres, to undermine Polish national influence, to effect the material and moral annihilation of the Polish national organs of authority, and finally to attain and institutionalize its own independent Ukrainian nation. In the course of the first two years

of the existence of the UVO, this work unfolded according to plan, the proof of which were many deeds.

By instituting its own detachments, the UVO was to create a real, although secret, Ukrainian army which could at the appropriate moment initiate an open war against the Polish occupant.¹²

The political platform of the OUN, worked out at its 1929 conference in Vienna, was based on the fascist doctrines of Dmytro Dontsov.¹³ Its policy toward the Second Republic of Poland was the same as that of the UVO. Its ultimate objective was to establish, through a revolution against the Polish state, an independent Ukraine under OUN control on all the so-called Ukrainian ethnolinguistic territories cleansed of "foreigners" ("Ukraine for Ukrainians"). The western borders of that envisioned independent Ukraine reached up to Warsaw and Cracow. Two pivotal documents emerged from that 1929 conference, documents which would provide the ideological basis for the removal of the non-Ukrainian population from southeastern Poland in the 1940s by means of a systematic campaign of ethnic cleansing. They read as follows:

> **Proclamation:** Only the complete removal of all occupants from Ukrainian lands will create the possibility for an expansive development of the Ukrainian people in the borders of their own nation.... In its internal political activity, the Ukrainian nation will strive to attain borders encompassing all Ukrainian ethnographic territories.
>
> **Resolution:** The complete removal of all occupants from Ukrainian lands, which will follow in the course of a national revolution and create the possibility for an expansive development of the Ukrainian people in the borders of their own nation, will be guaranteed only by a system of our own armed military forces and purposeful political alliances.¹⁴

During the interwar period, the UVO-OUN campaign of terror forced the Polish government to resort to various counter-measures aimed at this separatist threat. Poland was, after all, a very young and fragile democracy surrounded by enemies who were all too willing to exacerbate Poland's internal ethnic conflicts and to contribute to the nation's downfall. Be that as it may, by September 1939 most of the members of the OUN Provid (Leadership) and many rank-and-file members were serving time in Polish jails. Among the former were Stepan Bandera and Mykola Lebed, both of whom received a death sentence commuted to life imprisonment for their role in the 1934 assassination of Minister Bronisław Pieracki.

With the outbreak of World War II, all the Ukrainian Nationalists were released from prison and began immediately to actively support the German war effort in the hopes of securing an independent Ukraine in alliance with the victorious "Great German Reich."¹⁵

On February 10, 1940, the OUN split into two factions, one led by Andrii Melnyk (OUN-M), the other by Stepan Bandera (OUN-B). Shortly after the June 22, 1941, invasion of the Soviet Union by Germany, OUN-B declared Ukrainian independence and established its own Ukrainian "government" in Lwów, thus alienating the Nazis, who didn't like surprises. Repressions followed but OUN-B refused to withdraw its proclamation. At the beginning of July 1941 Bandera was arrested by the Germans and sent to Zellenbau, a special section in the Sachsenhausen, Germany, camp for political prisoners. Mykola Lebed replaced Bandera as head of OUN-B.

With tensions mounting and the prospects of German victory growing dim, OUN-B's plan to create its own military formation was formulated at its April 1942 (second) conference and implemented in the fall of that year in Wołyń with the founding of the (OUN-B) Ukrainian Insurgent Army (UPA). Initially, about 600 men from Sarny County were recruited for that army by Vasyl Sydor, a member of the Provid, sent to Wołyń by the OUN-B Central Provid for that very purpose. This recruitment of the Ukrainian people by OUN-B for its UPA continued until the end of the war and beyond.

A decision was also made to consolidate the various nationalist forces under one command and to mobilize the entire Ukrainian society and place it at the disposition of that unified army, the OUN-B UPA. It was thought that after the war a balance of power similar to that following World War I would emerge and that the presence of such a Ukrainian military force in "Western Ukraine" would assure its independence.

The mobilization of the Ukrainian society, ostensibly for the purpose of self-defense, took two forms: The assignment of all Ukrainians to one or another local organization whose principal task was to supply the UPA with various needed commodities and services; and the creation of the SKV units throughout Polesie and Wołyń. The SKV units were paramilitary brigades consisting of 30-50 Ukrainian peasants per unit who were to be "on call" for whatever task was demanded of them by the UPA. They were like an invisible self-supporting army. They lived in their villages with their families (the UPA inhabited the forests), but when the need arose they would arm at a moment's notice, do what was ordered, and return just as quickly to their villages. Their weapons consisted of the usual assortment of ordinary domestic and farm implements. By the spring of 1943, a veritable network of SKV units existed throughout Wołyń. The recruitment of simple and by-and-large illiterate Ukrainian peasantry for both types of UPA assistance fell to the unscrupulous OUN-B Security Service (Sluzhba Bezpeky, or SB), whose only policy was "join or die." As Maksym Skorupskyi put it, referring to Ukrainians, "Whoever hesitated to fulfill its [OUN-B's] demands to mobilize was shot together with his entire family and his home was burned."[16]

The consolidation of the various nationalist forces under the OUN-B UPA was also accomplished by brute force. Given the usual SB option of joining or being killed, many of the followers of Melnyk (who formed their own UPA units) as well as the followers of Taras "Bulba"-Borovets (a separate faction of nationalists, the first to use the designation "UPA") joined up. Eventually, the ranks of the OUN-B UPA were complemented by thousands of German-trained and German-equipped Ukrainian-Nationalist deserters from a variety of pro-German military and paramilitary formations. At the end of 1943, the OUN-B commanded a highly disciplined and formidable force — some 40,000 well-armed Ukrainian Nationalists — in southeastern Poland.

Meanwhile, to further its twin, inseparable, primary objectives (independence of Ukraine and unification of all Ukrainian ethnolinguistic territories), the Central Provid of the OUN-B (at whose head stood Mykola Lebed [1909-1998], *nom de guerre* "Maksym Ruban," organizer of the SB) made a momentous and tragic decision: It turned its military and paramilitary forces (the UPA and the SKV units subservient to it) against the "occupants" and "foreigners" living in "Western Ukraine." Just as the Jews became the proverbial scapegoat for the Nazis, so too the Poles became the very incarnation of evil for these fanatic "patriotic" Ukrainians. Ethnic cleansing followed.

Too much evidence has now been accumulated — in the form of testimonies (memoirs, oral histories, personal recollections, and court depositions), exhumations and forensic analyses, and Ukrainian, Polish, Soviet, German, and Jewish archival sources — to question the systematic nature of this campaign,[17] and it would be naive to believe that such a campaign could have been carried out without a direct order from the leadership of this highly integrated, disciplined, and authoritarian organization. That order was probably issued by the OUN-B Central Provid in the fall of 1942.

At the very beginning of it all, a son of a Ukrainian Baptist minister joined the UPA in good faith to fight for a free Ukraine. One day, his and other UPA units were assembled in Polesie, and an order was read requiring them to murder the Polish families that hosted them during their military exercises. When some of the men refused, they were summarily executed.[18]

Oleksandr Hrytsenko tells us that "The ruling Provid member [of the OUN-B], Maksym Ruban (Mykola Lebed), demanded from the leader of the Supreme Command of the UPA [that UPA which existed under the leadership of Taras "Bulba"-Borovets] ... the cleansing of the Polish people in all the territories of the insurrection."[19]

And Taras "Bulba"-Borovets tells us in his August 10, 1943 "Open Letter to Members of the Provid of the Organization of Ukrainian Nationalists of Stepan Bandera" that "Already during the talks [between Lebed and Borovets], instead of conducting actions in keeping with the agreed-upon course, military units of the OUN [Bandera faction] ... began in a horrid manner to exterminate Polish civilians as well as other minorities."[20] In 1981 Borovets wrote, "The officer corps of the new UPA received the following military assignment from Mykola Lebed's party in June 1943: Without delay and as soon as possible conclude the action of completely cleansing the Ukrainian territories of Poles."[21]

Polish Home Army (Armia Krajowa, or AK) field reports refer to such orders being issued; for example, the AK report for April 20, 1944: "In Wołyń, the UPA received an order to hide its weapons and, beginning in the summer, to leave the forests and to murder Poles and Soviets."[22]

Soviet field reports refer to such orders as well; for example, the March 30, 1943, field report of the Soviet unit, Shitov: "The Ukrainian Nationalists conducted a bestial action against the defenseless Polish people, setting themselves the task of completely exterminating the Poles in Ukraine.... In the Cumań region, UPA companies were ordered to exterminate all Poles and to burn their places of residence and colonies by April 15, 1943."[23]

German field reports confirm the existence of such orders; for example, a May 18, 1943, Army Group North, Ukraine, report states that the Germans are in possession of a Ukrainian order for the "shooting of Poles in villages"; a July 13, 1943, German military report confirms the "Ausrottung polnischer Siedler in Wolhynien" (extermination of Polish settlers in Wołyń).[24] On May 19, 1943, Nehring — reporting from Kamionka Strumiłowa on UPA-Wehrmacht cooperation — stated: "I personally do not see any possibility of positive cooperation since individual UPA groups, in all likelihood on orders of the UPA leadership, in a willful way continue to burn Polish villages and even landed property. I regard this destruction of property not only as intolerable during war but also, above all, as a crime that will burden the Ukrainian nation in the future."[25] In another German report dated March 13, 1944, regarding a previous UPA meeting with the Wehrmacht, Harasymovskyi (*nom de guerre* of Ivan Hryniokh, an OUN-B representative with plenipotentiary powers) is quoted as stating quite unambiguously that there was such an order and that it came from the OUN-B Provid. His admission follows a series of transparent rationalizations, fabrications, and sheer fantasies:

> [Harasymovskyi] attributes the responsibility for the continuing terror between the Ukrainians and the Poles exclusively to the Polish side. At the beginning of the occupation of the former Polish territories, there was peace and tranquillity between the

Poles and the Ukrainians. But later, under Warsaw's initiative, an unbridled terror emerged which touched many Ukrainian localities. At first, the OUN tried to convince the Poles to come to their senses and it put forth many constructive propositions. But the Poles underestimated the strength of the Ukrainians, especially that of the Bandera group. The escalation of the terror aimed at the Ukrainians forced the OUN-B to resist and *to issue an order* that military units should answer the Polish terror with retaliatory actions, for which the organization accepts full responsibility.[26]

As indeed it should!

Most incriminating, UPA field reports specifically refer to such genocidal orders being issued and to the success in carrying them out. A June 1943 secret directive from OUN Central Provid member and UPA commander, Roman Dmytro Klachkivskyi ("Klym Savur," "Okhrym," "Klym," "Krymskyi," "Omelian"), called for the liquidation of "the entire Polish population from 16 to 60."[27] In his June 24, 1943, field report another UPA commander, Iurii Stelmashchuk ("Rudyi," "Kaidash"), reiterated that "secret directive in the matter of a complete, universal, physical liquidation of the Polish people" and dispatched three UPA battalions to do the job.[28] "Lysyi," the commander sent to the Luboml area, reported back: "On August 29, 1943, I conducted an action in the villages of Wola Ostrowiecka and Ostrówki in the Hołowno region. I liquidated all Poles from young to old. I burned all the buildings and took the possessions and livestock for the needs of the battalion."[29] The combined losses in these two villages were enormous: at least 1,041 victims, half of whom were children. (In that area, some 1,700 persons were murdered at this time.) We have the names of these 1,041 victims, we have the testimonies of survivors, we have exhumation forensic reports, we have videotapes and photographs, we have the actual field reports of the executioners — much more than would be needed to establish a case for genocide in any world court.

Agnieszka Muzyka survived the massacre near the Ukrainian village of Sokół to which several hundred women and children from Ostrówki (and a few from Wola Ostrowiecka) were herded. She was among those who were made to lie down and were shot. She tells of an order being read prior to the execution: "He pulls out a piece of paper and reads that today, at this moment, all are to be shot."[30] That order had to be repeated once more when some of the shooters refused to go on with their ghastly task. After the second reading, reinforced by the threat of execution for insubordination, the shooters kept firing on the hysterical women and screaming children — they fulfilled their "patriotic duty," they finished the job. (Several other narrators in this work refer to hearing from their Ukrainian friends that such orders for the liquidation of Poles were being issued.)

On April 6, 1944, Orest Karat issued special instructions to his subordinate which began with the words: "I order you conduct a cleansing of the Polish element and Ukrainian-Bolshevik agents in your region without delay." He demanded that "the cleansing of the territory must be completed before our Easter so that we can celebrate it without the Poles." He then asked for a report containing "detailed information about the cleansing, how it is being conducted in your territory," and added, "conduct a hard battle with them without pardon. Spare no one." He ends with the words: "Take out your weapons. Death to the Poles."[31]

We also have an OUN order to SKV Provid leaders and administrators which mandates the annihilation of "everything that is Polish ... all walls of churches ... buildings of worship ... trees growing near homes ... all houses which were formerly inhabited by Poles." A military order from the OUN high command to kill "Polish" trees! This order was issued on February 9, 1944, after the majority of the Poles had already been murdered or fled. That final liquidation was to be completed by November 25, 1944, long after the Soviet front had passed. In my mind's eye I can see them now, with their bloodstained axes and the saws they had used to cut "half-Polish" children in two, coming into a former Polish settlement that had become a burned-out ghost town, and chopping down trees. This, at a time when a World War was drawing to a close, but a war that still demanded supreme efforts and sacrifices. What contribution to the war effort and the Allied victory did this chopping down of trees make? That OUN directive concludes with an explanation: "We call your attention once more, to the fact that if anything whatsoever remains that is Polish, the Poles will have claims to our lands."[32]

Some of the documents and accounts appearing in this work bear witness to this insane venture. One account from Łuck County states that in the Polish colony of Chrobów "there was nothing left; even the fruit trees had been burned."[33] Another account from the same county paints a similarly bleak picture: "We discovered that Andrzejówka was a wasteland: the orchards and wooded areas had been cut down, and only a few shrubs remained here and there."[34] In his letter of September 5, 1943, Stanisław Czekanowski of Hrubieszów, writes: "The villages to the east of the Bug [River] are empty. The Poles have either been massacred or have fled; the Ukrainians are sitting in the forests. The crops are not being gathered. The sight in the villages is uncanny: the livestock is all taken, only poultry roams here and there." And in his letter of February 24, 1944, he notes: "I just spoke with quite an intelligent person, a farmer from Łuck. Between Łuck and Uściług, for a few kilometers along each side of some 80 kilometers of road, not a single village remains. Everything is burned down, and the people have been either shot or they have fled."[35] Haunting photographs of verdant fields with captions like "This is where my village stood" provide a chilling commentary on the success of this final endeavor. A UPA political report of June 27, 1944, for the period June 13-28, 1944, states: "Poles. There are no Poles in our territory."[36] In the chronicle of one UPA unit we read: "Nothing has been moved by human hands on the Polish colonies for over a year. Everything is overgrown with luxuriant grass. It's a very sad sight."[37]

How is all of this to be accounted for?

Some Ukrainian historians maintain that the events in Wołyń can be explained, if not justified, by the previous slaughter of Ukrainians in the Lublin Province (especially in the counties of Zamość, Biłgoraj, Hrubieszów, and Tomaszów) by the Polish underground in 1942. We know that in November of the previous year (1941) the Germans began to remove Poles from that area and to bring in German settlers in an effort to extend their *Lebensraum* ("living space"). Similar campaigns occurred in October 1942, November 1942-March 1943, and June-August 1943. This was a part of Heinrich Himmler's Generalplan Ost: The planned expulsion of 31 million people from the eastern territories and for the colonization by 10 million ethnic Germans of 700,000 square kilometers of land — an ambitious plan that would more than double the size of 1938 Germany. Over 100,000 Poles succumbed to this German "resettlement" (brutal deportation) policy in the Zamość region (Zamojszczyzna).[38] We know that many Ukrainians were resettled on Polish properties by the Germans in the hope that they would protect the German settlers from Polish retaliation. We know that the collaborationist Ukrainian Central Committee (Ukrainskyi Tsentralnyi Komitet, or UTsK, established by the Germans in Kraków in the spring of 1940 and headed by Volodymyr Kubiiovych) did much to poison

Polish-Ukrainian relations in this region, to Germany's benefit. We know that the Ukrainian Nationalists — especially in their capacity as members of the militia, as village administrators (sing., *sołtys*), and as members of the Ukrainian police — assisted the Germans in this Nazi ethnic-cleansing campaign. We know that, in retaliation, the Polish underground issued a warning to the "Ukrainian People Living in the Area of Hrubieszów County" that "for every Polish village evacuated with the help of the Ukrainian police and militia, two Ukrainian villages will be burned immediately" and that "for every Pole killed by a Ukrainian, two Ukrainians will be killed immediately."[39] (This warning was issued on April 25, 1943.) We also know that that threat was implemented in May of that year, when several Ukrainian villages were put to the torch by the Polish underground.[40] The sequence of these events counterpoised with the Ukrainian-Nationalist ethnic-cleansing campaign, which began in Wołyń in the fall of 1942, belie the argument that the Poles began it all. Moreover, even if these allegations (that the Poles began it all in the Lublin Province) were true, why take it out on the innocent residents of Wołyń who had nothing to do with the events in the Lublin Province? And where is the proportionality of it all? According to the OUN-B propaganda brochure *Kudy priamuiut Polaky?* written by O. S. Sadovyi in 1944, 394 Ukrainians perished in the Chełm area in the years 1942-43.[41] In that same time frame, some 30,000 to 40,000 Poles perished in Wołyń!

As for the specious argument that it was the Poles of Wołyń who began it all, it is important to keep in mind that in 1931 the Poles represented 15.6 percent and the Ukrainians 69.3 percent (adjusted census figures) of Wołyń's total population of just over two million, and that although more Poles settled there after 1931, most of these colonists, together with a large number of the indigenous Polish residents (especially state officials, the educated, and well-to-do), were deported to the Gulag under the Soviet occupation (1939-41). Would it make sense for this Polish minority to initiate an all-out war against the substantially larger Ukrainian majority ... and to do so on their own without the backing of the Polish armed forces or the underground, which was still very weak at this stage in Wołyń?[42] (The Ukrainians also outnumbered the Poles 3:2 in 1931 in Eastern Galicia.

Moreover, despite Lebed's unfounded assertion that "among the Polish society of Wołyń there were many people who were blinded by historical hatred of the Ukrainian people" and that "therefore, the answer of the Ukrainian nation [*sic*] could only be: to clear the territory of the hostile Polish people,"[43] the Poles and the Ukrainians got along reasonably well in "peaceful Wołyń" during the interwar years. A moment's reflection tells us that if there was any "historical hatred"— and some of it was certainly justifiable — it was on the part of the Ukrainians, egged on by the Nationalists, toward the Poles. In any case, it is simply inconceivable that either side would have begun such a bloodbath there on its own.

Who, then, initiated that systematic ethnic-cleansing campaign in Wołyń? It was the long-frustrated Ukrainian-Nationalist leadership from Eastern Galicia. It was they, and Lebed foremost among them, who hated the "occupants" and "foreigners" in "Western Ukraine": the indigenous, settler, and refugee Poles, Jews, Russians, and all the other non-Ukrainian minorities. It was they, during Lebed's reign over the OUN-B, who began to "clear the territory" of "foreign elements." It was they, during Lebed's reign over the OUN-B SB, who killed their own people. As the previously-cited Stanisław Czekanowski put it in his letter dated February 26, 1944: "It began with the propaganda coming from [Eastern] Galicia for *samostiina Ukraina* (independent Ukraine), and it was that which produced these frightening results in Wołyń .... And it happened because our rich county was inundated by riffraff from [Eastern] Galicia, seemingly ideologically motivated but in reality only out for profit. Having valuable caretakers [the Germans], it was they who have poisoned our lives. Generally speaking, our [Ukrainian] peasants are not represented among them, and one can count on one's fingers those who have linked themselves to these activists."[44] This sentiment is echoed again and again in the narratives from Wołyń. It was not the locals, but the ideologically-oriented "strangers from Eastern Galicia," the "others," who were the problem.

The clearest and the most astute formulation of what was going on at the time as well as the reasons for it, is contained in the following German field report submitted to Gerhard von Mende, the director of the department in the Ministry of the Third Reich responsible for the affairs in the occupied eastern territories:

> Under the battle-cry of "revenge" for the Polish policy of extermination [sic] in the years 1918-39 and hostile disposition [of Poles toward the Ukrainians, [sic] under first the Soviet and then the German occupation, the OUN-UPA began a campaign of annihilation of the Poles which released all those instincts associated with vengeance stemming from age-old animosities and whose object was the wholesale physical destruction of all that was Polish in this territory. Irrespective of the stated reasons for this war ("Poles are the Soviet agents of destruction," "Poles are setting the Germans against the Ukrainians," and the like), one cannot deny that the objective of the leadership of the OUN-UPA was to cleanse the Ukrainian territory of everything which was Polish, or at least to destroy that which the Poles had achieved in this territory in the years 1918-39. The canvas of the map of nationalities, and foremost in Wołyń, is bound to change fundamentally as a result of this war.[45]

That prediction was dead right. In fact, the "canvas of the map of nationalities" of southeastern Poland — encompassing the provinces of Wołyń, Lwów, Tarnopol, and Stanisławów — had already been radically changed at the time of the submission of this German field report, November 2, 1944. Shortly thereafter, the Soviets would administer the final brush strokes to the new ethnic map of "Western Ukraine" by their massive population exchange program, probably a wise move given that the ethnic turmoil in that region was exacerbated, if not generated, by World War II.

The Ukrainian-Nationalist ethnic-cleansing campaign (initially concentrated in Wołyń) began in the fall of 1942 with the murder of non-Ukrainian (mostly Polish) individuals and families. This was followed by attacks on Polish villages and settlements at the beginning of 1943 in the Sarny region. In May 1943 the attacks multiplied in Sarny County, then spread to Kostopol, Równe, and Zdołbunów counties. In June 1943 they embraced the counties of Dubno and Łuck. At the end of that month, already 15,000 Poles were dead. In July, the height of this brutal campaign, the killings spread to the counties of Horochów, Kowel, and Włodzimierz. That August, villages in Luboml County were attacked.[46]

These attacks were not sporadic. They were well orchestrated (planned, organized, coordinated) to the very last detail. The following patterns (extrapolated from the accounts that follow and others that I have read), although not universally applicable, attest to the systematic nature of this campaign.

First, from the beginning of the ethnic-cleansing campaign, various notices were circulated by the OUN encouraging the Ukrainian population to kill Poles and to burn their property. At times this message was reinforced from the pulpits of Ukrainian churches by fanatic clerics who placed their allegiance to the ideology of the OUN above their loyalty to the Christian ideals of their profession. (This is not to say that the

Ukrainian clergy as a whole actively approved of these barbaric measures or that there were no genuine heroes among them. There were.)

Those Ukrainians who objected to the policy of ethnic cleansing were themselves terrorized. They were often labeled as "traitors," condemned by the so-called Revolutionary Court, and summarily executed.

In advance of the attack, mandatory meetings were held in nearby Ukrainian villages during which OUN-UPA ideological propagandists from Eastern Galicia attempted to convince the local Ukrainian population of the necessity of exterminating the entire Polish population. One slogan ran: "Exterminate the Poles unto the seventh generation, including those who no longer speak Polish."[47]

It was during these meetings (although at times separate meetings were held) that SKV members were assigned their respective tasks and the women were told to prepare their wagons in order to transport the booty. It was also during such meetings that Ukrainians sympathetic to the Poles learned of the imminent attacks and relayed this information to their Polish friends and neighbors, thereby putting themselves and their own families at risk.

Sometimes, in order to lull the Poles into a false sense of security, leaflets would be distributed a few days in advance of the attack encouraging Poles and Ukrainians to unite against the German and Soviet threats. Poles were assured that they had nothing to fear from the Ukrainians and were told that to leave one's village at this time would be taken as a sign of bad faith toward the Ukrainians.

Often several simultaneous attacks were planned on the same day and even at the same hour. Just as often, they were planned on specific anniversaries, such as the anniversary of the proclamation of Ukrainian independence (June 30), or Dmytro Dontsov's birthday (August 30), and on specific holidays, such as the Orthodox holiday of St. Peter and Paul, Polish Easter, and Christmas. On Christmas Eve 1943 Ukrainian-Nationalist attacks took place in Dworzec, Hnidawa, Ołyka, and Wólka — all in Łuck County. On Christmas day, Janówka, Lublatyn, and Radomle were attacked in the county of Kowel. The "Peter and Paul action" (beginning on July 11, 1943) involved a series of attacks on Poles while they attended Sunday church services, for example, in Kisielin and Koniuchy (both in Horochów County), Krymno (Kowel County), Chołoniewicze and Sokul (both in Łuck County), and Chrynów, Oktawin, Poryck, and Swojczów (all in Włodzimierz County).

In some instances, prior to the attack, Ukrainian peasants would bring their weapons (knives, axes, pitchforks, etc.) to their local church and have them blessed by the priest.

On the day of the attack, the Polish village would be surrounded, all escape routes would be closed off, and those attempting to leave their village, for whatever reason, were ordered to go back home.

In attacks on larger settlements, flares were used to coordinate the beginning of the siege.

The procedure for mass murder was almost always the same: UPA and SVK units would enter the village, round up the people in a central location — sometimes under some pretext (like holding a village meeting to convey "important information" regarding the "German threat"), sometimes by force — and either kill them then and there with grenades, machine guns, and rifles, or set fire to the building and burn them alive, or remove them a few at a time to an out-of-the-way location and then kill them. Such incidents transpired in the villages of Woronczyn (Horochów County), Majdan, Mielnica, Sucha Łoza, and Wólka Lubitowska (Kowel County), Ostrówki and Wola Ostrowiecka (Luboml County), Łamane

(Łuck County), and Huta Majdańska (Zdołbunów County). There were variations upon this scenario, to be sure: Sometimes the people would be separated by gender, sometimes there was resistance which had to be suppressed, sometimes it meant a house-to-house search, sometimes the victims would be told to lie down in front of prepared pits and shot in the back of the head (a technique learned by the former members of the Ukrainian auxiliary police from the Nazi Einsatzgruppen [mobile execution squads]), and so on.

The killings were almost always accompanied by a high degree of sadism toward the living, who would eventually be killed, and toward the corpses. This almost ubiquitous theme in the accounts lends credence to the many assessments of the *haydamak*-like character of this 20th-century barbarity. In Korytnica (Włodzimierz County), for example, Fr. Karol Baran was repeatedly stabbed by the Ukrainian Nationalists, then placed in a wooden trough and sawed in half.[48]

Each attack would be followed by wholesale looting of the possessions of those murdered. Witnesses report seeing wagonloads of their goods being transported, often by women, to Ukrainian villages. Once there, some of the goods would be taken by the UPA for their own use, and the peasants were allowed to keep the rest.

After being plundered, Polish homes and farm buildings would be burned, except those standing within 15 meters of Ukrainian dwellings. At times, all vestiges of the villages would be destroyed — such as orchards, schools, chapels, and churches — to erase even the memory of these Polish villages ever having existed.[49]

Then a hunt would begin for runaways and those hiding in fields, forests, marshes, but just as often in homes, barns, and makeshift hideaways provided by sympathetic Ukrainians. Those found would be immediately killed. The rescuers and their families would be beaten and often also killed, either on the spot or later by order of the SB or the "Revolutionary Court."

After it was all over, local Ukrainians would be forced to collect and bury the dead. There was no need for this, of course, in the case of victims thrown dead or alive into cisterns and wells — a frequent and universal practice throughout Wołyń.

After the attacks, a few Poles would inevitably return to their homes, farms, and villages. Others were encouraged to return, at times even by their own neighbors, who assured them that it was all over, that they had nothing to fear any more, and that they should come back to gather their crops. Still others, having no intention of returning but plagued by hunger or cold, would sometimes take a chance and return in secret to scavenge for food or clothing for themselves and their families. In most instances, whoever returned for whatever reason was killed.

In the event that the first attack failed, the village or settlement would be attacked a second time.

Even civilian defense centers, where Poles gathered for safety, were attacked. Although many such centers came into being throughout Wołyń, only a few were able to play a significant role in the rescue of the threatened Polish population.[50]

And finally, refugees fleeing in all directions were ambushed and killed.

There were cases when UPA units conducted attacks on the Poles under the guise of being Soviet partisan units. A UPA "Zahrava" field report attests to this practice: "The liquidation of 27 persons in the village of Puznia and a whole series of other liquidations and dirty work carried out at the expense of the Bolsheviks [that is to say, under the pretense of being Bolshevik partisans] were unmasked. This offended the local population and reflected negatively on our work."[51] Needless to say, the UPA often dressed in their old German uniforms as well.

According to the comprehensive 1990 study of Józef Turowski and Władysław Siemaszko, some 20,000 people perished throughout Wołyń just in July 1943. The count for July 11 and 12 alone was 12,000 victims.[52] The intensity of this campaign can be gauged by the fact that between July 11 and 19, 1943, the UPA attacked, for example, 103 places in Horochów County and 96 places in Włodzimierz County — two of the 11 counties in Wołyń.[53]

In the fall of 1943, this wholesale murder, this crime against humanity, this genocide, was exported to Eastern Galicia and later to the Lublin region. It is unknown just how many Poles were massacred by the OUN-B UPA/SKV/SB units — estimates range from 50,000 to 500,000. In 1993 Ryszard Torzecki provided the following estimates: Wołyń, 30,000-40,000; Eastern Galicia, 30,000-40,000; Polesie and Lublin area, 10,000-20,000.[54] In 1998, speaking only of Wołyń, Władysław Siemaszko and his daughter Ewa Siemaszko concluded on the basis of their long years of study that: "The number of documented murders of Poles in Wołyń between 1939 and 1945 is at least 34,700 persons, or 11 percent of the Polish population living in Wołyń in 1942. The murders occurred in at least 1,642 places, mainly in the villages, out of a total of 3,260 places inhabited by Poles. These figures may be revised upward as a result of further investigation. The true losses were significantly higher and could have exceeded 50,000 to 60,000 Poles [just in Wołyń]."[55]

Prosecutor Stanisław Kaniewski, vice-director of the Main Commission for the Investigation of Crimes Against the Polish Nation, issued a bulletin in 1997 in which he stated:

> On the basis of factual information considered thus far in its ongoing investigation, the Main Commission concludes that:
> In the winter of 1942-43, a veritable explosion of Ukrainian nationalism on a scale hitherto unheard of occurred in conjunction with the emergence of the Ukrainian Insurgent Army (UPA), the military arm of the Organization of Ukrainian Nationalists (OUN). This commenced a far-reaching action aimed at the destruction of everything that was Polish. The purpose of that action was to prepare for the takeover of the governance of these territories in the event of a Wehrmacht withdrawal. At the beginning, these sporadic murders were motivated by revenge. They were carried out against the administrators of estates and the forestry and highway service personnel. Gradually, they began to spread out and embraced the Polish people in general, mainly those living in the villages (colonies and settlements). The perpetrators of these bestial actions were the units of the Ukrainian police in the service of the Germans (Schutzmannschaft), the Melnykowcy [Ukr., Melnykivtsi; OUN members of the Melnyk faction], deserters, and ordinary bandits. With time, the murders and attacks grew in intensity and assumed the character of organized terror. In addition to the mounting attacks and the demands for Polish people to leave the territory, massive murders were committed when UPA units were involved. In time, this rebellion embraced all of Wołyń, Małopolska Wschodnia, and even the Lublin and Rzeszów regions. In the panic that followed, some 500,000 people fled from Wołyń and Małopolska Wschodnia in 1943-44. According to as yet incomplete data, murders transpired in 1,750 different locations, mostly in Wołyń. (There, about 40,000 to 70,000 persons were killed).[56]

Kaniewski categorizes these events as a crime against humanity. "Some historians claim," he writes, "that there was a battle and even a war going on between the Poles and Ukrainians at the time. That is not true. It was unequivocally an extermination or, in other words, almost a total murder of Poles in the former eastern territories of Poland and a partial murder of Poles in the southeastern territories which today belong to Poland."[57] After providing some existing estimates (ranging from 90,000 to 500,000) of the number of those killed, he continues:

The Main Commission agrees that the figure of 100,000 approximates the truth but does not wish to "dot the i" at this time.... It accepts 1,750 as the number of locations in which Ukrainian crimes had been committed, but the list may grow. Thus, on the basis of information compiled by the Association of the 27th Wołynian Division of the Home Army, the incomplete register of places in Wołyń where such crimes occurred includes about 1,000 locations; in the Lublin, Rzeszów and Zamość areas — 516; in the provinces of Lwów, Stanisławów, and Tarnopol — 250 locations where murders of Poles by Ukrainians had taken place. Without doubt, further investigation will most certainly increase the number of such places to 2,000."[58]

The Ukrainian-Nationalist ethnic-cleansing campaign in southeastern Poland was neither a function of the Polish government's interwar policies nor the territorial claims of the Poles. Although there were other minorities (Belorussians, Lithuanians) in Eastern Poland with territorial claims and interwar recriminations against Poland, and although individuals and organizations within these minorities collaborated with the Nazis, there was no ethnic cleansing in the Polish provinces inhabited by these minorities. Ethnic cleansing of Russians did not take place in German-occupied Soviet Ukraine either, where a greater reason existed (millions of Ukrainians perished there due to Soviet interwar policies). There was no ethnic cleansing of Poles or Czechs in the disputed Cieszyn region, nor was there ethnic cleansing in the Lemko area. Another factor, therefore, must have been at work in the case of the Ukrainian minority in southeastern Poland: the influence of the fascist ideology of the OUN. These large-scale atrocities occurred only in those areas under OUN-UPA control or influence and nowhere else. It is the same logic we use in regard to the Nazis and the extermination of the Jews.

The chief perpetrators of the genocide under discussion in southeastern Poland, therefore, were not the Ukrainian people as such within these territories, but the Ukrainian Nationalists and their collaborators. Members of the SS-Galizien, an OUN-M outfit, also committed atrocities against Polish civilians.[59] Although desiring independence and (according to both Polish and Ukrainian historians) generally supporting the Ukrainian-Nationalist movement, it can only be assumed that many ordinary Ukrainians in "Western Ukraine" neither participated in nor approved of these "revolutionary methods." Many, including protesting Ukrainian clergymen, were themselves victims of that fascist ideology. Thousands of Ukrainians, accused of "treason" by the OUN, were murdered by the SB.

Acts of "treason" included previous conversion to Latin-rite Roman Catholicism, being married to a Pole, refusal to join the OUN-UPA, desertion, refusal to carry out orders, refusal to participate in the murder of Poles, speaking out against the OUN-UPA, forewarning Poles of impending UPA attacks, and rendering assistance to Poles and Jews. The slogan ran: "All those who in Ukraine today are not with us, are not with our Leader — these are against us, these are our enemies."[60] Murders of Ukrainian "traitors" began in southeastern Poland during the interwar years; they continued until well after the Second World War. Relying on archival and other sources, Wiktor Poliszczuk sets the number of Ukrainians — mostly civilians — killed by the Ukrainian Nationalists at 36,000.[61] That being the case, it is extremely difficult to argue that the UPA was an "army of (Ukrainian) liberation."

One of these "traitors" was a young Ukrainian girl who committed the "crime" of exchanging a few words with a soldier of the Red Army. The Ukrainian Nationalists tied her feet to two saplings, bent to the ground for the occasion, and let her go — thus tearing the poor girl in half. The soldier she spoke to may very well have been Ukrainian.[62]

Another victim was Mykola, a Ukrainian who escaped from a Soviet prison in Żytomierz in 1944. He was suspected of collaboration and hung over a fire by the SB during an interrogation.⁶³

Wiktor Poliszczuk's paternal uncle was shot through the mouth because he dared to speak ill of the UPA. Poliszczuk's in-laws (father, Czech; mother, Polish) were warned by a young Ukrainian of an imminent UPA attack. For this "act of treason," the Ukrainian was hung in the village square with a sign on his chest that read: "This will happen to all traitors." No one was allowed to cut him down for several days.⁶⁴

In Zamlicze, Wołyń, the SB killed 16 Ukrainian families in the course of a single night.⁶⁵

The Ukrainian village of Netreba in Wołyń consisting of some 60 households was destroyed by the UPA in 1943 because many of its residents had converted to Roman Catholicism in 1937-38. Some of the residents were murdered and the rest fled into forests with the Poles from the surrounding villages.⁶⁶

On August 28, 1943, 12 Ukrainian youths were executed in Szepel, Wołyń, because they refused to join the UPA.⁶⁷ Mykhailo Senkiv, a Ukrainian now living in Florida, recalls another such incident: "My mind has retained a picture of the recruitment of 'volunteers' into the ranks of the UPA. At night, in the place of my birth, going from house to house, they gathered a hundred middle-aged and younger men. They led them all to a forest, stood them in ranks, and asked, 'Who wants to go back home?' Fifteen poor unfortunates raised their hands. They made them dig ditches, shot them, and buried them there. Among those killed were two of my cousins."⁶⁸

For desertion, reads one "Revolutionary Court" order, "the penalty is beheading in front of the unit."⁶⁹ Deserters were also shot.⁷⁰ Wiktor Poliszczuk tells of a woman of Belorussian-Lithuanian descent who "witnessed how one Ukrainian, who deserted from the UPA 'because he could not bring himself to commit murder,' was apprehended by the SB, tormented beyond belief (his hands and feet were broken, his tongue cut out, his ears and nose cut off) and then killed. That Ukrainian was 18 years of age."⁷¹

Generally speaking, torture preceded death. The idea was not only to eliminate deserters and "traitors" but also to set an example for all others. Mandrivnyk's order of November 9, 1944, addressed to Provid and SKV leaders, specifically mandates that "various agitators-propagandists of hostile ideas, when they act openly, should be arrested on the spot and publicly liquidated after being subjected to torture."⁷²

In 1990-91 the Rivne (formerly: Równe) archive published an incomplete register of Ukrainians murdered by the OUN-UPA in Wołyń. These documents contain the names, ages, and places of residence of 9,018 Ukrainian victims.⁷³ These documents also provide an estimate of the number of ethnic Poles murdered by the Ukrainian Nationalists in Wołyń: 50,000.

Wołyń was only the beginning. Vasyl and Anna Genek, good Ukrainian people who often helped the Poles, lived in Berezów Niżny, in the county of Kołomyja, the province of Stanisławów. They raised a fine son by the name of Antek, a Banderowiec (Ukr., Banderivets; member of the OUN-B) by force but one who helped the Polish people and ended up joining the Russian army. That final "act of treason" was a death warrant for his Ukrainian parents. They were executed in the "revolutionary manner." Helena Piotrowiak, whose Polish family was saved on several occasions by Vasyl and Anna, as well as by their son Antek, told the story:

> Sometime after their house was burnt, I saw two bodies hanging from a weeping willow. I ran over to see who they were because I thought that maybe the Ukrainians killed

my mother and my sister. There I saw Vasyl and Anna suspended from a single nail under a weeping willow tree. It was a very large nail, this thick [Helena showed me her little finger] and about this long [she measured off a distance of about 30 centimeters with her hands]. Vasyl was dangling from that nail, his feet barely touching the ground. Dried blood was caked on his face and his long matted whiskers were also drenched with blood. On his chest hung a sign: "*Za zradu batkivshchyny* [For betraying the fatherland]."[74]

In Uście Zielone, a small town in the county of Buczacz in the province of Tarnopol, a certain Slavko Hulub was hung and perforated with bayonets by the UPA for refusing to participate in the killing of Poles. On his chest was placed a sign that read: "*Khto ne z namy, toi proty nas*" (Who is not for us is against us).[75] In that same province, 55 Ukrainians, including converts to Roman Catholicism, were murdered by the Banderowcy (Ukr., Banderivtsi; members of the OUN-B) in the village of Potoczyska on October 10, 1944.[76] Many similar examples could be cited from that province as well as from the provinces of Lwów and Stanisławów.

In his field report of November 27, 1943, the leader of the "Ozero" region lamented: "The SB is working quite hard in dealing with informants, communists, robbers, and those who are harmful to our organizational work — and there are as many of them here as mushrooms after a rain. It cannot keep up with their liquidation."[77] Indeed, the "black lists" kept by the SB must have been very long.[78] Cheremshyna's order of May 29, 1944, had made it very difficult, even in those days, to count the victims of the SB: "The entire enterprise and the methods of the SB should be conducted in a conspiratorial, secretive way. It is forbidden to leave behind the liquidated corpses or other traces of the work."[79]

For these and other such reasons, Maksym Skorupskyi noted, "In general, the SB and its activity constituted the blackest page of history in those years ... that police was the law and the court. The Security Service was organized on the German model. The majority of the leaders of the SB were the graduates of the German police school in Zakopane from the years 1939-40. They were mostly Galicians."[80]

Mychailo Podvorniak, a Ukrainian Protestant minister from Wołyń, recalled that the Banderowcy "annihilated our people no less than did the occupants. During the day they sat in the forests, at night they came to the villages to ply their black trade.... SB — our people feared these two letters no less than they feared the NKVD or the Gestapo.... SB members, often dressed as Bolshevik partisans, would find an escaped prisoner of war in a village and would force him to go with them.... They took him to the forest and there they killed him.... It came to pass that our people rejoiced when, during an action, the Germans would decimate the partisans [i.e., Banderowcy]."[81]

These, then, were the conditions under which the Ukrainian rescuers operated, conditions which made their extraordinary acts of heroism all the more remarkable.

That the Germans neither objected to nor tried to prevent the OUN-UPA ethnic-cleansing campaign aimed predominantly at the Poles should surprise no one. For example, the German garrison consisting of about 1,000 Wehrmacht soldiers stationed in Janowa Dolina did absolutely nothing to prevent the UPA attack of April 23, 1943, that claimed the lives of about 600 Poles. The Germans simply stayed in their barracks. In this case, it is highly improbable that the UPA would have dared to attack Janowa Dolina without some prearranged understanding with the German command. At times the Germans supplied the Ukrainian Nationalists with arms and ammunition. At times they also supplied the Poles with the same. That, in fact, was a part of their "divide and conquer" strategy in the East. "I would like," said Reichskommissar Erich Koch in 1943 during one of his sessions with his underlings in Równe, "that when a Pole encounters a Ukrainian he would kill him, and vice-versa. And if, in addition to this, they also kill a Jew, that would be just what I need."[82]

Every time a village burned or a civil-defense center was attacked by the UPA, the partisans, and later the Polish Home Army, would be inevitably diverted from their prime anti-Nazi objectives to render assistance. The uneasy anti-Nazi alliance that characterized all the partisan groups in the East never embraced the UPA. They were a force unto themselves and much of their effort was directed to the slaughter of innocent civilian men, women and children both Polish and Jewish, Gypsy and Czech, Russian and, as we have seen, even Ukrainian.

Among the probable reasons for the extent and the barbarity of this slaughter in Wołyń and Eastern Galicia and for the relative absence of defensive strategies, the following are noteworthy:

- The 1940-41 massive deportations to the Gulag by the Soviets. (Of all people deported, ethnic Poles constituted an absolute majority.)
- The liquidation of the Polish intelligentsia and officers by the Soviets.
- The massive deportations of able-bodied civilians (Poles and Ukrainians) to Germany for forced labor after June 22, 1941. The Ukrainian Nationalists, on the other hand, were either in German uniforms or in the ranks of the UPA.
- The liquidation of the Polish intelligentsia by the Nazis.
- The continual recruitment of men into the armed forces on all fronts and into anti-Nazi partisan groups.

- The complete breakdown of previous governance and criminal-justice structures in towns and villages.
- The "crime" of bearing arms, punishable by death (while the Ukrainian Nationalists were legally armed).
- The gullibility of the Polish peasants, who, knowing themselves to be innocent, could not believe that they would be killed without reason. (This is a common refrain in many survivors' stories.)
- The Ukrainian-Nationalist propaganda, which even while leading civilians to their death, assured them that they had "nothing to fear" and that "nothing would happen" to them if they cooperated (another common refrain).
- The ability of the Nationalists to mobilize the local Ukrainians into SKV units for the task of ethnic cleansing. This was done through various manipulative techniques (e.g., appeals to patriotism, hatred, or greed), terror tactics, threat of execution, and outright murder.
- And finally, the already stated fact that the gullible, defenseless, and inexperienced civilians were confronted by German-trained and German-equipped Ukrainian military and paramilitary personnel. In addition to the *pokhidni hrupy* who arrived in Wołyń in July of 1941, some members of the Nachtigall and Roland battalions joined the UPA upon the expiration of their "service" contract on October 31, 1942. Among these was Roman Shukhevych, the organizer of the Nachtigall, the chief of the Ukrainian auxiliary police, and later the head of the OUN-B and the commander-in-chief of the UPA. It was no coincidence that the first murders in Wołyń began around this time as well. After mid-March 1943, some 5,000 members of the infamous Ukrainian auxiliary police who, under German command, had participated in the execution

of the Jewish population, joined the UPA. Likewise, the first *massive* murders of Poles in Wołyń began in that same month and year. "We have finished with the Jews," said the Ukrainian Nationalists, "now it's the Poles' turn."[83] In July 1944, after their defeat at Brody, some of the soldiers from the SS-Galizien division joined up as well.

Some plausible reasons why this ethnic cleansing of Poles began in Wołyń instead of Eastern Galicia, the cradle of Ukrainian nationalism, are as follows:

- The marshy, forested terrain of Wołyń was especially suitable for the guerrilla tactics of the UPA. Also of great significance (in 1938) were the 416,000 horses in Wołyń.
- There were fewer Poles in Wołyń, and their scattered villages were difficult to defend.
- In Eastern Galicia, the Polish underground was stronger and much better organized.
- Wołyń was a relatively backward province and housed a large percentage of uneducated Ukrainians who could be easily manipulated.
- The OUN could count on the support of the Orthodox Church because of the wrongs done to it in the interwar period, especially in the Chełm region of Lublin Province, where a number of old and mostly abandoned churches and chapels were destroyed in 1938-39.
- Taras "Bulba"-Borovets's *Poliska Sich* (Polesian Stronghold) had formidable forces in the north of Wołyń, forces the OUN-B wanted to incorporate and control — and did so by the fall of 1943. In fact, the name "UPA" itself was stolen from Borovets. At this time, an internal struggle for power characterized the OUN. Borovets leaned toward the OUN-M.
- For symbolic reasons, the Ukrainian Nationalists wanted to launch the revolution, whose aim was to create an independent Ukraine, on Ukrainian soil, that is, in Reichskommissariat Ukraine, which included Wołyń, rather than in the Generalgouvernement of Poland, which included Eastern Galicia.
- Soviet partisans were present in Wołyń, enabling the UPA to represent itself as an antipartisan force and thereby win German approval and support.
- Expecting a scorched earth in the aftermath of its actions, the OUN opted to destroy "Orthodox" Wołyń rather than its own homeland.
- The Ukrainian Nationalists did not want to jeopardize the relatively favorable treatment that they and the Ukrainian population received (achieved, worked out) in Eastern Galicia under Nazi Governor General Hans Frank. Their compatriots in Wołyń and Soviet Ukraine did not have it nearly so good under Erich Koch and therefore were more likely to join a partisan force.
- And finally, and most important, Eastern Galicia was the home of the organizational and propaganda departments of the OUN. A revolt there may very well have destroyed the organization itself. This area, after all, with its rich petroleum deposits, was under the special protection of Governor General Hans Frank. As the corridor to the east and Rumania, it was thought that any disruptive uprising in this area would have been brutally suppressed by the Nazi régime.

It was not until the summer of 1943 — when the Poles in Wołyń, in violation of direct government-in-exile orders, began to enter the German police (vacated by the Ukrainians) for self-defense and retaliation — that the civilians received some measure of paramilitary protection. Some Poles also signed up for the Soviet partisans for similar reasons. As one person whose account appears herein put it after learning that his mother and sister were murdered by the UPA, "I joined the partisans. I was not particular about which ones I chose as long as I was given weapons. Later, I joined the Polish army."

Aside from the AK Wołyń (the 27th Infantry Division of the Polish Home Army officially named in April 1944, but in formation since January 1944), the Polish underground lent some assistance, as did the Hungarian forces stationed in Eastern Poland (including Wołyń), the Soviet partisans,[84] and the Soviet-organized *istrebitelnyye* (destruction) battalions, formed after the Soviet liberation, which consisted both of Poles and Ukrainians under Soviet command — about 25 men to a village. There were even instances where Jews joined in the defense of Polish villages against UPA attacks.[85]

Regarding the question of retaliation — morality aside — it could be argued, granted that when the ethnic cleansing began, a decisive, all-out, retaliatory *and* preemptive strike on Ukrainian villages, followed by the slaughter of innocent Ukrainian women and children, by the Polish partisans would have dampened the desire on the part of the Ukrainian Nationalists to "cleanse the territory of Poles" and, moreover, would have reduced the overall number of victims. But would it have? Chances are the very opposite would have happened, and few on either side would have emerged unscathed from that universal bloodbath.

Neither the Polish government-in-exile, which was not always well informed as to what was going on in the field, nor the local AK commanders who were, followed this course of action. How different were their orders from those of the OUN Central Provid and its UPA commanders! Kazimierz Damian Bąbiński ("Luboń"), commander of the Union for Armed Struggle-Home Army, Wołyń (ZWZ-AK, "Hreczka"), for example, in his April 22, 1943, order to AK partisan units stated: "I forbid the use of the methods utilized by the Ukrainian butchers. We will not burn Ukrainian homesteads nor kill Ukrainian women and children in retaliation. The self-defense network must protect itself from the aggressors or attack the aggressors but leave the peaceful population and their possessions alone." On February 16, 1944, he reiterated his position: "Most categorically do I repeat the former injunctions and orders ... to the leaders of regiments and groups — that they refrain, both during and after the war, from doing harm to Ukrainian women and children. I will hold accountable, with all due severity, those leaders and soldiers who perpetrate such unworthy deeds."[86]

Although AK leaders forbade actions against Ukrainians on the basis of "collective responsibility," normal retaliation was allowed (i.e., measures against individuals and even villages which offered assistance to the UPA or served as UPA bases). On August 10, 1943, Władysław Filipkowski ("Janka"), Commandant of Districts, issued an order to the effect that all acts of retaliation against those who attacked Poles would be contingent on his approval. A similar order was issued by the commandant of the Lwów District, T. Tabaczyński ("Biegun"), as well as by the AK commanders in the Lublin area.[87]

Be that as it may, in the heat of the battle things did not always proceed in accordance with the best-intentioned orders issued by commanders. War, as we know only too well, follows its own inner logic. As could be expected, there were cases of vengeful retaliation against the innocent, and UPA POWs were not always treated with civility. Andrzej Żupański, for example, tells us that when his unit crossed the Bug River on March 9, 1944, and two days later attacked the UPA stronghold in the village of Korytnica in Włodzimierz County:

The Warsaw soldiers were surprised by the ferocity with which the soldiers from Wołyń engaged in the battle and the ruthlessness with which they treated the UPA members who were surrounded and taken prisoner. Our opposition to this and our demands that the prisoners be treated in a civilized manner were met with rebuttals. "Don't butt in. You didn't see your family burned in a barn," one of them said to us. Another said, "You did not see people being sawed in half while still alive." That being the case, our attempts at intervention could avail nothing.

I received my next lesson during a march into the interior of Wołyń, when our scouts caught two Ukrainians. One was about 20, the other, most probably the father, about 40. When the scouts ordered them to take off their boots, I knew what fate awaited them. In answer to my protest, the scout leader said to me, "You did not see your family murdered with knives." I left the place of execution as quickly as I could, but I also observed, meanwhile, that the Ukrainians were taking off their boots without any emotion. They were not afraid, there was no pleading for mercy or anything of the sort — as if they knew that what awaited them was inevitable.[88]

As the Ukrainian-Nationalist terror intensified, several patterns of self-preservation emerged among the Polish civilian population of southeastern Poland. Those living in the western sector fled beyond the Bug River. Some of those living along the 1921 Polish-Soviet border sought refuge in the predominantly Ukrainian villages of eastern Ukraine, where they were generally well received.[89] Those living in the interior were driven into the surrounding swamps and forests, where hunger, cold, and typhus awaited them. Some made their way to the large towns occupied by German garrisons — from which they were promptly dispatched to the slave-labor camps of Nazi Germany. Others became homeless and sought the protection of the Polish partisans in the civilian camps set up for fleeing refugees. Those who wished to remain on or near their own farmsteads joined one of the civil-defense centers organized in 1943 to protect the Polish people and their villages. And finally, some of them turned to their Ukrainian friends and neighbors for help, but just as often it was the Ukrainians who came to them with an offer of assistance.

This work is about those who received help, and those who gave it: the Polish victims in Wołyń, and the Ukrainians who helped them survive. Appendix B serves as grateful acknowledgment that there were also such Ukrainian heroes in the three provinces of Eastern Galicia, namely, Lwów, Stanisławów, and Tarnopol.[90]

1
Dubno County

The county of Dubno was divided into 12 village communes (*gminy*): Boremel, Demidówka, Dubno (county seat), Jarosławicze, Kniahinin, Malin, Młynów, Radziwiłłów, Sudobicze, Tesłuchów, Warkowicze, and Werba.[1]

Table 4
Population of Dubno County by Mother Tongue

Ukrainian	157,639
Ruthenian	534
Polish	33,987
Jewish	17,430
German	2,789
Czech	11,148
Russian	2,751
Belorussian	107
Lithuanian	8
Other	96
Unreported	220
Total	226,709

Table 5
Population of Dubno County by Religious Affiliation

Orthodox	172,674
Roman Catholic	27,638
Uniate	838
Protestant/Evangelical	3,545
Other Christian	3,664
Jewish	18,227
Other Non-Christian	12
Not Specified or Non-Religious	28
Unreported	83
Total	226,709

Dubno, together with the counties of Krzemieniec, Równe, and Zdołbunów, fell under the jurisdiction of the UPA "Eneia" region. The leadership corps of this region came from the German trained and equipped Ukrainian auxiliary police, ordered by the OUN-B Provid to desert their posts in mid-March 1943. The rank-and-file were recruited earlier from the local population. Three UPA battalions operated in the "Eneia" region, each consisting of three companies. They were: "Kruk" battalion, stationed mainly in Dubno County, under Ivan Klymushyn; "Maks" battalion under Maksym Skorupynskyi; and "Negus" battalion. In late fall, the Pidhaietska company (from Podhajce near Lwów) was stationed here as well.

In addition to these front-line military formations, several police companies—chiefly under the OUN-B SB—also operated in the region. There was even a prisoner-of-war camp headed by Commandant "Vovk."

The majority of the UPA attacks on civilians in Dubno County took place between March and August 1943.

People

KORCHAK from Załawie
From the account of Kazimierz Wąsek from Załawie, as transcribed by Henryk Komański:

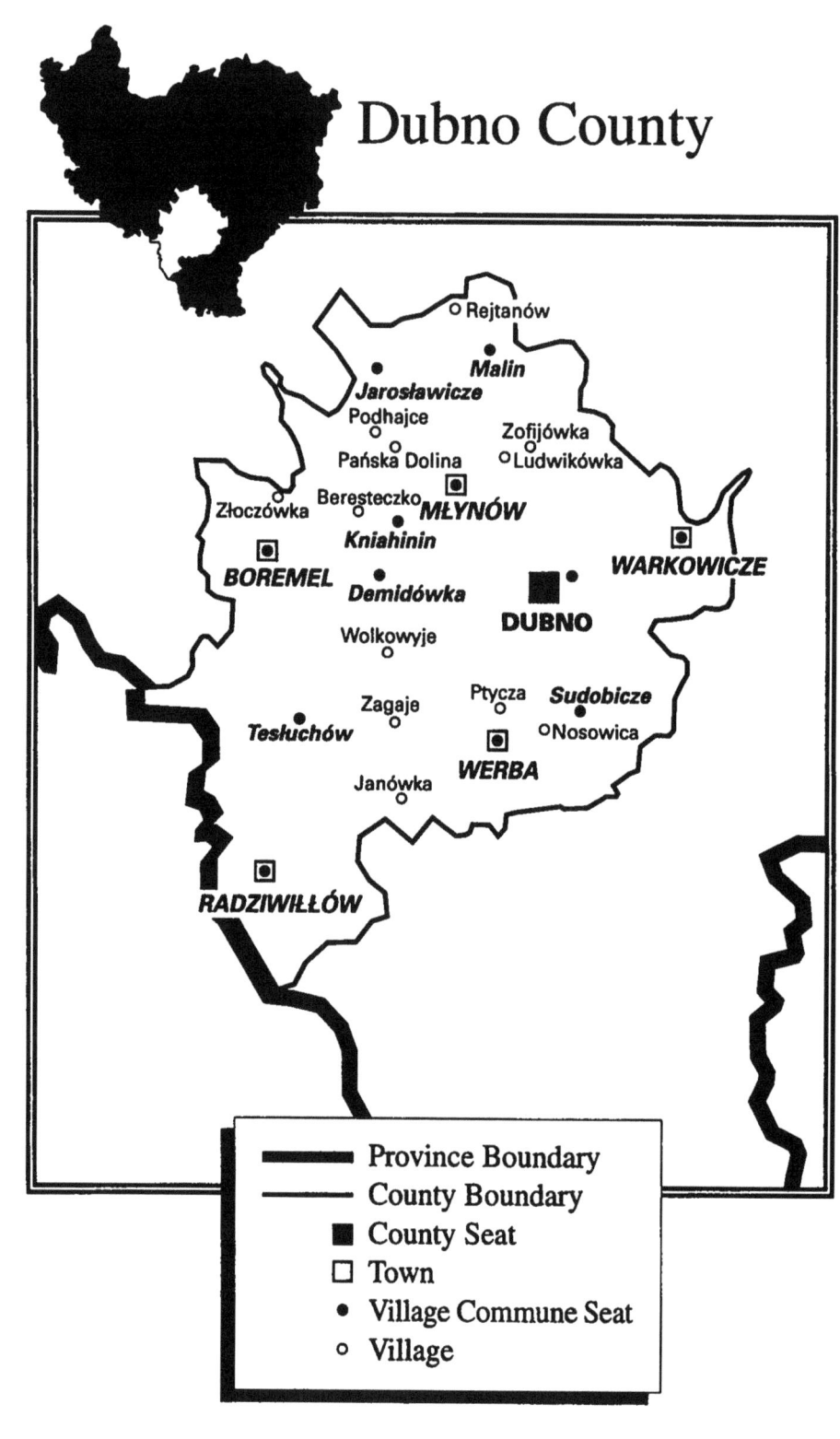

"The growing danger from the UPA bands forced the Poles of Załawie to flee to Łuck. My family was among them.

"On May 5, 1943, my father and my brother Bolesław left Łuck by wagon in order to reclaim some of the provisions which we had left behind in our home in Załawie. They were halted on the road near the village by armed men who claimed to be Soviet partisans, but in reality they were Banderowcy. They ordered my father to turn his wagon around and to drive it into the woods. There, they shot my brother and seriously wounded my father. My father lost consciousness and the murderers, thinking that he was dead, left him there. After regaining consciousness, my father crawled to the village. The Ukrainians in the village were afraid to help him because they feared reprisals from the UPA. Finally, our third neighbor, Korchak, took pity on him and gave him a night's lodging. The following day, he lent his horses and wagon to my brother Jan who brought my father to the hospital in Łuck. As a result of his injuries, my father became an invalid: he lost the use of his left hand and his jaw is partially paralyzed.

"That same day, the returning Stankiewicz family was also halted near our village. The entire family, consisting of five persons, was murdered and their bodies were flung into the Styr River. The seventh victim of the day was a local farmer named Paduch."[2]

Places

JAROSŁAWICZE
From the account of Mieczysław Jankowski from Jarosławicze:

"On May 22 [1943], beginning in the morning hours, a group of armed UPA bandits conducted a bloody massacre of the Poles living in Jarosławicze. They began with the farmstead of my uncle, Mikołaj Jankowski.... [A description of the murders follows.]

"The UPA butchers threw the bodies of my aunt, her daughter Zofia (20 years of age), and her 18-year-old son Antoni) into a well.

"After the attack on my uncle's family the bandits went to the Feliks Żukowski farmstead, located near the village ... all three [the parents and their 16-year-old daughter, Anna] were axed to death....

"Next, the bandits went to the Kwiatkowski farmstead, located in the center of the village. That family consisted of an elderly couple, their son (an invalid), and their daughter with her husband and four-year-old child....

[The family was transported to a prepared pit on the outskirts of the village at the edge of a forest. The invalid, a cripple, was tied to the wagon and made to run. When his strength gave out he fell and was dragged to the place of execution.]

"They quickly dispatched this family with axes and threw their bodies into a pit.

"Then they went to the Jachemek family consisting of five people. This family lived by the mill in the center of the village. When the bandits reached the small residence standing by the mill near the river, they found only Stasia, a beautiful and personable 18 year old. Like wild animals they threw themselves on her and took turns raping her. Afterwards, they took her out into the yard, tied her feet to a beam and lowered her head first into a well...."

[Sometime later they captured Stasia's 21-year-old brother, Stefan Jachemek, as well as his friend, Kazimierz Żukowski. They bound them and tried to force them into the cog-wheel of the mill. Failing in this, they killed them with an ax. They placed all of the bodies, including Stasia's, on a wagon and proceeded to the previously mentioned pit. On their way they forced an older couple, Suk, out of their home and killed them as well. After dumping the bodies, the murderers crossed the river and came to the Przewłocki residence.]

"The following members of the Przewłocki family were home at the time: the mother (70), her daughter Jadwiga (30), and her son with his wife and daughter Lucia (18). Dobrowolski, who lived with his wife and two children nearby, was there as well. He served as an official in the Jarosłwicze commune for a few years. They bound all six of them and took them to the woods for execution. When they got there, they engaged in a horrible orgy with Jadwiga and Lucia, raping them in front of the rest. Dobrowolski took advantage of this moment of debauchery and bolted through the trees to his house, which was about two kilometers away. When he ran out onto a field road, he met an old Ukrainian who, with tears in his eyes, unfastened the ropes on his hands and giving him a blessing said, 'Flee brother as far as your eyes can see because terrible things are happening around here.' Dobrowolski ran home, took his wife and two children, as well as Mrs. Komińska and her two children who lived there, and the seven of them ran to the main road called Dubieńska, about three kilometers away. There, they were picked up by the Germans....

"And so, May 22, 1943, in a tragic and cruel way, entered the historical annals of the Polish families who had lived in Jarosławicze. Three persons died in the Jankowski family, six in the Żukowski family [only four are recorded above], six in the Kwiatkowski family, two in the Jachemek family, two in the Suk family, and five in the Przewłocki family. These 24 persons were brutally murdered in broad daylight in the name of the UPA struggle for *samostiina Ukraina* [independent Ukraine].

"I have attempted many times to record this genocide, but believe me, I could not do it. It was beyond my strength. Now that I have reached an advanced age, I am determined to leave some trace of the bloody deeds that took place in my own village. That nightmare, despite the passing of over half a century, still haunts me in my sleep. Although I try not to think about this great tragedy, my thoughts return to it with ever greater intensity. They have been imbedded deeply within my memory. I sympathize with all those from Wołyń who must continue to live with this terrible burden. Whoever did not live through this will not understand, because such things are truly difficult to understand, and more difficult still to live through."[3]

NOWA NOSOWICA
From the account of Zbigniew Wojcieszak (b. 1925) from Młynów, Boremel, and other locations:

On Holy Saturday, 1943, the Spałek family (parents and three sons) was warned by a Ukrainian of an impending UPA attack. "Do not sleep in your home tonight," he said, "because they are going to kill Poles." Sixty people were killed in Nowa Nosowica that April.[4]

ZŁOCZÓWKA
From the account of Danuta Chiniewicz from Złoczówka:

In April-May, 1943, the Polish residents of Złoczówka were warned by local Ukrainians of a possible UPA attack. The attack came on the night of May 14. Twelve Poles were killed, including Franciszek Kantor and his wife, aged 70 and 69, respectively. Franciszek was thrown into his burning house after being severely wounded; his ailing wife, Weronika, burned to death in her own bed. The village was attacked again on July 12, and 38 people were killed.[5]

2
Horochów County

The county of Horochów was divided into seven village communes: Beresteczko, Brany, Chorów, Kisielin, Podberezie, Skobełka, and Świniuchy. The town of Horochów, located in the Brany commune, was the county seat.

Table 6
Population of Horochów County by Mother Tongue

Ukrainian	83,119
Ruthenian	1,105
Polish	21,100
Jewish	9,993
German	4,977
Czech	1,222
Russian	403
Belorussian	15
Lithuanian	13
Other	8
Unreported	90
Total	122,045

Table 7
Population of Horochów County by Religious Affiliation

Orthodox	85,273
Roman Catholic	17,675
Uniate	2,060
Protestant/Evangelical	5,199
Other Christian	1,672
Jewish	10,112
Other Non-Christian	1
Not Specified or Non-Religious	20
Unreported	33
Total	122,045

Horochów County, together with the counties of Luboml, Łuck, Kowel, Włodzimierz, and Kamień Koszyrski (part of Polesie before the war but tacked on to the Reichskommissariat Ukraine), belonged to the UPA "Turiv" region. The head of this region, Iurii Stelmashchuk ("Rudyi," "Kaidash"), was a graduate of the German school for reconnaissance and diversion in Brandenburg.

The following UPA units were stationed in the "Turiv" region: Zavydivskyi battalion under "Slavko," replaced later by Oleksyi Brys ("Ostap"), divided into three companies, namely, those of "Moskalenko," "Iurko," and "Holub," who was replaced later by "Kniazhenko"; a munitions and provisions detachment consisting of 235 men stationed in the Sadów forests; and the "Mochul" company from the Svynarynskyi (Świnarzyn) battalion under Porfyrii Antoniuk ("Sosenko").

Between March 15 and July 11, 1943, Polish activists in the county as well as former military personnel capable of assuming positions of leadership were liquidated by the UPA. During this time, in June, numerous private and state properties were destroyed by fire, including schools, railway stations, bridges, and telephone lines. Various product contingents were requisitioned by the UPA, including medical supplies from apothecaries. All skilled laborers, irrespective of nationality, were rounded up to

work for the UPA. The Polish craftsmen were murdered sometime before July 11, 1943.

The "Peter and Paul action" (also called "Action on Peter and Paul") — the systematic, massive slaughter of non-Ukrainian civilians that began on this Orthodox holiday — took place between July 11, 1943, and July 1944. This action was preceded by the UPA's blocking of all evacuation routes in the area under attack. On July 11, 1943, Petro Vlasiuk, a company commander from the neighboring county of Kowel, attacked the church in Kisielin, "Iurko" attacked the church in Poryck as well as the village of Orzeszyn, and "Moskalenko" destroyed Liniów. On July 12 Vlasiuk destroyed the villages of Rudnia and Wólka Sadowska, "Moskalenko" destroyed ten Polish colonies in the Wólka Markowiecka-Kremasz-Krzemieniec area, and "Iurko" destroyed Zagaje. On July 15 Vlasiuk murdered the inhabitants of Woronczyn, and "Moskalenko" murdered the Polish inhabitants in the mixed villages near the Zawidów Forest. On July 16 "Iurko," with the help of the "Holub"/"Kniazhenko" company, attacked and destroyed the villages of Nowe Gniezno, Lulówka, Boroczyce, Kupowalce, and Szerokie. The latter company, together with SB and SKV forces, was responsible for the murders and wanton destruction of the Polish villages lying along the Horochów-Lwów border. The last two places that succumbed to their terror were the colony of Jasiniec (August 28) and the colony of Warszawska (September 15). Such was the nature of the UPA "Peter and Paul action," launched purposefully to "cleanse" the territory of "foreigners" and "occupants."

People

BAMBYLO, Petro, and his family, from Liniów. *See* Ivan Sheremeta (Chapter 7, Łuck County).[1]

CHORNYI, Iukhym, from Horochówka
From the account of Helena Włosowska (née Golisz, b. 1931) from Horochówka:

In July 1943, after spending a night in the home of a Ukrainian, Iukhym Chornyi, the Golisz family started back to their own house. When Edward, aged 11, ran out onto the road, he saw an armed Banderowiec. At the same time, a crippled Ukrainian woman who was in the yard motioned to the rest of the family to hide. They decided to return to Iukhym Chornyi's house, where they remained for a few hours before setting out again. Later, the UPA rounded up all the Poles they could find. They locked the men in a cellar and kept the women and children in the yard. That evening, the men were killed, and the women and children were taken to a house packed with straw. Helena recalls:

"Just as they were about to light it in order to burn us alive, a Ukrainian from Rogowicz — my mother's neighbor when she lived there — rescued us and took us to our home. He locked the doors and windows and told us to sit quietly. He then went in the direction of the building containing the women and children that was already on fire. To this day I cannot forget the cries, the shrieks, the laments, and the screams of those who were being burnt alive....

"After the fire had died down, a Ukrainian led us to the cellar of Kopryian, where there was a group of older people and children.... In the evening, we were all taken out of the cellar by the Banderowcy and told to kneel as they prepared to shoot us. And again we were saved by the same Ukrainian who rescued us the first time. He came riding on a horse, gave one of the bandits some papers, ordered us to be taken back into the house, and left....

"I must note that the Ukrainians terrified us until the very end. But there were also those with whom one could live, like my mother's neighbor from her younger days, who saved us several times, or the one who took us to the transport leaving for Poland."²

DATSIUK, Nykon, from Kisielin
From the account of Adela Preis (née Ziółkowska, b. 1926) from Kisielin:

At the request of Adela's mother, Nykon gave shelter to Adela's father, wounded in the UPA attack on Poles gathered for services in the church at Kisielin on July 11, 1943. During the attack, over 60 men, women, and children were killed.³

LUKASH from Rudnia
From the account of Leokadia Jakubowska (née Garczyńska) from Jesionówka Colony:

"I would also like to mention the story of my uncle's [Jan Garczyński's] daughter, Władysława, who was in Rudnia during the attack of July 12, 1943. My uncle gave a team of horses and a wagon to a Ukrainian [from Zaturce] who brought his wounded daughter back to Zaturce. This Ukrainian was a very good man. During the attack, two of my father's [Feliks Garczyński's] sisters were killed. One was named Jakubowska; the other, Zienkiewicz. They, together with 18 others, hid in a rather large shelter. The Banderowcy ordered them out and fired into the shelter. My two aunts were killed, but Władysława Garczyńska was only wounded and lay under the corpses pretending to be dead. In the evening she went to see Lukash, a Ukrainian who served in my Aunt Zienkiewicz's home for many years. Lukash hid her and cared for her until the aforementioned Ukrainian took her back to Zaturce."

During the attack on Rudnia, about 100 people were killed.⁴

PADLEVSKYI, Viktor, from Kisielin
From the account of Sławosz Dębski from Kisielin:

After the attack on the church in Kisielin, Sławosz recalls:

"Then I hear, yes, I hear distinctly that someone is calling my name.... If I do not answer, no one will find me and I will most certainly die. I cry out again, but the calling dies away. My breath is taken away by fear. Before me stands a Ukrainian acquaintance, Viktor Padlevskyi. 'This is the end,' I think to myself, 'and so much effort in vain.' I close my eyes. I open them after a while and see that Padlevskyi is crying; he is obviously crying. He is cursing his fellow-countrymen for what they had done to the people there by the church wall and to me, reduced as I was to a bleeding scrap of humanity.

"Then, at Anielka's [the narrator's fiancée] request, her father came with a wagon. They loaded me on and took me to the home of another Ukrainian, Parfeniuk.

"There I lay the entire next day. On Tuesday morning, both Ukrainians took me to the hospital in Łokacze."⁵

PARFENIUK from Kisielin
From the account of Teresa Siedlicka (née Świderska, b. 1929) from Zapust:

Parfeniuk warned Teresa and her parents, Szymon and Janina Świderski, all three of whom were being sheltered by another Ukrainian, Syrotiuk, after the UPA attack on their village of Zapust. Teresa states:

"On the last Sunday in September 1943, a Ukrainian by the name of Parfeniuk came to us from Kisielin and warned us that the [UPA] bands were already on their way to our village to murder the Poles. With tears in his eyes he said, 'Go to the forest belonging to Witwicki one at a time, in old clothes, without any baggage. Take a pitchfork or a scythe with you to give the impression that you are Ukrainians going to do some work in your field. God help you if you do not escape in time!'

"I did not manage to leave with my parents. When I came out of my hiding place the bandits were already in the village.... I heard wild shouts and curses bemoaning the fact that the Poles had escaped.... They came to the Syrotiuk residence, turned the stacks of hay upside down, stuck bayonets into them, and beat up the couple, accusing them of warning the Poles.... They searched the Syrotiuk residence several more times but found nothing.... They also beat the old man and his son Mykola, but they did not betray me."[6]

PAVLIUK, Iurko, and his family from Lulówka
From the account of Jolanta Dudkowska (née Sawicka, b. 1929) from Lulówka:

Iurko Pavliuk sheltered 21 Poles who came to his house begging for assistance during the UPA attack of July 16, 1943, on the village of Lulówka. The narrator of the following account, 14 years of age at the time, sustained seven puncture wounds in her chest, stomach, and hands during the attack. She writes:

"When I regained consciousness, I didn't know where I was. My whole body hurt, my hair was mangled, my dress was torn, and I was bleeding all over. I was very thirsty. I felt feverish. Although my head was spinning, I managed to get up. I began to walk, not knowing where to go. Along the road I saw human remains; I knew some of them personally. I approached some houses. Many of them were still on fire; some were already burnt.

"I went further and saw the property of Iurko Pavliuk, a Ukrainian. His family knew us. When I entered the house, I told them that I was a Markowska rather than Sawicka. I knew that this Ukrainian knew my Uncle Markowski very well. At that moment, Pavliuk's wife began lamenting and pleading with me to go on, not to remain with them. She said that they would also be killed for helping the Poles. She gave me some bread and some milk and cleaned and bandaged my wounds.

"Although these Ukrainians weren't pleased about it, I remained with them anyway. I simply did not have the strength to go any further. I then discovered that other Poles were being sheltered there as well, and that among them were my younger sisters: Alina, who was 12, and three-year-old Krystyna. In all, 21 Poles were there. We hid in the wheat. We slept among the raspberry bushes. We knew that if we were found here, we and the Pavliuks would perish."

These 21 Poles remained with that good Ukrainian family for a full three weeks.[7]

SHKUROPATKA from Niedźwiedzie Jamy
From the account of Teresa Siedlicka (née Świderska, b. 1929) from Zapust:

After being sheltered by a Ukrainian family (Syrotiuk), and after being warned of an imminent UPA attack by another Ukrainian (Parfeniuk), Teresa, a survivor of the attack on both the church in Kisielin and her village of Zapust, decided to make her way to Zaturce, where a German garrison was stationed. She was 14 years old at the time. She recalls:

"I left the Syrotiuk home on a rainy October night. I ran through the fields of our village and through the village of Żurawiec near the cross where the residents of that village, murdered on July 14, 1943, were buried. After that, I did not know the way. I knew that I had to travel south over fields and avoid villages. I also knew that Zaturce was a large village on a hill with brick buildings housing Germans. At dawn I found myself in an open field and did not know whether to proceed any further. I had to ask someone where I was and how to get to Zaturce. I was afraid to enter the nearby villages, so I sat down and began to cry.

"Suddenly, I saw a woman coming my way and I recognized her. It was Shkuropatka, a Ukrainian from Niedźwiedzie Jamy. I became all the more frightened because I knew that she did not take kindly to Poles. She also recognized me and asked me what I was doing there. I lied, saying that I was going to my village and got lost. I told her that I wanted to return to Zaturce but did not know the way. She then said, 'There are so many of them around these parts, how ever did you get here without being seen? Come with me, girl. Don't be afraid. I'll show you how to go so that you can save your life. They're all over the place.'

"She threw her own kerchief around my head, led me to her home, prepared me a bowl of borsch, and told me to eat in a hurry. I did not touch the soup. I stared at the doorway from beyond which came the songs and laughter of drunken Banderowcy.

"'Don't worry,' she said quietly, 'they will not come in here. Eat. I will lead you out shortly.'

"Seeing that I was very much afraid, she gave me a large scarf with flowers, such as Ukrainian women wear, led me outside into a field, and showed me the way to Zaturce. At the time, I could not believe that she would not betray me. Now, I know the truth."[8]

SYROTIUK family from Zapust
From the account of Teresa Siedlicka (née Świderska, b. 1929) from Zapust:

Syrotiuk gave shelter to his young neighbor, Teresa, and to her parents, Szymon and Janina Świderski, from July 11, 1943, (the day of the attack on the church in Kisielin) to October 23, 1943.[9]

TKACHUK family from Kupowalce
From the collective account of Danuta Goszczyńska from Szeroka and the residents of Kupowalce: Irena Łaszczewska (née Gilewicz), Leokadia Konopko (née Gilewicz), Filipina Sawicka (née Gilewicz), Wincentyna Rozalewicz, Eugeniusz Gilewicz, Halina Markowicz (née Gilewicz), and Roman Witkowski:

The Tkachuk and Tsipiukh families were among those Ukrainian families who either sheltered Poles or gave them assistance during the July 16-17, 1943, attack on the villages of Kupowalce, Szeroka, Nowe Gniezno, Boroczyce, and Lulówka. These attacks were organized by Ukrainians from other villages than those named herein but were carried out with the assistance of local members of the UPA.[10]

TSIPIUKH family from Kupowalce. See Tkachuk family.

VOITOVYCH family from Lulówka
From the account of Aleksandra Głowińska from Lulówka:

"I lived — together with my parents, my 12-year-old brother, my grandmother, and a 15-year-old boy-servant — in the village of Lulówka, the county of Horochów. Our household and that of our nearby neighbor were cut off from the village by a narrow wooded strip of land.

"July 16, 1943, was warm and sunny. Everyone on the farm was busy pursuing their usual daily routines. My father and the neighbors were processing grain in the barn. My mother was working in the garden and I, a seven-year-old girl, was with her. My grandmother was in the kitchen. Suddenly, our neighbor burst into our house and shouted, 'They're murdering!'

"Panic seized us and we all began to run around aimlessly. My mother ran into the house and began to pack a suitcase. With suitcase in hand, she ran out of the house into a stand of poppies and hid it there. I ran everywhere that she ran. Then all of us together — my parents, my brother, the servant, and I — ran toward the forest. From the forest we ran to a field of grain. Shots rang out; screams and moans were heard. We crawled through the field. Along the way we met my 12-year-old cousin, who was also fleeing, and he joined our company. We then encountered other people; among them, a hysterical woman with a severed ear. We went further and further.

"After a while the firing ceased, but the wailing and groaning of the wounded remained. We sat in the grain near the edge of the road. I think that we had intended to cross that road in order to reach the field on the other side because my father stuck his head out of the grain to look around. At that very moment, a patrol happened to be passing by.

"'Halt!' rang out a command.

"They asked my father if he was alone. He could not lie because we were sitting right behind him and it was impossible not to notice us. They told us to come out and to return to our house. There were six of us and two of them. My mother felt weak. Since she had a hard time walking, they pushed her along and abused her with shouts. When they saw us being led away, two more Banderowcy ran up from across the way.

"When we entered our house, we found it in shambles. In a doorway leading to another room stood a man with an arrogant demeanor. He was probably the ringleader since he was the most heavily armed of them all. My mother went up to him and began to plead with him not to kill us. He growled, 'Don't speak to me.'

"Mother began to cry and a shot rang out. Next thing I knew, I was lying on the floor. I lay there very still. I could hear how they paraded through the house, kicked at things with their boots, and spoke among themselves. I did not feel being hit or shot. I must have fainted because when I came to, I thought I had awakened from a deep sleep. I was very thirsty. Although feeling very weak, I got up and went outside. I did not pay any attention to anything. My only objective was to reach the watering trough and to lay down in it because I knew that water was there and I that would feel good. But there was no water in the trough, and I felt nauseous again. When I regained consciousness, I was inside the watering trough. Thirst hounded me. I crawled out and noticed a bucket of water near the well. I scooped the water up with my cupped hands and brought it to my mouth. It was tepid but I drank it anyway.

"I returned again to my house, lay down in the exact same spot on the floor where I had been previously struck down, and fell asleep immediately. When I awoke again, I felt better. I began to walk around to see where those who were killed lay. My father was draped across the bed, his face toward the sheets. His entire shirt was drenched with blood. My mother lay next to the table, my brother behind it, my cousin under the bed, and next to him lay the servant boy. My grandmother was killed in the yard. She did not flee with us; rather, she hid herself in a pile of dried twigs near the house. But I think that when she heard what was happening she must have come out, and that's when they killed her.

"Blood was everywhere, and I was also drenched with blood. My dress and hair stiffened with it. I had the urge to change my clothes. I chose my mother's blouse, the one that I liked very much. Since my left arm was shot through at the elbow and the short sleeve of my blouse had a cuff which was above my elbow, I knew that if I tried to remove my dress it would hurt. I therefore decided to cut off the sleeve. I took the scissors down from the sewing machine, sat down on our doorstep, and tried to cut the fabric. I was too weak, however, even to lift the scissors. Whenever I would raise them, my arm would swing down again. While attempting this task, I must have fallen asleep once more because I dreamed that all those who were killed got up and left the house. After a while, they came back in again and Mother, entering last, came over to me, laid her hand on my head and said, 'Sit here, Olesia, sit.'

"At that moment I looked around behind me and ascertained that everyone lay exactly where they had lain before. This at least was no dream because I remember precisely how the wound in my right shoulder hurt when I turned to look. I finally lost interest in that endeavor of trying to cut off my blouse and went out into the yard. I strained to hear what was happening at the neighbor's house. They had a large family, but no one was walking about the yard. Only the dogs howled. That's how I knew that no one was left alive over there either. Standing there, I suddenly felt that I was all alone in the whole world. I imagined that I would now somehow become reincarnated as a different person and that everything would be as it was before.

"I became hungry. I went into the kitchen. I poured some cherries from the basket into a bowl, covered them with sour milk, and began to eat a little. I went out into the yard again. I saw immediately that two men were approaching the house from the direction of the woods. I quickly ran back into the house and lay down in the same place where I had been before. As I lay there, I kept my eyes open and watched. They came over to the window, and one of them told me not to be afraid. I did not move an inch. They came in, looked around, and left.

"After a while one of them returned, came over to me, took me by the hand, and led me outside. The second man was standing in front of the house throwing up. They walked about the yard and searched here and there as if they were looking for something. They asked me if I knew whether my father had buried anything. Next, they began to dig a ditch in the flower bed. After they were finished, they led me behind a currant bush and told me to sit there. Then they went back inside the house. I was curious about the ditch that they had dug, so I went over to it. After a while, the two men brought out the victims, which were now wrapped, and lowered them into the grave. They hid me behind the currant bush because they thought that I was going to cry. But I did not cry. I simply stood there without any emotion.

"After they covered the grave, they took me by the hand and we went toward the woods. Along the way, I began to regurgitate the cherries. In the forest, one of the men remained with me while the other one walked away. He returned after a while and said that it was safe to go on.

"We now headed toward some house with a garden. A woman opened a window and I was quickly transported inside. There was a bowl of water in the middle of the kitchen. They cut the dress off me. They also cut off my hair; it was caked with dry blood and was brittle. They washed me and dressed my wounds—I had eight of them: my head was cracked in two places; the remaining wounds were on the right side of my rib cage and along my left arm. The bandits probably confused the left side of my body with my right and so missed my heart. After they bathed me and disinfected my wounds with iodine, they placed me on a straw mattress in the pantry.

"The master of the house took care of me for the most part: He changed my bandages, fed me, and taught me to pray in Ukrainian and to make the sign of the cross in the Ukrainian way. Since I was already familiar with the Ukrainian language due to the fact that Ukrainians used to visit my father, I soon forgot my Polish and began to speak in Ukrainian. I called my caretakers 'Daddy' and 'Mommy.' They had one 17-year-old daughter, Nastusia, and a son who was absent at the time. (My cousin maintains that he was in the UPA.)

"When I got better and began to go out, my guardians told their acquaintances that I was their niece. After some time, 'Daddy' brought home a 17- or 18-year-old girl that he had found in the woods. She could not walk. I believe that she was suffering from an inflammation of her joints. She used to lay in the barn and groan in pain. Whenever I brought her food or water I spoke to her in Ukrainian. She became very upset at this and wanted to know why I didn't speak to her in Polish. She was called Wacka, and she knew both me and my parents. But being just a child, I did not know her. She currently lives in Poznań.

"My Ukrainian 'Mommy' usually took me to the Orthodox church. As I recall, no one took a particular interest in me; it was 'Daddy' who chiefly took care of me. Their daughter Nastusia and I pastured cows together. I now know that my stay with the Voitovych family (for so they were called) was a public secret. Because of threats, they were finally forced to part with me. They put me into a wagon and covered me with hay. With 'Mommy' at the reins, we left the house.

"We arrived in the neighboring village of Burzany. A Polish family named Strutńyski lived there, and they knew my parents. This was probably all pre-arranged because two women stood in front of the house when we arrived. My Ukrainian 'Mommy' took me into her arms and without saying a word placed me into the arms of these two women. With tears in her eyes, she quickly got into the wagon and cracked the whip. (I can hear the clatter of the departing wagon even today.) I began to wail terribly and screamed, 'Mommy, don't leave me,' in Ukrainian. I cried for a very long time, and they could not console me for the world. The next day they took me to some village charlatan who performed some magic over me, said some prayers, poured out an egg, and threw pieces of coal into water. She then confirmed that I was terrified.

"After a short time, I left with them for Lublin Province. Once there, my aunt (my mother's sister) located me. She managed to escape from Lulówka with her six-year-old daughter. Her oldest daughter, 17-year-old Jolanta, suffering from wounds all over her body, sat six days in a field of grain. When she was completely famished and thin as a rail, she went to a Ukrainian family in the same locality where I had been, fell down in their yard and fainted. A Ukrainian took her under his protection and brought her to Horochów to her mother.

"Jolanta's 12-year-old sister, Alina, and her three-year-old sister, Krysia, sat in the field for two days. The older sister fed the younger one with seeds and water gathered from dew drops on leaves. Unable to take it anymore, she decided to go to a Ukrainian farmer. She walked right on the road not caring any more. She only forbade her younger sister from speaking to anyone at all for fear of revealing to them that she was Polish. Alina went to school with Ukrainians and spoke the language beautifully.

"As they were going along that road, a wagon with a few Banderowcy was passing by. They halted and asked her where she was going. She told them that she was on her way to her aunt's house. They also asked her younger sister, but Kyrsia kept quiet. One of them wanted to get off the wagon. He aimed his rifle at them shouting that they were Poles and threatening to shoot them. But another one told him to leave them alone, cracked the whip, and drove away. When the girls reached the first farmhouse, a Ukrainian woman first began to yell at them, but then gave them some water and bread anyway. She also showed them the road to Horochów, where the other refugees went. They arrived there safely and found their mother. Their brother was murdered along with my family since he was in our house at the time of the attack. Their father was killed in the field.

"In 1945 another aunt (my father's sister — their whole family returned from

Germany to where they had been deported) took me in because it was difficult for the aunt with whom I was staying to raise me; she was a widow and had very many children of her own. It was while living with my second aunt that I completed my education and became independent.

"In the spring of 1977, after 34 years, I found out that my 'Ukrainian Mommy' had been searching for me for many years. She had been asking everyone whom she had met from Poland who had returned to those parts where she lived whether they knew where I was. By lucky coincidence, she met a man who knew my aunt, and that's how I obtained her address. The Voitovychs still live where they had lived before. In the past, I had often wanted to make inquiries as to their whereabouts and to make contact with them, but I was advised not to do so since that might cause them harm. (Various opinions were expressed on these matters at that time). I now immediately wrote her a letter. In answer, I received an invitation for a visit that this 82-year-old 'Mommy' arranged personally for me. After attending to the formalities, I went to visit them with my husband and daughter.

"We arrived at the designated address. In front of the newly built house, I was greeted by a woman who reminded me, without doubt, of 'Mommy'—but it was her daughter Nastusia. Shortly thereafter, an 82-year-old woman ran out of the house and this was 'Mommy.' She, in turn, called out to me using my mother's name — because it seemed to her that I was that woman. (I do resemble my mother.) She took me by my hand, sat me down on the bench by the house, and began to examine my head parting my hair this way and that. When she found the scar, she embraced me and through her tears she said, 'Now I believe that it's you, Ola!'

"It was difficult for her to believe that it was me. The last time she saw me I was a seven-year-old child; and here before her stood a 41-year-old woman. While there, I found out that when 'Mommy' returned from delivering me to Burzany, she found her husband dead. Supposedly, it was the 'Russians' who killed him. They were still afraid to talk about these things.

"In planning my trip, I had intended to visit the grave of my dear ones. We went there in the company of 'Mommy,' Nastusia, her husband, and the grandchildren. A vast field of grain murmured over the land on which my home once stood and over the graves. We halted the horses next to my woods. I had planned to get down from the wagon and at least to kneel in that place; my courage, however, left me. I was gripped by fear and did not do it. Perhaps next time."[11]

VOITSEKHIVSKYI from Liniów. *See* Olha Chervak (Chapter 7, Łuck County).

Places

BERESTA
From the account of Maria Gulak (née Paluszyńska) from Beresta:

After a visit from the Banderowcy, Maria's father was hidden in a hay wagon by friendly Ukrainians and transported to the village of Zaturce. He returned later for his family, but rather than leaving with them, he decided to stay on his property in the predominantly Ukrainian village of Beresta.

"My parents made a big mistake," comments Maria, who was in a German forced-labor camp at the time. "As a result of the crimes of the Banderowcy, I lost my father [Grzegorz], my mother [Zofia], and my sister [Stanisława]."[12]

KISIELIN
From the account of Elramina Kieraszewicz from Kisielin:

"I am one of the few that was saved from death by axe, bullet, and grenade.

That irreparable atrocity was committed by the UPA on July 11, 1943, in the Roman Catholic church in Kisielin in Wołyń. The slaughter of innocent children, unarmed adults, and old people began after the celebration of the Mass by Fr. Witold Kowalski, the pastor, and lasted for 12 hours.

After 55 years, it is difficult to return to these painful memories. I will try, although briefly, to describe what had happened there.

"The services were coming to an end, the priest intoned the Angelus, and the people began to leave the church. I noticed a strange commotion by the main doors. Frightened people were backing up and were closing the doors. I heard a shout: 'The Ukrainians have attacked! The church is surrounded!'

"I run through the church and chapel to the rectory. The first shots fall here. A wounded person calls out for help. The people hide in the corners. I make my way to the stairs leading to the second floor of the rectory where several people have gathered. We begin to knock and to call out. The doors open and we go inside. Down below, we hear more and more shooting. The people down there are groaning and sobbing. The priest is giving them absolution. It grows quiet inside. Bullets fly through the windows more frequently. The priest is wounded in the left side of his face. Self-defense is organized. A battle rages to prevent the bandits from entering the church. They attack the doors with axes and toss in a grenade. The grenade is tossed back, and the explosion injures the attackers on the staircase. The attack on the windows continues. More people are wounded. They suffer without proper assistance and die from loss of blood. The stairs are on fire, so are the first floor of the rectory, the church, and the farm buildings. We assist in the defense by taking apart the walls and the stoves for the bricks. A fierce rain begins to fall. After midnight the attackers form ranks and march off singing, counting on the fact that we will perish in the fire. There is silence.

"After a short consultation a mattress is launched down the stairs, and on it ride women and children. I and three of my friends were in the first group. I ran through the gardens and meadows and reached my empty home. My parents were hidden that night by a Ukrainian neighbor, and I didn't see them until the morning. This neighbor helped us to reach Zaturce, where a German convoy was stationed. The Kisielin area burned for quite a while throughout that day and night.

"We never returned to my family's town, but we did have contact with the family that helped us, or rather, that saved us in the face of death."[13]

KISIELÓWKA

From the account of Piotr Procajło (b. 1934) from Kisielówka:

"In July 1943 a Ukrainian woman whom we knew came to our house, told us what had transpired [in Kisielin], and advised us to leave as soon as possible."[14]

WATYNIEC

In July 1943, two 70-year-old men, Piotrowski and Dobrawski, were murdered in the village of Watyniec and their homes were burned. After fleeing from the UPA, the Polish families of Grynowicz and Tarasiewicz decided to return to their homes that September. A few days later, both families were murdered and their bodies were tossed into a well. Maria Tarasiewicz, a 12-year-old who was axed in the head but was still alive, was the last to be thrown into the well and lay on top of the rest. A Ukrainian Baptist fetched her out and delivered her safely to her aunt in Łuck.

The Ukrainian Baptists often helped the Poles. They themselves were threatened by the UPA and regarded as "traitors" because of their religious affiliation. Often they fled together with the Poles to the larger towns for safety.[15]

ZAMLICZE
From the account of Bogusława Nowicka (née Krysiak, b. 1936) from Zamlicze:

During the first UPA attack on the village of Zamlicze on July 11, 1943, when 118 Poles were murdered, the Krysiak family (mother and four children under 14 years of age) hid in a swamp. Their 84-year-old grandmother, who refused to leave the house believing that she would not be harmed, was dragged into a cowshed with the wounded and dead, drenched with petroleum, and burned alive. After spending two nights in the swamp, when all had quieted down, the Krysiak family returned to their home only to find it robbed of all their possessions. Bogusława Nowicka remembers:

"It was harvest time and deceptively peaceful. During the day, the Poles worked the fields and were helped by their Ukrainian neighbors. [The attackers were said to have been strangers.] At night, however, the Poles gathered in a large barn of a Ukrainian whose name I do not recall....

"At the end of August or beginning of September — I do not remember the exact date — there came the tragic night. As we were sleeping in the barn, suddenly we were awakened by terrible cries and Ukrainian voices. The barn door swung open and in came the bandits yelling and screaming at us. We all huddled together for safety.

"There was a Ukrainian family staying with us as well. The Banderowcy told them to get out. As she was leaving with her children, the Ukrainian woman also took my brother and oldest sister with her. Unfortunately, these bandits came from our village; they recognized my brother and sister and killed them with crowbars by the threshold of the barn. Then the pogrom began. They did not shoot; rather, they attacked us with crowbars, spades, pitchforks, and God knows what else. My mother was struck in the head with a crowbar and fell on top of me, covering me entirely. The next blows landed on the left side of her body. I also received a blow to my left side. I remember the ungodly shrieks, the pleading followed by moaning, the death rattles, and finally the absolute silence. I don't know how long it all lasted. At one point, I felt my mother stir. Shaking with fear, I whispered to her not to move because they would kill her. She lay there a while longer, then got up slowly, took me by my hand, and we crawled out of the barn.

"No one else survived. We crawled over a potato field and when my mother's strength gave out, we dropped into a deep furrow so as not to be seen. We lay there for three days. My mother's body was all bruised and puffy. Because the sun was fierce, she began to lose consciousness. The night, cool and damp, brought us some relief. I plucked potato leaves and placed them on my mother's wounds. The dew slacked our thirst somewhat. On the third day, near dusk, a Ukrainian woman came to dig potatoes and saw us. She recognized me and signed with her hand for us to stay put. That night, she returned to us with a large pitcher of milk, bread, scarves for our heads, and a shirt for my mother. She told us that we must flee because the Ukrainians were preparing an action against the Polish survivors in hiding. Moreover, when those in the barn were being buried, our absence was noted. If we were found on her field, her entire family would also be murdered by the Banderowcy.

"The final day for the cleansing of Poles was dawning, but God did not abandon us. We lay in that field for another sweltering day. That night was fortunately cloudy and very dark. The Ukrainian woman's husband came for us together with Adam Szeletowski, the son of a Polish woman who had managed to escape from the flaming cowshed in July. We left together and proceeded in the direction of the nearest town, Łokacze. The Ukrainian led us through the wetlands; it was the safest route. The flames of burning Polish villages lit our way. When we finally neared our destination, our savior returned home and the three of us continued on through a meadow with mounds of hay, on the other side of which lay the town....

"[Later] when the Germans conducted an action against Zamlicze that resulted in the capture of the bandits' ringleader, he turned out to be a not-so-distant neighbor of ours."[16]

ŻURAWIEC COLONY
From the account of Jan Łopuszyński (b. 1917) from Żurawiec Colony:

"We were still living at home in August 1943. We found out from our well-meaning Ukrainian neighbors that the Nationalists belonging to the UPA planned to murder the rest of the Poles who remained alive after the first pogrom. We had to flee."[17]

3
Kostopol County

The county of Kostopol shared a common border with Soviet Ukraine. It was a forested, marshy terrain through which two rivers, Horyń and Słucz, flowed. The county was subdivided into six village communes: Berezne, Deraźne, Ludwipol, Małyńsk, Stepań, and Studyń. The town of Kostopol was the county seat.

Table 8
Population of Kostopol County by Mother Tongue

Ukrainian	103,980
Ruthenian	1,366
Polish	34,951
Jewish	10,481
German	7,545
Czech	216
Russian	588
Belorussian	212
Lithuanian	none recorded
Other	44
Unreported	219
Total	159,602

Table 9
Population of Kostopol County by Religious Affiliation

Orthodox	102,609
Roman Catholic	34,450
Uniate	1,303
Protestant/Evangelical	6,694
Other Christian	3,643
Jewish	10,786
Other Non-Christian	6
Not Specified or Non-Religious	1
Unreported	110
Total	159,602

Until the formation of the OUN-B UPA in the fall of 1942, this territory was under the control of Taras "Bulba"-Borovets's UPA. The largest unit of the Bulbowcy (Ukr., Bulbivtsi; members of Borovets's organization) was stationed in Chmielówka, near Ludwipol. Eventually, OUN-B forces penetrated this area, attacked Borovets's men, and forced them to join their UPA—a name which they stole from Borovets. The headquarters of the OUN "UPA-North," which operated in this area, was in Studyń Wielki. Roman Dmytro Klachkivskyi ("Klym Savur," and other *noms de guerre*) was its commander. Among those on his general staff were the chief of the SB squad, Mykola Lebed ("Maksym Ruban"), the prosecutor "Bezridnyi," and his deputy "Mitla," called by his men "the biggest cutthroat" in Wołyń.

Kostopol County belonged to the UPA "Zahrava" region under the general command of Ivan Lytvynchuk ("Dubovyi"). "Ostryi" was the military commander; his deputy was Petro Huzuvatyi. The UPA battalion operating in this region consisted of about 480 men subdivided into four companies: those of "Hrabenko," "Tsygan," "Voronyi," and "Iarmak." The Kostopol

battalion quartered in the villages of Złotolin, Japołoć, Stepań, and Wielka Lubasza. In Japołoć, the UPA ran a hospital, a nursing school, and an officers' school. Colonel Stupnytskyi, a former Petliura officer, was the founder of these schools.

People

BAZYLUK, Petro, from Butejki
From the account of Mieczysław Słojewski from Borek:

Mieczysław Słojewski, whose wife Marcelina was murdered and whose daughter Helena was severely wounded on the night of July 16, 1943, hid with his small son Edward (seven years of age) until late fall in a shelter in the marshes near Butejki. They were found on the verge of starvation by a Ukrainian, Petro Bazyluk, and taken to his house, where they remained until the arrival of the Red Army at the beginning of 1944. Prior to sheltering Słojewski and his son, Bazyluk was wounded by a Pole from Borek while he was pasturing his cows. This, however, did not deter him from rendering assistance to other Poles.[1]

FESIUK family from Płoteczno. *See* Arsen Kolba.

KOLBA, Arsen, and his family, from Płoteczno
From the account of Katarzyna Karpińska (née Łączyńska, b. 1934) from Płoteczno:

"We heard shots and immediately left our house and hid in the marsh until the next morning. There were ten of us in all. To prevent my two-and-a-half-year-old sister from crying, my mother thrust her breast into her mouth. On the other side of the marsh lived the Dobrowos family. We could hear and see how the bandits were murdering them. Whoever jumped out the window was axed to death.

"In the morning when things quieted down, we returned to our house grimy and hungry. We then went over to our Uncle Bolesław Konopacki and were in for a real shock. The entire family (my Uncle Bolesław, my Aunt Weronika, and their three daughters: Antonina, Helena, and Teodozja) were murdered with axes. We buried them with the approval of our Ukrainian neighbors."

When the family of another uncle of Katarzyna, Adam Konopacki, returned after the first attack because of the reassurances of local Ukrainians that nothing would happen to them (a common refrain in many accounts), they were also murdered. That family consisted of the parents and four children. Eventually, three of the Łączyński children were separated from their parents. Katarzyna continues:

"We stayed with our Ukrainian neighbors: I with the Arsen Kolba family, my brother with the Kozhushko family, and my sister with the Fesiuk family. (Mr. Fesiuk maintained contact with the bands.) The bandits came inquiring about me several times, but I could speak Ukrainian and my protector always told them that I was her niece....

"When the front passed, my mother returned for us with a soldier and, thanking the Ukrainian families for protecting us, took us with her under Soviet escort."

Katarzyna concludes her narrative with an episode concerning a bunker that she had discovered quite by accident in the nearby woods. From that bunker, Soviet soldiers flushed out a large number of Ukrainian Nationalists. After they were interned at the railway station in Mokwin, Katarzyna and some other children went to observe them as they were being shaved. "Many of them," she comments, "were neighbors whom we knew well but hadn't seen for a very long time."[2]

KOPERNYK, Serhii, from Borówka
From the account of Mieczysław Kobyłecki from Borówka:

"Then came 1943. The incidents in the villages became more frequent. The Poles began to seek shelter in the towns and Polish self-defense centers. I knew Stanisław Dąbrowski. He lived in the village of Czudwy near the Horyń River in the Deraźne commune. There were two Polish families living in that village. One day, Dąbrowski took some wheat to the mill owned by another Pole, Franciszek Brocik. (The entire Brocik family was later murdered by the Bulbowcy.) Dąbrowski brought the flour home, and his wife was just about to knead the dough for bread when a group of Bulbowcy broke into their house. They grabbed Dąbrowski's child out of his arms and threw the child against the wall. When his wife began to cry, a Ukrainian struck her. Then they bound Dąbrowski's hands and led him outside. When his wife saw that her child was dead and that they were murdering her husband, she jumped out the window and began to run to the nearby swamp. They shot at her and she fell. The Bulbowcy thought they had killed her. She lay there half a day and in the evening went to her parents in the Borówka Colony.

"During that time, Antoni Romaniuk and his family were leaving Borówka. They were all murdered after they passed the colony and neared the woods....

"I went to Janowa Dolina and told everything to [Stanisław] Pawłowski. It was decided to send a group of men under Pawłowski's command to Borówka. I was in that group. Bypassing the villages and sticking to the woods, we arrived there safely. During that first night, as we kept guard over the colony, we noticed that the Bulbowcy were up to something. We counseled the people to flee. While we were conveying this message to one of the residents, a Ukrainian came to his house. He did not notice us since we were in another room. He advised, almost pleaded with the homeowner, 'Get out, and I will go with you because they are going to kill all the Poles.'

"That Ukrainian, Serhii Kopernyk, whose two brothers belonged to the Bulbowcy, was engaged to a Polish girl. That's why he even revealed where the ambush was to take place....

"The Poles who did not want to leave with us and remained in Borówka and Józefina were murdered. [The attack on these two villages occurred in March 1943. About 29 Poles were killed and the villages were burned.]

"We were returning to Janowa Dolina.... During the few days of our absence many refugees from the surrounding territory had gathered there. They figured that the German garrison stationed there would come to their assistance in case of an attack. Unfortunately, it did not turn out that way. On Good Friday, the Bulbowcy attacked Janowa Dolina and only a few Poles emerged alive out of the slaughter that followed. The Germans never left their quarters."

Janowa Dolina was attacked on April 23, 1943. In 1939 about 11,000 persons lived there. In 1943 its population doubled because of the Polish refugees. The German garrison consisted of about 1,000 Wehrmacht soldiers. About 600 Poles died in the course of that UPA attack. The Germans remained in their barracks.[3]

KOSTIUK from Kamionka
From the account of Jan Chołodecki from Budki Kudrańskie:

After the UPA attack on Horoszówka, Kostiuk assisted several Polish families to get to Bystrzyce.[4]

KOZHUSHKO family from Płoteczno.
See Arsen Kolba.

MATUSHEVSKYI from Kruk Colony
From the account of Jan Chołodecki (b. 1933) from Budki Kudrańskie:

Matushevskyi warned Poles of planned UPA attacks on Horoszówka. Two of his three sons were members of the Banderowcy.[5]

NYCHYPIR from Kamionka
From the account of Jan Bagiński from Kamionka:

"News began to reach us regarding the murder of Polish people in the surrounding villages. Groups of armed Banderowcy and Bulbowcy also marched or rode through our village at night. We lived in constant fear for our lives. We spent the nights in the fields or thickets away from our house. At times, our Ukrainian neighbors provided us with shelter, especially on rainy and cold nights. All around us Polish properties and villages went up in smoke. We waited anxiously for our turn.

"On July 23, 1943, a group of Banderowcy rode into our village and halted at the house of our Ukrainian neighbor. Our neighbor listened to what they had to say and then sent his children to us with the warning that we should flee immediately. We decided to flee to the town of Bystrzyce, located on the Słucz River, where a large German garrison was stationed. At one point during our flight my great-grandmother, Michalina Bagińska (82 years of age), refused to go any further. She turned around and went back home. There, she was slain by the Banderowcy, who brought her to the Protestant cemetery in Kamionka and pierced her with bayonets.

"My relatives, the Burawski family, remained in their home. The family consisted of seven persons: Maria (60), Stefania (59), Zofia (40), Władysław (18), Jadwiga (20), Stanisława (28), and Bolesław (23). All of them were murdered with axes and knives. Their remains were left in the field. After a few days had passed, one of their Ukrainian neighbors buried them next to their home.

"Other Polish families — among them Fajfer, Miller, Sozański, and Gdowski — were warned and managed to escape to Kostopol. The Gdowski family was transported there by their Ukrainian neighbor, Nychypir. For this, he and his family paid with their lives. [After killing him] the Banderowcy led his wife, his daughter, his son-in-law, and his two small grandchildren to some shrubs near the house and there choked them with horse tethers....

"During our flight [to Bystrzyce], I saw the outline of the former Polish village of Niemilia. It was completely burned down and only the chimneys and parts of some buildings remained standing. I heard from the people I met that there were only two wounded survivors from that village. The rest perished under the axes and knives of the Banderowcy. Estimates as to the number of victims ranged from 150 to 200."[6]

SEVRUKOV from a farm near Pieńki
From the account of Włodzimierz Drohomirecki from Deraźne:

On March 18, 1943, Pieńki Colony, Pendyki Duże, and Pendyki Małe in the Deraźne commune were attacked by the UPA and about 180 people were murdered. Fleeing a subsequent manhunt the narrator, his mother, his younger sister, and another woman whose husband was just killed ran into a Ukrainian neighbor's (Sevrukov's) barn and hid in the hay. At dusk the barn door opened, someone came in, and they heard a quiet voice say, "I know that you are in here. I was standing near my home when you ran in. Come out, they are gone."

The four survivors crawled out from beneath the hay and were told by Sevrukov to remain in the barn until he came for them. He came back that night and advised them to flee, saying, "Please proceed slowly and confidently, and if you meet anyone along the way do not panic and run. In your place, Ukrainians would not be afraid and would not run. Such a bearing on your part will testify that you are Ukrainian and no one will bother you."

Upon leaving the barn, they traveled along a river bed and over fields to the village of Pieńki, about two kilometers away. Near Pieńki, the refugees hid in a chicken coop next to a cowshed that was subsequently set on fire. When they were discovered, although they claimed that they were Ukrainians, they were nevertheless placed under guard. The narrator continues:

"Suddenly an old Ukrainian resident of this village appeared, came over to us, embraced my mother, and said in Ukrainian, 'My dear, why did you leave the house?' He then said to the guard, 'These people are ours,' and led us away. Seeing this the guard went to join his companions in robbing the farmstead.

"This old man was poor, had a paralytic wife and lived by begging. Whenever he came to Deraźne, he would always stop by our house and we would feed him and give him some food or clothing to take back with him. He was the only Ukrainian living in Pendyki. When we entered his house he said in Polish, 'You always took me in and fed me, so I will do the same for you until they leave.' He told us to crawl behind the stove and hide there. Meanwhile, he kept guard, at times going outside to look around. There we remained until the next day.

"In addition to us, this Ukrainian was also sheltering a small Polish girl whose family had fled to the woods. He told us that he would try to find her family and return her to them, but if he couldn't locate them, he would raise her as his own."

The narrator's family then left for Stepań, where his mother's family lived. On their way they had a harrowing encounter with the Banderowcy, who suspected them of being Polish until the narrator's baby sister (Wanda, but called Marushka for the occasion) said during the questioning, "Mama, I want something to eat"—in Ukrainian! That child's simple request satisfied the killers.

"You're dressed like a Pole," said one of them, "and we were thinking of killing you. But it turns out that you're a Ukrainian after all."

The narrator continues:

"In the evening we arrived in the village of Studyń Wielki, a large, prosperous Ukrainian village. We went to the center of the village, where a Ukrainian family that we knew lived, but we did not know how we were going to be received by that family.

"I opened the gate and led the horse and wagon into the yard. The mistress of the house, who was observing us through a window, came out to greet us and [addressing one of the women] in a loud voice proclaimed in Ukrainian, 'My dear sister!'

"We took the horse into the barn and entered the warm house. The Ukrainian woman greeted us quietly in Polish, inquired about my father, and said that they would be able to provide us with food and shelter only for a night because the penalty for sheltering Poles was death. We were awakened before dawn, and the horse was already hitched to the wagon. We thanked them and left. The gate closed behind us immediately. The village was still asleep. We heard the crowing of roosters and the barking and howling of dogs.

"Not being detained by anyone, we arrived in the town of Stepań in the afternoon. From Deraźne to Stepań was about 50 kilometers. The way we traveled, along side roads, it turned out to be more like 70 kilometers. We arrived at the house of Anna Vloshchynska, my aunt. She was my mother's sister and her husband was Ukrainian."

The Drohomirecki family saga continued in Huta Stepańska, a large self-defense center which was successfully attacked by the UPA between July 16 and 18, 1943. Three battalions ("Rubashenko," "Ostryi," and "Shavul") numbering 2,000 men participated in this attack. In addition, another 3,000 local Ukrainians joined in the fray. About 40 Poles were killed in this prolonged siege. When the rest of the 16,000 to 18,000 refugees decided to break out of the encirclement, an additional 300 were killed. The narrator then tells us what happened to Anna's Ukrainian husband: He was hung upside down until he expired because he refused to murder or to betray his Polish wife.[7]

SMULKA, Hryhorii, from Kazimirka (Kazimierka). *See* Małyńsk and n.

TYKHON from Głuboczanka Colony
From the account of Bronisława Murawska-Żygadło from Głuboczanka:

"It was Whit Sunday, June 1943. A group of armed UPA members surrounded our small colony. We were all home at the time: my father, Antoni; my brothers, Marian (16) and Adam (nine); my sister, Basia (two); and I (15). My mother had just gone over to my uncle, Aleksander Murawski, who lived next door.

"The UPA murderers found my father outside, led him into the house, and made him lie on the floor. I can still remember his pale face. He whispered to us, 'Lie down children, they are going to rob us.'

"At that moment I heard a gunshot. I was holding my sister Basia in my arms. I jumped up and leaped out of the window. Basia fell out of my arms. Shots ran after me. I ran like mad towards the open field. I fell among the tall stalks of rye and that saved me.

"My brother Marian tried to jump out of the window after me but was shot twice: once in the shoulder and once in the lower mandible. He fell back into the room and slumped over the cradle near the window. The murderers went up to the cradle, grabbed him by his hair, and lifting his head barked, 'Die Pole!' Marian still remembers these words.

"I began to run again, not knowing where I was going but thinking that I had to get away as far as I could from the Banderowcy. Finally, when my strength gave out, I collapsed. As I sat there thinking and sorrowing over was happening to my family, I saw a Ukrainian acquaintance, Myshko Unyshchuk, coming towards me. When he stopped, I told him about the murder of my family. He listened to me patiently and sympathetically. Although he was a Ukrainian, I was not afraid of him. He then told me that he had seen my wounded brother Marian lying under a hazel bush by the ditch near our house.

"I don't remember how much time elapsed before I gathered enough courage to return to my home. There, I saw my father lying in a pool of blood by the entrance to the house. Not too far away lay the butchered remains of my brother, Adam. Two-year-old Basia lay outside by the window. She was also dead, pierced through either with a bayonet or a knife. I found my mother's lifeless body next door in my uncle's yard; her head was cut to shreds. Not far away lay my Uncle Aleksander, murdered together with his two daughters aged seven and nine. This was my very first confrontation with death, and it was the death of all of my loved ones. Confusion and chaos filled my brain. I was seized by a strange paralysis of mind and body. I don't know how long I remained in that state of shock.

"I was brought out of my stupor by the voices of the survivors who were returning to our village. By that time it was almost evening. Everyone was searching for members of their families. We wanted to know who died and who survived.

"I found my brother Marian near the hazel bush, just as Myshko told me that I would. The lower part of his face was in tatters. He could not speak. He signed for something to write on. When I gave him the paper and pencil, he wrote:

'Get out quickly! Save yourself. I will probably die.'

"Before darkness fell more and more survivors returned to search for their relatives.... I was taken in by the Jadowski family and spent the night in the field with them without any hope of being delivered from this living hell. Everyone said that we had to flee to Bystrzyce, where a German garrison was stationed. A Ukrainian acquaintance, Tykhon, placed my wounded brother on a wagon and in the evening transported him to a German military doctor in Bystrzyce. However, since the doctor refused to see him, Tykhon brought him back to us. I and the Jadowski family took care of him.

"The following day several dozen German soldiers arrived. They looked over the victims and made some notes. They told us to bury the dead quickly. Under their protection the people brought the bodies of their loved ones and buried them in a mass grave: there were 28 victims. I turned to the leader of the German unit and asked for his help in transporting my wounded brother. He ordered one of the wagons to be emptied out and we laid Marian on it.

"All the survivors were then taken to Bystrzyce by the Germans. There, the conditions of life were very primitive. Such conditions did not allow for an operation on my brother. Thanks to the initiative of the German doctor, my brother was taken to the hospital in Berezne, where he was treated by Polish doctors. I remained in Bystrzyce literally without any means of support. I was barefooted and my only possession was the dress in which I was clad. Fortunately, some good-hearted people came to my assistance and to the assistance of all the refugees from Głuboczanka Colony. Although I was only 15 years old at the time, the first grey hairs appeared on my head.

"In spite of his serious condition, Marian's fortune turned for the better. After a complicated operation in the hospitals in Równe and Kiev, his wounds healed and he regained his ability to speak. He currently lives near Wrocław and has a son, a daughter, and two grandchildren.

"I survived that frightening nightmare of my youth. My fortune also improved in later life. I have raised children and have grandchildren. The memory of those terrible days in 1943, however, has never left me. I have written this account in the hope that someone may eventually publish it as a warning to those who follow us. May they always be on guard lest the days of blind hatred toward people who are of a different nationality or faith return. Such a threat is present today in the resurgence of those who have inherited the legacy of the UPA."[8]

VLOSHCHYNSKYI from Stepań. *See* Sevrukov.

Places

LIPNIKI
From the account of Tadeusz Bagiński:

"After the massive murders in Lipniki on March 25-26, 1943, my father, Gracjan, my brother, Ignacy, and I hid for four months (until August 14, 1943) in an underground shelter which we had dug out. We survived because of the help we received from our friendly Ukrainian neighbors."

In that attack on Lipniki, 141 individuals (of whom 104 were women and children) were murdered. On May 5, 1943, Lipniki was attacked again by the UPA and 16 people were killed. The total number of victims in Lipniki was 182, of whom 157 are known by name. Sometimes entire families were wiped out; for example, the Murawski family consisting of 18 members, 10 of whom were small children.[9]

MAŁYŃSK

From the account of Kazimierz Boruta (b. 1912) from Małyńsk:

"After a while, the Ukrainian *sołtys* from the village where Paweł taught school before the war came to us and warned us that difficult times lie ahead for the Polish people. He either did not want to or could not elaborate on the nature of that threat. He told us that someone from the village of Bronne would come to us with an offer of protection; however, we were not to agree to his proposition, otherwise the same fate would befall us as that which befell the Horodecki family. [On the night of January 30, 1943, that entire family was murdered with axes by the UPA not far from the narrator's place of residence.] I took note of what he said. Sure enough, a man arrived from Bronne proposing that we go with him and assuring us of provisions and protection. Paweł wanted to do so, but I protested and so we remained. After a while, we found out that the *sołtys* was murdered for warning us. That *sołtys* also told us that the Banderowcy were mobilizing the Ukrainians with promises of an independent Ukraine and that they were telling them that the lands left behind by the Poles would become their property."[10]

MEDWEDÓWKA

On September 16, 1943, a group of Banderowcy surrounded the village of Medwedówka, where half of the residents were Polish and half Ukrainian. In this attack over 30 Poles were massacred and 68 properties were burned. Eighteen names of the victims and their ages are known. During this vicious attack, one of the sadists hoisted a small child aloft on a pitchfork and sported the child about for a while in front of the mother. The mother was also murdered later. One of the eyewitnesses to this atrocity was a Polish teenager who spoke Ukrainian fluently. The Banderowcy, uncertain whether she was Polish or Ukrainian, decided to take her along with them. She was rescued by a local Ukrainian woman who knew her. The woman ran up to the Banderowiec who held the girl and tore her out of his grasp shouting, "Don't you have enough Polish blood on your hands that you want to kill this Ukrainian girl as well?"

This brave gesture on her part saved the Polish girl's life.[11]

TUR COLONY

In the attack of July 18, 1943, on Tur Colony by the UPA, about two dozen people died. Jan Milewicz (a cripple) and his wife, unable to flee with the other survivors, hid in a thicket. After several days, they were found by a Ukrainian who transported them both to Rafałówka, where they remained until the end of the war.[12]

WERPCZNA

From the account of Franciszka and Roman Piotrowski from Wyrka:

"Between July 15 and 18, 1943, almost all the neighboring Polish villages were attacked simultaneously and therefore could not offer assistance to one another....

"I cannot omit the fact that among the Ukrainians were also very good and sympathetic people. Unfortunately, I do not know the names of those Ukrainians who rescued Jadwiga Dziekańska, a six- or seven-year-old Polish girl from Wyrka. Here is her story.

"During their flight from the UPA, the girl became too exhausted and had to be carried by her mother. While in her mother's arms, Jadwiga was shot in the thigh and the bullet lodged in her mother's breast. Her mother, Franciszka, died instantly. Jadzia bandaged her wound with a rag and waited by her mother for rescue. The girl spent the next ten days near her mother. At night she slept in a wrecked wagon full of comforters and pillows. She nourished herself with seeds from the field and quenched her thirst with water from a puddle. One day, a Ukrainian came to harvest the field left behind by the Poles and found her. A Ukrainian family then took her with them to the village of Werpczna. The village council pressured the family to kill the child 'left behind by the Poles.' But another Ukrainian, a teacher from the same village, interceded in her behalf and took her to live with him. With proper nourishment and care Jadwiga regained her strength.

"The Russians arrived in the region in 1944. In the course of a teachers' conference in Sarny, the former director of the elementary school in Wyrka, Kazimierz Karpiński, met the aforementioned Ukrainian teacher who told him that he was raising a Polish child that had survived the massacre in Wyrka. Karpiński, moved by a strange feeling, went to visit this Ukrainian. As he entered his home, Jadwiga called out joyously, 'Our *pan* has arrived!'

"She knew him very well because she used to play with his daughter, Lala. That is how Jadwiga wound up with the Karpiński family. She was returned to her father after he was released from German bondage. Presently, Jadwiga lives in Gdańsk and is a schoolteacher herself."[13]

4
Kowel County

The county of Kowel bordered with Polesie. Three rivers — Prypeć, Turia, and Stochód — flowed through this picturesque, partially wooded, partially wet terrain. The county was divided into 15 village communes: Datyń, Górniki, Gródek, Hołoby, Krymno, Kupiczów, Lubitów, Maciejów, Maniewicze, Niesuchojeże, Ratno, Siedliszcze, Stare Koszary, Turzysk, and Wielick. The town of Kowel was the county seat.

Table 10
Population of Kowel County by Mother Tongue

Ukrainian	182,807
Ruthenian	2,433
Polish	36,720
Jewish	26,476
German	1,813
Czech	1,062
Russian	3,120
Belorussian	237
Lithuanian	3
Other	99
Unreported	325
Total	255,095

Table 11
Population of Kowel County by Religious Affiliation

Orthodox	185,305
Roman Catholic	35,191
Uniate	2,412
Protestant/Evangelical	3,398
Other Christian	1,833
Jewish	26,719
Other Non-Christian	9
Not Specified or Non-Religious	47
Unreported	181
Total	255,095

In the latter part of March 1943, two UPA battalions emerged in this area. The first was formed from the Ukrainian youth and the auxiliary police in Kowel under Fedor Shabatura. Led by "Holobenko," a prewar officer of the Polish army, this battalion was subdivided into four companies: those of "Honta," "Kniaz," "Rozvazhnyi," and "Krylatyi." The second battalion consisted of volunteers and the auxiliary police from the southern sections of Włodzimierz, Horochów, and Kowel counties. Porfyrii Antoniuk ("Sosenko") was the commanding officer. The battalion's three companies were led by "Pidkhmurnyi," Holod ("Sliusar"), and Petro Vlasiuk. They operated in the southern part of Kowel, central Włodzimierz, and the northern part of Horochów.

In time, "Sosenko" added the "Sich Svynarynska" (Świnarzyn Stronghold) to his battalion. This unit consisted of two companies: that of the SB Army Field Gendarmerie, led by "Vorona"; and an Uzbek Legion that deserted its German post, led by "Solomianyi." Numerically, the Sich was larger than "Sosenko's" original battalion.

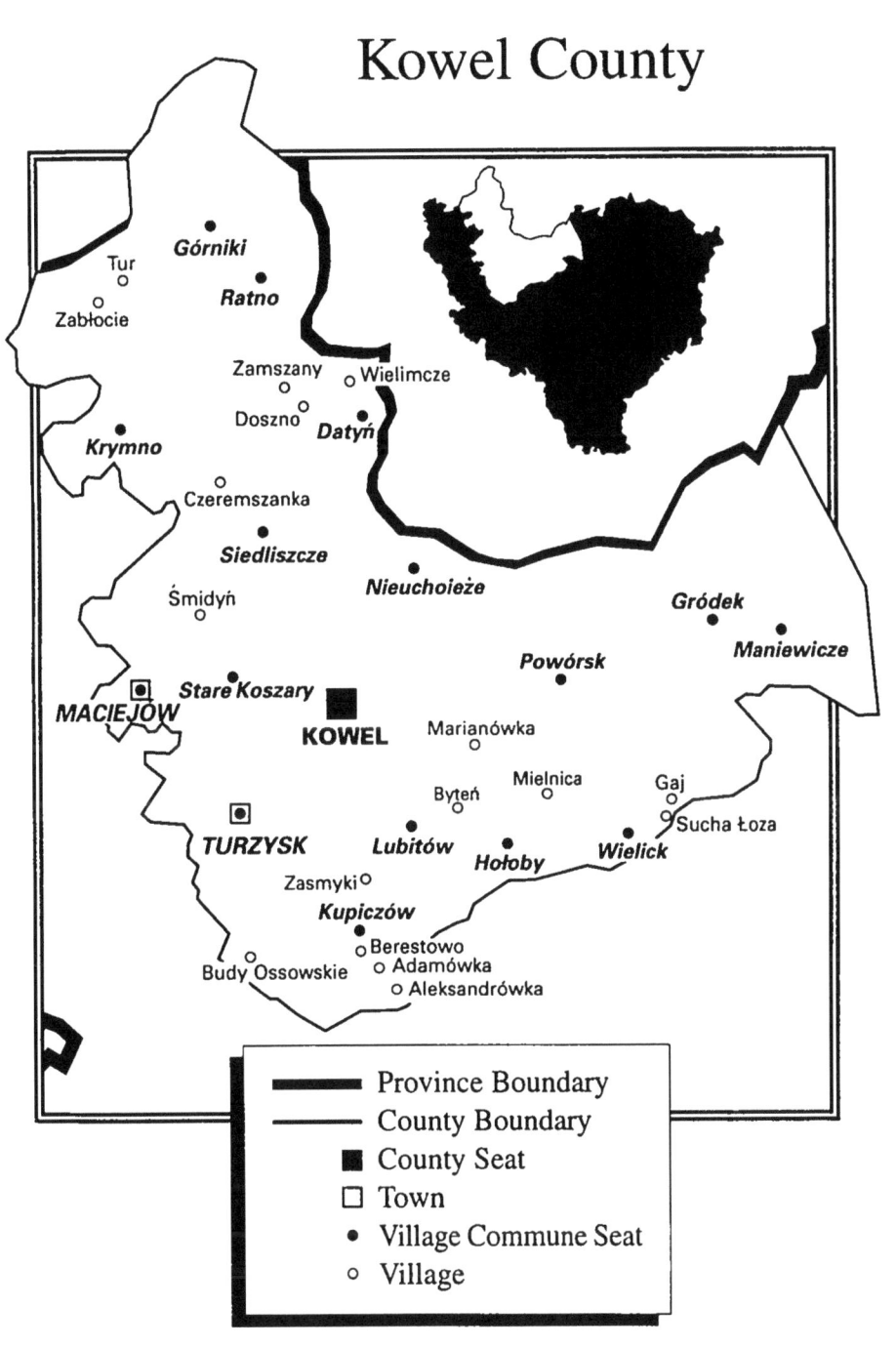

Kowel County was also the site of the UPA "Turiv" regional headquarters.

From March 18 to July 11, 1943, the UPA in Kowel County engaged in the murder of Poles as individuals in attacks on their farmsteads and forest dwellings. These attacks intensified especially around the (Polish) Easter holidays. July 11 marked the beginning of "Peter and Paul action" in this area and elsewhere. Another round of massive murders occurred toward the end of August. Although the fall months brought some relief, the murderous campaign dragged on until the Christmas holidays, when such villages as Radomle, Janówka, and Stara Dąbrowa fell. In addition to the military forces mentioned above, the "Nazar" battalion from Kamień Koszyrski County joined in the fray.

People

BOICHUN, Omelian, from Rewuszki
From a letter of Wacław Chmielewski from Kowalówka Colony, addressed to the Ukrainian Ambassador in Poland:

"February 13, 1997
Dear Ambassador:
"I turn to you with a special request for a favor which is in keeping with the current trend toward mutual forgiveness and unification.

"I was born in Kowalówka Colony in the commune of Turzysk. I lived there with my family until the end of August 1943. On August 29, 1943, late in the evening, a man came to our house and tapped on our window. Since we were in hiding, no one opened the door for him. Finally, his persistence forced my father to leave our hiding place in order to find out what he wanted. It was Omelian Boichun, a Ukrainian from the neighboring village of Rewuszki. He informed my father that a liquidation of Poles was planned for the following night in the colonies of Kowalówka, Marszałówka, and Brodyszcze, as well as in the Polish village of Budy Ossowskie. Omelian said, 'You are not my enemy. Take your families and flee.'

"My father became very agitated at this news; however, by the time he rejoined us in our hideout, he had already worked out a plan of action. He relayed Omelian's message to his nearest neighbors and cousins, and they in turn informed others. Some took Omelian's warning seriously whereas others did not.

"Our family and cousins (there were 16 of us in all) left our farms that same night. Those who delayed found themselves in a great deal of trouble because on the following evening a horde of murderers did arrive. They were surprised to find empty houses and became very angry. They sought revenge for their humiliation and found it when someone betrayed our informant. They grabbed him, persecuted him, and brought him to the village of Nowy Dwór, where they murdered and buried him. His wife was hounded by her husband's enemies and passed away shortly thereafter. Their children were sent to a faraway place for safety.

"The tragic death of that noble man weighs on my conscience. I am the last of the Poles who can turn to you in order to repay our debt to him. Formerly, we did not have an opportunity to do so.

"Today, in an era of good relations between our two nations and during the ongoing process of forgiveness and unification, I turn to you, Mr. Ambassador, for your help in restoring to Omelian Boichun his humanity, dignity, and honor. Omelian loved life and the people for whom he sacrificed his own young life. Since he perished as a 'traitor' to Ukraine and as 'an enemy of the Ukrainian nation,' his family as well as the Ukrainian people deserve to be told the truth in the interest of restoring his good name.

"He was a hero and took a stand against the thousands of Nationalists who pined for blood. He did not want to participate in the killing of innocent people and his unarmed neighbors.

"September 1998 will mark the 55th anniversary of his death. This will be perhaps my last chance to make such a request in his behalf for a posthumous rehabilitation. [Chmielewski then requests that a "remembrance and unity" memorial be erected to commemorate both Omelian Boichun and the Polish victims of the colonies and village mentioned in his letter.]
— Wacław Chmielewski"

From the response of the Ukrainian Embassy in Poland to Chmielewski's letter:

"May 29, 1997
Dear Mr. Chmielewski:
"... After an investigation of the facts presented by you, it has been ascertained that O. Boichun voluntarily deserted a partisan group of which he was a leader and went into hiding in the village of Iwaniwka. He then proceeded to his family in the village of Rewuszki. According to witness depositions, the circumstances surrounding his death are not known. It is only known that he died at night while going from Iwaniwka to Rewuszki. His place of burial is also not known. No archival materials have been found to validate the truth of your statements.

"Witnesses, however, did verify the fact that O. Boichun had helped several Polish families and thereby saved their lives. The national Administration, therefore, does not object to the erection of a memorial on the Rewuszki cemetery as long as the cost is born by the 'Polish-Ukrainian Association' [of which Chmielewski was a member].
Teodozyi Starak"[1]

BORKNIUK from Nowosiółki

In July 1943 Borkniuk warned a local Polish schoolteacher and his family of a UPA attack, thus saving their lives.[2]

BRYCHKA, Hordii, from Aleksandrówka
From the account of Rev. Jan Kurdybelski:

"The first individual murders of Poles began in the spring of 1942. In May 1942 some residents of Staryki discovered the massacred bodies of three men on the road to Jamne. Their tongues were torn out, their eyes were gouged out, their noses and ears were cut off, and all of these body parts were laid on the chests of the victims. On their foreheads, a cross was carved. At the time we did not know who was responsible for this. Two weeks later, a small group of Ukrainians launched several attacks against the Polish households in Staryki. The men were beaten but not murdered. [The following year, on May 29, at least 90 people were murdered in Staryki.] We heard of similar Ukrainian attacks in other regions as well. There was peace in Rokitno, however, because of the presence of Germans.

"The massive attacks against the Polish people by the Ukrainians began in the spring of 1943.... [Examples follow.]

"On May 22, 1943 — it was Friday evening — a Ukrainian from Aleksandrówka, Hordii Brychka, informed Franciszek Hanuszewicz (whose home had been attacked in March) that 'It will go badly with you tonight.' However, he did not want to provide any details of what was to happen. The women, children, and old men immediately fled by wagon to the forest, where they spent the night. The village was guarded only by the young men who remained there. A torrential rain fell that night, but nothing happened.

"Those who spent the night in the forest returned to their village around 5:00 A.M. As they were changing their clothes, the Ukrainians, who were hiding in the fields and awaiting the return of those in the forest, attacked. They fell upon the village and began to spray the homes with machine-gun fire. Eighteen people were killed in the course of this attack, including men, women, and children. Two severely wounded persons were taken to the hospital in Rokitno. There were also many less severely wounded people. The village was robbed and burned; scarcely four homes survived the fire. The victims were buried in a mass grave in the Rokitno cemetery. The funeral was conducted by an old priest from Sechów. The survivors of Aleksandrówka fled to Rokitno. From there they came back in secret to their village in order to gather the crops and to bring back something to eat. While doing so, eight more of them were killed."[3]

CHERNYK family from Mielnica. *See* Mielnica.

DANYLIUK, Trokhym, from Czerniejów
On August 6, 1943, several Polish families were murdered in Czerniejów by local Ukrainians. Władysław Zubkiewicz survived because he was warned of the attack by Trokhym Danyliuk.[4]

DAVYD from Uhły (Kuty)
From the account of Stanisław Popek (b. 1927) and Mieczysław Popek (b. 1930) from Nowy Gaj:

"The simultaneous attacks on Stary and Nowy Gaj were organized by the Banderowcy on August 30, 1943, at sunrise. [During that attack, about 600 people were killed]. The village and colony, which together numbered over 200 houses, were surrounded by a cordon of UPA members armed with guns, pitchforks, axes, scythes, clubs, and knives. Earlier, a few friendly Ukrainians had warned the Poles about the threatening danger, but their warnings were disregarded. And furthermore, no one had bothered to organize a self-defense center there to protect the civilian population. About one month before the attack, the UPA leaders had called a meeting of all Polish farmers and demanded that they turn over their weapons. All present signed some kind of a document attesting to the fact that they did not possess arms. People were also asked whether there was a Polish partisan unit in the area and whether anyone belonged to the underground. And now, the Banderowcy, fully armed, entered every home at the same time. The Poles were axed and knifed; those who ran were fired upon.

"Our family decided to flee since there was no chance for defense, and besides, we had nothing to defend ourselves with. Our father, Mikołaj (52), hid in a sheaf of grain. He had a revolver and was able fire a few rounds at the attackers. Who knows how many he killed or wounded? It was probably when he ran out of ammunition that our Ukrainian neighbor, Stepan, pierced him with a pitchfork. He suffered in agony for a few hours before dying. Fornal, our neighbor, hiding in the adjoining sheaf, saw the whole episode. Our father, being a wealthy man (he had, among other possessions, two windmills: a cereal mill and an oil mill), had often helped Stepan's family in difficult times and saved them from starvation and death. And this was how Stepan repaid him.

"In our family we lost our sisters: Kazimiera (18), Marianna (20), Zofia (21), and Helena (22), who had a nine-month-old son named Antoni. Our sisters perished by the Stochód River, where they were axed and pierced to death with bayonets.

"Stanisław ran away and hid at the home of a Ukrainian acquaintance, Davyd from Uhły, and when the Banderowcy began to search for hidden Poles, he ran off to Maniewicze and later made his way across the Bug River.

"Mieczysław fled together with Antoni Fila, Janina Fila (six), and Teresa Ramza (14). They hid in a meadow and saw the armed Banderowcy pass by. With them marched our Ukrainian neighbors from the surrounding villages armed with axes and pitchforks. The wounded Poles, together with those found in hiding, were murdered on the spot. Luckily, the four of them survived.

"Our mother, Franciszka, was able to run out of the house in time and hide in the cherry tree nearby. She saw how the Banderowcy exited our house, cursing and swearing because no one was there. Later, another group began to rob the premises. They did not approach the cherry tree because of the vicious dog on a chain near it. In the evening our mother fled to Arsenowicze, a neighboring Ukrainian village. After a few days she went back to our house in a wagon driven by Pototskyi, a Ukrainian from Arsenowicze, with the hope of finding some clothes or food there. When she entered the house, she noticed immediately that everything was either robbed or destroyed. Suddenly, a few young Banderowcy appeared in the yard. They dragged our mother out of the house intending to kill her by one of the walls. She was saved from certain death by Pototskyi, who told them that she was a good woman, that she helped many Ukrainians, and that he could vouch for her himself. Mother survived and in great haste made her way with Pototskyi back to Arsenowicze, and later to Maniewicze.

"Our brother Mieczysław, while fleeing, discovered our sister's, Helena's, body among the lupines. She was pierced with a bayonet. By her breast lay the body of her young son, Antek, also pierced with a knife or bayonet. Near Maniewicze, the group of refugees encountered some Banderowcy who were hunting fleeing Poles. The entire group survived thanks to Antony Fila, who had a gun and was able to fend off the attackers. It became apparent that these UPA 'soldiers' fought most eagerly only with defenseless women and children.

"During the attack [on Gaj], Bolesław Greguła was pasturing horses in the meadow with some of his Ukrainian friends who were between 12 and 15 years of age. These Ukrainian lads had decided to kill him. He received 20 gashes in his back and chest, and his arms were cut in many places. Miraculously, Bolesław survived. He owes his life to a German soldier who gave his own blood to save him while he was bleeding to death in the hospital in Kowel.

"When we were in Gaj, in May 1996, we could still see the bones washed up by the rains from the mass graves in the former firing range near the school.... Local Ukrainians say that there could be as many as 1,000 victims buried in that firing range."[5]

HARASYM, Semen, from Łuczyce Colony

In August 1943, after two elderly woman were killed in Łuczyce Colony, the Polish population fled to Kowel and Zasmyki. The five member Denys family, not having transportation, hid in the home of their Ukrainian neighbor, Semen Harasym. When a group of Banderowcy came to his house with the intention of killing the Polish family, Semen stood in the doorway with an axe in their defense. Later that night, he led the family out in the direction of Włodzimierz Wołyński.[6]

KORIN, Mykola, from Aleksandrówka.
See Pavlo Kyts, second account.

KOSIAK from Byteń

On March 18, 1943, the village of Byteń was pacified by the Germans and the Ukrainian police. On the basis of a list prepared by Vasyl Kolchak, a Ukrainian-Nationalist leader, the victims were gathered in a former Jewish residence from which they were taken one at a time behind a barn and killed. In all, 46 people were murdered including children. Risking his own life, a Ukrainian named Kosiak hid a Polish boy from the Jagliński family, thus saving his life.[7]

KOSYNSKYI, Nykanor, from Doszno
From the account of Antoni Zarzycki from Doszno:

"I was 13. Early on the morning of that tragic day, I put the cows out to pasture and returned home around noon. I saw my father hanging on the fence; he was dead. My mother was also dead; in her head was an iron tooth which had broken off a cultivating hoe. My sister and brother were also slaughtered. I don't remember how I reached the yard of Nykanor Kosynskyi, a Ukrainian. We lived in the colony; they in the village. His daughter, Nastka, assured me that she would take care of me. When she left, her father opened the window and said, 'Son, get out of here because she will annihilate you.' I knew then that she had ties with the Ukrainian bands. I ran to my Grandfather Leon. I found him in the garden, massacred beyond belief. I hurried to my second grandfather, Piotr. By his house lay the desecrated body of my Grandmother Michalina. I ran to the woods near the lake. By the lake I chanced upon Leonka Szymonowicz and then Tańka Rubinowska. We took our horse and wagon and headed for Ratno....

"Today, it is difficult for me to speak and write about the tragedy that befell my own family."[8]

KOZEL and his wife, from Ratno. *See* Hrymuchyi Romanko.

KYTS, Pavlo, from Aleksandrówka
First account. Kamila Ostasz (née Ziółkowska, b. 1928) from Aleksandrówka Colony:

"The Ukrainian bands began to prowl in June and July 1943. News of attacks on Polish homes and of the murder of entire families began to arrive more and more often.

"Our colony of Aleksandrówka was attacked for the first time a week after the attack on the church in Kisielin. [The church was attacked on July 11, 1943.] It was getting dark. A Ukrainian by the name of [Pavlo] Kyts came by and told us not to spend the night in our home because something evil was in the air....

"[One month later] we returned. We were afraid to sleep in our homes. We spent the nights in a barn that stood on a hill, and during the day we would come down and work the fields. One morning, we looked through a slit between the barn boards and saw the bandits walking and riding to Michałówka. The blades of their scythes were set on end in an upright position. They carried pitchforks and axes."[9]

Second account. Teresa Radziszewska (née Adamowicz, b. 1934) from Aleksandrówka Colony:

"A week after the attack on the church [of Kisielin], some armed people appeared in the woods. [Pavlo] Kyts came to us and counseled us not to spend the night in our house because one never knows what might happen. It would be better, he told us, if my mother and the children slept over at his house. Since dusk was approaching, we went over to Kyts's house; my father remained at home. We scarcely arrived at the property of this Ukrainian when shots rang out on the other end of Aleksandrówka. Kyts led us to [Mykola] Korin's house, which was next door, and we were hidden in a room which was then locked with a key. Another door led out of the room to the garden by the road. Through the slits in the door, I could see the Bulbowcy as they ran, shouted, and fired shots. We almost died of fright when the bandits entered the house in which we were staying and asked whether any Poles were there. After they were told that there weren't any, they went away. There were four of us children in that room: I was nine, my brother Jan was five, my sister Stasia was three, and my baby brother was one-and-a-half. We all sat without moving, scarcely daring to breathe.

"When the band left, Korin led us to a hiding place he had prepared in the barn. It was in a corn bin which was lined with hay in such a way as to leave a path to an open space near one of the walls. Night had fallen by then, and the light from the burning houses of the Poles shone through the cracks between the barn boards.

"The place where the murders occurred was across from the home of my uncle, Franciszek Adamowicz, who hid in a thick hedge and was a witness to the tragedy. 'The people who were rounded up were killed in various ways,' he told us. 'One bandit tore a child from the arms of its mother and holding it by its feet, smashed its head on the fence so that the child's brains spilled out. The mother was screaming, so another one stabbed her with a pitchfork. They threw the smaller children into the well. The older ones were herded into a potato cellar and buried. Older people were beaten with clubs, hacked with axes, and pierced with pitchforks....'

[The next attack on Aleksandrówka took place in August 1943.]

"On September 4, 1943 (my 75-year-old grandmother told me to remember this date), my parents decided that we would try to get to the other side of the Bug River, to the Zamość region where the rest of our family lived. We retrieved our warmer clothes, such as overcoats and sweaters, from Kyts, who kept them safe for us, but we could not find my shoes; and so I had to walk barefooted.

"It was raining when we set out for Ośmigowicze. We arrived at the property of Prokop, a Ukrainian, and rested in his barn. This good-hearted man proposed that I and my grandmother remain with him. My brother Jan said that he was afraid and that he wanted to go with my father.

"My last and final separation from those dear to my heart took place in Prokop's barn. I remember that a torrential rain was falling. My parents said their good-byes and left with Stasia and my baby brother in that great downpour. My brother Jan followed behind them with lowered head. I watched as they were disappearing, and wept, and kept hitting my head against the barn door until they vanished behind the trees. The Prokops tried to cheer me up; they kept talking to us. After a while, a shot rang out and my grandmother said, 'Ah — Our children are perishing!'

"As it turned out, they were indeed shooting at them. Mr. Prokop left, but when he returned he did not want to tell us what had happened right away. Finally, Grandmother asked, 'Are our children lost? Tell us so that we may know.'

"'The sons-of-bitches killed them,' he replied.

"In 1989 I began to search for the graves of my parents through the Red Cross and the Red Half-Moon in Moscow, Kiev and Lutsk [Łuck]. In 1990, when I returned to Ośmigowicze for the first time in 47 years, a Ukrainian woman who witnessed the events told me what had happened.

"'They came to my parents,' she said, 'in order to get warm and to dry out because it was raining and there were small children and a pregnant woman. After them, came the Ukrainian Maninkhvast with a gun and ordered my father and a neighbor to hitch up the horses. They took them to the swamp. Your mother pleaded with him not to kill them. Then she begged him to kill the adults first, so they wouldn't have to watch their children being murdered. When they all knelt down and began to pray, that's when he shot them. The residents of Ośmigowicze were able to identify the burial place of these Poles because a wild rose took root there.'

"On May 18, 1991, I retrieved the remains of my dear ones and buried them next to the grave of my grandparents in Białowola [near Zamość].

"In 1943, while I was still in Prokop's barn, I tore out a hiding place high in the hay near a beam, and I and my grandmother took refuge there. We did not have to wait long for the search. The 'soldiers' came; they walked over the hay and pierced it with their swords and pitchforks. Fortunately, they stabbed the beam near which we were hiding, and so we were saved.

"Mrs. Prokop gave my grandmother a Ukrainian skirt and an apron, and we left on a bright and sunny day. We went to Kyts's home, hid in a flax field, and waited for one of the family members to appear. Around noon, Korin's children saw us as they were driving their cows out of the woods. After a while, Mrs. Kyts came to us and informed us that our grandfather, who was staying with them, would come for us that evening."[10]

LUKAICHUK, Harasym, from Aleksandrówka

From the account of Leokadia Skowrońska from Aleksandrówka:

"I lived with my parents until I was ten years old. On July 15, 1943, at about nine o'clock in the evening, the Banderowcy attacked our village. They were armed with pitchforks, axes, knives, and guns. They surrounded the village and began to gather the people in one place. My parents bid us a hurried good-bye. My father gave each of us a bottle of distilled liquor and told us to run wherever we could. It was already dark. I ran toward our barn and then into the field. A shot rang out, and I felt a terrible pain in my foot. The bullet went right through; it knocked me off my feet. I began to crawl through the wheat field toward the ridge of unplowed land that separated our field from that of our neighbor. There, I dug myself in until morning. All through the night I heard the frightening cries of people and the sounds of shooting. My foot hurt more and more. I made a bandage, soaked it in the liquor, and applied it to my foot....

"Days passed. I drank the liquor and gathered seeds for food. Hunger troubled me more and more. After one week, I heard some voices in the village. I crawled out and reached the yard of our Ukrainian neighbor, Uliana [Sydor], whom I asked for a piece of bread. She looked at me and shrieked, 'You Polish brat! Are you still alive?' She then grabbed a hoe which was near her. In my fear, I forgot about my wounded leg, got up, and ran back to my hiding place in the wheat field. I did not leave that place again. My leg swelled and hurt so much that I could no longer move. I lived only on the seeds.

"After 11 days, the Ukrainians decided to clean up after the attack. They walked the fields and when they came across some corpse they would bury it. They came closer and closer, and I didn't know what to do. Suddenly, above me, I heard the voice of Harasym Lukaichuk, a Ukrainian with whom my parents were on good terms. He approached me slowly and said, 'Do not move from here, perhaps they will not see you. I will come for you this evening. Your brother is staying with me.'

"He then moved on. Just as he promised, he came for me, put me in a sack that he slung over his back, and brought me to his house. He then examined my wounded leg; it was all swollen and red. He said that we could not wait, that we had to go to the hospital in Kowel right away. He put a scarf on me and placed me in a bag used for feeding horses. He then covered me with some chaff and put me in a wagon. He seated my brother next to him, and we started out. When we reached the woods, some bandits ran out, approached him, and began to inquire where he was going and why. He explained to them that he was taking his gravely ill son to the doctor and motioned to my brother. They let us go.

"Harasym brought us to the hospital in Kowel. They took us in and performed an operation. My brother got better sooner than I, and he was released. I stayed longer. After 20 days, my mother came to see me. Later, the doctor informed me that my leg had to be amputated because it wasn't healing. That same day, Harasym came to the hospital and told me that my parents and siblings were murdered. That news just about finished me off."[11]

MARCHUK, Helena, from Aleksandrówka.

From the account of Józefa Brudzińska (b. 1926) from Aleksandrówka:

"There was terrible shooting around sundown. The armed attackers came from the direction of the Woronczyn woods and fell on the defenseless Poles. The bullets flew like hail as we lay in the potato field and waited to see who would be the first to die. But it was God's will that we survived. This was the first attack....

"I went with my mother. A terrible sight greeted us by the Dzięsław home. In the garden by the linden tree, a pit was dug. In it lay about 70 murdered, half-buried people. The blood, which flowed like a river onto the road from the pit, was now congealed. They threw the children into a potato cellar and covered them with dirt. Those still alive were finished off with clubs that still lay nearby, all bloody. Dead children floated in the well. The buildings were burned to hide all traces. We went further to look for my sister....

"We finally found her. She was killed on her way to our cousins, the Zalewski and Kański families, who lived near the woods. They were all dead. Upon hearing the news, my brother, brother-in-law, and father went there, buried them, and placed a cross on the graves. From the time of that attack and murders we did not sleep in our house; rather, we slept in the orchard so that it would be easier to run away in case of trouble.

"The next attack of the murderous UPA took place on Sunday. The weather was beautiful. That is why we could see the butchers coming at a distance. They stopped by our house. They had guns. At that time, I was in the barn. I heard seven shots, then silence. I waited, full of terror. Suddenly, the barn door swung open and in came our Ukrainian neighbor, Helena, the daughter of Vasyl Marchuk. She said to me, 'Józia [an endearing diminutive of Józefa], you are an orphan. We buried your parents and brother Witek with his children in the orchard and placed a piece of sheet metal over them. You must get away from this place because there's no room here for the Poles.' She then gave me some pierogi to eat.

"I went out on the road. More and more of us were gathering: first, Kamila and Witek Ziółkowski (they hid out at Pakhomas), Franciszek Adamowicz (he hid out at Prokops), and my brother Stanisław; then Feliks Ziółkowski, Maria, Leokadia, Stanisław Adamowicz, and Bogusław Ziółkowski. While we were discussing what we should do, Mrs. Prokop came out and brought us some bread and salt pork. She told us we could go wherever we wanted to.

"We left. We crawled on our bellies through a field and lay in the cereal grasses until evening. The rest of the journey was terrible. Never had I been so far without my parents. We walked day and night through swamps. Some of us sank into the mud up to our waists. There was no clean water to drink. With the last ounce of our strength we reached Ozierany and found the home of a Ukrainian named Kovalchuk, an acquaintance of Ziółkowski. We hid behind his barn in a wheat stack. But there were UPA members there, and they killed Maria Ziółkowska when she approached the house without exercising caution. So we had to leave there immediately and hide in the cemetery. After many more difficulties we finally arrived in Zasmyki, where a self-defense center was forming. When we approached this village, a battle was in progress between the Poles and the Ukrainians, who were continually on the attack....

"We found out later that the bandits had gathered all those who did not have time to hide and those who believed that they were going to a meeting at the home of Dzięsław, which stood near the wayside shrine, and murdered them there."[12]

OLSZAŃSKA, Mrs., from Adamówka
From the account of Zbigniew Jakubowski (b. 1939) from Adamówka:

"I survived two UPA attacks. The first one occurred on July 11, 1943, at 9:30 A.M., on Adamówka.... Thirty-two Polish families and three Ukrainian families lived in Adamówka....

"The second attack of the UPA took place in the early hours of the morning of August 8 on Dunaj. We were still sleeping. We were awakened by gunfire coming from the Kamieniecki residence near the forest. We began to flee over the fields in the direction of Turzyce, where there was a self-defense center. I was ten years old at the time. I started running as soon as I awoke; the Banderowcy ran after us shooting. My father was carrying my four-year-old brother, Walerek, in his arms. After sustaining a wound in his shoulder, he left Walerek in the field crying 'Daddy, Daddy.'

"My mother fled with my older sister, Mirka, who was eight years old. Mother was also shot, in her right shoulder. She went to the Olszańskis and was hidden by the proprietress, a Ukrainian married to a Pole, in the attic of the cowshed. Mrs. Olszańska did not betray my mother even though the bandits beat her."[13]

PAKHOMA family from Aleksandrówka. *See* Helena Marchuk.

POTOTSKYI from Arsenowicze. *See* Davyd.

PROKOP family from Aleksandrówka. *See* Pavlo Kyts (second account) and also Helena Marchuk.

ROMANKO, Hrymuchyi, from Wielimcze
From the account of Franciszka Kosińska from Doszno, as transcribed by her daughter:

Doszno, August 28, 1943. "My husband and his younger brother slept in the barn for several nights now. At home, there remained our in-laws and my husband's three sisters. When it was already light, I walked over to the window, cradling my child in my arms. I saw Józef Sawicki running along the lake shoreline and behind him, a Ukrainian on a horse brandishing a sword. Just as the horse passed the runner, the rider swung the sword and Sawicki's head dangled over his shoulders.

"In the next moment, I bolted with my child over the dirt road by my house and found myself in the wheat. It was probably around noon when my daughter, glued to my neck, whispered, 'Mommy — drink.' It seemed to me that all was quiet in the village, so we went there and were allowed into a Ukrainian home. But before they could give us some water, about 30 to 40 bandits on horseback halted by the house. One of them asked from the entrance way, 'Which one of you is the Polack Frania?'

"I stood directly in front of him, and looking intensely into his eyes, I answered in Ukrainian, 'If I am Polack Frania, don't I have a right to live?'

"My child, still clinging to my neck, whispered into my ear, 'Don't speak Polish, don't speak Polish.'

"Continuing to look straight into his eyes, which I will never forget, I prayed. I prayed to the Blessed Mother to hide me even under a tiny piece of her mantle. I prayed with my whole soul and every inch of my body. I saw that mantle; saw how I hid my head and my child beneath it.

"Meanwhile, my host informed the inquiring Ukrainian that no Polack by the name of Frania was there. 'She's sick in the head,' he said pointing to me.

"'And where did she get married?' the Banderowiec pressed on.

"'What do you mean where? In the Orthodox church — where else?' replied the host.

"Throughout the entire time this bandit never took his eyes off me, all the while slapping his whip against his tall boots. I knew him by sight, and he knew me too. He lived near the Datyń Colony. He waved his hand and said, '*Zhyvy*' ["*Hai zhyve!*" or "Cheers!"]. He withdrew into the yard, was handed his horse, waved his hand before saddling up, and the bandits left. I saw an axe fastened to his saddle with shreds of cloth and hair still clinging to it.

"Then I heard a loud noise behind me; its source was the master of the house, who in trying to sit down in a chair, landed on the floor. At that point I went into convulsions. The rest of the family stood there as if in a hypnotic trance. I prayed continuously, but for how long I don't know. Finally, another Ukrainian neighbor entered the room and said, 'Well, the butchers have gone.'

"I ran out of the house and went next door to the two-story building belonging to my relatives. I found my uncles, Florian and Piotr Rubinowski, and my cousin, Kazimierz Jedynowicz, lying face down, pinned to the floor with bayonets. Near the entrance, under the apple tree, lay my aunts and the children. Gienia still held her youngest in an embrace; both her head and that of her son were cleaved by an axe. My Aunt Sabina's head was also split and she was naked; her children, the eight-month-old twins, rested by her breasts. I saw the grandmother; she was pinned to the wall with a bayonet and died in that position. She was bent over a bit but still standing.

"I ran to my parents' house in the colony. My father lay face down near the bed in his underclothes; he was also pierced with a bayonet. My sister Janina lay crumpled under a table in one of the rooms; she was shot through the heart. I searched for my mother. None of the Ukrainians could tell me where she was.

"I ran further on through the colony to my three old aunts. Michalina was in the potato field; her hands and feet were severed and she was already dead. Stasia and Hania were murdered in the yard of a Ukrainian in the village; they were pierced to death. In the pantry, I found the desecrated remains of my aunt, Karolina Jedynowicz (a widow), her son Tadeusz, and her stepdaughter Józefa; their hands were bound with barbed wire. Her second stepchild, Bronisław, lived with his wife and three children elsewhere. They were all taken to the barn and killed. In that barn I discovered their bodies desecrated beyond description: their eyes were gouged out, their heads were split open, their tongues were cut out.

"Maria, the wife of Kazimierz Jedynowicz, seeing many people in the yard of her Aunt Karolina, told her children to remain in the house and went to see what was happening. During her absence, her oldest son brought one of the children, a cripple, out into the yard. Seeing their mother being brought back and pushed along by strangers, the three healthy children ran over to a Ukrainian neighbor. They remained there until the evening. He gave them some bread and salt pork and showed them the road to their grandmother's house who, with her husband, later transported them to town. The children's mother and her crippled child were found in the yard with split heads.

"My relative Ewa Rubinowska was married twice under the tsars, both times to

Ukrainians in an Orthodox church. She was therefore considered to be one of them. She had two sons, one from each marriage. The third time, in the interwar years, she married my cousin Leon Rubinowski. Even though the wedding took place in a [Roman Catholic] church, she, like her sons, considered themselves to be Ukrainians. Her husband Leon was murdered in her presence and in the presence of her sons. Later they took her youngest son, 17 years of age, to show them the Polish households and to participate in the murder of Poles — in order to prove that he was a Ukrainian. He helped them to kill Karolina Rubinowska, her mother, and three children — and then fled. He went to Ratno and never returned. In their fury, the bandits killed his half-brother, who was a cripple. I found his mangled body outside the home of Paulina Rubinowska, my aunt. Her daughter Antonia's body was also there. She was 18 years of age.

"And so I ran all day long from house to house with my two-year-old daughter in my arms. It wasn't until that evening that my husband dragged me and my daughter away to the woods near the cemetery. When it was dark, he brought my mother and my first cousin, Józia, there as well.

"That night some Ukrainians — Baptists — came to us from Wielimcze. They brought milk for my child and food for all. They promised that they would bury all the dead before dawn. In the gray morning hours, they brought a wagon full of corpses. At my mother's request, they took some boards off our home and made coffins for my father and sister. The others were buried in a mass grave lined with linen. The children were laid next to their mothers. The bodies were then covered with the linen and buried.

"We hid in the forest for ten days, and the Ukrainians from Wielimcze took care of us. One of them, Savluk, to avoid transporting us as a group, took my mother and Józia to Ratno. In the morning, another Ukrainian, Hrymuchyi Romanko, brought me, my child, my husband, and my husband's cousin there as well.

"In Ratno, Kozel and his wife, both Ukrainians, took care of and provided for all of the refugees from Doszno."[14]

SARADKO from Budy Ossowskie Colony. *See* Petro Stelmashchuk.

SAVLUK from Wielimcze. *See* Hrymuchyi Romanko.

SENECHKO from Obeniże
In August 1943 the fleeing Polish population of Łuczyce Colony was assisted by the Ukrainians of Obeniże. One of these was Senechko, who provided shelter for an elderly couple, Piotr Bartoszewski and his wife.[15]

SENKEVYCH family from Mielnica. *See* Mielnica.

STELMASHCHUK, Petro, from Budy Ossowskie Colony
In the August 30, 1943, UPA attack on Budy Ossowskie Colony, 205 persons, including 80 children, were murdered. Because of the warning they received about the impending attack from two Ukrainians, Saradko and Petro Stelmashchuk, some of the residents left the village in time and survived.[16]

VIDYNSKYI family from Mielnica. *See* Mielnica.

ZHUK family from Mielnica. *See* Mielnica.

Places

ALEKSANDRÓWKA
From the account of Stanisław Adamowicz from Aleksandrówka:

"The Ukrainian bands attacked our colony in June 1943. A number of residents were killed at that time, including my mother, who went to our cousins living near the forest. Others survived by hiding in various places: in the wheat fields, in farm buildings, or in the homes of Ukrainian acquaintances."

On September 4, 1943, Teofil and Bronisława Adamowicz, together with their three children, were murdered by the Ukrainian Nationalists in Aleksandrówka. They were being given shelter by the local Ukrainians at the time of their tragic deaths.[17]

BERSTOWO
From the account of Wadiusz Kiesz from Boremel:

The Werner family was warned by their Ukrainian neighbor half an hour before the UPA attack of April 9, 1943. Taking his advice, "they lay in their field and watched as their home and possessions were burned."[18]

DOSZNO
From the account of Władysław Rubinowski from Doszno:

"I was 17. That night, as in the preceding nights, I slept at a Ukrainian neighbor's home. My sister, Józia, also slept in another Ukrainian household. Very early one morning I was awakened with the words, 'Get away, they're murdering the Poles.'

"I ran toward the woods. A Ukrainian on horseback saw me. He began to chase me and to shoot, but I managed to escape. In the woods, I met Jan Rubinowski, his sister Antonia, and Alina. When it became dark, Jan and I went to Wielimcze and obtained bread and cottage cheese from some Ukrainians. In the morning, I and the others reached Ratno. There, I learned that my mother, Paulina, and my sister, Antonina, were murdered. After a few days I joined the partisans. I was not particular about which ones I chose as long as I was given weapons. Later, I joined the Polish army. I visited Doszno at the beginning of the 1970s."[19]

GAJ
From the account of Jan Ferszt from Gaj, as recorded by Leon Karłowicz:

"I am often surprised by those Ukrainians. We know very well what kind of atrocities they committed and how many thousands of innocent people they murdered for nothing. How much suffering they caused their former neighbors! Supposedly, it was done for their nation's freedom. But to resort to such methods! And at the same time, you must believe me, in part I owe them my life. A few of us from Gaj actually survived. Perhaps it was God's will that someone could testify to the truth of what happened in those days, about which I will tell you. But now, I'd like to say something about those decent Ukrainians.

"There was such a Ukrainian family in our village. They were very patriotic. They dreamt of having their own free country. They sighed openly about independence. But when those from the Bandera contingent came to them one time, the head of the house asked them, 'Why do you kill Poles?' And he continued, 'When the time comes we will be free anyway; we must prepare for that time in another way! The children in cradles pose no danger, neither do those who barely walk with the help of a cane. Let's fight for independence with clean hands against our true enemy — and him we know well!'

"That's what he said! I know this from an eyewitness. And do you know what they did? They came back two days later and they murdered them all! Not a single person survived from that family, and it was a very large family. They killed their own!

"Here is another example. We know very well that the Ukrainian priests also bear responsibility for this slaughter. They blessed the knives, gave provocative talks, and encouraged the people to commit murder. But there was a Ukrainian priest near us who did not agree with their program of killing all the Poles and refused to bless both the exploits of the bandits and their knives, bayonets, and guns. He even told them that they would never achieve anything in that way, that they would turn the nation and other nations against themselves, and that they should not expect praise for their deeds from their compatriots. And the same thing happened to him as to the other family. They murdered him, his wife, and their two children because he had the courage to tell them the truth to their face. Whoever refused to murder the Poles became the object of murder. There were those who preferred to die rather than to become bandits themselves....

[Jan Ferszt describes his escape from the slaughter in Gaj. Running from UPA bullets, he was advised by a Ukrainian acquaintance to escape over a footbridge to the other side of the Stochód River.]

"In the evening, I left my hiding place. It was quiet and deserted. I survived, but my ears still rang from the screaming and shooting in Gaj. I wanted to go over there, but I was afraid that they may be lying in wait for me. After all, they knew that I had escaped. I managed to regain my self-control, even though my heart was still pounding. I crawled into a thicket and remained there for quite a while. A few days later, when the partisans — or perhaps they were the men from the self-defense center in Rożyszcze — arrived, I went back to my farm. Even today, after so many years, it is still difficult for me to talk about what I saw....

"Murdered people were lying around everywhere: in entranceways, houses, yards, and by-ways. Some were buried by their families in shallow graves and covered with a thin layer of dirt. About a hundred bodies, perhaps more, were taken to the nearby firing range. There, I found my daughter. I saw people who were decapitated. Some of the victims had their arms and legs hacked off. They were all pierced, probably with pitchforks and knives. Their faces were all blue. They were axed while still alive. Their limbs were cut off. How they suffered before they were allowed to die! One could see it all in their terribly contorted faces....

"This will remain with me for the rest of my life. How they must have felt knowing that help was not forthcoming! And the murderers standing around, shooting at everyone who tried to escape, and in every yard a few of them in a mad frenzy hitting and stabbing, axing children while mothers watched, torturing parents while children watched. Satan himself could not have thought up something like this. I could not then, and cannot now, understand whence came that sudden cruelty in the Ukrainians who lived among us for so many years in peace, often in friendship. After all, we helped each other in our work, did things for one another, played together, socialized ... and now some help me escape, show me the way to run, do not inform on me to those on the other side of the river, while others come and systematically kill family after family! And they eat bread from such fields! And how many such villages were there in Wołyń? How many graves? They live there now, as if on a cemetery!"[20]

LUBLINIEC
From the account of Tadeusz Kotarski from Rużyn Colony:

"The murder of Poles by the UPA began in the summer of 1943 and reached its apex in the fall of that year. The first tragedy occurred on July 10, 1943: the terrible murder of Zygmunt Rumel, Krzysztof Mazurkiewicz [Markiewicz], and Witold Dobrowolski. These men were sent by the regional Government Delegate, Kazimierz

Banach, to engage in the second series of peace talks with the UPA.

"The second tragedy occurred on August 17, 1943, in Rużyn. On that day, in full view of the residents of the Rużyn Colony and village, eight young Poles were abducted from that colony as well as the colony in Truskoty....

[They were bound with barbed wire and killed. The narrator then addresses the October 1943 execution of the Ukrainians sentenced to death by the Polish underground court for provoking a German attack on a Polish self-defense center. He also tells of a Pole who on his own shot two of his Ukrainian neighbors (both women) for supposedly failing to warn the village of a UPA attack, and because of their nationalist sympathies. This incident, the narrator adds, was universally condemned by the Polish society.]

"The third tragedy in my life occurred on November 11, 1943....

[This was the murder of the narrator's friend from childhood, Stefan Skowron, an orphan who was 18 years old. When found, his entrails were pulled out and his eyes were pierced.]

"The fourth tragedy concerned the death of the Ukrainian Ivan Oksiutych and his son Serhii in the fall of 1943. Ivan, an older man, lived in peace for years with his Polish neighbors and had the courage not to support the UPA fascists. He was murdered in the village of Klewieck with the assistance of his nephew, Lonka, who also chose the manner of his uncle's death: to be cut in half with a saw. His son's death was less painful: he was shot.

"At this time my parents lived with my Grandfather Michał in the village of Lubliniec. Our Ukrainian neighbors begged my father and mother to flee to Kowel, where their brothers lived near the German barracks, because they [the neighbors] did not want their deaths on their conscience.

"The fifth tragedy for me was the death of the Konopacki family. Like my parents, they were warned and advised to flee to Kowel. The mother and son did so; the father and two daughters remained behind, only to be murdered by the Ukrainian residents from the neighboring village of Dołhonosy."[21]

MIELNICA
From the account of Józefa Cyniak from Sucha Łoza:

The village of Sucha Łoza was attacked by the UPA on the same day and hour as the village of Gaj: August 30, 1943. The narrator's brother, Czesiek, was among those rounded up in Sucha Łoza for execution, but he managed to escape. As he was returning to his village, he met a Ukrainian acquaintance who entreated him to run away because he would be killed. "Your mother, father, brothers and sisters," the Ukrainian told him, "are all dead." Czesiek went to Hołoby instead.

Having escaped to Hołoby with her husband and several other Polish families, the narrator was told by eyewitnesses that the residents of Sucha Łoza were herded into the yard of her neighbor, Wybult, and were killed and buried in a clay pit. Out of 108 residents, only 12 survived.

Józefa recalls that after the liberation by the Red Army in 1944, "Some Ukrainian informed those of us in Hołoby that there were orphaned Polish children in Mielnica [another village attacked in the summer of 1943]. Evidently, they were being cared for by some Ukrainian family there. Mrs. Jasińska, together with some other women, went to the Soviet commander and requested a transport under guard to retrieve the children." They received the transport and the guard, and brought the children safely back to Hołoby.

The village of Mielnica was pacified by the Germans with the assistance of the

Ukrainian police on March 18, 1943. In all, about 80 persons from 19 Polish families were dragged out of their houses, taken in the direction of Wielick, and murdered. On April 24, 1943, Mielnica was pacified again by the Germans and the Ukrainian police. This time, 93 persons were shot. On August 29, 1943, Mielnica was attacked by the Ukrainian Nationalists. The remaining Polish residents were gathered in a school and more than 100 were murdered. However, some Ukrainian families in Mielnica, such as the Chernyk, Vidynskyi, Zhuk, and Senkevych families, manifested goodwill toward the Poles. Two daughters of the last family, who were medical students, were murdered for refusing to cooperate with the Ukrainian Nationalists.[22]

RATNO
From the account of Stanisława Krasińska from Doszno:

"I was 13 years old. We lived at the end of the village alongside some Ukrainians with whom we got along well. News reached us that a Ukrainian band had formed and that it was murdering Poles for the sake of establishing their own nation....

"[On the morning of August 28, 1943:] Mother called out to us, her three daughters, to run to the woods. Our brother remained behind since he was a cripple. We kept running around in the woods without stopping because it seemed to us that they would be able to find us everywhere. We finally reached the sprawling forest swamps. Although we felt hungry around noontime, we were afraid to leave. We chanced upon our cousin, Jan, who had been searching for his nephews. He found them and informed us, 'They're all dead. They've all been hacked to death.'

"Toward evening our oldest sister, Weronika, found us and took us home. In the yard, a horse and wagon was waiting. By taking various winding roads we finally arrived in Ratno. There, the residents — although they were Ukrainians — helped us and gave us food. They sympathized with us greatly....

"The *sołtys* of the village at that time was Stanislav Khrapchynskyi, a Ukrainian. After the murders in our village by the Ukrainian bandits, he took his wife and son and left. After the war he lived in Poland. Although my mother knew his address, she never wanted to meet him again.

"It was said that the large village of Wielimcze was settled by Ukrainian nobility before the war. No one from Doszno has ever heard that the residents of that village took part in the atrocities; on the contrary, they assisted the Poles. They hid five teachers: three Poles and two Russians. However, the bandits still managed to murder three of them. According to my mother, among those who survived was Cholewa. The bandits also murdered the Polish operators of the mill, but Płaskociński survived.

"All the surviving residents of Doszno spoke very highly about the village of Wielimcze. Those who by some miracle were able to live through those terrible times benefited in some way, great or small, from the people in that village."[23]

ŚMIDYŃ

Four members of the Eum family were murdered by the Ukrainian Nationalists in Śmidyń on September 1, 1943. Two brothers from this family survived because on their way home they were warned by their Ukrainian neighbor of the danger that awaited them. The local Ukrainian priest wanted to bury the bodies of the victims in the Orthodox cemetery, but the leaders of the UPA forbade him to do so. They were buried in the orchard instead.[24]

5
Krzemieniec County

Krzemieniec County, the southernmost in Wołyń through which three rivers — Horyń, Ikwa, and Wilia — flowed, shared a common border with Soviet Ukraine. Its 12 village communes were: Bereźce, Białokrynica, Białozórka, Dederkały, Katerburg, Krzemieniec (county seat), Oleksiniec, Poczajów, Szumsk, Uhorsk, Wiśniowiec, and Wyszogródek.

Table 12
Population of Krzemieniec County by Mother Tongue

Ukrainian	195,817
Ruthenian	183
Polish	25,758
Jewish	18,679
German	118
Czech	301
Russian	1,754
Belorussian	56
Lithuanian	13
Other	86
Unreported	267
Total	243,032

Table 13
Population of Krzemieniec County by Religious Affiliation

Orthodox	194,517
Roman Catholic	25,082
Uniate	716
Protestant/Evangelical	1,195
Other Christian	2,571
Jewish	18,751
Other Non-Christian	5
Not Specified or Non-Religious	14
Unreported	178
Total	243,032

All three factions of the Nationalists (Borovets's, Melnyk's, and Bandera's) operated within this county. It was also the headquarters of the OUN-B "Eneia" region. Ivan Klymushyn ("Kruk") was in charge of the 200-man battalion formed there.

The Polish genocide in Krzemieniec County was initiated by the two-company battalion of "Negus." Its march led from the Antonowce Forest toward Kąty (Kuty) and toward Krzemieniec. Although the murders of individuals in this area began shortly after mid-March 1943, the massive exterminations of the Polish people there took place during Holy Week and on Easter Sunday of that year. For example: on April 20 Uhorsk was destroyed, on April 22 Mosty fell, and on April 23 Baszkowce and Czuhale were attacked. This "Easter Action" embraced many other counties as well, especially those in the "Eneia" and "Zahrava" regions.

On May 5, 1943, many places throughout Wołyń succumbed to UPA attacks. Kąty and its parish church were among these, as were the surrounding villages of Huta Antonowiecka, Majdan, Dąbrowa, and Zabara.

In June the attacks subsided somewhat only to be resumed with resolute vigor and hellish intensity during the "Peter and Paul

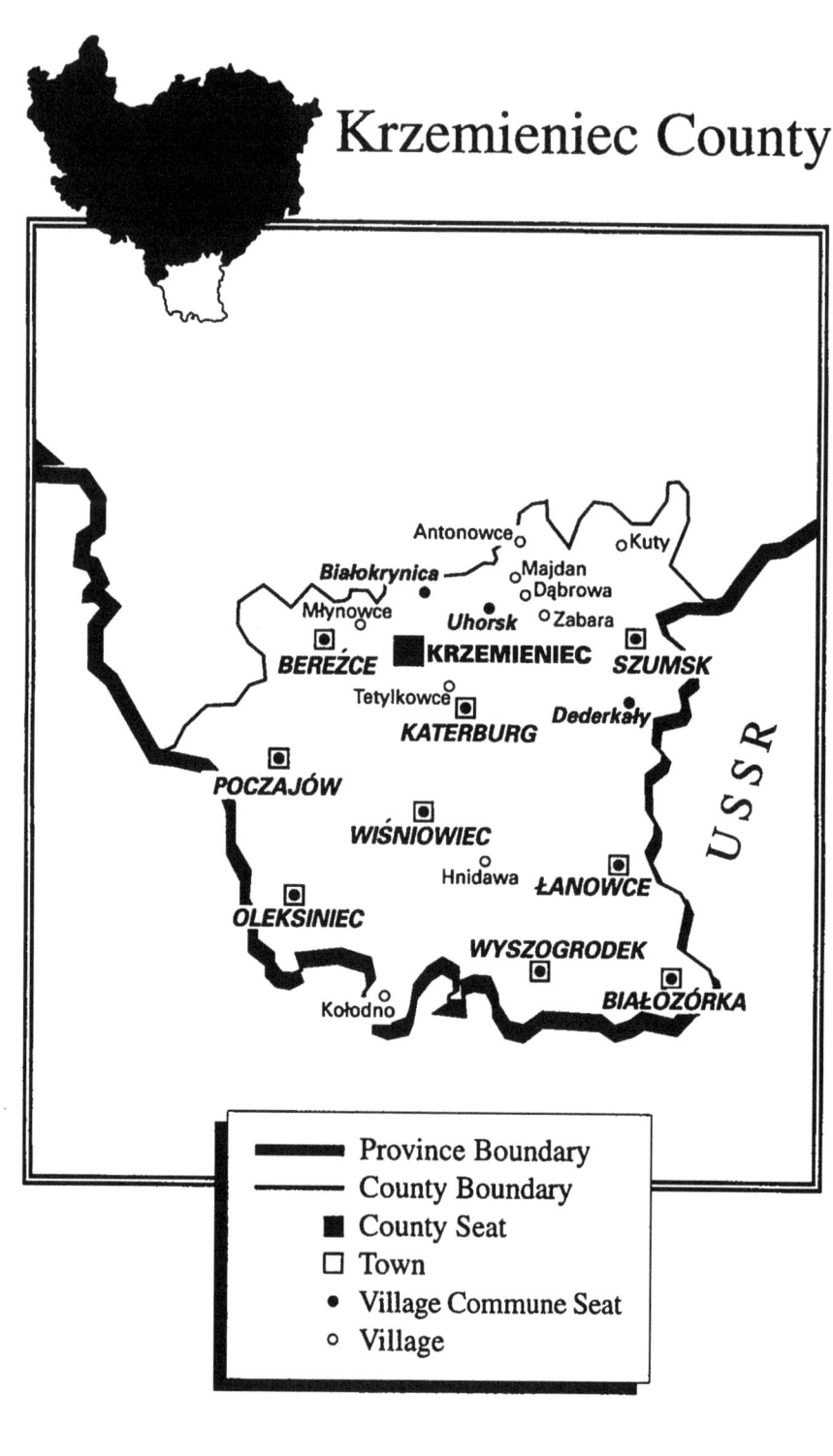

action" of July. Every county in Wołyń except Luboml was affected by that "action." In Krzemieniec County, over 19 places were attacked and the civilian population brutally murdered. The town of Wiśniowiec was one of these. When the gullible Poles opened the town gates, believing in the guarantee of safety proffered by the Melnykowcy, they were slaughtered.

Although the ethnic-cleansing campaign diminished in intensity after August 1943, it nevertheless continued until the end of the war and beyond.

People

BOBOSHKO, Mrs., from Mołotków
From the account of Helena Kulczycka (b. 1921) from Mołotków, as recorded by Władysław Wolski:

"I was born in 1921 in Mołotków in the commune of Białozórka, the county of Krzemieniec, the province of Wołyń. My village was large: over 300 houses. About 25 percent of the population was Polish, the rest was Ukrainian. Before the war, both ethnic groups lived in peace. After the Soviet invasion of September 17, 1939, the Ukrainians took over the governance structures. Generally speaking, there was still peace.

"In 1941, after the German invasion of Wołyń, the Ukrainians began to collaborate with the new occupant, who promised them an independent Ukraine. They arrested some Poles, including my brother. They also organized the roundups of youth for forced labor in Germany — mainly Poles, but the Ukrainians also had to go since there were more of them.

"The attacks on Poles by the Ukrainian Nationalists began toward the end of 1942. At that time, these attacks were regarded as the personal settling of scores. This created some mistrust and put people on alert, especially in regard to strangers.

"My parents got along well with their Ukrainian neighbor, Boboshko. They entrusted their clothes to her for safekeeping, and we spent the nights in her home when the attacks escalated....

"One day, several Ukrainian bandits came to the house. [This incident took place in the village of Płoska, a few dozen kilometers from Mołotków.] They were no men at home at the time because of a warning by a friendly Ukrainian who urged them to go into hiding because the bandits were coming for them. In the house, therefore, there remained only the women and children. The bandits began to hit us hard and demanded that my sister reveal the whereabouts of her husband. They struck us in the face. When I fell face down on a pillow after being slapped, the assailant struck me in the back between my shoulder blades with some dull object. For a while, I could not catch my breath and thought that was the end of me. After a minute, I began to breathe slowly. Upon leaving, the attackers ordered us all to be home the next day. After that beating, my brother-in-law's mother and I had black and blue faces for two weeks. I thought my face would always remain like that."[1]

HALIA family from Wiśniowiec Stary
From the account of Maria Stemplowska-Niezgoda (b. 1912) from Wiśniowiec Stary, as recorded by Leon Popek:

"About 50 Polish families lived in Wiśniowiec Stary in 1939....

"When the UPA began its bloody trek, the people from the surrounding villages gathered in the Carmelite monastery in Wiśniowiec. The monastery was attacked several times, both by the Melnykowcy and the Banderowcy. The people defended themselves as in the Middle Ages, pouring hot water over the walls and throwing bricks and stones at the invaders. The UPA did not dare to attack while the Germans were stationed there. However, when the Germans left in January 1944 and the Hungarians began to withdraw to Zbaraż, fear gripped the defenders. The Hungarian army allowed about 100 people — one person per wagon — to leave with it. In the monastery, there remained about 300-400 people.

"On the night of February 12, 1944, the monastery was attacked in a perfidious manner. UPA members, posing as Polish refugees, begged for the monastery gate to be opened. After the gate was opened, the Banderowcy made their way into the courtyard and monastery. The people immediately began to flee; they ran out of the monastery and hid in the adjoining buildings. The bandits murdered everyone, mainly by shooting them. Neither women nor children nor old people were spared. Only a few were able to save themselves by running away or hiding. The monks (except for the one who died in 1976 in Lublin) also perished. One of the Holy Fathers was choked to death with a towel. The bodies of the murdered victims were taken to the monastery cellars and covered with sand....

"The next organized attack on the Poles took place on Saturday, February 26, 1944. The surviving Polish families (28 people in all) included the Stemplowski, Królikowski, and Dudkowski families. They were hidden by the following Ukrainian families: Natalka, Soroka, Halia, and Kniaz. On the night of February 26, 1944, the bandits came to Soroka and demanded that the Stemplowski children (ten-year-old Helena and five-year-old Piotr) be handed over. Mrs. Soroka replied that she would hand the children over only to their parents and that she would not relinquish them to strangers and foreigners. Then the UPA members, knowing that Józef Stemplowski (aged 44) and his son (Dominik, aged six) were hidden at the home of the Ukrainian Halia, went there, and threatening Józef with a gun, led him back to Soroka's house. Hearing the voice of the father, Mrs. Soroka opened the door and let them all inside the house. The Sorokas were told to dress the children and to take them outside. When the children were awakened and were being dressed, ten-year-old Helena began to cry. The murderers, who stood in the vestibule, began to scold the child and to laugh. 'Why are you crying?' they asked.

"The girl answered, 'Should I not cry over my own death?'

"Józef took his son Piotr in his arms saying 'My child' and went for his third child, Dominik, who was still with Halia.

"All three children were left at the Halia residence under guard lest they tried to escape. Józef was then forced at gunpoint and blackmailed (his children's safety was at stake) to go from house to house in order to find his wife Maria (who was hiding with her daughter, Jadwiga) by calling out her name. Maria, however, upon hearing the voice of her husband, did not come out. She suspected a trick and remained in hiding.

"Then the Banderowcy took the sleigh and horses and decided to abduct Maria's brother, Józef Królikowski. The brother managed to escape, but his son Bolesław (16) remained at home. Threatened and probably beaten, Bolesław said through his tears, 'I want my father.' The UPA members promised to take him to his father if he showed them where he was hiding. The father, hearing the crying and the voice of his son, gave himself up to the Banderowcy.

"The rounded-up party of Poles was then loaded on the sleigh and taken to the home of the aunt of one of the bandits, Protsiuk. The home lay near some woods about five kilometers from Wiśniowiec in the direction of Krzemieniec. There, it was proposed that Józef Stemplowski axe to death Maria's brother and thereby save himself and his children. The father refused; the brother objected as well.

"So they took them all to a settler's well located about 50 meters from Protsiuk's buildings. There, the Poles were murdered with an axe: first the men, then the women, and finally the children. The children watched as their parents and the other adults suffered and died. The murders were accompanied by an exceptional sadism: the arms and feet were hacked off 'so the Polish pigs would suffer all the more' — thus testified Myshko Protsiuk (18 years of age), the chief executioner, at his trial in Krzemieniec in August or September 1944. Twenty-eight persons from the Stemplowski, Królikowski, and Dudkowski families, as well as 47 others from Wiśniowiec and the vicinity whose names are not known, were thrown into a well seventy meters deep....

"[Meanwhile:] Maria, in despair, was constantly searching for her husband and children. She wanted to know at least the place of their burial and about the last moments of their lives. A few days after the murders in Wiśniowiec she met a group of Banderowcy. Not mindful of danger, she walked up to them with her daughter and said, 'You took away my husband, take me and the child as well.'

"She was saved from death by a UPA messenger who arrived just then with some important news for his comrades. They immediately scattered in all directions. At that very moment Soviet soldiers appeared. All this was observed by an old Ukrainian woman, Medzarykha. She began to plead with Maria not to expose herself to danger and to be concerned about her own safety and the safety of her child; she could do nothing for her husband. She led Maria and the child to her home, fed them, and gave them shelter for the night. That night, the UPA came to murder Maria and her child. They were defended by Medzarykha's son, a Banderowiec, who refused to allow this sequential murder.

"Shortly thereafter, the Soviets began to recruit men for the front. A wife of one of the Ukrainian recruits, Halytskyi, in her grief over her husband's departure, said that she knew what happened to Maria's husband and children. Pressed by the NKVD [Soviet security police], she named Protsiuk as the chief culprit and he was shortly arrested. During the investigation, he revealed that the bodies of the victims were in the well. The Soviets decided to conduct a local investigation in order to verify his statement and to determine the cause of death.

"In the company of Soviet officers, a doctor, and the *sołtys*, Maria went to the well at the beginning of June 1944. With the help of a rope, Protsiuk's father was lowered into the well from which he retrieved the body of five-year-old Dominik, Maria's son. At the sight of her child, she fainted. The inspection revealed that he had been axed to death. The child's teeth were knocked out, his arms and legs had been broken and cut, his stomach was slashed open....

"On a return visit in 1967, Maria saw thousands of human bones and entire skeletons in the basement of the church in Wiśniowiec Stary....

"On her third visit in 1990, Maria noticed that the church was completely destroyed ... [and that] the bones of the dead lay scattered everywhere....

"In 1996 Maria went back to Wiśniowiec with her daughter Jadwiga and her grandson. On the obelisk commemorating the tragedy, with the permission and assistance of the local authorities, she placed a small cross."[2]

KNIAZ family from Wiśniowiec. *See* Halia family.

MAKAR from Hucisko Horodyńskie
From the account of Feliks Jasiński from Kąty (Kuty):

"The villages of Marynki and Hucisko Kowalowe, located in the middle of a group of Polish villages, did not have many casualties. Almost everyone from these locations sought shelter in Kąty (Kuty). After the exodus, only two elderly people remained in Marynki. One of these was Józef Listowski, who was hiding in the home of his Ukrainian friend, Makar, in Hucisko Horodyńskie. He worked for him that summer and fall; that winter, he was murdered. The second person who remained in Marynki was a woman, an invalid and a beggar, who in all probability did not fear death. She was murdered and left by the side of a road."³

MEDZARYKHA, Mrs., from Wiśniowiec. *See* Halia family.

NATALKA family from Wiśniowiec. *See* Halia family.

SKAKALSKA, Mrs., from Tetylkowce
From the account of Olga Kucewicz from Krzemieniec and later Tetylkowce:

"March 19, 1943, and the days that followed have imbedded themselves in my memory as if on a photographic plate so that today I am able to describe in detail what I and my loved ones had lived through....

[A description follows of how the narrator's family was attacked, made to lie on the floor, bound and robbed. Only the narrator with her three-and-a-half-year-old daughter, her aunt, and a female servant were not tied up.]

"The bandits ordered everyone to get up and get into the wagons. My daughter, meanwhile, fell asleep. I went out with my family onto the porch. The night was bright and the full moon lit up the house. We did not want to get into the wagons, knowing that death and perhaps torture awaited us. Jan Kucewicz, the owner of the estate, and his family got on the first wagon and were driven off. We all stood around and did not budge. My husband said that we would not get on the wagons.

"Then a series of shots were fired in our direction. Everyone fell onto the porch floor. I felt a temporary constriction in my neck. When I touched it, it was wet. It turned out to be blood. I ran into the bedroom and wrapped my neck in my child's flannel blanket knowing that I would bleed a lot. I heard the moans of the dying. I went out onto the porch. Leon Czepielowski (senior) and his wife Regina [narrator's visiting in-laws] lay there without moving. He was struck in the forehead; she, in her left side, perhaps the heart.

"My husband and his younger brother, Tadeusz, seemed to be in good shape. My husband asked me to untie his hands. I couldn't do it, so I ran through a small hallway into the kitchen for a knife. I returned with it to the porch. When I finally freed my husband, a bandit in a dark uniform appeared out of the shadows beyond the porch. I froze and heard these words: 'You're still alive, you brat?'

"I was paralyzed with fear. He placed his revolver to my breast and pulled the trigger. It misfired. I immediately unfroze and with one leap found myself in the anteroom, then in the dark hallway leading to the dining room, then in the kitchen, and finally in the servant's room, where in great fear I hid under the bed. Behind me fell a volley of shots aimed either at me or the survivors on the porch.

"When it became quiet after a while, I crawled out of my hiding place with the knife still clutched in my hand and went back to the porch. It was there that I noticed that Tadeusz's white shirt turned red and that blood ran from his mouth. He got up by himself and went inside. My husband, who had on a thick sweater, seemed to be all right, but he could not get up. I dragged him inside and propped him up in a sitting position against the wall....

"I realized that I had to take the wounded to the hospital as soon as possible.... I sent Hania, the servant, with the request to have the wagons prepared for transport. Unfortunately, the field hands were all gathered in one place and had orders from the bandits not to go anywhere; perhaps they simply did not want to help.

"In one part of the estate there lived a Ukrainian woman, Skakalska, who had some kind of a quarrel with the directors of the high school in Krzemieniec and as a result did not want to move out. Hania asked this woman for the horses. Since Skakalska's husband was taken to Germany for forced labor, she hired a young Ukrainian boy to help her out with the farm. She now told the boy to hitch up the horses, spread the wagon with hay, and take the wounded to Krzemieniec. The boy prepared everything, but refused to drive to the town claiming that he was afraid of the bandits — so I had to handle the team myself. With the help of the servant, I added some blankets and pillows to the wagon and placed the wounded on top of this bedding. We left the house, still bathed in moonlight so bright that no lantern was needed. As we left, the blood of the victims was still flowing down the porch steps and our part-wolf dog was sniffing the bodies of our slain relatives."

The narrator's husband died in the hospital in Krzemieniec from three gunshot wounds. While convalescing in the hospital, Olga met many other wounded people brought there from the surrounding Polish villages and recalled and recorded in her account a few of their tragic stories, including the incident of the discovery of the headless body of Stański, murdered on the night of March 19, 1943, the same night her family was attacked.[4]

SOROKA family from Wiśniowiec. *See* Halia family.

Places

BIAŁOZÓRKA
From the account of Edmund Bosakowski from Białozórka:

"We must also acknowledge that not all Ukrainians were badly disposed toward the Poles. There were those who befriended the Poles and warned them of danger...."

One of these Ukrainians warned Fr. Terlikowski, who then stopped having church services in order to avoid gathering the Polish people together. After receiving a second warning at the beginning of July 1943, he closed up his church and left for Podole.

On August 1, 1943, another Ukrainian warned the Centkiewicz family of the UPA's intent to murder the Poles in that village. The news spread. Nevertheless, five Polish families were murdered on that date in Białozórka.[5]

UHORSK
Wiktor Poliszczuk states:

"My wife's parents lived in Polesie before the war. Her father was Czech; her mother, Polish. At home they spoke Polish. When the massive murders of Poles began in southern Polesie in 1942, her family went to live with the family of her father in the village of Uhorsk near Dermań in the county of Krzemieniec. In 1943 a Ukrainian acquaintance informed my wife's father that the UPA intended to murder his family. They fled to Krzemieniec. But someone witnessed the talk between the young Ukrainian and my wife's father. Accusing him of 'treason,' they [the Banderowcy] hung that Ukrainian in the center of the village with a sign on his chest that read: 'This will happen to all traitors.' They did not allow his body to be taken down for several days. The Banderowcy also shot my father's brother in the village of Lipa for speaking ill of the UPA. They shot him through the mouth."[6]

WIŚNIOWIEC
From the account of Irena Sandecka from Krzemieniec:

After emerging, under German escort, from the monastery cellars filled with corpses, Irena recalls:

"I thanked the Germans who were with me for their help and dedication. They answered that it was not pleasant to look at the corpses. Meanwhile, Konopacki did not waste any time. Finding a Ukrainian acquaintance on one of the streets of Wiśniowiec, he inquired whether there were any Poles hiding in the area. The Ukrainian answered, 'I'll search.' After a while, Gąsiorowski, quite unshaven, was found. It turned out that he was in hiding with the above-mentioned Ukrainian. He told of terrible things, but we ourselves could see that all of the Polish homes in Wiśniowiec were destroyed from top to bottom."[7]

6
Luboml County

Bordering on the Bug River and the Lublin Province to the west, Luboml County—a forested terrain broken by numerous lakes, marshes and the Prypeć River—shared its northern border with Polesie. The county's seven village communes included: Bereżce, Hołowno, Huszcza, Luboml (county seat), Pulmieniec, Szack, and Zgorany.

Table 14
Population of Luboml County by Mother Tongue

Ukrainian	65,741
Ruthenian	165
Polish	12,150
Jewish	6,818
German	8
Czech	8
Russian	371
Belorussian	114
Lithuanian	none recorded
Other	4
Unreported	12
Total	85,507

Table 15
Population of Luboml County by Religious Affiliation

Orthodox	65,578
Roman Catholic	10,998
Uniate	107
Protestant/Evangelical	930
Other Christian	931
Jewish	6,861
Other Non-Christian	2
Not Specified or Non-Religious	6
Unreported	94
Total	85,507

A two-company UPA battalion was organized in this county at the end of March 1943 under the command of "Lysyi." One of these companies was responsible for the August 10, 1943, attack on Kamień Koszyrski.

On the night of August 29, 1943, a number of villages were attacked simultaneously in Luboml County, including: Kąty (not to be confused with Kąty, also called Kuty, in Krzemieniec County), where out of 282 inhabitants, 141 were killed, including 64 children; Jankowce, where 79 persons (out of 762 residents) were murdered, of whom 18 were children; Czmykos Colony, where 42 Polish families (about 240 persons) were murdered; Borki Colony, where at least 55 people in 12 families perished; and Ostrówki and Wola Ostrowiecka, where enormous losses took place—at least 1,041 victims whose names are known, half of whom were children.

In Wola Ostrowiecka, 79 families were completely wiped out and in 37 families only one person survived. At least 664 people in 121 families lived in Ostrówki at the time of the attack. Out of that number, at least 469 persons (or about 70 percent) were killed. Among the victims were 145 women and 179 children under the age of 16. In that area, an estimated total of 1,700 persons

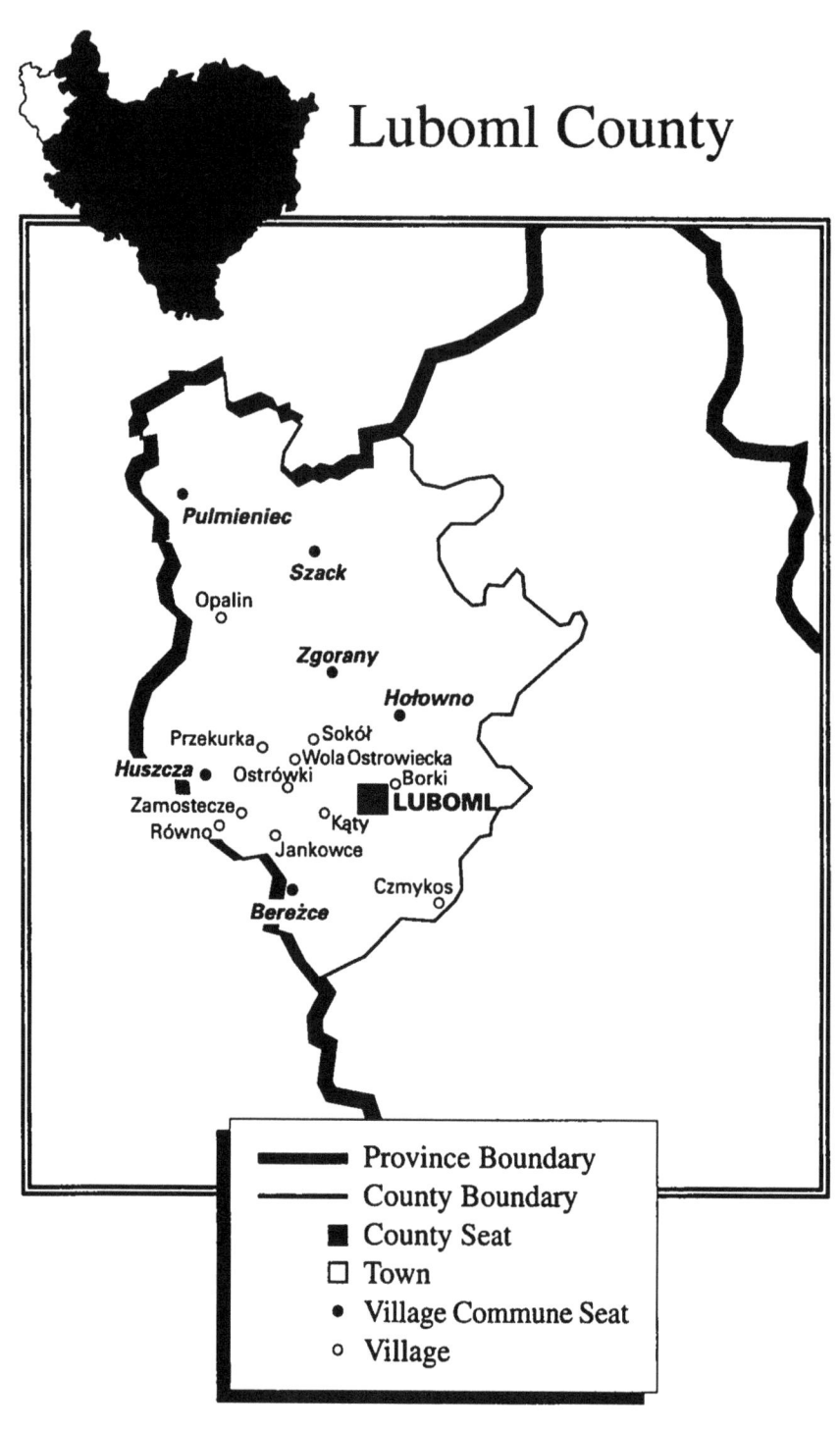

were murdered. And there were numerous other victims as well at this time throughout Wołyń. (For a field report and court testimony of Iurii Stelmashchuk and a field report of "Lysyi" regarding their part in the massacres, see Appendix C: Excerpts from Documents, Ukrainian — "Report of Iurii Stelmashchuk ['Rudyi,' 'Kaidash'], Commander of UPA 'Turiv' Region, to Mykola Lebed ['Maksym Ruban'], June 24, 1943"; "Court Testimony of Iurii Stelmashchuk ['Rudyi,' 'Kaidash'], Commander of the UPA 'Turiv' Region, February 20, 1945"; and "UPA ['Lysyi's'] Field Report of September 1943 on the Destruction of Ostrówki and Wola Ostrowiecka.")

This August "action," which began in Równe County and ended in the county of Luboml, was meticulously prepared by the UPA and even involved the blockading of escape routes. In Luboml County this was done by "Lysyi's" men, members of the UPA cadet school located at Biały Lake, and the SKV.

In terms of its widespread coverage, the alarming number of victims, and short duration, this was undoubtedly the most efficiently conducted and the most effective campaign ever undertaken by the UPA. Significantly, this massive genocidal action took place *after* the OUN-B's August 21-25, 1943, Third Great Conference of the Organization of Ukrainian Nationalists (VZOUN) during which it ostensibly "abandoned" its fascist orientation in favor of democracy and minority rights.

People

MAKAR family from Przekurka
From the account of Czesław Kuwałek (b. 1927) from Ostrówki:

"The Banderowcy entered the village [Ostrówki] at dawn reassuring the people and herding them into the school for a meeting — first the men and then the women and children....

[The following two sentences are out of sequence. They appear in a later section of this account: "Janina Fotek, a young girl 18 years of age, ran over with tears in her eyes saying that her mother had been wounded. A UPA officer turned to the nurse and said, 'Tamara, go take care of her wounds.'"]

"Both of them left in a westerly direction. I don't know how far they got, but I do not believe that they ever reached the girl's wounded mother. However, the officer's words served to quiet the crowd, which then entered the school with confidence....

"Upon hearing a German voice, I left my hiding place. I met my father and a few other people, including my school friend Bolesław Trusiuk, who spoke a little German. He began to plead with the Germans to rescue the women and children [being led just then to the Ukrainian village of Sokół for execution]. When this didn't work, he asked them to lend us some weapons since the women and children being led away were no more than 500 to 600 meters from the village. Unfortunately, they refused this request as well and shoved him away with a smirk. During that time, I discovered that the remains of my great-grandfather, Władysław Kuwałek, who was 98 years of age, as well as the remains of some children were in Trusiuk's well. (They shot the men in Trusiuk's yard.) The children were later removed from the well, but they were beyond all recognition....

"There were also incidents when the Ukrainians behaved decently toward the Poles. My uncle, Bolesław Kuwałek, lived with his family near the Przekurka border and became acquainted with two Ukrainian families. One of them was named Makar; the other, Mykolus.... They sheltered my uncle's family for about three days after the attack and then took them to Wilczy Przewóz, where they could cross the

Bug River. There, they handed them over to my uncle [who was not with his family at the time].

"It is difficult for someone who has lived through it all and has lost everything and everyone nearest and dearest to him to write about these matters. It's like reopening an old wound that has scabbed over. I carry this sorrow within my breast constantly. It haunts me at every turn. I have to swallow my tears every day."[1]

MYKOLUS family from Przekurka. *See* Makar family.

SANURYK, Pelahiia, from Przekurka
From a March 25, 1992, court deposition of Nestor S. Kots (b. 1907) from Borowe, near Przekurka:

"To answer the question put before me, I attest that the Petruk (also commonly called Prystupa) family lived on an estate in Przekurka not far from our house.

"I know that in the fall of 1943 a sub-unit of the UPA, the Masliuk company, exterminated that family. They killed the father, Petruk, near the village of Sokół. They killed his son, Piotr, in the woods near Przekurka. His mother and two daughters hid for a short time in the village of Przekurka in the home of Pelahiia Sanuryk (who died over ten years ago.)"[2]

Places

BORKI
From the account of Edward Soroka (b. 1930) from Wola Ostrowiecka Colony:

"During the war I lived in Wola Ostrowiecka Colony.... After sunrise [on August 30, 1943] I noticed a strange thing. No one from nearby Wola Ostrowiecka was taking their cows to pasture. We did not know then that the village was surrounded by the Ukrainians just before dawn and that they did not allow anyone out....

"I was sprayed with machine-gun fire in Ostrówki Colony by a Ukrainian who sat on the roof of one of the buildings. Being near the cemetery, I saw women and children on the road. I thought that they were on their way to Wola Ostrowiecka. Wanting to warn them, I ran out onto the road. It was then that I noticed that they were guarded by armed Ukrainians. [This was the death march to the Ukrainian village of Sokół, where several hundred people, predominantly women and children, were executed in a Nazi-like "open-air" shooting.] Being still unnoticed, I hid in the bushes again.

"I decided to find myself a better hiding place. I saw a nearby hayrick, crawled beneath its lowered roof, kept perfectly still, and fell asleep out of fear. After a few hours had passed, I awoke and left my hiding place. I saw the burning village and heard occasional gunfire. I met Jan Palec, who was wounded in his right hand. We went together in the direction of Jagodzin. In the woods of Borki we met a Ukrainian, the wife of the forester. I asked her for help for my wounded friend. After a while, she brought some water and bandages. After dressing the wound, she told us that she could not show us the way to Jagodzin because she didn't know it. When she left, we hid again.

"From afar we observed the garden in the field. That evening, we noticed that our Ukrainian friend was explaining something to her husband who had just returned home. We suspected that she was telling him about us. When we emerged from our hiding place, both of them came up to us and told us that they would take us to Jagodzin themselves. The forester brought us as far as Jagodzin Colony, a colony that was inhabited by Poles."[3]

OSTRÓWKI
First account. Janina Martosińska (née Kuwałek, b. 1930) from Ostrówki:

"It was Sunday, August 29, 1943, and the day was full of tension. Some Ukrainians warned their [Polish] acquaintances that on that night Polish people were to be killed. Those warned, in turn, passed the message on to other villages so that their residents could be on guard. In our county, there were two Polish villages: mine (Ostrówki) and Wola Ostrowiecka. The rest were mixed....

"While our village was dozing—one could not call it sleeping—the Ukrainians let out a volley of shots; some of the bullets were incendiary. A terrible panic gripped the village. People grabbed whatever they could and fled into the fields or forests. Some of them got away, but most of them were turned back to the village by the Ukrainians. The men were herded into a school; the women and children into a church. Meanwhile, pits were being dug near these two locations....

"The Ukrainians began by murdering the men. They were piercing them with pitchforks and axing them to death. My great-grandfather, Władysław, who was about 90 years old, was thrown into a well....

"The women and children were then driven out of the church into the square. They told us to leave everything behind and herded us in the direction of the cemetery. When the Germans [at some distance] began to shoot, we were told to march faster through the marshes toward the [Ukrainian] village of Sokół. They were probably afraid that the Germans would rescue us....

"On our death march, the women and children sang religious songs such as 'Dearest Mother,' 'Under Your Protection,' and many others. There was no thought of escape because the Ukrainians were a legion. They were armed in various ways: some had guns and rifles, others carried shovels, axes, and pitchforks. They were also dressed variously: in Russian, Polish, and German uniforms as well as in civilian clothing.

"There were two women in our group dressed in black; they were referred to as nuns. They begged the Ukrainians to kill them, but to release the rest of us. To this, one of the bandits replied, 'Why in hell do you bore us?'

"When we reached the destination, the two women pleaded again for our safety. Another Ukrainian replied, 'In 1918 you did this to us.'

"Then all hell broke lose.

"They drove us from the clearing into a field of stubble. There, they took a few people at a time, made them lie down, and shot them. Entire families of women and children were brought out. I waited until I could go with my own family, which was large and included my father's three sisters with their children. (One had three daughters; another had two sons who were two-and-a-half and four years old.) I was 14, my brother was 12, and my mother, Marianna, was in the last weeks of her pregnancy. With us were two of the above-mentioned aunts: one with her sons Stanisław and Edward; the other, an unmarried aunt, with her brother and mother. We could not find our third aunt.

"There were about 300 to 400 of us in all, mostly women and children from Ostrówki but also a few from Wola Ostrowiecka. One of the Ukrainians killed about half of us. His comrades snickered on the side at his courage. Finally, he got fed up, threw down his rifle, and said, 'Since I'm doing all the killing, the entire responsibility will fall on me.'

"Then a few more of them came over, and they continued the killing. Not many of us remained alive, and now it was our turn.

"We went to our death together. We lay down on the ground: I, next to my mother and brother, and next to us, our aunts with the boys. One of the aunts held Stanisław, the other held Edward. The boys did not want to lie down and began to cry hysterically. Both my aunts begged them to lie down but they wailed all the louder. I will remember their frightening screams for the rest of my life. There was a shot, and one of the children was silenced; then another shot, and the other child was stilled as well. I prayed, 'God grant that he will kill me, rather than wound me.'

"When he shot my brother, a faint waft of gunpowder reached my nostrils. He shot me next. I felt no pain and hoped he would kill me quickly so that I wouldn't have to keep smelling that gunpowder. I fell. I did not realize that I had been shot. I lay there a long time, and although I was quite resigned to it all on the march to my death and was not afraid, I was now paralyzed by fear. A strange feeling came over me which is difficult to describe.

"I was wounded between 12:00 and 1:00 P.M. When I finally lifted my head, it was already around 8:00 P.M. I felt an acute pain in my left shoulder and in the palm of my right hand. I looked about me. They were all dead. I was left alone, and I was wounded in the shoulder, the palm and, as I discovered later, in my head.

"I saw our neighbor nearby. She was about 28 eight years old. Next to her lay her ten-month-old baby. The baby was dead. Being severely wounded, my neighbor asked me to help her get up. She wanted to go to the railroad station in Jagodzin. I tried to help her but I was too weak, and she herself had no strength left at all.

"Among the murdered sat a small girl about seven years of age who was sound and in good health. She wept bitterly because her mother, three sisters, and brother were slain. Her father was killed in the school. Evening fell and I gave up trying to reach the railroad station...."

[Later, on the road between Ostrówki and Wola Ostrowiecka, the narrator met her grandmother.] "When my grandmother saw how I looked, she began to cry. She then took me to my uncle, who was being hidden by Ukrainians, and we all went to Luboml...."

[A brief description follows concerning the events known to the narrator about the simultaneous attack on nearby Wola Ostrowiecka.]

"My friend from school hid with her younger brother during the attack. After the slaughter, they came out to look for their parents. Suddenly, a Ukrainian appeared who took them by the hand and told them to hide again. And so, they survived."

The narrator concludes her story by relating incidents she had heard about, while recuperating in the hospital in Luboml, from the hospitalized survivors of the UPA attacks on Kąty and Baranowicze.

Aleksander Pradun (from Ostrówki, b. 1931) and Agnieszka Muzyka (from Ostrówki. b. 1918) also survived the massacre near Sokół. Both were among those who were made to lie down and were shot. The speed with which this massive execution was carried out no doubt accounted for their survival. Evidently, a German contingent was on the way and their machine-gun fire could be heard. Describing how the loved ones next to him were being killed, including his mother (whose blood splattered his head and neck) and his aunt, Aleksander Pradun adds, "This all lasted but a short time because the Ukrainians were shooting everyone in double time. They were in a great hurry."

Agnieszka Muzyka states that toward the end, several grenades were thrown among the living and dead. Nevertheless, the murderers still took the time to gather up the victims' clothing and to finish off most of the wounded before departing. Agnieszka also recalls that prior to the execution, a man on horseback rode up and read an order which condemned the Poles to death by shooting. Evidently, after a while, some of the shooters refused to go on with their ghastly task. "The Ukrainian leader read the order again," states Agnieszka, "and said that those who do not carry it out will be shot." The threat proved to be effective and the massacre continued.

While the women and children were being herded toward Sokół, the men of Ostrówki were taken out of the school ten at a time and marched to the barnyards of Trusiuk and Suszek, where they were axed to death.[4]

Second account. Antoni Ulewicz (b. 1912) from Ostrówki:

"They told me to go toward Trusiuk's barnyard, where they were murdering the Poles who had been led out of the school. After a while, a Banderowiec whom I recognized came riding up on a horse. I said 'Good morning' to him, but there was no reply. At Trusiuk's, I saw a pit in which naked people were lying. I was told to lie down with them. I stretched out my hand to my friends in greeting and simultaneously to bid them good-bye. One of them was Julian Kudan. Three Ukrainians stood over us; the rest circulated in the yard. Among them was someone I knew. I began to beg him to kill me with a bullet, rather than an axe or some other instrument. Julian heard me and said, 'You'd be better off praying because there's no use in talking to him. They're animals, not people.'

"After a moment of reflection, the Ukrainian acquaintance came up to the ditch, gave me his hand, and told me to get up. When I crawled out of the pit, he gave me a hat and a coat and told me to follow him; we went in the direction of my house. When we reached the Pińkowski residence, he cast a backward glance. He pointed out a narrow concrete tunnel under the road and told me to hide in there. With some trouble, I squeezed myself inside. Upon leaving, he told me to remain there quietly because if they found me I would be killed and the village would be burned.

"After a while, I sensed that someone else was trying to crawl into my hiding place. Since I lay inside head first, I couldn't tell who it was. I thought it might be the one of the bandits. Then I was asked to identify myself. By his voice I knew that it was our school director, [Józef] Jeż. It turned out that the same Ukrainian brought him there as well.

"Germans on their way to Luboml from Borowe found us. One of them noticed Jeż sticking out and shouted, 'Bandit!' Soon we were standing in front of him with a rifle pointed at us. The German took us to Fotek's house, located at one end of the village. At the intersection by the cross stood a few women and men. A Ukrainian policeman in the service of the Germans came up to us. His name was Iakiv Rohovskyi. I had known him for many years. I asked him what they were going to do with us. He said that they were going to shoot us. I asked him to shoot us himself rather than have the Germans do it. He thought a bit and then began talking to the German who stood next to him. He convinced the German that we were not bandits, but rather, his neighbors. The German told us to flee to Jagodzin, otherwise the bandits would kill us. That's exactly what we did."[5]

PRZEKURKA
First account. Aleksander Lubczyński (b. 1937) from Wola Ostrowiecka:

"On the night of September 29 [1943] the Ukrainians surrounded Wola Ostrowiecka. Early in the morning one of my two brothers ran into the house shouting, 'Get out!'

"There were four of us there: my father, Stanisław; my sister-in-law, Zofia, with her two-week-old baby; and I. We ran outside and headed in various directions. I hid in the bean field. As it turned out, I was noticed by the Ukrainians. After a while two of them came up to me; both had rifles. They told me to get up and go to the school for a meeting. Since I resisted, one of the Ukrainians took me there by force. There were a lot of people in the square already and among them were my oldest sister,

Józefa Soroka, as well as my sister-in-law with her child. The meeting was scheduled for 10:00 A.M.

"After a while the Ukrainians tightened the encirclement, and the people realized that they had fallen into a trap. A great tumult arose, and the people began to sing religious songs and to pray. [After herding most of them into the school] the Ukrainians removed ten men at a time and led them to Strażyc's barn. When no more men were left, they threw grenades into the school in which only women and children remained. Then they piled straw on the porch and set it on fire. When the building caught fire, one of the Ukrainians shouted, 'Polish bitches, we should have done this to you a long time ago!'

"The Poles, not wanting to be burned alive, began to jump out of the windows into the yard, where the Ukrainians picked them off with rifles. When I jumped out, I heard some shots. I landed near the window; the women with whom I jumped landed on top of me. I thought they were alive, but it turned out that they had all been killed. Pretending to be dead myself, I waited until the Ukrainians left.

"When I got up, the school was entirely consumed by flames. Above Wola Ostrowiecka a German airplane was circling. It flew low, circled the schoolyard three times, and then flew off toward Luboml. I went to the road and there I found my sister and sister-in-law still clutching her child. They were both dead. When I reached the Strażyc residence, I heard someone's plea for help. It was the voice of Wiktoria Harmata, a young girl from our village whom I knew; she was burned badly. With the assistance of her first cousin, who also survived, I pulled her out from beneath the pile of bodies. Terrified by what I saw, I then ran and hid in a nearby thicket. I sat there without food or water for three days; all I could do was sleep. On the fourth day, when I became weak from hunger, I went to the Ukrainian village of Przekurka. The Ukrainians I met gave me some milk and bread and instructed me to run to the village of Dorohusk. But I decided to go to a Polish family who lived near Przekurka."

At the time it was burned, the school in Wola Ostrowiecka contained from 150 to 200 women and children. Only a handful survived. Before this incident, a group of about 40 additional woman and children — for lack of space in the school — were locked in the nearby barn belonging to the Jesionek family. This barn was also set on fire. There were only two survivors.

The men who were taken from the school to the barn of Aleksander Strażyc were murdered outright. Out of approximately 250, only one survived: Władysław Soroka (from Wola Ostrowiecka, b. 1900). He describes the events and his survival as follows:

"For the fifth time, the Ukrainians took away another ten men. I was led out with the seventh group. They surrounded us outside the school and demanded our weapons and watches. They led us to the property of Aleksander Strażyc. One of the barn doors was open, just like the one in the cowshed. The Ukrainians told us to sit down and to remove our clothes in preparation for a medical examination. The bandits then took the men behind the closed door of the barn, where a pit had been dug, and killed them there with axes.

"I was dressed in a torn shirt and a pair of pants with a wide belt; I left my best clothes at home on purpose. The Ukrainians told me to get undressed. When I got down to my underwear and shirt, one of the bandits said, 'That's fine, let him go in.'

"Behind the door, on the left side, I saw a pile of clothes by the corn-bin. On the right side was a pile of shoes. I backed up.

"'No, no, not there — here!' barked one of the Ukrainians and gave me a shove.

"The pit was lined with guards. They were hitting the victims in the head with axes and dumping their bodies down below. I jumped between the butchers and ran out through the open door into the field....

"[After being wounded twice] I ran in a zig-zag fashion while the pursuing Ukrainians shot at me the whole time. Luckily, I reached the forest.... During the slaughter, the Ukrainians killed my three sons and my wife in the school. I and my mother were severely wounded."

There were 866 people living in Wola Ostrowiecka in 197 family units at the time of this UPA attack. At least 572 (or 66 percent) were murdered. Among them were 158 children.[6]

Second account. Maria Pendel (née Jesionek, b. 1927) from a colony near Przekurka:

"Our home stood in a colony near the Ukrainian village of Przekurka.... A red flare appeared over Ostrówki, then a green one. A while later, the school in Wola Ostrowiecka began to burn. We were terrified. We grabbed the most needed articles and fled to a thicket near our house. Alders and pines grew there and for ten days we hid among them....

"Two Ukrainian families knew about our hideaway, and they provided us with food and drink throughout that time. On the tenth day after we fled our home, a Ukrainian came to us and said to my father, 'Listen, Bronek, I have some good news for you today. There was a meeting at our house last night and five partisans were in attendance. They said that if there were Poles still left alive, they could return to their farms.'"

The Ukrainians also offered to return the family's livestock. Maria's family returned to their home only to be beset by the murderers that same evening. The father was severely beaten and the premises were robbed. The family was spared only because Makhonko from Hupał, the leader of this group of 30-40 Ukrainians, was their pre-war acquaintance. At one point, the narrator's mother said to him, "Makhonko, dear fellow, we once danced together at my brother's wedding, and now you come to kill us?"

To which Makhonko replied, "Today, there are no acquaintances. Boys, take whatever you want."

He then told the Jesioneks that nothing would happen to them that day, but that they would come back the following day and kill them. The narrator continues:

"The two Ukrainian families that took care of us for those ten days came over with food and water. One of the Ukrainian women advised us to flee to Stary Jagodzin because the Polish people in Nowy Jagodzin were being harassed by the Ukrainians."[7]

Third account. Franciszek Soroka (b. 1939) from Wola Ostrowiecka:

"I am aware of instances where Ukrainians gave shelter to the Poles. Two such families lived in the village of Przekurka; another two lived in the village of Sokół. Unfortunately, I cannot recall their names."[8]

Fourth account. Helena Twaróg (née Przystupa, b. 1914) from Wola Ostrowiecka:

"On Sunday, August 29, 1943, troubling news reached us. I therefore took my children and went to my godmother, Paulina Pogorzelec, who lived in Wola Ostrowiecka. We spent the entire night hiding in the lupine field....

"After I returned home with my children and cow, I went to a Ukrainian family in Przekurka, and we were hidden by them in the forest [for five days]. Their son belonged to the UPA."[9]

SOKÓŁ

First account. Agnieszka Łysiak (née Harmata, b. 1912) from Wola Ostrowiecka:

"We spent the night [of the attack on Wola Ostrowiecka] in the thicket near our house. In the morning, my stepmother and a neighbor went to a Ukrainian acquaintance in Sokół. They complained to him that one of his buddies, Kostia, did not return my stepmother's horse and wagon. When he heard this, the Ukrainian said, 'They took everything you had and now they will kill you too.'

"Just then, the Ukrainian's wife saw her kinsmen approaching the house. My stepmother and the old woman who came with her were hidden in a closet. The Ukrainians came into the house and asked, 'Where are the Mazovians [*Mazury*, that is, Poles]?'

"They received the answer, 'Those were our own old women who left to buy some oats.'

"When the visitors departed, the Ukrainian woman let the two ladies out of the closet, gave them a loaf of bread and some salt pork, and told them to flee to Jagodzin."[10]

Second account. Ewa Palec (née Jesionek, b. 1921) from Wola Ostrowiecka:

"Knowing that the Ukrainians intended to murder the Poles in Wola Ostrowiecka, I hid near the cemetery in Ostrówki. There, I met a boy from Ostrówki, Bonifacy Muzyka, who fled when the murders began. The Ukrainians walked the fields looking for Poles in hiding. '*Kasiu, Jagusiu*,' they called out [in Polish], 'come out because everything is over and we are going further.'

"They found us both. They shot Bonifacy on the spot and took me to the church in Ostrówki. There were only women and children from Ostrówki and Wola Ostrowiecka in that church. After a while, they led us toward the Ukrainian village of Sokół. There, we were ordered to lie on the ground and they shot us in the head. I was shot in the face. The bullet entered my upper jaw and came out through my ear. After regaining consciousness, I went to the railroad station in Jagodzin....

"A small child, Czesław Lubczyński, also survived the pogrom near Sokół. He was taken in and raised by a Ukrainian family. When his father, Jan, found out about the fate of his son, he returned after the war to the other side of the Bug River and took the boy to Poland."[11]

RÓWNO
From the account of Tomasz Muzyka (b. 1921) from Ostrówki:

"I spent the night of August 29, 1943, in Równo [not to be confused with Równe]. After the church services [in Ostrówki], my parents asked me to take some money [to Równo] for tax payment on my mother's property. Besides her family (Wawrzyk), about 30 other Polish families lived there as well.

"I handed the money over to my uncle, and in the evening his son and I went to see a Ukrainian girl whom we knew. He stayed over but I returned to my sister-in-law's (Stasiuk's) house. Before I left, we had agreed that I would call on him in the morning prior to my departure to Ostrówki. But it didn't happen that way. His mother came that night and took him away. The Ukrainians had warned her to flee because they had received orders to murder the Polish population of Równo. They were to do this either at night or during the day at the Barański residence in the colony. The attack never materialized because the Germans from Wilczy Przewóz intervened."[12]

ZAMOSTECZE COLONY
First account. Julian Grzesik from Lublin:

"Ewelda Pakuła (née Ryl), who together with her father, Gustav, survived the murders in the village of Zamostecze, now lives in Lublin. Her mother (née Popek), brother, and sister were killed in that attack. Stanisław Ryl, a witness to these murders, now lives in Dobryłów, in the Chełm Province. His family was warned of the attack by a Ukrainian family. Thanks to that, he survived."[13]

Second account. Zofia Ryl (b. 1908, family background: Dutch) from Zamostecze Colony:

"At three o'clock in the morning on August 30, 1943, we were awakened by a banging on the door of our house. My husband got up and opened it. Three Ukrainians dressed in civilian clothing barged into the kitchen (the first room) and ordered my husband to lie down on the floor. Yelling, they killed my 14-year-old son and my 21-year-old sister. Shortly thereafter, one of them opened the door to one of the rooms and threw in a grenade which thankfully failed to explode. My husband ran into my room and shouted, 'What should I do?'

"I lay in my bed throughout this time since I was very ill. I did not see how my son and sister died. In the confusion, my father-in-law was able to flee and survived by hiding in a potato cellar.

"My husband jumped out the window but was shot in the thigh. Then one of the butchers struck him in the head with a butt of his rifle and left him in the field believing that he had been killed.

"The Ukrainians set fire to our house; smoke was everywhere. With difficulty, I crawled outside and was approached by two Ukrainians. One of them wanted to shoot me, but the other said, 'Leave her, she'll die anyway.'

"I sat on the ground and watched my home go up in smoke. I did not react even though my sister and my small son were inside that house. It burned to cinders. We never found a trace either of my child or Lodzia [Leokadia, the narrator's sister]. There was no funeral.

"After a few hours, when things quieted down a little, a woman, our Ukrainian neighbor, came out onto the field and bandaged my husband's bloody leg. Then our cousin came with horses and took us both to a doctor in the nearest village. On the way, my husband died. I remained in the hospital for about one week....

"In my family, 13 persons (they all had the name of Ryl) were murdered by the Ukrainians."[14]

7

Łuck County

Centrally located, the county of Łuck was cut in half by the winding Styr River. There were 13 village communes: Czaruków, Kiwerce, Kołki, Łuck (county seat), Medweże, Ołyka, Poddębce, Połonka, Rożyszcze, Silno, Szczurzyn, Torczyn, and Trościaniec.

Table 16
Population of Łuck County by Mother Tongue

Ukrainian	171,793
Ruthenian	245
Polish	56,446
Jewish	34,142
German	17,619
Czech	6,107
Russian	3,909
Belorussian	220
Lithuanian	14
Other	141
Unreported	169
Total	290,805

Table 17
Population of Łuck County by Religious Affiliation

Orthodox	176,461
Roman Catholic	55,802
Uniate	916
Protestant/Evangelical	18,982
Other Christian	4,110
Jewish	34,354
Other Non-Christian	55
Not Specified or Non-Religious	61
Unreported	64
Total	290,805

A Ukrainian "agricultural school"—a paramilitary unit organized along the lines of a battalion—under Stepan Koval ("Rubashenko") quartered in Łuck County. On March 20, 1943, the unit deserted and was reorganized into a UPA battalion. The first murders in this county occurred well before the desertion of the Ukrainian police in mid-March 1943. That March, they escalated in the "Turiv" region to which Łuck belonged, as well as in the neighboring regions of "Zahrava" and "Eneia," and culminated in the "Easter action" of April 24-25, 1943. As in the rest of Wołyń, the months of July and August were the worst. During these months, nearly every Polish village, colony, hamlet, and family was the object of a UPA attack.

People

BOICHUK, Kostiantyn, from Koszów.
See Ivan Sheremeta.

CHERVAK, Olha, from Koszów
From the account of Sabina Królikowska (née Tarnawska, b. 1935) from Koszów:

"The village of Koszów belonged to the Torczyn parish. The Poles murdered in Liniów (Horochów County) lie buried in that town's cemetery. Among them were my relatives: my sister-in-law and her children.

Although wounded, my brother [Dominik Tarnawski] managed to escape. He was assisted by a Ukrainian whose name I do not remember since I was only eight years old at that time. That good man brought my brother to the hospital in Łokacze. (My brother passed away 25 years ago.)

"As I recall, it was Monday after Low Sunday (April 19, 1943) and it was a warm day. A Ukrainian from Liniów came to my parents and said, 'Your children are murdered.'

"My father and mother hitched up the wagon and went off, leaving me at home. I was greatly afraid that they would be murdered as well and that I would be left all alone in the world. And so, crying, I ran after them. When they turned around and saw me, they stopped and took me with them. On the way they explained to me that I should not be going there.

"When we arrived in Liniów, I saw a frightening spectacle: All the buildings of my brother and of his neighbor, Maćkowiak, who lived on the other side of the road, were burned. As my brother told me later, after being wounded he hid in the bushes and saw it all. The Maćkowiak family was burned alive. When we got there, their parents were already gathering their bones for burial.

"Helena, my brother's wife, had 12 holes in her body, which were made either with a bayonet or a knife, and her legs were broken. The bandits threw her into the well along with her oldest daughter Władzia, a 12-year-old child whose head was smashed in. Her younger children, Edzio (six) and Gienia (three), were also thrown into the well while still alive. This we knew because the youngsters' hands were full of mud and their fists were closed so tightly that it was difficult to straighten them out.

"My parents immediately went for a well-sinker, a Ukrainian, and with his help hauled all the corpses out of the well. For his assistance, the Ukrainian took the piglets which were suckling at the nipples of a dead sow. (The sow lay in the field near one of the buildings; her stomach was ripped open.) My parents then took the bodies of their loved ones to their home, washed them, made some wooden caskets, and buried them in the cemetery at Torczyn.

"After the burial they attempted to discover whether their son was still alive. They decided to go to the hospital in Łokacze. On their way they were accosted by five UPA bandits dressed in German uniforms. But when the bandits saw that some wagons for gathering wood were traveling behind them with a German escort, they told us not to say anything about their being there and ran off into the woods.

"My brother was indeed in the Łokacze hospital. His ribs were broken and he was shot in the head. When he got better (it was not until August), he came to our village and took us to Łokacze, where there were many Polish refugees and a small German outpost. Since the Ukrainian Nationalists conducted raids on that town quite often, the Germans — to protect themselves — gave the Poles some weapons. During the attacks, we hid in the church. Later, the Germans took us to Włodzimierz, where our armed men joined the Polish partisans in Bielin....

"I must mention that my father's sister gave a lot of money to the Ukrainian *sołtys* for a safe passage to Torczyn. Unfortunately, her family got only as far as the woods before they were murdered. The victims included: Michał Sztyk, Julian Synich with his wife and child, Dionizy (a bachelor), and Czesław, who was 11 years of age. My aunt remained at home and thus was saved....

"I must also mention a certain Ukrainian girl named Olha Chervak. Although her brothers were bandits, she saved my life. One day, when Olha had just turned 13, I went with her to a Ukrainian church in Sadów. Something unusual was happening there: Ukrainians were bringing axes, pitchforks, and knives, and the Ukrainian priest was blessing them for the killing of Poles—an action which was to bring about a free Ukraine. Olha then led me out of that church, showed me a path, and told me to run away as quickly as I could.

"Why did I write that my friend's brothers were bandits? Because my father noticed that one of them was wearing my brother's watch, and because the horse belonging to my brother, whose family was murdered by the Ukrainians, stood tied behind Olha's house.

"Finally, I must say a word about the Ukrainian who appropriated our grain after we had fled from our house. When we were in Łokacze, he brought us one quintal [100 lbs.] of wheat and one quintal of rye saying, 'You, Marian, have no bread, so I brought this to you because I took your grain.'

"On his way back home, this Ukrainian was accosted by the Nationalists and beaten so hard that he died. He received a terrible punishment for bringing bread to my father, a Pole. This Ukrainian had a Polish name: Wojciechowski [Voitsekhivskyi]."¹

CHERVAK, Petro and Ivan, from Koszów. *See* Ivan Sheremeta below as well as Olha Chervak and the accompanying note above.

DONETS, Kostiantyn, and the residents of Jezioro. *See* Jezioro.

DRZEWIECKA, Mrs., from Taraż
Zenobiusz Janicki states:

"Zygmunt Drzewiecki headed up our intelligence. He stayed with his 30-year-old son in Przebraże [a large Polish self-defense center], while his Ukrainian wife remained with the younger children in Taraż, near Kołki, on their farm. It was well known what type of conditions the UPA imposed on couples in mixed Polish-Ukrainian marriages. In order to avoid the worst, that is, death at the hands of the Bulbowcy, Zygmunt had his wife pass the word around that he and his son had fled to join the *Lakhy* [Poles]. His wife resisted the Bandera [OUN-B] order to kill her Polish husband. The husband and wife arranged to meet in specified places from time to time. In order to avoid being caught, they used a pre-arranged light-in-the-window signal at those places. From Przebraże to Kołki was 25 kilometers. Zygmunt would go out at night along familiar forest roads and paths, would meet his wife in the prearranged place, and would receive information from her that came directly from the UPA headquarters. His wife's brothers were highly placed UPA leaders; therefore, the information received by Zygmunt from his wife was trustworthy. After returning to Kołki, Zygmunt would convey the latest news to the Polish leaders. That news was troubling."²

FUKS, Kalina, and her family, from Jeziorany Szlacheckie
From the account of Henryk Komański from Jeziorany Szlacheckie:

"I was a witness to the annihilation of the village of Jeziorany Szlacheckie. In the course of four days [June 19-23, 1943], this Polish village with its over 200-year history was wiped off the face of the earth. About 30 percent of its inhabitants were killed by the OUN-UPA, and the losses would have been even greater if there had been no attempt to put up an armed resistance....

"The residents of Jeziorany Szlacheckie did not confine their social relations only to their village. They maintained direct and close contacts with the surrounding Ukrainian population. The majority of the residents knew the Ukrainian language and used it often in their conversations with neighboring Ukrainians. The Ukrainians likewise knew and used the Polish language. Both groups cooperated in a neighborly fashion when it came to sowing and reaping the harvest. There was mutual lending, borrowing, and barter. Various festivals were held in common, and each side invited the other to its religious and family celebrations.

"Nine Ukrainian families lived in the village and harmonious neighborly relations prevailed. None of these families, as it turned out, took part in the attacks on the residents of Jeziorany, and one of them provided shelter for a time to one of the Polish survivors of the pogrom. Tomasz Czajkowski, a Pole married to a Ukrainian women, converted to Orthodoxy during the Russian partition and attended the Orthodox church. His sons married Polish women and considered themselves Roman Catholics and Poles. During the interwar years in the 1930s, Kazimierz Rudnicki also entered into a mixed-marriage. He kept his faith (Roman Catholic) and his wife kept hers (Orthodox). The son was baptized in the Catholic church and the daughter, if there happened to be one, was to have been baptized in the Orthodox church. And so, there were no religious or ethnic conflicts in this region until September 1939....

"It should be pointed out that [during the Soviet and German occupations] certain groups of Ukrainians defended the Poles and opposed the prevalent chauvinistic campaign. Unfortunately, that group of people became more and more isolated.

"Already at the beginning of 1942, such sayings as '*Lakhy* beyond the Bug,' 'Death to the *Lakhy*,' and 'We will annihilate the *Lakhy*,' became louder and more frequent. In 1942 news began to arrive in the village concerning the murders of individual Poles and sometimes entire Polish families in other villages. These murders were said to have been carried out by the Ukrainian Nationalists called Bulbowcy, but more often by the Banderowcy. These facts instilled unrest in the men and the Polish youth.

"Toward the end of June 1942 the home of Józef Budkiewicz was robbed; in August, that of *sołtys* Stanisław Biernacki; in March of 1943, that of Bolesław Tchórzewski. All these were armed robberies....

"The first major attack [by approximately 50 armed Banderowcy] on the village and colony took place on June 19, 1943, between the morning hours of 9:00 and 10:00....

[A description follows.]

"On that memorable morning of June 23, 1943 [the concluding date of the attack], the Polish village of Jeziorany Szlacheckie in effect ceased to exist.... [The narrator points out that several dozen Polish families were slaughtered during this attack. Another 43 Poles were killed during the second major attack on the village on July 11, 1943.]

"Given this background of UPA terror and bestial murders, the heroic acts of those Ukrainians who, at the risk of their own lives, rescued individual Poles and even entire Polish families deserve a special mention. Here is one example. After surviving the first pogrom of June 19, 1943, Jan Marmucki, a resident of Jeziorany, hid in a field of grain near his property. When it became safe, he made contact with a friendly Ukrainian family by the name of Fuks. This family consisted of two brothers and their sister, Kalina. She undertook the task of hiding Marmucki. A shelter was dug for him in the orchard and its entrance was camouflaged. He remained there during the day, but at night one of the Fuks family members would accompany him on walks. This lasted for some time. The Banderowcy in the neighboring village, meanwhile, began to suspect that the Fuks were hiding someone, and one or another of them would suddenly appear at various times asking whether they perchance knew of any Poles in hiding. Feeling threatened, the Fuks decided to take Marmucki in secret to nearby Nieświcz, where a German garrison was stationed. Kalina again was in charge of this undertaking. Marmucki was placed in a wagon and covered with straw and sacks of grain. In this way Kalina delivered Marmucki, as 'grain contingent,' to Nieświcz."³

HRODSKYI, Ivan, from Koszów. *See* Ivan Sheremeta.

IEVCHUK from Kozakowa Dolina
From the account of Leokadia Zawilska from Aleksandrówka Colony:

"In 1943 the colony in which I lived [Aleksandrówka] had 18 farmsteads and about 70 residents....

"At the beginning of 1943 we became aware of a growing threat from the Ukrainian Nationalists from the village of Kozakowa Dolina. At night hidden weapons would be retrieved and nightly watches were kept. At the end of March a Ukrainian from Kozakowa Dolina named Ievchuk warned Paweł Zawilski that an ambush was planned for his brother Apolinary, but Paweł did not take this warning seriously....

"On the evening of April 3, 1943, when the men were sitting at table, several Banderowcy armed with rifles and an automatic fell into the room. They shot four men: Marian, Apolinary, and Mieczysław Zawilski, and Bronisław Ukraiński. Marian, whose body was perforated with bullets, fared the worst. Supposedly, he attempted to defend himself with a gun. Apolinary's 12-year-old son was dragged off the stove and stabbed to death. Only three persons survived that attack: Apolinary's wife Julia, who hid behind a window curtain and went unnoticed, and her son Ignacy and daughter Helena, both of whom jumped out the window in the adjoining room.

"During this time, my brother Paweł Zawilski left our house and headed in the direction of Apolinary's home, thus escaping the grenades that were thrown in through the window. The shrapnel severely wounded my mother, Anna, our guests, and me....

"After the attack the Banderowcy immediately withdrew from our colony. Our home caught fire but Paweł, with the assistance of some neighbors, was able to save it....

"This was one of the first murders in our area. After that the residents of the colony relocated to the village of Sienkiewiczówka and returned to work on their farms only during the day. But this, too, was dangerous. In May, Amelia Lisowska was murdered on her way back to Sienkiewiczówka. The same thing happened to Adela Zawilska (32) in June.

"In mid-June, the Banderowcy robbed and burned our colony to the ground."⁴

IATSURA, Semen, from Koszów. *See* Ivan Sheremeta.

LUKASH from Usicze
In March 1944 a UPA unit riding through the village of Usicze rounded up many Poles and took them away. They were never heard from again. A Polish blacksmith, Stefan Rajewski, was saved from this fate by Lukash, a Ukrainian.⁵

MAVZELEPA, Laktion, from Bukowce. *See* Kharyton Pasteruk.

PASTERUK, Kharyton, from Bukowce
From the account of Jan Rodziewicz from Bukowce:

"On June 22, 1943, a group of armed UPA fighters attacked our home. My parents, Hipolit and Justyna, were in the orchard at the time. The attackers ordered them to lie down on the ground, bound them both with barbed wire, and shot them in the back of their heads. One of the murderers was our neighbor, Valerian Kravchuk.

"Next, they set fire to all the buildings: our house, the stable, cowshed, and barn. After annihilating everything, the murderers left. I was 27 years old at the time. I was in the garden, which was quite a distance from the house, and was not noticed. The following Ukrainians assisted me in hiding: Kharyton Pasteruk, Zakhar Pots, Laktion Mavzelepa, and Vychyniuk. Two Czechs, Antonín Pokorny and Josef Balada, assisted me as well. Our Ukrainian neighbor, Ulian Kravchuk, wrapped the bodies of my parents in sheets and buried them in a flower bed in front of our burned house.

"In spite of my being sought after by the UPA, no one betrayed me. My neighbors hid me for eight weeks and three days at the risk of their own lives. I grew a beard and a mustache. Dressed as a carpenter, with carpentry tools, pretending to be looking for work, I reached Łuck. There, I lived with my uncle, Ferdynand Brzeżniakiewicz. On March 18, 1944, I joined the Polish army."[6]

POTS, Zakhar, from Bukowce. *See* Kharyton Pasteruk.

SAPOZHNYK, Makar, from Koszów. *See* Ivan Sheremeta.

SERVYTNIUK, Ievhen, from Ławrów
From the account of Jadwiga Wilkowska (née Buczyńska, b. 1929) from Ławrów:

"It was spring 1943. Polish villages were burning all around us and grim death gathered an abundant harvest. The Poles perished en masse at the hands of criminals, the Ukrainian Nationalists.

"On one of these terrible days, in the morning hours, our nearby neighbor, Ievhen Servytniuk, crawled to us through the wheat field in order to avoid being spotted by the other residents and said, 'Władek, get out today. I have defended you up to now, but that's over. You are marked for death.'

"My father, Władysław, after a brief consultation with my mother and grandmother, loaded up the wagon with necessities and two sheep and tied a cow to the wagon's ladder. Father, Mother and I (14 years of age at the time) went to Łuck.

"At home, there remained my grandmother, my father's sister who was crippled from birth, and a nine-year-old boy. The boy was an orphan who was living with us.

"Near Ławrów there was a colony called Kościuszkowo. It was initially inhabited by Polish military settlers who were deported to Siberia in 1940. The Germans established an animal-husbandry farm in that village. The uncle of one of my parents, Karol Jaskut, lived there with his family and worked there.

"After we left, Jaskut — with the permission of my grandmother — moved his eight-member family into our house. Three weeks thereafter, on July 14, some Ukrainians came by on a wagon. They were dressed in civilian clothes and carried rifles with bayonets ready. They came into the house, told everyone to lie down on the floor, and began to stick them with the bayonets. Meanwhile, Jaskut's 12-year-old daughter Kazia and the nine-year-old orphan Stasio dove under the bed. The girl raised her body up on hands and feet so as not to be seen, and the boy slid behind the washtub that was kept there. One of the bandits noticed their hiding place and jabbed Kazia 11 times, wounding her feet, thighs, and chest. Fortunately, none of the injuries were fatal.

"After the executioners left, the children jumped out the window and fled into a field. They went (Stasio helping Kazia) to the village of Ratniów, to a well-disposed Ukrainian family that they knew. There, Kazia's wounds were attended to and she was put to bed.

"The following day Stasio ran into my father, who had returned for some food, and told him about the murder of his uncle's family (seven persons) and my grandmother and aunt. Father took Kazia to a hospital in Łuck. After a week he returned once more, under German protection, to mow his field. It was then that he found out that the bodies of the murdered had been thrown into the well. He retrieved the bodies and dug a pit next to the well. Therein he buried the victims of this crime."⁷

SHEREMETA, Ivan, from Koszów
From the account of Irena Justyna from Koszów:

"The UPA began to prowl around Polish villages more and more often. Each night we left the house for the restless and uncomfortable quarters of fields and thickets. Each morning, still tired and afraid, we returned to our homes for some food and rest. Our nearby Ukrainian neighbor, Ivan Sheremeta (called Ivasyk by everyone), came to us one day and informed us that he had made a hiding place for us among the fruit in his barn where we could sleep. A loose board in the wall facing the garden would enable us to escape at a moment's notice. He was a very good lad, modest and of short stature for his age. In the company of Ukrainians he pretended to be dull-witted and uninterested in anything, but in reality he caught their every word and conveyed to us news of everything that was going on in the village.

"It was he who brought us the news that the bandits were preparing to kill all the Poles on June 29 [1943]. We took counsel with our poor Poles from Koszów as to what to do and where and how to escape so as not to fall into the hands of the murderers. A few Polish families managed to leave for Skurcze and from there go to Horochów, where Polish self-defense centers were organized. We ourselves had no means of transportation since the bandits had already stolen our horses and wagon. In the morning we crawled out of our hiding place, taking care not to be noticed and not to betray the Ukrainians who provided us with shelter. We buried our more valuable possessions: sheepskin coats, boots, quilts, pillows and good clothes. As it turned out, it was all a waste of effort because everything was dug up and stolen anyway.

"One day an armed group of bandits pulled up to our property. After a short consultation, one of them jumped down from the wagon and aimed his revolver in our direction. We froze in fear. He chased us into the house. My mother had enough strength and courage to ask him to allow us to pray before our death. We knelt down and began reciting out loud the prayer 'Under Your Protection, O Lord.' After the prayer, my sister Relunia began to cry loudly and said to him in Ukrainian, 'For what reason do you want to kill us? What have we ever done to you?'

"I also began to entreat him, looking straight into his eyes. Large tears rolled off our faces. Only Janina stood as if she was made of stone. She had an obstinate countenance and said not a word. When we finished praying, suddenly the bandit's hand began to shake and the gun fell onto the floor. He picked up the gun, and a sudden change came over him. It was as if a different man stood before us. He then said, 'I cannot kill you,' and counseled us to run away quickly because the others would come and kill us for sure. 'I would gladly help you, especially you,' he said pointing to me. After saying these words he turned around quickly and left the house without looking back. Wasn't this a miracle? It certainly was....

"In the evening, a young Ukrainian came to us. He was the son of a forester who worked for my father before the war. If I recall correctly, his name was Petro Bambylo. My mother recognized him and let him into the house. When his father found out that the Poles were going to be killed that night, he sent Petro to bring us to his family in Liniów, a neighboring village. We did not deliberate for long. We took our ever-ready bundles, some food and other necessities, and went with Petro along paths and over fields to his home in Liniów. There, we were sheltered by his family during that 'Night of Cain,' June 23, 1943.

"There were very noble people among the Ukrainians who were against this criminal action and who more than once risked their own lives to save the Poles. The best example is Petro Bambylo and his parents. They awaited us with great anxiety, wondering whether Petro would be able to accomplish his task. Fortunately, we arrived safely and found that everything had been prepared for us in advance. Our hiding place was high up in the barn under a large beam. We ascended to it by means of a tall ladder which Petro's parents removed afterwards. He, however, remained with us for the entire time and kept guard. We will never forget these kind people.

"It was well after midnight when the bandits began their attack. Knowing that several Polish families were trying to reach Skurcze by traveling through the neighboring village of Liniów, they ambushed them there. A hail of bullets greeted the refugees. The crying of frightened children made the manhunt that followed all the more successful. Fires raged all around, terrible screams of people in agony could be heard, often silenced by pistol shots. It is simply impossible to describe it all in words....

"The hunt continued all through the night and into the next day until evening. We spent two days in our shelter in shock and fear. Finally, after looking around, Petro informed us that everything had quieted down for the time being and that the Banderowcy withdrew to the forest. Evidently a small AK unit from Skurcze and some men from the self-defense center arrived and began firing at the bandits, causing them to leave the village....

"A few Polish families managed to reach Skurcze.... Julek Sokołowski and his six-year-old son were among these. His wife, fleeing with her two-year-old son, was beset by the bandits who killed her child and wounded her. She survived because she fainted and the bandits, took her for dead. She was also rescued by some Ukrainian family which subsequently took her to a hospital in Łuck. The majority of those who remained in their houses were tortured and murdered: Their arms and legs were broken, their stomachs were slit open, and the dying, while still alive, were thrown into wells.

"Another victim was the 77-year-old midwife from Koszów who was renowned in the area. Her name was Boguszewska. Her brother and his wife were also murdered. Boguszewska's daughter, whose husband Venek was Czech, and her two beautiful children, aged six and eight, were also killed in a bestial manner. The girls were held by their feet and their heads were smashed against a tree. Afterwards, they were thrown into a well. Kajetan Biernacki and his wife, both around 78, also perished. Their son, Marceli, perished on May 8, together with [his wife?] Wandzia.

"Dominik Tarnawski lived in Liniów near the forest. The butchers attacked his family at night and, knocking down the door, began to take out the victims. Dominik managed to jump out the window and headed for the forest. His wife Helena, aged 32, was in her eighth month of pregnancy. She was subjected to a singularly cruel death. She was found lying near the well into which her three children were thrown. Her stomach cut open and her poor unborn baby lay next to her. The Siatecki family was attacked in a similar manner.

"Besides these unfortunate Polish families, two Ukrainian brothers, Petro and Ivan Chervak, were also murdered. Their older brother Roman was wed to Boguszewska's [the midwife's] daughter, Aniela. They had a eight-year-old son. When the bandits came for them, neither

Roman, nor Aniela, nor their son were at home. The Banderowcy, therefore, took it out on Roman's two brothers because of his marriage to a Polish girl. Petro and Ivan refused to reveal the hiding place of their brother's family, and so had to die instead. They were also thrown into the well.

"There were several Ukrainian families in Koszów who sympathized with us during these cruel times. Makar Sapozhnyk was among these. His daughter, Shura, was also murdered by the Ukrainian Nationalists. His son survived and today lives in Torczyn. We were especially helped by Semen Iatsura, Ivan Hrodskyi, and Kostiantyn Boichuk, who still live in Koszów. But there were others who were opposed to these criminal deeds as well.

"I do not remember how much longer we suffered and hid in our unfortunate and, at the same time, beloved Koszów. We grew up there, and there we spent the days of our youth. As I recall, at the beginning of August we heard the motor of an approaching vehicle. We managed to hide in our shelter, which we built with the help of our Ukrainian neighbor, Kostiantyn Boichuk."

Fortunately, the vehicle was driven by Poles, Dominik Tarnawski among them, who had come back to rescue the survivors.[8]

VYCHYNIUK from Bukowce. *See* Kharyton Pasteruk.

Places

ANATOLIA COLONY
From the account of Zenon Dagoński from Anatolia Colony:

"Although we had a farm in Anatolia Colony, our father worked on the railroad. In March 1943 we began to feel that our lives were threatened by the UPA. Our father procured a residence for us in Łuck and commuted to his place of work at the Anatolia station. My father's mother, Katarzyna, did not want to live in Łuck and remained at home to take care of the farm. She spent the nights with a neighboring Ukrainian family.

"One day this Ukrainian family was visited by their son-in-law from Korszów and several armed Banderowcy. They murdered Katarzyna as well as four members of the Ukrainian family with whom she stayed. Only one of their sons survived; he happened to be away at the time.

"Under the second Soviet occupation in 1944, my father continued to work on the railroad and would, from time to time, visit our farm in order to do some work there. On October 4, 1944, he went to his farm and never returned. My mother searched for him for over three weeks. Finally, she was told by some of her female Ukrainian acquaintances where he was buried. When she found him, around his neck was a telephone wire tightened by a stick. His murderer was Shulhyn, one of our Ukrainian neighbors."[9]

ANDRZEJÓWKA COLONY
From the account of Aleksandra Ostrowska from Andrzejówka Colony:

"Only Poles lived in Andrzejówka Colony. At the beginning of the war the colony consisted of 46 farmsteads and 187 residents....

"On the night of June 29, 1943, the Banderowcy attacked Andrzejówka. They had a small-caliber cannon which was not very effective. Only one shell found its mark, damaging a corner of a building. Three German civilians and several dozen Poles set up a defense. After four hours, the Banderowcy withdrew. They had suffered losses: some dead, others wounded. Nine Poles were also killed, those who did not seek shelter in the school that night....

"On January 14, 1944, due to the approaching front, the Germans organized a large convoy for the Polish people from

Andrzejówka, Nieświcz, Podberezie, and Skurcze (regions in which there were properties under German management). The convoy left in the direction of Włodzimierz with the intention of crossing the Bug River into central Poland. It was guarded by several dozen German civilians and Poles armed by the Germans.... The convoy with the refugees was halted by the German border police at the boundary of Wołyń and the General Government and diverted back to Włodzimierz....

"After the departure of the convoy, the UPA descended on the colony, robbed it, and set all the buildings on fire....

"My mother, my sister, and I did not join the convoy. We remained in Łuck. The Germans moved out of Łuck on February 2, 1944. After the Soviet armies arrived, we continued to live there. That summer, we set out for Andrzejówka to gather the harvest.... We discovered that Andrzejówka was a wasteland; the orchards and wooded areas had been cut down, and only a few shrubs remained here and there. We obtained permission from a representative of the Soviet authorities, a Ukrainian, to gather potatoes and grain. That Ukrainian, together with his entire family, was murdered by the Banderowcy....

"Piejak and his father continued to live in Andrzejówka. They were hidden by an acquaintance, a Ukrainian Baptist. After the entry of the Soviets, Piejak was accused by local Ukrainians of collaboration with the Germans. He was a member of the Polish self-defense and had German permission to bear arms. He was given a prison term of ten years [by the Soviets]."[10]

BEREZOŁUPY

In the Kaliszewski family, both parents and their son were murdered in August 1943. Their daughter, however, was hidden by their Ukrainian neighbor and survived. After the attack, she was turned over to the Polish people.[11]

CUMAŃ

From the account of Maciejewska (a fragment from a memoir):

"Once, while passing near a Ukrainian church, I saw a large announcement plastered on the fence. I read it but did not believe my eyes. It was a proclamation signed by some Ukrainian committee calling on the Ukrainian people to slaughter the Poles and to burn their settlements. I thought that some crazy person must have written it and that it would go unheeded. But on the following night, I saw the glow of a fire in the sky coming from the direction of the forest. In the morning, one of the Polesian settlers brought the bodies of his young wife and two children, murdered during his absence, in order to bury them in our cemetery. From that time on, every night the glow of fires would appear in two, three, and sometimes more places near the forest.

"The residents of my village, although Ukrainians, were good people. They had known me well for several years and liked me. One day they said, 'We will not harm you, but when the others, the strangers, come, they will kill you.'

"My [Ukrainian] landlady was afraid to spend the night with me in the same house. She went to the neighbors each night so that she would not be killed for renting to a Pole. I was therefore left alone at night and would go to bed without undressing. Then I would lie awake and count the number of fires which I could see from my cottage window facing the forest. At each footstep on the path outside, my heart would stop beating and I would imagine that the murderers were already here, or that some kind soul was running to warn me with the words, 'Flee, because they are coming for you.'

"The Poles who worked in the sawmill spent their nights there with their families because the mill was guarded by the Germans.

"In one Polish settlement, during an attack, a resident Polish doctor was rendering medical assistance to the wounded in the barn. The bandits set fire to the four corners of that barn, and all those inside, including the doctor, burned to death.

"In another village [Poryck, in Włodzimierz County], they broke into a church during the services, threw grenades into the congregation, shot the priest by the altar, and ran off. The priest, who was severely wounded, requested that an old Ukrainian priest would be summoned to hear his confession and to grant him absolution. After the confession, the Ukrainian priest ordered the wounded cleric to be brought to his own [the Ukrainian priest's] house. But on their way back, the bandits finished him off. The name of this young Catholic priest was Fr. Bolesław Szawłowski....

"In one corner of Łuck, in a suburb called Hnidawa, the Ukrainian bandits broke into a house on Christmas Eve, when the table was already set for the *wigilia* [vigil — traditional Christmas Eve meal and rituals]. The residents were able to hide themselves in a deep cellar, but they left a baby covered with a sheet in his crib in the bedroom. They were afraid that if they woke the child, he would give them away with his crying. Those beasts, the Ukrainians, carved up that baby, laid his remains on the plates which were to have been used for the traditional supper, and ran off.

"It was in such conditions and in such terror that we Poles lived for long months.

"'Go among your own people,' my Ukrainian landlady finally told me because she was afraid for her own life. But, since I was alone in the world, where and to whom could I go?"[12]

JEZIORANY CZESKIE
From the account of Danuta Wierzbowska-Robaszko (b. 1928) from Łuck:

"We had heard that the Ukrainian Nationalists engaged in terrible murders, but we did not believe that they would come for us.

"One Sunday in 1943 — it was either in May or June — a Ukrainian acquaintance came over to see us. He behaved rather strangely, kept looking around, and asked for my father. My mother told him that my father had fallen asleep after supper. The visitor said nothing and left in a hurry. When my father found out about this visit, he immediately reached the conclusion that it was not a good sign, that the Ukrainian had come to warn us. He went to Vladislav Kopecký (a Czech), spoke with him, and when he returned he told us to pack....

[When the Ukrainian Nationalists came looking for them, they were already in hiding with the Czech family under the floor in a structure used for drying hops. Vladislav attended to all their needs and in the evening brought them the news of the day.]

"One day, he informed us that the richest Polish family living in nearby Jeziorany Polskie had come to his brother Karol. They had a writ of safe conduct from the UPA, paid for dearly, to the effect that they could live in Jeziorany Czeskie. No sooner had they arrived with a few wagons at Karol's barn, than three young Banderowcy appeared. They took the Poles behind the barn, bound them, and murdered them there. The women's breasts were severed and their bellies were slit open.

"The Czechs were surprised most of all by the passivity of the Poles. After all, they were armed and few of them looked strong and healthy. They could have quickly dealt with those three young attackers....

"I have asked myself why these Polish people didn't defend themselves. Perhaps they didn't want to place the Czech family at risk, or perhaps they didn't believe that they were going to be murdered.

"Our stay with the Kopecký family became more precarious. The murderers knew that many Poles were in hiding with the Czechs and they began to search them out. We had to therefore leave that relatively good hiding place and go into the grain field. There, in a designated place, Vladislav would bring us food and take back the empty containers. Our stay in the field, especially for us children, was macabre. Fear, rains, storms, heat, and darkness — all took their toll.

"We lived in that field for three weeks, until the Czech informed us that the Bulbowcy were combing the fields on horseback. After this news, when about ten of us gathered in the field, we decided to go to Łuck, about 18 kilometers away. We traveled by night and avoided the main roads.

"The night we left was horrendous. Weaving through the fields we hit the dirt and lay motionless in response to every sound. Fortunately for us, these sounds turned out to be those made by pasturing horses or snapping twigs. Guessing our way over the terrain, we lost our orientation during that short summer night. When morning came we saw some houses, but it was not Łuck. After surveying the territory, the men informed us that we were in Ławrów, a Ukrainian village next to which lay a large German settlement. Were the Germans still there? We did not know. We were frightened. While we sat in the wheat near the road, the adults took counsel as to what was to be done.

"Just then, a Ukrainian woman who was passing through the field chanced upon us. Fear gripped us as we realized that the minutes of our lives could be numbered. She was surprised to see my father, whom she knew. She told us that the Germans were still there and showed us the way to go, but warned us to approach with a white flag raised aloft so as not to be shot by the guards. She also told us not to go right away, but to wait until her men-folk came onto the field. We didn't know whether this was a trap, but having no alternatives, we sat down and waited.

"After a while, the Ukrainian woman came back with a liter of milk hidden under her apron and gave it to us children. We drank it all. She then informed us that it was now safe to proceed, and so we went in the direction that she indicated. The Germans let us in because the harvest was just beginning and they needed the extra hands."[13]

JEZIORANY POLSKIE COLONY
From the account of Genowefa Kołcowska (née Kułakowska, b. 1918) from Jeziorany Polskie Colony, as transcribed by Henryk Komański:

"The first person to be murdered in our colony was Antoni Kołcowski (30 years of age). This happened at the beginning of May 1943. His naked body was discovered lying in the bushes....

"The second murder took place toward the end of May 1943. The five-member family of Józef Bober lived near the forest. The Banderowcy attacked at night and killed: Józef's wife, Marianna (30); Marianna's mother, Maria Kułakowska (55); and two small children aged four and eight. Józef was able to escape and, in the darkness, saved his life.

"On June 19, 1943, news of the attack on Jeziorany Szlacheckie, during which 40 persons were killed, reached our colony. The third murder in our colony took place on the following day; the Kułakowski couple and their child were killed near the forest.

"There was no organized self-defense in our village; no underground organization operated there either. Individuals, the youth in particular, had some weapons and ammunition. These weapons were well hidden in great secrecy even from family and neighbors. We feared Ukrainian police searches, arrest, torture, and death. Friendly neighbors kept watch at night. We often went to the school in Maczkowce to sleep. The majority of the people, especially the older generation, was convinced that we could survive this period of 'anarchy,' just as we did during the First World War when there were also robberies and murders. Hardly anyone realized the growing danger. No one knew of the criminal ideology of the OUN. That name, like the name of the UPA, was not known to the residents of our colony. The murderers — the Banderowcy — these were Ukrainians from other, faraway villages. The neighboring Ukrainians were not referred to in these terms. No one believed that they were capable of murdering women, children, and the elderly. Some of our Ukrainian neighbors even warned us of approaching danger. My father's friend said to him on several occasions, 'Kułakowski, take your family and flee because the Banderowcy will come and kill you all.'"

When the murders began, Genowefa's family, like so many others, initially sought safety in the fields. Later, they set out on foot to the town of Łuck, 25 kilometers away. During the flight, 17 residents of the colony perished at the hands of the Banderowcy. Five others were ambushed and killed near the village of Górka Połonka. In all, 30 residents of Jeziorany Polskie were murdered. In Łuck, where about 270 of them gathered, about 20 were conscripted for forced labor in Germany. At the beginning of 1945, the remaining survivors were transported to the "recovered territories" of Poland.

"The buildings on our property," concludes Genowefa, "were not burned. This was a rare exception. Later, Ukrainians from neighboring villages, mainly from Radomyśl, settled there."[14]

JEZIORO
According to Zenobiusz Janicki:

The Ukrainian village of Jezioro lay alongside Przebraże. When Przebraże was later transformed into a self-defense center (some 25,000 refugees eventually gathered there for protection), a Ukrainian delegation headed by Kostiantyn Donets, a Ukrainian priest, came to Przebraże from Jezioro with a proposal. The Ukrainians promised that no attack would be launched by the residents of Jezioro against the self-defense center and that, furthermore, Przebraże would be warned by them of any approaching UPA bands. It is to the credit of the Ukrainian residents of Jezioro that they honored both of their pledges to the very end.

"In relating the story of the Ukrainians of Jezioro and of other places known to me," states Zenobiusz Janicki, "I can vouch for the fact that there would have been more victims among the Polish people were it not for these better Ukrainians who helped and warned the Poles."

Several Ukrainian families living along the road that separated Przebraże and Jezioro had even asked to be incorporated into the perimeter of the self-defense center. They also opened their homes and barns to several dozen Polish refugee families.[15]

LENIEWO
From the account of Genowefa Modrzejewska (née Sobczyńska, b. 1938) from Leniewo:

"I lived with my parents in Leniewo, a mixed Polish-Ukrainian village in Łuck County. I was five years old when my parents were murdered — by our Ukrainian neighbors. On my mother's orders, my sister Emilia and I hid in the doghouse. Some of our friendly Ukrainian acquaintances found us and took us to our grandfather, Paweł Sobczyński, who lived in the village of Kołbyń. This happened in July 1943, just before the harvest. After all the Polish families in Leniewo were murdered, their relatives from the surrounding area gathered in Kołbyń and decided to go to the Polish village of Skurcze, where there was a civil-defense center.

"The Poles in Skurcze defended themselves for a few days against the overwhelming strength of the Banderowcy. In the end, they began to flee one at a time through a prepared tunnel under the cemetery. Thanks to the help of good-hearted Ukrainians, wandering children were reunited with their families in Łuck."[16]

RUDNIKI

On November 13, 1942, the Ukrainian police under Sachkovskyi, a former schoolteacher, murdered about 50 women and children in a barn in Obórki. The 17 men taken as prisoners from Obórki, were shot in Cumań. Three Soviet partisans were also killed.

When Stanisława Trusiewicz (one of the five women sent to Cumań to inquire about the fate of the men) returned, she found her village not only empty, but also destroyed by fire. She went to a Ukrainian friend in Rudniki, who placed her under the protection of another Ukrainian in Bogusława. That Ukrainian transported her to Silno and left her with a third Ukrainian, with whom she remained throughout that winter of 1942. The following spring, he brought her to the civil-defense center in Przebraże.[17]

SŁAWOTYCZE

From the account of Dominik Kowalski from Czetwertnia, as narrated by Zenobiusz Janicki:

"The third survivor [of the April 14, 1943, UPA attack on the convoy from Przebraże to the village of Czetwertnia for provisions] was Dominik Kowalski. Dominik stated that when the UPA left the barn, the noose had not yet tightened around his neck. Grasping the rope from which he hung, he was able to extricate himself and fell on the straw beneath him. He had a fractured skull from being severely beaten with a stick and a sword. Battered and bleeding, he lay on the straw and moaned.

"That evening, a Ukrainian returning from the mill passed by the property and heard the moaning coming from the barn. Finding the wounded man, he took him to his own house in Sławotycze and hid him in his barn. On the evening of the second or third day, exercising extreme caution, with the help of his trusted neighbors, the Ukrainian brought Dominik to Przebraże....

"In Czetwertnia, of the 22 persons detained [by the UPA], 19 were murdered."[18]

8
Równe County

Bordering on Soviet Ukraine, Równe County was crossed by the largest river in Wołyń, the meandering Horyń. Its nine village communes were: Aleksandria, Diadkiewicze, Hoszcza, Klewań, Korzec, Majków, Międzyrzec, Równe (county seat), and Tuczyn.

Table 18
Population of Równe County by Mother Tongue

Ukrainian	160,371
Ruthenian	113
Polish	36,990
Jewish	37,484
German	7,458
Czech	5,817
Russian	4,093
Belorussian	140
Lithuanian	11
Other	85
Unreported	225
Total	252,787

Table 19
Population of Równe County by Religious Affiliation

Orthodox	166,469
Roman Catholic	36,444
Uniate	501
Protestant/Evangelical	7,752
Other Christian	3,686
Jewish	37,713
Other Non-Christian	34
Not Specified or Non-Religious	22
Unreported	166
Total	252,787

Although Równe County belonged to the UPA "Eneia" region, no specific battalions were organized there. Rather, the ethnic cleansing of Poles was conducted by the well-organized SKV units and the SB units—with the assistance of the "Kruk" and "Negus" units of "Eneia," the "Zahrava" units from Kostopol under "Ostryi," "Hroznyi," and later, Stupnytskyi (a Podhajce company), and the UPA units from Zdołbunów under Volodymyr Lukashchuk ("Kropyva"). Initially, the mission of the last-mentioned units was to penetrate into Soviet Ukraine.

Among the many places in Równe County where atrocities occurred were: Korzec and Józefówka on April 22, 1943, during Holy Week; in the communes of Diatkiewicze, Tuczyn, and Korzec that June; in the communes of Korzec, Międzyrzec, Tuczyn and Równe that July; in the communes of Tuczyn and the towns of Aleksandria and Klewań that August; and in various towns from September on, including the November 1943 attack on Aleksandria by the UPA Podhajce company, which came to Równe County from Lwów. Needless to say, in these brutal attacks on innocent and by-and-large unarmed civilians, thousands perished—including my relatives in the village of Leonówka and our neighbors in Ryświanka Colony.

People

BEZUKHY from Mikołajówka. *See* Spyrydon.

KRAVCHUK, Paraska, from Klecka Wielka Colony

In March 1943, on behalf of a group of Poles hiding in a forest, Paraska Kravchuk brought a petition to the Germans in Korzec requesting assistance. A contingent of 50 soldiers were dispatched, under whose protection the group was safely transported to Korzec, and from there to the Hołownica estate.[1]

PASICHNYK family from Ryświanka
from T. Piotrowski's family recollections:

"Bear with me now as I relate the sad story of the Leonówka massacre, which also involved members of my extended family. It is but one more instance of the insanity which ruled our land at that time. Far be it from me to claim that this was the worst incident of the war or even in the history of my family. But it is representative of those days of terror in our immediate vicinity.

"Picture in your mind's eye two quaint East-European villages strung out along the same winding, quiet, country road within a mile and a half of each other: Leonówka, a small Polish village of some 30 numbers, with a store, a school, people in the streets, and many, many children; and Żalanka, a Ukrainian village of similar description, but without a school. That the relationship between these two villages was cordial before the war can be surmised from the fact that Żalanka's children were always welcome in Leonówka's red-brick schoolhouse, where Zofia Sigda taught grades 1–3, and her husband, Tomasz, taught grades 4–7 in the Polish language.

"My own family of orientation lived in Leonówka for some time before moving to Amelin and finally settling down in Ryświanka. My two surviving brothers were born there. Two of my father's brothers still lived there with their families in the early 1940s. One of these was Władysław, who passed away quite unexpectedly on February 2, 1942, after a severe asthma attack, and who left behind him his wife, Marcelina (née Bagińska), and seven children.

"The date, fixed forever in the annals of human iniquity, was August 1, 1943. It was a Sunday. Marcelina went to her parish church in Tuczyn that day to attend Mass and to pray for her recently deceased husband. She also prayed for her children: Stanisława (called Stasia), a young lady of 18 summers; Mirosława (13), Zofia (11), Władysława (nine), Romualda (seven), Stefan (five), and her fair-haired child with an angelic face and long baby curls, named (at the insistence of his sisters) Waldemar — after a popular romance novel hero of that day. He was only three.

"Not all the Piotrowski children were home that day. Stasia, the oldest, had been staying with her aunt, Franciszka Kuczyńska (her mother's sister), who lived near Aleksandria. She recalls that one day the Gestapo came to her aunt's house looking for Jews and human slaves; they also raped young girls. Being well hidden, after their departure she was sent to a friendly Ukrainian's house in the village of Remel, where she was to remain overnight in case they should return. She went, but, becoming frightened by the constant whispering in the household, she left the Ukrainians and made her way back on foot to her own home in Leonówka, some 16 kilometers away. Just before August 1, she was sent to stay with Pawlina Prokopowiec, married to a German by the name of Bitner, who lived in the village of Kwasiłów on the other side of Równe.

"Zofia, her sister, was also absent. That afternoon she had gone to her cousin's house (Adolf Bagiński) and had decided to remain there overnight. So at home there remained only Marcelina, her four youngest children, her daughter Mirosława, and her daughter's two visiting friends — a boy, Gienek Paśnieski (15), whose family lived on the outskirts of the village, and a girl, Władzia Bagińska (13), who lived next door.

"It was that very night, at about eleven o'clock, that the cohorts from Żalanka descended upon sleeping Leonówka. Whether this particular group of men consisted of the actual residents of Żalanka (as my cousin, Stasia, believes), or whether it was a contingent of the UPA using Żalanka as its base of operation, will perhaps never be known for certain. In any case, these hundred or so Ukrainians came well equipped with grenades, field rifles, and an assortment of axes, scythes, and swords.

"Posting some men around the village, the rest threw themselves upon the first Polish household of Leonówka, the one closest to Żalanka, the home of Jan Bagiński, his seven-months-pregnant wife and eight of their children (their ninth, Władzia, was spending the night next door with the Piotrowskis.) A live grenade was flung through the window into the home of the sleeping family, and as the panic-stricken survivors emerged, they were slaughtered one by one. Only two children, Halina and Władysław, survived the carnage, by hiding in the fields. On that particular night they slept in the hayloft of the barn.

"The exploding grenade awakened Marcelina, her family, and their two young visitors. In horror, they saw their next-door neighbor's house go up in flames. In utter disbelief, they heard the death screams of the parents and the children with whom they played that very day. They all knew full well that they would be next.

"As Mirosława, Gieniek, and Władzia (whose family was being burned and slaughtered next door) dove through an opening under the [makeshift] altar into the cellar, crawled through the tunnel, and ran out into the fields, Marcelina threw each one of her darling babies out the nearest window, then dove out after them into the yard. Even as she scrambled to gather her dear little ones around her before running for safety, she perished. An axe-wielding Ukrainian cut her in half, and then in half again. Stefan, too, was killed outright, and fell beside his mother. Waldemar, the fair-haired child, the three-year-old named after the romantic hero of his day, was caught by a flying saber on the side of his head and fell bloody and unconscious to the ground. Romualda ran into the barn, where she had hidden so many times before, and there was pierced to death with an ordinary pitchfork. Władysława ran as fast as her little legs could carry her into the family orchard, only to be slaughtered by another scythe-wielding henchman.

"Then, after the house and barn were both put to the torch, one of the men remembered that he had seen some children running toward the fields. The child-hunt began.

"Mirosława and her two friends thought they could hide from the butchers by burying themselves deeply in the fresh-cut hay stacked up like sentry-shelters by their house. (How transparent to adults are the secret hiding places of our youth!) The terrible hunters searched every inch of the terrain, thrusting pitchforks into the hay stacks and turning them inside out as they went along. First, they found Gienek, the 15-year-old boy, and he was killed without a word of protest. Next, they found Władzia, the 13-year-old girl, and although she pleaded with them for her young life, she too was cut down with a bloodstained sword. Mirosława alone, somehow, managed to survive the carnage and lived to tell about it.

"And so they proceeded from house to house, from family to family, from child to child until the entire village was utterly destroyed. Only those from the village and the houses beyond who were able to conceal themselves in the fields, woods, and the nearby marshes managed to survive. Stanisław Piotrowski (my father's brother), his wife, Marynia, and their four children were among these. Somehow, they were able to flee their home, reach the swamp, and thus, submerged waist-deep in mud and water, save their lives.

"At approximately 2:00 A.M., when the butchery was over and all of Leonówka stood in flames, the leader of those who called themselves 'partisans' sounded a long victorious whistle which signaled the end of the siege, or rather the slaughter, and the return of the men to Żalanka; Żalanka which, in the Polish language, means 'grief, sorrow, and anguish'; Żalanka which meant home and safe haven to the Ukrainians.

"After the Ukrainians departed and all grew still as death, Mirosława left her shelter, bypassed her two slain childhood friends, and fearfully made her way back to her burning home. There, she beheld — and this memory of hers has never dimmed — the bloodied and dismembered bodies of her mother, her brothers, and her sisters. Amid the ocean of sorrow which overwhelmed this 13-year-old child, the only fleeting moment of joy — if that is the appropriate word to describe such an emotion — was the discovery that her youngest brother, Waldemar, with his bloodstained angelic face and his matted baby curls, was still alive. She lifted this feather of a child off the ground and pressed him to her sheltering bosom. Thus, they remained alone amid the fires of hell; sister and brother joined forever in that last heart-rending embrace ... for even as she held him fast in her loving arms, his body went limp, and his little soul flew up to heaven.

"As it was August and the barns were full of harvested grain and hay, the flames could be seen from far away. Zofia saw them from her cousin's house three kilometers away. We saw them, too, from about the same distance, rising above the treetops of *Las Ryświanecki* [Ryświanka Forest]. Stasia claims that, while at Pawlina's house, she had a dream that night about her mother, and that her house was on fire. When she awoke and looked in the direction of her home, she saw that the sky in the vicinity of Leonówka was all red, like a bright glowing ember in the night. She knew then that her own village was on fire. Perhaps it was the glow of her Leonówka that she saw at a distance of some 33 kilometers ... but it also could have been the glow of any one of the many Polish villages burning, burning, burning night and day throughout Wołyń in those terrible months of July and August.

"In the morning, when people from the surrounding countryside arrived in the village that was Leonówka to bury the remains of the deceased, the Ukrainians returned once more to drive them off. The bodies of the dead were left to lie there where they fell, under the red sky of August....

"In our vicinity, as elsewhere, stories abounded of Polish mothers being held by the Ukrainian Nationalists and forced to watch as their families were dismembered piece by piece; of pregnant women being eviscerated; of vivisected pregnant women having cats sown into their bleeding abdomens; of Ukrainian husbands murdering their own Polish wives; of Ukrainian wives murdering their own Polish husbands; of Ukrainian fathers murdering their own sons in order to prevent them from murdering their own Polish mothers; of sons of Polish-Ukrainian heritage being sawed in half because, the Nationalists said, they were half-Polish; of children being strung up on household fences; of helpless infants being dashed against buildings or hurled into burning houses. Were these, then, the worst instances of cruelty in the war? And if these were not, then what were?

"And so we were afraid, afraid for one another and for ourselves, knowing neither the day nor the hour of our own final sacrifice. Each night and day new fires were visible, rising high above our ever-darkening landscape, and each day and night they grew more numerous and brighter. Nothing could deliver us from our growing fears save death itself. If they did not come for us yet, it was because Ryświanka was a Ukrainian village and the few Polish families scattered among its colony were not worth the effort. Our turn would surely come after the larger pools of Polish blood dried up ... perhaps sooner....

"The Leonówka massacre (just three kilometers away) convinced us that we must consider the unthinkable. Immediately afterward, most of the Polish families in our neighborhood decided to abandon their homesteads and head for Tuczyn where, it was said, a German garrison was stationed. Such was our fear of the Ukrainian bands that we preferred to take our chances with the Nazis! Moreover, what other alternative did we have? To stay put would have meant certain death.

"Since we were without any means of transportation, it was decided that Stasia [my sister] would go with the Domalewskis (she and Felek planned to marry upon their arrival in Tuczyn), and that Anna [my sister] would go with the Gruntkowskis and return for us with their team of horses on the following day.

"After their departure, only my 51-year-old mother, my two brothers, Franek (12) and Janek (ten), and I remained at home. I was of the same age as my poor cousin Waldemar. Our situation was ominously similar to Marcelina's. With these thoughts in her mind, my mother asked our Polish neighbor to the east, Filip, if we could spend the night with his family. Since his house stood next to a Ukrainian home, it was unlikely that it would be burnt. Our kind neighbor was more than gracious with his hospitality. He assured us that he and his four daughters would spend the night as sentries in case of an attack. He, too, was much troubled by what had been transpiring in our area.

"At about eleven o'clock that night, as we all tossed and turned uneasily in our beds, Filip's daughters ran into the house, yelling and screaming that our home and barn were on fire. So this was the day and the hour!

"All was instinct now. In the twinkle of an eye there was not a living soul left on the premises. My mother grabbed me, still asleep, and we all ran out and kept on running until we collapsed in a potato field some 60 meters from the conflagration. We saw then that our flaming house was completely surrounded by Ukrainians ... and that they had axes.

"We were so close we could feel the heat and hear the mournful lowing of the cattle and the unearthly sounds of the other animals trapped within the barn. They were desperately thrashing about. They were being burnt alive. We heard the sound of broken glass. We saw our house and barn disintegrating before our very eyes. We smelled the awful scent of burning flesh.

"It was at that most inopportune moment that I, frightened as I was, began to cry. The night was clear and the moon was so bright one could find the proverbial needle in any one of the many haystacks surrounding our house; and if one could find a needle in a haystack, one could all the more easily find four crouching figures in a potato field. Moreover, the flaming house and barn were like two huge torches which lit up the whole countryside and turned the night into day.

"What mother does not know the fine art of quieting a despairing child? And so Maria Piotrowska began to tell me a story about sheep. I am told that as a child I entertained a healthy respect for those wooly creatures. At the age of three the terror of sheep had more power to deter my tears than the events of the night had to inspire them. So, despite the felt agitation of my family, the night, the black fields, the shrieking animals, and the burning barn and house, I stopped crying. For the moment, at least, we were safe.

"I have often wondered what she was thinking then, my poor, dear mother, seeing her own home going up in smoke and flames — that home that she swept daily and nurtured like her own child. How she loved that house! How many memories did she lose that night — or gain? Our homeless *Burek* [our dog] — where was he now? Our dear *Bociek* [our stork] — where will he build his nest? Our cruel swallows — barns were so scarce these days! The work, the joy, the grief, the sorrow, all mingled with the flames and smoke rising, rising to the moon and stars.

"'What shall we do now?' she must have thought. 'And where shall we go? ... And where is my husband? ... And what has become of my four oldest daughters? ... And what am I to do with these three young boys of mine? ... And will they ever reach full manhood?'

"Did she perhaps think of poor Marcelina, and Waldemar, and Stefan, and Romualda, and Władysława, and Hilary, and Paweł, and his wife, and their slain children?

"Did she sing? My mother always sang. Did she sing 'Gorzkie Żale' [Bitter Lamentations]?

"Did she think of the time when she was almost devoured by the hungry wolves, or of the old *babusieńka* [granny] with her amulets and herbs, or God, or the devil?

"Did she become a little girl again, playing in the sweet memories of her bygone 19th-century days?

"*Mother, what did you think out there in that potato field, seeing your home go up in flames and knowing that only by the grace of God were we* here *in this desolate field and not* there *inside the house? How I wish I could ask you that one question now! I have never in my life known, nor will I ever know, a more important question. Oh Mother, please tell me the story of the sheep once more.*

"I think it was my brother Franek who disturbed her quietly racing thoughts with the sobering news that we were still at risk. It was so bright; shelter must be found.

"We did not go very far from where we were, when my mother suggested that we hide in one of the haystacks in our field. (Perhaps she did not want to leave at all.)

"'No, Mother, they will surely find us here. It is still too close. Remember Gienek and Władzia,' someone must have said.

"And so we went on into the night a little further until we reached the small forest bordering our property, called *Ochrona*, which means 'Shelter.' There, we fell beneath the sprawling branches of an evergreen tree — the type that spreads its limbs low upon the ground for little frightened animals to hide beneath, the type under which *krasnoludki* [gnomes] dwell, the type which children often use in their games of hide and seek. Yes, that was the type!

"At about midnight (but who could say exactly when it was?) we heard the sounds of hurried footsteps coming in our direction along the road which separated *Ochrona* from our potato field. We held our breath in panic as six armed men ran past our hiding place in the direction of our house. They, too, must have been Ukrainians zeroing in for the final kill. God only knows how they missed seeing us, for at the time, we did not realize just how close we were to the road.

"After several more attentive hours, as the fire continued to dance in the pupils of our unblinking eyes, the gruff voices of the men mingled with the soft murmuring of the pines, then faded in the distance. When all grew silent as the grave, some of us finally surrendered ourselves to the welcome tides of sleep in the vain hope that upon awakening, all this horror would prove to have been nothing more than a bad midsummer night's dream.

"We remained in our forest shelter the whole night through, until the first rays of sunlight appeared over the horizon and fell on the smoldering ashes which had been our house and barn only the day before. Even then we were in no hurry, as we no longer had anywhere to go. Now, the whole wide world was our home: everywhere and nowhere. The road was no more than two meters from the tree, so we followed that to our neighbor's house, where we planned to spend the night.

"When we arrived at Filip's we found that, although all the windows were broken, no one was hurt and the house was still intact. They were much relieved to see us safe and sound.

"The time had finally come to bid farewell to our Ryświanka. We could no longer even think of waiting for Anna to return with Gruntkowski's team of horses. Perhaps she would never come. We would walk. We urged our neighbor to come with us, since he and his family would most certainly be the next target of attack — but to no avail. He was of an unyielding disposition. Neither he nor his family, he said, would ever abandon their ancestral home. They were resolved to stay and confront the devil that they knew, rather than the unknown demons to the west. Since we were all doomed anyway, they preferred to die here in Ryświanka. So be it. We embraced them all there, near their doorstep, near their fields and meadows, on the graveyard of their own choosing, and prepared for our departure.

"As we hurried to dig out our emergency provisions from fields and woods, we realized that our cache did not contain extra footwear. Who would think of hiding *trepy* [wooden shoes]? No matter, we would walk barefooted, as we had the evening before to Filip's house.

"At the very moment of our departure, the unimaginable transpired. We saw a lone, unarmed figure coming slowly toward us all.

It was our Ukrainian neighbor, Pasichnyk. And just when we thought that we finally caught a glimpse of the devil that we knew, he metamorphosed before our unbelieving eyes into an angel of mercy.

"He was a mild-mannered man, a compassionate man, a man of genuine sympathy and good will. We could all see the painful expression in his face as he drew nearer. We could feel his deep sorrow for our recent tragedy. We could sense his heartfelt regret for what his people had done. He was a good man — like the passer-by who once put down his basket of eggs to help our Savior bear his cross. It was he who saved our lives that day.

"Mr. Pasichnyk offered to take us to Tuczyn himself, but when his wife saw him harnessing the horses and realized what he was about to do, she said to him in the presence of my mother, 'You will not get anywhere because the road you must take leads through the forest where the bandits are lying in ambush and you will perish along with them.'

"It was a sobering thought, and although the eight-kilometer trip was very long by foot, we all realized that it was much safer to proceed that way. Before we left, [Pasichnyk] warned us not to take the main road through the woods:

"'Do not go that way, Piotrowska!' he said. 'The woods are full of bandits! You will be killed! Rather, take the winding footpath through the fields, the one which skirts the forests and the Ukrainian village on the other side. It is much longer but it is much safer too.'

"The forests he referred to were our own *Ochrona* and *Las Ryświanecki*; the village was our own Ryświanka. So, we took his neighborly advice and left. Never will we forget our kind Ukrainian [neighbor and] friend."[2]

SPYRYDON from Mikołajówka
Z. Ch. from Mikołajówka states:

"The Banderowcy attack [on Mikołajówka] took place at dawn on April 29,

1943. Returning from Kobylnia [Kobylnica], they fell on the Polish families of Bruchlewski and Zagładów.

"The Banderowcy entered our house and began to murder us with bayonets. They brought some hay inside and set it on fire. I was pierced with a bayonet, lost consciousness, and fell on my aunt. Just as the flame reached me, I came to and jumped out the window. (By that time the Banderowcy had left.) A Ukrainian, Spyrydon, heard my moans. He carried me to another Ukrainian, Bezukhy, who took me by wagon to the hospital in Korzec. Fourteen people died in this attack.... [Names and ages follow.] Among them was a 20-year-old woman who was pregnant."³

Places

BASOWY KĄT
From the account of Ryszard Majer (b. 1925) from Równe:

"In 1928 my father bought a small parcel of land in the village of Basowy Kąt, now located within the borders of the town [Rivne, formerly Równe]. We lived there until July 1943, that is, until the time that we were forewarned by a Ukrainian resident of the village to flee immediately to the town. That warning was delivered to us while we were having supper.

"My sister and I, followed by my father and mother, fled from our home, leaving almost everything to the Banderowcy for the taking. I know that for a period of two weeks, the UPA awaited our return. I have remembered the following facts from the days of the massive murders:

"1. In August 1943 the Germans laid out dozens of bodies of terribly massacred children, women, and men on the main street of Równe. The victims were the residents of the small town of Aleksandria lying in the middle of a forest by the Horyń River, about 18 kilometers from Równe. Being afraid of a UPA attack, the residents of Aleksandria organized a communal getaway to Równe. Four kilometers before reaching the village of Bamki, they were beset upon and horribly murdered with axes, pitchforks, and knives. The sight of the murdered victims will remain with me for the rest of my life. They were buried in a large mass grave in the cemetery in Równe on Dubieńska Street."⁴

9
Sarny County

The most sparsely populated of the 11 counties in Wołyń (33 people per square kilometer), Sarny County bordered both Polesie and Soviet Ukraine. Three rivers flowed through its forested terrain: Styr, Horyń, and Słucz. Among its nine village communes were: Antonówka, Bielska Wola, Dąbrowica, Horodziec, Kisorycze, Klesów, Niemowicze, Rafałówka, and Włodzimierzec. Sarny was its county seat.

Table 20
Population of Sarny County by Mother Tongue

Ukrainian	128,284
Ruthenian	1,353
Polish	30,426
Jewish	16,019
German	922
Czech	85
Russian	2,765
Belorussian	1,183
Lithuanian	17
Other	57
Unreported	173
Total	181,284

Table 21
Population of Sarny County by Religious Affiliation

Orthodox	132,241
Roman Catholic	28,192
Uniate	450
Protestant/Evangelical	1,700
Other Christian	2,478
Jewish	16,088
Other Non-Christian	5
Not Specified or Non-Religious	8
Unreported	122
Total	181,284

Judging by numerous testimonies of survivors, it was probably Taras "Bulba"-Borovets's UPA which began the genocide in Wołyń in this region in the fall of 1942. The February 9, 1943, slaughter in Parośle was no doubt its doing. Wishing to consolidate the military strength of the various nationalist factions in Eastern Poland, the more powerful Bandera faction attacked Borovets's men in June 1943, murdered the officers, and forced the rank-and-file soldiers into its own UPA—a name stolen from Borovets.

Several UPA companies operated in Sarny County, including the original UPA units of Serhii Kachynskyi ("Ostap") and Ivan Perehiiniak ("Dovbeshka-Korobka"), established in October 1942.

In addition to the many lesser attacks on Polish individuals, families, and settlements by both UPAs, the OUN-B UPA launched two major assaults in Sarny County. The first began on July 16, 1943, when the "Rubashenko" (Stepan Koval's) battalion in its march on Huta Stepańska, a large Polish self-defense center, wiped out the villages of Iwańcza, Wyrobki, Soszniki, Szymonisko, and Hały. [See Appendix C: Excerpts from Documents, Ukrainian, "Court

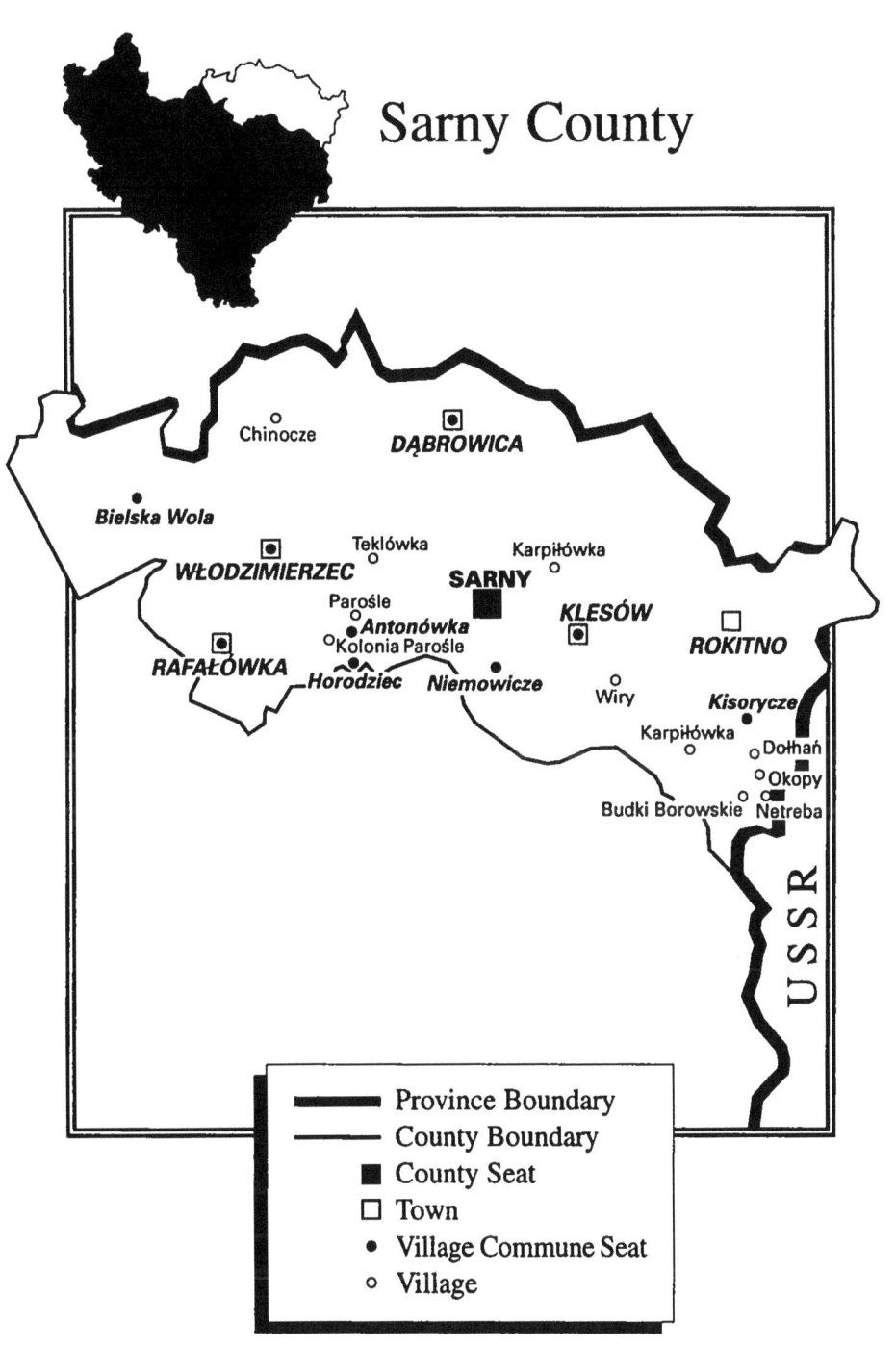

Testimony of Battalion Leader Stepan Koval ('Rubashenko,' 'Burlak') in the 'Zahrava' Region."] The second "action" transpired on July 31, 1943, when "Iarema's" battalion first blocked all escape routes and then proceeded to decimate 11 Polish settlements.

People

DMYTRUK, Trofym, from Okopy
Bronisław Janik writes:

"On December 5 [1943], as some men were gathered in the home of Franciszek Koziński, there was a knock on the door. It was Trofym Dmytruk. He came with another warning that the Bulbowcy were preparing to murder them. Not everyone believed him.

"'This is not the first time that Trofym has warned us,' said 'Prymak.' 'He warns us and warns us, but the Bulbowcy do not attack. They evidently want to keep us in suspense and fear.'

"'Don't talk nonsense, Józef,' said Maria Żelazko. 'I do not believe Trofym wholeheartedly, but since he comes and warns us we should be on guard....'

"The night was peaceful, and by morning the people began to put less and less faith in Dmytruk's warning....

"On December 6, 1943, the residents of all three villages [Budki Borowskie, Dołhań, and Okopy], feeling a little better, went to bed; some even slept in their own houses.... Suddenly a flare lit up the sky and revealed hundreds of Bulbowcy shouting, 'Kill the Poles!'....

[After the massacre.] "In the morning the refugees made their way to the forest shelters of their neighbors from Netreba; after all, they had to feed their children and provide them with warmth. The residents of Netreba, whose village had been burned down in July, welcomed them with open arms. [This Ukrainian village was destroyed by the UPA in 1943 because many of its residents converted to Roman Catholicism in 1937-38. The survivors fled to the forests for safety.] By this time the residents of Netreba were able to build shelters and adjust to living in the forest. Leontyna Ciołkowska, who — together with her mother, Aniela Romaniewicz, and her six-year-old daughter, Stefania — knocked on the forest home of Mykola Sheremeta, can attest to their goodwill. Sheremeta not only received them graciously and offered to share his humble abode with them but also provided for them for a long time. Sheremeta's wife even took solicitous care of Leontyna's daughter when her mother was severely ill."[1]

KORENCHUK, Volodymyr, and his family, from Borowe
According to Leon Żur:

During the December 6, 1943, UPA attack on Budki Borowskie, Michalina (née Kozińska) — the Polish wife of Oleksandr Korenchuk, a Ukrainian who converted to Catholicism after marriage — was shot through the mouth by a Bulbowiec [Ukr., Bulbivets; member of Borovets's organization] and left for dead. The family of Volodymyr Korenchuk (Oleksandr's relatives) rescued her and took her to a doctor on the following day.[2]

PARASKA from Długowola
From the account of Władysław Żarczyński (b. 1924) from Czudła:

"One day — this was in May 1942 — our former servant, Paraska, came to us. She ran all the way from the village of Długowola, about six kilometers away, and she was out of breath and in a state of great excitement. She was in a hurry because she was afraid that her husband might notice her absence. To my mother she said, 'Aunt, the Ukrainians are holding meetings over our way, and they plan to kill the Poles. I came to warn you. Oh, God, what will happen?'

"My mother became frightened and told her that it would be better if she did not bring us such news. However, Mother relayed the message to our neighbors and friends. Although they did not believe it, they nevertheless began to organize guard duty in their villages and colonies....

"Already at the beginning of 1943 news began to arrive in our village that Ukrainian bands were killing and robbing the Poles in various parts of Wołyń."

The narrator then describes the various murders of which he is aware (beginning on February 8, 1943, in Włodzimierzec) and the Ukrainian-Nationalist attacks on various Polish villages and colonies, e.g., Parośle, Brzezina, Huta Stepańska, Poroda (Porada), Prurwa (Przerwa), Stachówka (attacked twice), and Choromce (a Polish self-defense center attacked three times). The refugees who gathered in Choromce were finally rescued by Germans who came to their assistance from Włodzimierzec. Later, about 300 of the survivors, including the narrator, were taken to Germany for forced labor. Władysław concludes, "It is worth mentioning that as one enemy, the Ukrainians, were attacking us, another enemy, the Germans, ironically came to our assistance and placed us under their protection. Such were the times."[3]

SHEREMETA, Mykola, and his wife, from Netreba. *See* Trofym Dmytruk.

SUDRAK, Mykola, from Struga
From the account of Antoni Przybysz from Antonówka:

"Early in the morning on July 31, 1943, Mykola Sudrak, a Ukrainian from Struga, warned a resident of Perespa, Antoni Piotrowski, that there would be an attack by the Banderowcy that night. Some of the residents immediately took their families to Antonówka, where a German unit was stationed....

"That night the Ukrainian Nationalists attacked the Polish villages and colonies....

"During the Banderowcy action, a young Ukrainian named Volodymyr Iashchuk, who worked on our farm, was asked why he didn't return to his family in Teklówka. He replied, 'I have worked for the Przybysz family for several years now, and I have it good here. I feel like a Pole [i.e., a Polish citizen] and am revolted by those Ukrainians who are murdering the Polish people.'"[4]

Places

ANTONÓWKA

In March 1943, when Józef Ejsmont came by wagon to the mill in Antonówka, the Ukrainian mill owner warned him of imminent danger. Józef immediately turned around and headed back home. On his return trip he was beset by the Ukrainian Nationalists, who tied him to a post, plucked out his eyes, cut out his tongue, and cut him in half with a saw.[5]

10
Włodzimierz County

Located in the southwestern part of Wołyń and bordering with the Lublin Province, Włodzimierz County was subdivided into seven village communes: Chotiaczów, Grzybowica, Korytnica, Mikulicze, Olesk, Poryck, and Werba. Włodzimierz was the county seat.

Table 22
Population of Włodzimierz County by Mother Tongue

Ukrainian	87,212
Ruthenian	962
Polish	40,286
Jewish	17,236
German	2,778
Czech	490
Russian	1,228
Belorussian	77
Lithuanian	2
Other	16
Unreported	87
Total	150,374

Table 23
Population of Włodzimierz County by Religious Affiliation

Orthodox	88,005
Roman Catholic	38,483
Uniate	1,636
Protestant/Evangelical	2,965
Other Christian	1,926
Jewish	17,331
Other Non-Christian	3
Not Specified or Non-Religious	9
Unreported	16
Total	150,374

As they attacked Taras "Bulba"-Borovets's men in July 1943 and forced them into their own ranks, so the OUN-B also attacked and incorporated the followers of Andrii Melnyk in that same month. The rank-and-file soldiers of the OUN-M were assigned to the Svynarynskyi (Świnarzyn) battalion, also known as the Włodzimierz battalion. As already mentioned (cf. Chapter 4, introduction to Kowel County), Porfyrii Antoniuk's ("Sosenko's") three-company battalion and his "Sich Svynarynska" also operated out of Włodzimierz. In addition, a company of the Zavydivskyi battalion was stationed there as well for a time.

As elsewhere in Wołyń, the initial UPA acts of terror were aimed primarily against individuals and Polish families. Later, entire villages and village complexes were attacked and destroyed. For example, on July 11, 1943, 34 locations in the county of Włodzimierz, including the churches in Poryck and Chrynów, were attacked by the UPA. (According to an AK field report, "60 Polish villages in the counties of Horochów and Włodzimierz were annihilated" on July 11 and 12. See Appendix C: Excerpts from Documents, Polish, "Other Home Army Field Reports on the Ethnic-Cleansing Campaign," the first entry.) This massive action was followed by a second one on August 29 and 30, 1943. These dates figure prominently in the testimonies of many survivors.

People

BALYTSKYI, an Orthodox priest from Lachów
From the account of Jadwiga Krajewska from Lachów:

"I will begin my sad narrative with March 20, 1943. On this Saturday, around 8:00 P.M., Ukrainians in German uniforms entered our house and arrested my father and the forester, Dołwiat. After about an hour, they returned and informed us that my father and the forester had escaped. We found their remains the next day under a sheaf of grain. They were dressed only in their underclothes. They were buried in Poryck because the church and cemetery were there....

"On May 11, 1943, my mother and I were awakened by the sound of hoofbeats and the glow of fires. On that occasion farmsteads were set on fire and horses and cattle were robbed. Shortly thereafter, the roof of our house was also set on fire and we lost almost everything. We moved in with an Orthodox priest, Balytskyi. He was a good man but was disliked by the Ukrainians because he conducted the services in the Russian [probably Old Church Slavonic], rather than the Ukrainian language. Besides us, he was also sheltering a Jewish doctor....

"On July 11, 1943, the Ukrainians attacked the church in Poryck.... [A description follows].

"Shortly thereafter, a column of wagons passed through Lachów loaded down with the goods of the murdered Poles. Meanwhile, we were forewarned by Pokydko, a Ukrainian teacher, to flee immediately. She instructed us not to take anything with us and to dress as if we were going for a Sunday walk. This we did. The road ran along the woods, and although we imagined seeing all kinds of dangers along the way, we finally reached the railway station in Iwanicze."[1]

BRANYTSKYI, Myta, from Bielin. See Mykola Kordashuk.

BUGAI from Zofiówka
From the account of Stanisław Fedorowicz (b. 1926) from Zofiówka:

"In 1943 all hell broke loose. Murders and fires abounded. In our colony alone, in July and August 1943, over 20 people were murdered. We survived thanks to the help of our Ukrainian neighbor, Bugai, who was a good man. His daughter married our Polish neighbor before the war and emigrated to America."[2]

DUBENCHUK, Iakiv, Katia, and their family, from Swojczów. See Swojczów, fourth and fifth accounts.

GONTAR from Mosur. See Mosur, second account.

HARKYS, Artem, from Poryck. See Poryck, first account.

HAVRYLIUK, Semen, from Mosur. See Mosur, first account.

IADZIUK, Moisei, from Sielec
After the April 23, 1943, UPA attack on the village of Sielec, two Ukrainians (Moisei Iadziuk and Oleksandr Zakharuk) helped to transport the few remaining survivors across the Ługa River and brought them to the railway station in Bubnów. From there, the survivors were safely transported to Włodzimierz Wołyński.[3]

IEVHEN from Swojczów. See Swojczów, fourth account.

IUKHNO from Sielec. See Sielec, first and second accounts.

KATIA, NATASHA, and their family, from Niebrzydów
From the account of Teresa Guz (née Persona) from Niebrzydów:

"On Sunday, August 29, 1943, the

Banderowcy attacked our village of Niebrzydów. The following members of my family were killed: my father, Kazimierz Persona (45); my mother, Aniela (née Parcheta, 35); my sister, Bogumiła (14); my brother, Aleksander (12); my brother, Piotr (ten); and my sister, Krystyna (three).

"That I survived was almost a miracle. I stayed with the Ukrainian family of Katia and Natasha.... That family, at the risk of their own lives, took care of me and looked after the graves of my loved ones for many years after the tragedy.... To this day the local Ukrainians refer to the place where the graves are located as 'Persona Field.'"[4]

KORDASHUK, Mykola, from Bielin
From the account of Edward Kondracki from Bielin:

"A total of 43 persons were killed [by the Ukrainian Nationalists] in my family and the family of my wife....

"We survived thanks to two Ukrainians: Mykola Kordashuk, the *sołtys* [village head], and Myta Branytskyi, the vice-*sołtys*. In the fall of 1942, I do not remember the exact date but it was on a raw Sunday, a band of butchers came to our village carrying scythes, axes, pitchforks, and every tenth one had a gun. In all, there were over 2,000 of them under the leadership of Mykola Dubytskyi, who lived in Hajki. Evidently on that day the population of Bielin was to be exterminated. However, the above-mentioned two Ukrainians — after a prolonged discussion with the leaders of the butchers — prevented the murders from taking place. Our village was completely destroyed by the Germans on Easter, 1943."[5]

KOVALUK, Vasyl, from Kałusów
From the account of Julian Grzesik from Lublin:

"During my stay in Ukraine, I obtained some information regarding the events under the German occupation. This information concerns the murder of about 180 persons by the Banderowcy in a colony near the present-day village of Hrady [formerly Kałusów], a few kilometers from Novovolynsk.

"According to A.K., a resident of Hrady, the Banderowcy appeared in that colony in Polish uniforms and ordered the Poles to gather in two barns (the women in one, the men in the other one) under the pretext of distributing arms to them with which they would be able to defend themselves [against the Germans], or as the current version has it in those parts, with which to 'murder Ukrainians.' With the exception of one woman and her child, both of whom hid under a threshing machine, all of them were then killed and buried nearby. The Poles in the remaining colonies fled to Włodzimierz Wołyński. The families of the murdered victims set up crosses on the graves. The Banderowcy tried to force the local Baptists (including Andrei's father, Pavlo) to break the crosses and to level the graves, but the Baptists refused to do so.

"In Hrady there lives a Polish widow [Antonina Kovaluk, née Szostek], originally from Rzeszów, who was saved by her now deceased [Ukrainian] husband, Vasyl Kovaluk. [Vasyl had also rescued several other Poles]. She is still spry enough mentally to relate the whole incident, and the local people can point out the place where the murdered victims are buried....

"From the slaughter in Kałusów itself, a small child survived because it was taken by Platon, a Ukrainian, into his own home. When the Banderowcy came to kill the child, Platon protected it with his own breast. The mother of the child hid in the hemp field, and the father jumped into a dry well. In this way, all three were saved. Platon later returned the child to the parents in Włodzimierz."[6]

KRASHKEVYCH from Poryck. *See* Vasyl and Anysia Siokh.

KULAI, Mitko, from Poryck. *See* note to Vasyl and Anysia Siokh.

KULAI, Volodymyr, from Pawłówka. *See* Poryck, first account.

KUSHNERUK, Aleksy, from Głęboczyce Colony

On August 29, 1943, Głęboczyce Colony was attacked by the UPA, and about 200 Poles were murdered. Two children, a six-year-old boy and a two-year-old girl, were rescued by a Ukrainian named Aleksy Kushneruk. Aleksy handed them over to the Polish Red Cross in 1944.[7]

KYSLYI, Iukhym, from Poryck. *See* Poryck, first account.

LASHUK (widower) and his daughter, Halushka, from Swojczów. *See* Swojczów, fifth account.

MALASHKA from Duliby
From the account of Anna Szyjkowska (née Kunysz) from Wiktorówka:

"On Sunday, August 16, 1943, the Banderowcy murdered all the Poles in the village of Wiktorówka. In the colony of Grabina they killed: Maria Kunysz, my brother's pregnant wife; Zygmunt Kunysz, her seven-year-old son; Ludwika Kunysz, three years of age; and Aniela Kaczorowska, the 23-year-old sister of my brother's wife.

"My brother, Bronisław Kunysz, was helping his friend, Józef Rolak, with the harvest in the neighboring village of Soroczyń and spent Saturday night at his house. Awakened that Sunday by some shots, he headed for the barn. From the barn loft he could see some people armed with guns and sharp implements coming across the field. He also noted that they surrounded the households. He hid in the barn for two days while the bandits searched the buildings several times a day looking for the residents and stealing their belongings. Afterwards, traveling at night through fields, Bronisław returned home. No one was there. In the flower garden he noticed a spot where the ground had been recently turned over. There, he uncovered the bodies of his wife, her sister, and his sons.

"Since the Bulbowcy continued to penetrate the area, the unfortunate widower hid himself in a nearby pasture in some willow bushes. He remained there for another five days after the tragic death of his loved ones, not daring to look for food or water. By that time he was weak, unshaven, and ill. It was in this state that he was found by Malashka, a Ukrainian acquaintance who came over to pasture her cows from the nearby village of Duliby.

"'You look like Jesus Christ,' she told him and drove the cows back home.

"After a short time she returned to the pasture with her animals and in her basket was a bottle of milk. While she kept a lookout, Bronisław took a few swallows of the milk and immediately vomited; his contracted stomach would not accept the milk.

"Malashka told the poor man to steal to her house at night and to hide in her attic. This he did knowing that she was a good woman from having worked for her in the past. Although she lived together with her daughter-in-law and granddaughter, she didn't tell them about her guest for security reasons. She looked after him herself. Knowing about folk medicine, she fed him various brews from the field thinking that she was dealing with typhus. In any case, the remedy worked and the patient recovered his health.

"He remained with this family for another half a year. In the end, Soviet troops arrived in Duliby and the population had to be evacuated because of the [approaching] front."[8]

MROCHKO, Petro, from Przewały
From the account of Ludwik Zalewski (b. 1922) from Święte Jezioro:

"The Ukrainian band did not attack our village [Święte Jezioro] because we were warned by the refugees from the other villages that were attacked on August 29, 1943. The victims in those villages were predominantly the ill, the old, invalids, women, and children. It was at this time that my mother and grandmother were murdered in a neighboring village. I was informed of this by my brother-in-law, Michał Użyński, who escaped being killed but who saw these two unfortunate women after they had been decapitated. In addition, their home was completely robbed and their livestock was stolen. My brother-in-law fled without taking any extra clothing or food. He received these items from us when he joined the refugees on their way toward the safety of a German outpost.

"The residents of our village constituted a large group to which I and my family attached ourselves. Avoiding the main roads, we traveled through fields and forests until we reached Przewały, where we stayed for one day. We did not see any young people in that village, not even Ukrainians. An elderly Ukrainian whom we knew quite well came over to us and said, 'Come to my house, nothing will happen to you today.'

"His name was Petro Mrochko. In spite of his assurance that we were safe, we posted a guard at night. The next day Petro said, 'Wait here, and I will go and find out what the situation is like in the village.'

"He came back a few hours later and declared, 'Get going because I will not be able to defend you.'"[9]

MUZYKA from Gucin Colony
On July 11, 1943, a group of several hundred Ukrainian Nationalists gathered about 140 Polish residents of Gucin Colony in a blacksmith shop which was then locked, doused with gasoline, and set on fire. Some of those inside were able to escape under the cover of smoke by knocking down a part of the wall; the majority, however, perished in the flames. An old Ukrainian woman managed to rescue Jan Krzysztan's three children. Unfortunately, they were taken from her by force on the following day and drowned in a well. Apolonia Traczykiewicz survived by hiding in a field of grain. A Ukrainian woman named Muzyka took care of her for a while. After her son was murdered by the UPA for refusing to kill Poles, the Ukrainian woman urged Apolonia to flee to a more distant shelter.[10]

POKYDKO from Lachów. *See* Balytskyi.

PLATON from Kałusów. *See* Vasyl Kovaluk.

PROKOPIUK from Strzelecka Colony
From the account of Rozalia Wasilewska (née Hojarska, b. 1924) from Strzelecka Colony:

"After hearing the news about the Banderowcy attacks, in July 1943 we and our Polish neighbors left our colony by wagon and headed for Stężarzyce, where there was a self-defense center.

"At the beginning of August 1943 the Polish guard unit was replaced by a Ukrainian one. As a result, all the Poles left by wagons to Uściług. My parents and I returned to Strzelecka Colony for the harvest and remained there until November 1943. My mother paid dearly for this with her life. She was murdered by the Banderowcy on November 17, 1943. I was forewarned by our Ukrainian (female) neighbor, Prokopiuk, that we were also to be killed. The following day, my father and I escaped by wagon along forest roads to Uściług."[11]

ROMANIUK from Orzeszyn Colony. *See* Orzeszyn Colony, first account.

SECHERCHUK, Dr., from Poryck. *See* note to Vasyl and Anysia Siokh.

SHOSTACHUK, Vladyslav, and his parents, from Sielec. *See* Sielec, first and second accounts.

SIOKH, Vasyl, Anysia, and their family, from Poryck
From the letters of Kamila Kamińska (née Cybuchowska) from Poryck, and Bronisław Terpin from Wolica (near Poryck):

Nineteen-year-old Kamila Cybuchowska miraculously survived the UPA slaughter of the Polish congregation gathered for services in the church in Poryck. She writes:

"I survived by hiding in various nooks and crannies in the interior of the church, especially in its upper quarters. After the slaughter, I saw how the Ukrainians brought an artillery shell and some straw into the church, and how they laid the shell on the straw, which they then set on fire. When the shell exploded the windowpanes of the church were blown out. That's when those who could made their escape amid the smoke and dust.

"After the conclusion of that whole Dantesque scene, when the air cleared somewhat, I looked out from the choir loft and saw my nine-year-old cousin, Elżbieta Sarżyńska, standing in a corner. I decided to go down to her. As I descended the choir loft, I had to move the bodies on the steps to avoid stepping on them. Elżunia [diminutive of Elżbieta] stood over the body of her murdered mother, my Aunt Tekla. Tekla was caught by machine-gun fire and her side was ripped open by a grenade. Elżunia was wounded and carries a piece of shrapnel in her upper arm until this day. She now lives in Kraków and goes by the name of Elżbieta Zając.

"The attack came during the Mass being said by Fr. Bolesław Szawłowski. He was severely wounded. I know that later he was taken to someone's home and that an Orthodox priest came and administered the last rites over him. They were not able to save him, however, because some Ukrainians found him and murdered him.

"Upon leaving the church, I found my mother and handed Elżbieta over to her own father, Leon Sarżyński, who also had a five-year-old son, Ryszard. The three of them went to the home of a friendly Ukrainian named Krashkevych who protected them as best he could. In times of danger, he even placed the children in a doghouse.

"I and my mother, Stanisława Cybuchowska, spent two nights in a field of grain and in the underbrush — until Vasyl and Anysia Siokh found us. They first hid us in a shed, and then in a bin next to their house. Vasyl's father knew of the rescue; Vasyl's younger brother Adam, a member of the UPA and a murderer, did not. When Adam would stop by or sleep in his home, we were warned by his father and told to keep very quiet. If Adam had found us, no doubt a tragedy of unknown proportions would have befallen us all. My mother and I, together with the three other Poles that Vasyl and Anysia were sheltering, would most certainly have been killed by him.

"We remained in hiding with the Siokhs for a period of about two weeks. During that time, either Vasyl's father or the younger Ukrainians would bring us food and take away the buckets containing our waste material. Eventually things quieted down so much so that we were able to return to our own house and, together with Sarżyński and his children, plan our departure from Poryck to Lwów. It was at this time that all the Poles had decided to leave that place of slaughter, Poryck.

"Our departure was organized with the knowledge and assistance of the Germans. We took up a collection as payment, and they provided us with a train car with a military escort. We left from the railway station in Iwanicze and arrived in Lwów without any serious mishaps.

"I do not know who buried the remains of those slaughtered in the Poryck church. The body of my Aunt Tekla was recovered from the church by some distantly related Ukrainians and buried in one of the Polish cemeteries on the outskirts of Poryck. I do not remember the names of these Ukrainians, and I probably did not know them personally.

"That is all that I remember of those cruel times. Perhaps my recorded memories will serve as a memento mori [a reminder of death]. May they hail a beginning of the return to normal relations between the Poles and those Ukrainians who were and are decent human beings, not murderers. I hope that time will heal our injuries and cleanse our minds.

"Vasyl and Anysia Siokh are still alive. We correspond with them and pay them visits. We do not dare, however, to ask them whatever became of Adam."

Bronisław Terpin visited Kamila (now residing in Kraków) in 1994. He also visited Poryck and, at Kamila's request, conveyed to the Siokh family her best wishes. He stated in his letter to me:

"While I was in Poryck, I also looked up Bronisława Ryś, with whose family I had lived while attending the Poryck school. When I relayed the episode about the Siokh brothers to her, she told me that her own father had been killed by the younger brother, the murderer Adam.

"I also wanted to find out what happened to the Jews of Poryck. Bronia told me that one day, after the German occupation, as she was on her way to church, she encountered a convoy of Ukrainian militiamen herding a group of Jews to the marketplace. In that group of Jews was her nearby neighbor. She was carrying her twins in her arms. As Bronia and the others watched this death march, the Jewish mother lost her grip on one of the twins and he fell onto the pavement. As she struggled to pick up her baby, a Ukrainian militiaman came up and kicked the child into the middle of the road. Then other militiamen joined in the fray and began to amuse themselves by kicking the child around as if he were a ball. When the Poles, instead of going to church, began to gather into a crowd, they were ordered by the militiamen to go back home.

"After reaching the marketplace the Jews were loaded on German trucks, taken to the nearby Czacki Forest located to the south of Poryck, and murdered there. Their bodies were dumped into the defense trenches dug the previous year by Soviet soldiers.

"Enclosed you will find the addresses of Stefan and Kamila (née Cybuchowska) Kamińska, Elżbieta Zając (née Sarżyńska), Bronisława Ryś, as well as the address of Stanisław Filipowicz, whose account I have included herein along with the account of Tadeusz Wojewódka. Stanisław, Tadeusz, and I went to school together in Poryck."[12]

SIUNIA, Tymish, from Wólka Swojczowska. See Kyrylo Stolariuk.

STANKO, a Jehovah's Witness from Głęboczyce Colony
From the account of Konstancja Szczepańska (née Małecka) from Głęboczyce Colony:

"On the night of August 29, 1943, I stayed in the home of Eliasz Małecki, my father. It was still gray when my husband, Władysław, came running to us and shouted, 'Get out; they're murdering everyone!'

"My sisters Adela and Karola, my brother Wacław, and I immediately set out toward the Turia River. Having my two-year-old child with me, I was forced to hide behind a haystack. My sisters and brother, however, ran as fast as they could toward the river. They were chased by men on horseback with guns. They shot at my siblings but fortunately missed them.

"After a while, the UPA bandits returned. Hidden deep inside the hay, I could hear their conversation. One of them ordered the men to stick together. On their heads, the attackers wore berets with badges similar to Polish emblems.

"When they departed, I came out of the haystack. I saw my father. His head was split in half and his large, lifeless eyes were wide open. My sister's child was walking in the field and crying. A Ukrainian acquaintance, a Baptist, took the child to her house.

"I fled with my child to the forest, where we lived in hiding for three weeks. There, I met a ten-year-old boy, Maszko. I do not know his first name. There was a provisional shelter in the forest in which several men were staying. They did not want to take me in because of my child, who might give them away by crying. At twilight, I would come out of the forest to look for something to eat.

"After three weeks, during one of those trips, I encountered a UPA bandit who wanted to kill me. But a Ukrainian acquaintance came to my defense. He suggested that I would be useful as a spy and could be used to inform them about what the Poles were saying....

"After he brought me out of the forest, this acquaintance took me to a Ukrainian neighbor, Irina Tsykhosh, and asked her to give me something to eat. She refused. As we were leaving, her son Petro said, 'You should all have been killed a long time ago.'

"My guide then took me to the home of a Jehovah's Witness, Stanko [a woman], whom I knew. Fortunately for me, Germans arrived in our village from Włodzimierz and with them came Polish workers....

"I will only add that the murdered victims were buried in the places of their death: on their farms. The Ukrainian Jehovah's Witnesses, who did not want to participate in the murders, were forced to perform this task. The bandits murdered their victims with axes and shot at those trying to escape."

There are seven other eyewitness accounts from Głęboczyce Colony in the work by Debski and Popek. One of these is that of Katarzyna Ograbek (née Krakowiak, b. 1922). After describing the murder of her parents, she relates what happened to her sister Ania, an 11-year-old who sat on a stump, watched as her Ukrainian neighbor and other Ukrainians from the neighboring villages were burying her parents and eight-year-old brother, and cried terribly:

"Suddenly, a Banderowiec rode over on his horse, yelled to the workers to hurry up and finish, and was about to move on to the next property when he noticed my sister Ania. He got off his horse, began to yell at her, and asked (and I quote), 'Don't you know where your place is today?'

"He then grabbed her by her hair, dragged her to the ditch, and told her to lie down on top of the corpses of our parents. But she refused. He then hit her in the head with a shovel. She lost her balance and fell into the ditch, but she was still alive. They finished throwing dirt on the grave anyway. Then they went to the next property, that of our neighbors, the Sławskis. I saw how they buried eight of the murdered victims. The most terrible sight was when one of the butchers caught a small child by the feet, smashed its head on a stump, and threw it into the ditch."

Katarzyna observed these events through a hole made by her husband in their thatched roof.

In this same colony, a sick child was removed from a shelter by the mother to protect the rest in hiding. Eugeniusz Sobieraj tells the story:

"I entered the hideaway. About 20 persons were already there hiding from the bandits. Among them was a woman with a sick child that cried incessantly. Everyone inveighed upon her to do something to quiet the child, otherwise the Ukrainians would hear and murder them all. The mother left the hiding place with the child and a milk container. Soon, she returned alone.

"I left the hideaway in the morning and saw something on the ridge which looked like a fresh grave on top of which lay the container. I also saw an old Ukrainian crawling about Wyka's yard and listening for sounds of Poles. I remained alone in this world, barefoot and practically naked."

Who murdered and buried this innocent child? His own mother? The old Ukrainian?...

Another such tragic story is told by Maria Piast from Sucha Łoza (Kowel County):

"In Gaj [also in Kowel County] there was a hideaway into which chanced two families and Józefa Kociołek with her infant. Out of fear that the child would give away the hiding place, they choked the infant. The mother, after her escape, died from a heart attack as a result of all her troubles."[13]

STOLARIUK, Kyrylo, from Wólka Swojczowska

On July 11, 1943, the Ukrainian Nationalists murdered 88 adults and 28 children in Teresin Colony. The Krakowiak family survived this massacre because it was hidden by Kyrylo Stolariuk, a Ukrainian from Wólka Swojczowska. Another Ukrainian, Tymish Siunia, from the same village provided shelter for Stanisław Bydychaj and his mother. After the slaughter, Tymish showed them the way for a safe flight to Włodzimierzówka.[14]

VAKOLUK family from Poryck. See Poryck, first account.

ZAKHARUK, Oleksandr, from Sielec. See Moisei Iadziuk.

Places

BUBNÓW

From the account of Zuzanna Sebestiańska and Halina Hilbrecht (née Sebestiańska) from Chrobów Colony (Łuck County):

Chrobów Colony consisted of ten Polish families, four Ukrainian families, and one Czech family. The first murder in the colony, that of Jan Michałek, occurred on June 8, 1943. The crime was reported to the German gendarmerie stationed in Nieświcz. In turn, the Germans came and burned the households of two Ukrainians suspected of the deed, but the culprits were not caught. After that, the Polish residents of Chrobów Colony dispersed to various other Polish villages for protection. The Sebestiański family first went to Marianówka to stay with the father's sister. On June 19, 1943, during the attack on Jeziorany Szlacheckie, three Polish women (Skowrońska, Kurek, and Tuńska) who remained in Chrobów Colony were murdered by one of the UPA groups. After a few days the Sebestiański parents reparted to the colony for provisions but deturned empty-handed after being shot at. Meanwhile, the Banderowcy began to burn the abandoned houses. When Marianówka was threatened, the Sebestiański family fled to Skurcze, and then to relatives in Bubnów. The father, however, went to stay with his cousins in Bakonów in the county of Horochów. The narrators continue:

"Suddenly, on the night of July 11, 1943, someone began to hammer violently on our door. It was our Ukrainian neighbor. He warned us of an impending attack and urged us to flee immediately. We hid in the fields. That night, the Polish farmsteads were burned. My aunt's home was spared probably because her family belonged to the Stundites [Baptists]. Several of her Ukrainian neighbors also belonged to that sect. On the following day we, together with our aunt, hid in a nearby Ukrainian village among the Stundites. After a few days, one of them ran to us from the field and told us to hide in the hemp field because the Banderowcy were coming. The Banderowcy searched the premises and warned everyone that the penalty for sheltering the *Lakhy* was death. At night, we returned to our aunt's property and hid in the barn."

Dressed as Ukrainians, the family returned to Skurcze once more, where they met many other refugees from the area. A makeshift hospital was set up in the Skurcze rectory for the wounded victims of the UPA. One boy, whose entire family had been murdered and who suffered from a head wound and shock, had to be tied to his bed and watched constantly. The narrators conclude:

"In September Halina and Mother returned to Chrobów, 20 kilometers away. There was nothing left; even the fruit trees had been burned. The fields were not harvested, and the provisions buried in our garden were stolen by thieves. They returned without anything, thankful to be still alive....

"Sad news reached us by turns: how the Banderowcy murdered our mother's parents, her brother, her sister's two children, and some of our other relatives and friends. Finally, the most tragic news arrived, the news regarding the death of our father. He was burned alive in a barn in Bakonów in July. With him perished five of his cousins. In the spring of 1944, Mother and some of our cousins retrieved the remains of our grandparents and uncle. They were buried in a single coffin in the Łuck cemetery. No one buried the remains of our father and his cousins."[15]

BUŻANKA
From the account of Roman Naklicki (b. 1933) from Bużanka, as transcribed by Stanisław Piwkowski:

"Not all Ukrainians were murderers of Poles in Wołyń. Four Polish families lived in the Ukrainian village of Bużanka, near Uściług, in the county of Włodzimierz Wołyński. Władysława Adamska (37), my cousin, belonged to one of these families. She married Naklicki and had two children by him: Irena (eight) and Roman (ten).

"In Bużanka, the Polish and Ukrainian families coexisted in peace and there were no misunderstandings among them. In July 1943 a unit of Bulbowcy arrived in this village and murdered 14 Poles.

"My family was saved in the nick of time by their Ukrainian neighbors. My cousin and her daughter were hidden by one family; her husband and son by another. They were able to survive in this way for about three months.

"Unfortunately, among the local Ukrainians were those who reported the hiding place to the Bulbowcy. One night, the bandits surrounded the home where my cousin was staying. An armed Bulbowiec entered the house and demanded that the landlord hand over the Poles in hiding. The landlord, however, insisted that everyone in the household belonged to his family. The bandit seemed to believe him and left. But once outside, the local traitors told him exactly where to look. He came back in and walked over straight to the bed in which the terrified mother and child were lying. He led them outside and proceeded to torture them: he cut off my cousin's breasts. Despite her terrible agony, she tried to protect her daughter by hugging her tightly. And so, they were both murdered. They were buried under a tree in the orchard. In punishment for hiding them, the entire Ukrainian family was severely beaten by the bandits.

"The following day, the Ukrainian who was hiding the father and the son informed them of this terrible episode and told them that he could no longer continue to provide them with shelter since he and his whole family were now at risk. The following day, early in the morning, he loaded up his wagon with hay and told the refugees to make a bed for themselves in it. He then covered them with a thick layer of hay. In this way he brought them to a shallow place in the Bug River, where they could cross over to the other side. Then with tears in his eyes this good man wished them a safe journey on their way to their family in Izbica in the county of Krasnystaw."¹⁶

GRZYBOWICA
From the account of Zygmunt Stański from Holendernia, a part of Poryck:

This part of the account is prefaced by a description of events following the UPA attack on the church of Poryck.

"There were also instances when the Ukrainians defended the Poles. In Grzybowica commune in the county of Włodzimierz, the land-steward was Polish. One day, three armed Ukrainians in civilian clothes barged into the chancellery. Present in the office was also the bookkeeper, whose wife was Ukrainian. The two men were searched and told to proceed to the woods. They resisted and the situation was becoming critical when suddenly a shot rang out. At that moment, the bookkeeper's wife ran into the room and the surprised attackers desisted from their previous designs."¹⁷

HAJKI
From the account of Edward Rosa from Kolonia Wielka, Dubniki, and Włodzimierz:

"Józef Lemiecha, my mother's brother, hid in the underbrush and swamps. He had a Ukrainian friend in the village of Hajki, and she brought food to his hideaway. One day her son followed her, chased my uncle out of the swamp, and shot him while he was running away.

"My Aunt Konstancja [Józef's wife] and her children, Stanisław and Marysia, were hidden by another neighbor, also a Ukrainian, in her cellar.

"Both Konstancja and her six-year-old son, Stanisław, became mentally disoriented when they heard about Józef's death. They were brought to us in Włodzimierz. Little Staś kept repeating, 'Grandmother is carrying a child. Grandmother is carrying a child.' He developed a fever a few days later and, without medical attention, died. I do not know what happened to my benignly mentally ill aunt. I heard that she married and now lives in Szczecin. I also heard that Marysia had died in Chełm before her mother's remarriage.

"Jan Lemiecha, my mother's younger brother from the village of Liski, hid in his barn. On Sunday, July 11, 1943, he was dragged out by his own neighbors and killed with an axe. While sleeping in their beds, his wife Jadwiga and her three children were also axed to death by these same neighbors."¹⁸

JASIONÓWKA
From the account of Anna Świderska (née Manias), as recorded by Alfreda Głowińska-Krawiec:

"In August 1943 the Banderowcy conducted a bloody campaign against the residents of Jasionówka, located not too far from Pniaki. The news concerning this slaughter was brought by a four-year-old child from the Hardzik family. She hid among the hemp plants growing near her house and sat there — hungry, frightened, and barely alive — for three days. She remembered only how her family and neighbors (the Przybylski family) were killed. She was in such a state of shock that she was unable to say anything else. From other sources it was learned that near the murdered families lived a Ukrainian woman with children and that she maintained close contacts with the Poles to the very end. She was among the victims of the bandits for the sin of associating with the Poles. Her children were murdered as well."¹⁹

MARIANÓWKA
From the letter of Bronisława Rosa from Marianówka to Edward Rosa:

"A few words about your grandmother, my mother-in-law. After her husband's [natural] death, she moved in with her daughter Aniela. Since she did not want to sleep in the house, she slept in the barn. The Ukrainians came to the barn and, finding only my mother-in-law there, kicked her to death.... [A description follows of the UPA attack on Aniela's house and the murder of two — aged 21 and five — of her five children. Aniela was not home at the time.]

"As far as we are concerned, thanks to a Ukrainian who warned us about the [planned] murder of Poles in Marianówka, we fled to Włodzimierz.... This was in the summer of 1943."[20]

MOSUR

First account. Gustaw Surmacz (b. 1930) from Mosur:

"Until 1939 Polish-Ukrainian relations were cordial and in many instances even friendly. The following fact may serve as an example: My mother [Maria Surmacz] was the godmother of over 30 Ukrainian children, and my father's older sister, Maria Łagodowska, was the godmother of still a greater number of Ukrainian children....

"The following Polish families were murdered:

"1. The Czechowski family: Stanisław (about 75 years of age); his wife Aniela (75); her sister Maria; and Urszula, the two-year-old daughter of Wacława [Czechowska, whose story was recounted previously in the narrative]. I will only add here that Wacława was married to Ievhen Hul, a Ukrainian, and that Urszula was the child from that marriage.

"2. The Dragan family: three people. These three, namely the mother and her two children, were the first victims in the village.

"3. The Janicki family: Antoni (father), Hanna (mother), and their four children — Helena (about 16), Stanisława (about 14), Antoni (about 12), and Gustaw (about eight). Their parents were killed after August 13, 1943, near the home of Feliksa Zielińska, located in the middle of the village. The Janicki children survived for a time because their grandmother (Hanna's mother), who was Ukrainian, took them in. However, on Orthodox Christmas Eve, January 6 [5], 1944, these children were murdered and buried in a cowshed belonging to their parents.

"4. The mother in the Lipian family.

"5. Maria Łagodowska (née Surmacz), the previously-mentioned godmother of well over 30 Ukrainian children ... and her son Mieczysław. Her older daughter was the widow Jadwiga ... who had a four- or five-year-old daughter by the same name. She also had an infant by a Ukrainian, Petro Misiuk (called Dychka in the village), with whom she lived in an informal arrangement.... Maria and her son Mieczysław were murdered toward the end of August 1943.... Petro Misiuk, a.k.a. Dychka, brought their bodies from the field and buried them in the orchard near the house. After Maria's and Mieczysław's murder in the fall of 1943, her daughter Jadwiga and the infant were also murdered. These murders were committed by Petro Misiuk, a.k.a. Dychka, who buried their bodies in a field next to the Łagodowski residence....

"In all, 23 persons from among the indigenous Poles in Mosur were murdered by the Ukrainian Nationalists in 1943 and January 1944."

The narrator also describes the murders in the village of Ziemlica and provides a list of 35 names of the victims. He adds: "No one was recognized among the Ukrainian murderers. It is also noteworthy, that according to witnesses of these events, a Ukrainian from Mosur came to Władysław Wawryszuk in secret, informed him of the intentions of the UPA to murder the Poles [in Ziemlica], and urged him and his family to save themselves by fleeing."

In another segment of this account, the narrator states that the *sołtys* of Mosur as well as other friendly Ukrainians from the village, such as Semen Havryliuk, sent his father (Władysław Surmacz) signals, albeit weak ones, about the threat to his family from the UPA.[21]

Second account. Anna Prymas (b. 1929) from Grabowiec, near Hrubieszów:

Anna's grandparents (Stanisław and Aniela Czechowski, both 75 years of age, of the family mentioned in the account above) lived in Mosur. Anna states:

"When the slaughter began, my grandparents were hidden by a Ukrainian named Gontar. However, under threat of death, he had to hand them over to the Nationalists."[22]

NOWOSIÓŁKI

In March 1944 the Ukrainian Nationalists murdered most of the villagers in Nowosiółki. The survivors of this pogrom, assisted by some older Ukrainians, fled to Włodzimierz Wołyński.[23]

ORZESZYN COLONY

First account. Honorata Zarębska from Orzeszyn Colony:

"In 1921 a new colony was established in Orzeszyn in the county of Włodzimierz Wołyński. It lay between two villages inhabited predominantly by Ukrainians: Samowola and Gruszów, near Poryck and Sokal. The colony, comprised of 48 farmsteads, consisted almost exclusively of [Polish] military settlers, but a few Ukrainians lived there as well.

"The family of Antoni and Helena Zarębski were among the Poles who settled in this newly established colony. Their next-door neighbors, the Romaniuks, were Ukrainian. There were five children in the Zarębski family, the youngest of which were cared for by a Ukrainian woman from the village of Samowola. The Zarębskis and Romaniuks were on good terms despite the fact that two of Zarębski's sons were members of a distinguished unit in the Polish army in the 1930s and that two of Romaniuk's sons were known to the locals because of their illegal activities in the Organization of Ukrainian Nationalists. Toward the end of 1936 and at the beginning of 1937, Romaniuk often spoke with Zarębski about the international political situation, including the situation in Poland, and warned Zarębski of anticipated and planned anti-Polish disturbances on the part of the Ukrainian Nationalists. During one of their talks Romaniuk said in so many words, 'Zarębski, get out because our people are going to slaughter the Poles.'

"Zarębski, being in addition the *sołtys* of the colony, did not take these warnings lightly and resettled a part of his family toward the end of 1937, and the rest at the beginning of 1939, in the Radom region. By that time, one of his sons was already married to a Ukrainian girl whose parents remained in Samowola. Since they had given away their daughter to a Pole, they must not have harbored ill will towards them. They were murdered with sickles in 1943 by the Ukrainian Nationalists and their farmstead was burned. The residents of Orzeszyn were decimated in June [July] 1943 in the church of Poryck. They were cut down with scythes as they were fleeing the church, and when they barricaded themselves inside, the church was set on fire. The rest of the residents were slaughtered in July in Orzeszyn, and the colony was put to the torch. Today, Samowola and Gruszów still stand, but no trace remains of Orzeszyn or of the church in Poryck. The Romaniuks perished in 1944."[24]

Second account. Stanisława Dąbrowska-Brzozowska from Orzeszyn Colony, as transcribed by Genowefa Stachów:

"I ran into the grain field, made my way to my sister [Zofia Kowalska] and said, 'Let's get out of here! There's no one left in the village!'

"We took my sister's three children, her brother, father-in-law, and my son and immediately set out for the Józefatka settlement, where German soldiers were stationed. Over 30 survivors from our village came with us. We did not know at that time that 300 people were murdered in the nearby woods. Among them were the following members of our family and the family of my brother-in-law: [Twenty names follow; one of them, entry number 15, is that of Władysław Leśko].

"15. Władysław Leśko. He was home that day with his wife who was giving birth. The assisting village midwife was Ukrainian. After removing the father from his house, [the bandits] threatened to return for the mother and her new-born. A Ukrainian woman helped the mother to escape and even went with her. That child, named after his father, was born on July 11, 1943, in the very hours that his father was being murdered."[25]

PORYCK

First account. Tadeusz Wojewódka from Poryck:

"On Sunday, July 11, 1943, after the 9:00 A.M. Mass, Pastor Bolesław Szawłowski informed his altar boys that there would be an attack on the church [in Poryck] during the High Mass later that morning. He wanted us to warn our dear ones. We found out later that it was a Ukrainian, Volodymyr Kulai from Pawłówka, who had conveyed this information to the priest.

"After the services, around 10:00 A.M., I set out for home and met my family as well as many acquaintances on their way to High Mass. I told them about Fr. Szawłowski's warning, but they dismissed it, thinking that this was simply another rumor, and went to church.

"A few minutes before High Mass, three Ukrainians — Pylyp Mazurok ["Fylyp Mazurok" in the copy of the original account in my possession] from Stary Poryck, Shtukalko ... from Żaszkiewice, and a third unknown person — entered the church. In all likelihood, they came to check out the place and to plan their strategy for the murderous action. The people panicked. Those who recognized the threesome fled outside after their departure. The bandits shot at them from automatics, and also at the congregation through the open door and windows. There were many wounded. One could hear groans, shouts, and the crying of children. Prayers were offered to God pleading for help.

"Fr. Szawłowski was wounded for the first time in his hand. Even so, he assisted the others by bandaging their wounds with strips torn from his cassock and administered the last rights to the dying.

"Then the Banderowcy threw grenades into the nave of the church and began to spray the congregation with handguns and machine guns, thus forcing them all to hit the floor. After this cannonade the bandits entered the church and finished off those showing signs of life with shots to the head. Many survived by pretending to be dead.

"Fr. Szawłowski was wounded again, this time in the stomach. He lay on the steps of the altar and pretended to be dead when they were killing the wounded.

"After this massacre the henchmen brought straw, set the church on fire, and placed explosives under the walls. The explosives failed to knock down the walls. That evening a torrential rain not only put out the fire but also helped the survivors to escape.

"After the murderers left, the dying Fr. Szawłowski asked for his confession to be heard. A local Ukrainian Orthodox priest was asked to come. He came dressed in his liturgical vestments and fulfilled the wish of the dying Catholic priest. A while later, Fr. Szawłowski passed away, thus complementing the group of about 500 persons who perished that day in the church and its environs.

"Only about 20 persons survived that pogrom; among them was my family. With the first round of gunfire my parents, Bronisław and Jadwiga, hid in a vault beneath the church....

"My brother Czesław hid in the sacristy in a large chest containing the liturgical vestments....

"My sister Janina was in the choir loft during the services. When the church was set on fire, the steps leading to the choir burned; so there was no way of getting down. With a few others, she climbed out a window, made her way to the top of the vault, and hid there. After two days of calling for help, during a lull in the murder of Poles, she was brought down with the help of a ladder and ropes. She was rescued by some local Ukrainians sympathetic to the Poles. My sister was then taken to the home of a Ukrainian named Iukhym Kyslyi, where she remained in hiding for two weeks....

"On July 12, 1943, the Banderowcy attacked Poryck and the surrounding areas once more. Many of those wounded the previous day in the church were killed in their homes....

"In Kłopoczyn near Poryck, local Ukrainian Nationalists fell on the home of a Polish family by the name of Musionka, where several dozen Poles took shelter right after the July 11 attack on Poryck. I wound up there as well. When I saw the armed Banderowcy approaching, I jumped out the window and hid in the grain field. As I was running, I heard shots. Whoever was not able to escape from that house was murdered. In all, 15 Poles were killed there, including the Musionka family (four persons).

"In the evening, around eight o'clock, I went to a Ukrainian family that I knew. Artem Harkys, the landlord, gave me something to eat, put me in his barn, and went to my house to fetch my parents. When they arrived, they were completely drenched. Being very tired, they wanted to remain there. But this kind and virtuous Ukrainian acquaintance of ours could not provide us with shelter simply because, for a year now, he had been hiding five Jews. My mother went to another sympathetic Ukrainian family for help, the Vakoluk family. She was hidden by that family in their attic for two weeks. I and my father set out that night in the pouring rain in the direction of Sokal....

"Nowadays, during various family gatherings, we often return to our memories of those tragic times. At such times, important questions emerge.

"How did it come about? How could such barbaric murders take place after so many years of mutual coexistence and good social relations?

"What political forces, which religious leaders were behind this murderous action, this extermination of the Polish people by the Ukrainian Nationalists?

"What role did the German occupation authorities play in these territories during the time when these crimes were being perpetrated?

"Why didn't the government of the [postwar] Polish People's Republic, a sovereign state recognized by all nations, investigate the murders of so many thousands of Poles in the eastern borderlands? Why did it not indict, convict, and punish the perpetrators?

"What is the position of the present-day leadership of the Third Polish Republic with respect to the extermination of the Polish people in Wołyń between 1939 and 1945 by the Ukrainian Nationalists? Where does it stand on the issue of redressing the material and moral wrongs done to those people?

"I am but one of many who were able to escape. Leaving the land of our fathers, we left everything behind: our homes, farm buildings, property, personal items, livestock, and other valuables for which entire generations of our forefathers worked....

"In conclusion, I wish to underscore the fact that I harbor no wish for revenge or hatred toward the Ukrainian people. My intention is only to convey the truth about this crime on the basis of which the murderers will be judged before the tribunal of justice.

"At the same time, I wish to thank those Ukrainian individuals and families who, risking their own safety and lives, saved my family by helping us during our flight."[26]

Second account. Janina Gruszka from Radowicz:

"One of those who survived the July 11, 1943, attack of the Banderowcy on the Poles gathered for Mass in the church of Poryck, was my husband's mother, Zofia Gruszka, from Radowicze near Poryck.

"Although she was buried beneath the bodies of the dead, she herself was unharmed. She managed to reach the choir loft, where she joined the few that remained alive. After the bandits left, when she was returning home covered with blood, a small Ukrainian boy warned her to take a different road because they were murdering people along the one she was traveling. Thanks to this child, she did not fall into the hands of the bandits. She had nightmares about that tragedy in the church to the end of her life."[27]

Third account. Bolesław Dorociński:

In mid-September 1943, Bolesław Dorociński, together with a priest, another man, and an armed Polish escort, went to the home of an Orthodox priest in Poryck to retrieve the liturgical vestments and paraphernalia that were placed into his custody after the tragedy and fire in Poryck's Catholic church. On the way back, the Catholic priest (Kapturkiewicz from Włodzimierz) relayed to the men the information he had received from the Orthodox priest regarding the fate of the pastor of Poryck, who had been hidden in the attic of the Orthodox priest. Unlike most other eyewitness accounts that state that the pastor was in the church at the time of the massacre and was wounded there, this account places him in the rectory just before Mass. According to Bolesław, upon hearing the shooting and shouting, the priest hid, and later that evening went to the Orthodox priest for shelter. He continues:

"The UPA murderers, discovering that the pastor survived, began to search for him without results. Finally, the suspicion fell on the Orthodox priest. After a week, they searched his home thoroughly, found Fr. Szawłowski, and murdered him. The Orthodox priest performed the last rites over the pastor just before his death."

Apparently, several versions exist regarding Fr. Szawłowski's wounding and death.[28]

SIELEC
First account. H. D.:

"On Tuesday July 14, 1943, the Ukrainians killed two elderly people, Józef Wiktowski and his wife Stefania, in the village of Sielec, county of Włodzimierz Wołyński. They shot them in their own home, which they subsequently set on fire. The older children fled to Włodzimierz Wołyński the day before, but the older people did not want to abandon their homes.

"In the afternoon of that same day, the Banderowcy murdered with axes another elderly couple named Michałowicz, their seven-year-old granddaughter, a third elderly couple named Gronowicz, and the priest's housekeeper, Zofia. Ivan Shostachuk, a corporal in the Polish army before the war and a convert to Roman Catholicism, took part in these atrocities. His younger brother, Vladyslav, who was of Orthodox persuasion, warned the Morelowski family (father and four daughters) and the Michałkowicz family (father and two daughters) and thereby saved their lives. Iukhno, a Ukrainian, was also a member of the band and killed Poles; his father, however, rescued the Styczyński family.

"Relations between the Poles and Ukrainians were good before the war. They began to deteriorate at the beginning of 1943, when Ukrainian agitators arrived in Wołyń from the provinces of Lwów and Stanisławów and began to radicalize the youth and to promise them a free Ukraine. Not all succumbed to this propaganda, least of all the older Ukrainians.

"They drowned Mariia Sokolov, a Russian elementary-school teacher and wife of the director of the school sent to Sielec from the USSR. She was thrown down a well together with her husband, mother, and one-year-old son, Slavek. Some of the young people fled from the village; the older ones were killed. In the Morelowski family, they murdered the daughter, Irena, who married Józef Powszek [Papowszek] and lived with her [husband's] family near Łuck. The Banderowcy killed the parents, Apolonia and Stanisław [Papowszek], their daughter-in-law Irena (19), and son Józef (20). All of them, except Irena, were killed near the forest. Irena was taken to the home of the leader of the band, held in the cellar, raped, and then tossed into a well. She was pregnant. The Banderowcy did not order the Poles to leave the village; on the contrary, in one instance, the Ukrainian Nedzelskyi did not allow the Morelowski family to leave the village. They also killed mixed [Polish-Ukrainian] families."[29]

Second account. Stanisława Jóźwiak (née Morelowska) from Sielec:

"I am a Wołynian from Sielec, a village that lay about eight kilometers south of Włodzimierz Wołyński. My parents lived in Wołyń from time immemorial and my mother's family lived in Sielec for generations. I went to elementary school in Sielec.

"The war found us in Sielec. Here we survived a terrible ordeal in 1943, especially between July 11 and 13....

"Our family, together with several other residents, quartered in the Sielec schoolhouse since June 1941. This was because on June 24, 1941, many houses in the Polish section of the village were destroyed during a battle between the Germans and the Russians.

"On June 29, 1943, a group of Ukrainians came to our village at night, woke us all up, and told us to remove our belongings because they had an order to burn down the school. And that's just what happened. By the next morning the large, brick, two-story schoolhouse no longer existed. We should have gone to Włodzimierz then and there, but not being aware of the danger, we stayed put.

"On Sunday, July 11, 1943 ... the Ukrainian bandits conducted pogroms against the Polish people in many churches.... The news of the pogrom in Chrynów was brought to Sielec by my cousin, Edward Stanisławski. In the afternoon of that same day, he evacuated his family to Włodzimierz. With him went Fr. Kamiński, the pastor of the Sielec church. Several other families also left; our family, however, remained.

"We finally left on Monday, July 12, by wagon for Włodzimierz. As we passed the home of Nedzelskyi, a Ukrainian known for his nationalistic convictions, we were halted. Nedzelskyi, together with another Ukrainian that we knew well from a neighboring village, became indignant at our attempt to flee and tried to calm us saying that we had nothing to fear. They even resorted to blackmail, saying that since we wanted to leave it meant that we must be friendly with the Germans. They tried to convince us that we should not leave the place of our roots; they even turned our horse around. And so, we had no choice but to go back to the burned-out schoolhouse.

"In the afternoon of that same day, the Ukrainians murdered the Poles in nearby Maria Wola Colony. [About 200 people were killed in that colony. Some 30 of them were thrown into wells and stoned to death.] Columns of black smoke rose on the horizon, but we were told that it was a German pacification action. My classmate, Witek Osuchowski, perished that day. He was cut in half with a saw. Only the father of that family survived. He hid in a shelter, and although a Ukrainian looked inside, he was not noticed. The father heard the inhuman cries of his own son but could not help him. Tadeusz Adwent, who was sitting in his doorway repairing some boots, was also killed. I only mention these two persons because I knew them.

"We were horrified at the sight of Maria Wola Colony, but were still unaware of personal danger. Then Vladek [Vladyslav] Shostachuk, a Ukrainian whose father was the director of the Sielec school in 1942-43, came running over to us and told us to get out because there's an order to kill all Poles without exception. Unfortunately, there was no longer an opportunity for escape. We therefore went to a shelter which was constructed in case the Germans would enter our village. The Shostachuk family knew about this shelter because we built it together. Asked by my father whether we could spend the night there, after a short pause Vladek responded, 'Go ahead. I do not wish to have your death on my conscience.'

"Vladek was 16 years old. Ivan, his older brother, who was a corporal in the Polish army before the war and a Roman Catholic, was a member of the band and participated in the pogrom in Maria Wola Colony on July 12. At dawn on July 13, after having been advised by [Vladyslav's] Shostachuk's wife, who came to pasture her cow, that all was quiet and that it was safe to depart, we went to Włodzimierz on foot.

"There still remained some old people in Sielec who did not want to travel; moreover, they did not believe that they would perish. On Tuesday, July 12, the following persons were murdered before noon: Józef and Stefania Witkowski, my grandparents, shot and burned in their own home; an older couple named Gronowicz; another older couple named Michałkiewicz, together with their granddaughter Alicja who was about ten years of age; and Zofia, Fr. Kamiński's housekeeper, axed to death in the yard of the rectory. All the houses were burned. Ivan Shostachuk participated in these actions.

"Next, Maika [Mariia] Sokolov, who was a Russian schoolteacher and wife of the director of the school in Sielec in 1940-41, her mother, and her three-year-old son, Slavek, were murdered and their remains were tossed into a well.

"Another Ukrainian [Iukhno's father, according to the previous account] hid the three-member Styczyński family under some hay and transported them by wagon to Włodzimierz. The son of that Ukrainian belonged to the band. Apparently, for rendering assistance to his Polish neighbors, the father paid with his life.

"The Ukrainians also murdered the family of Iukhno [the same as above?], a known Communist who operated a mill in Sielec in 1940-41. Iukhno himself was thrown onto the mill's grinding wheel.

"My younger sister, Irena, was married in August 1942 and lived with her husband's family in Iwańczyce near Łuck.... In July 1943 my sister Irena (18), my brother-in-law Józef Papowszek (19), and his parents, Stanisław and Apolonia, were all murdered."[30]

STĘŻARZYCE
From the account of Helena Bitner from Stężarzyce:

"That year [1943] on Whit Sunday the Banderowcy held a meeting of all Polish men in a field surrounded by a high barbed-wire fence. The field belonged to one of the Ukrainians. No one was murdered, however, because a Soviet partisan unit rode into the village. During their stay in Stężarzyce we could finally sleep in peace for a few days.

"On Sunday, July 11, 1943, the Bulbowcy planned to attack our church during services. It didn't come off because my Ukrainian girlfriend begged me not to go to church that day. She also insisted that I tell no one about this because she was afraid of her father. But my mother warned the priest, and he hung a notice on the church doors to the effect that there would be no services that Sunday due to his illness.

"Around midnight on July 13, 1943, well-armed UPA members rode into our village on horseback and in wagons, fell on some families, took away the few men they found at home, and murdered them. They did not touch the wives and children. They also abducted the pastor. Most of the Poles went into hiding at this time in the grain fields or among the thickets.

"The following day we left our home. We left without taking anything at all, not even a piece of bread. By traveling through the underbrush we managed to reach the Polish colony of Edwardpole, and from there we went to Włodzimierz. All the Polish families who remained in Stężarzyce were murdered toward the end of September.

"They killed a pregnant woman. They cut open her stomach, took out the infant, and impaled it on a thick stick with a sign that read: 'The Polish Eagle.' They hoisted this woman and her child up on a wayside pear tree. They threw some families alive into wells.

"What I have written here is a part of my most tragic life experiences."[31]

SWOJCZÓW
First account. Zofia Michowska (b. 1935) from Swojczów:

"The Poles were ill-informed about the danger. They often thought that they themselves would not be attacked — and so, they stayed put. They ran only at the last moment. It was already evening when a well-wishing Ukrainian ran up to my father and shouted, 'Stach, get out because tonight they are going to murder you all!'"[32]

Second account. Petronela Władyga-Rusiecka from Swojczów:

"We all hid wherever we could. Our hideout was safe and we liked it, except for the plague of fleas which tormented us constantly. Today, we joke about whether it was the dog or we who brought them there.

"On August 29, 1943, my father went to a designated place by the woods and met with a Ukrainian who informed him that a decision had been made in Gnojno to finish up the massive murder of Poles. They received an order to have their instruments of death blessed in the Ukrainian churches in order, as the Gospel says, to 'separate the chaff from the wheat and cast it into the fire.' On the 29th, they had their instruments blessed, drank, and waited until dark to begin murdering the Poles. That friendly, virtuous Ukrainian — there were such — told my father, 'Rusiecki, if you do not flee today, you will all be killed.'"

The Rusiecki family wasted no time leaving. As they neared the woods, they heard someone shouting, "You did not volunteer to fight and now you're hiding Poles." Then they heard shooting and the loud barking of dogs.[33]

Third account. Władysława Główka (née Bdychaj) from Swojczów:

"In their church in Swojczów, the Ukrainians had their axes, scythes, and pitchforks blessed. With these weapons they proceeded to murder the Poles. I remember specifically our Ukrainian neighbor, Holubytskyi, who married a Polish girl. He murdered his own in-laws and told his comrades to kill his wife and children. It was he who murdered his neighbors, Karol and

Karolina Rusiecki; they were my grandparents. Here are the names of the Poles who were murdered by the UPA in 1943.... [A list of 82 names of those murdered in Swojczów and the vicinity follows.]

"I saw the bodies of the murdered victims when they were brought back: a pregnant woman whose stomach had been cut open, and near her, a baby with its umbilical cord still intact; women with severed breasts; a scalped man (his ears had been sliced off, his hair with the skin lay on his left shoulder); a young man with a hole in his back into which a sheet had been packed; and many people with broken arms and legs, cut throats, and severed heads. I saw Włodzimierz Szurkowski taking photographs of these murdered victims."[34]

Fourth account. Stanisława Sobczuk (née Rusiecka, b. 1932) from Swojczów:

"My father and mother, Józef and Julia, owned a grocery store in Swojczów. I had a sister named Jadwiga. She was nine years old. Our tragedy began on July 11, 1943. We were awakened in the morning by a tremendous explosion. We learned shortly thereafter that our church was mined and blown sky high.

"In the village panic erupted. The people began to hide wherever they could. My parents ran to our neighbor, Dubenchuk, a Ukrainian. I, my sister, and our grandmother, who was living with us at the time, were hidden by a Ukrainian named Ievhen. His son, the 17-year-old Volodka, went to kill the Poles. The father, on the other hand, told my grandmother to climb up on the stove and to sit quietly. I and my sister were supposed to go up into the attic; instead, being curious, we went to the road on the other side of which was our home. There was also a field of wheat. An unplowed ridge, some 100 meters away, separated this field from the next. It was on that ridge that we saw our father for the last time. He looked at us, we at him, and he went on to a Ukrainian who lived still further away. His first cousin ran behind him. They both thought that they would be better off there, or so our mother explained to us seeing their anxiety.

"The farmer who hid us told us later what had happened. When they reached the second Ukrainian's home, the owner told them to remove their gold rings. He took my father's watch and some five-zloty notes as well. Then my father, sensing that this was his last hour, began to implore him, 'We are your neighbors. How in good conscience could you kill us?'

"But the Ukrainian shouted back, 'I am not your neighbor now,' and shot them both.

"My father's cousin left behind five children between the ages of one-and-a-half and 12. They came over to us and we all stood beside the road together. One passing Ukrainian woman saw our little group and remarked, 'You are still walking around here and your mothers are already in the cemetery.'

"Today, I would understand that to mean that they were no longer alive. But at that time, it seemed to us children that the words meant that our mothers were still alive and waiting for us in the cemetery. And so, we set out through the fields to that everlasting place of rest about two kilometers away. Of the entire group, I spoke Ukrainian the best. I therefore forbade the rest of them to speak in case anyone started to ask questions.

"Haystacks were standing in the fields. I had on a dress with pockets and in one of them, a picture of Our Lady of Swojczów. When we would reach a haystack, I would place the holy card behind the hay-rope, kneel down, and pray to see our mothers again. There was a thicket of small trees by the cemetery. A Ukrainian riding on a horse saw us near it and sprayed us with his machine gun. The bullets hailed around us but did not hit us. We quickly hid in that thicket.

"When we reached the cemetery, a terrible sight greeted us: many corpses and open graves in which they were to be buried. I led our group back to the village. On its edge lived the grandmother of my cousin Zofia. We entered the house. On seeing us, the old lady began to cry and asked, 'Why did you come here? All of our people have gone into hiding, but I don't care. It's all the same to me....'

"I asked her for some water because the younger children [the narrator was 11 years old at the time] were thirsty. She gave us the water. She told us to hide in the staked beans, beyond which was a cabbage patch, and further still, a wire fence separating the garden from the property of an Orthodox priest. His house was located on that property as well.

"As we were hiding, four Ukrainians on horseback rode into the old woman's yard. They began to yell that they would find those 'Polish bastards'—meaning us. Meanwhile, the grandmother had lain down behind a small mound about two meters away. We could see her whole body very well; so could one of the Ukrainians on horseback. He rode up and shot the old woman. He then looked up and down and sideways, but somehow he seemed not to see us at all. We were seven, and we had to cross the cabbage patch in order to reach the fence. In all probability, Our Lady, to whom we prayed constantly along the way, helped us because the Ukrainian rode away.

"I lifted the wire and, after the children had slid under it to the other side, I joined them. I ordered the younger children not to say anything. When the Orthodox priest saw the seven of us, he asked us who we were and where we were from. I answered that I and my sister were Ievhen's children and that the rest were the children of Stepan. I pretended that we were Ukrainian children. In order to convince the priest all the more, I took his own crying child into my arms and began to sing in Ukrainian. The *batiushka* [priest] was either convinced or simply pretended to be convinced. His home was located on one side of the village; his pigsty on the other, near the Orthodox church. I asked him to take us with him and leave us off near our house. He agreed.

"I remember that as he was bringing us by wagon, the Ukrainians — this was already after the slaughter of the Poles — stood in formations of four on the road, and that at the head of the column was our *sołtys,* named Tsebula. He watched us for a very long time but said nothing. We got off the wagon at the agreed-upon place and met our grandmother. She told us that our father had been killed and that our neighbor had explained to her how he died. I began to cry and asked what were we to do now.

"It was getting dark. Our mother came for us. Her legs were swaying. She said that she would not go anywhere; let them kill her because what would she do without father. My grandmother was more clear-headed. She explained to my mother that she had children and that she had to live for their sake.

"We decided to flee to Włodzimierz under the cover of night. A Ukrainian woman gave us some bread and salt-pork. Mother made a bundle out of that, threw it over her back, and tied the ends on her chest. In that way, her hands were free to hold ours.

"We set out through the fields, ditches, bushes, and grasslands. We reached a swamp wherein my grandmother, being stout, began to sink. I and my sister managed to pull her out. While on our journey that night, we saw fires all around us; the sky was glowing. It was the Banderowcy burning all the Polish villages."[35]

Fifth account. Zofia Hasiak from Włodzimierz Wołyński and Swojczów:

"I [a widow] found myself among strangers and was grateful to everyone for their help and kind words.

"One day, as I was walking to church with Mrs. Skosalas and my son Ryszard, we encountered two of our Ukrainian neighbors, Katia and Iakiv Dubenchuk, sitting on one side of the ditch. Ryszard, on passing them, bid them a good morning in his resonant voice and bowed politely to them. When we reached them, I also said, 'Good morning, what a nice day for sitting in the sun to warm oneself.'

"They responded in kind, but that Mrs. Skosalas, in a voice that the Ukrainians could hear, said, 'Zosia, how can you bow to these cads?'

"I answered that they were such pleasant neighbors. That 'Good morning' saved both me and my son. When the Poles in Swojczów were being murdered on August 30, 1943, Katia came running to me and said, 'You must get away! Come, we will hide you.' By that time, her brother Iakiv had already made a deep hole inside a stack of hay for us. They hid me and my child there and secured the opening.

"That stack of hay stood just behind the building, and I heard how the murderers entered the house, dragged out Mrs. Skosalas [the narrator's landlady], stabbed her with bayonets, and held her down until she died. I can hear her terrible shrieks even today. I can hear her pleading, 'Kill me already! Stop torturing me!'

"Her husband was axed to death inside his house.

"All night long and the next day I heard terrible groans, curses, and shouts. In the evening, Katia sent a small girl, Halushka, to our hiding place under the pretense of getting some hay for the cattle; she brought us bread and water. That lasted for several days, but we could not continue to hide there because the bandits began to stick the haystacks with pitchforks looking for Poles. We were hidden deep within, but they also burned suspected haystacks as well as buildings.

"I had the good fortune of meeting Ukrainians with a good heart. They began to hide me in various Ukrainian buildings until the murderers became convinced that there were no more Poles left. They hid me and my son in cellars and in attics. They dressed me as a Ukrainian. I always wore a scarf which hid my face, and also a blouse, skirt, and an apron. I could speak Ukrainian, but since Ryszard could not, he pretended to be dumb. Katia told everyone that she had brought a Ukrainian woman from the Russian border who 'may make a nice girl for Lashuk'—Halushka's father, who was a widower.

"They set up sewing machines in the Lashuk household and Ukrainians came there to alter the clothes stolen from the Poles. Often I could tell to whom these clothes had belonged. When they brought in the suit of my grandmother, Karolina Rusiecka, who had helped me so much in these difficult times, I began to shiver and to shake. A Ukrainian woman asked me, 'Sonia [that is the name Zofia went by while in hiding], what is the matter with you?'

"I answered that I was ill and could not do this work. I heard how they bragged about murdering the Poles. While hiding behind a large stove, I heard Volodia say, 'A neighbor came running over to me. She was a friend to whose house I used to go from time to time. She begged and pleaded: "Volodia save me." And after her, another Polish girl ran in. So I grabbed them and knocked their heads together until the blood came squirting out, and that was the end of them both.'

"I heard them talk about how they had killed small children and had thrown their bodies on the dump, where they had been covered over by whatever trash was there to avoid having to dig graves. Sometimes they would brag about who had done the killing, and how, and with what results.

"I heard how they had murdered my grandfather, Karol Rusiecki, who had emerged from hiding after a few days and had come over to Jędrych Rusiecki's yard.

They laughed that he had been so concerned lest they burn down his house. They had driven all the animals out of the cowshed and had searched for buried objects and valuables. They had tortured him cruelly until he finally admitted where it was all buried. The murderer Korchak added to all this bragging: 'When I saw that it was Karol Rusiecki that they were beating, I came over and struck him in the belly so hard that I cut him in half and his guts spilled out. Then we threw him into the pond.'

"Listening to this, I imagined that my grandfather must have been cut in half with a large knife since Korchak said 'I slaughtered him.'

"I heard that my grandmother, Karolina Rusiecka, had been shot in the garden and that she had been buried under a tree.

"I prayed earnestly that when the time came for my death I would be shot together with my son. I never thought that I would be able to survive for eight-and-a-half months living in constant fear.

"That winter all the buildings, both Polish and Ukrainian, were burned in Boża Wola. The Ukrainians moved into the Polish homes in Swojczów. *Sołtys* Tsebula moved into Stanisław Rusiecki's home, located in the middle of the village. Stanisław had a store before the war and a house with two porches next to the Ukrainian church. I often went to that church, stood near the miraculous portrait of the Blessed Mother of Swojczów [translocated there from the Roman Catholic church], and prayed for my sufferings to be shortened. *Sołtys* Tsebula seemed to recognize me because he spoke with me about how I had sold things in the store after my uncle's death. Although I was dressed as a Ukrainian, he could have figured it out.

"One day in late fall he came over to Lashuk and asked him about his 'girlfriend's' whereabouts. Lashuk became frightened and told him that I traveled all over the village and sometimes came over to his house to sew. The *sołtys* handed Lashuk the beautiful apples that he had brought with him and told him to give them to me and to instruct me to meet him by the gate to the orchard at a certain hour.

"After the *sołtys* left, Lashuk sent his daughter Halushka to Katia and Iakiv with the message to hide me and my child somewhere else because we were no longer safe in his house. I did not go out to meet the *sołtys*....

"[Some time later] After a few days in Włodzimierz, Katia's brother, who had helped me survive, came looking for me. I can still recall that scene. I came into the room and someone was sitting in a chair. Next to him was my son and that Ukrainian, Katia's brother, was kneeling by them. He entreated and begged me to leave Włodzimierz immediately because now the murderers would find me. 'Just as I found you within a few days,' he said, 'so they will also find you and kill you because you are a witness to their murders.'

"I left Włodzimierz."[36]

WŁODZIMIERZ

First account. Regina Śliwa (née Kowalska, b. 1934) from Zapust (in Horochów County):

"On July 11 [1943] the Ukrainians began to murder the Polish people, beginning with the attack on the church in Kisielin. We left our village [Zapust] just as we were without taking any personal articles with us. We arrived in Włodzimierz. After a while, my mother returned to our house for food because we were without any provisions whatsoever. On the way back, she was caught by the Banderowcy and murdered....

"Strangers took us orphans in and our ways parted. Being the youngest, I was taken by a lady to babysit her children.

"While I was there, the front moved closer. The Germans used the civilian population to dig their trenches. Because the lady I stayed with was sick, I took her place. One day while at work, a young woman expressed surprise that my mother would send me (I was nine years old then) to dig trenches. When I told her that I was an orphan, she invited me to dinner, and later gave me some salt pork and bread. She was the daughter of an Orthodox priest."[37]

Second account. Edward Rosa from Kolonia Wielka, Dubniki, and Włodzimierz:

"My sister [Honorata] was taken to Frankfurt am Main. In May 1945 she returned from Germany to Włodzimierz not being aware of what had happened to the Poles there because German censorship prevented the news of the murder of Poles by the UPA from reaching her. She arrived at her friend's house, a Ukrainian who was living in a post-Jewish home. When Vasyl Soroka, husband of the already-mentioned Julia, came by, my sister's friend hid her under the table. Perhaps he only wanted to find out about his Julia, or perhaps he had other intentions because he was, after all, Vasyl the Ukrainian and not some romantic Romeo. The Ukrainian woman who hid my sister was our and his neighbor. She probably knew what Vasyl was doing during the slaughter of Poles in Wołyń, and that's why she hid my sister when he came over."[38]

ŻASZKIEWICZE
From the account of Kazimierz Kaszuba:

Among those who survived the attack on the church in Poryck were Kazimierz's Aunt Żmudzka, her nine-year-old daughter, and her 13-year-old son. They lived in the village of Żaszkiewicze, located about three kilometers from Poryck. The rest of the Żmudzki family (the father, a four-year-old daughter, a 16-year-old son, and a 92-year-old grandmother) were later axed to death in their home by the Ukrainian Nationalists and buried behind their barn.

Upon returning to her village, the mother and her two children were hidden by a Sobotnik [Seventh-Day Baptist] in the attic of his chicken coop. "There was a sect of Sobotniks in the village," writes Kazimierz, "and they were forbidden to kill."

After five weeks, when things had quieted down a bit, the Ukrainian rescuer decided to take them to Żmudzka's brother, who lived 15 kilometers away and who was married to a Ukrainian woman. The children were placed in a wagon and covered with hay. Their mother was given a large shawl and sat next to the Ukrainian. If stopped, he would say that he was taking his ill wife to a doctor.

They arrived safely and were immediately put up in the attic of an "abandoned" Polish house by the brother, his Ukrainian wife, and her father. They remained in hiding for another seven weeks, until they were rescued by a passing Polish patrol.

This second rescue is all the more remarkable because Żmudzka's sister-in-law's brother was a leader of one of murderous bands of Nationalists. Fortunately, he never found out about the refugees hiding in the attic. Żmudzka's brother also escaped death because he was under the solicitous protection of his Ukrainian wife and father-in-law.[39]

11
Zdołbunów County

Bordering Soviet Ukraine and crossed by the rivers Horyń and Ujście, Zdołbunów County was subdivided into the following six village communes: Buderaż, Chorów, Mizocz, Nowomalin, Sijańce, and Zdołbica. The town of Zdołbunów was the county seat.

Table 24
Population of Zdołbunów County by Mother Tongue

Ukrainian	81,561
Ruthenian	89
Polish	17,826
Jewish	10,787
German	856
Czech	4,521
Russian	2,405
Belorussian	56
Lithuanian	9
Other	21
Unreported	203
Total	118,334

Table 25
Population of Zdołbunów County by Religious Affiliation

Orthodox	86,750
Roman Catholic	17,901
Uniate	198
Protestant/Evangelical	1,064
Other Christian	1,438
Jewish	10,850
Other Non-Christian	11
Not Specified or Non-Religious	13
Unreported	109
Total	118,334

Before being transferred to Dubno County, the "Kruk" battalion of Ivan Klymushyn quartered in Zdołbunów County. After the transfer, its place was taken by the "Negus" battalion. In addition, a company of Georgians — deserters from the German police — was stationed there. For a time, this county served as headquarters for the general staff of the "Eneia" region.

The UPA reign of terror in Zdołbunów County followed the same pattern as in all of Wołyń. There too, the majority of the atrocities were committed in July and in August of 1943. On January 16, 1944, just before the Soviet offensive, the UPA succeeded in attacking the town of Ostróg, where many refugees had gathered. Thirty-eight people were murdered and the rest, having formed a self-defense center, held out until the arrival of the Red Army on March 2, 1944. Unfortunately, instead of being liberated, the survivors became the object of NKVD persecution.

People

POTERIUKHA, Iaryna and her brother Petro, from Tajkury
From the account of Rev. Podhorodecki, a son of a colonist in Tajkury:

"Restrained, good Ukrainian families, and even those who loved the Poles also existed. Iaryna Poteriukha, a cripple, a fine individual, sent us packages to Siberia because we left many things with her. But she always insisted, 'Do not write to me because they [the Banderowcy] will kill me!' Her brother, Petro, sheltered an old woman, Wojciechowska, during the murders ... and brought her hidden in a wagonload of peas to Równe. Some Ukrainian from Tajkury saw him do this and reported it to the bandits. When Petro returned, he was bound and gagged and roasted on a spit like a lamb."[1]

Places

ZIELONY DĄB
From the account of Ambroży Wereszczyński (b. 1931) from Zielony Dąb:

"We slept in the forest for many months irrespective of the weather. Since that proved to be very uncomfortable, Father built us a camouflaged underground shelter in the orchard. We were all in that shelter during the first attack of the Banderowcy on our village. The attackers did not notice our hiding place, and our friendly Ukrainian neighbors did not betray us. The glow of flames could be seen over the nearby Polish villages.

"One very chilly day in May, my parents decided for the sake of us [eight] children to spend the night at home but took proper precautions. In the middle of the night our neighbor, a Ukrainian woman, came running over and informed us to get out immediately because the Banderowcy were coming. In great hurry we took shelter in a gully in the forest some distance away, and although it was cold, we failed to bring any warm clothing with us. After a short while, we heard despairing cries and saw the glow of flames over the Polish village of Hurby.

"Bestial scenes of the murder of Poles became an everyday occurrence. Women and children, the old and the young perished in terrible agony.... [Descriptions of the attack on the narrator's family, his father's murder, the attack of July 1943 on Zielony Dąb, and his escape follow.]

"Taking every precaution, we [the narrator and several other survivors] decided to return to the scene of the crime in order to see who was murdered and how. We first decided to go to my property. On the floor of our barn, I saw the burnt remains of about 40 victims. I recognized my mother because her skeleton was intertwined with the bones of my two youngest brothers....

"We went to Pasieca to a Ukrainian acquaintance who gave us some food to eat. It must be remembered that the Banderowcy punished their own people with death for rendering assistance to the Poles. My aunt, Jasińska, also procured some milk for her two young children at great risk to all concerned.

"The following day my brother, Jan, and my uncle, Stanisław, joined our group. All of us lived in the forest, changing locations constantly. We had neither blankets, nor warm clothing, nor provisions, nor matches. We suffered from hunger and cold.

"One night the adults among us hurriedly dug a grave in our orchard wherein we buried the bones of the murdered. No cross was set up, no markers....

"[After spending some time in the forest] I decided to go to the village in order to obtain something to eat. No sooner did I emerge from the forest than I saw armed Banderowcy on horses on the road. Taking advantage of the fact that on the other side of the road there were some Ukrainian children pasturing cows, I joined them and asked them not to betray me. Some of them knew me. The bandits rode over to our group and asked each one of us our names. They asked me to say a prayer. I recited it in Ukrainian because I knew the language. Satisfied, they rode away."[2]

Appendix A: Ukrainian Victims By County

Dubno County

People

BEBEL from Złoczówka
From the account of Danuta Chiniewicz from Złoczówka:

In January 1943 Bebel was murdered by the local Ukrainian Nationalists because he was a former member of the Communist Party of Western Ukraine (KPZU).[1]

BROŻEK, Mrs., and her children from Ptycza
From the account of Zbigniew Wojcieszak (b. 1925) from Młynów, Boremel, Werba and other locations:

In 1943 the UPA murdered Mrs. Brożek (a Ukrainian) and her children. They were all decapitated on the threshold of their home. Since Mrs. Brożek's husband, a Pole, had died previously, her Ukrainian neighbors assured her that nothing would happen to her and her children.[2]

DĘBSKA, Veronika, from Czarna Łoża
In April 1943 Veronika Dębska, the Ukrainian wife of the owner of the Tartak estate, was murdered by Ukrainians when she returned to her village after her husband's death.[3]

GONTA from Werba
From the account of Zbigniew Wojcieszak (b. 1925) from Młynów, Boremel, Werba and other locations:

In 1943 Gonta and Tsentkevych were conscripted by the UPA. Nevertheless, they both returned to their administrative posts in the town of Werba, and later to their own families in the adjoining village by the same name. On the night of their reunion with their families, a group of young Ukrainians (members of the SB) that they knew led them out of their homes in their night shirts while ordering their families to stay put. They were secured to fence posts with barbed wire around their neck and bled to death. On their chests signs were hung that read: "For betraying Ukraine."[4]

KONOPLANKO, an Orthodox priest from Lubieszów in Polesie, murdered in Dubno. See Dubno below, first account.

MELNYCHUK, Mykola, from Złoczówka
From the account of Danuta Chiniewicz from Złoczówka:

Mykola was murdered by the UPA on July 12, 1943, during its attack of Złoczówka. Two reasons have been advanced for his murder: 1. his refusal to participate in the massacre of Poles; 2. his conversion to Roman Catholicism in 1939.[5]

TSENTKEVYCH from Werba. *See* Gonta.

ZHERDYTSKYI family from Jarosławicze

In June 1943, 39 persons were murdered by the UPA during its attack on the village of Jarosławicze. Four persons in the Ukrainian family of Zherdytskyi (Andrii, 48; Mariia, 45; their son Seriozha, 24; and daughter Nadia, 19) were also murdered for rendering assistance to the Poles. Before the war, Andrii was the village *sołtys*. Seriozha was married to a Polish girl.[6]

ZONKA and her mother, from Rejtanów

Fearing for their lives, a young Polish-Ukrainian family fled to Łuck. In May 1943 the wife's mother, a Ukrainian, was murdered by Ukrainians in the village of Wierchówka while on her way to Łuck with some provisions for the couple and her granddaughter. The following week, her daughter Zonka was strangled with a rope in her own house. Zonka's brothers as well as her older sister were married to Poles.[7]

Places

DUBNO
First account. Zbigniew Małyszczycki from Lubieszów in Polesie:

"I did not notice any ethnic antagonisms [in Lubieszów] until the beginning of the war....

"I attended our elementary school for six years. We — Jewish, Ukrainian, and Polish — students knew that there were differences in our religion and language, but that meant very little to us. We respected one another.... Truly, we lived in harmony.

"I am looking at a photograph taken during our trip to Pińsk in 1935. We had no idea then of the terrible tragedy that would befall us in just a few years. Serhii Horshchar was murdered by the UPA at the end of 1943. Borys Feldman vanished without a trace in a Soviet battalion. Litman Serchuk saved himself by fleeing to the interior of the USSR in June 1941. Mitia Veremiichuk unintentionally found himself in a Ukrainian Schutzmannschaft battalion, but he did not join the UPA in 1943. He was sent to a forced-labor camp in Austria and after the war, as a result of being falsely accused of belonging to the UPA, spent about ten years in prison and died shortly after his release. Ivan Horshchar was murdered by the UPA at the end of 1943. Halyna Konoplanko was the daughter of an Orthodox priest who was transferred to Dubno before the war and murdered there in 1943 by the UPA for refusing to bless their instruments of death in his church. Hela Kurhanowicz was in the partisans for one year. In 1943 the Soviets murdered her father. Irka Demianenko collaborated with the Germans and was a lover of a German officer. Szklarz, together with his parents, emigrated to Palestine in 1936. Ela Pawlaczyk [ówna] was the daughter of a policeman. In 1940 she, her younger brother, and her mother were deported to Kazakhstan. No one knows what happened to her father. I don't know what happened to Tamara, the daughter of a Ukrainian priest in Buczyn. My own head is visible between Ivan and Halyna. I spent a year in the partisans. My father was burned to death by the UPA.

"There are six Ukrainians, three Jews, and three Poles in that photograph. But there were more of us in my sixth grade: fourteen Jews, six Ukrainians, and five Poles. Only about half of us went on that trip to Pińsk."[8]

Second account. Wiktor Poliszczuk from Dubno:

"In the summer of 1943 my aunt on my mother's side, Anastazja Witkowska, went with her Ukrainian neighbor to the village of Tarakanów, about three kilometers from the town of Dubno. They spoke in Polish because my aunt, being the only aunt and coming from Lublin Province, never learned Ukrainian. Since my aunt had six children to feed, they went to the market in order to exchange some things for bread. Neither she nor my uncle, Antoni Witkowski — both illiterate — had ever mixed in politics, nor had they the slightest notion of what it was all about. My aunt as well as her Ukrainian neighbor were killed either by the UPA or the SKV only because they spoke in Polish. They were killed in a bestial way with axes and tossed into a roadside ditch."[9]

MŁYNÓW
From the account of Zbigniew Wojcieszak (b. 1925) from Młynów, Boremel and other locations:

In July 1943 the UPA killed a Ukrainian driver by mistake. The intended victim was Czesław Fedorowicz, commander of the local self-defense center and local AK unit.[10]

Horochów County

Names

*VOITOVYCH from Lulówka
From the account of Aleksandra Głowińska from Lulówka:

The Voitovych family adopted Aleksandra as their "niece" after her whole family was slaughtered. Because of threats, Aleksandra's "Ukrainian Mommy" transported her to a Polish family in Burzany for safety. When she returned home, she found that her husband was murdered.[11]

*VOITSEKHIVSKYI from Liniów
From the account of Sabina Królikowska (née Tarnawska, b. 1935) from Koszów:

Voitsekhivskyi was murdered by the Banderowcy on his return home after bringing sacks of wheat and rye to the family of Marian Tarnawski in Łokacze.[12]

Places

ZAMLICZE
The SB murdered 16 Ukrainian families in the course of a single night.[13]

Kostopol County

People

BEDNARZ, Mrs., from Mosty
Paweł and Stanisław Bednarz had Ukrainian wives. In March 1943 they and one of the wives were murdered by the Ukrainian Nationalists. The second wife, Natasha, managed to survive.[14]

MISHCHANIUK, Mykhailo, from Antolin
In August 1943 Mykhailo was ordered to kill his Polish wife (Genowefa, née Szyndrów) and their one-year-old child. Because he refused, he and his family were murdered by their own neighbors.

In this same village of Antolin there was another mixed Polish-Ukrainian family. In that family, the Ukrainian wife (née Vovk) killed her Polish husband.[15]

*NYCHYPIR family from Kamionka
Nychypir, his wife, his daughter, his son-in-law, and his two small grandchildren

---

*The asterisk indicates that the entry or a reference to this entry also appears in the main text.

were killed by the Banderowcy for transporting the Gdowski family to safety in Kostopol.[16]

OLHA from Głuboczanka

In June 1943, on Whit Sunday, 28 people were murdered by the UPA in Głuboczanka and 20 homes were burned. Among those killed was a 50-year-old Ukrainian woman named Olha. She was murdered with an axe.[17]

OLIINYK from Deraźne

In May 1943 the Ukrainian Nationalists murdered 300 Poles in Deraźne. They also killed a Ukrainian teacher, Oliinyk, for calling for good relations with the Poles.[18]

*SMULKA, Hryhorii, from Kazimirka (Kazimierka)

From the account of Stanisław Domalewski from Karaczun, based on a personal interview:

"Kazimirka was a small, predominantly Ukrainian village lying to the north of us [i.e. T. Piotrowski's family] between Kostopol and Sarny. This ancient village was renowned for its magnificent Roman Catholic church with its three ponderous bells (the largest of which could be heard for many kilometers) and its famed painting of the Blessed Mother. Like Our Lady of Częstochowa and Our Lady of Ostra Brama, Our Lady of Kazimirka was said to possess miraculous powers which she often used to alleviate the trials and tribulations of suffering mankind. Quickened by the majestic pealing of the bells, the faithful—not only from Wołyń, but from Polesie and Podole as well—flocked to the village church in order to avail themselves of her good graces.

"In October of 1942, Grzegorz Smulka [Hryhorii Smulka], the Ukrainian *sołtys* of the village of Kazimirka, was ordered by the atheistic philistines of the Third Reich, in the name of their own Unholy Trinity, to have the bells taken down and brought to Stepań for immediate transport into the heart of Germany—the Krupp [industrial] foundries, no doubt. All that precious metal was not to be wasted on pious ringing while there was a two-front war going on! Smulka dutifully relayed his orders to the Polish priest but added, on the side, that he would not be surprised if, in the course of that very night, the bells should happen to 'disappear.'

"The ecstatic clergyman needed no further prompting. At midnight, Stanisław Domalewski and seven other husky men from the nearby village of Karaczun met in secret at the belfry of the church. With them, they brought four of their village's strongest horses and two sturdy wagons. In no time at all, the ancient bells were muffled, dismantled, loaded on the wagons, and transported posthaste not to Stepań, but to Karaczun, where they were solemnly blessed, sprinkled with holy water, and buried in a field belonging to one of the men, about half a kilometer from the village. On the following morning, the entire area was plowed and sown over with winter wheat and rye to cover the traces of this strange funeral.

"The secret of the bells was faithfully preserved during the remaining two and a half years of the war. The bells were saved! However, in 1945, when (after Yalta) Wołyń became a part of the Ukrainian Soviet Socialist Republic, the resurrection of the bells was indefinitely postponed by those involved, in the hope of Wołyń's eventual reunification with Poland and Poland's subsequent liberation from the Soviet Bloc. It was a vain hope, but the secret of the bells of Kazimirka, interred somewhere near the village of Karaczun, remained hidden throughout all these many years. For all Stanisław Domalewski knows, they are still there, ringing silently deep within the bowels of Mother Earth for the deceased and the displaced people of Wołyń.

"Shortly after this incident, Grzegorz Smułka, at a village meeting involving the Ukrainian delegates from Kazimirka, Karaczun, and Krzeszów, publicly voiced his opinion regarding the senseless fratricide which was going on in that vicinity.

"'Brother Ukrainians,' he said, 'let us stop killing the Polish people in Wołyń. As we lived among them in peace for these 20 years, so now let them live in peace among us.'

"The very next day, Smułka — the Ukrainian *sołtys* of Kazimirka — was found brutally murdered."[19]

*VLOSHCHYNSKYI from Stepań
From the account of Włodzimierz Drohomirecki from Deraźne:

The Ukrainian husband of Anna Vloshchynska was hung upside down until he expired for refusing to murder or betray his Polish wife.[20]

Places

JANÓWKA

In August 1943 the Banderowcy killed a Polish child and two Ukrainian children who were being raised (and *because* they were being raised) by a Polish family.[21]

Kowel County

People

*BOICHUN, Omelian, from Rewuszki
From a February 13, 1997, letter of Wacław Chmielewski from Kowalówka Colony, addressed to the Ukrainian Ambassador in Poland:

Omelian was murdered in September 1943 by the Ukrainian Nationalists for warning Poles about an imminent attack on the colonies of Kowalówka, Marszałówka, and Brodyszcze, as well as the Polish village of Budy Ossowskie.[22]

HNAT, Volodymyr, from Sucha Łoza. *See* Ivan Mroz.

MROZ, Ivan, from Sucha Łoza
On July 13, 1943, the UPA rounded up the residents of Sucha Łoza for a "meeting" at the residence of Józef Wybulta, behind whose house was a large clay pit. In all, 97 persons — including about 50 children — were murdered and tossed into the pit. There were 22 survivors. Ivan Mroz and Volodymyr Hnat, two Ukrainians who protested this slaughter, were among the victims.[23]

*OKSIUTYCH, Ivan, and his son Serhii, from Rużyn Colony
From the account of Tadeusz Kotarski from Rużyn Colony:

In the fall of 1943, Ivan, the father, was sawed in half for his pro-Polish sympathies and his anti-UPA stance. The manner by which he was to die was chosen by his nephew, Lonka, a co-participant in this brutal execution. Ivan's son, Serhii, was shot.[24]

*SENKEVYCH sisters, from Mielnica
The Senkevych family assisted the Poles of Mielnica during their repeated trials and tribulations. Two of their daughters, who were medical students, were murdered for refusing to cooperate with the Ukrainian Nationalists.[25]

Places

*GAJ
From the account of Jan Ferszt from Gaj, as recorded by Leon Karłowicz:

A large Ukrainian family was murdered for opposing the UPA attacks on Poles. A Ukrainian priest, his wife, and their two children were also murdered for the same reason.[26]

LITOGOSZCZ

On March 11, 1943, several Ukrainian families were murdered by the Ukrainian Nationalists in this village for voicing their opposition to the killing of Poles.[27]

Krzemieniec County

People

ISHCHUK from Szumsk

One of two Ukrainians murdered by the Nationalists on March 20, 1943, for befriending the Poles. The name of the other Ukrainian was Kravchuk.[28]

KRAVCHUK from Szumsk. *See* Ishchuk.

MYKOLUK, Tetiana, from Białozórka

In April 1943 Tetiana was murdered by the UPA because she had a child by a Pole.[29]

WITKOWSKA, Mrs. Marcin, from Hucisko Pikulskie

From the account of Feliks Jasiński from Kąty (Kuty):

Marcin (a Pole) was certain that his Ukrainian wife would defend their family as well as the two Jasiński families from Mała Iłowica who were hiding in the cellar. But pleas did not help. Marcin's wife and 11 other people perished. After this murder, the bandits were seen washing their knives by a well.[30]

Places

ANTONOWCE

From the account of Feliks Jasiński from Kąty (Kuty):

In the village of Antonowce the UPA murdered a forest inspector, the son of a Ukrainian priest.[31]

BIAŁOZÓRKA

In April 1943 two Ukrainian sisters were murdered for warning Poles of danger.[32]

*UHORSK

A young Ukrainian acquaintance who warned Wiktor Poliszczuk's wife's father of an UPA attack on his family was hung by the Banderowcy in the center of his village with a sign on his chest that read: "This will happen to all traitors!" No one was allowed to cut his body down for several days.[33]

Luboml County

Names

KRASOVSKYI, Volodymyr, family from Kąty

From the account of Janina Bijas (née Prończuk, b. 1932) from Kąty:

"On August 30, 1943, I was at my uncle's (Jan Prończuk's) house in the village of Sawosze, located about two kilometers from my house in Kąty. That morning I heard that Kąty was on fire. Around 6:30 A.M. a group of Banderowcy numbering a few hundred men (they perpetrated the murders in Kąty) passed through Sawosze heading in the direction of Jagodzin. Their wagons were full of the goods robbed from the Polish households. Among the booty were cattle and horses. In Sawosze they killed a 20-year-old woman who was pasturing some cows by the road. [Janina did not know her by name, but she did know that this young woman was mentally retarded.]

"After the band had passed, Uncle Jan, my sister Stanisława, her husband Jan Sawosz, and I went to my family's home. The door to the house stood ajar. Inside, everything was trashed; the chests were open and the best things were stolen. The farm animals were also let out. Our neighbor Ivko (first name probably Stanislav) came over. Following the trail of blood behind the house, we came to the well of Józef Prończuk, my father's brother. The following people lay by the well: Marcin (50), my father; Karolina (50), my mother; Jan (16), my brother; Franciszek (14), my brother; Helena (eight), my sister; and Józef's daughter, Teresa (seven). They were fished out of the well by our neighbors, the Ivko family.

"Ivko told us what had happened. When the Banderowcy showed up, around 3:00 or 4:00 A.M., they led my parents out of the house. Uncle Józef, however, would not let them into his home and told his family to flee. He was wounded in Ivko's orchard and died in the hospital in Luboml. The Banderowcy waited on the other side of the house and caught them all. They threw my Aunt Maria (57), her daughter Anna (about 22), her son Józef (14), her son Jan (six), and her daughter Teresa (seven) alive into the well. Only Józefa-Zofia, my uncle's daughter, who now lives in Sielce near Chełm, was able to escape. They then threw a feeding trough into the well. They murdered my parents with an axe behind their house and threw their bodies on top of the trough. Those who were thrown alive into the well — my uncle's family — survived because the water was shallow. Only Teresa died. She had a broken arm.

"We took the bodies of my parents back to our yard, wrapped them in bedlinen, and buried them in shallow graves with the hope of giving them a proper burial later. It was only a provisional burial in threatening circumstances. The bodies of my family have remained there until this day. A wooden cross marks their grave.

"We then went to some neighbors whose name I do not recall. They lived at the entrance to the village; ours was the third house. We saw the parents (both in their 20s) and their son (nine or ten) lying on the barn floor. They were axed to death. A baby girl about six weeks old still evidenced signs of life. Her head was swollen as if she had water on her brain, as if she was smashed against a wall or a post. The child died the next day, and they were all buried together by the Ivkos in their yard.

"I then went to Sawosze, to my Uncle Jan's family. Along the way, I saw corpses in many (at least five) different wells. I lived there for about two months. During all that time the bands were on the prowl.

"In Sawosze there were two incidents of Ukrainian husbands killing their Catholic wives as well as two children."

In the August 30, 1943, UPA attack on the village of Kąty located in Luboml County (there are villages with this same name in other counties as well), 141 of 282 residents, including 64 children, lost their lives. Entire families were tossed into wells. Among the victims was Paweł Prończuk, who left his hiding place in order to defend his mother. He was placed on a bench, his hands and legs were cut off, and he was left there to die in his agony. The Ukrainian family of Volodymyr Krasovskyi with two small children was also among the victims.[34]

SHPAK, Nina, from Jankowce

During the August 30, 1943, UPA attack on Jankowce — a village consisting of 762 residents — 79 people were killed, including 18 children and Nina Shpak, a Ukrainian woman who was with child.[35]

Łuck County

People

BLASHCHUK, Valerii, family from Katerynówka
From the account of Hieronim Wardach from Katerynówka:

"On May 7, 1943, a band of Ukrainian Nationalists attacked the village of

Katerynówka.... Twenty-seven people were murdered....

"In the evening, we put all the victims on a wagon and, together with those who remained alive, we left Katerynówka forever. Among those murdered were Dunia and his wife (both Poles) as well as the Ukrainian Blashchuk family: Valerii, his wife, child, and his old mother. They were taken with the rest of the victims to Kiwerce and buried in a mass grave."[36]

*CHERVAK, Petro and Ivan, from Koszów
From the account of Irena Justyna from Koszów:

These two Ukrainian brothers were killed by the Banderowcy because they would not reveal the whereabouts of their third brother's (Roman's) family. Roman was married to a Polish girl. They had an eight-month-old son.[37]

GARLICKI, Stanisław, family from Czartorysk

In April 1943 several Polish families were murdered by the Ukrainian Nationalists. Among them was the Garlicki family. Stanisław Garlicki was married to a Ukrainian girl.[38]

LIPCZYŃSKA, Mrs., from Łyczki

On July 5, 1943, the Ukrainian wife of Lipczyński (a Pole) was murdered along with seven other Polish citizens.[39]

OSTROWSKA, Mrs., from Józefin
From the account of Wacław Ostrowski (b. 1921) from Hołodnica:

The Ukrainian wife of Stanisław Ostrowski was murdered for being married to a Pole; so were her parents for being Stanisław's in-laws.[40]

*SAPOZHNYK, Shura, from Koszów
From the account of Irena Justyna from Koszów:

Shura Sapozhnyk was murdered by the UPA because of her pro-Polish sympathies.[41]

SYLOVIAK, Pavlo, from Rokitnie Nowe

In March 1943 the Ukrainian Nationalists murdered Pavlo Syloviak, a Ukrainian married to a Pole named Zofia Grys.[42]

TROFYMCHUK, Petro, from Klepaczów

On May 5, 1943, in the UPA attack on the village of Klepaczów, 42 Poles ranging in ages from two (Wanda Markowska) to 77 (Tekla Markowska) were killed. During the attack, a Ukrainian, Petro Trofymchuk and his Polish wife were also murdered.[43]

TSISAR family from Dębowa Karczma Colony
From the account of Leokadia Grzybowska (née Zawilska, b. 1924):

"Between Aleksandrówka and Łuck lay a large colony called Dębowa Karczma, as well as a railroad station by the same name. Next to them was Leonówka [not the same as in Równe County].... In Dębowa Karczma Colony lived a mixed Polish-Ukrainian family named Tsisar. The mother was Polish; therefore the daughters were baptized in a Roman Catholic church and the sons in an Orthodox church. The children were raised by the mother to cherish their Polish background. The boys belonged to the Polish boy scouts, the Sharpshooter Association, and Krakus. A terrible fate met them all. All eight children were murdered while the parents were forced to watch. Then the mother was killed. Old Tsisar hung himself out of despair....

"The last *wójt* [headman] of the village of Żabecznik was Jan Szuryński from Olgin Colony. His son, Mieczysław, was brutally murdered. His tongue was ripped out, his eyes were plucked out, splinters were driven under his fingernails, and he was burned alive. The same thing happened to Józef Szuryński, his relative. This was done by their Ukrainian buddies with whom these boys went to school."[44]

Places

*ANDRZEJÓWKA COLONY
From the account of Aleksandra Ostrowska from Andrzejówka Colony:

After the Soviet liberation of Andrzejówka Colony in February 1944, a Ukrainian in the service of the Soviet authorities and his entire family were murdered by the Banderowcy.[45]

*ANATOLIA COLONY
From the account of Zenon Dagoński from Anatolia Colony:

When Zenon's father moved his family from Anatolia Colony to Łuck for safety, Katarzyna Dagońska, his father's mother, decided to remain behind to mind the farm. She spent the nights with a neighboring Ukrainian family. Both Katarzyna and four members of the Ukrainian family with whom she stayed were murdered. The perpetrators were the Ukrainian family's son-in-law from Korszów and his Banderowcy companions.[46]

KOSZYSZCZE
On March 15, 1942, the Germans—with the assistance of the Ukrainian police—murdered 145 Poles, 19 Ukrainian communists, seven Jews, and nine Soviet prisoners of war who were in hiding.[47]

KOTÓW
From the account of Mrs. Falkowska from Palcze, as transcribed by Jędrzej Giertych:

"The village of Palcze lay between Równe and Łuck. In that village 18 members of Mrs. Falkowska's husband's family were murdered by the Ukrainians in several attacks. [The village was attacked in March, July, and on September 14, 1943.] On one occasion, seven persons were murdered in one household. They were first tortured (their tongues were torn out and they were subjected to other indignities as well), then killed and burned. The house was also set on fire. They cut one 80-year-old blacksmith into strips. They nailed children to the wall. One person was cut in half with a saw. Some people's ears were cut off....

"In the village of Kotów, not far from Palcze, there was a Ukrainian married to a Polish woman; they had two children. His brother was ordered by the Ukrainians to kill everyone in that family. As the family was fleeing from Kotów to Palcze, they were accosted by Ukrainians, among whom was that brother. They killed them all: the children, the Ukrainian father, and the Polish mother. The brother participated in the murders....

"In the village of Zwierów, a Polish family was murdered by the Ukrainians. Later, some Poles discovered a baby which was still alive; it was sucking the breast of its murdered mother."[48]

ŁYCZKI
The five-member Zawadzki family as well as several other persons were killed by the Ukrainian Nationalists in the village of Łyczki in July 1943. Among the victims was a Ukrainian girl whose husband was Polish.[49]

SZEPEL
On August 28, 1943, 12 Ukrainian youths were executed because they refused to join the UPA.[50]

UKRAINIAN VILLAGE NEAR THE STYRE RIVER
Zenobiusz Janicki states:

"When our patrol returned from Jezioro to Przebraże, the watchman reported to

[Commandant Ludwik] Malinowski that the soldiers from the first company had brought a prisoner, a Bulbowiec, to the barracks. We went to see that prisoner....

"Malinowski asked the Bulbowiec if he had murdered a lot of Poles.

"'Not a single one, Sir Commandant.'

"'Did you see how they murdered the Poles?'

"'I saw how they murdered Ukrainians.'

"'Who murdered them?'

"'Ukrainians.'

"And he began to relate how a unit of Bulbowcy rode out beyond the Styr River in order to procure some cattle and pigs for the needs of the company. When they tried to take the livestock away, they encountered resistance from a few of the Ukrainian farmers.

"'You take everything,' said the farmers, 'food, clothes — and still there is no Ukraine. Przebraże still stands and it is we who have to leave our farms and flee over the Styr.'

"In the course of the argument, the Ukrainians in the village shot three of the Bulbowcy. When the rest returned and told their story, the UPA company commander ordered a punitive expedition against that village. Our prisoner was a member of that expeditionary force. They arrived at the village, and those who had been there earlier indicated the farms on which their three buddies were shot. Then the Bulbowcy shut up the residents in their houses, doused the premises with gasoline, and set them on fire. Several dozen persons perished in the flames. This is how the UPA dealt with its opponents.

"Ludwik Malinowski then asked the prisoner whether he joined the UPA voluntarily or whether he was conscripted. The prisoner replied that he had been conscripted in the region of Kołki. Those mobilized in that region were sent to Łuck for training, and then to Kołki — probably to prevent them from deserting. Our prisoner was a deserter."[51]

Równe County

People

DZIABAK (Diabuk), Nestor, family from Piotrowice
From the account of Jan Bagiński from Piotrowice:

"When the murders of Poles began in August 1943, a Ukrainian forester named Makar came to Aleksander Żukowski in Piotrowice and explained that there was no need to flee because everything would pass.

"But at night, the Nationalists came to Zofia Dziabak, a neighbor whose husband was Ukrainian. They called out her husband and ordered him to kill his wife, his two children, and his mother-in-law, Stanisława Guzowska, and to join them. They gave him three days to carry out the orders. Nestor Dziabak (or Diabuk) hitched up his horses at night with every intention of taking his entire family to the town of Tuczyn, where Germans were stationed. But on the way, near the village of Kraśnica, he was assailed by the Ukrainian Nationalists, told to dig a ditch, and killed together with his entire family....

"As it turned out, the previously mentioned Makar was one of the ringleaders of the bandits."[52]

ONUFRII from Gródek
In April 1943 several Polish families and a Ukrainian named Onufrii were murdered by the Nationalists. Onufrii was killed because he befriended the Poles.[53]

*PASICHNYK family from Ryświanka Colony
Based on hearsay evidence related to me by my brother, Franciszek Piotrowski, Pasichnyk and his family were murdered by the Ukrainian Nationalists for befriending our family and providing us with assistance. (See Chapter 8, Równe County, "Pasichnyk," and the accompanying note.)

SOLOVEI from Gozdów (Hwozdów). *See* Wiry (Sarny County) below.

TYMOSHCHUK from Szubków
From the account of Zbigniew G. Studułł from Jazłowce, and later, Tuczyn:

"My 'uncle' (or so I called him) remained in Szubków. He was a completely Polonized Ukrainian married to my aunt. He was almost 70 years old. Until our evacuation, I never even gave it a thought that 'Uncle' Tymoshchuk was Ukrainian. He remained behind in order to say good-bye to his brother, who lived a few kilometers from the Agricultural School. We learned later that he was murdered, but under what circumstances we never found out.

"A Ukrainian man married to a Pole or a Ukrainian woman married to a Pole were regarded as *Lakhy*, and many people in such mixed marriages were murdered."[54]

Sarny County

People

CHORNA, Olena, and her two children, Semen and Zhenia, from Budki Borowskie
Leon Żur recalls:

"The first UPA attack on Budki Borowskie took place on June 12, 1943.... The second attack took place in late fall 1943....

"On the night of December 6, 1943, the Ukrainian Nationalists attacked the Polish villages of Budki Borowskie, Dołhań, and Okopy and murdered all the people that they found. Over 50 persons perished....

"I will remember that night until the end of my days. Władysław Januszkiewicz and I were staying at his Uncle Antoni Januszkiewicz's house, located about one kilometer from my own. When we fled from there, my home was already burning brightly. We ran through the village, then through the woods near Netreba, and woke up everyone along the way so that they could save themselves. The attackers chased us on horseback, but a tall barbed-wire fence halted their pursuit. They shot at us but missed. We spent the rest of the night in a haystack in the woods of Dermańka.

"In the morning we retraced our steps. I remember that we did not have enough time to awaken the family of Oleksandr Korenchuk. Now, in their yard, we saw the bodies of Kamila and Bronisław Skobelski and their child. Inside the house lay the rest of the murdered residents, including a Ukrainian woman and her children. She was the wife of Stepan Chornyi, a Nationalist. Only her eight-year-old son survived, by hiding in a corner of the house under some rye stalks that his mother had brought home to dry, thrash, and cook for her children. The boy was a witness to the death of his mother and siblings. He told us, 'Mother said that she was Ukrainian, that her husband was shot by the Soviet partisans. She begged for her own life and the lives of her children. Nothing helped. She was shot.'

"In that same house, the several-months-old infant of Michalina Korenchuk was killed with a knife, and Michalina was shot through the mouth and severely wounded. The exiting bullet left a gaping bloody hole on the back side of her neck. Oleksandr Korenchuk's two young sons were decapitated. Their little heads lay on the earthen floor among the scattered kitchen pots and pans....

"Among the over 50 persons of these three villages who were murdered by the Banderowcy-Bulbowcy bandits on the night of December 6, 1943, were: from Budki Borowskie — Olena Chorna, a 30-year-old Ukrainian woman along with her two sons, three-year-old Semen and two-year-old Zhenia; Janina Januszkiewicz (around 25); and Fedora (Teodora) Nyzhynska (around 33), also of Ukrainian background."

Other names from Budki Borowskie, Dołhań and Okopy follow, along with brief descriptions of the manner of their tragic deaths (e.g., "axed to death," "shot," "pierced through the abdomen with a stake and pinned to the ground," "torn apart (a small child) and thrown into a well.")

In addition, the names of two other Ukrainian victims are given: Serhii Kryzhov, a member of the (V. I.) Chapayev partisan unit who was murdered by the UPA in April 1943 while on a reconnaissance mission in Horochów, and Adam Sheremeta from Netreba, murdered one month later.

After the bodies of the residents of these three villages were buried in a mass grave in the cemetery in Okopy, "both the Poles and the Ukrainians who remained alive after the December pogrom hid in the woods of Dermańka and Janowa Dolina. They did not remain there for very long because they feared that the Bulbowcy would finish up their deeds even in the forest. The Polish self defense continued to be weak and the partisans were not returning from the places of their concentration. So a hundred of us Poles, both young and old, gathered together and proceeded eastward across the former Polish-Soviet border for protection and salvation among the Ukrainians who lived there. We were received well in the village of Perevysianka; we were sheltered in various homes and cottages, provided with warmth, and given food.

"My family was placed with Marko Los [who also provided shelter for a Jewish woman, Gienia, and a lay brother, Karol Dziemba]. How different was the behavior of these Ukrainians who were not infected with nationalism! They were, after all, related by blood to our Polish Ukrainians living near the border."

In May 1989 the narrator, Leon Żur, visited the places of his childhood horrors and spoke with local Ukrainians, including Volodymyr Korenchuk.

"Volodia remembered that night very well," continues Leon, "when the Bulbowcy from Karpiłówka fell on Budki Borowskie, Dołhań, and Okopy. At the time he lived with his family on the Ukrainian side of the village of Borowe. He said, 'I was a witness to the burning of Polish properties. I heard how the cries of those being murdered, the desperate moaning of the dying, and the calls for divine assistance tore the night asunder.'

"I asked, 'Why were the Ukrainian people also killed that night, like your neighbor Fedora Nyzhynska, Olena Chorna and her children, and others?'

"He replied, 'Fedora, because at that time a Pole, Janina Januszkiewicz, was living with her. And Olena quartered two Polish families, the Korenchuks and Skobelskis.'

"At this point, it may help to explain that our neighbor, Oleksandr Korenchuk, was a close relative of Volodymyr Korenchuk. When Oleksandr married Michalina Kozińska, a Pole, he converted to Catholicism. Michalina [as stated above] was severely wounded that night. The Bulbowiec shot straight into her open mouth and left her for dead. Volodymyr's family rescued her and took her to the doctor the following day."[55]

KOSTIUK, Andrii, from Borowe
From the account of an older Ukrainian resident of Borowe, as recorded by Leon Żur:

Since Poland's independence, Leon Żur has set out several times for Wołyń from Giżycko, Poland, both for sentimental reasons and to do research. He was especially interested in the fate of the pastor from Okopy, Fr. Ludwik Wrodarczyk, at whose side he had served as an altar boy.

On the morning of December 7, 1943, just after the previous night's attack on the villages of Budki Borowskie, Dołhań, and Okopy by the UPA quartered in the village of Karpiłówka, "where every third resident was connected with the UPA," Fr. Wrodarczyk was abducted from his village and taken to Karpiłówka for "interrogation." That was the last anyone had seen of him.

In the spring of 1992, on his third trip to Wołyń, Leon Żur and his companions were staying with the family of Petro Kostiuk in Borowe, a village near Karpiłówka. On that particular day, several Ukrainians had gathered at the Kostiuk residence to welcome the visitors from Poland. Leon informed Petro that he planned to visit Karpiłówka the next day to interview some eyewitnesses regarding Fr. Wrodarczyk's disappearance and asked whether Petro knew anything about it. Petro replied that he did not know much. He also avoided speaking about the fate of his own brother, Andrii Kostiuk, who assisted the Poles and worked on behalf of the Soviet partisans. (The Polish underground and the Soviets partisans consisting of Russians, Ukrainians, and others, were allied at that time against Nazi Germany.) One of the older residents of Borowe, however, courageously volunteered the following information regarding Petro's brother, which Leon transcribed and published:

"'I know,' [the older Ukrainian] began his story, 'that Andrii loved the truth and that he perished for the truth. The Bulbowcy abducted him more than once. The first time it was like this. He was returning from Rokitno through Karpiłówka with some interesting information for the partisans. He was also bringing them some things which he had bought, like razor blades, matches, and flint for lighters. The UPA members asked him where he had gotten these things and how he had managed to pay for them. He replied that he had found some money and that he was bringing these things with us, the residents of Borowe, in mind. He admitted nothing. He was then lashed mercilessly.

"'They sent for him a second time after the meeting between the UPA and the leader of the Slovak unit, Capt. Nalepka. The purpose of this meeting [arranged by Andrii] was to ease the tensions between the Ukrainians and Poles. They interrogated Andrii in the home of our neighbors. They wanted to know how he was able to establish contact with the Slovak partisans. They beat him mercilessly that time as well. They beat him with a rifle ramrod and with everything else that was available in that farm kitchen: potato beaters, pokers. They beat him so much so that he lost consciousness. Then they threw him outside behind the house and left him for dead. He lay there for who knows how long and, upon regaining consciousness, crawled back to his house.

"'The neighbors [in whose house he had been tortured] thought that Andrii's family had taken his body away and buried him. He was unable to walk. His wife nursed him with various herbs. After a while he regained some of his strength and, with the assistance of two long forks used to take pots off the stove, he began to walk. Since he had to leave his house from time to time to answer nature's call, the neighbors saw him. This was already after the Red Army had occupied these territories, and they [the neighbors] were afraid that he would report everything to the Soviet authorities. The woman of the house where he had been interrogated was especially worried because she encouraged the butchers to beat him. She therefore immediately informed the Bulbowcy in Karpiłówka that they had not killed him, that he not only lived, but was even walking.

"'A young Banderowiec named Mykhailo Dovhal came to Andrii's house. He still lives in Karpiłówka today. He halted in front of the house and called out from atop his horse, 'Andrii, come out. I come to you on urgent business.'

"Andrii did not want to come out, so he said to his son, 'Go tell that uncle that I am sick and cannot walk.'

"The son did as he was told, but the rider insisted, 'Andrii, come out. Show yourself but for a moment.'

"Andrii instructed his son once more, 'Go tell him that I cannot come out; I don't have the strength, and I am lying down.'

"The son left the house, ran up to the man, and in a pleading voice said, 'Uncle, my father cannot. He is sick and lying down.'

"But the Banderowiec would not listen and called out again, 'Andrii, I don't want anything from you, only a little tobacco for a cigarette. Come out, even if you have to do it slowly.'

"Andrii, feeling helpless by this time, took out two packets of tobacco and made his way to the threshold of the house. When Mykhailo saw him, he cried out, 'Look at that! They said that Andrii is no longer alive, and here he is walking about.' And he rode off.

"At dusk, several Banderowcy came over, surrounded the house, and ordered Andrii to come along with them. Andrii did not want to go and told them so. But they said that he would not have to go far, only to show them the way. Andrii's wife began to cry. She refused to let him leave the house. She begged them to leave her husband alone. But nothing helped. They told him to get dressed and that was that.

"So, with the help of his wife, Andrii put on a sheepskin coat, went up to his children, gave them a big hug, and kissed them dearly. That's how he said good-bye. Upon seeing this, they made fun of him saying, 'Look what a fool he is! He's saying good-bye to his children. We never do that with our families when we go somewhere. He's only going to lead us a little way, show us the road, and come right back home.'

"When they took him from the house, they did not allow anyone outside. I don't know; they either placed him on a wagon or led him away or dragged him with their horses. We never found that out. Later it was said in the village that he stayed in the Zababa forest range. They held him for another two days and interrogated him about his contacts with the Poles and the Soviet partisans. In all probability, they tortured him severely. Finally, they laid him on a stump in which there was a hollow and pierced his stomach with a sharp wooden stake. The point of the stake went into the stump, and there he suffered until he expired."

Leon Żur then relates what the Ukrainian residents of Karpiłówka had told him regarding the fate of Fr. Ludwik Wrodarczyk:

"'We lived right here,' said one of the [three sisters from Karpiłówka], and points to a small wooden house consisting of a foyer, kitchen and a separate bedroom....

"'In this kitchen,' said Fedosia, 'on the right, stood a large stove for baking bread. The icons hung in that far corner. As soon as he was brought in, Fr. Ludwik went right up to the icons, made a sign of the cross, and began to pray. That's when they threw themselves on him, tore him away from the icons, and forbade any further prayers. Next, they shoved him into the bedroom, where they began to beat and interrogate him. We were then in the kitchen and could hear the sound of the blows and the cries of the captive. After a while, they led him out of the house, laid him naked on the snow, and murdered him.'

"At this point of the story I wonder at her use of the word 'interrogate.' Why and about what did they interrogate him? Suddenly, one of the residents of the village comes over to me and says in a hushed voice, 'Go over to that man in the hat and ask him how it was done [i.e., how Fr. Ludwik was murdered].' I go and ask. He replies:

"'Well, they tore his heart out of his chest. It was done in this way. They laid Fr. Wrodarczyk undressed on the snow. One UPA member stood on his hands, another held his feet, and the third cut open the chest cavity of the priest and took out his pulsating heart. Oh, he shrieked! He shrieked!'

"I ask him his name and date of birth. I have neither the strength nor the courage to ask for more.

"Meanwhile, Hanna Brychka takes Fr. Ludwik Kieras and Franciszek Wrodarczyk [the other members of Leon's party, both related to Fr. Wrodarczyk] into the torture room. She shows them Fr. Wrodarczyk's dry blood stains, still visible on the wall. Later, Fedosia and Hanna relate how they had buried the body behind the barn on the following day....

"Upon my return from Karpiłówka, I go to the residents of Borowe in order to share with them the new information that I had received about the death of Fr. Wrodarczyk. As if to confirm this version of the story, they tell me that in fact there was such a UPA member who 'specialized' in 'opening up people's chests.' He would take out the pulsating heart of the victim and then, gathering a group of people around him, he would pierce it with an awl and time the duration of the agony on his watch, that is, the time up to the point at which the heart stopped beating."[56]

KRYZHOV, Serhii, from Budki Borowskie. *See* Olena Chorna.

NYZHYNSKA, Fedora, from Budki Borowskie. *See* Olena Chorna.

SHEREMETA, Adam, from Netreba. *See* Olena Chorna.

Places

*NETREBA
From the account of Rev. Jan Kurdybelski:

"The Ukrainian village of Netreba consisted of about 60 households. In 1937-38 Fr. Bruno Wyrobisz accepted most of these Ukrainians into the Roman Catholic faith. In reprisal, the entire village was burned down [by the UPA] in 1943. Part of the residents were murdered and part fled with the Poles."[57]

WIRY
From the account of Julian Grzesik from Lublin:

"During my numerous trips to the East, where I stayed among circles of [Baptist] believers, I have obtained much information regarding the events linked to the fate of the Polish people from that area....

"In full view of fellow believers and residents, the Banderowcy — using axes — cut off the heads of two young Baptists in the village of Wiry in the county of Sarny and of a third in the village of Bogusze for refusing to join the UPA. Before their death the victims asked the murderers to be allowed to face their friends who assisted in the execution. It is said that a rock splattered with their blood is located in the house of prayer in Wiry. I have also heard that the breasts of young Ukrainian women who refused to cooperate with the UPA were severed, and that many people were killed by being thrown into wells.

"The youngest member (a minister) of the Tsaruk family told us how the Banderowcy brought a young Pole to their house and, despite the protest of his father, tortured him and led him outside. It is unknown what happened to him after that.

"While he was in Lublin, Mykola Tsaruk told us how the slaughter of Poles began in Polesie. The Banderowcy, during their stay in Tynne [a village by Sarny], tried to force him into their ranks. Being a believer, he refused. When they ended their badgering and left, one of them — who stood aside and was silent — remained behind. He admitted that he was the son of a Baptist minister of some congregation and that he had joined the UPA in good faith in order to fight for a free Ukraine. One day the UPA units were concentrated in an area supposedly for military exercises. His unit took up quarters among the people in some Polish colony and became acquainted with the local girls.

"After a series of exercises the units were assembled in one place and an order was read requiring everyone to murder the Polish family with whom they were staying. The men in the ranks began to protest that they were supposed to fight for Ukraine, not kill unarmed people. So the commander asked those who refused to follow the order to step forward; about 80 men left the ranks. The commander then, going from one to another, shot five of them. When the rank-and-file protested all the louder that they were killing their own people, the officers took up counsel and announced that those who refused to take part in the operation could leave the unit and go back home. The son of the minister, fearing for his life, did not join those who left — a fact he later regretted. He now admonished Mykola not to enter the UPA....

"The Banderowcy physically punished and killed those Ukrainians who did not want to join their ranks. That's what they did with Solovei, Anastasiia Fedorovych's half-brother in Gozdów [or Hwozdów, near Korzec in Równe County]."[58]

WŁODZIMIERZEC
From the account of Franciszek Skurzyński from Dołhań, as recorded by Leon Żur:

"In mid-1944 our unit received orders to take Włodzimierzec, located about five to seven kilometers from the railway station in Rafałówka on the Sarny-Kowel line....

"After taking Włodzimierzec, we confirmed the fact that the Banderowcy had penetrated the settlement after the departure of the Germans. We entered one of the Ukrainian homes on the perimeter of the settlement with the intention of quartering there. Inside the house the couple was in tears. In response to our question of what had happened, the landlord opened the door to the adjoining room, showed us a large bloodstain on the floor, and said, 'They killed my son, those who wear the trident on their hats [i.e., the UPA].'"[59]

Włodzimierz County

People

DZIDUKH, Vladyslav, family from Maria Wola Colony

In the July 12, 1943, UPA attack on Maria Wola Colony, 200 persons of all ages were murdered. Of these, about 30 were thrown alive into a well and killed with large rocks. Those who ran off into the countryside were hunted down like animals. These included 18 children between the ages of three and 12. After being caught, they were transported by wagon to the Ukrainian village of Czestny Krest and were murdered there with pitchforks and axes. During this "action" on Maria Wola Colony, Vladyslav Dziduhk, a Ukrainian married to a Polish girl, was ordered to kill his wife and two children. He refused; consequently, he, his wife, and the children were murdered.[60]

*IUKHNO family from Sielec

According to one account, Iukhno — whose son belonged to the UPA — rescued the Styczyński family.

Another account refers to a Ukrainian (evidently the same Iukhno, but no name is given) whose son belonged to the UPA, who hid and transported the Styczyński family to Włodzimierz, and who supposedly paid for it with his life. This account continues: "The Ukrainians also murdered the family of Iukhno a known Communist who operated a mill in Sielec in 1940-41. Iukhno himself was thrown onto the mill's grinding wheel."[61]

***MUZYKA from Gucin Colony**

After the July 11, 1943, UPA attack on Gucin, the son of Muzyka — a Ukrainian woman who sheltered Apolonia Traczykiewicz — was murdered by the UPA for refusing to kill Poles.[62]

Places

*JASIONÓWKA

From the account of Anna Świderska (née Manias), as recorded by Alfreda Głowińska-Krawiec:

In August 1943 the UPA carried out a bloody campaign against the village of Jasienówka. A Ukrainian woman who maintained contact with the Poles and associated with them was also murdered, along with her children, for this "treasonous" action.[63]

*SAMOWOLA

From the account of Honorata Zarębska from Orzeszyn Colony:

The parents of a Ukrainian girl married to a Pole were killed with sickles in 1943 by the Ukrainian Nationalists and their farmstead was burned.[64]

SUCHODOŁY

From the account of Bronisława Pieczykolan (b. 1921) from Nowojanka, later a resident of Smołowa:

"The massive murder of the Polish people by the Ukrainian Nationalists began in July 1943. From that time on, none of us ever slept at home; rather, we hid in the fields or in farm buildings or in the forest. If we went to our homes in Smołowa, it was always in secret in order to feed our animals or to get something to eat.

"Our neighbor Tomasz Kozidło, being concerned for the lives of his two daughters and grandson, turned to a Ukrainian acquaintance by the name of Kharyton to take them to Włodzimierz. Having packed their wagon with essential clothing and food, the Kozidło family awaited the arrival of Kharyton. He came but told them that for safety's sake he would not take the main road from Suchodoły to Włodzimierz, but rather another, less-prominent road.

"The parents, bidding farewell to their five-year-old daughter Jadwiga, their 20-year-old daughter Stefania, and her three-year-old son, were happy that at least they would be safe in Włodzimierz. After a while, three shots rang out from the direction of their departure. Being concerned, Tomasz Kozidło's wife decided to follow her family. From a hill, in the distance she saw some bodies lying by the side of the road. When she came nearer, she realized that they were the bodies of her two daughters and her grandson, whom she had just sent off with Kharyton. As a result of this shock, she suffered a stroke; although she could still make some strange noises, she was unable to speak for the rest of her life.

"Kharyton, the Ukrainian whom they considered to be their friend, turned out to be a bandit.

"A few days later, the Banderowcy murdered Józef Pieczykolan (the brother of my husband), his sister Zofia, and her husband, who came from a mixed marriage. His father was a Ukrainian; his mother, Polish. Zofia lived in the village of Suchodoły and was in her ninth month of pregnancy; she was expecting her child to be born at any moment.

"Although they spent the nights hidden in haystacks rather than in their house, the bandits discovered them. They were hauled out and led back to their house. There, Zofia's husband was ordered to kill his Polish wife or himself be killed. He and his wife begged the bandits on their knees to spare their lives. Their pleas were to no avail. They were both killed cruelly with some blunt object."[65]

Zdołbunów County

People

HRYTSAIUK (forester). *See* Vasyl Huk.

HUK, Vasyl, and his mother, from Zielony Dąb
From the account of Feliks Jasiński from Kąty (Kuty):

"I am horror-struck at what happened in Zielony Dąb, the last village in our parish. The residents of that village were better off than others. The Poles constituted about one-half of the residents; the Ukrainians, the other half. The Ukrainians assured the Poles that they could remain there in peace and mouthed the same arguments as those used to fool the residents of Huta Majdańska. On June 25 [1943], three weeks after the attack on the neighboring village of Hurby, came the terrible attack on Zielony Dąb. The bandits burned 46 people in buildings and murdered nine more. The victims constituted 46.2 percent of all resident Poles. Such naïveté! They believed that their neighbors would defend them, or at least warn them of an impending attack. They did not know that the idea circulated among such as their neighbors that if there were no Poles in Wołyń, every Ukrainian would receive nine tithes [1.1 hectares] of land. If the Poles fled from their properties, they could always return. But in this way [i.e., by being killed], they would never come back.

"Vasyl Huk, a Ukrainian married to a Polish girl, was a hero in Zielony Dąb. The Banderowcy threatened him with death unless he obey their order and kill his wife. Vasyl, without even reflecting on the matter, took his wife to Szumsk and there entered the police, received a gun, and participated in excursions. For this, the Banderowcy killed his Ukrainian mother in her home and spied on him in order to kill him too. He was shot on a dam in Szumsk from a great distance....

"The Banderowcy killed their own people without trial on the spot: on the merest suspicion, for talking with a Pole or a German; for the smallest gesture, such as giving permission to drink water by a well. The leaders terrorized those under their command and punished them by death for the slightest infraction.

"The Germans had to evacuate from the eastern front and that made them furious. The Ukrainian Nationalists were repaid for their attacks by terrible expeditions, which razed entire villages and farmsteads; half of the large village of Dermań was burned. That state of affairs lasted until the middle of 1944, that is, until the arrival of the Red Army and the institution of the Soviet administration. But this was not easy to do; whenever some Ukrainian took over some function, he was shortly thereafter killed in secret....

"We are aware of the destiny of several butchers and seven upright Ukrainians. The UPA shot Pavlo Kirychuk—a high-ranking Banderowiec murderer in Stara Huta, and destroyer of the church in Kąty (Kuty)—for desertion. Young Lishchuk was killed by his compatriots while they were dividing up the booty. So was Samolei, under similar circumstances.

"The upright Ukrainians included: Stepanyda Kirychuk, for her work in a military kitchen; the forester Hrytsaiuk, for various assistance; and the five-member family of Shmatkovskyi. He, his wife, and their three children were thrown into a well for being loyal to the Soviet authorities."[66]

KIRYCHUK, Stepanyda. *See* Vasyl Huk.

PANKOWSKA Mrs., from Huta Majdańska
From the account of Cezary Wereszczyński (b. 1930) from Huta Majdańska:

"I come from a 13-member family. We lived in Huta Majdańska in the county of Zdołbunów until July 12, 1943. On that day, around three o'clock in the morning, the Banderowcy (black company) attacked our village. Kovalchuk and Kuryluk were their leaders. They murdered, pierced with bayonets, and burned. Children were impaled on fence posts and thrown into wells. The whole village, consisting of 46 [house] numbers, was wiped out: about 200 persons died. Only a few people survived, including my neighbor and myself. The UPA assured us beforehand that they would not attack our village because its Polish residents were peaceful — and they did just the opposite.

"Pankowski and his two sons also survived. Their mother was Ukrainian, and they [the UPA] murdered her."[67]

POTERIUKHA, Petro, from Tajkury
From the account of Rev. Podhorodecki, son of a colonist in Tajkury:

After sheltering an old Polish woman named Wojciechowska and taking her in a wagonload of peas to Równe, Petro was betrayed to the Banderowcy by a Tajkury resident. Upon his return, he was bound, gagged, and roasted on a spit.[68]

SHMATKOVSKYI family. *See* Vasyl Huk.

Appendix B: Three Stories from Eastern Galicia

Lwów Province

Helena Wysocka (née Pilch) was born on June 7, 1925, in the village of Konotopy, near the county town of Sokal, in the province of Lwów. Konotopy was located on the Bug River, which in that area marked the infamous German-Soviet line of demarcation. Konotopy was on one side of the river, Sokal on the other. A bridge spanning the Bug connected them.

Helena's father, Wojciech Pilch, was a military settler, that is to say, a land-grant recipient from the Polish government for his years of military service to the country. Her mother's maiden name was Józefa Dórak. They raised a large family: five sons and five daughters.

Helena recalls that the problem with the Ukrainians in that region began in 1938 in the suburb of Sokal, called Waławka, when Janek, a young man in his twenties whose Ukrainian father had passed away, had decided to join the Polish sharpshooters. His Polish mother recalled that one day some Ukrainians knocked on her door at about midnight, woke up the family, and ordered her son to hitch up the horses and to take them (the Ukrainians) over the bridge to the Sokal railway station. As all learned later, this was only a pretext because in reality the visitors had murder on their minds. Poor Janek was killed on the bridge which spanned the Bug, and his body was dumped in the river. Many people from the vicinity, including Helena, attended this young man's funeral and tried to console his grieving mother.

Then came the war, and despite the needs of their large family, the Pilchs rendered what assistance they could to the retreating Polish soldiers, as well as to the Jewish refugees streaming eastward to get away from the Germans.

Just after the Soviet invasion of Eastern Poland on September 17, 1939, but before the Red Army reached Konotopy, Helena remembers that some local Ukrainians went on a pyromaniacal spree and burned down about eight to ten Polish residences. Fortunately, Helena's house was spared, and more important, no one was killed because a small contingent (ten to twelve men) of the Polish police arrived from Sokal to investigate the reason for the fires that could be seen from that county town.

After being told that it was the Ukrainians that set the fires, the police left. Soon, Ukrainian homes were burning. Later, a friendly Ukrainian neighbor told Julia Adamarek, a Polish resident of Konotopy, that were it not for the arrival of the police, the Poles in this mixed village would have been murdered that very night. Many, therefore, began to avoid sleeping in their houses after this event as a precaution.

When the Soviets arrived a short time later, they were greeted by the local Ukrainian population with a triumphal arch, and bread and salt. Their stay in Konotopy, however, was short. After about two weeks, the Red Army marched out and the Germans marched in. They were also greeted with a triumphal arch that one German on a motorcycle purposefully kicked over in disdain as he rode by. From that time until the Soviet counteroffensive in 1944, Konotopy found itself under German rule.

Meanwhile, from the date of the attack on Konotopy until March 1943, when Helena was deported to a forced-labor camp in Mühlhausen, Thüringen, many more Polish homes were burned by the Ukrainian Nationalists and many Poles were killed in her region. For example, a woman was shot on the bridge as she was making her way back home to Konotopy from Sokal, and a visitor from Łańcut was shot through the window of Trąb's, their neighbor's, house. Be that as it may, Helena missed the worst part of Konotopy's tragic history, a history which she later heard from her mother after their postwar reunion.

That history began in early summer 1943 with a Ukrainian-Nationalist attack on the village of Wazów, located about two kilometers from Konotopy. Wazów was reduced to ashes and about 120 of its Polish residents were brutally murdered. As the survivors gathered in the Konotopy cemetery to bury their dead, the Nationalists struck again, throwing live grenades into the crowd of mourners and adding to the list of those murdered previously.

That same evening, a Ukrainian acquaintance named Vozhniak visited the Pilch household and told Helena's father to get out with his family as soon as he could because "something might happen to you tonight." Wojciech, in turn, immediately warned his neighbors and left with his wife and his remaining children (the seven who were not deported) for the West. From her family and the other refugees that she met later in Poland, Helena learned that their Ukrainian friend's warning was a godsend, as many Polish villages — including Opulsko, Bojanice, and Zawiśnie — were attacked right after that warning and many Poles were killed.

After the war Helena became a displaced person, and rather than returning to her family in Poland and live under the Communist régime, she decided to emigrate. She came to Canada alone in February 1948. She now lives with her husband, Antoni, within the shadow of Mont St-Hilaire near Montreal. But the real shadow in her life has always been, and will continue to be, the shadow of the war with all of its tragedy and sad memories of lost youth in Konotopy, Poland.[1]

Stanisławów Province

Emilia Krupka (née Englot) was born on May 15, 1927, in the village of Ludwikówka, the township of Bursztyn, the county of Rohatyn, the province of Stanisławów. Her parents were Władysław and Franciszka (née Maćków). She had three brothers: Józef Kochman (her half-brother from her mother's previous marriage), Franciszek, and Filip. Emilia did not begin with her own story.

In September 1939, shortly after the Soviet occupation, some Ukrainians attacked the Polish residents living in the village of

Krasnolesie. One of Emilia's relatives, Katarzyna Zembroń (her husband, Florian, was in the Polish army), and her four children (ages 16, 12, 6, and 4) were among the victims. Frightened by the commotion and the sight of burning houses, Katarzyna ran out of her home and in her panic just stood there in the middle of the yard, covering her eyes with her hands. The attackers beat and stabbed her 13 times and left her for dead in a pool of her own blood. Somehow, she managed to crawl away from the place of her torment and hide in a stack of hay.

She was still conscious when the Ukrainians murdered her two oldest children. She saw how they plucked out their eyes and witnessed how the children's throats were cut with a straight razor. Katarzyna's two youngest children were more fortunate; they were hidden by their Ukrainian neighbors and survived the slaughter. This all happened under the veil of night.

On the following day the attackers came and apologized to those who remained alive, claiming they had made a mistake. They said that they were supposed to have murdered some other family by the name of Zembroń. "But they were killing all the Poles in the village" explained Emilia. "Even the Uniate priests urged them to make order while there was still time."

"Why did they apologize?" I inquired.

"Probably because some of the people they came to kill survived and could identify them," replied Emilia.

Hearing what had happened, Katarzyna's brother came from Ludwikówka and took her and her surviving daughters away. She was placed in a monastery converted into a hospital in nearby Bursztyn. Thinking her condition was beyond all hope, the two doctors present at that "hospital" did not try to save her. But Katarzyna hung on to life, and after three days she finally received such treatment as they had to offer.

After recuperating, Katarzyna and her two daughters moved in with her brother in Ludwikówa, where, as we will see shortly, her troubles were far from over. Today, Katarzyna Zembroń lives in Rzeszów, Poland. She is 98 years old. Her deformed hand bears witness to the Ukrainian attack on her village and to her near-death experience.

"Before I tell you about Ludwikówka," said Emilia, "I have to tell you about another incident that happened in Bursztyn. Bursztyn, our town, lay on the Gniła Lipa River. It was inhabited by Poles, Ukrainians, and Jews. Two priests, Fr. Władysław Porębski and Fr. Stanisław Stankiewicz, served Holy Trinity parish, and they lived in separate buildings. At the beginning of July 1943 [she did not recall the exact date], the Banderowcy knocked on the door of the home of Fr. Porębski, the younger of the two priests, and informed his mother that they came to search the premises for hidden arms. Upon hearing them enter, Fr. Porębski immediately jumped out the window and hid in some lilac bushes. When his mother tried to explain that her son was not at home, they barged in and proceeded to search the rectory. Not finding their intended victim, they murdered his mother in cold blood, beat his father to a pulp, broke both his hands, and went on their way."

After burying his mother, Pastor Porębski and his father left for Przemyśl. Fr. Wojciech Olszowski was his replacement in Bursztyn.

Emilia ended this part of the story that she had prepared to tell me with the words: "Such attacks on Polish priests, teachers, and other learned persons took place in other locations throughout Eastern Galicia." She then told me the tragic story of her own family.

"Ludwikówka lay about two kilometers from Bursztyn," she began. In 1944 there were about 200 households in Ludwikówka, a village that had already celebrated its centennial. Except for the five or six mixed (i.e., Polish-Ukrainian) households, all the families there were Polish. Before the war the residents of Ludwikówka supported themselves by the weaver's craft, supplying the adjoining, predominantly Ukrainian villages, such as Korostowice, Nastaszczyn, Kuropatniki, Jezierzany, Stasiowa Wola, and many others, with yarn and cloth. Relations between the local Poles and Ukrainians in this area were rather cordial.

There were also villages further removed from Ludwikówka, such as Żylibory, Dykietyn, Sarnki Dolne (Lower), Sarnki Górne (Upper), and of course Sarnki Średnie (Middle). "In one of these Sarnki," added Emilia, "the Banderowcy also killed a Polish priest, but I do not remember his name." (Fr. Wiktor Szklarczyk was murdered in Sarnki Dolne during an attack on the rectory on February 19, 1944.)

On the night of February 15, 1944, the Banderowcy killed one of two Polish guards whom they encountered while passing through Ludwikówka. "Władysław Szyndlar was buried on Thursday afternoon, the 17th of February," remembered Emilia, "and on that same day, around 7:30 P.M., gunfire sounded in the village. It was the Banderowcy again. They surrounded Ludwikówka and began to destroy both the village and the inhabitants. In a short while, all of Ludwikówka was in flames." Those who tried to run from their homes were shot. Emilia still recalls the names of some of those who died on that tragic night, and the manner of their deaths.

Among those who ran out into the fields barefooted in their nightshirts and froze to death (it was below zero) were Janina Kochman and her sister, and Jadwiga Harmazij and her sister. Paweł Filar was shot; so were Antoni Krzysztyniak, Władysław Kuźniar, Józef Maćków, Jan Trojniar, Antoni Zembroń (Katarzyna Zembroń's brother-in-law), Genowefa Żywer, Wojciech Gargała, as well as Bronisława Gargała and her son Franciszek, who were hiding in their potato cellar. (Franciszek's wife had passed away in September 1943.) His two children, aged two and five, who were hiding in that same potato cellar with their father and grandmother, somehow survived the slaughter and were immediately adopted — together with their eight-year-old brother, who was visiting his uncle at the time — by their mother's brother, Franciszek Zembroń. Walerian Cwynar, his wife, and their two daughters and son were burned to death in their own home; so were Józef Baran and his wife and children; and Stanisława Żywer (Genowefa's sister-in-law) and her four children. Twenty-two-year-old Augustyn Korbecki was hacked to pieces in the barn of Jan Gargała. Józef Kochman (Emilia's half-brother) ran to the home of a friend named of Bielecki. There, as he set his back to the door to prevent the Banderowcy from entering the house, an axe split the door and his skull. Witnesses hiding in the bushes nearby — they had to stuff their baby's mouth with a rag — saw how poor Józef ran for about 30 meters before collapsing in death.

"In all about 100 persons were killed in Ludwikówka and some 30 were injured," said Emilia.

When only two houses remained standing between Emilia's home and the nearest conflagration, the Englot family decided to take their chances outdoors. They ran out and, joined by members from three other families, made their way to the village cemetery and barricaded themselves in the mortuary (*trupiarnia*).

"In this group of 11 people," said Emilia, "were a 16-year-old girl, my mother, my two brothers [Franciszek (15) and Filip (13)], and myself. I stood by the door holding a pillow next to my body for protection because my father had always said, '*Kula przez pióra nie przejdzie.*' (A bullet will not pass through feathers)." And for the first time since our session began, having repeated this spurious admonition, 70-year-old Emilia evidenced a slight smile — albeit an embarrassed one — at her own naïveté at age 16.

"We also prayed in silence," she added. When their work was done, the Banderowcy, numbering around 100 men, withdrew from the village but halted by the cemetery, located some 80 meters from the burning houses.

"Perhaps they saw our footprints in the snow," said Emilia. "We then heard some voices calling for benzine."

"Let's burn down that house," she heard them shout.

Others, a minority, said, "'We ought not burn this down; this is a cemetery, this is a mortuary.'"

"Thanks to our prayers," remarked Emilia, "our lives were spared and the Banderowcy proceeded on their way."

The group spent the entire night in the mortuary. When they exited in the morning, they congregated with the remaining survivors who had returned to their village. Out of 200 homes, only about 15 remained intact.

"Many people died in those homes, and many cows, horses, pigs, chickens, and rabbits also lost their lives in the barns and various farm buildings at the hands of these Ukrainians," remarked Emilia. Miraculously, although their barn was still smoldering, the Englot house was not among those destroyed.

That same morning (February 18, 1944), the Gestapo and the Ukrainian Police arrived to investigate the incident. When they discovered that some people were still alive, orders were given to the local Ukrainians to transport the survivors to the county town of Rohatyn and to bury the dead. The bodies were placed in three mass graves in one corner of the cemetery. Three concave areas mark the spot today. The village of Ludwikówka is no more.

Rather than wait, one of Emilia's brothers stopped a young Ukrainian on the road and asked him for transport to Rohatyn. With tears in his eyes, this good-hearted Ukrainian said that he would gladly take the family as far as Bursztyn. But he would not take them to Rohatyn (17 kilometers from Bursztyn) because the road to that town led through several Ukrainian villages where death awaited them all. He encouraged them to pack such provisions as they would need for their journey and helped them with the task himself. He then transported them to their acquaintances in Bursztyn: Anna (née Lytvyniuk, a Ukrainian) married to Wojciech Stasik (a Pole). With his father's help, the young Ukrainian made a second trip to retrieve the rest of their provisions. They stayed with the Lytvyniuks (Anna's parents) by night for over a week, and after Anna and Wojciech moved to central Poland, they stayed in the Stasik house with Wojciech's old mother until June 29, 1944, that is, until the time when they were loaded on a train and transported to the village of Czudec near Rzeszów. From Czudec, Emilia came to Canada alone in 1964.

At this point of the story, Magda, a young Polish university student who had been assigned to assist me while I was in Toronto and who had been listening to *Pani* Emilia's story, perked up a bit and said, "I am from Rzeszów too." I had invited her to sit in on our interview with a purpose in mind, and I was happy to see that Emilia oriented herself mostly to her younger counterpart throughout the interview. I now wonder what exactly this young woman had learned from that intense session. It is a part of her country's history that she had never heard about in any classroom in Poland.[2]

Tarnopol Province

Adela Katarzyna Socha (née Zacharko) was born on October 10, 1935, in the village of Boków, the county of Podhajce, the province of Tarnopol.[3] On February 11, 1944, as family and friends gathered at the home of Karol and Marcelina Szymkowicz to celebrate someone's birthday, they were informed by one of the residents, Kazimierz Kołaczkowski, that he had heard that trouble was brewing and that they should be on the lookout. As a precaution, the men placed a few guards in the perimeter of the property, but the folks continued their celebration. By that time, such warnings came often and besides, the Szymkowicz house was probably the safest place in the entire area in which to be in case of trouble. It was a sturdy brick structure with a fire-proof tin roof, a stone wall, and a locked gate. The windows were grated. People often spent the night there in situations such as this.

Just before midnight, Adela recalled, someone ran inside and shouted that the home of one of the neighbors, Adam Cywiński, was on fire. Needless to say, the party came to an abrupt end as the hosts and guests hurriedly began to make what preparations they could for the expected onslaught. The Ukrainian Nationalists, meanwhile, broke through the fence gate and entered the courtyard.

"*Panowie*," they said in sterling Polish. "Please come outside. Nothing will happen to you."

Since their polite demand went unanswered, they broke down the front door and made their way to the locked and barricaded doorway leading to the attic, where by this time everyone had gathered. To force them out, a fire was started in the hallway. As the smoke thickened, those inside began to hack their way out through the tin roof, the only escape route left. Among those who found themselves on top of the house was Adela's mother, Eugenia, who, being afraid to jump, was pushed off the roof by her husband, Wiktor. She fell into the waist-deep snow, and as she scrambled to make her way to the orchard, she was shot. Wiktor then yanked Adela up through the rafters and in the process was himself mortally wounded. Adela was also shot and fell onto the roof. The dum-dum, a flat soft-nosed bullet engineered to explode upon contact, left a large, jagged wound in her arm. There she lay throughout the horror of the night — an eight-year-old child, orphaned so cruelly and suddenly, and in undescribable pain.

In all, 39 persons perished in that UPA attack in Boków. Their names appear in one of the issues of *Na Rubieży*.[4] In his work *Oko w oko z banderowcami (Eye to Eye with the Banderowcy)* Stanisław Jastrzębski describes the attack as follows:

> When the entreaties [for the occupants to leave the building] failed, they [the UPA] brought straw and set it on fire in front of the door. To make it even more effective, gasoline and kerosene were poured on the straw. The billowing smoke forced the occupants to flee the house. The desperate shrieks of the women and children had no effect on the Banderowcy.
>
> The people went mad. They tried to free themselves from that hell. Since the doorway was blocked by the fire, they sought escape through the roof and attic windows. The women who had to jump with infants in their arms were in a state of shock; their pleas were in vain. Those who remained on the roof saw how those who had jumped were axed to death and either thrown into the flames, or strewn about the courtyard and along the road leading to the house.[5]

When peace returned to Boków, Adela Zacharko, still on the roof, heard the voice of her father's cousin, Adela Szymkowicz, calling out if anyone was still alive. Having survived the attack, she and her sister Anna, who was slightly wounded, were now looking for other survivors. Hearing a familiar voice, Adela Zacharko answered that she was on the roof and jumped into the snow when told to do so by her 20-year-old cousin. At the break of day, she and Aleksander (Oleś) Pilichowski — a seven- or eight-year-old boy who survived a throat-slashing — were taken by the cousins to the house of Adela Zacharko's grandfather.

When Marcelina Zacharko saw her granddaughter's and Oleś's predicament, she immediately went to the Ukrainian *wójt* and demanded a police escort to the hospital in Podhajce. The *wójt*, evidently sympathetic to the Poles, obliged. Under police escort, they all arrived safely in Pohdajce and were met at the hospital by a resident employee from Boków, Wiktor Jaźwiński. It was Dr. Ferenc, the family doctor, who amputated Adela's arm.

"And to think," she remembered him saying, "that six years ago I vaccinated you on the thigh so as not to disfigure that arm!"

This particular hospital consisted of four wings, three of which were reserved for German casualties and the fourth for civilians and occasional AK members — never, of course, identified as such.

At this time, Podhajce was caught in a game of see-saw between Soviet and German troops. Once, when the Germans reoccupied it, the Ukrainian Nationalists struck again (either in March or more likely April 1944) to finish off the survivors of their previous attacks now convalescing in the hospital. During that siege Wiktor Jaźwiński and Sister Janina, the head nurse in the hospital, gathered all their patients (predominantly children) into one room, barricaded the door, and began to pray.

As the Ukrainian Nationalists hacked away at the door, shots rang out in the rear of the hospital and shouts were heard in the Russian language. Under Soviet threat, the UPA abandoned its attack and retreated. Adela remembers clearly that their rescuers, and in particular the captain of this Soviet scouting party, were ecstatic to find them all still alive. She also remembers that the captain not only gave them food, but also money (rubles) as well. And so Adela was saved for the second time.

After this incident, Adela and the other children were taken to an orphanage in Podhajce by Sister Janina of the Congregation of Franciscan Sisters of the Family of Mary. Due to the constant threat from Ukrainian Nationalists, the head nun of the orphanage, Sister Helena Chmielewska, decided to evacuate her young charges — which included at least two Jewish children[6] whose names Adela could recall — to Lwów. This proved to be a difficult task, however, since the Ukrainian Nationalists attacked every train suspected of evacuating Polish refugees to the west, and there were many of them. (What does this tell us about the claim on the part of current OUN-UPA apologists who maintain that the objective of the OUN-UPA was not to exterminate the Poles but only to drive them out, to "de-Polonize" "Western Ukraine"?) Even the trip to the train station had to be carefully planned: members of the group were driven there two at a time so as to make it appear that they were ordinary families on normal trips. Once in the station, the children and the nuns were placed in the basement and told to wait without making any sounds whatsoever.

Fortunately, both the stationmaster and the engineer were Polish, and they had worked out a system of communication just for such occasions. The engineer would telegraph ahead and ask if everything was in order. The response "All is quiet" meant that there were refugees to be picked up, but the train would never stop. It would only slow down at the station, thus enabling the refugees to jump onto the passing freight cars.

With children, however, this tack was simply out of the question. The solution was provided by the stationmaster. Gathering some young men for the purpose, he wrapped the 15 children and the four nuns in heavy blankets. As the train slowed by the station, he tossed them into the open cars like so many sacks of potatoes. Thus, their lives were snatched from the hands of their determined would-be murderers for the third time.

They arrived in Lwów on June 13, 1944. Once there, Adela remembered her grandmother's address, written down for her on a playing card while she was at the Podhajce hospital by Antonina Szymbowicz, a nurse in the AK wing of the hospital. "Remember this address! Remember this address! Remember this address!" Antosia told her. And Adela did.

About a month later Adela was told that the Mother General of the Congregation was planning to take the orphans to a small village in Poland near Kraków. She decided to go with them. In December 1945 her uncle found her and took her to Bytom in Upper Silesia, where she was finally able to rejoin her mother's family.

Today Adela lives on a steep slope overlooking the Tappanzee Bridge in Upper Grandview, New York, where she is a practicing psychotherapist. As I left her home, without thinking I gave her a tight embrace from the left side, an embrace that she could not reciprocate. As I embarked on my five-hour trip back to New Hampshire, I wondered about Adela, the orphaned girl and the woman, and her mother, still lying in Boków in the white snow besmirched with blood, and her father, still lying there on the cold tin roof of the Szymkowicz residence. And I wondered how many other Zacharko families there are in the world whose heart-wrenching stories will never be told. And I wondered about the enormity of that tragic story of war-torn Eastern Poland and about man's inhumanity to man.[7]

Appendix C: Excerpts from Documents

UKRAINIAN

Osyp Dumyn's June 17, 1926, Report, "Die Warheit über die ukrainische Organisation (The Truth About the Ukrainian [UVO] Organization)," to the German Ministry of Foreign Affairs

The mission of the UVO was to conduct an incessant and uncompromising war with Poland. The objectives of the UVO were to destroy Polish rule in all Ukrainian spheres, to undermine Polish national influence, to effect the material and moral annihilation of the Polish national organs of authority, and finally to attain and institutionalize its own independent Ukrainian nation. In the course of the first two years of the existence of the UVO, this work unfolded according to plan, the proof of which were many deeds.

By instituting its own detachments, the UVO was to create a real, although secret, Ukrainian army which could at the appropriate moment initiate an open war against the Polish occupant.

Source: Osip Dumin [Osyp Dumyn], "Prawda o Ukraińskiej Organizacji," written in May 1926, received in Berlin on June 17, 1926, trans. from German, *Zeszyty Historyczne* (Paris) 30 (1974): 104.

Great Commandments of the Revolutionary-Fighter

1. Never do anything that may benefit the enemy.
2. Always and everywhere do what will bring harm to the enemy.
3. Consolidate your spiritual and physical forces.
4. A struggle without arms must be waged not only by individual groups of revolutionary-fighters but also by the entire people. The revolutionary-fighters are only the advance guard in this protracted conflict.

Source: Surma, March 2, 1927, quoted in Alexander J. Motyl, "Ukrainian Nationalist Political Violence in Inter-War Poland, 1921-1939," *East European Quarterly* 19 (March 1985): 53.

Decalogue (Dekaloh)

1. Attain a Ukrainian State or die in battle for It.
2. Do not allow anyone to defame the glory or the honor of Your Nation.
3. Remember the Great Days of our efforts.
4. Be proud of the fact that you are an heir of the struggle for the glory of Volodymyr's [St. Vladimir's] Trident.

5. Avenge the death of Great Knights.
6. Do not speak of the cause with whomever possible, but only with whomever necessary.
7. Do not hesitate to commit the greatest crime, if the good of the Cause demands it.
8. Regard the enemies of Your Nation with hate and perfidy.
9. Neither requests, nor threats, nor torture, nor death can compel You to betray a secret.
10. Aspire to expand the strength, riches, and size of the Ukrainian State even by means of enslaving foreigners.

Source: Alexander J. Motyl, *The Turn to the Right: The Ideological Origins and Development of Ukrainian Nationalism, 1919-1929* (Boulder, CO: East European Monographs, 1980), p. 142. These ten commandments, composed by Stepan Lenkavskyi, were used as a set of guidelines by the Union of Ukrainian Nationalist Youth (SUNM) established in 1926. This "Decalogue," with some modifications, was adopted by the First Congress of Ukrainian Nationalists at their conference in Vienna in 1929 as the creed of the OUN (i.e., OUN members were required to swear by it). The modifications were: the addition of Dmytro Dontsov's invocation ("I, the ancient elementary Spirit, who rescued you from the Tartar deluge and placed you on the border between two worlds to create new life:"); the replacement of the word "efforts" by the phrase "struggle for freedom" in commandment no. 3; and the deletion of the phrase "even by means of enslaving foreigners" in commandment no. 10.

First Congress of Ukrainian Nationalists (also called the First Great Conference of Ukrainian Nationalists — Velykyi Zbir Ukrainskykh Natsionalistiv, or VZUN), Vienna, January 28-February 3, 1929

Proclamation: Only the complete removal of all occupants from Ukrainian lands will create the possibility for an expansive development of the Ukrainian people in the borders of their own nation. Rejecting the orientation on historical enemies of the Ukrainian Nation, but remaining in alliance with the nations that are hostilely disposed toward the occupants, the national dictatorship that will be created in the course of a national revolution will guarantee, in difficult times, the might of the Ukrainian Nation....

In its internal political activity, the Ukrainian nation will strive to attain borders encompassing all Ukrainian ethnographic territories and to ensure appropriate economic self-sufficiency and strategic security....

In recognition of these principles, the Organization of Ukrainian Nationalists opposes all party and class groupings and will strive, by bringing under its control the whole of Ukrainian life in all Ukrainian lands and abroad, to expand the Ukrainian-nationalist forces as much as possible and to guarantee the great Ukrainian Nation its rightful place among the other national states.

Resolution: The complete removal of all occupants from Ukrainian lands, which will follow in the course of a national revolution and create the possibility for an expansive development of the Ukrainian people in the borders of their own nation, will be guaranteed only by a system of our own armed military forces and purposeful political alliances.

Source: Petro Mirchuk, *Narys istorii Orhanizatsii Ukrainskykh Natsionalistiv 1920-1939* (München: Ukrainske Vydavnytstvo, 1968), pp. 93, 98, and *Rozbudova natsii* (Prague), no. 3-4, 5, 1929, quoted in Wiktor Poliszczuk, *Integralny nacjonalizm ukraiński jako odmiana faszyzmu*, vol. 1 (Toronto: n.p., 1998), pp. 120, 122.

Novyi Shliakh, January 1939

We acknowledge only one banner; all others must give way because Ukraine is and will be nationalist.... Our program of liberating Western Ukraine and defeating Poland makes us, and only us, the sovereign leaders of the battle in all its stages and leads us directly to power without even any tentative provisions.

For this, a swift and certain victory is needed.... We persuade or annihilate.

Source: *Novyi Shliakh* (Winnipeg), (January, 1939), quoted in Ryszard Torzecki, *Kwestia ukraińska w polityce III Rzeszy 1933-1945* (Warszawa: Książka i Wiedza, 1972), p. 178.

Second Congress of Ukrainian Nationalists (also called the Second Great Conference of Ukrainian Nationalists, or VZUN) in Rome, August 26-27, 1939

Ukraine for Ukrainians. We will not leave one inch of Ukrainian land in the hands of enemies and foreigners.... Only blood and iron will decide between us and our enemies.

Source: Petro Mirchuk, *Narys istorii Orhanizatsii Ukrainskykh Natsionalistiv 1920-1939* (München: Ukrainske Vydavnytstvo, 1968), p. 581.

Second Congress of the OUN-B (also called the Second Great Conference of the Organization of Ukrainian Nationalists, or VZOUN) in Kraków, April 1941

The Jews in the U.S.S.R. constitute the most faithful support of the ruling Bolshevik regime and the vanguard of Muscovite imperialism in the Ukraine. The Muscovite-Bolshevik government exploits the anti-Jewish sentiments of the Ukrainian masses to divert their attention from the true cause of their misfortune and to channel them in time of frustration into pogroms on Jews. The OUN combats the Jews as the prop of the Muscovite-Bolshevik regime and simultaneously it renders the masses conscious of the fact that the principal foe is Moscow.

Source: *UPA v svitli nimetskykh dokumentiv* (Toronto: Litopys UPA, 1983), 41, quoted in Philip Friedman, "Ukrainian-Jewish Relations during the Nazi Occupation," in Michael R. Marrus, ed., *The Nazi Holocaust: Historical Articles on the Destruction of European Jews. Vol. 5, Public Opinion and Relations to the Jews in Nazi Europe*, vol. 1 (Westport, CT: Meckler, 1989), 364. Also in Roman Drozd, *Ukraińska Powstańcza Armia. Dokumenty—Struktury* (Warszawa: Burchard Edition, 1998), pp. 33-34.

Note Signed by the Bandera Group

Long live a greater independent Ukraine without Jews, Poles, and Germans; Poles behind the River San, Germans to Berlin, and Jews to the gallows.

Source: Einsatzgruppen report, July 16, 1941, quoted in Yitzhak Arad et al., eds., *Einsatzgruppen Reports: Selections from the Dispatches of the Nazi Death Squads' Campaign Against the Jews, July 1941-January 1943* (New York: Holocaust Library, 1989), p. 210. OUN's negative disposition toward the Jews was reflected in its numerous articles published throughout the war. The Jews were hated by the Ukrainian Nationalists not only because they were regarded as "the most faithful support of the ruling Bolshevik regime and the vanguard of Muscovite imperialism in the Ukraine" but also because they were Jews and "foreigners." On July 10, 1941, OUN-M and other nationalist groups pledged Hitler their "most loyal obedience" in creating a Europe "free of Jews, Bolsheviks, and plutocrats." From an Einsatzgruppen report of July 7, 1941, quoted in Alexander Dallin, *German Rule in Russia, 1941-1945: A Study of Occupation Policies*, 2d ed. (London: Macmillan, 1981), p. 121, n. 3.

Instruction of OUN Provid to Local Organizations, July 1941

All attempts at indirect or direct sabotage, disobedience to the authorities, and actions directed against the Ukrainian State are to be punished most severely on the spot.

Organization of Ukrainian Nationalists

Source: Central State Archives of the October Revolution, Organs of State Government and State Management of the Ukrainian SSR, fund 4620, invt. 3, file 378, p. 52, quoted in Yu. Yu. Kondufor et al., eds., *History Teaches a Lesson*, trans. from Russian by Vadim Piatkovsky (Kiev: Politvidav Ukrainy, 1986), p. 219.

Items 22 and 27 of the April 1942 Second OUN-B Conference

[Missing. The proceedings of this conference — with the exception of these two, probably incriminating, items — have been published. Item 23 refers of the necessity of controlling the impulse of the Ukrainian masses from carrying out spontaneous actions against the Germans. Item 26 foresees the necessity "to conduct war against the nationalistic tendencies of the Poles and their appetites regarding Western Ukrainian lands."]

Source of quote: OUN v svitli postanov Velykykh Zboriv, Konferentsii ta inshykh dokumentiv z borotby 1929-1955 (München, 1955), p. 70, quoted in Wiktor Poliszczuk, *Legal and Political Assessment of the OUN and UPA*, English trans. by Tadeusz Piotrowski (Toronto: n.p., 1997), p. 34.

Third Conference of the OUN-B, February 17-21, 1943

Point 12, no. 2. We conduct a fight to inaugurate a Ukrainian-Nationalist Revolution that, at the moment of crisis [Stalingrad] in the present war, will lead to the removal of the occupants from Ukraine.

Source: Wiktor Poliszczuk, *Fałszowanie historii najnowszej Ukrainy* (Warszawa-Toronto: n.p., 1996), p. 80.

UPA Military Activity, March 1943

In March 1943 a UPA unit liberated 40 prisoners in Łuck. They all joined the UPA....
    UPA operations in the Krzemieniec region.... In the Szumsk area, the Polish colony in the village of Kuty was burned (86 farmsteads) and the people were liquidated for collaborating with the Gestapo and the German authorities....
    UPA operations in the Dubno region.... In the Werba area, the Polish colony of Nowa Nowina [?] (40 farmsteads) was burned for collaborating with the German authorities. The people were liquidated....
    UPA operations in the Kostopol region. Near the village of Biczal [?] in the Deraźne area, an encounter took place between a UPA unit and the German police consisting of 200 persons. The enemy scattered in panic leaving a great number of weapons and much ammunition behind. The [German] losses were two killed and seven wounded. The UPA unit did not record any losses. The captured [German] soldiers were released. For active collaboration with the Germans, the Polish colony in this same village was annihilated.

Source: Kiev archives, quoted in Grzegorz Motyka, "Ukraińska orientacja," *Karta* (Warszawa) 23 (1997): 54-55. The bracketed question marks are Motyka's. This document is one of 15 cited by Motyka in the second part ("Niemcy a UPA: Dokumenty," pp. 54-73) of his article. The note on page 54 states that these documents come predominantly from the Central National Archive of the Higher Organs of Government and Administration of Ukraine (TsDAVOVU), set 3833, invt. 164, as well as the Central National Archive of Social Organizations of Ukraine (TsDAHOU), set 4628, invt. 1, vol. 10. Many of these documents contain references to the Ukrainian-Nationalist atrocities against the Polish people. Excerpts from the Polish and German documents found in Motyka's article have been included under the respective headings ("Polish," "German") in this appendix. The Ukrainian documents (excerpts) appear below in proper chronological order.

OUN Order to Vacate Official Posts and Police, April 4, 1943

TO UKRAINIANS IN OFFICIAL POSTS AND THE POLICE

In consideration of the political situation brought about by the Germans that could eliminate the intelligentsia and leadership of the Ukrainian nation, the OUN orders [all persons] to immediately vacate their present posts, link themselves up with the OUN, and disappear in the territory. Whoever does not leave his position by April 15 and does not come to an understanding in this matter with the OUN will be punished in the revolutionary manner.

4.IV.1943

Glory to the Ukraine
Glory to the Heroes
Iaroslav Chornomorets

Source: Mikołaj Siwicki, *Dzieje konfliktów polsko-ukraińskich* vol. 2 (Warszawa: n.p., 1992), p. 111.

OUN-B Mobilization Order, April 5, 1943

TO ALL UKRAINIANS WHO HAVE LEFT THEIR POSTS AND ARE WANDERING AT LARGE

It has been ascertained that many Ukrainians who have left the police and civil service have not joined the OUN and are sitting quietly at home or wandering about the territory not realizing the gravity of the moment.

Therefore, the OUN decrees that:

All Ukrainians who have left the police and civil service and are wandering about the territory should immediately join the OUN and submit themselves to its orders.

After April 20 the OUN will catch and shoot as deserters all those who will be wandering about the territory.

5.IV.1943

Glory to Ukraine!
Glory to the Heroes!
Iaroslav Chornomorets
Okr. Dca. OUN

Source: Antoni Szcześniak and Wiesław Szota, *Droga do nikąd: Działalność Organizacji Ukraińskich Nacjonalistów i jej likwidacja w Polsce* (Warszawa: Ministerstwo Obrony Narodowej, 1973), p. 482.

Blank Mobilization Card from Wołyń

MOBILIZATION CARD

Ukrainian Insurgent Army, Eneia Group, no. _____ Mobilization Card
Last name _____ first name _____ village _____ region _____
Calls you into the ranks of the Ukrainian Insurgent Army (UPA). On _____, 1943, you are to report to the designated place as specified by the bearer of this card. In the event you do not fulfill this order, you will be subject to the Revolutionary Court of the UPA.
Given _____, 1943.

Glory to Ukraine!
Glory to the Heroes!
Leader of Group UPA — Eneia

Source: National Archive of the Rivne Oblast (Derzhavnyi Arkhiv Rivnenskoi Oblasti, henceforth: DARO), f. R-30, op. 2, spr. 15, ark. 51, quoted in Wiktor Poliszczuk, *Pojęcie Integralnego Nacjonalizmu Ukraińskiego* (Warszawa: n.p., 1997), p. 25.

Litopys UPA on the Destruction of Janowa Dolina (April 23, 1943)

About two-thirds of the buildings were burned during the capture of a strong Polish nest, or rather a Polish center, in Janowa Dolina in the county of Kostopol. The battle lasted several hours. Poles list their losses at 500. The number of Germans killed is unknown. Our losses were minimal.

Source: Peter Potichnyj and Ievhen Shtendera, eds., *Litopys Ukrainskoi Povstanskoi Armii*, vol. 5 (Toronto: Vydavnytstvo Litopys UPA), p. 20, quoted in Władysław Filar, ed., *Przed akcją "Wisła" był Wołyń* (Warszawa: Światowy Związek Żołnierzy Armii Krajowej, Okręg Wołyń, 1997), p. 31. Janowa Dolina was attacked on April 23, 1943.

Secret Directive Issued and Signed by Roman Dmytro Klachkivskyi ("Klym Savur," "Okhrym," "Klym," "Krymskyi," "Omelian") Commander of UPA "Pivnych," June 1943

We should undertake the great action of the liquidation of the Polish element. We should take advantage of the occasion, before the German forces withdraw, to liquidate the entire Polish population from 16 to 60.... We cannot lose this battle and without counting the cost we should diminish the Polish strength. Forest villages and those near forests should disappear from the face of the earth.

Source: Archive of the Security Service of Ukraine, Volyn Oblast (Sluzhba Bezpeky Ukrainy Oblast Volynskyi, henceforth: SBUOV), directive no. 11315, vol. 1, part 2, p. 16, quoted in Władysław Filar, ed., *Przed akcją "Wisła" był Wołyń* (Warszawa: Światowy Związek Żołnierzy Armii Krajowej, Okręg Wołyń, 1997), p. 33.

Report of Iurii Stelmashchuk ("Rudyi," "Kaidash"), Commander of UPA "Turiv" Region, to Mykola Lebed ("Maksym Ruban"), June 24, 1943

Drukh Ruban!

I wish to inform you that in June 1943 the representative of the Central Provid, the leader of UPA "Pivnych" [North, or the northern region], "Klym Savur," imparted to me a secret directive in the matter of a complete, universal, physical liquidation of the Polish people.... To fulfill this directive please prepare yourself in earnest for the action against the Poles, and I am appointing the following responsible persons: in the Burzany region, battalion leader "Lysyi"; in the Turzysk, Owadno, Oździutycze regions and the rest, "Sosenko"; in the Kowel region, "Holobenko."

Glory to Ukraine!
Commander of UPA "Turiv"—"Rudyi"
June 24, 1943, Stavka

Source: SBUOV, directive no. 11315, vol. 1, part 2, p. 16, quoted in Władysław Filar, ed., *Przed akcją "Wisła" był Wołyń* (Warszawa: Światowy Związek Żołnierzy Armii Krajowej, Okręg Wołyń, 1997), pp. 33-34.

Taras "Bulba"-Borovets's Open Letter, August 10, 1943

Already during the talks [between Lebed and Borovets], instead of conducting actions in keeping with the agreed-upon course, military units of the OUN [Bandera faction] ... began in a horrid manner to exterminate Polish civilians as well as other minorities.... Can a true revolutionary-statesman submit himself to the leadership of a party which beings the construction of the nation with the extermination of national minorities and the mindless burning of their buildings? Ukraine has more formidable enemies than the Poles.... What are you fighting for? For Ukraine, or for your OUN? For the Ukrainian State, or for the dictatorship in that state? For the Ukrainian people, or only for your party?

Source: Otaman Taras Bulba-Borovets, "Open letter [of August 10, 1943] to members of the Provid of the Organization of Ukrainian Nationalists of Stepan Bandera," *Ukrainskyi Istoryk* 27, no. 1-4 (1990): 114-19.

Pastoral Letter of Metropolitan Andrei Sheptytskyi, August 10, 1943

We even have been witnesses to terrible murders whose perpetrators were young people, committed perhaps with good intentions but with terrible consequences. We sometimes saw people who conveyed to our youth as if orders from national leaders to kill someone for the good of the cause.

Source: Lvivski Visti (August 15-16, 1943), quoted in Wiktor Poliszczuk, *Apokalipsa według Wiktora Ukraińca* (Warszawa-Toronto: n.p., 1996), pp. 104-05.

UPA Field Report, September 10-20, 1943

Information from the field. September 10-20, 1943.... On September 10, 1943, in the village of Bystrzyce in the Ludwipol region, our insurgents ... burned a Polish center to the ground.

Source: DARO, f. R-30, op. 2, spr. 15, ark. 5, quoted in Wiktor Poliszczuk, *Pojęcie Integralnego Nacjonalizmu Ukraińskiego.* (Warszawa: n.p., 1997), pp. 22-23.

UPA (Laidak's) Order No. 4, September 28, 1943

Order No. 4

I order Commander Huk to send two detachments to the Galicja Colony in order to destroy five Polish families living there.

September 28, 1943
Laidak

Soruce: DARO, f. R-30, op. 2, spr. 28, ark. 2, quoted in Wiktor Poliszczuk, *Pojęcie Integralnego Nacjonalizmu Ukraińskiego* (Warszawa: n.p., 1997), pp. 23-24.

UPA ("Lysyi's") Field Report of September 1943 on the Destruction of Ostrówki and Wola Ostrowiecka

On August 29, 1943, I conducted an action in the villages of Wola Ostrowiecka and Ostrówki in the Hołowno region. I liquidated all Poles from young to old. I burned all the buildings and took the possessions and livestock for the needs of the battalion.

Source: SBUOV, directive no. 11315, vol. 1, part 2, p. 16, quoted in Władysław Filar, ed., *Przed akcją "Wisła" był Wołyń* (Warszawa: Światowy Związek Żołnierzy Armii Krajowej, Okręg Wołyń, 1997), p. 34.

UPA ("Lysyi's") Field Report on the destruction of Ziemlica

All the [Ukrainian] residents with their axes and pitchforks from the surrounding territories were brought to the village of Mosur where *Drukh* Zukh explained to them that, under the leadership of his armed unit, they were go to the village of Ziemlica in order to settle accounts with the Poles and demanded that they show no mercy to anyone they find there. The village was surrounded at night; at dawn, all the residents were gathered in the center of the village. The elderly, the children, and the ill who could not walk on their own — these they killed on the spot and threw them into a well. Those gathered in the center of the village were made to dig their own graves. They killed them by hitting them in the head with an axe. Those who attempted to flee were shot. All the residents of Ziemlica were liquidated; their possessions were taken for the needs of the UPA; the buildings were burnt.

Source: SBUOV, d. No. 11315, vol. 1, part 2, p. 30, as quoted in Władysław Filar, *"Burza" na Wołyniu: Z dziejów 27 Wołyńskiej Dywizji Piechoty Armii Krajowej* (Warszawa: Rada Ochrony Pamięci Walk i Męczeństwa, 1997), pp. 51-52.

UPA Field Report, September 1943

The SB conducted a liquidation of enemy activists. Sixty-five communists and about 25 informants and Poles were exterminated.

Source: DARO, f. R-30, op. 2, spr. 35, ark. 9, quoted in Wiktor Poliszczuk, *Pojęcie Integralnego Nacjonalizmu Ukraińskiego* (Warszawa: n.p., 1997), p. 23.

Chronicle of the UPA Kolodzynskyi Unit, November 11, 1943

November 11, 1943. On orders of Commander Laidak, one platoon at the head of the Nedatypolskyi [?] unit is on its way to liquidate the Polish colony of Chwoszczowata. At 10:30 P.M. the 20-man platoon surrounded the colony of Chwoszczowata. The *Lakhy* [Poles] are only equipped with rifles and there weren't many of them. When the Cossacks began to encircle the colony, the *Lakhy* began to return fire, but when they heard machine-gun fire, they began to run away. Orlenko's unit was stationed on the other side to which the *Lakhy* fled. He began to address them in Polish, and they thought that it was their unit. Orlenko says to this one, "Who's shooting?" A big *Lakh*, about 45 years of age, came up and answers, "Don't know, it's probably the Bulbowcy." When he drew nearer and became aware of who it was that he approached, at about six steps he wanted to shoot, but it was too late because he was cut down by a well-aimed bullet from a Medved rifle, but he was only wounded, he began to beg the Cossacks despairingly saying, "Sirs hatchet men, do not shoot." The entire colony was burned down, ten *Lakhy* were killed.

Source: DARO, f. R-30, op. 2, spr. 88, ark. 16, quoted in Wiktor Poliszczuk, *Pojęcie Integralnego Nacjonalizmu Ukraińskiego* (Warszawa: n.p., 1997), p. 23. Bad grammar and run-on sentences are in the original.

OUN Order to SKV Provid Leaders and Administrators, February 9, 1944

OUN. Order to Provid leaders and administrators....

    7. Liquidate all traces of everything that is Polish....

        a) Destroy all walls of churches and other Polish buildings of worship.

        b) Destroy trees growing near homes so that not even a trace remains that anyone had lived there (do not destroy fruit trees by roads).

        c) Before November 25, 1944, destroy all houses which were formerly inhabited by Poles (if Ukrainians are living in the houses, it is imperative that they [the houses] should be taken apart and converted into dugouts); if this is not done, the homes will be burned and the people who live in them will have nowhere to spend the winter. We call your attention once more to the fact that if anything whatsoever remains that is Polish, the Poles will have claims to our lands.

        Postii [Stopover].
        February 9, 1944
        Mandrivnyk

Source: DARO, f. R-30, op. 2, spr. 16 ark. 95, quoted in Wiktor Poliszczuk, *Pojęcie Integralnego Nacjonalizmu Ukraińskiego* (Warszawa: n.p., 1997), p. 24; and "OUN i UPA u druhii svitovii viini," *Ukrainskyi Istorychnyi Zhurnal* no. 5 (1995): 105-07, quoted in Grzegorz Motyka, "Od Wołynia do akcji 'Wisła,'" *Więź*, no. 3, 473 (March 1998): 116-17.

From an article by Iaroslav Halan, March 24, 1944

For the second year in a row, Wołynian soil flows with streams of hot, human blood. For the second year in a row, such occurrences transpire there as would turn the hair of young maidens grey. Armed from head to toe bands of Ukrainian Hitlerites surround Polish villages at dawn, burn homes, and axe the people fleeing from the burning huts. They do this carefully, solicitously, so that not a single soul would survive the terrible slaughter.

    And not only Polish villages. At the hands of the yellow-blue Hitlerites already perished thousands of Ukrainian peasants suspected of having sympathy for the partisans and the Red Army. In a single night the Hitlerite Ukrainians butchered the entire population of a village near Rożyszcze — 800 people.

Source: Iaroslav Halan, "Na dnie," *Wolna Polska* (Moscow), no. 11/52, March 24, 1944, quoted in Antoni Szcześniak and Wiesław

Szota, *Droga do nikąd: Działalność Organizacji Ukraińskich Nacjonalistów i jej likwidacja w Polsce* (Warszawa: Ministerstwo Obrony Na-rodowej, 1973), p. 170. See also n. 84. Halan, a Ukrainian communist, was axed to death by the UPA on October 24, 1949.

Orest Karat's Special Instructions, April 6, 1944

Strictly secret   Glory to Ukraine

Special Instructions

I order you to conduct a cleansing of the Polish element and Ukrainian-Bolshevik agents in your region without delay. This cleansing is to be carried out in the areas which are scarcely settled by Poles. To this end, you are to create a combat unit consisting of our members whose task will be to liquidate the above-mentioned elements. The larger areas will be cleansed of this element by our army units even in broad daylight.

As I stated in my order of April 5, I now remind you once more to acquaint yourselves systematically with your territory so that you may be able to track down the Bolshevik bands. You must send a courier with a report to our unit daily. If no manoeuvres take place, we want to know this as well. These daily reports are to be sent to Sokal in care of comrade (*drukh*) Orel. The reports should provide answers to the following questions:

1. The place where the Bolshevik band is quartered.
2. The length of its stay and where it came from.
3. The numerical strength of the band.
4. The type of heavy weapons it possesses.
5. The direction in which it departed and where it came from.

All members, including the youth and women, are to be mobilized in the interest of performing this task. All instructions are to be fulfilled precisely and immediately. Why do you continually neglect to do this? The cleansing of the territory must be completed before our Easter so that we can celebrate it without the Poles. Remember that if the Bolsheviks find us on our lands together with the Poles, they will murder us. [This sentence is meant to play on the Ukrainian fears that after the arrival of the Soviet forces the Poles would inform on them to the NKVD (Soviet Secret Police) for welcoming the German armies in 1941.] Act quickly and intelligently. In this matter we have the full backing of the Germans. There is no need to exercise caution to the detriment of action. Why don't you ever inform me about fulfilling the orders and various instructions that I send you? After fulfilling every order, a report must be submitted specifying the dates and other pertinent information. I want to have it all.

Send me detailed information about the cleansing, how it is being conducted in your territory. The 10th [of April] is approaching, and I remind you about the monthly reports. Do not send me statistical reports until I order otherwise. Inform me in detail about Polish manoeuvres and their evacuation of our territories. Conduct a hard battle with them without pardon. Spare no one. In the case of mixed marriages, drag the Poles out of the house but do not liquidate the Ukrainians and children in these homes. I remind you once more that this has to be done before our holidays.

Retrieve all your weapons and ammunition because they are now needed. Do not let the weapons lie in your attics. This is, after all, a revolution, and it has reached a high degree [of development] throughout the entire land.

Take out your weapons. Death to the Poles.

Glory to the heroes!
Postii. April 6, 1944
Orest Karat (—)

P.S. Forward immediately all statistical reports to Orel's unit. Inform me immediately about every movement of armed people. Do not warehouse those persons capable of bearing arms.

Source: Kiev archives, quoted in Grzegorz Motyka, "Ukraińska oriеntacja," *Karta* (Warszawa) 23 (1997): 65-66.

Political Report for the Period of April 7-15, 1944

Sokal region

... Poles. The Poles are the worst plague in the territory. They serve all the devils in the world in order to destroy the Ukrainians. They join up with the Bolshevik partisans and, through the Volksdeutsche [ethnic Germans living as nationals in nations other than Germany], they assist the Germans through various denunciations. Last month they endeavored to extend their imperialism and to secure it in the Chełm area. They burned either entirely or partially 30 Ukrainian villages and murdered 3,000 Ukrainian people, predominantly women and children. Their bandit-like exploits in the Chelm region were halted by our military units, UPA-Z [UPA-North] and UPA-S [UPA-East], and by the (smaller) self-defense units. The anti-Polish action conducted in Galicia has forced the Poles into the towns where, under the protection of the Germans and the gendarmerie, they are forming fighting units. Only our concerted action in that sector can drive them out of the towns. The Poles who remain are beginning to convert to the Greek Catholic [Uniate] faith. The cleansing of the territory is made more difficult in the zone of war activity.

Source: Kiev archives, quoted in Grzegorz Motyka, "Ukraińska orientacja," *Karta* (Warszawa) 23 (1997): 66-67. The passage dealing with the Chełm region in this report refers to the Polish offensive action of March 1944, when the AK attempted to prevent the repetition of Wołyń's tragedy in the Chełm region. In the course of the offensive, over 20 Ukrainian villages were burned (e.g., Sahryń, Bereść, Łasków) and over 1,000 Ukrainians perished. Although AK orders forbade the killing of civilians, excesses no doubt did occur.

Excerpts from UPA Field Reports, May 1, 1944

May 1, 1944

On March 16, 1944, Group "L" and Group "Garkusha" of 30 men exterminated 25 people and burned down a house in Solotvino.

On March 17, 1944, Group "L" and the district combat team carried out an action in the village of Nadorozhye by Tovmach. Thirty men were annihilated. Houses weren't set on fire but were destroyed.

On March 19, 1944, Group "L" and the district combat team carried out an action in the village of Bogorodchik. Fifty farmsteads were burned down and 46 persons killed.

On March 27, 1944, Group "L" and the district combat team of 23 men carried out an action in the village of Zelenovka (Tovmachina). Thirteen farmsteads were burned down and 16 persons killed.

On March 28, 1944, the group commanded by Sulima numbering 30 men annihilated 18 persons and burned down 4 houses in the settlement of Zhebrach (Volosov).

On March 29, 1944, Group "L" carried out an action in the village of Baby (Otiniyshe). Twenty-four farmsteads were burned down, nobody was killed because all people had taken to the woods. The purpose of the action was to punish the local population for threatening to fight all nationalists by joining hands with the Bolsheviks after their comeback.

On March 29, 1944, the group commanded by Semen annihilated 12 persons and burned down 18 farmsteads in Pererosl. Another 6 farmsteads were burned on the same evening.

On March 29, 1944, the district combat team burned down 12 farmsteads and killed 3 persons in the village of Grabovets (Bogorodchany). The rest of the inhabitants had left the locality before the action.

On March 30, 1944, the group commanded by Zheleznyak burned down 30 farmsteads and killed 11 people in the village of Tarnovka Lesnaya.

On April 5, 1944, the district group under Zheleznyak carried out an action in Porogy and Yablonka. Six houses were burned down and 15 persons annihilated.

On April 6, 1944, the group under Zheleznyak killed 14 people and destroyed 6 farmsteads in the village of Rosilnoye.

On April 6, 1944, the group commanded by Zheleznyak carried out an action against the inhabitants of Solotvino. Fifteen farmsteads were destroyed and 9 persons killed.

On April 7, 1944, the group under Zheleznyak killed 5 persons and burned down 2 huts in Zvenyachy.

On April 8, 1944, the detachment under the command of Iskra killed 15 people and burned down a hut in the village of Maidan by Rosilnoye.

On April 9, 1944, the group under Nechai exterminated 25 people in the village of Pasechnaya. The rest were able to flee to Bitkov and Nadvornaya.

On April 9, 1944, the group under Zheleznyak burned down 5 farmsteads and killed 5 people in the villages of Zhuraky and Monasterichy.

On April 11, 1944, the group under Dovbush exterminated 81 people in Rafailov.

On April 16, 1944, the group under Dovbush exterminated 20 persons in the village of Zelenaya.

On April 23, 1944, the groups commanded by Iskra and Komar burned down 16 farmsteads and killed 14 people in the village of Viknyany.

Source: Central State Archives of the October Revolution, Organs of State Government and State Management of the Ukrainian SSR, fund 4620, invt. 3, file 378, pp. 43-44, quoted in Yu. Yu. Kondufor et al., eds., *History Teaches a Lesson*, trans. from Russian by Vadim Piatkovsky (Kiev: Politvidav Ukrainy, 1986), pp. 233-35.

Order from the Main OUN Provid to County Provid Members, May 5, 1944

"Troian," May 5, 1944
Strictly secret
Response to the ORKP Order No. 7/44

To the County Provid Members — Order

... In view of the Polish government's official position in the matter of cooperation with the Soviets, we ought to remove the Poles from our lands. Please understand this in the following way: Give the Poles notices to remove themselves in a course of a few days to their own native lands. If this is not done, send in the fighting units to liquidate the men and burn the houses and landed property (take them apart). I call your attention once more to the procedure of giving the Poles notices to leave the territories and then liquidating them, and not the opposite. (Please pay close attention to this.) In particular, we ought to chase out those Poles in mixed villages who have no intention of assimilating. On the other hand, we ought not touch those who have Ukrainian families and do not lean especially toward the Poles but only profess their religion. Eviction notices can take the form of leaflets (local) without our organizational signature. They should underscore the Polish government's and the people's position [of collaboration with the Soviets] in the territories occupied by the Bolsheviks.

(Forward detailed protocols of anti-Polish actions to the Regional Provid Leaders of the OUN.)

Source: TsDAVOV of Ukraine, set 3833, invt. 1, vol. 3, k. 53, quoted in Grzegorz Motyka, "Ukraińska orientacja," *Karta* (Warszawa) 23 (1997): 71.

Evacuation Injunction

Poles!

You are ordered to leave the Western Ukrainian lands immediately [and go] beyond the San [River].

Whoever does not leave within 48 hours will be liquidated.

Ukrainian Insurgent Army
Postii. April 4, 1944

Source: Jerzy Janicki, *Towarzystwo Weteranów... 2. Alfabet Lwowski* (Warszawa: Polska Oficyna Wydawnicza "BGW," 1994). Photocopy of an original UPA notice in Cyrillic which ordered the Polish people to leave Eastern Galicia or perish. This notice was nailed to the door of Michał Kozar, who saved it.

Evacuation Injunction

Injunction

You are called upon as a Polish family to leave the village within 48 hours and to depart from Ukrainian lands westward beyond the San [River].

In the event that you do not comply with this order, you bring upon yourself a death sentence, and your possessions will be burned.

Postii. May 11, 1944

Source: Biuletyn (Koło Lwowian), 3 (June, 1982): 8. Photocopy of an original Ukrainian-Nationalist notice in Cyrillic.

Evacuation Injunction

Because the Polish government and the Polish people collaborate with the Bolsheviks and are bent on destroying the Ukrainian people on their own land, [name] is hereby called upon to move to native Polish soil within 5 days.

Source: Antoni Szcześniak and Wiesław Szota, *Droga do nikąd: Działalność Organizacji Ukraińskich Nacjonalistów i jej likwidacja w Polsce* (Warszawa: Ministerstwo Obrony Narodowej, 1973), p. 173.

Political Report of June 27, 1944, for the Period June 13–28, 1944

... Poles. There are no Poles in our territory. Only mixed families are left and those who have brought their baptismal certificates to Greek Catholic churches and want to become assimilated. These are ordinary people who have never come out actively as Poles and whose only sign of Polishness was their Roman Catholic religion

The Poles who fled to Sokal are frequently returning to the village with the Volksdeutsche in order to dig out their belongings and, while they are at it, they rob and threaten the Ukrainians.

After the "reception" prepared for them in Komarów on June 15, 1944, the Poles no longer appear in the village. There are Poles from Poznań in the German units. They are very interested in knowing who it was that killed the Poles, and they worry about the fate of the Poles who left the western lands of Ukraine.

Glory to Ukraine!
Ref. Prop. (Robert)
Postii. June 27, 1944
Pow. P. [illegible signature]

Source: Kiev archives, quoted in Grzegorz Motyka, "Ukraińska orientacja," *Karta* (Warszawa) 23 (1997): 72–73.

OUN-B Proclamation

Ukrainian nation!... Know! Moscow, Poland, Hungarians, Jews — these are your enemies. Destroy them!... Your leader is Stepan Bandera.

Source: DARO, f. R-30, op. 1, spr. 19, ark. 26, quoted in Wiktor Poliszczuk, *Pojęcie Integralnego Nacjonalizmu Ukraińskiego* (Warszawa: n.p., 1997), p. 23.

Order to the OUN-B Security Service (SB)

6. Instigate hatred among the people for the Poles (*Lakhy*) and destroy them at every turn.

Source: DARO, f. R-30, op. 2, spr. 15, ark. 53, quoted in Wiktor Poliszczuk, *Pojęcie Integralnego Nacjonalizmu Ukraińskiego* (Warszawa: n.p., 1997), 22.

UPA Field Report — Group Zahrava

UPA, Group Zahrava K.Z.V.N.
Field Report No. 1

Drukh Leader,

I am submitting a field report from the Stolin

region. 1) The general state of affairs in the region is mixed. One encounters traces of cruel terror everywhere on the part of the Germans, the Reds, as well as needless maneuvers on the part of our own (the regional Provid, the underground).... The liquidation of 27 persons in the village of Puznia and a whole series of other liquidations and dirty work carried out at the expense of the Bolsheviks [that is to say, under the pretense of being Bolshevik partisans] were unmasked. This offended the local population and reflected negatively on our work.

Source: DARO, f. R-30, op. 2, spr. 35, ark. 98, quoted in Wiktor Poliszczuk, *Pojęcie Integralnego Nacjonalizmu Ukraińskiego* (Warszawa: n.p., 1997), p. 24.

Chronicle of a UPA Unit

May 26. Nothing has been moved by human hands on the Polish colonies for over a year. Everything is overgrown with luxuriant grass. It's a very sad sight.

Source: DARO, f. R-30, op. 23, spr. 88, ark. 1-48, quoted in Wiktor Poliszczuk, *Pojęcie Integralnego Nacjonalizmu Ukraińskiego* (Warszawa: n.p., 1997), p. 24.

Taras "Bulba"-Borovets's Statement

The officer corps of the new UPA received the following military assignment from Mykola Lebed's party in June 1943: Without delay and as soon as possible conclude the action of completely cleansing the Ukrainian territories of Poles.

Source: Otaman Taras Bulba-Borovets, *Armiia bez derzhavy: Slava i trahediia ukrainskoho povstanskoho rukhu. Spohady* (Winnipeg: Tovarystvo "Volyn," 1981), p. 272.

Court Testimony of Iurii Stelmashchuk ("Rudyi," "Kaidash"),

Commander of the UPA "Turiv" Region, February 20, 1945

In March 1943 I received an order to desist from organizational work and to take up the task of creating the UPA. At that time, the name "UPA" did not exist.... There were units variously named. The UPA finally formed in July 1943.

In June 1943 I was appointed as the leader of a unit which contained 450 persons. That June 1943 I met "Klym Savur." "Klym Savur" gave me an order to exterminate all Poles in the Kowel region. The entire leadership, including myself, protested against this, but "Savur" threatened us with court-martial. The situation was difficult. I did not have the right to refuse to follow an order, but my own convictions did not allow me to fulfill it. I remained in that state until August 1943. While I was conducting the talks, "Holobenko" from my unit burned a Polish colony....

In August 1943 "Savur" and "Oleh" called me to them again and demanded the annihilation of the Poles.... Because to refuse any longer was not possible, I agreed.

I divided the Kowel region into three parts. I appointed "Lysyi" for the Bużanka and Luboml regions, "Sosenko" for the Tur region, and "Holobenko" for the Holoby region. The SB was to undertake the annihilation of Poles in Kowel. This annihilation was to take place from August 25 to August 30, 1943.

The assignment was carried out in all regions except Tur. "Sosenko" appointed "Besket" to carry it out, but he was afraid to engage the Poles, having found out that in the Tur region a unit of Poles consisting of 1,500 people was organized and that they were armed and ready to defend themselves.

In my region about 3,000 Poles were destroyed. In addition, about 1,500 to 2,000 were destroyed by the SB. Thus, in the Kowel region, a total of about 5,000 Poles were destroyed. Naturally, these figures are not exact because we were not allowed to keep statistical records.

We took the possessions and food of those killed for the band; the buildings were burned. The order to burn the buildings came from me.

In October 1943 the commander of the "Pivnych" region, "Klym Savur," came to Wołyń and ordered the destruction of the Poles in the Tur region. I gathered 700 people. But the Poles were not annihilated because the Germans brought 1,500 soldiers into the Tur region....

On August 29 and 30, 1943, in keeping with the order of the leader of the "Oleh" region, together with a unit consisting of 700 armed bandits, I exterminated the entire Polish population to the last person in the territories of Hołoby, Siedliszcze, Maniewicze, and the Luboml region. I confiscated all the movable assets and burned all the immovable ones.

In all, on August 29 and 30, 1945, I butchered and shot over 15,000 civilian residents among whom were the elderly, women, and children.

We did it in this way: We rounded up the entire Polish population in one place, surrounded them, and began the massacre. Next, when not a single person was left alive, we dug mass graves, threw the corpses into it, covered them up and, in order to hide the traces of these terrible grave sites, we set huge fires and went on. In this way, we went from village to village until we exterminated all the people — over 15,000.

Source: "Svidchat dokumenty," *Dialoh* (Lviv), no. 49 (December 1993), quoted in Leon Popek, Tomasz Trusiuk, Paweł Wira, and Zenon Wira, comps., *Wołyński testament* (Lublin: Towarzystwo Przyjaciół Krzemieńca i Ziemi Wołyńsko-Podolskiej, 1997), pp. 170-71.

Court Testimony of Battalion Leader Stepan Koval ("Rubashenko," "Burlak") in the "Zahrava" Region

In the summer of 1943, in keeping with the order of the commander of UPA "Pivnych," "Klym Savur," I conducted an operation of annihilation against the Polish people in the Równe region. The UPA detachment under my command destroyed the villages of Rafałówka and Huta Stepańska inhabited by Polish people. In keeping with the order of "Oleh," the commanders of my companies, "Moroz," "Bohdan," and "Rybak," received orders in the summer of 1943 to liquidate the Polish colonies and the peaceful residents living in them; namely, commander "Moroz" with his UPA company was to destroy the Poles in the Marianówka Colony.... The "Bohdan" company was to liquidate the Polish people in Wólka Kotowska Colony and Aleksandria.... The company of "Rybak" was to liquidate the Polish people in the Zofiówka Colony.... Two days were allotted for this action, and the companies carried out the undertaking. After the action in the above-mentioned colonies were completed, the companies were to proceed to the village of Przebraże in the Kiwerce region in order to participate in the liquidation of the Polish people in that area.

Source: SBUOV, Acts of Court Proceedings Against Stepan Koval, quoted in Władysław Filar, ed., *Przed akcją "Wisła" był Wołyń* (Warszawa: Światowy Związek Żołnierzy Armii Krajowej, Okręg Wołyń, 1997), pp. 34-35.

Court testimony of Ohorodnychuk, a.k.a. Mykola Kvitkovskyi

On the morning of July 12, 1943 [during the "Peter and Paul action"], together with a UPA unit consisting of about 20 persons, I entered the church during the services in Pawłowka [Poryck] in the Iwanicze region and, in the course of 30 minutes, killed the citizens of Polish background. During this action we killed 300 people, among whom were children, women, and the elderly. After killing the people in the church in Pawłowka, I went with the unit to the nearby village of Radowicze as well as the Polish colonies of Sadów and Jeżyny, where I took part in the massive liquidation of the Polish people. In these colonies we killed 180 women, children, and the elderly. All the homes were burned and the possessions and cattle were seized.

Source: SBUOV, Acts of Court Proceedings Against Ohorodnychuk-Kvitkovskyi, quoted in Władysław Filar, ed., *Przed akcją "Wisła" był Wołyń* (Warszawa: Światowy Związek Żołnierzy Armii Krajowej, Okręg Wołyń, 1997), p. 35.

Court Testimony of Mykola Havryliuk ("Fedos," "Arkadii"), Chief of the SB of the OUN Provid in the Kowel Region

In the course of my activity as the commander of the regional SB Provid, under my personal leadership, with the participation of a UPA battalion, the following Polish colonies in the Łuck region were completely annihilated: Kościuszkowo, Ozierany Polskie, Bunasiówka, Antonówka, and others. About 1,000 Poles were killed, and only a small percentage of the people were able to hide and escape to Łuck.

Source: SBUOV, Acts of Court Proceedings Against Mykola Havryliuk, quoted in Władysław Filar, ed., *Przed akcją "Wisła" był Wołyń* (Warszawa: Światowy Związek Żołnierzy Armii Krajowej, Okręg Wołyń, 1997), p. 35.

Court Testimony of Arsenii Bozhevskyi, Member of the SB

During my service in the UPA SB, I personally killed 15 persons. I remember that in July 1943 our unit arrived at the former property of Count Koszewski, where about 100 Poles lived and whom we liquidated without mercy with firearms. We liquidated entire families without sparing the elders, women, or children. The children cried. The women, mothers, begged us to spare the lives of their children. But we paid no attention to these pleas and killed them anyway using firearms and knives. During this action, I personally killed seven people with a rifle.

Source: SBUOV, Acts of Court Proceedings Against Arsenii Bozhevskyi, quoted in Władysław Filar, ed., *Przed akcją "Wisła" był Wołyń* (Warszawa: Światowy Związek Żołnierzy Armii Krajowej, Okręg Wołyń, 1997), p. 35.

UPA Field Reports Regarding the Liquidation of Ukrainians

I

Sentence: June 23, 1943. The Extraordinary Session of the Field Court-Martial of the UPA Group Eneia, having verified the case of Mykola Martynovskyi-"Mukha" from the Berkut unit, states as follows: the accused Mukha was arrested on June 20, 1943, for conducting provocative activity within the ranks of the OUN and UPA from January 18, 1942, to June 20, 1943. After a thorough investigation [lasting two days], it became apparent that Martynovskyi was a provocateur who knew what he was doing. Mykola-Mukha Martynovskyi is condemned to death by beheading in front of the UPA unit.... The sentence was carried out ... in front of the UPA unit at noon on June 24, 1943.

Source: DARO, f. R-30, op. 2, spr. 36, ark. 108, quoted in Wiktor Poliszczuk, *Ukraińskie ofiary OUN-UPA* (Warszawa: n.p., 1998), p. 7 (paper presented at a symposium in Wrocław, July 12, 1998, and subsequently published); and Wiktor Poliszczuk, *Pojęcie Integralnego Nacjonalizmu Ukraińskiego* (Wars-zawa: n.p., 1997), pp. 25-26.

II

[November 27, 1943, "Ozero" region] The SB is working quite hard in dealing with informants, communists, robbers, and those who are harmful to our organizational work — and there are as many of them here as mushrooms after a rain. It cannot keep up with their liquidation.

Source: DARO, f. R-30, op. 2, spr. 22, k. 35, quoted in Wiktor Poliszczuk, *Ukraińskie ofiary OUN-UPA* (Warszawa: n.p., 1998), p. 7.

III

[Notification] For desertion, for not carrying out the orders of their leaders, for disseminating hostile propaganda ... in keeping with the decision of the Ukrainian Revolutionary Court, the following were shot: Vasyl Khropot, Roman Karpiuk, Ivan Korchak, Leon Hubetskyi, Viktor Kolada. They were shot on November 29, 1943. Warning: order and discipline must be maintained in the ranks of the UPA.... Death to all who harm the Ukrainian nation in its revolutionary struggle.

Source: DARO, f. R-30, op. 2, spr. 16, k. 262, quoted in Wiktor Poliszczuk, *Ukraińskie ofiary OUN-UPA* (Warszawa: n.p., 1998), pp. 6-7.

IV

Arrested:	307 persons
a) for communism:	111 persons
b) for informing:	59 persons
NKVD:	67 persons
Families:	70 persons
Total	307 persons

Condemned to death — 306 persons (three hundred six); freed — 1 person (one). All liquidated possessions, after being inventoried, were turned over to the agricultural unit; a part was given to the unit.

Glory to Ukraine!
Postii. May 5, 1944
Glory to the Heroes!
Chornyi

Source: DARO, f. R-30, op. 3, spr. 32, k. 51, quoted in Wiktor Poliszczuk, *Ukraińskie ofiary OUN-UPA* (Warszawa: n.p., 1998), p. 8. This SB report for the "Ozero" region covers the period from January 13 to May 4, 1944.

V

The entire enterprise and the methods of the SB should be conducted in a conspiratorial, secretive way. It is forbidden to leave behind the liquidated corpses or other traces of the work.

May 29, 1944
Cheremshyna

Source: DARO, f. R-30, op. 2, spr. 37, k. 48, quoted in Wiktor Poliszczuk, *Ukraińskie ofiary OUN-UPA* (Warszawa: n.p., 1998), pp. 8-9.

VI

[To Provid and SKV leaders] Various agitators-propagandists of hostile ideas, when they act openly, should be arrested on the spot and publicly liquidated after being subjected to torture.

Postii. November 9, 1944
Mandrivnyk

Source: DARO, f. R-30, op. 2, spr. 16, k. 141, quoted in Wiktor Poliszczuk, *Ukraińskie ofiary OUN-UPA* (Warszawa: n.p., 1998), p. 9.

VII

UPA. Z.G. Postii. November 24, 1944. I report that the following [six Ukrainian names follow] have been punished with the death penalty by shooting [for desertion].

Source: DARO, f. R-30, op. 2, spr. 26, ark. 27, quoted in Wiktor Poliszczuk, *Pojęcie Integralnego Nacjonalizmu Ukraińskiego*, (Warszawa: n.p., 1997), p. 25.

VIII

[Mizocz region] In Nowa Moszczanica the regional SB publicly executed eight peasants suspected of communism.

Source: DARO, f. R-30, op. 2, spr. 39, k. 29, quoted in Wiktor Poliszczuk, *Ukraińskie ofiary OUN-UPA* (Warszawa: n.p., 1998), p. 8.

Court Testimony of Ivan Vasiuk, UPA Member, regarding the Murder of Poles and Ukrainians

We left the bodies of the killed men, women, old people, and children in their homes, which we later set on fire. If Poles and Ukrainians lived together in a given village, and if the Ukrainians did not belong to Banderowcy organizations, we dealt with them the same as with the Poles. Our unit, that is, our company, killed about 1,500 people of all ages in three villages.... The murders were carried out with axes; some were killed with knives. I personally killed 19 people.

Source: TsDAHO of Ukraine, f. 1, op. 70, spr. 237, kk. 1-3, quoted in Wiktor Poliszczuk, *Ukraińskie ofiary OUN-UPA* (Warszawa: n.p., 1998), p. 10.

From the Register Containing the Names of 9,018 Ukrainians Murdered by the OUN-UPA in Wołyń [Volyn], Published by the Rivne [Równe] Archive in 1990-91

Dubno region. On May 11, 1944, at 10:00 P.M., the leader of the village council, Solovei, together with his family, consisting of seven persons, was shot in the village of Diadkiewicze [Diatkowicze, Didowicze]. The corpses were burned in the house, which was set on fire.

On May 13, 1944, Nataliia Mykhailivna Barabash was killed in the village of Iwanie because her husband was conscripted into the Soviet Army. Five SB members from the UPA tormented her.

On June 6, 1944, a pit was discovered in the village of Zarudzie, in which were found 18 local residents murdered by the UPA as enemies.

On the night of August 6, 1944, the band "Viun" murdered two militiamen in the village of Ołyka.

That same night the OUN murdered Hanna Shumylo and her ten-year-old son, Dorofei, together with a seventy-year-old man named Dankevych.

During the first days of August 1944, a UPA band broke into the home of Hofman in the village of Mołodawo-Ukraińskie and robbed him. The homeowner complained to the authorities. Two days later the UPA came back, told everyone in the house to lie down on the floor, and shot them. Only a five-year-old boy, whom Hofman took in as his own, survived.

On July 11, 1944, the regional commandant of the SB. "Mamai," murdered Hanna Bodnarchuk and two of her daughters in an ambush near the village of Wolica.

Source: DARO, f. R-30, op. 2ff, quoted in Wiktor Poliszczuk, *Ukraińskie ofiary OUN-UPA* (Warszawa: n.p., 1998), pp. 9-10. According to these documents, in addition to the Ukrainian victims, approximately 50,000 ethnic Poles were also murdered in Wołyń by the OUN-UPA.

Appeal of the Ukrainian Committee of Wołyń

People come to your senses. What are you doing? The enemy has murdered the Jews using Ukrainian hands. He has shown films of these murders to the world, films in which the Ukrainians are portrayed as the worst despots of all. None of us had protested at that time against these inhuman deeds of murder and pillage. When Jews became scarce, the enemy of the Slavic people—the Russian and German—in order to prevent understanding and cooperation, directed these same heroes against their own and other Slavic nationalities.

The planned murder of Poles is the most monstrous crime of the Ukrainians. How can one not see it, not feel it—and do such great harm to one's own nation; become such a despicable tool of the enemy? By murder, by robbery of neighbor by neighbor, by the burning of villages—we blacken ourselves before the whole world. We dig for ourselves a terrible grave.

Benefiting from our naiveté and our idiocy, one enemy builds a road for a more certain return, while the other lays the groundwork for agitational work.

Thanks to our "partisans," the Germans are strewing bombs on our villages instead of on Orel and Belgorod. Derwań [Dermań], Ludwikówka, and Malińsk-Czeski [Malin Czeski] are burning; Tajkury, Tuliczów, and other villages have already burnt.

In such a way, in the twentieth century, our nation is winning its freedom.

Villagers. Ukrainian intellectuals. Father, talk to your son, and if needs be, do battle with him.

Never again enter on the path of evil along which travels your deluded son. History will neither forget the father nor the foolish son. In a little while, the power of reason and truth will triumph over evil. The Ukrainian Committee of Wołyń, seeing the tragic state of affairs of the Ukrainian people and knowing where it will lead, calls upon all Ukrainians to unite and to turn the whole potential of Your nation in the right direction. History will condemn and curse all those who resort to murder and pillage, irrespective of whether they do so knowingly or not.

Remember, we must emerge out of this war with clean hands; consider the nature of the road that we are building.

Our only way out lies in joining our nearest Slavic peoples in mutual work.

So desist, while there is still time, from this fratricidal slaughter, this vile work.

The good of Your Fatherland demands this of You.

Ukrainian Committee of Wołyń
(—) Grab
(—) Dzhum

Source: CA KC PZPR AM 1640/12 vol. 202/III/132 k. 253, quoted in Władysław Filar, *"Burza" na Wołyniu: Z dziejów 27 Wołyńskiej Dywizji Piechoty Armii Krajowej* (Warszawa: Rada Ochrony Pamięci Walk i Męczeństwa, 1997), pp. 262-63.

OUN Letter to the Military Public Prosecutor's Office in Warsaw, March 19, 1947.

OUR ANSWER

The Polish press, controlled by Bolshevik propaganda instructions and orders, often publishes articles and news reports full of lies about the Ukrainian Insurgent Army and the Ukrainian independence movement in general. The lies promoted most frequently by Bolshevik propaganda in the Polish press against Ukrainian insurgents are as follows:

1) That the Ukrainian independence movement is a fascist movement.
2) That it was pro-German and pro-Hitler, and that it collaborated with the German occupants.
3. That the military operations of the UPA are conducted by German officers.
4) That Ukrainians took part in putting down the Warsaw Uprising.
5) That Ukrainian insurgents murder Poles, burn their villages, and torment the Polish civilian population.

All these accusations are figments of the imagination and lies....

1. The Ukrainian independence movement, manifesting itself mainly in the activities of the UPA, directed and represented by the UHVR [Ukrainska Holovna Vyzvolna Rada, or Ukrainian Supreme Liberation Council], is not and never was a movement of the fascist variety....
2. The Ukrainian independence movement is not and never was pro-German and pro-Hitler. The Ukrainian independence movement, from its very beginning, fought with the German occupation....
3. All accusations that UPA forces are directed by German officers are also fabrications of Bolshevik propaganda. No German officer ever was, or is now, a commander of any UPA unit....
4. The accusation of the alleged participation of Ukrainian units in the quelling of the Warsaw Uprising has not been substantiated by any facts and does not rest on any concrete evidence. The Ukrainian society, therefore, regards this accusation as one of the most vicious lies. As of now, no political Ukrainian activist is aware of any Ukrainian participation in the quelling of the Warsaw Uprising.... We do not know of any Ukrainians who assisted the Germans in the pacification and destruction of Warsaw, and if it turns out that there were such, they were ordinary German lackeys similar to the Polish Volksdeutsche or current individuals or other traitors....
5. One of the most frequently repeated lies in Polish-Bolshevik propaganda is the accusation that the Ukrainian insurgents burn Polish villages and murder Polish people, sparing neither women nor

children. Such claims and even alleged concrete news reports of a similar nature are being carried daily in the Polish press. There is not one iota of truth in these reports.

In the first place, the UPA — although it is a partisan army — attempts to follow all humanitarian rules pertaining to the conduct of war in respect to the soldiers of enemy armies as well as the civilian population. In conjunction with this, the UPA even frees all Soviet and Polish prisoners of war who are not personally guilty of outrages and murders.... All the more so in regard to the civilian population, even those persons sometimes ill-disposed to us. The UPA follows the principle of the greatest tolerance and humanitarianism....

We never engage in terror against anyone anywhere, since we ourselves fight against terror....

The accusation that we are anti-Semitic is also a groundless figment of the imagination. This is another one of those sequential tricks of Bolshevik propaganda. We have never taken part in any anti-Jewish manifestations anywhere. There is not even a trace in our ideology of any Hitlerite racist, misguided, cannibalistic theories.... No one will ever find a single word against the Jews in our newspapers, political brochures, leaflets, or other writing either during the German or the Bolshevik occupation.

Source: Roman Drozd, *Ukraińska Powstańcza Armia. Dokumenty—Struktury* (Warszawa: Burchard Edition, 1998), pp. 199-206.

POLISH

Capt. Mikołaj Kunicki on the Massacre in Wysock in the Second Half of January 1943

In the second half of January 1943, we moved a large amount of arms and ammunition in supply wagons toward Stolin, where we remained for about a week. While there, I received information that some band, probably Soviet, chased the Germans out of the town of Wysock [in Polesie], some 24 km south of Stolin, and that it had murdered civilians. I conducted an investigation. It turned out that the murders were committed by a UPA band. We moved out immediately, encountered the UPA unit and after a short fight took Wysock.

In Wysock I noticed a medical shield with a Polish name on one of the buildings. I entered the building and saw a pile of mutilated corpses of naked and dressed children, women, and men. The floor was covered with dried blood. I encountered the same situation in the homes of other Poles; there were about 30-40 Polish homes in Wysock. I called my company together and explained that the murders were committed by Ukrainian bandits and that we must take action against them. The Ukrainians in our unit did not like what I said. They informed the Germans, and the Germans called a general meeting the next day during which they laid the blame for the murders on the Soviet partisans.

Source: Mikołaj Kunicki, *Pamiętnik "Muchy"* (Warszawa: MON, 1959), p. 17.

Order of Kazimierz Damian Bąbiński ("Luboń"), Commander of the Union for Armed Struggle-Home Army, Wołyń (ZWZ-AK, "Hreczka"), to AK Partisan Units, April 22, 1943

Order No. 2.

A few weeks ago the Polish people in Wołyń became the object of barbaric massive murders perpetrated against entire family units by Ukrainian butchers. I know the hand that pushes the Ukrainian people to this suicidal battle with their co-citizens of Polish origins in this territory which we share in common. I know who benefits from these internal conflicts: the German occupant for whom it becomes easier to enslave the nation when individual groups fight among themselves. The Soviet partisans who operate within the territories of the Second Republic also have an easier time to grasp the leadership role for themselves. Only the Poles and Ukrainians, the custodians of this land, suffer losses. Understandably, I cannot remain neutral to the Ukrainian rape and murder of the Polish people, to the facts that neither women nor children are spared and that farmsteads are burned. A well-focused retaliation has been initiated against the Ukrainian Provid members whose political activity is aimed at agitating the Ukrainian society against their Polish co-citizens in Wołyń. However, this type of retaliation will not protect the Polish people from further murders entirely. In connection with this, I hereby order:

A) The emerging self-defense system in the threatened territories of Wołyń will prevent or at least inhibit the attacks by the butchers. I place the responsibility for undertaking the organization of self-defense measures in the hands of commanders of every rank, but [they should act] without exposing their own underground organizations. As the leadership corps, it is our duty and responsibility to protect the Poles in Wołyń, where Polish blood has been spilled through no fault of ours.

B) I forbid the use of the methods utilized by the Ukrainian butchers. We will not burn Ukrainian homesteads nor kill Ukrainian women and children in retaliation. The self-defense network must protect itself from the aggressors or attack the aggressors but leave the peaceful population and their possessions alone.

C) I forbid any sort of cooperation with the Germans in the interest of self-defense. It is forbidden to join the German militia or any other guard or service units for a mess of porridge disguised as armaments. It is permitted and even mandated to obtain firearms from the Germans, but only in an independent manner if circumstances allow it.

D) I forbid initiating cooperation with the Soviet partisan units. I do not deny them their right to be on our land as long as the war lasts.

"Luboń"

Source: ZWZ-AK Wołyń field report no. 123/III, April 22, 1943. UW library, sygn. 3312, quoted in Władysław Filar, ed., *Przed akcją "Wisła" był Wołyń* (Warszawa: Światowy Związek Żołnierzy Armii Krajowej, Okręg Wołyń, 1997), pp. 50-51. See also "Order of Kazimierz Damian Bąbiński ('Luboń'), Commander of the Union for Armed Struggle-Home Army, Wołyń (ZWZ-AK, 'Hreczka'), to AK Partisan Units, February 16, 1944" below.

Home Army Field Report of General Stefan Rowecki ("Grot") to Central Headquarters: Anarchy in Wołyń—Murder of Poles (Radiogram), May 4, 1943

Wanda 6
O. VI L. dz. 2366/43
May 4, 1943
Received: May 12, 1943
Read: May 15, 1943

The Situation in Wołyń

In March [1943] the province of Wołyń was engulfed by anarchy that began at the end of February due to the activity of the nationalist anti-Soviet bandits of Bulba-Borovets in the county of Sarny. They spread to the Kostopol County, reaching a numerical strength of 4,000. This action was aimed primarily against the Poles: foresters and settlers. The toll of those murdered is estimated at 800.

The Polish people are seeking shelter mainly in Sarny, Kostopol, Janowa Dolina, and Łuck.

Under German pressure, the Bulbowcy withdrew into the forest, where they fight the Soviet partisans.

Between March 19 and 25 [1943] Ukrainians in the Schutzmannlandesdienst and Bahnschutz—about 6,000 in all—absconded into the forests. The wave of desertions began in the east. On March 14 the Ukrainian police school left Maciejów.

The security service has ceased to exist. Reinforced German garrisons protect only railroad tracks and administrative centers.

The Bulbowcy are deserting the police and peasants are attacking government properties and Polish settlers. About 200 Poles were killed.

Up to now things have been quiet in the western counties.

The Germans are taking almost no steps to control the anarchy. They are issuing proclamations to the deserters calling for their return and offering amnesty until April 25. They have appealed to the Poles to join the police — negative reaction.

The Poles have gained control over the initial panic. They have placed the children in the larger settlements. People capable of work and defense continue their spring field work [farming].

The commander of the region is organizing self-defense centers. In answer to the Ukrainians, he has declared a willingness to live in peace with them. At the same time, he warned them that in the event of a repeat performance on their part, repressions would follow.

The Wołynian Ukrainian intelligentsia repudiates these actions, calling them escapades of youth.

I am investigating the reasons for these actions.

The German version attributes these outbreaks to the Banderowcy, whose organizational network was threatened by the anticipated disarming of the Ukrainian police.

Undoubtedly, the influence of Soviet propaganda that is persistently urging the national elements in the occupied territories to launch a premature uprising is also at play here.

Kalina 693

Source: Home Army field report, quoted in Tadeusz Pełczyński et al., eds., *Armia Krajowa w dokumentach 1939-1945*, vol. 3, April 1943-July 1944 (London: Studium Polski Podziemnej, 1976), pp. 4-5. Many other AK field reports in this collection comment on the situation in Eastern Poland. See the following entry. (The page numbers in brackets that follow refer to Pełczyński's work.)

Other Home Army Field Reports on the Ethnic-Cleansing Campaign

[August 19, 1943] During the period covered by this report, March to May, 3,000 Poles were murdered [by "Ukrainian extremists"] and 5,000 were deported to the Reich....

On July 11 and 12, 60 Polish villages in the counties of Horochów and Włodzimierz were annihilated [pp. 58-59].

[August 25, 1943] The slaughter of Poles by Ukrainians continues in Wołyń in the counties of Kowel, Horochów, and Włodzimierz.

In Małopolska Wschodnia [Eastern Galicia] secret murders [take place]. The Ukrainians are demanding that the Poles leave Galicia [p. 63].

[August 31, 1943] Events in Ukraine: the slaughter of Poles in the district of Wołyń and neighboring territories....

The conditions for self-defense are grim; the power of the occupant is everywhere. In the southern territories, the numerical preponderance of the Ukrainians and their armaments preclude results [pp. 64, 68].

[No date — received December 27, 1943 by headquarters] The political director of the UPA in his November 16 directive calls on the Poles to leave Ukrainian lands and remove themselves beyond the Bug. He threatens to annihilate those who resist, citing by way of example the fate of the Poles in Huta Stepańska [p. 217].

[March 1, 1944] The armed escapades of the Ukrainian bands which were active during the past half year in Wołyń have now been transferred to the entire district of Lwów. The initiative has been taken over by organized units of the UPA, well-armed and supported by the Germans. Many Polish villages and properties have been burned, the goods confiscated, and the people murdered. The Polish self-defense organized by our regional command posts has curtailed these Ukrainian attacks somewhat, but we suffer from a catastrophic lack of weapons....

Due to the entry of the Soviet armies into the Wołyń district and the progressive movement of the front southward, the armed Ukrainian bands which had previously operated in Wołyń have now begun to arrive in Małopolska Wschodnia. This moment has been exploited by Ukrainians intent on waging war with the Poles as well as by the units of the Ukrainian Insurgent Army, the so-called

UPA, to begin an armed action against the Polish people.

The worst murders occurred in the district of Tarnopol and in the southeastern parts of the district of Lwów. Armed bands and UPA units numbering into the hundreds [of persons] attacked Polish villages and murdered and annihilated the entire population: men, women, and children. In this way, they intend to exterminate the Polish element within these territories.

To illustrate the Ukrainian atrocities, I am including the number of those killed in the region of Tarnopol: 45 in August 1943; 61 in September 1943; 93 in October 1943; 127 in November 1943; 309 in December 1943; and 466 in January 1944. The figures for February will be several times higher [than those in January]. In the Przemyślany and Rohatyn districts, there were 13 attacks between February 20 and February 25, and the number of victims was over 300.

On February 18, 89 persons, including 30 women and 30 children, were murdered in Firlejów in the district of Rohatyn....

In order to oppose this extermination action on the part of the Ukrainians, the regional command has ordered the immediate establishment of self-defense as well as pacification counteraction. Detailed instructions have been issued in the district, and — through handbills and word-of-mouth — the Polish people have been instructed on their course of conduct. The organization of self-defense action is patterned on the one utilized in Wołyń in the past half year. The Polish people living in smaller settlements should group themselves in larger ones which will become defense centers. In case of a more intense escalation of murders, retaliatory pacification actions have been ordered against Ukrainian settlements. Self-defense efforts heretofore have brought about some results. Many bloody battles have been conducted, resulting in large losses for the attackers. A serious difficulty in our action is the catastrophically small number of weapons and, above all, of ammunition....

Generally speaking, the Germans not only do not intervene actively against the Ukrainians but often also enter the threatened Polish centers after a successful defense effort, conduct a search, confiscate weapons, and arrest the men.

In the last days of February such actions took place in Karczunek, where over 170 men were arrested. In Bieniów (Złomczów [Złoczów] County), a search was conducted and two wounded men were taken away. In Trościaniec (Zborów County), after a search, three persons were abducted. In Majdan Wielki (Złoczów County), the village was surrounded and 140 Poles were taken.

[We have also noticed] the active appearance of units of the Ukrainian division SS "Hałyczyna" [SS-Galizien] against which the action of our small self-defense units is futile. The appearance of this SS division has caused panic among the Poles....

During the Christmas holidays a new wave of hostile armed action on the part of the Ukrainians against Polish centers erupted in the entire territory of Wołyń. Strong UPA units and divisions armed with machine guns and cannons struck at our defense bases unexpectedly. The Ukrainian units were assisted by large numbers of the local Ukrainian rabble armed with axes, pitchforks, and scythes. Although caught off guard by the Ukrainian units dressed in German uniforms, our bases in the regions of Kowel, Równe, and Łuck fought bravely and defended themselves while inflicting severe losses on the Ukrainians in terms of their dead, wounded, and their loss of military equipment [pp. 325-26, 346-47, 349].

[April 14, 1944] A concentration of UPA forces numbering about 4,000 persons is taking place in Małopolska Wschodnia in the regions of Dolina, Stryj, and Żydaczów. The activity of the UPA in Wołyń is diminishing [p. 404].

[April 20, 1944] In Wołyń, the UPA received an order to hide its weapons and, beginning in the summer, to leave the forests and to murder Poles and Soviets.

There's an increase of murders by Ukrainians in Małopolska Wschodnia, especially in the regions of Mościska ... and Złoczów, as well as in the Rawa Ruska – Tomaszów Mazowiecki – Sokal triangle. Our units are conducting retaliatory actions [p. 417].

Appendix C: Excerpts from Documents

[April 27, 1944] As a result of the loosening of the German administration, the UPA is in partial control of Małopolska Wschodnia. It is mobilizing the youth and requisitioning [product] contingents. OUN organizations have embraced the majority of the village populace.

The slaughter of Poles is spreading to Lwów's meridian. It is estimated that 8,000 have been massively murdered: [in] Podkamień (almost 1,000), [also in] Zawuń near Sokal [pp. 436-37].

[May 4-5, 1944] The burning of [Polish] settlements by Ukrainians continues in Małopolska Wschodnia and is moving to the Drohobycz and Przemyśl counties.

In the county of Kamionka Strumiłowa, UPA leaflets have been distributed on April 2 calling on the Poles to leave Western Ukraine by August 6 under penalty of annihilation and burning.

In the Chełm and Hrubieszów regions there is incitement to slaughter. Attacks on Poles are taking place and settlements are being burned.

Desertion of the SS-Galizien to the UPA [is taking place] [p. 430].

[May 13, 1944] German assistance to and cooperation with UPA units has been confirmed....

The slaughter by Ukrainians is being directed by the Germans in Przemyśl and Drohobycz regions.

In the Hrubieszów region: 21 persons were murdered in Maziarnia; six in Putnowice; two in Nowy Majdan [pp. 443, 445].

[May 18, 1944] The battle with our self-defense and the partisan units rushing to render assistance has heated up. As a result, 40 villages have been completely burned down. In this same period of time we note the flow of UPA units from Małopolska Wschodnia towards the Tomaszów County [p. 447].

[May 24, 1944] The murders by Ukrainians, generally preceded by evacuation notices given to the Polish people, continue in the Chełm region and in Małopolska Wschodnia [p. 460].

[June 1, 1944] The intensity of the UPA attacks is not diminishing; it is spreading to the San region....

Murders by Ukrainians continue. In Derżów near Stryj, several dozen Polish children were burned in a church....

The Poles of Lwów are against giving any concessions to the Ukrainians. There's a massive exodus of Poles to the West [pp. 465-67].

[June 7, 1944] The attacks of Ukrainian bands have ceased in the Lublin region because of our countermeasures. They continue in the Lwów region [p. 473].

[June 14, 1944] The task of arming the UPA by the Germans and of concentrating them in the Hrubieszów and Biłgoraj regions is taking place....

There is local anti-Soviet cooperation between the UPA and the Wehrmacht. Germans from Soviet Ukraine are organizing a Ukrainian army of liberation. In the counties of Hrubieszów, Tomaszów, and Zamość, the Germans are issuing leaflets calling on the Ukrainian units from [Eastern] Galicia and Wołyń to move beyond the Bug River and there to fight the Bolsheviks....

The UPA has 40,000 armed [persons] and is continuing to mobilize. Its main concentration is in the Carpathian Mountains. The slaughter [of Poles] does not cease. The police have called for the evacuation of Jarosław, Przemyśl, Sanok, and Biłgoraj.... About 300,000 Poles have fled from Małopolska Wschodnia, including 45,000 from Lwów [pp. 480-83].

[June 28, 1944] Several thousand UPA members have arrived from beyond the Bug River to the regions of Hrubieszów and Chełm County. Lately there have been reports of serious confrontations between the UPA and our forces [p. 493].

[July 13, 1944] Since May there have been sporadic anti-Polish excesses on the left bank of the San under the motto: "Great Ukraine up to [the River] Wisłok" [p. 544].

[July 21, 1944] With the agreement of the Germans, a part of the UPA remained in Wołyń [p. 570].

Source: Home Army field reports, quoted in Tadeusz Pełczyński et al., eds., *Armia Krajowa w dokumentach 1939-1945*, vol. 3, April 1943-July 1944 (London: Studium Polski Podziemnej, 1976), pages as noted in entries above.

Letter to Archbishop Adam Sapieha, Metropolitan of Kraków, June 7, 1943

Krzemieniec, June 7, 1943

Most Venerable Father:

An opportunity presents itself to send you a few words through a person who is escaping the knives of the Ukrainians. What is happening here and now, the slaughter and torment of Polish families, defies all words. The descriptions in [Henryk] Sienkiewicz's *With Fire and Sword* or [Zofia] Kossak-Szczucka's *Conflagration* pale in comparison to present events.

Almost all the Poles in the villages of the county of Krzemieniec have been butchered, and those who were able to escape the haydamak knives and bullets have sought shelter in Krzemieniec and Wiśniowiec, where there are still German units. In other places, such as Szumsk, Dederkały, Kuty [a.k.a. Kąty] and Łanowce, the weaker units were either destroyed or fled before the larger bands of Ukrainians.

I will submit a few examples in a chronological order so as not to be accused of exaggeration. The murder of Poles began already last November and continued through the winter, but these were sporadic occurrences — for example, in one village a family was butchered; in another, two or three more. Massive murders began only after Easter [1943] and with each day gather force. Immediately after the holidays, about 600 people were killed in the villages around Szumsk, and the rest sought shelter in Krzemieniec. Later, Kuty was attacked. This was the largest parish (4,000 souls) in Krzemieniec County. When the murders began, the people and their parish priest barricaded themselves in a church. There, they defended themselves all through the night. In the morning, the women and children went to Krzemieniec, and the men remained to defend the church. The following night, more numerous hordes arrived, destroyed the church, and butchered the 200 Poles who were in it. Not a single soul remained of those in the parish. The church in Krzemieniec was converted into a shelter for the refugees. Later, the Germans came and deported the young people for forced labor in Germany; the old people continue to suffer in dire poverty.

At the beginning of May two parish priests from Oleksiniec and Kołodno came to our refuge. Almost all the Polish parishioners from the Oleksiniec parish were robbed and killed. The parish priest, having nothing to do, left us yesterday for the General Government; so did the pastor of Kołodno. Almost daily one can see fires; they are burning Polish settlements and murdering those who do not escape in the most bestial manner.

On the night of May 15, the honorable Kuś family was attacked in Młynowce. Two daughters and a twenty-one-year-old son were killed; the rest of the family managed to escape. The attackers, after thoroughly robbing the house, threw the murdered victims into it and burned it down.

All the refugees are fleeing to Wiśniowiec, where they are living in the monastery in terrible conditions and utter poverty. One's heart bleeds at the sight of their poverty and over the stories of their experiences.

Every morning there is news: there, they were killed; there, robbed; there, another house was burned together with its occupants. And thus one day follows another in suffering and our nerves are constantly on edge because there is no doubt that on the first night after the German unit leaves Wiśniowiec (castle) all the Poles will be murdered. Whoever can, therefore, flees to the GG [General Government] because these haydamaks swear that not a single Polish foot will remain in Wołyń. Wiśniowiec, once consisting of Jewish houses, has almost vanished. Every single Jew was killed there last year, and the Ukrainians took apart all their houses and sheds. Only the castle, monastery, commune office, and pharmacy still remain — the rest was knocked down. On the outskirts of town, only the homes of the haydamaks remain.

You, Reverend Father, can imagine what our life is like from this description — we are prepared to die because only a miracle and the special protection of Our Lady can save us now. We therefore plead earnestly for your holy prayers so that the Lord Jesus would have mercy on us and all would quiet down again. The Poles here, whose only fault was that they were born Poles and are Catholics, are truly experiencing a terrible crisis. Even those Ukrainians who converted to Catholicism during the Polish times are being killed.

Ending once more, we humbly ask for your holy prayers so that our peace of mind may be restored and that we may be able, in accordance with God's will, to endure these moral and perhaps even physical torments.

I humbly kiss the holy scapular and once more beg for your prayers.

Brother Cyprian [Jan Lasoń]

Source: *Karta* (Warszawa) 8 (1992): 65. Also in Jerzy Dębski and Leon Popek, *Okrutna przestroga* (Lublin: Towarzystwo Przyjaciół Krzemieńca i Ziemi Wołyńsko-Podolskiej, 1997), pp. 356-57. Brother Cyprian Lasoń, together with Fr. Kamil Gleczman and 47 others, was murdered in Wiśniowiec by the Banderowcy in February 1944.

Appeal of the Home Political Representation of the Polish People (Krajowa Reprezentacja Polityczna Narodu Polskiego, or KRP) to the Ukrainian People, July 30, 1943

Warszawa
July 30, 1943

Appeal of the KRP
"To the Ukrainian People"

The end of the war is near. The ocean of blood spilled in the defense of freedom and justice and the sacrifice of the millions of victims will not have been in vain. Poland, whose participation in the war is so great and whose suffering and sacrifices are so enormous, will emerge out of this war victorious and will take part, together with the Allies, in the reconstruction of a new and better world.

Unfortunately, the Ukrainian society — under the influence of hostile propaganda and confused by those who today want to be considered as the leaders and the exponents of the will of the Ukrainian people — has, in great measure, embarked upon a different road than that taken by the Poles, the road of cooperation with the occupant. The first months of the war, however, had already indicated that this "cooperation" rested on a blind obedience and assistance to the occupants in their war against the Polish nation and people.

The Ukrainian people are already paying dearly for this naive and slavish political orientation. The final evaporation of all delusions regarding even the most modest form of political independence, the forced slave labor on behalf of the war machine in Germany and the Fatherland, the merciless economic exploitation, and, lastly, the "privilege of spilling blood" in the auxiliary formations of the German army — this is the balance sheet of the four-year-long Ukrainian-German collaboration. In the external forum, isolation — in particular with respect to the Allies — is the most important result of that political orientation.

The Ukrainian people have also a living memory of their "cooperation" with the Soviet occupant. Those two years of the Bolshevik rule have left behind them nightmarish memories. Arrests, massive deportations, and, in the last phase, executions — these are the stages traversed by the Bolsheviks to achieve the "liberation," so they claimed, of the Ukrainian people from the "Polish yoke." The Ukrainian people have also become acquainted with the results, in this same period of time, of the Soviet twenty-five-year rule in Soviet Ukraine — a rule that had brought about the extermination of the intelligentsia of the Ukrainian nation, the ruinous assimilation of the proletariat, and finally, the Russification of large segments of the Ukrainian society.

It would seem that these experiences should have brought the Ukrainian people to their senses and forced them to reexamine their heretofore-held positions. The glimmer of this realization is already evident in a wide proportion of the masses of the Ukrainian people, but the continuing collaboration with Germany and the acts of cruelty and lawlessness perpetrated recently by the Ukrainians against the Polish people on the territories of the Republic — acts that have been allowed to take place by the occupants but have often been carried out on their own [Ukrainian] initiative — continue to dig a chasm between the Polish and Ukrainian people and, at the same time, to dig a grave for their dreams. A great historic hour is dawning on the clock of history: the hour of the final victory of justice. Whoever cannot feel it, renders judgment on himself.

As the Home Political Representation of the Polish people, we turn to You at this historic moment: Turn off this dead-end street; break off your humiliating dependence on the occupant; condemn the bestiality of the mass murders perpetrated on the Polish population of Wołyń by the Ukrainian people who are egged on by the Germans or the Bolsheviks; desist from all acts of hostility against the Polish people and nation; condemn the recruitment [of Ukrainians] to the Ukrainian [SS] division and agitate against it; erect with us a solid defense against the annihilating action of the occupant and thereby actively confirm the stand of the Ukrainian people against the enemy.

We have common enemies; therefore stand at our side in the battle with them. Only the blood spilled in a fight against our common enemies — one of which, namely Germany, oppresses both of our nations; the other, namely Russia, extends an avaricious hand toward our lands, inhabited by both Poles and Ukrainians — can smooth over the chasm dividing our two nations and create a basis for further cooperation between Poles and Ukrainians under the motto: "For Your freedom and Ours."

We understand and appreciate the aspirations of the Ukrainian people in regard to the creation of an independent Ukraine. We declare, however, that we will not give up the eastern territories of the republic in whose southern parts Poles have lived side by side with Ukrainians from time immemorial, lands to which the Polish people in the course of centuries have made great civilizing and economic contributions. These lands should, in the final analysis, become a place of brotherly coexistence of both nationalities.

We therefore guarantee the Ukrainian people a full and free development on these lands in keeping with the principles of freedom as well as equality under the law and the obligations of citizens. Along this road the Ukrainian people will find full understanding and support of the Polish people as well as their magnanimous readiness to forget about previously sustained transgressions and injuries.

KRP

Source: CAW 392/62/53, quoted in Władysław Filar, *"Burza" na Wołyniu: Z dziejów 27 Wołyńskiej Dywizji Piechoty Armii Krajowej* (Warszawa: Rada Ochrony Pamięci Walk i Męczeństwa, 1997), pp. 263-65.

Letters (January 24, 1943-March 25, 1944) of Stanisław Czekanowski of Hrubieszów

[August 6, 1943] Beyond the Bug [River], in the county of Włodzimierz, a mindless slaughter of Poles by demented Ukrainians [is taking place]. They [refugees] speak of two girl-students from the village of Grzybowica, attending the high school in Włodzimierz, who are participating in the butchery. A total insanity [prevails] of murdering even neighbors with whom the best of relations obtained. Here [in Hrubieszów], we also hear of scheming and plotting. The Galician Ukrainians are behind it all. One is reminded of the times of Gonta and Zalizniak [a reference to Taras Shevchenko's work, *Haydamaks*]. You won't believe this and I, myself, who have been accused of and am being accused of Ukrainophilism, did not believe that this wild bloodbath was perpetrated by the "Ukrainians." But the facts from the county of Kostopol, and now also from the county of Włodzimierz, convince me that this curious and talented people is wild and without any political sense. A cruel rabble.

[September 5, 1943] Refugees are arriving here daily nonstop from beyond the Bug. Now, the Ukrainians, fleeing from punitive expeditions, are also trying to cross over.

The villages to the east of the Bug are empty. The Poles have either been massacred or have fled; the Ukrainians are sitting in the forests. The crops are not being gathered. The sight in the villages is uncanny: the livestock is all taken, only poultry roams here and there.

[September 17, 1943] When I arrived here [in Hrubieszów], our entire county was engulfed by fires and murders.... It is impossible to count the murders of Polish peasants and collectivized workers.

[February 1, 1944] In Hrubieszów, I met an old deacon from Łuck. Nothing remains of his seven parishes: the faithful have been killed or ran away, and the churches and rectories have been burned.

[February 24, 1944] I just spoke with quite an intelligent person, a farmer from Łuck. Between Łuck and Uściług, for a few kilometers along each side of some 80 kilometers of road, not a single village remains. Everything is burned down, and the people have been either shot or they have fled. We do not see fires there any more, rather, as I write this letter, I hear artillery fire.

[February 26, 1944] Except for one Polish center in Bielin in which about 500 people held out and, it seems, are still holding out, there are no Polish people left in the county of Włodzimierz for sure as well as in another county. Whoever did not flee was murdered. (Addendum: It seems that there are two such centers in the county of Włodzimierz.) I have given some serious thought to, but cannot understand, the origins of such cruelty in Wołyń, the likes of which is comparable to the slaughter in Humań [another reference to Shevchenko's poem]—in Wołyń, where such peace prevailed in former days. It began with the propaganda coming from [Eastern] Galicia for *samostiina Ukraina* (independent Ukraine), and it was that which produced these frightening results in Wołyń. Our county has also become involved in all of this, and, with the exception of the peaceful Chełm region consisting of a similar population mix as here, nothing like it has happened anywhere else. And it happened because our rich county was inundated by riffraff from [Eastern] Galicia, seemingly ideologically motivated but in reality only out for profit. Having valuable caretakers [the Germans], it was they who have poisoned our lives. Generally speaking, our peasants are not represented among them, and one can count on one's fingers those who have linked themselves to these activists....

P.S. The unfortunates from beyond the Bug are streaming in again. It's horrible! How these people suffer.

[March 7, 1944] How strange these Ukrainians are. They come here with every bad intention, demand to be fed; they eat, drink, engage in friendly discussions with the homeowner and then tell him to leave his house and murder him near his doorstep—that same homeowner whith whom they had just been conversing and smiling. This happened yesterday, but I have heard of it very often before. Their cruelty is known from the time of Khmelnytskyi and Humań—nothing has changed. Also, unbelievable cruelty has transpired in Wołyń until the last days. About Wołyń, about the heroic actions of the Polish groups there, volumes could be written. Really miraculous events are happening even today in the county of Włodzimierz.

Source: Towarzystwo Rolnictwa Hrubieszewskiego, sygn. 1251, APL, quoted in Jerzy Dębski and Leon Popek, *Okrutna przestroga* (Lublin: Towarzystwo Przyjaciół Krzemieńca i Ziemi Wołyńsko-Podolskiej, 1997), pp. 349–55.

Letter from the Polish Social Welfare Committee in Chełm to the Polish Main Social Welfare Council in Lublin, September 10, 1943

In answer to the inquiry of September 4, 1943, No. 1168/43, concerning the refugees from Wołyń, we inform you that we have the following current statistics:

From August 31, 1943, to September 9, 1943, over 15 transports with about 1,509 persons arrived in Chełm. In addition, families arrived on foot and by wagon. These numbered about 500.

In the Świerże commune: a) in Okopy, about 315 persons; b) in Świerże, about 775 persons.

In the Turka commune: a) in Dorohusk, about 525 persons; b) in Barbarówka and region, about 427 persons.

The Sobibór commune: a) in Uhrusk, about 295 persons; b) in Rybga and region, about 315 persons; c) in Zbereże, 100 persons. Total: 2,752 persons.

Source: Jerzy Dębski and Leon Popek, *Okrutna przestroga* (Lublin: Towarzystwo Przyjaciół Krzemieńca i Ziemi Wołyńsko-Podolskiej, 1997), photocopy of letter, p. 428.

Letter of Irena Kozłowska, a Teacher from Wola Ostrowiecka, December 9, 1943

The children cuddle up to us in such a way that we can't bear to look at them. Other children are crying, yelling, but ours are quiet. There are fewer and fewer men now. Lolo [Leon] wants to go, but I don't let him. He begs me to let go of him because we will be together again shortly [in death]. Five minutes won't make a difference. Well, eventually he also has to leave. He bids us farewell. The children begin to cry, cuddle up, plead, "Daddy, don't go." And he looks at us stoically. I cry and he begs me, "Irel [Irena], don't cry because in a little while we will be together again forever." I can't control myself. He bids us farewell and goes out. Four Ukrainian bandits take him away.

My heart is torn by sorrow, the children cry and beg to go to their Daddy. "Let's go home," they say. I calm them by telling them that we will go to our home forever. They are already taking the women and the children out. I procrastinate, knowing that I will have to go sooner or later. I stay a bit longer. I pray with the children and ask for an easy death. There are about 50 of us. I hear a grenade being tossed in. They are closing the classroom doors. I see that the school is banked by straw. Fire. A second and a third grenade is thrown in. I place the children under a school bench. I cover them with my own body. Terrible smoke. We are beginning to choke to death. Janeczek [Jan] runs off. He does not want to lie still. He runs all over the classroom. There's already a few corpses. He runs to the door. Fire explodes there. I grab him. He runs off to the people who are looking for rescue. He runs into another classroom. The fire is even stronger there, and he perishes in the flames. I have no strength left. The suffering of that child destroys my self-composure. Another loved one perishes and in such a terrible way. I see nothing now. Black smoke bites and chokes me. I look through another window. No one is there. I grab my children, throw them out of the window. We hide beneath the fence among the lilacs. Sparks fall and burn me but that's nothing. I only want to save these two children and myself.

Suddenly, a woman appears and falls near us. Ukrainian hoodlums are behind her. They discover us, take us out, lead us away. They bring us to a fork in the road near the cross which stands by our house. A shot rings out. I fall down out of fear; some other woman is killed. Another shot. Haneczka [Anna] falls into my arms. Her skull shatters and she covers me with blood. Andrzej calls out "Mommy" and falls on my back. He dies. His blood flows over me. I feel sullied. I wait for my turn. Shots are fired, but into others. I no longer fear death from a bullet. It becomes quiet. They return, stand over me and say, "*Ot dumala shcho nam vteche. Svoloch. Dumala shcho bude Polshcha. Ot maie vzhe Polshchu.*" [She thought that she would get away from us. Idiot. She thought that Poland would exist. Here's her Poland.]

I sink to the ground, hold my breath, wait. They leave. I lie there a long time—about two hours. Silence. I lift my hand, look at my children, strike my head against the earth, howl in an inhuman way, and decide not to remove myself from this spot. I do not have the strength. I cannot think. I long for death. Lying there I reach the conclusion that I am alive and that I cannot lie here. I look around and see my poor Haneczka. Her skull is in pieces. Andrzej is in the same condition. I cover them with kisses. I crawl to the garden. I want to go back to my children, to bury them. But with what? I do not have the strength. I want to see my dear Leon. He died such a terrible death. But it is a little too far for me to walk, and they are still milling around there. I gather my courage and set out for the fields. I meet a woman. We creep along and meet eight other persons, but no one from among the educated class. Everything's gone. Out of 800 people, I alone survived from that school. I make my way eight kilometers to a Polish village (Jagodzin).

There were no murders here, yet. It's evening. The local people are gathering near the railroad station. In the morning, I meet some of my fellow teachers. They take care of me, and I am transported by car to Luboml. I go to my acquaintances. With them I come to Warsaw. From there, I write to my dear brother Leon. He comes and fetches me. I am here since October 15.

Source: Leon Popek, Tomasz Trusiuk, Paweł Wira, and Zenon Wira, comps., *Wołyński testament* (Lublin: Towarzystwo Przyjaciół Krzemieńca i Ziemi Wołyńsko-Podolskiej, 1997), pp. 86-87. The note at the bottom of p. 87 reads: "Irena Kozłowska was a teacher in Wola Ostrowiecka. Her husband, Leon, was a public official in Zgorany. This account is a fragment from a letter dated December 9, 1943, sent from Chorosznica to Ricarda (no further information is available). The letter was provided by Aleksander Korman from Wrocław."

Order of Kazimierz Damian Bąbiński ("Luboń"), Commander of the Union for Armed Struggle-Home Army, Wołyń (ZWZ-AK, "Hreczka"), to AK Partisan Units, February 16, 1944

Most categorically do I repeat the former injunctions and orders issued during the briefings of the leaders of the inspectorates and partisans in the days of covert operations and later, after surfacing, to the leaders of regiments and groups — that they refrain, both during and after battle, from doing harm to Ukrainian women and children. I will hold accountable, with all due severity, those leaders and soldiers who perpetrate such unworthy deeds.

Source: Ryszard Torzecki, *Polacy i Ukraińcy: Sprawa ukraińska w czasie II wojny światowej na terenie II Rzeczypospolitej* (Warszawa: Wydawnictwo Naukowe PWN, 1993), p. 289, n. 125.

Anonymous Account of a Member of the Polish Schutzmannschaftsbataillon 202, March 1944

Daily we hear about the bestial murders of the Poles in the neighboring villages. We give them first aid, that is, the children and the young men who managed to escape are given food and lodging for the night. Next, we send them to Łuck where the German authorities are supposed to continue taking care of them. After every notification we proceed immediately to the scene of the crime. But these actions are an aimless waste of time. We arrive on our wagons fully armed (three howitzers, two medium machine guns, seven light machine guns) but our leader has no plan; rather, he avoids confrontation since the Germans are deathly afraid of the Ukrainians. We enter the village while the Ukrainians all run off across the fields in the opposite direction, and we are not allowed to shoot them. Only old men and women remain who cannot flee and with tears in their eyes lament and curse their sons and brothers. It all ends with our requisitioning two or three pigs and a couple of cows and horses from their empty houses and our return by caravan. Every excursion is conducted in this way.

One day a 12-year-old girl ran over to us with tears in her eyes and informed us that all her siblings had been murdered and that around 20 Polish families are wandering in the fields and forests. We quickly sound the alarm and leave by wagon for the place. It's the village of Stryłki, four kilometeres from Klewań and we are confronted with a horrifying sight. The ruins are still smoldering. The attack took place at 2:00 A.M. We got there at 11:00 A.M. After our arrival, those who were able to flee began to gather. Lamenting, they fall near their small children who are lying in pools of blood. The majority of those murdered have been burned in the rubble. We also discover many victims lying near homes. They have all been tormented in a cruel way: The men have severed genitalia; the women have bottles and rocks shoved up. Their fingers, tongues and noses are severed; wodden stakes are dirven into their skulls or necks. There's no way of determining the number of those murdered.

Source: "Relacja policjanta," *Karta* 24 (1998): 129-40. An anonymous account of a member of the Polish Schutzmannschaftsbataillon 202 created in May-June 1942 in Kochanówka near Dębica. The quoted section appears on pp. 133-34. This account was written in March 1944 in Lwów. A three-page introduction, "Polski policjant na Wołyniu," by Grzegorz Motyka, precedes the account.

A Delegation for the Homeland Report on the Slaughter in Podkamień

Slaughter in Podkamień

Presently, a detailed report has reached us regarding the events in Podkamień [in Tarnopol Province] that, in their monstrosity, belong to one of the most tragic and, at the same time, the most vivid examples of the cooperation between the Ukrainian bands and the Germans, without whose help there would have been no slaughter in Podkamień.

Source: Instytut Studiów Politycznych PAN, Collection of Wojciech Bukat, Report from the Eastern Territories, no. 41. k. 4., quoted in Grzegorz Motyka, "Ukraińska orientacja," *Karta* (Warszawa) 23 (1997): 62-63.

Diary of Zygmunt Klukowski

[March 17, 1944] I was told about the terrible things taking place in Hrubieszów County. Ukrainian nationalists are torturing and murdering Poles, singling out large farmers and ranchers. In retaliation the Polish underground is killing Ukrainians....

[May 9, 1944] Yesterday and today many Polish escapees from Rawa Ruska arrived in our town. There, the Ukrainians are the law. Ukrainians set May 10 as the day by which all Polish families must leave.

Source: Zygmunt Klukowski, *Diary from the Years of Occupation, 1939-44* (Chicago: University of Illinois Press, 1993), pp. 310, 324.

Home Army Field Reports Regarding the Activities of the SS-Galizien

[March 23, 1944] Murders increase especially in Tarnopol. The participation of the SS-Galizien (the name of the Ukrainian unit) in these murders is verified. Our self-defense is limited by the lack of weapons. Often the Germans arrest and deport our men after a successful defense against the bands. The murders make it easier for the Germans to break the resistance of the Poles to evacuation.

[May 13, 1944] After the German bombardment in the region of Rejowiec, Ukrainian SS men come and massacre the Poles: April 24-30— Pawłów ... Żużlin, Borowno.

[May 18, 1944] Lately, there appeared in the [region] of Hrubieszów units of the division SS-Galizien, which began their terrorist activity by exterminating the people. Six Polish villages were burned.

[May 24, 1944] The terrorist activity of the Ukrainian division SS-Galizien and the UPA in Chełm region [is being] restrained only by our self-defense and partisan units.

[July 7, 1944] Terrorist activity on the part of the SS-Halychyna [Galizien] Division in the Lublin region has increased.... Cruelty of the Ukrainian SS [is noted] in southern Lublin Province during food requisition.

Source: Tadeusz Pełczyński et al., eds., *Armia Krajowa w dokumentach 1939-1945*, vol. 3, April 1943-July 1944 (London: Studium Polski Podziemnej, 1976), pp. 383, 445, 447, 458, 507-08.

Letter from the County Elders of Lubaczów to the Ministry of State Administration in Warsaw, April 12, 1945

The Ukrainian revolutionary bands of Banderowcy [are] murdering the remaining [Polish] population in a bestial manner ... and burning their possessions. Daily there are dozens of murders; the same is true in the eastern part of the county of Jarosław. The battalion of the Polish army stationed in Lubaczów ... is not in a position to control the situation in the county, which is getting worse every day. The detachment dare not leave the town even for one moment for fear that it would be immediately attacked by the Banderowcy and the unarmed Polish population murdered.... [The letter then noted the burial on that day of two militiamen and 28 Polish soldiers who were attacked by the UPA as they were trying to bring arms and ammunition to the battalion stationed in Lubaczów.] If this situation lasts any longer this entire county and part of Jarosław County will be under the control of the Ukrainian bands and the remainder of the Polish population will perish.

Source: Zdzisław Konieczny, ed., *Źródła do dziejów regionu przemyskiego w latach 1944-1949* (Przemyśl: Wojewódzkie Archiwum Państwowe w Przemyślu, 1979), p. 67.

SOVIET

Field Report of the Soviet Unit I. I. Shitov, March 30, 1943

The Ukrainian Nationalists conducted a bestial action against the defenseless Polish people, setting themselves the task of completely exterminating the Poles in Ukraine.... In the Cumań region, UPA companies were ordered to exterminate all Poles and to burn their places of residence and colonies by April 15, 1943.

Source: CAMO FR, f. 1, op. 23, spr. 523, p. 44, quoted in Władysław Filar, ed., *Przed akcją "Wisła" był Wołyń* (Warszawa: Światowy Związek Żołnierzy Armii Krajowej, Okręg Wołyń, 1997), p. 36.

Field Report of O. F. Fedorov, Commander of Unified Partisan Units in the Równe area, to the Ukrainian Partisan Movement Headquarters, May 28, 1943

The chief activity of the Nationalists in the last phase is directed at the annihilation of the Polish people, Polish villages.... In the regions of Stepań, Deraźne, Rafałówka, Sarny, Wysock, Włodzimierz, Klewań, and others, the Nationalists are conducting massive terror campaigns against the Polish people, and it should be emphasized that the Nationalists do not shoot the Poles, but that, rather, they butcher them with knives and axe them with hatchets irrespective of their age or gender. In the village of Tryputnia they axed 14 Polish families and then they dragged the murdered victims into a house and set it on fire.... In the villages of Bereźne, Czajkowo, and Cechy (in the region of Włodzimierz and Wysock), the Nationalists annihilated everyone and burned over 200 buildings. In the region of Parośle, 21 Polish families were liquidated.

Source: TsDAHO of Ukraine, f. 1, op. 22, spr. 75, ark. pp. 37-43, quoted in Władysław Filar, ed., *Przed akcją "Wisła" był Wołyń* (Warszawa: Światowy Związek Żołnierzy Armii Krajowej, Okręg Wołyń, 1997), pp. 36-37.

Partisan Report, June 19 to August 18, 1943

The chief task of the Ukrainian Nationalists at the present time is to gather forces and clear the occupied territories of Poles. The Nationalists conduct themselves in a bestial manner with the Poles: They burn people alive, butcher them, shoot them. They confiscate their possessions and burn their buildings.

Source: Party Archive of the Institute of the Party's History of the Central Committee of the Ukrainian Party, "Separate section — Secret part," f. 57, op. 4, spr. 191, p. 118, quoted in Władysław Filar, ed., *Przed akcją "Wisła" był Wołyń* (Warszawa: Światowy Związek Żołnierzy Armii Krajowej, Okręg Wołyń, 1997), p. 36.

Field Report of O. F. Fedorov to the Secretary of the Central Committee of the Communist (Bolshevik) Party of Ukraine, Nikita Khrushchev, January 21, 1944

[Fedorov tells Khrushchev that during his tenure in the Wołyń region between June 1943 and January 1944 he had no evidence to substantiate the fact that the Ukrainian Nationalists were waging war against the German occupant there. On the contrary, his facts indicated that the Nationalists had entered German service right from the very beginning and that they had constantly impeded, in a variety of ways, the Soviet partisan movement against Germany. At the same time, they had conducted "wild and bloody actions, annihilating completely the Polish and Jewish people.... They burn, kill, butcher with axes.... All these bandit groups (called UPA, under the direction of the OUN) are preoccupied with robbing and murdering the peaceful population."]

Source: TsDAHO of Ukraine, f. 1, op. 2. spr. 75, ark. pp. 48-55, quoted in Władysław Filar, ed., *Przed akcją "Wisła" był Wołyń* (Warszawa: Światowy Związek Żołnierzy Armii Krajowej, Okręg Wołyń, 1997), p. 44.

GERMAN

Diary of Admiral Wilhelm Canaris

I would have to make appropriate preparations with the Ukrainians so that, should this alternative [the incorporation of Galicia as a nominally independent state under the Third Reich] become real, the Melnyk Organization (OUN) can produce an uprising which would aim at the annihilation of the Jews and Poles.

Source: Alexander Dallin, *German Rule in Russia, 1941-1945: A Study of Occupation Policies*, 2d ed. (London: Macmillan, 1981), p. 115.

K-Organisation Ost-Galizien Document

[This document states that on the eve of the war, 4,000 Galician Ukrainian-Nationalist agents trained by German counterintelligence (Abwehr) in sabotage and diversion infiltrated central and southern Poland, incited the minorities, and participated in acts of violence against the Polish people.]

Source: Andrzej Szefer, "Dywersyjno-sabatażowa działalność wrocławskiej Abwehry na ziemiach polskich w przededniu agresji hitlerowskiej w 1939 r.," *Biuletyn Głównej Komisji Badania Zbrodni Hitlerowskich w Polsce* 32 (1987): 317.

Dr. Otto Korfes's Report, July 3, 1941

[Złoczów, Tarnopol Province] I saw that in the ditches, about 5 meters deep and 20 meters wide, stood and lay about 60-80 men, women, and children, predominantly Jewish. I heard the wailing and screaming of the children and women — hand grenades were bursting in their midst. Beyond the ditches waited many hundreds of people for execution. In front of the ditches stood 10 to 20 men in civilian clothes who were throwing grenades into the ditch.... I found out from the SS soldiers that they were Bandera's people.

Source: Antoni Szcześniak and Wiesław Szota, *Droga do nikąd: Działalność Organizacji Ukraińskich Nacjonalistów i jej likwidacja w Polsce* (Warszawa: Ministerstwo Obrony Narodowej, 1973), p. 110 and n. 134. Otto Korfes was a former general of the Wehrmacht.

Report of the Chief of the SS and Police to the Commander of Communications Zone South on the Structure and Leadership of the Nationalist Bands, June 30, 1943

June 30, 1943
Intelligence and Counter-intelligence Department (1c)
Recordbook 51/43
Kiev
Secret

The general command of the Ukrainian nationalist bands is doubtless in the hands of the OUN-Bandera movement. The previous supposition of Taras Bulba (Borovets) taking over the general leadership of the Ukrainian nationalists' bands hasn't been confirmed.

The following band leaders are known at present:

Taras Bulba — undoubtedly the most prominent figure who since recently calls himself the commander of the Ukrainian Insurgent Army. His most active assistant is Shpak from Kostopol.

Adam Rudyk from Ludvipol — leader of a 700-men-strong band in the Kostopol area.

Fiel — formerly a police commandant, commands a band in the area of Sarny.

Bobruga — son-in-law of the Ukrainian priest Trefka from Belozotsovka, leader of a 1,000-men-strong band in the area 20 km north of Ludvipol, Kostopol District.

Rozolovsky — leader of a band in Kremenets District (allegedly killed by his political adversaries).

Karpo — supposedly a former major, commands a band in the area of Stydin (50 km north of Rovno [Równe]).

Shvorobey — leader of a band in the area of Kostopol.

Skuba and Shaburevsky — commanders of two bands in the Derazhne area (north-west of Rovno [Równe]).

Stobnitsky — allegedly a former Ukrainian general, commands a band in the area of Trostyanets (30 km north-east of Lutsk).

Lopatin (alias Zubenko) leader of a band in the Letishev area (60 km east of Proskurov).

Voloshin (of Galician origin) — leader of a 700-men-strong band in the area of Lokachi–Kizilin (50 km west of Lutsk).

Levkovich — formerly a squad leader in the local police force, commands a 500-men-strong band in the Druzkopol area (10 km south of Gorokhov).

Subordinate commanders are mostly defected local policemen and former prisoners of war.

Organization Inside the Districts and Tasks:

It follows from the captured documents that the bands' commanders are planning to introduce a strict village-wise organization of all population fit for military service. Each village band is headed by a section leader every three village bands, by a squad leader; and the whole band of a district, by an executive who is a member of the control headquarters. Even though this organization hasn't yet been established all over the place, the emergence and activities of bands in certain areas point up the fact that this structure is already well developed.

(Signature)

Source: Central State Archives of the October Revolution, Organs of State Government and State Management of the Ukrainian SSR, fund CMF-8, invt. 2, file 494, pp. 30-31, quoted in Yu. Yu. Kondufor et al., eds., *History Teaches a Lesson,* trans. from Russian by Vadim Piatkovsky (Kiev: Politvidav Ukrainy, 1986), pp. 227-28.

Abwehr (Counterintelligence) Report, July 13, 1943

[This German report confirms the "*Ausrottung polnischer Siedler in Wolhynien*" (extermination of Polish settlers in Wołyń). Since the Polish settlers were deported to the Soviet Union in 1940-41, this passage can only refer to the Polish peasants left behind.]

Source: Militararchiv, sygn. H 3/474, (Amt Ausland Abwehr Dienststelle Walli III, nr D 5800/43 g/B/AUSW. 273) Feststclungen zur Bandenlage, Q.U. den 13.7.1943, in Peter

Potichnyj and Ievhen Shtendera, eds., *Litopys Ukrainskoi Povstanskoi Armii*, vol. 6 (Toronto: Vydavnytstvo Litopys UPA), pp. 260-61, as summarized in Władysław Filar, ed., *Przed akcją "Wisła" był Wołyń* (Warszawa: Światowy Związek Żołnierzy Armii Krajowej, Okręg Wołyń, 1997), p. 36, and Ryszard Torzecki, *Polacy i Ukraińcy: Sprawa ukraińska w czasie II wojny światowej na terenie II Rzeczypospolitej* (Warszawa: Wydawnictwo Naukowe PWN, 1993), pp. 262-63.

Commissar (of Wołyń and Podole) Heinrich Schöne's Talk with Archbishop Polikarp (Sikorskyi), May 28, 1943

The Nationalist bandits reveal their activity by attacking and murdering defenseless Poles. According to our estimates, about 15,000 Poles have been murdered. The colony of Janowa Dolina no longer exists.

Source: DARO, f. R-30, op. 2, spr. 16, ark. 198-201, quoted in Wiktor Poliszczuk, *Pojęcie Integralnego Nacjonalizmu Ukraińskiego* (Warszawa: n.p., 1997), p. 24.

Report of SS-Sturmbannführer Pütz, Chief of Police and Security Service (SD), to SS Gruppenführer Heinrich Müller, Chief of Gestapo, September 14, 1943

IV-A-53/43
Łuck, September 14, 1943
Secret. State Security

To Chief of State Security SS
SS-Grupennführer and Generalleutnant of Police
Personal. Secret. Berlin

One of the leaders of the Bandera faction of the OUN informed us during the September 12, 1943, meeting that detachments of Ukrainian Nationalists conducted massive actions between August 29 and 30, 1943, aimed at the liquidation of the Poles in Wołyń.

According to his information, the UPA subunits annihilated over 15,000 Poles in the province of Wołyń.

Chief of Police and SD
of Wołyń and Podole
Pütz

Source: Document No. IV-H-53/43, Łuck, September 14, 1943, quoted in Władysław Filar, *"Burza" na Wołyniu: Z dziejów 27 Wołyńskiej Dywizji Piechoty Armii Krajowej* (Warszawa: Rada Ochrony Pamięci Walk i Męczeństwa, 1997), p. 53. See also Leon Popek, Tomasz Trusiuk, Paweł Wira, and Zenon Wira, comps., *Wołyński testament* (Lublin: Towarzystwo Przyjaciół Krzemieńca i Ziemi Wołyńsko-Podolskiej, 1997), p. 168.

Abwehr (Counterintelligence) Report, September 15, 1943

September 15, 1943
Orderbook
16 668/04010/43 III G2
Zdolbunov
Secret

An officer of Abwehr Section III in Zhitomir has received the following report from his agent:

In mid-June 1943, the 3rd Conference of the OUN (Organization of Ukrainian Nationalists) [the Third Great Conference of the Organization of Ukrainian Nationalists, or VZOUN, was held between August 21 and 25, 1943] took place in Western Ukraine, attended by representatives from other Ukrainian political groups. It is quite probable that among the participants were certain groups of the Melnik [Melnyk] movement, groups of former military adherents of UNR (Petliura), some top military experts from different Ukrainian groups, as well as non-party people.

On the initiative of the OUN (Bandera), prior to the conference discussions had been held aimed at the creation of an All-Ukrainian union of military character.

The following has been learned about the conference from Ukrainian circles not directly interested in the OUN:

1. In its resolution the conference rejected the OUN claims to the exclusive management of Ukrainian affairs.

2. A central command of purely military nature was formed under the name "Supreme Command of the Ukrainian Insurgent Army" (UPA). It is founded on All-Ukrainian representation, non-party principles and political independence from Bandera's OUN and other political groupings. The Supreme Command is staffed mostly with representatives of Bandera's OUN and military experts from other groups. Taras Bulba refused to be placed under the UPA, after which some 200 of his supporters must have left him and joined the UPA.

3. The structure of the OUN has undergone radical changes in consequence of the renunciation of its fascist character, which outwardly manifests itself in the abolition of the fascist salute and a change in the existing national emblem.

The work of the UPA Supreme Command focuses on strengthening the organizational and combat activity of nationalist bands in all regions where the influence of Bandera's OUN is felt. In Western Ukraine an officer and NCO school is being set up. Three striking forces named North, Middle, and South have been raised, aimed at advancing from Western Ukraine in the direction of the Dnieper. Already at the end of July 1943 there appeared on the outskirts of Zhitomir units of 500-800 men each, which had moved there through the area Korosten–Radomyshl–Makarov.

(Signature)

Source: Central State Archives of the October Revolution, Organs of State Government and State Management of the Ukrainian SSR, fund CMF-8, invt. 2, file 234, pp. 93-94, quoted in Yu. Yu. Kondufor et al., eds., *History Teaches a Lesson,* trans. from Russian by Vadim Piatkovsky (Kiev: Politvidav Ukrainy, 1986), pp. 230-31.

Summaries of Other Field Reports and a German Leaflet

May 17, 1943. A Chief of the SS and Police report in the General Government speaks of the "burning of properties and the beating and shooting of Poles" by "Ukrainian partisans" in April of that year. It also states that the Ukrainian Central Committee (Ukrainskyi Tsentralnyi Komitet, or UTsK) provided the UPA with arms and food.

May 18, 1943. An Army Group North, Ukraine, report states that the Germans are in possession of a Ukrainian order for the "shooting of Poles in villages."

May 31, 1944. A Fourth Panzer Army report states: "*Der Polnischen Bevölkerung O. des S. hat sie* [UPA] *wie schon im Bericht darauf hingewiesen, schärfsten kampf angesagt. Die UPA fordert nach wie vor kategorisch, daß das Polentum die Ukraine bis zum San räumt. Infolgedessen halten die Brandstiftungen an polnischen Siedlungen und Ermordungen der polnischen Bevölkerung in unmindertem Umfange an.*" (As reported, it [the UPA] initiated a hard battle with the Polish people west of the [River] San. The UPA categorically demands, as previously mentioned, that the Poles leave the Ukrainian territory up to the San. As a result, there follow the burning and murder of the Polish population in its settlements which does not diminish in scope and range.)

In a leaflet (*Under Einsatzraum: Ost-Galizien*) distributed to German units we read: "Although the leadership of the UPA has no intentions of fighting against the German army, acts of sabotage against German administration do occur. Above all, however, [there is] the barbaric extermination of the Poles by the UPA."

Source of summaries: Ryszard Torzecki, *Polacy i Ukraińcy: Sprawa ukraińska w czasie II wojny światowej na terenie II Rzeczypospolitej* (Warszawa: Wydawnictwo Naukowe PWN, 1993), pp. 263, 283, n. 78.

Otto Wächter's Congratulatory Speech to the SS-Galizien, February 22, 1944

While you, full of hope, openly engage in battle against the Bolsheviks, the enemy of the world, the people from the green cadre [UPA] murder innocent men, women and children. In this way they sink all the more into crimes and chaos, covering their nation's name with shame. In the battle for the future of one's country and a better world, one does not kill in treachery but fights in the open, in a disciplined way, as a soldier at the front of this unique war.

Source: Archiwum Zakładu Historii Partii, Delegatura Rządu RP na Kraj, 202 AM/1640/10, quoted in Ryszard Torzecki, *Kwestia ukraińska w polityce III Rzeszy 1933-1945* (Warszawa: Książka i Wiedza, 1972), p. 326, n. 14.

Report on a UPA Meeting with the Wehrmacht, March 13, 1944

March 13, 1944
Strictly secret
Of national importance

To the Leader of the Security Police and SD in the General Government Oberführer SS and Col. of Police, Bierkamp (personal) Kraków

On March 5, 1944, a meeting took place between my official N. with a certain Ukrainian who presented himself as Harasymovskyi [pseudonym of Ivan Hryniokh] and stated that he had plenipotentiary powers from the central command of the OUN-B to conduct talks in the name of the political and military sectors of that organization which represented all the territories inhabited by Ukrainians....

[Harasymovskyi] attributes the responsibility for the continuing terror between the Ukrainians and the Poles exclusively to the Polish side. At the beginning of the occupation of the former Polish territories, there was peace and tranquility between the Poles and the Ukrainians. But later, under Warsaw's initiative, an unbridled terror emerged which touched many Ukrainian localities. At first, the OUN tried to convince the Poles to come to their senses and it put forth many constructive propositions. But the Poles underestimated the strength of the Ukrainians, especially that of the Bandera group. The escalation of the terror aimed at the Ukrainians forced the OUN-B to resist and to issue an order that military units should answer the Polish terror with retaliatory actions for which the organization accepts full responsibility. The terror against the Poles will be curtailed immediately as soon as all obstacles are removed toward the attainment by that organization of its chief objective: battle with the Bolsheviks — provided that the Ukrainians will receive a German guarantee of protection from Polish terror.

Source: TsDAHO of Ukraine, set 4628, invt. 1, vol. 10, quoted in Grzegorz Motyka, "Ukraińska orientacja," *Karta* (Warszawa) 23 (1997): 56-59. Harasymovskyi's claim that "under Warsaw's initiative, an unbridled terror emerged which touched many Ukrainian localities" is pure fantasy. The rest of his claims are also beyond belief, except for his admission that an order had been issued by the OUN-B — not for "retaliatory actions," but for ethnic cleansing.

Telegram of the Chief of the Kraków Police (Bierkamp) to the Chief of the Lwów Police, March 15, 1944 — Two Versions

Version I

March 15, 1944
Lwów
Telegram BdS [leader of the security police]
Kraków

The chief of the order police submitted the following report to the higher command of the SS and police:
On March 12, 1944, from the gendarmerie unit ... [the ellipsis is in the original document] came the following report from the gendamerie post:
On March 11, 1944, in the vicinity of Podlamia [Podkamień] ... 200 members of the Ukrainian independence movement declared that they would fight against the Bolsheviks alongside the German Wehrmacht. On March 12, 1944, their number rose to 1,200 persons.

They come from RKU [Reichskommissariat Ukraine] and most of them are armed. In the monastery in P[odkamień] there are about 500 Polish fugitives.

On March 12, 1944, this monastery was fired upon with howitzers by the Ukrainian freedom fighters. Furthermore, they attempted to break into the monastery, but did not obtain permission to do this from the Wehrmacht. The gendarmerie post was not able to ascertain what happened next....

BdO [BdS] and SD in the General Government Oberführer Col. of the Police — Bierkamp

---

Source: Kiev archives, quoted in Grzegorz Motyka, "Ukraińska orientacja," *Karta* (Warszawa) 23 (1997): 62.

Version II

March 15, 1944
Secret

On March 11, 1944, in the environs of Podlamia (P293) [Podkamień] 200 participants in the Ukrainian Freedom Movement [UPA] declared themselves ready to join hands with the German Armed Forces in fighting Bolshevism. In the course of March 12, 1944, their number reached about 1,200.

On March 12, 1944, the monastery in Brody was shelled from grenade launchers by the Ukrainian freedom fighters who also attempted to break into the monastery.

Major Dr. Giebel, officer of the intelligence and counter-intelligence section of Operational Team Brody, confirmed this information and stated that the army had supplied the armed band with weapons and dressings. To my mind, he should have used the term "friendly troops" instead of "armed band."

Maj.-Gen. of the Police
(Signature)

Source: Central State Archives of the October Revolution, Organs of State Government and State Management of the Ukrainian SSR, fund 4620, invt. 3, file 378, p. 88, quoted in Yu. Yu. Kondufor et al., eds., *History Teaches a Lesson*, trans. from Russian by Vadim Piatkovsky (Kiev: Politvidav Ukrainy, 1986), p. 232.

Report on a UPA Meeting with the Wehrmacht, March 24, 1944

March 24, 1944
Lwów
Of national importance
Strictly secret

Report

The second meeting with Harasymovskyi began late....

1. OUN is ready to cease immediately all actions which are injurious to German interests and to end all terror against the Poles....

OUN-B also feels that it ought to receive permission to conduct military campaigns using its own forces against the Polish bands operating beyond the pale of groupings of people and gives full guarantee that this action will be directed only against the Polish bands and that it will in no way spread to the Poles living in a given area or to the nearby Polish villages which have nothing in common with the bands. After each encounter with a Polish band, the OUN is prepared to present proof that that band perpetrated atrocities against Ukrainians, and to inform [the Germans] how and under what circumstances it was disposed of.

Obersturmführer SS and commissar of the Criminal Police (—)

Source: TsDAHO of Ukraine, set 4628, invt. 1, vol. 10, quoted in Grzegorz Motyka, "Ukraińska orientacja," *Karta* (Warszawa) 23 (1997): 63-64.

Report on a UPA Meeting with the Wehrmacht, April 8, 1944

April 8, 1944
Lwów
Of national importance
Secret

In accordance with the agreement of April 7,

1944, a meeting took place in the residence of the county elder, Nehring, between the undersigned and the leader of the UPA band, Orel, in the village of Kamionka Strumiłowa....

I presented Orel the following demands from which he was not allowed to deviate a single step.

1. Full loyalty in respect to German interests.

2. The cessation of terrorist activity against the Polish people. I began by saying that Orel and his UPA unit is not prevented, on their own initiative, from fighting with the Polish band in the forests. That fight, however, cannot in any case spread to the Polish settlements and villages or to those Polish men, women, and children who do not belong to the band. If Orel can prove that the local Polish men and women are acting illegally or that they are supporting the band, he should present that intelligence report to the security police, which will avail itself of the information and hold the accused Polish men and women accountable.

3. To resign from exerting any pressure on the Ukrainian police.

4. To resign from exerting any pressure on the Galician SS infantry division.

Orel, without wasting words, declared that he is ready to abide by these four demands, except for the stipulation contained in point number 2, which deprives him of punitive action against suspected or guilty local Polish men and women and their settlements. On that point, he first wishes to obtain the consent of his superiors and to discuss it once more in a subsequent meeting.

Obersturmführer SS and criminal commissar (—)

Source: Kiev archives, quoted in Grzegorz Motyka, "Ukraińska orientacja," *Karta* (Warszawa) 23 (1997): 67-68.

Appendix to Operative Dispatch of the Chief of Security Police and SD in Eastern Galicia, April 8, 1944

April 8, 1944

SS-Sturmbahnführer Schmitz (Chief of intel-[ligence] & cint. [counterintelligence] section of Prützmann's Combat Team), whom I invited to discuss the negotiations with the UPA, reported on arrival that with a view to expanding his intelligence network, he had made contact with small groups of bandits in order use them for conducting intelligence and sabotage against Soviet partisans and the Red Army.

This cooperation has brought in signal [i.e., remarkable] results.

He doesn't know whether SS-Obergruppenführer Prützmann has informed the Reichsführer of this cooperation, but he believes that such things are usually not reported.

The said cooperation gave him the impression of the UPA honestly trying to support German interests as much as possible.

I presume that Schmitz has built, with the help of the UPA, a good intelligence net, but it seems that he and his subordinates rather overestimate the gained results.

(Signature)

Source: Central State Archives of the October Revolution, Organs of State Government and State Management of the Ukrainian SSR, fund 4620, invt. 3, file 378, p. 85, quoted in Yu. Yu. Kondufor et al., eds., *History Teaches a Lesson,* trans. from Russian by Vadim Piatkovsky (Kiev: Politvidav Ukrainy, 1986), p. 233.

Report on the UPA Contact with Wehrmacht, April 15, 1944

April 15, 1944
Main State Security of the Reich
Gruppenführer SS Müller (personal)
Berlin
Of national importance
Secret

Contents: UPA contacts with the Wehrmacht, police and civilian administrative institutions.

Toward the end of January 1944, numerous units of the UPA began to seek direct contacts with the (Wehrmacht) military units....

Although Harasymovskyi, as the official representative of the leadership of the OUN-B, continually assures us that that organization will give imminent orders forbidding actions against German interests, subversive activity continues to be conducted against the Ukrainian police that has remained in German service as well as against the voluntary infantry division SS "Galizien"; so does the ruthless Ukrainian terror against Polish women, children, and entire settlements. These activities of the UPA units in the district of Galicia do not attest at all to the fact that they have received directives from the central leadership of the directorate which are in keeping with the understandings stemming from the talks between official N. and Harasymovskyi

Moreover ... the Ukrainian terror directed against the Polish people who have congregated together is continually on the increase.

Source: Kiev archives, quoted in Grzegorz Motyka, "Ukraińska orientacja," *Karta* (Warszawa) 23 (1997): 68-69.

Report on the UPA Contact with Wehrmacht, April 21, 1944

April 21, 1944
Lwów
Main State Security of the Reich
Gruppenführer SS Müller (personal)
Berlin
Strictly secret

Contents: UPA contacts with the Wehrmacht, police and civilian administrative institutions

In spite of this [the promise of OUN-B to "curtail its terror against the Poles" made during German—OUN-B negotiations], the German side is forced to conclude that the UPA bands continue their punitive actions against the Poles and continue to accept deserters into their ranks from the Ukrainian police and the volunteer SS "Galizien" Division.

Source: TsDAHO of Ukraine, set 4628, invt. 1, vol. 10, quoted in Grzegorz Motyka, "Ukraińska orientacja," *Karta* (Warszawa) 23 (1997): 69-70.

Nehring's Report, May 19, 1944

Kamionka Strumiłowa
May 19, 1944
Leader of the group
Khmil

2) On the remaining questions, I personally do not see any possibility of positive cooperation since individual UPA groups, in all likelihood on orders of the UPA leadership, in a willful way continue to burn Polish villages and even landed property. I regard this destruction of property not only as intolerable during war but also, above all, as a crime that will burden the Ukrainian nation in the future.

Source: Kiev archives, quoted in Grzegorz Motyka, "Ukraińska orientacja," *Karta* (Warszawa) 23 (1997): 72.

Field Report from the Eastern Territories to Gerhard von Mende, Director of the Department of Affairs in the Occupied Eastern Territories, Ministry of the Third Reich, November 2, 1944

In the interest of realizing its objectives, the UPA — beginning in 1944 — has launched a growing initiative to link its plans to the local units of the Wehrmacht. At the same time, orders were given to its units to support the activities of the Wehrmacht and to cease attacks on individual German soldiers or smaller units of the army for the purpose of obtaining firearms or other supplies. The adequate preparation of the groundwork among the Ukrainian population and the removal of the political obstacles against military cooperation with the Germans have resulted in a unique type of general cooperation between the UPA and the Wehrmacht in August 1944.

Regarding the extent and the means of conducting this cooperation, evidently serious contentions have arisen between the directorate of the OUN and that of the UPA because various military necessities arising from the battles with the Red Army did not always fit the politics of the OUN. That organization has kept itself in the background, and it matters a great deal to it that its military cooperation with Germany, and in particular with the Wehrmacht, does not come to light.

Just as the relationship of the UPA to the Germans, so too have its relations to the Poles and the smaller nationalities of the Soviet Union remained under the influence of the political concepts of the OUN. While a war of extermination had been declared against the Poles because of the age-old tensions between these two nations, regarding other nationalities of the Soviet Union, a policy of coalition has been embarked upon based on the foundation of a mutual war of liberation to be waged against the Soviet Union, or rather, Russia, which found its expression also in the organizational phase (by incorporating individual units of these nationalities into the UPA)....

The UPA conducted its activity on three levels:

    a) anti-German
    b) anti-Polish
    c) anti-Soviet

Ad b) Under the battle-cry of "revenge" for the Polish policy of extermination in the years 1918-39 and hostile disposition under first the Soviet and then the German occupation, the OUN-UPA began a campaign of annihilation of the Poles, which released all those instincts associated with vengeance stemming from age-old animosities and whose object was the wholesale physical destruction of all that was Polish in this territory. Irrespective of the stated reasons for this war ("Poles are the Soviet agents of destruction," "Poles are setting the Germans against the Ukrainians," and the like), one cannot deny that the objective of the leadership of the OUN-UPA was to cleanse the Ukrainian territory of everything which was Polish, or at least to destroy that which the Poles had achieved in this territory in the years 1918-39. The canvas of the map of nationalities, and foremost in Wołyń, is bound to change fundamentally as a result of this war.

Source: Bundesarchiv-Abteilungen Potsdam, R 6, No. 150, pp. 6, 11, quoted in Leon Popek, Tomasz Trusiuk, Paweł Wira, and Zenon Wira, comps., *Wołyński testament* (Lublin: Towarzystwo Przyjaciół Krzemieńca i Ziemi Wołyńsko-Podolskiej, 1997), pp. 168-69.

JEWISH

Leon Weliczker Wells

December 6, 1943; in the evening.

I should like to tell about the Polish and Ukrainian underground. On the whole, the Ukrainians in this section of Poland [Lwów], in the beginning, joined the Germans, and took a very active part in the murder of the Jews. After a time, seeing that the Germans were not going to give them an independent Ukraine, a group of them became partisans, under the leadership of one Bandera; for this reason they were known as the Banderowcy. Their fight was not against the Germans but for a "General Peace Conference." Their aim was to prove that they were an absolute majority in this area. To become an absolute majority they had to get rid of the Poles. The Banderowcy would catch an important Pole, cut him to pieces, and place him in a public place for other Poles to see and take note; they wanted to force the Poles to move out of this part of the country. The Jews were even more afraid of the Banderowcy than the SS....

Christmas passed. It was now the New Year. At the start of of year 1944, all-night shootings began between Ukrainians and Poles.

Source: Leon Weliczker Wells, *The Janowska Road* (New York: The Macmillan Company, 1963), pp. 236-37. The author kept a diary during the war.

Deposition of M. V. (b. 1912 in Tomaszów Mazowiecki), Gathered by the Jewish Historical Commission of Poland, Recorded in Landsberg, Bavaria on April 10, 1946

This happened in 1943, when the Germans were

staggering from their first big defeats. That was also the year Ukrainian nationalists became very active. They were convinced the time had come for a German withdrawal which would leave in its wake an independent Ukrainian national state upon the Ukrainian earth.

During this year, I was still in the Polish village of Kurdyban-Warkowiecki, fifteen kilometers from the county capital of Dubno [in Wołyń]. The village was built on adjoining hills, and straddled the highway connecting Dubno and Rovno [Równe]. The huts stretch on for a distance of two kilometers, with huge gaps from one to the other. Seventy percent of the inhabitants were Poles, the rest Czechs and Ukrainians. Until June 1941, when the German-Soviet war broke out, I was the principal of the local school, so the villagers weren't exceptionally hostile to me. This was how, in the terrible year of 1943 when the Jews in the Ukraine had long been exterminated, I was able to save myself through forged "Aryan" papers. I was also put up by different peasants, who, to tell the truth, did it with great reluctance. Besides me, twenty-two other Jews found refuge in the village, staying with two Czech farmers. Two Jews also stayed with Poles. Altogether, twenty-five Jews found hiding places in this village, and all of them survived till Liberation.

Every night of that whole year of 1943, the village faced great danger. As soon as night fell, a barrage of shots ripped through the village, and wherever the eye turned—fires. These were the Polish villages set ablaze by the *Banderovtsy* [Banderowcy] Ukrainian gangs. The Poles were shot and butchered.

Our village maintained a constant death watch, especially the Jews who were hiding here, because the end could come any second—if not at the hands of the Ukrainian gangs, then surely through betrayal by the Poles. For the Poles, there were the cities to flee to, but Jews—where could we run? Gradually, the village armed itself. The peasants had sixty rifles, twelve automatics, six heavy automatics, and up to 400 grenades in their possession. The Jews who stayed with Poles were also armed—including myself and two others—and sometimes, the Jews who stayed with the Czech farmers also got guns.

The attacks came at us in steady waves, but the tightly organized defense didn't break to let the brigands through. I took an active part in the defense. I also used to write proclamations for the peasants on organizing defense and I tried raising the combat morale of the defenders. I'll give you a copy of one of these proclamations. I've also preserved the originals.

The other armed Jews also kept watch at night and took part in the defense of the village. The attitude of Poles to Jews in this village was tolerant as long as they felt their own skins in danger.

For a whole year, practically, we never slept during the night. We were on constant alert. There were pitched battles many times and during one exchange, two people fell—the Pole Antek Wiezinski, and the Czech, Jorko Studenny. Similar bravery was shown by the fighting Jews alongside the Poles in the defense of the Polish village of Bortnica, eleven kilometers from Dubno. The bloodiest fighting in this village broke out on Christmas eve, December 25 [*sic*], 1943, which was only six weeks before the Red Army came. Fifteen Poles and eight Jews, all from Dubno, took part in this battle. This small unit held out in two houses against an invading force of 400 men. The battle lasted all night and ended tragically for the defenders after they used up all their ammunition. The eight Poles and two Jews were overrun and killed. The others got away and avoided falling into the hands of those savages. The strongest Jewish resistance was put up in defense of the Polish village of Panska Dolina, near the town of Młynów, Dubno County.

This village recruited 160 Polish combatants and had an autonomous Jewish strongpoint one-and-a-half kilometers outside the village, by the wooded area. Kuna Gutenberg, born in Dubno in 1911, a painter by profession, told me the following facts about the defense of Panska Dolina:

> The Jewish stronghold, which was a part of a larger Polish one, was manned by fifty Jews, most of them heavily armed. The guns were gotten from the Poles by our liaison men. They requisitioned their own food. During attacks, the two groups

united and defense was carefully coordinated. For the most part, the Jews were the first to fight off the marauders, since they also operated from the forests. The Poles built concrete trenches and had modern, low-caliber weapons and even machine guns. On a certain day in July, almost 3,000 rebels attacked, but the small number of Jews fought back with such fury that the Ukrainians fled in panic, leaving hordes of dead behind them on the battlefield—five wagonloads of corpses were filled, not counting those who had jumped into wells, and the wounded. But despite the vigorous organized defense, almost the whole village went up in smoke. The combatants didn't pull out, but lived to see the Red Army arrive.

A joint defense by Poles and Jews was also organized in the village of Zemówka, which was situated between the renegade Ukrainian villages of [names inaudible]. On the fourteenth of July, 1943, when everyone was out working at gathering the harvest, the village was suddenly put to the torch. I could go on about other battles where there was joint defense of Polish villages.

Source: In Isaiah Trunk, *Jewish Responses to Nazi Persecution: Collective and Individual Behavior in Extremis* (New York: Stein and Day, 1979), pp. 250-52. The initials of the person deposed (M. V.) most probably stand for Moshe Weissberg. See Shmuel Spector, *The Holocaust of Volhynian Jews 1941-1944* (Jerusalem: Yad Vashem—The Federation of Volhynian Jews, 1990), p. 267 and n., 33. Spector renders the village of Zemówka as Żeniowka.

From the Accounts of Jewish Children Transcribed between 1945 and 1949

[Seweryn Dobroszklanka, b. 1931] One night, we were awakened by some Jews who came from town and told us that there's an action in Bereźne (in the province of Wołyń), and that the Germans were coming for us. Without taking time to dress, we all ran off to the forest....

One day, the Banderowcy surrounded the forest and found three Jewish bunkers and shelters. They threw a grenade into one of them and no one came out of it alive. A mother with five children was in that bunker. Her name was Fisch. One of her daughters was pasturing cows at the time and thus survived. In another bunker, there was a family also consisting of five persons. The grenade which was thrown in failed to explode and, as the people tried to flee in all directions, they were shot at by the Banderowcy. In all, 20 persons were killed that day. We were not in the forest at the time. Some people came and told us about the attack. The following day, several persons went to the forest to see what had happened. Some had fled, leaving their families behind. What they saw there was terrible. Parts of human bodies lay on the ground. The Banderowcy often conducted these types of attacks and killed very many Jews. There were about one hundred Jews in the forest from Małyńsk. Of these, about 50 survived; the rest were killed by the Banderowcy.

Three families of Polish settlers remained in the colony in which we were staying. These settlers were armed and although their rifles, in comparison to the overwhelming strength of the attackers, didn't do much good, they did not want to leave the place. They said that they preferred to die there, rather than to go to Germany. These Poles helped us.

The Ukrainians spread the rumor that they would not murder Jews and Poles. At that time, I worked for a Ukrainian peasant and pastured his cows. The Banderowcy saw me, but did me no harm. The Jews hiding in the forest found out about this and began to come out. It turned out that the rumors were only a trap set by the Banderowcy. They attacked three Polish homes, in which there were also Jews, and killed twelve Jews and ten Poles. They entered the house in which my mother was staying. One of them stood by the door. My mother and several others managed to escape. The rest did not even try to escape because they knew these Ukrainians and did not believe that they would be killed by them. The Banderowcy ordered the people to lie on the ground and shot them with a machine gun. Then they took the victims' boots and their better clothes and set fire to the house....

I did not leave the forest for three months.

We did not know what was happening in the world or where the front was. In December we often heard cannon fire but did not know what it meant.

The last two weeks were the worst. Running before the Banderowcy, we had no time to take any possessions with us. We could not light any fires during the days and, since it was very cold at that time, we froze miserably.

One day, two of our people went on reconnaissance and met the Russians nearby. It was January 20, 1944.

[Szyja Flajsz, b. 1930] During the occupation I lived with my parents and sisters in Bereźne until the summer of 1942. The last "action" took place in August 1942. My father was no longer alive. The Ukrainians brought my mother, my sisters, and me to the square — but I immediately ran away. They found me and brought me out again, but I ran away once more. I ran away three times and three times they found me, but the fourth time I hid under a bed and they did not discover my whereabouts. I lay on my side for the whole day and did not move. The Ukrainians searched and the German dogs trained to seek out Jews ran through the room twice, but they did not find me....

The Ukrainians began to search the bushes looking for Jews in hiding. One older Jew who joined us later told us that we had to go further, to where the Poles lived. We went by forests nourishing ourselves on berries; we begged for bread in the villages. We arrived in Woronówka and stayed there until spring 1943....

There was a farmer there, Zygmunt Kuriata, and he took me in to pasture his cattle. He knew that I was a Jew but was not afraid because the entire village consisted of Kuriatas and Torgońs and they were all related. I had it very good with him.... Later, the Bulbowcy and Banderowcy began to attack our village and we had to flee to the forest with our possessions each time. When the Soviet army arrived, the Kuriata family went to Lower Silesia, but not before signing me up on their evacuation card. When I left them, they were sad and cried. This was in December 1946.

[Leon Gewandter, b. 1932] During the occupation, I lived with my parents in Bukaczowce, in the county of Rohatyn, the province of Stanisławów.... We had to go to Rohatyn because all the Jews were chased out of Bukaczowce.... I wanted to return to Bukaczowce for our belongings.... A Ukrainian took me into his house, allowed me to wash up, and fed me. From there, I went to a Polish peasant who had our belongings in his keeping and remained in his attic for a few months — until they began to round up the people for forced labor in Germany. The people rebelled. They did not want to go. The Ukrainian fascists and the Germans then set the village on fire....

The front drew nearer.... We went a few at a time, in between German encampments, to the Dniestr and Świerz. There were already many Poles there who had fled from the Ukrainians. The Banderowcy were murdering the Jews and the Poles at that time. I remained by the river until the Soviet armies arrived.

[Mieczysław Korman, b. 1937] One day, a fire broke out. The Ukrainians set the village [Niedzieliska, in Lwów Province] on fire because only Poles lived there. Everyone ran off grabbing their possessions and cows, and we went with them. We fell into a ditch. The Ukrainians shot at the people, and thinking that we were dead, went on. When they left, we fled.... On the following day, we returned to Niedzieliska and went back to the Wojtków [the family with whom the Kormans were staying]. Except for the Wojtków house, almost the entire village was destroyed by fire.

Source: Stanisław Wroński and Maria Zwolakowa, eds., *Polacy Żydzi, 1939-1945* (Warszawa: Książka i Wiedza, 1971), pp. 324-25, 327-28, 330. These excerpts come from the recollections of Jewish children transcribed between the years 1945-49 by the Historical Commissions under the Jewish Committees in Poland. They may be found in the following archival collections in the Jewish Historical Institute (ŻIH): Sygn. 1222, 2739, 3655, and 3751.

From the account of Karolina Heuman (b. 1928)

I was born in the town of Nowy Sącz.... The war found us in Truskawiec [near Lwów].... In the winter of 1941-42, we were deported to the ghetto in Drohobycz.... We managed to escape.... My brother and I were placed by Father in the cloister of the Sisters of Charity in Czerwonogród.... My brother perished during a raid on the cloister by the followers of Bandera. He was then nine years old. Here is how, at the time, I described the events of this horrible day:

> It was the second of February 1945, at eleven o'clock. The night was dark and terrifying, filled with some inhuman menacing mystery. I was in the cloister of the Sisters of Charity in Czerwonogród. There were three of us young girls and my beloved brother Jędruś [Andrzej]. I woke up with a start during the night and heard terrible shooting all around the cloister. There was often shooting going on at night, but it never made the same impression on me as then. I got up and walked up to the window. It seemed to me that it was strangely bright outside. I lay down again, but some inner voice would not let me lie. I started to get dressed, and I dressed my brother. All of us girls were already dressed when Sister Władysława walked in and said that Czerwonogród was in flames and that we were surrounded by Bandera's followers. We were terrified.
>
> Right away, we went over to the bedroom of the Sisters, and there, by the window, we stood for three hours, watching the terrible tortures of people who were fleeing in panic from the flames. The inhuman barbarians ran around furiously with flares in their hands and set fires to one hut after another, and whenever they saw someone, if they could, they grabbed him alive, and if not, then they would shoot him on the spot. They captured one family in our village and all that was later found of the children were fragments of burned-up bones, and the father's skin had been ripped off from his stomach all the way to his head. We, the girls, stood all the time by the window, waiting for what would happen next. We felt that our own lives, too, were hanging by a thread. We said that they are leaving us for dessert.
>
> Soon, our suppositions came to pass. At three o'clock in the morning, we heard terrible knocking on the front gate, which seemed to foretell our approaching end. Sister Władysława called us into the chapel and began to pray and prepare us for death. We knelt in front of the altar for perhaps ten minutes. During that brief moment, my life as it had been, and the life to which I thought I was soon to pass, stood before my eyes.
>
> I had no regrets about dying because until then I had not experienced contentment on earth. I just felt very sorry for my brother. I knew that he was still but a child and that one day he would forget about everything. I wanted him to grow up into a good human being, and it was really for him that I lived. However, unfortunately, it did not happen as I had thought. All my hopes faded into nothingness. In the last moment, when the glass of the windows in the lower corridor started falling onto the floor with a loud crash, Sister Superior hid us under the altar.

Those who survived repatriated to Poland.

Source: Wiktoria Śliwowska, ed., *The Last Eyewitnesses: Children of the Holocaust Speak*, trans. from Polish by Julian and Fay Bussgang (Evanston: Northwestern University Press, 1998), pp. 187-89. This annotated work consists of Jewish oral histories assembled by the Association of the Children of the Holocaust in Poland. Karolina Heuman's account was composed between February 8, 1992 and February 18, 1993. The indented passage above prefaced by the sentence containing the phrase "at the time" was apparently written just after the UPA attack on the cloister. Other references to UPA atrocities can be found on pp. 64-66, 85, 162, 173-74, and 284. In the account of Karol Galiński (p. 173) from Mosty Wielke in the province of Lwów, we read:

> When we recovered, we entered a nearby Ukrainian village, and in one of the homes we asked for something to eat and that they show us the road to Stanisłówka. Of course, we said that we were Poles and that the Ukrainians had chased us. An old woman burst out crying over us, saying, "What are they doing to you; how can they have no fear of God?" As can be seen, among Ukrainians there were also decent people.

A description of the UPA attack on the Polish village of Stanisłówka follows.

UNITED NATIONS WAR CRIMES COMMISSION

Letter

[Page stamped:] 1412
United Nations War Crimes Commission
[blocked out section]
Church House
Great Smith Street, S.W.I.

Dr. Litawski:

Reference Polish charge 6697 it seems certain that the "3rd Schützen Division" referred to in line 2 of page 1 is 14th SS (galizische) Division, which was formed in Poland in 1943 from Polish [sic] and Ukrainian volunteers and was trained in Galicia.

According to the U.S. "order of facts" it was commanded by General Fritz Freitag (Brigadeführer).

I have contacted the War Office who confirm the above. They have nothing about General Kapuscianski.

Signature
(Illegible)
31-10
[Page 1, stamped:] 1413

United Nations War Crimes Commission Polish Charges Against German War Criminals of Ukrainian Origin

Registered Number: 6697/P/U/1124.
Case No. 1124.
Date of receipt in Secretariat:
October 23, 1947.
Transmitted by: The Polish
Representative on the U.N.W.C.C.,

Name of accused, his rank and unit of official position (Not to be translated):

All members of the 2nd Coy of the Ukrainian Army and 4th Coy of the 3rd Schuetzen-Division "Hałyczyna," in particular against the following persons:

KUBIJOWICZ; MELNYK, Col.; PYNDUS, eng.; MARTYN; BARANOWSKI, Jarosław; FREYTAG–Gen.; ZAPOROZEC, Michał; SUSZKA, Colonel; KIRYLOZUK, Patia; BARWINSKI, Colonel KAPUSCIANSKI, Gen.

Date and place of commission of alleged crime:

September, 1942–February, 1944
District Zamosc in Poland, in particular villages Borek, Hamernia, Socha, Palikrowa, Huta Pieniacka, Pawłow niear [near] Radziechow and Pawłow near Rejowiec.

Number and description of crime in war crimes list. References to relevant provisions of national law:

Wanton devastation and destruction of property
Complicity in deportation
Systematic terrorism
Putting hostages to death
Complicity in mass-murder

SHORT STATEMENT OF FACTS

The above listed persons took part in organising – according to the instructions issued by the Hitlerite authorities – of U.P.A. (Ukrainska Powstanesa Armia – Ukrainian Insurgent Army) and SS-Schuetzen – Galizien, later called "Hałyczyna". Both were used for deportation of civilian Polish population, for destruction of whole villages and for murdering their inhabitants.

[Page 2, stamped:] 1414

PARTICULARS OF ALLEGED CRIME

On 26/27 February, 1944, the 4th Coy of a certain battalion of the SS-Schuetzen Division Galizien cordoned off a Polish village "Huta Pieniacka", Brodzki District. The inhabitants of this village were herded in a church and then led to sheds where they were burned alive. Those who tried to take refuge at home were killed with knives regardless of sex and age (many women and children were thus killed). Approximately 500 persons were killed in this action and their homes set on fire.

On 10th March, 1944, both 2nd Coy of UPA and 4th Coy of the SS-Galizien cordoned off the villages Podkamien & Polikrowy and slaughtered their inhabitants (approx. 800 persons). Scores of persons were killed in the villages Pawłow near Radziechow and Pawłow near Rejowiec by the same companies for the sole reason that their inhabitants were Poles of catholic creed. The same happened in the following villages: Socha, Borek, Hamernia and several other places in Zamosc District.

Murders of Polish civilians became so frequent that Himmler found it necessary to issue a special instruction which forbade murdering of civilian population unless specially ordered to.

As it transpires from the documents in the possession of both the Polish Institute of National Memory (Polski Instytut Pamięci Narodowej) and the Polish Main National Office for War Crimes, as well as from other documents, reports and evidence, the accused Kubijowicz, Melnik, Pyndus, Martyn, Suszka and Baranowski were for both political education aiming at arousing of racial and national hatred towards Poles and for direct supervision of murdering of innocent people, putting hostages to death and setting whole villages on fire.

[Page 3, stamped:] 1415

PARTICULARS OF EVIDENCE IN SUPPORT

The Director of the "Instytut Pamięci Narodowej" Dr. Stanisław [illegible] in his report on the activities of both the UPA and the SS–Division Galizien otherwise "Hałyczyna" stated that Kapuscianski, Kubijowicz, Col. Melnyk, Col. Sushka, Pyndus, Martyn and Baranowski not only did nothing to prevent the crimes committed by the subordinates but took part in organising their units and in training the men for the purpose of annihilation and destruction of Polish villages and their inhabitants.

The Gefreiter Grzegorz MELNIK during the interrogation conducted by the interrogating officer, JESKE, and in presence of Andusikiewicz, stated the following: —

Grzegorz MELNIK: — A Ukrainian from Poland. During the war was in the USSR and immediately after the German invasion volunteered for the German Army. He was attached to the SS-Galizien. He stated that during his service with the a/m Division he was constantly imbued with hatred towards Poles and was urged to commit several atrocities on the Polish civilian population. Melnik himself as well as 19 other members of his unit were (4th Coy) awarded special orders for carrying out their duties which consisted of murdering civilians, setting their villages on fire and shooting at fleeing victims. Melnik further stated that his officer commanding, Cpt. KIRYLOZUK Patia gave orders to murder civilians, burn the villages and fire at civilians who tried to escape from the burning sheds. The whole unit carried out those orders.

This statement was confirmed by ZAPOROZEC Michał.

The following persons gave evidence about murdering of Apolonia Bozek, the family of Uszejec, about burning alive Buczakowa with her daughter, the family of Bełzow and Kucow in Suchowola, Anna Smyk, Marcela Pyrzek, Agnieszka Szałacka and hundreds of other Poles during burning and deportation to Germany for forced labor by 2nd Coy of UPA and 4th Coy of SS-Galizien:

A. Tkaczyk–Nowa Wies; Wł. Guza–Roslop; J. Budzynski–Płock District; A. Więcek–Nielisz; M. Sieklucki–Krasnobrod; Bogdan Kłosinski–Zamosc District; Jan Gębala–Zamosc District; J. Jesionkiewicz–Zamosc District; M. Krel–Zamosc District

and several other persons who were interrogated by the Polish Main National Office for War Crimes in Warsaw. The relevant detailed reports are being printed now in the IInd Part of Biuletyn No. 2 of the Polish Main National Office for War Crimes. In the possession of the Polish Main National Office for War Crimes are also original reports made by the chief of the security police in the District of Zamosc which describes the original activity of the accused units.

Polish Response

Reply to the reply
November 3, 1947
Main Commission for the Investigation of War Crimes in Poland
3024/47
Warsaw

The investigation of our complaint against the "SS-Galizien" Division and "Hałyczyna," as well as certain units of the UPA has been suspended by the United Nations War Crimes Commission in London until specific information is provided regarding the position, the level of authority, and the time span in office of the following major figures accused of committing crimes against the Polish people in the Zamość and Chełm regions and in Wołyń.

1. Gen. Kapuscianki
2. Col. Melnyk
3. Eng. Pyndus
4. Ed[itor] Martyn
5. Ed[itor] Jarosław Baranowski
6. Col. Szuszka
7. Lt. Col. Barwinski

I request that you forward all the facts in your possession pertaining to the above-mentioned persons as soon as possible.
Verte.

Seal
Signature
(Illegible)

Source: United Nations War Crimes Commission. Polish Charges Against German War Criminals [added in script: of Ukrainian Origin]. Registered Number: 6697/P/U/1124. Case No. 1124. Date of receipt in Secretariat: October 23, 1947. Transmitted by: The Polish Representative on the U.N.W.C.C. The first letter and the indictment are written in English. The "Polish response" is in the Polish language. For additional evidence regarding atrocities committed by the SS-Galizien and its police battalions, see Piotrowski, Tadeusz. *Poland's Holocaust.* Jefferson, NC: McFarland, 1998, pp. 229-32.

Appendix D: Chronology

January 25, 1918—Ukrainian Central Council *(Rada)* in Kiev passes a resolution establishing the Ukrainian National Republic (Ukrainska Narodna Respublika, or UNR). The resolution is backdated to January 22.

April 29, 1918—The fall of the UNR.

October 9, 1918—Ukrainian National Rada in Lwów passes a resolution establishing the Western Ukrainian National Republic (Zakhidno-Ukrainska Narodna Respublika, or ZUNR). The ZUNR is not connected to the Ukrainian integral nationalist movement which begins with the founding of the Ukrainian Military Organization (UVO) in 1920.

November 1, 1918—ZUNR government is established in Galicia.

November 13, 1918—ZUNR constitution is approved.

November 1918-July 1919—Polish-Ukrainian (Galician) war.

January 1919—A union of the UNR and ZUNR is ratified and proclaimed but never implemented.

June 25, 1919—Eastern Galicia is placed under the military control and administration of the Second Republic of Poland by the Supreme Council of the Four Powers, which authorizes "the forces of the Polish Republic to pursue their operations as far as the river Zbruch [Zbrucz] (which separates Galicia from East Ukraine)."[1]

June 28, 1919—Poland, as part of the formal recognition of the Polish state, signs the League of Nations' supplementary Treaty of Versailles on the Protection of Minorities. Many Poles regarded the Supreme Council's demand for its acceptance as an affront and as an infringement on their sovereign rights as a nation to manage their own internal affairs. Nevertheless, Poland voluntarily incorporates many of the rights guaranteed by the Treaty into its 1921 Constitution. The Minorities Treaty is unilaterally abrogated by Poland in 1934.

April 21, 1920—Poland and Ukraine sign a treaty of alliance against the Soviet Union. The Ukrainian Directorate led by Symon Petliura agrees to abandon its claim to "Western Ukraine," that is, to the western part of Volhynia and to Eastern Galicia.

April 25, 1920—Combined Polish-Ukrainian forces attack the Bolsheviks in the hope of securing Ukrainian independence. Kiev falls on May 7. This endeavor almost ends in a disaster for Poland. In its counteroffensive, the Red Army reaches the suburbs of Warsaw before being turned back.

August 30, 1920—Ukrainian Military Organization (UVO) is founded in Prague with Ievhen Konovalets at its head. In an article written in 1929, Konovalets gives the impression that the UVO was founded at the meeting of the Sharpshooters' Council in July 1920, when the Sich Sharpshooter Organization (*striltsi*) "in fact ceased to exist." Whether these words mean "*officially* ceased to exist" and whether the UVO was formally established at that meeting as Konovalets implies, are questionable. Szcześniak and Wiesław Szota maintain that the UVO was founded at the August 30, 1920, Prague meeting of the representatives of the Nationalist military organizations. The meeting was called by Konovalets, Andrii Melnyk, and Roman Sushko.[2]

March 18, 1921—Treaty of Riga determines the border (Zbrucz River) between Poland and Soviet Ukraine.

1921—According to Alexander Dallin: "Under Colonel Eugene [Ievhen] Konovalets the OUN and its predecessor organizations had cultivated ties with German intelligence from as far back as 1921."[3] In that year, Richard ("Riko") Jary establishes contact with the Reichswehr and Alfred Rosenberg, Hermann Göring, and Ernst Röhm.[4] Later, Jary is placed on the German intelligence payroll.[5]

Jary, of mixed Ukrainian-Austrian descent, was a journalist as well as a military and political leader. He had been a cavalry officer in the Ukrainian Galician Army (Ukrainska Halytska Armiia, or UHA). He became chief of UVO intelligence, founding member (in 1929) of the OUN, member of the OUN-Bandera faction Provid and, together with Sushko, its Berlin liaison. In March 1939 he arranged for Germany to deliver arms to Ukrainian Nationalists in Transcarpathia and was the coordinator of the assistance provided by the Abwehr to Ukrainian-Nationalist military formations.[6]

1922—Ievhen Konovalets begins to court the German General Staff and moves his place of residence from Eastern Galicia to Berlin, then to Geneva and Rome, where he remains until 1929.

In 1922 Andrii Melnyk assumes the home command of the UVO in Galicia.

Also in this year, the UVO launches a terrorist campaign against the Second Republic of Poland and its citizens. (See also entry for July 1–November 30, 1930.)

1922-1927—Training courses are established by German military and intelligence circles in Munich (1922-23), Preußisch-Holland (1924-25), Breslau (1926), and near Berlin (1927). The intent of these training courses is to prepare young Ukrainian intellectuals for espionage service before their recruitment into the Polish army.

March 15, 1923—Council of Ambassadors recognizes Poland's sovereign rights over the eastern provinces, including "Western Ukraine."

April 5, 1923—The United States seconds the above-mentioned decision of the Council of Ambassadors.

1923-1924—Dmytro Dontsov, at the request of Konovalets, edits the UVO organ, *Zahrava*.

1924—Abwehr's (German military counterintelligence service headed by Wilhelm Canaris) interest in supporting the intelligence-gathering service of the UVO prompts the UVO leadership to initiate a request for financial assistance through Richard Jary. To persuade Germany of UVO's usefulness, a decision is made to assassinate Poland's Head of State, President Stanisław Wojciechowski. Since no qualified or willing assassin could be found, a young student, Teofil Olshanskyi, a son of a Uniate priest, is recruited for the job. He is given a badly designed bomb (which fails to explode) and a revolver without a firing pin. Since no money was given him for cab fare, he has to use the trolley. After the unsuccessful assassination attempt he receives political asylum in Germany. Stanisław Steiger, a Jew, is accused of the assassination attempt, tried, and found innocent. Only toward the end does Germany (not the UVO) reveal Olshanskyi's role in this affair.[7]

1925—A Berlin-sponsored officers' school is established in the Free City of Danzig (Gdańsk) and graduates 110 active UVO members.

June 17, 1926—Osyp Dumyn, the director of UVO Intelligence Department in behalf of Germany, submits his report (composed in May) "Die Warheit über die ukrainische Organisation (The Truth About the Ukrainian Organization [UVO])" to the German Ministry of Foreign Affairs. (See the first document in Appendix C: "Osyp Dumyn's June 17, 1926, Report....")

1926—Dmytro Dontsov publishes his *Natsionalizm*. The work is manufactured in a printery operated by Greek Catholic (Uniate) Basilian Fathers.

According to Dontsov, in the attainment of a sovereign state (the be-all and end-all of mankind's existence), the will is omnipotent. The following statements appear in that work: "Fanatics created history";[8] "On this will (not reason), on dogma (not established truth), on authentic not derived postulates, on a groundless impulse must our national idea be founded if we are to stay afloat on the surface of cruel life";[9] "*The strengthening of the nation's will to live, her will to rule, her will to expand*—these I have designated as the chief foundation of nationalism.... The second foundation of the idea of a healthy nation should be *the aspiration to war, the awareness of its necessity without which heroic deeds are impossible as is an intensive life or faith in it or the triumph of any new idea* which seeks to change the face of the world."[10]

Among his terrible heroes was Italian fascist dictator Benito Mussolini, who gathered about him his 10,000 followers "willing, when it came to their native land and fascism, not only to make their voice heard in elections, but also to kill others and themselves."[11] The following statements also come from Dontsov: "I do not mean here to advertise fascism or Bolshevism .... I am not concerned with their internal politics, but rather with their methods of garnering the power of the state and its maintenance (the same task confronts us!)—and in this matter, both fascism and Bolshevism are current examples of how this is to be done";[12] "Egoism ... hatred, raw impulse, anger, the aspiration to conquer—these are the principles which animate the world";[13] "Only Philistines can absolutely dismiss and morally condemn war, murder, brute force—Philistines or people with a deadened instinct for life."[14]

In 1926 the UVO Supreme Command moves the its headquarters to Berlin and receives political and financial support from the German General Staff.

Also in this year, the Union of Ukrainian Nationalist Youth (Soiuz Ukrainskoi Natsionalistychnoi Molodi, or SUNM) is established in Lwów.

March 2, 1927—*Surma* publishes the four "Great Commandments of the Revolutionary-fighter." (See the second document in Appendix C: "Great Commandments of the Revolutionary-fighter.")

November 3-7, 1927—Conference of Ukrainian Nationalists is held in Berlin.

1927—The UVO organ, *Surma*, is published in Berlin.

April 8-9, 1928—Second Conference of Ukrainian Nationalists is held in Prague.

June 25, 1928—Fascist Ukrainian organizations which emerged in Italy, Czechoslovakia, Germany, and Galicia—including the Association of Ukrainian Fascists—coalesce into the Association of Ukrainian Nationalists headquartered in Berlin.

1928—*Surma* is moved from Berlin to Lithuania to offset Polish complaints that the UVO is on Germany's payroll.

January 28-February 3, 1929—First Congress of Ukrainian Nationalists (also called the First Great Conference of Ukrainian Nationalists—Velykyi Zbir Ukrainskykh Natsionalistiv, or VZUN) convenes in Vienna and creates the OUN. The OUN, under Ievhen Konovalets, will eventually subsume the UVO, also headed by Konovalets.

At this conference Dmytro Dontsov's fascist doctrine (derived eclectically from Niccolò Machiavelli, Charles Maurras, Georges Sorel, Arthur Schopenhauer, Friedrich Nietzsche, and others) is adopted by the directorate of the OUN and becomes the movement's ruling ideology, the ideology of Ukrainian "integral" or "active" nationalism. According to that ideology, the future Ukrainian nation-state—led by a supreme *vozhd* (*führer* or leader) whose authority is unlimited and unquestionable—is to be Fascist (a "national dictatorship"). It is to be ethnically pure ("Ukraine for Ukrainians"). It is to be established on all ethnolinguistic Ukrainian lands ("Greater Ukraine"). And it is to be achieved through compulsory mass action ("creative coercion") in an armed struggle first with Poland and then with the Soviet Union.[15]

At this conference, a slightly modified version of Stepan Lenkavskyi's "Decalogue" is adopted as the creed of the OUN, and proclamations are issued calling for the "complete removal of all occupants from Ukrainian lands." (See Appendix C: Excerpts from Documents, Ukrainian, "Decalogue (Dekaloh)" and source note, as well as "First Congress of Ukrainian Nationalists (Also Called the First Great Conference of Ukrainian Nationalists—Velykyi Zbir Ukrainskykh Natsionalistiv, or VZUN), Vienna, January 28-February 3, 1929.")

1929—Ievhen Konovalets visits America and Canada. Subsequently, at the beginning of the 1930s, the Organization for the Rebirth of Ukraine (Orhanizatsiia Derzhavnoho Vyzvolennia Ukrainy, or ODVU) is established in the U.S., and the Ukrainian National Federation (Ukrainske Natsionalne Obiednannia, or UNO) is founded in Canada.

May 1930—Combined conference of the OUN and UVO convenes in Lwów.

June 1930—Second combined conference of the OUN and UVO is held in Prague. In the course of that conference, the UVO is subsumed under the OUN and becomes its military arm.[16]

July 1-November 30, 1930—1,739 Ukrainians suspected of terrorist activities are arrested in Eastern Galicia. Their 1929-30 subversive campaign alone had resulted in some 2,200 serious acts of sabotage.

The UVO-OUN made unsuccessful attempts on the life of Marshal Józef Piłsudski (1921), President Stanisław Wojciechowski (1924), and school superintendent Godomski (1933) and assassinated the minister of the interior, Bronisław Pieracki (1934), as well as Stanisław Sobiński (1926), Tadeusz Hołówko (1931), Emilian Czechowski (1932), and Jerzy Ciesielszuk (1933). The attaché at the Soviet consulate in Lwów, Aleksei Mailov (1933), was also killed. Among the Ukrainians labeled as "traitors" and executed on OUN command were Sydor Tverdokhlib (1933), a writer, and Ivan Babii (1934), the well-known and respected director of the prestigious Ukrainian *Gymnasium* in Lwów. According to Alexander Motyl:

> The OUN was particularly active in eliminating its real and perceived political opponents. At least sixty-three actual or attempted killings are known to have occurred between 1921 and 1939. (The real figure is probably higher, since unreported killings in backwater regions must have also taken place.) Of this number, at least two-thirds were the work of the OUN. Only eleven cases can be considered significant as assassinations or attempted assassinations of prominent Polish and Ukrainian figures. The vast majority of the remaining 52 killings and attempted killings were of Ukrainians believed to be collaborators (informers and minor officials enjoying good relations with the authorities, or publicly opposed to nationalist tactics) and of Polish policemen, undercover agents, and suspected informers. A breakdown by nationality reveals that successful and unsuccessful attempts were made on the lives of 36 Ukrainians, 25 Poles, one Russian, and one Jew. Of this number, two Communists—one Ukrainian and one Russian—were assassinated.[17]

These acts of terror were intended to provoke the Polish authorities to retaliation.

Another type of provocation consisted of the so-called "Cult of Tombs of the Fallen." According to Petro Mirchuk: "The occupation authorities [that is to say, the Second Republic of Poland] quickly understood the political nature of this cult. Consequently, confrontations with the [Polish] police followed. This was precisely what the OUN wanted."[18]

September 16-November 30, 1930—Polish authorities undertake a ten-week "pacification" campaign against some Ukrainian villages in Eastern Galicia in response to continuous terrorism on the part of the UVO-OUN.

The League of Nations, in its January 30, 1932, response to Ukrainian-Nationalist protests regarding this "pacification," while not approving the methods used, recognized that it was the Ukrainian Nationalists themselves who were to blame for consciously inviting this response by their "revolutionary actions" and maintained that this was not a governmental policy of persecution of the Ukrainian people. The *Encyclopedia of Ukraine* states: "The Council of the league issued a statement as late as January 1932 in which it stated that the Polish actions could be justified because of Ukrainian sabotage activities."[19]

April 1933—A conference convenes in Berlin at which Ievhen Konovalets and Richard Jary agree to the assassination of interior minister Bronisław Pieracki. Stepan Bandera, son of a Uniate priest, orders the assassination, Mykola Lebed organizes it, Roman Shukhevych assists in its preparation.[20]

1933—Richard Jary signs a contract with Ernst Röhm. On the basis of this contract, a number of Ukrainians are accepted to the Brown-shirt Storm Troopers (Sturmabteilung, or SA). Ievhen Konovalets and Jary officially engage in talks with the Gestapo regarding collaboration and financial support.[21]

Also in this year, Oleksandr Kuts, an OUN member, is arrested, tried, and convicted for his several unsuccessful attempts to assassinate Henryk Józewski, the Polish provincial administrator of Wołyń who was well disposed toward the Ukrainians. The plot was organized by the OUN.[22]

June 15, 1934 — Minister Bronisław Pieracki is assassinated by Hryhorii Matseiko.

December 18, 1935-January 13, 1936 — Trial of those responsible for the murder of Bronisław Pieracki.

Among those convicted were Stephan Bandera and Mykola Lebed, each of whom received a death sentence commuted to life imprisonment. Although arrested for his role in the assassination of Pieracki, Roman Shukhevych was not convicted for this crime due to a lack of evidence. In 1926 Shukhevych also took part in the assassination of the Lwów school superintendent, Stanisław Sobiński.[23]

May 1936 — Trial of the leadership of the OUN. Among those indicted were Stepan Bandera, Roman Shukhevych, Volodymyr Ianiv, and Iaroslav Stetsko. Bandera was condemned to death for the second time, and again his sentence was commuted to life in prison. Shukhevych was sentenced to four years' imprisonment for being a member of the OUN. His sentence was then reduced to two years by an amnesty. He was released in 1937.

April 1938 — Henryk Józewski is dismissed from his post. He is replaced by Aleksander Hauke-Nowak, the last Polish *wojewoda* (provincial administrator) of Wołyń.

May 23, 1938 — Ievhen Konovalets is assassinated by a Ukrainian NKVD agent, Norbert Valuch-Ianenko.

June-July 1938 — According to official information received in London from Warsaw on August 4, 1938, during this period the Polish authorities demolish 91 Eastern Orthodox churches, ten chapels, and 26 houses of prayer — all in the Lublin Province.[24]

Under tsarist rule, the Uniate population had been forcibly converted to Orthodoxy. In 1875, at least 375 Uniate (i.e., Eastern-rite Roman Catholic) churches were converted into Orthodox churches. The same was true of many Latin-rite Roman Catholic churches. In 1905, when voluntary conversion was allowed (but not to the Uniate rite), some 200,000 Orthodox reverted to Latin-rite Catholicism. Hence the Polish "revindication campaign" — the closing and even destruction of old, often abandoned, Orthodox churches or their reconversion into Roman Catholic churches during the interwar years. The use of the Polish army in 1938 to accomplish this end gave this action the appearance of an anti-Ukrainian campaign. The Roman Catholic hierarchy (notably Bishop Marian Leon Fulman of Lublin) did not support this government action.[25]

1938 — An extensive network of training centers for the Ukrainian Nationalists is established by the Abwehr; for example, the one near Lake Quenz in Austria in the Wiener-Neustadt region.[26]

February 1939 — The leader of the OUN Andrii Melnyk, writes:

> Today ... at our side stand other nations — Germany, Italy, Spain, Japan — whose victories aim at the final annihilation of the common enemy. In this battle the leading task falls to Ukraine. The quick conclusion of this battle depends on the strength and tenacity of the Ukrainian nation.[27]

March 1939 — Massive arrests of OUN members (including Lev Rebet) by Polish authorities.

In this month and year, Ukrainian Nationalists surface in the ephemeral Transcarpathian government. Sol Littman writes:

> A little-known sidebar to Ukrainian history is the brief period of a few weeks in which the nationalists took over the

government in Transcarpathia before Hitler took it away from them and assigned it to the Hungarians. Mykyta Kosakivs'kyy's [Mykyta Kosakviskyi] description of this blip on history's screen reveals that the Ukrainian regime was marked by severe legislation against the Jews, the end of freedom of the press, the abolishment of all competing political parties, and the establishment of German-style concentration camps.[28]

Summer 1939— A regiment of OUN members, known as the Nationalist Military Detachments (Viiskovi Viddily Natsionalistiv, or VVN) but officially called Mountain-Peasants' Help (Bergbauernhilfe, or BBH) by the Abwehr, who organized it, is placed under the command of Roman Sushko in Austria.

The mission of this secretly formed unit of some 200 men (sometimes also referred to as Sushko's Ukrainian Legion) working hand in glove with the Abwehr and the SD, was to participate in the war effort against Poland both as a legion[29] and as the instigator of a bloody uprising in the east directed against communists, Jews, and Poles after the attack on Poland. The attack never materialized because, by virtue of the August 1939 Agreement (see following entry), Eastern Poland fell to the Soviet Union.

After the Polish campaign, the legion was reorganized into a Ukrainian police unit and served as a border patrol guard (Grenschutz) in the Carpathian Mountains (the Polish-Slovak border). Its main task was to prevent Poles and Jews from escaping and to attack Polish civilians and straggling Polish soldiers.[30]

August 23, 1939— Germany and the Soviet Union sign a Non-Aggression Pact. The secret protocols contained in the pact call for the fourth partition of Poland along the Ribbentrop-Molotov line of demarcation.

August 26-27, 1939— Second Congress of Ukrainian Nationalists (VZUN) convenes in Rome. Andrii Melnyk is elected as the head of the OUN.

Eve of the war— According to the estimate of Orest Subtelny, the membership of the OUN on the eve of the war reaches about 20,000.[31]

The great majority of the rank-and-file members were teens and young adults, mostly students. They were led by the "Galician schoolmaster's son" from Berlin (Ievhen Konovalets) and his cadre of "hardened conspirators."[32]

Also on the eve of the war, according to a German document ("K-Organisation Ost-Galizien"), 4,000 Galician Ukrainian-Nationalist agents trained by the Abwehr in sabotage and diversion infiltrate central and southern Poland, incite the minorities, and participate in acts of violence against the Polish people.[33]

September 1, 1939— Germany invades Poland, marking the beginning of World War II. In the million-man Polish army, tens of thousands of Ukrainians take part in the defense of Poland.

September 5-10, 1939— After their release from Bereza Kartuska, a Polish concentration camp for political prisoners (among them many terrorists and subversives), Stepan Bandera and other Ukrainian Nationalists contact the Abwehr.

September 17, 1939— The Soviet Union invades Poland. Of the 200,000 to 250,000 Polish POWs taken to the interior of the Soviet Union, from 20,000 to 25,000 were of Ukrainian background. After the mid-1941 "amnesty," several thousand Ukrainians joined either Władysław Anders's army or Zygmunt Berling's Polish army.[34]

After the Polish Campaign— In preparation for the attack on the Soviet Union, the help of the Nationalists is enlisted by Germany. A German Abwehr officer responsible for subversive activities revealed at Nuremberg:

> It was pointed out in the order that for the purpose of delivering a lightning blow against the Soviet Union, Abwehr II ... must use its agents for kindling national antagonisms among the people of the Soviet Union.... In carrying out the above-mentioned instructions of [German generals] Keitel and Jodl, I contacted Ukrainian Nationalist Socialists who were in the German Intelligence Service and other members of the nationalist fascist groups.... Instructions were given by me personally to the leaders of the Ukrainian Nationalists, [Andrii] Mel'nyk [Code Name "Consul I"] and [Stepan] Bandera [Code Name "Consul II"] to organize ... demonstrations in the Ukraine in order to disrupt the immediate rear of the Soviet armies.... Apart from this, a special military unit was trained for subversive activities on Soviet territory.[35]

September 28, 1939— The German-Soviet Boundary and Friendship Treaty is signed.

This treaty provided for the return of ethnic Germans, Belorussians, and Ukrainians to their respective countries. This, in turn, greatly facilitated the movement of pro-Nazi Ukrainian Nationalists out of German-occupied central Poland into Soviet-occupied Eastern Poland.

October 15, 1939— With German permission, the Ukrainian Committee (a social welfare agency headed by Volodymyr Horbovyi, a close associate of Stepan Bandera), is established in Kraków to deal with the question of Ukrainian refugees from Soviet-occupied Eastern Poland as well as Ukrainian POWs who had served in the Polish army.

The committee then forwarded a resolution to the German authorities demanding the reunification of all Ukrainian lands, including the Chełm and Lemko regions, into a Ukrainian nation. This committee was later transformed into the Ukrainian Central Committee ((Ukrainskyi Tsentralnyi Komitet, or UTsK).[36] (See entry for June 1940.)

October 22, 1939— Soviet-style "elections" are held in Eastern Poland. The Polish territories, now officially called "Western Belorussia" and "Western Ukraine," are incorporated into the Soviet Socialist Republic on November 1 and 2, respectively. After these dates, all residents in these territories, whether they wanted to or not, became Soviet citizens.

November 1939— Nazi General Governor Hans Frank receives a delegation of local Ukrainians, thanks them for their warm reception of the German armies, and promises — according to the wishes of the Führer — to create for them favorable conditions for their national and social development.

A year later, on the occasion of the first anniversary of the creation of the General Government, Frank thanks the Ukrainian people for their loyalty to the Third Reich.[37]

Fall 1939— Volodymyr Kubiiovych establishes contact with the Abwehr.

Kubiiovych's father was Ukrainian; his mother was Polish. Polish was spoken at home; his father taught him Ukrainian. He married a Polish girl in 1929 who bore him two daughters. During the war, he abandoned his family and broke off all contacts with the Polish community.[38]

December 1939— A secret Gestapo police-espionage training school is established in Zakopane.

The training lasted five months, after which the graduates were deployed to various districts as prison and camp guards. Among the "students" were 120 Ukrainians. The school was run by Walter Krüger and his assistant Wilhelm Rosenbaum. Mykola Lebed was in charge of the Ukrainian unit.[39]

February 10, 1940— Stepan Bandera, with the backing of some other young radicals, such as Mykola Lebed, Roman Shukhevych, and Iaroslav Stetsko, challenges the leadership of Andrii Melnyk and establishes a rival Revolutionary Directory with himself in charge. After a bitter conflict, OUN splits forever into two uncompromising and mutually antagonistic factions. Bandera's group came to be known as OUN-B; Melnyk's, as OUN-M.

April 19, 1940— In a meeting between representatives of both factions of the Ukrainian Nationalists and Hans Frank in Kra-ków's Wawel Castle (there were several such meetings), the Nationalists issue a declaration of loyalty to the Third Reich. To prove their good will, they donate 38 church bells to German foundries, participate in various festivities organized by the Germans in the Generalgouvernement ("General Government" of Poland), and more important, support the delivery of product contingents demanded by the Germans and assist in the deportations of people for forced labor.[40]

May 20, 1940— Germans turn over a former Uniate cathedral in Chełm to the Ukrainians and restore to them over 20 Orthodox churches. During the interwar years, these churches had been turned over to the Roman Catholic Church by the Polish authorities. (See entry for June-July 1938.)

June 1940— The Ukrainian Central Committee (UTsK), headed by Volodymyr Kubiiovych, is established in Kraków and is officially recognized and funded by German occupation authorities. (According to Madajczyk, the UTsK [formerly the Ukrainian Committee] was established in April 1940.[41])

September 1940— Hans Frank instructs his subordinates to maintain a proper distance vis-a-vis the Ukrainians and even to treat them as friends.[42]

Beginning of 1941— During a conference between OUN-B representatives and the emissaries of German intelligence (Abwehr), an agreement is reached to organize and equip a Ukrainian legion.

Its soldiers (about 700 men) were recruited from the Ukrainian units formed earlier by German authorities, including Roman Sushko's demobilized Ukrainian Legion. Camouflaged under the harmless name of Reichsarbeitsdienst (Reich work service), it trained in such places as Krynica and Dukla. That May, the legion was divided into two OUN-B regiments: Nachtigall and Roland. Collectively, these two regiments are also known as Units of Ukrainian Nationalists (Druzhyny Ukrainskykh Natsionalistiv, or DUN).

Early 1941— Under German auspices, both OUN-B and OUN-M form and train their own so-called *pokhidni hrupy* (marching or expeditionary groups) to follow on the heels of the German army after its invasion of the Soviet Union.

The soldiers for these formations were recruited from German-occupied Galicia, Rumania, Bukovina, and the Nationalist central and western bases. In all, they numbered between 5,000 and 8,000 men. The destination of the OUN-B marching groups (assembled and trained in the San and Lemko regions) was Soviet Ukraine. OUN-M forces (assembled in Hrubieszów, Krystynopol, Jarosław, Radymno, and Sanok) permeated Wołyń and continued eastward as well. The mission of both units was to set up local administrations, militias and the auxiliary police, organize OUN cells, recruit new members to the OUN, and "combat Jews and Communists." Later, some of the leaders and members of the

OUN-M forces joined Taras "Bulba"-Borovets's partisans.⁴³

Spring 1941— An agreement is reached between the Wehrmacht and OUN-B that strengthens Stepan Bandera's hand. Under the terms of that agreement, his faction is allowed to engage in political activities in "Western Ukraine" in exchange for military and clandestine collaboration.⁴⁴

April 18, 1941— The UTsK sends Hans Frank a petition asking that the Ukrainian ethnolinguistic territories in the Lemko and Chełm regions be so designated and separated from Poland, and that the Polish population in these regions be resettled.

The main objectives of the UTsK as envisioned by Kubiiovych were: 1) to eliminate all Polish influence in the Ukrainian ethnolinguistic territories; 2) to elevate the level of Ukrainian national consciousness in the local populace residing there; 3) to agitate in favor of reclaiming the "lost" territories.⁴⁵ This UTsK program put Poles and Ukrainians in this area on a direct collision course that would be subsequently exploited by the Germans during their own resettlement plans for the Zamość region.

April 1941— Second Congress of the OUN-B (also called the Second Great Conference of the Organization of Ukrainian Nationalists — VZOUN) convenes in Kraków.

In this month and year, Germany begins recruiting Ukrainian Nationalists into its armed forces and paramilitary organizations. Military and police training is provided by German instructors in Kraków, Krosno, Zakopane, Sanok, and Tarnów.

May 1941— OUN-B issues the following instructions to its leading members regarding the role to be played by the OUN in the coming war with the USSR:

In the first days of the war, when the Soviet army is still unshaken and holds on with determination, the OUN will not join the battle with arms in hand.... [During this time, its members are instructed to disseminate propaganda, create an armed force, an army and militia, and take over local administrative offices and cultural centers.]

When the Soviet army begins to sway, when the régime is weakened, when the Red Army is no longer able to put up a protracted defense due to its being caught unawares — the OUN will then engage in an armed battle, in an armed uprising, in a TOTAL war.

This means that the OUN will openly enter the arena of life. The Ukrainian Revolution begins.⁴⁶

June 12, 1941— Ten days before the invasion of the Soviet Union, OUN-M forwards Hitler a detailed plan for its administration of the Ukraine and states therein that Hitler could rely on Melnyk's group as the "sole counterweight" to the Russian and Jewish influence.⁴⁷

It is interesting to note that whereas the German Ambassador to Moscow (Friedrich Werner von der Schulenburg) was never officially forewarned about the impending invasion of the Soviet Union, both factions of the Ukrainian Nationalists were not only informed about it months in advance, but also had a plan of action and a comprehensive proposal for the governance of Eastern Poland and Soviet Ukraine.⁴⁸ (See also the entry above as well as the entry for Early 1941.)

June 15, 1941— A "Memorandum of the OUN on the Solution to the Ukrainian Question" states that the "natural alliance" between Germany and Ukraine (that is to say, the Ukrainian Nationalists) demands not merely "tactical collaboration" on the part of OUN members but "sincere friendship" with the Third Reich:

Since the interests of both nations demand a natural alliance, German-Ukrainian relations must be based on sincere friendship.... Conclusion: An independent Ukrainian military power which corresponds to the spiritual attitude of Ukraine will warrant the German-Ukrainian alliance.[49]

June 22, 1941—The Nazi war-machine races across the Ribbentrop-Molotov line and invades the Soviet Union.

On this same day, OUN-B holds a conference in Kraków. The conference, led by Volodymyr Horbovyi, is attended by 113 Ukrainian representatives. On the initiative of the OUN-B, the Germans permit the Ukrainian Nationalists to establish a short-lived Ukrainian National Committee in Kraków consisting of all nationalist group representatives except Melnyk's. General Volodymyr Petriv is elected as the head of this committee in absentia. A manifesto, calling for the unification of Ukrainian lands, is issued and forwarded to Hans Frank. Provisions are also made for the establishment of a "Ukrainian government."[50]

Also on this day, Richard Jary sends a telegram to Hitler requesting that Nachtigall and Roland, units that fought alongside the Wehrmacht, be included in the Wehrmacht.[51]

June 23, 1941—Stepan Bandera sends a letter to Hitler in which he argues the case for the establishment of an independent Ukrainian state.[52]

June 25, 1941—On direct orders from Himmler, the Germans create the Wachmannschaften des SS- und Polizeiführers im Distrikt Lublin.

Members of this unit as well as other Wachmannschaften units were recruited from local police and Soviet POWs and schooled in Trawniki. (See entry for August-November 1941.)

June 30, 1941—The Nachtigall unit, having crossed the border near Przemyśl eight days earlier, enters Lwów together with the first battalion of the Brandenburg regiment and other German units, several hours in advance of the regular German army.

Also on this day in Lwów, OUN-B unilaterally (without informing the OUN-M and without German permission or knowledge) declares Ukrainian independence by the "Act of June 30, 1941." "The newly created Ukrainian nation," reads one version (there are several versions) of the declaration, "will work closely with the national social Germans who, under the leadership of their leader, Adolf Hitler, are creating a new order in Europe and the world." It ends with the following salutation: "Long live free Ukraine. Long live the Great German Reich and its leader, Adolf Hitler!"[53]

The usurpation of the power of government by OUN-B is carried out as follows: OUN-B creates a Ukrainian National Committee which, in turn, formally grants OUN-B the "right" to proclaim Ukrainian independence and to assume the role of "government" within that state.[54] (See entry for June 22, 1941, above.)

Beginning of July 1941—Massive pogroms of Jews ("Petliura Action") and Poles begin in Lwów. Thousands die—among them, 25 university professors and their families. Many sources state that the atrocities against the professors were carried out on the basis of lists prepared by young OUN members (former students?) before the invasion. That these lists were prepared well in advance (perhaps already in 1939) is corroborated by the fact that several of the professors whom the Gestapo came to arrest had already died during the war.

July 1, 1941—Metropolitan Andrei Sheptytskyi's pastoral letter is read in St. George Uniate Cathedral in Lwów. At least two versions (translations?) exist of one excerpt from that letter:

John A. Armstrong: "We greet the victorious German Army as deliverer from the enemy. We render our obedient homage to the government which has been erected. We recognize Mr. Iaroslav Stetsko as Head of the State Administration of the Ukraine."[55]

Central State Archives of the October Revolution, Organs of State Government and State Management of the Ukrainian SSR: "We welcome the victorious German army as our liberator from the enemy. We shall duly abide by the rules of the established authorities. We recognize Yaroslav Stetsko as President of the Administration of Ukraine's western regions."[56]

July 2, 1941—After interrogations in Kraków by German authorities, various Ukrainian-Nationalist leaders including Stepan Bandera, are placed under house arrest. Eventually, Bandera, Iaroslav Stetsko, Roman Ilnytskyi, Dmytro Iatsiv, Lev Rebet, and Volodymyr Stakhiv wind up in Sachsenhausen in Zellenbau—a special section of the camp for political prisoners which included such notables as the Chancellor of Austria, Kurt von Schuschnigg; the leader of the "Iron Guard," Horia Sima; and, from July 1943, Home Army General Stefan Rowecki ("Grot").

The conditions of life in this section were not comparable to those in the rest of the camp. In Zellenbau, the political prisoners not only ate well, they were also were exempted from the gruelling daily roll calls, could receive packages, and had access to newspapers.[57] Alexander Dallin states that while there, Bandera was "treated with deference."[58]

July 3, 1941—Dr. Otto Korfes, a former general of the Wehrmacht, describes one of the many crimes committed against the Polish and Jewish civilian populations by the OUN-B in Złoczów, Tarnopol Province. (See Appendix C: Excerpts from Documents, German, "Dr. Otto Korfes' Report.")

July 4, 1941—Iaroslav Stetsko, the "Head of the Ukrainian State," on behalf of the "Ukrainian Government," addresses a formal letter to Hitler from Lwów in which he expresses his gratitude to and admiration for the German army, extends his heartfelt wishes for a complete German victory that will enable Hitler to extend his "planned construction of new Europe also to her Eastern Part," and thanks him for allowing the "opportunity to the Ukrainian people as one of the full and free members of the family of European nations to take an active part in the implementation of this great plan in its sovereign Ukrainian state."[59]

July 6, 1941—Andrii Melnyk sends Hitler a declaration of utmost loyalty. His letter ends with these words: "We request that we be allowed to march shoulder to shoulder with the legions of Europe and with our liberator, the German Wehrmacht, and therefore we ask to be permitted to create a Ukrainian military formation."[60]

July 7, 1941—The Nachtigall and Roland units are directed to the front by (German) General Canaris. The former goes to Vynnytsia, the latter to Odessa. From there, on August 27, 1941, Nachtigall is sent to Neuhammer in Silesia and Roland to Saubersdorf near Vienna. Both are then directed to Frankfurt on the Oder.

July 10-23, 1941—Talks take place in Sulejówek near Warsaw between the leadership of OUN-B (Richard Jary, Ivan Ravlyk, I. Iavnyi, Ievhen Stakhiv, and Karpo Mykytchuk) and Abwehr representatives (Georg Gerulis and others). There, the OUN-B learns that Hitler is opposed to the declaration of independence, that Galicia will be incorporated into the Generalgouvernement, and that the remaining Ukrainian territories will become a part of the Reichskommissariat Ukraine.[61]

July 30, 1941—Prime Minister Władysław Sikorski and Soviet ambassador in London Ivan Maisky sign an agreement which unites Poland and the Soviet Union in the fight against Germany.

July 1941—The Bukovinian Battalion of 1941, consisting of about 1,000 men, is created by OUN-M.

Members of this volunteer battalion fought in the ranks of German auxiliary forces against Soviet partisans in Belorussia. Later, some joined the Ukrainian-Nationalist underground while others, after being transferred to the French front in 1944, joined the French Resistance.[62]

In this month and year, the provisional Ukrainian administration in Łuck forms the Ievhen Konovalets battalion under M. Meleshko ("Virlyk").

Under the German administration, this battalion was disbanded and reformed into an agricultural battalion under Major Kaizer. Its members were provided schooling in matters pertaining to the maintenance and administration of German farms established in that area.[63]

Also in July 1941, Mykola Lebed ("Maksym Ruban") assumes command of OUN-B after Bandera's arrest. He also establishes and heads the OUN-B Security Forces (SB). He maintains his position until he is replaced by Roman Shukhevych at the August 21-25, 1943, Third Great Conference of the Organization of Ukrainian Nationalists (VZOUN).

In July 1941 the OUN-B *pokhidni hrupy* arrive in Wołyń.

July-August 1941—During this time the Einsatzgruppen and the Ukrainian auxiliary police murder over 13,000 Jews in Wołyń.[64]

August 1, 1941—In his appeal to the Ukrainian people, Iaroslav Stetsko reminds them that "in its first declaration, the [OUN-B] government announced its close cooperation with the German State and the German Army which had entered the Ukrainian territory." He expresses the hope that after the German victory over Bolshevism, the "German government will favor our national aspirations and establishment of friendly mutual relations between the Ukrainian Independent Representative State and the great German Reich."[65]

Also on this date, by Hitler's decree, Eastern Galicia becomes incorporated into the General Government.

August 3, 1941—Stepan Bandera, referring to himself as "Führer der Organisation Ukrainischer Nationalisten—OUN," sends a letter to the Führer of the Third Reich in which he expresses his disappointment at the placement of Galicia, North Bukovina, and Bessarabia into the orbit of the General Government and hopes that this "division of the Ukrainian states [is] a temporary arrangement and that His Excellency would soon reunite these territories with the Motherland."[66]

August 8, 1941—Volodymyr Horbovyi, a member of the Ukrainian government liquidated by the Germans, asked whether in light of the negative disposition of the Germans to Ukrainian independence he intends to change his own disposition to the Germans, replies, "The Ukrainian society will continue to support the Germans and to profess a pro-German orientation.... The display of ill will and disillusionment obviously cannot be avoided, but the duty of the leadership will be to prevail upon the [Ukrainian] society to curtail its anti-German manifestations."[67]

August 14, 1941—An OUN-B proclamation favors a policy of continued cooperation with Germany: "The OUN supports further close cooperation with Germany and is of the opinion that the dissolution, or rather the disavowal, of the Ukrainian government established in Lviv [Lwów] would only place unnecessary burdens on this cooperation."[68]

German reports for this day indicate that the OUN-B *pokhidni hrupy* are engaging in intensive propaganda in the interests of "creating an independent and unified Ukrainian state ... are attempting to filter into the political administration and are trying to awaken among the people aspirations for the idea of an independent and unified Ukraine."[69]

August 1941— Metropolitan Sheptytskyi sends a letter to Hitler on the occasion of the fall of Kiev to German troops in which he wishes "Your Excellency my warmest congratulations as regards the occupation of the capital of the Ukraine" and imparts the following blessing on the Führer and the Third Reich: "I will pray to God to put his blessing upon the victory which shall be the guarantee of enduring peace for Your Excellency, the German Army and the German nation."[70]

On this same date, Taras "Bulba"-Borovets contacts the Wehrmacht and secures an authorization to form his Polesian Stronghold (*Poliska Sich*)— a diversionary, military unit which is armed by the Germans and participates in the German pacification of Soviet partisans and Jews in Wołyń during that autumn. This unit consists of approximately 3,000 men. Borovets's troops are the first (in December 1941) to use the designation "Ukrainian Insurgent Army" (UPA).

August-November 1941— Trawniki, a training center for concentration camp guards, is established in the Lublin district, then under the control of Odilo Globocnik.

Although Russians, Lithuanians, Latvians, and the Volksdeutsche from Poland (including a handful of ethnic Poles) were among the camp recruits, Trawniki was predominantly a training center for Ukrainian guards. All training (lasting 3-4 months) was done in the German language under the leadership of Volksdeutsche and noncommissioned Ukrainian officers from Galicia. After the completion of their training course, the graduates were used as concentration camp guards, as ghetto guards, and as auxiliaries of the SS. In all, about 2,000 Ukrainians trained for the SS-ukrainische Wachmannschaften. The recruits who deserted the unit after training were interned in concentration camps. Other training camps, similar to Trawniki, existed in the district of Lublin; for example, Wólka Profecka, where the Schutzmannschafts-Ersatz-Bataillon 203 was stationed. These were also run, in part, by Ukrainians from Galicia.[71]

One of the Trawniki-trained battalions participated in the liquidation of the Warsaw ghetto in the spring of 1943. The Trawniki graduates also constituted the major guard forces at Bełżec, Sobibór, Treblinka, and Trawniki, but other concentration camps employed Ukrainians as well.

September 11, 1941— The head of the Council of Trust of Wołyń, Stepan Skrypnyk, writes a letter to the Reichscommissar for Ukraine. An excerpt from that letter reads:

> Since long ago the Ukrainians have been aware of the integrity of their destination with that of the great German people, especially in the struggle for the new order. The Ukrainians are supporting the glorious German troops in their war against Bolshevism in the full conviction that the Great Germany and Ukraine share a common destiny, that the Ukrainian state can become strong only after Germany's ultimate victory and that the Great Germany will have all the backing of Ukraine in establishing the new order in Europe's east.
>
> As Head of the Ukrainian Council of Trust which expresses the feelings of the nationalist-minded Ukrainians of Volyn, I am aware of the military requirements and war needs of the Great Germany whose victory we are trying to facilitate as best we can. We know quite well that some of the main

branches of administration, particularly in the economic field, must be managed by German authorities, the Reich's government possessing the necessary plenary powers as a guarantee of Ukraine's security and territorial inviolability. We are also sure that the German administration will incorporate Ukrainian functionaries in leading positions that will never be occupied either by Poles or by Russians, and that only the German and Ukrainian languages will be used in German institutions for official written and oral communication. We are also convinced that the German authorities in Volyn will take into account the opinion of the Ukrainian Council of Trust in major economic and state matters. At the same time we firmly believe that scrupulous and methodical formation of all other Ukrainian departments is not contradictory to the above requirements and needs of the Great German Reich, but is desirable since it will foster healthy national and social life of the Ukrainian folk and strengthen its heartfelt trust in the new order pursued by the Great Germany in Europe.

Under these conditions, I can take upon myself the responsibility to my national conscience and the government of the German Reich for further successful management of the Ukrainian Council of Trust of Volyn.

> Stepan Skrypnyk,
> Head of Ukrainian Council
> of Trust of Volyn[72]

In May 1942, on the instructions of Erich Koch, Skrypnyk is ordained as bishop of the Ukrainian Orthodox (Autocephalous) Church. He assumes the name of Mstyslav.

September 12, 1941— Imprisonment of OUN-B members increases dramatically after a Berlin meeting on this date between the representatives of the Abwehr (Hans Koch, Gerhard von Mende) and the leaders of OUN-B (Stepan Bandera, Iaroslav Stetsko, and Ievhen Stakhiv), who refuse to change their political direction and withdraw the June 30, 1941, proclamation.

September 17, 1941— The General Staff of German Army "South" orders all OUN-B agents associated with the *pokhidni hrupy* to be arrested and handed over to the disposition of the Security Service (SD) in Lwów.[73]

September 1941— First OUN-B Conference convenes. The proceedings of this conference have not been published.

October 5, 1941— On the initiative of OUN-M, a Ukrainian National Council is set up in Kiev under Mykola Velychkivskyi.

October 1941— OUN-M attempts to establish a central Ukrainian government in Kiev. This effort is thwarted by the Germans; OUN-M leaders are arrested.

November 15, 1941— Erich Koch calls upon Taras "Bulba"-Borovets and his men to lay down their arms and to dissolve the Polesian Stronghold. In its place, a regional command post of the Ukrainian police, with Borovets as commandant, is established. In May and June 1942 Borovets forms another group of partisans from the remnant of the dissolved Polesian Stronghold.

November 1941, October 1942, November 1942-March 1943, June-August 1943— Massive German resettlement campaigns of the Polish population in the Zamość district are conducted with the assistance of local Ukrainian administrators and Ukrainian Nationalists from Galicia (initially as members of the SS-ukrainische Wachmannschaften and later as members of the SS-Galizien police regiments). The area is colonized by ethnic Germans. On the perimeter, Ukrainians are resettled on vacated Polish properties.

End of November 1941-beginning of 1942— The roundups of predominantly young OUN-M intellectuals commences in the Lwów, Prague, and the Dnieper areas.

December 16, 1941—In a speech to his subordinates, Hans Frank states: "Ukrainians are especially useful as a counterweight in [our] dealings with the Poles.... Every German that I plant here becomes a pebble in the construction of a progressive road for the German nation that leads eastward.... We must also remember, above all, about Galicia."[74]

In his diary, Frank writes: "I must stress that it is in the interest of German politics to maintain strained relations between the Poles and Ukrainians. The four and a half to five million Ukrainians which we have in the country are an especially important counterweight to the Poles. That is why I have always attempted to keep them in a state of contentment, out of political considerations, in order to prevent them from joining up with the Poles."[75]

In addition, according to David Littlejohn, unlike every other nationality group, including their compatriots from Soviet Ukraine, Galician forced-laborers in Germany were not required to submit to the indignity of wearing the humiliating and detested identification tags or badges which signified their national origin.[76]

Beginning of 1942—OUN-B disseminates leaflets in Wołyń encouraging Ukrainians to support the Germans materially and morally in their fight against Bolshevism.[77]

January 1, 1942—A letter in the same vein as the one mentioned in the following entry is sent to Hitler by Tymish Omelchenko, president of the OUN-M controlled National Union of Ukrainian emigrés in Germany, the UNO.[78]

January 14, 1942—A letter, signed by Metropolitan Sheptytskyi, Andrii Levytskyi, M. Melichevskyi, Omelianovych-Pavlenko, and Andrii Melnyk, "Führer of the Ukrainian Nationalists in Berlin," is sent to Hitler. In their letter, these Nationalist leaders assure Hitler of their continued loyalty and desire to do battle "shoulder-to-shoulder with the German army," bemoan the placement of Eastern Galicia in the orbit of the General Government, remind Hitler that "as soon as the German troops captured Ukraine's capital, Kiev, the leading Ukrainian circles took steps to establish cooperation with the German administration in this country," and "assure Your Excellency [Hitler] that the leading circles of Ukraine are ready for the most close cooperation with Germany in order to continue struggle against the common enemy by joint e ort of the German and Ukrainian peoples and establish the new order in Ukraine and in the whole of Eastern Europe."[79]

March 15, 1942—The village of Koszyszcze (Łuck County, Wołyń) is pacified by the Germans and the Ukrainian police. There are 180 victims.

Similar pacifications by the Germans and the Ukrainian police occurred, for example: on December 16, 1942, in Jezierce (or Ozirce) (Kostopol County)—280 victims; on February 2, 1943, in Brzezina near Chinoczy—600 victims; on February 22, 1943, in Kostopol—the 50 persons arrested in this county seat were murdered in Równe on March 9, 1943; on February 23, 1943, in Berezówka, Bober, Korecka Huta, Koziarniki, Myszakówka, Nowa Huta, Ochotniki, Poźniary, Rudnia Łęczyńska, Rudniki Wojtkowickie, Siwki, and Szopy (all in Kostopol County)—680 victims; on March 18, 1943, in Dąbrowa (three families), Byteń (46 victims), Chobut (ten victims), Gończybród (13 victims), Porsk Duży (12 victims), and Wielick (45 victims)—all in Kowel County; on March 18 and April 24, 1943, in Mielnica (Kowel County)—80 and 93 victims, respectively; in April and July 1943 in Mołotków (Krzemieniec

County)—100 and several dozen victims, respectively; and on July 15, 1943, in Ludwikówka (Dubno County)—172 victims.[80] This listing is not meant to be all-inclusive, only illustrative. (See also entry for November 13, 1942.)

March 23, 1942— DUN, consisting Nachtigall and Roland, are placed under Erich von dem Bach-Zelewski, whose Schutzmannschaften Bataillon 201 was then engaged in the brutal pacification of Belorussia.

March 27, 1942— Metropolitan Sheptytskyi promulgates a pastoral letter in which he condemns, threatens with anathema and excommunicates those who take part in Jewish atrocities. He forbids the youth to enter the ranks of the Ukrainian auxiliary police.

March 1942— Germans arrest many OUN-B members in Równe, Krzemieniec, and other Wołynian towns.[81]

April 1942— Second OUN-B Conference convenes. Ryszard Torzecki believes that this conference constitutes a declaration of war on the part of the Ukrainian Nationalists against Poles.[82] (See Appendix C: Excerpts from Documents, Ukrainian, "Items 22 and 27 of the April 1942 Second OUN-B Conference.")

During this conference a decision is made to unify all Ukrainian military formations under the OUN-B. After the conference, Vasyl Sydor, a member of the Provid, is sent to Wołyń by the Central Provid to organize what would become the OUN-B UPA.

May 24-25, 1942— Third OUN-M Conference convenes in Poczajów.

June 22, 1942— On this first anniversary of the invasion of the Soviet Union, Andrii Melnyk, in the name of the Ukrainian Nationalists, sends a letter to Alfred Rosenberg expressing his eternal gratitude to the "great German ally."[83]

Summer-Fall 1942— Military Self-Defense units (SKV) are established in Polesie and Wołyń.

These brigades of Ukrainian peasants were recruited both on a voluntary basis and by force (the "join or die" policy) by OUN-B to be "on-call" for the task of ethnic cleansing.[84]

Mid-1942— The leadership of Taras "Bulba"-Borovets's Polesian Stronghold contacts the Polish underground in Wołyń in an attempt to normalize Polish-Ukrainian relations during the war. Bronisław Chodorowski is the intermediary. However, no talks materialize.[85]

July 1, 1942— Mykola Maksymchuk-Kardash, the head of the regional Provid of Wołyń, is killed by the Germans.

August 10-October 15, 1942— The height of the Jewish Holocaust in Wołyń.

An estimated 150,000 Jews were murdered by the Germans and their collaborators during the liquidation of the ghettos.[86] The Jews who fled the ghettos and hid in the forests were hunted down and murdered by the UPA throughout 1943.[87]

August 14-15, 1942— OUN-M Home Conference of the Ukrainian Nationalists is held, possibly in Kiev.

September and November 1942— Taras "Bulba"-Borovets reestablishes contact with Wehrmacht officials.[88]

September 1942-December 1942— Representatives of the Soviet partisan unit under Dmitri Medvedev conduct a series of talks with Taras Borovets in Stara Huta. Agreement is reached only on mutual neutrality and the exchange of passwords.[89]

October 5, 1942—5,000 Jews are murdered in Dubno. This is but one of the many places where such atrocities ("open-air shootings") took place.

October 14, 1942—Founding date of the OUN-B UPA. On that day, the first units of this army come into existence in Sarny County in Wołyń: those under Serhii Kachynskyi ("Ostap") and those under Ivan Perehiiniak ("Dovbeshka-Korobka"). That fall, about 600 persons are recruited for the UPA.[90]

October 31, 1942—DUN contract (they were paid collaborators) expires and is not renewed by the Germans.

October 1942—Volodymyr Kubiiovych, pens a letter to Otto Wächter, the Gauleiter of Distrikt Galizien, stating, "We have fulfilled our obligation to provide product contingents commendably. The Ukrainians can always be counted on."[91] In 1985 Kubiiovych explained, "We in the UTsK appealed to our people to persevere in their stations, not to provoke the Germans, and to remember that anti-German action helps the Bolsheviks."[92]

Fall 1942—The order for the ethnic cleansing of Poles is probably issued at this time by the OUN-B Provid headed by Mykola Lebed. Murder of Polish individuals and families commence in the Sarny region of the province of Wołyń. They are perpetrated by Taras "Bulba"-Borovets's men and OUN-B members. This is the prelude to the full-scale genocide which began the following spring after Easter.

November 13, 1942—About 50 Poles are murdered by the Ukrainian police in the village of Obórki, located near Łuck in Wołyń Province.

November 21, 1942–December 1942 Germans initiate a series of talks with Taras "Bulba"-Borovets in the village of Mokwin in the Bereźne region. The German side is represented by the chief of security for Wołyń and Polesie, Pütz, and later by the Gebietskommissar of Równe, Bayer. No agreement is reached and the talks are discontinued that December.[93]

November 25, 1942—A member of the main Provid, together with a regional leader, Dmytro Myron, is assassinated on the streets of Kiev.

November 1942—Metropolitan Sheptytskyi's pastoral letter, "Thou Shall Not Kill," is promulgated. In addition to the murder of Ukrainians by Ukrainians (the fratricidal conflict within the OUN factions), the Metropolitan specifies three other types of murders that he considers particularly abhorrent: the killing of children by parents, abortion, and suicide. There is no unambiguous reference in this letter to the Polish-Ukrainian "fratricidal conflict": to the killing of Poles by Ukrainians, or the killing of Ukrainians by Poles.

December 1, 1942—The Nachtigall and Roland units are formally dissolved. The officers and enlisted men, after serving in the Schutzmannschtaften Bataillon 201, join the ranks of the UPA.

Second half of January 1943—UPA massacres Poles in Wysock in Polesie. (See Appendix C: Excerpts from Documents, Polish, "Capt. Mikołaj Kunicki on the Massacre in Wysock.")

January 18, 1943—Andrii Melnyk writes a letter to Hitler expressing his continued support.[94]

January 31, 1943—The German Sixth Army meets with disaster at Stalingrad, following a lengthy siege.

February 9, 1943—Ukrainian Nationalists murder 173 Poles in Parośle near Sarny.

February 17-21, 1943—Third Conference of OUN-B issues the following proclamation: "We conduct a fight to inaugurate a Ukrainian-Nationalist Revolution that, at the moment of crisis [Stalingrad] in the present war, will lead to the removal of the occupants from Ukraine."[95] This is regarded by Wiktor Poliszczuk as the marching order for the systematic ethnic-cleansing campaign aimed against all non-Ukrainians, and in particular the Polish population, in the so-called Ukrainian ethnolinguistic territories.

Ryszard Torzecki is also of the opinion that the decision to launch an open attack on the "occupants" of the Ukrainian territories was made at this conference but maintains that the words "open attack" do not necessarily imply physical extermination.[96]

March 8, 1943—Volodomyr Kubiiovych contacts Hans Frank with the proposition of establishing a voluntary Ukrainian military unit to fight alongside the Third Reich. Frank contacts his subordinate, Otto Wächter, the Gauleiter of Eastern Galicia, who contacts Heinrich Himmler, head of the SS, who gives his consent on March 28, 1943. Wächter formally announces the formation of the division on April 28; Kubiiovych pens his passionate "Appeal to Ukrainian Citizens and Youth by the Central Committee President on the Formation of the Ukrainian Division" on May 6; and the recruitment begins that month. Of the 80,000 volunteers, 50,000 are selected, 42,000 appear before the commission, 27,000 qualify, 25,000 are called up, 19,000 are accepted, and 13,200 report for duty. Of these, 11,600 receive military training. The remainder of the 80,000 volunteers are absorbed into the five (numbered 4-8) Police regiments connected with the division. By 1944 all the police regiments were incorporated into the SS-Galizien.

Membership in this division, called the SS-Galizien, was limited to Galician Ukrainians. Waffen-SS General Felix Steiner referred to these volunteers as "cannon fodder." According to Ryszard Torzecki, some 32,000 Ukrainians passed through the ranks of the SS-Galizien throughout its existence.[97]

According to John A. Armstrong, "To form the Division, virtually all major Ukrainian political factions eventually accepted (at least tacitly) renewed collaboration with the Germans."[98] It may be added that the only "political factions" in "Western Ukraine" at this time were the OUN factions. Surprisingly, in addition to the secular Nationalist leadership, both the Ukrainian Autocephalous Orthodox Church and the Greek Catholic (Uniate) Church supported this élite Nazi formation as well.

The SS-Galizien is often regarded as an OUN-M organization. There is, for example, a late 1944 UPA (OUN-B) leaflet which protests the forcible recruitment of OUN-B members for the SS-Galizien. The usual reason given for this lack of support on the part of OUN-B is the fear that such a formation would discredit the OUN in the eyes of the people. But there was another reason: the fear that the mobilization of the SS-Galizien would detract from the OUN-B efforts to form its own military arm, the UPA. As it turns out, a secret German report based on the testimony of the volunteers indicates that it was the OUN-B controlled UPA that had ordered them to enlist in the first place! In fact, to forestall an OUN-M monopoly over SS-Galizien membership and for other reasons as well, the UPA intended to have half of the Galician youth join the UPA and the other half, under its aegis, the SS-Galizien.[99]

According to Major Wolf-Dietrich Heike, Chief of Staff of the SS-Galizien and author of *The Ukrainian Division "Galicia," 1943-45: A Memoir*, during the training period the UPA "opposed the Division and tried to stop the flow of young Ukrainians into the Division." Two sentences later, he states: "During each leave the Division's soldiers were used by UPA cadres as instructors for their partisans. Generally, at the end of their leave, the UPA would let the soldiers return."[100]

Moreover, Roman Shukhevych, the head of OUN-B military staff since May 1943 — soon to be the supreme commander of the UPA — personally encouraged Ukrainian youth to join the division for the sake of the military training they would receive and even ordered "a considerable number" of OUN-B members to enter its ranks where they were to occupy prominent positions. Other OUN-B members gladly volunteered without authorization.[101]

In his study, *Galicia Division: The Waffen-SS 14th Grenadier Division, 1943-1945*, Michael O. Logusz, states: "From this former [UPA] intelligence officer [Ostap Vashchenko], I learned what I had always suspected — that the UPA had totally infiltrated the Division."[102]

Units (perhaps the police regiments) of the SS-Galizien were used by the Germans to pacify Polish villages in both eastern and central Poland.[103] (See Appendix C: Excerpts from Documents, United Nations War Crimes Commission.) After the battle at Brody some of the SS-Galizien soldiers joined the UPA. (See entry for July 13-22, 1944.)

March 15, 1943 — OUN-B Provid orders the Ukrainian police to desert their posts with their weapons and to join the UPA. About 5,000 men do so by March 25. More join in the months ahead. (See Appendix C: Excerpts from Documents, Ukrainian, "OUN Order to Vacate Official Posts and Police, April 4, 1943," as well as "OUN-B Mobilization Order, April 5, 1943.") The order for desertion may have been prompted by a fear of an anticipated disarming of the Ukrainian police (consisting mostly of OUN-B people) by the Germans and the consequent weakening of the OUN-B, especially given the formation of the OUN-M SS-Galizien.

March 20, 1943 — The "agricultural school" in Łuck — a paramilitary unit consisting of 320 persons under Stepan Koval ("Rubashenko") and organized along the lines of a battalion — absconds to the Sadów forests. From there it proceeds to the Kołki region, where it is armed and reorganized into a UPA battalion.

April 28, 1943 — An excerpt from the address of Kubiiovych that appeared in the newspaper *Lvivski Visti* on this day reads:

> The highest authorization for raising SS Infantry Division "Galizien" to be composed of Galician Ukrainians is to us a mark of distinction and special honor. We are aware of the important consequences this highest authorization will have. Therefore, we wish to do everything we can to make the division as efficient as possible. For us, the formation of the Galician-Ukrainian division as part of the SS is not only a distinction but also an obligation to continue active collaboration with the German state bodies up to the ultimate victory in this war.[104]

April 29, 1943 — Metropolitan Sheptytskyi's treasury receives the sum of 360,000 occupation zloty from the Nazi Administration of the Generalgouvernement. The letter of transfer states: "My Office does not require an account for this money."[105]

April 1943 — OUN-M forces at this time consist of about 2,000-3,000 armed men; OUN-B forces number 8,000-10,000 armed men; Borovets's forces consist of some 4,000 armed men, with a capacity to mobilize an additional 10,000.[106]

Spring 1943— OUN-B issues an appeal to the Ukrainians of Wołyń to begin mobilizing an underground army (i.e., to join the UPA) to fight for the creation of a Ukrainian state. Many Ukrainians join, only to desert when they realize that the "creation of a Ukrainian state" also necessitated their participation in ethnic cleansing. The deserters were regarded as "traitors" and, when caught, were executed by OUN-B SB squads.

May 1943— Roman Shukhevych becomes the head of the OUN-B military staff. Massive attacks are launched by the UPA against Polish villages and self-defense centers throughout Wołyń. The attacks begin in the Sarny County, then spread to Kostopol, Równe, and Zdołbunów counties. In June 1943 they embrace the counties of Dubno and Łuck. In July they spread to the counties of Horochów, Kowel, and Włodzimierz. That August, villages in Luboml County are attacked.[107]

June 22, 1943— OUN-M observes the second anniversary of the occupation of the Soviet Union with great fanfare.[108]

June 1943— In his 1981 work, *Armiia bez derzhavy* (Army Without a State), Taras "Bulba"-Borovets states: "The officer corps of the new UPA received the following military assignment from Mykola Lebed's party in June 1943: Without delay and as soon as possible *conclude* the action of completely cleansing the Ukrainian territories of Poles."[109]

July 1, 1943— An estimated 15,000 Poles have already been murdered in Wołyń by the UPA as of this date. (For example, 28 villages had been attacked in Włodzimierz County, 23 in Horochów County, and 15 in Dubno County.) The total number of Polish residents of Wołyń who had been killed, wounded, become refugees, or deported to Germany for forced labor as of this date is estimated at 150,000.[110]

July 10, 1943— On this date Krzysztof Markiewicz (representing the AK), Zygmunt Rumel, and Witold Dobrowolski (both representing the Polish Government Delegation for the Homeland) set out for a meeting with the Ukrainian side. Despite assurances of safe conduct, they are murdered in the village of Kustycze near Kowel.[111]

July 11, 1943— The beginning of the "Peter and Paul action": the systematic, massive slaughter of non-Ukrainian civilians, but especially the Poles, in Wołyń. The ethnic-cleansing campaign of the OUN-UPA reaches its highest intensity during this month.

July 20, 1943— After the name "UPA" was stolen from him by OUN-B, Taras "Bulba"-Borovets founds and becomes the head of the Ukrainian National Revolutionary Army (Ukrainska Narodna Revoliutsiina Armiia, or UNRA).

July 1943— OUN-B attacks OUN-M and coerces most of its members under penalty of death to join the Stepan Bandera ranks. Between July and August, most of Taras "Bulba"-Borovets's men are also incorporated into the OUN-B.

In this same month and year, paramilitary units called Ukrainian National Self-Defense units (Ukrainska Natsionalna Samooborona, or UNS) are formed in Eastern Galicia. The UNS units were similar in structure and function to the SKV formed in Wołyń in the summer and fall of 1942.

Summer 1943— Between 1,500 and 2,000 Poles are recruited for the police by the German occupation authorities in the east to replace the Ukrainian policemen who deserted that March. Prohibitions on the part of the AK notwithstanding, many Poles welcomed the opportunity to bear arms in order to protect Polish settlements against Ukrainian-Nationalist attacks as well as for purposes of retaliation. The Polish police deserted their posts in January 1944.

August 10, 1943—Taras "Bulba"-Borovets issues his open letter to the OUN-B Provid in which he accuses the military units of the OUN-B of ethnic cleansing.[112]

Also on this date, Metropolitan Sheptytskyi issues a pastoral letter in an attempt to restrain the slaughter. After reading his letter from the pulpit, some Ukrainian priests announced that "A letter is a letter; such are politics, but the Poles have to be exterminated anyway."[113]

August 13, 1943—Volodymyr Kubiiovych, head of the Ukrainian Central Committee, calls for a cessation of the fratricidal hostilities (as does the Ukrainian Committee of Wołyń) without results.[114]

August 19, 1943—OUN-B and SB forces attack Taras "Bulba"-Borovets's headquarters and arrest some of the leaders of the UNRA and "Bulba"-Borovets's wife, Anna. They are tortured and killed. The remainder of "Bulba"-Borovets's men are forced to join the OUN-B.

August 21-25, 1943—Third Great Conference of the Organization of Ukrainian Nationalists (VZOUN) is convened during which OUN-B ostensibly abandons its totalitarian orientation in favor of democracy and minority rights. The UPA attacks on defenseless Polish villages, however, continue unabated until the end of the war and beyond.

At this conference, Roman Shukhevych, the head of the OUN-B military staff since May 1943, is chosen to replace Lebed as the head of the OUN-B Provid. Now, the entire political and military power of the OUN-B is concentrated in the hands of one individual. (Shukhevych was made the commander-in-chief of all UPA forces on November 22, 1943.)

August 27, 1943—Roman Dmytro Klachkivskyi ("Klym Savur," "Okhrym," "Klym," "Krymskyi," "Omelian"), the regional OUN-B military commander, issues an order to establish army group UPA-North, with himself in charge. He also establishes the following military regions: the northern "Zahrava" region covering the counties of Sarny, Kostopol, Stolin, and Pińsk—under Ivan Lytvynchuk ("Dubovyi"); the northwestern "Bohun," or "Eneia," region covering the counties of Równe, Zdołbunów, Dubno, and Krzemieniec—under Petro Oliinyk ("Eneia"); and the "Turiv" region covering the counties of Łuck, Horochów, Włodzimierz, Kowel, Luboml, Kamień Koszyrski, Kobryń, and Brześć—under Iurii Stelmashchuk. These three regions were located in Wołyń and Polesie and fell within the jurisdiction of UPA-North. The fourth, the "Tiutiunyk" region—under Fedor Vorobei ("Vereshchak")—embraced the territories to the east of Poland in the Zhitomir area. Lytvynchuk, Stelmashchuk, and Vorobei were all products of Nazi diversionary schools, and were German agents.

In addition to army group UPA-North, three other groups were envisioned: UPA-West in Eastern Galicia, Bukovina, Transcarpathia, and the Chełm regions—under Vasyl Sydor ("Shelest," "Vyshytyi"); UPA-South in the Kamianets-Podilskyi/Vynnytsia region—under Omelian Hrabets ("Batko"); and UPA-East in the Kiev, and central and eastern Ukraine regions. Of these three, only UPA-West was formed. In other words, the UPA had no impact on Soviet Ukraine.[115]

August 30, 1943—The UPA attacks Wola Ostrowiecka, Ostrówki and many other

Wołynian villages. In all, about 1,700 Poles perish in the area, which included Wola Ostrowiecka and Ostrówki.

A partial exhumation of mass graves was conducted on August 17, 1992. A forensic expert, Dr. Roman Mądro, from the Medical Academy of Lublin examined the skeletal remains and wrote a lengthy report.[116] Photographs were taken. Witnesses were interviewed. A gruesome documentary was made on videotape. Referring to the videotape shown on Polish TV, Mikołaj Siwicki, a Ukrainian, commented: "The video did not provide an answer to the question of what these Poles perished for. The producers avoided this topic. Because there could only be one answer, not farfetched, but true — for the Polonization of a foreign land."[117]

In 1992, on the 49th anniversary of the slaughter, the remains of the Polish victims of the "reformed," "democratic" OUN-UPA were reinterred.

Late summer 1943 — The UPA transfers its terrorist activities to Eastern Galicia and then to the Lublin and San region.

October 1943 — OUN-B issues an official communiqué in which it places the blame for all the massacres on the shoulders of the Poles and denies that it had any part whatsoever in the murders.[118]

November 22, 1943 — A central command for all UPA forces is established under Shukhevych as commander-in-chief.

Also on this date, Taras "Bulba"-Borovets is brought to Warsaw by the SD for a "meeting." There, he is arrested and detained with the other political prisoners in Sachsenhausen in the Zellenbau section.

November 1943 — The Ukrainian Nationalists hold a conference of the captive nations of Eastern Europe and Asia in order to form an anti-Soviet block. Thirty-nine delegates representing 13 nations attend. Poles are not invited to participate in this conference.

Also on this date, in a swearing-in ceremony in France, the Ukrainian soldiers of the SS-Galizien division of the Waffen-SS pledge their personal loyalty to Hitler. The text of the oath reads as follows:

> I swear by God this sacred oath that in the struggle against Bolshevism I will give unconditional obedience to the Supreme Commander of the German Wehrmacht, Adolf Hitler, and that, as a courageous soldier, I will always be prepared to give my life for this oath.[119]

In his speech to the newly initiated SS-Galizien soldiers, Wächter made a point to clarify the meaning of that solemn declaration:

> Since today you pledged your oath to Adolf Hitler, you are now, Galician volunteers, triply obligated to him. In the first place, as the Führer and the Leader of the German Armed Forces. In the second place, you are obligated to Adolf Hitler as the Führer of the Reich.... In the third place, you are obligated to Adolf Hitler as the Führer of the whole of Europe.[120]

End of 1943 — Various German reports indicate that the total UPA strength at this time is about 40,000 armed men.

January 15, 1944 — The commander of the Wołyn region (*okręg*) orders a concentration of AK forces in the northern part of the province in anticipation of the planned "Burza" uprising. This date is taken as the beginning of the formation of the 27th Wołynian Infantry Division of the Polish Home Army.[121] (See entry for April 4, 1994.)

January 26, 1944 — Andrii Melnyk and many of his closest followers are arrested by the Gestapo.

February 11, 1944 — Równe is liberated by the Soviet army.

February 22, 1944—Otto Wächter congratulates the members of the SS-Galizien for their valor and uprightness. (See Appendix C: Excerpts from Documents, German, "Otto Wächter's Congratulatory Speech to the SS-Galizien.")

February 28, 1944—German forces, with the assistance of the police regiments of the SS-Galizien and the UPA, attack Huta Pieniacka. There are 500-800 victims. The SS-Galizien police regiments bear the main responsibility for the pacification actions conducted in the surrounding villages at this time.

March 5, 1944—The first of a series of meetings is held between the OUN-B and the Wehrmacht. (See Appendix C: Excerpts from Documents, German, "Report on a UPA Meeting with the Wehrmacht," for March 13, March 24, and April 8, 1944.)

March 8, 1944—The last of a series of meetings between OUN-B and the Polish Delegation for the Homeland and AK representatives takes place on this date.[122] Like all the former meetings, so also this one ends in an impasse. The Polish side does not agree to a change in its prewar borders after the war, and the OUN-B side vows to continue its fight for Ukrainian independence on all Ukrainian ethnolinguistic territories.

March 12, 1944—The UPA, together with the police regiments of the SS-Galizien, attacks the Dominican monastery in Podkamień near Brody, where the local civilian Polish population has taken shelter. More than 1,000 Poles are slaughtered in the monastery and in the nearby localities of Palikrowy, Maliniski, and Czernica. (See Appendix C: Excerpts from Documents, Polish, "Other Home Army Field Reports on the Ethnic-Cleansing Campaign" for April 27, 1944; and "A Delegation for the Homeland Report on the Slaughter in Podkamień." See also the German section in Appendix C, "Telegram of the Chief of the Kraków Police (Bierkamp) to the Chief of the Lwów Police, March 15, 1944—Two Versions.")

April 4, 1944—The 27th Wołynian Infantry Division of the Polish Home Army, in formation since January 15, 1944, is accorded the status of a regular unit of the Polish armed forces and receives its official name. The order confirming this comes on April 12, 1944.

It is estimated that the overall strength of the 27th Division consisted of about 6,500 to 7,300 soldiers. It fought against the UPA and the Germans.[123]

May 4-5, 1944—An AK field report notes: "Desertion of the SS-Galizien to the UPA [is taking place]." (See Appendix C: Excerpts from Documents, Polish, "Other Home Army Field Reports on the Ethnic-Cleansing Campaign" for May 4-5, 1944.)

May 10, 1944—An AK field report states: "It has been confirmed that the Germans are helping and are cooperating with UPA units."[124] (See Appendix C: Excerpts from Documents, German, "Report on the UPA Contact with Wehrmacht" for April 15, and April 21, 1944. See also entries for June 14, 1944, September 4, 1944, and November 2, 1944.)

May 16, 1944—Himmler's talk in Neuhammer. According to Himmler, as of January 1, 1944, there were some 25,000 Ukrainian soldiers in the Waffen-SS.[125] This means that a substantial number of Ukrainians served in SS divisions *other* than the 14. Waffen-Grenadier-Division der SS (the SS-Galizien).

May 24, 1944—Rosenfeld (secretary at Goebbels's Ministry of Propaganda) sends a message to the Chief of the Operations

Section of the Reichsministry for Occupied Eastern Territories that contains the following excerpt, submitted to Berlin on September 19, 1943, by Dr. Frederic (a security service agent):

> Monsignor Sheptitsky [Sheptytskyi] has approved and supported the idea of creating a Ukrainian army. It should consist of SS divisions which are to be concentrated in training camps for instruction. The Metropolitan's brother said in this connection that the "volunteers" of this army would not be volunteers in the true meaning of the word but would have to be coercively recruited by the German authorities.
>
> Beyond all doubt, Metropolitan Sheptitsky with his enormous influence in Galicia is the only available big figure ready to use that influence in the interests of cooperation with Germany. He has rendered us and is rendering still immense services.
>
> Dr. Frederic[126]

June 14, 1944— An AK field report states: "There is local anti-Soviet cooperation between the UPA and the Wehrmacht. Germans from Soviet Ukraine are organizing a Ukrainian army of liberation. In the counties of Hrubieszów, Tomaszów and Zamość, the Germans are issuing leaflets calling on the Ukrainian units from [Eastern] Galicia and Wołyń to move beyond the Bug River and there to fight the Bolsheviks.... The UPA has 40,000 armed [persons] and is continuing to mobilize. Its main concentration is in the Carpathian Mountains. The slaughter [of Poles] does not cease. The police has called for the evacuation of Jarosław, Przemyśl, Sanok, and Biłgoraj.... About 300,000 Poles have fled from Małopolska Wschodnia [Eastern Galicia], including 45,000 from Lwów." (See Appendix C: Excerpts from Documents, Polish, "Other Home Army Field Reports on the Ethnic-Cleansing Campaign" for June 14, 1944.)

July 11-15, 1944— First Congress of the Ukrainian Supreme Liberation Council (Ukrainska Holovna Vyzvolna Rada, or UHVR— an OUN-B outfit with Roman Shukhevych as secretary general) convenes in the Carpathian Mountains in the county of Sambor. Like the decrees of the OUN-B Third Great Conference of the Organization of Ukrainian Nationalists, or VZOUN (August 1943), the pronouncements issued by the UHVR also bear a stamp of democracy and speak of minority rights with an eye, no doubt, toward the western Allies. At the end of July, the UHVR signs an agreement with the Germans for a unified front against the Soviet threat.[127] (See also the entry for November 2, 1944.)

July 16, 1944— *Ridna Zemlia*, an OUN-M newspaper out of Lwów, publishes an editorial which states:

> The war will last until the Germans will be victorious together with all of Europe, until the dark forces perish, until Bolshevism together with Anglo-American imperialism fall to pieces.... The enemy will not break the spirit of Germany and Europe!... We Ukrainians must take our example from the German nation, from its spiritual determination to survive until the last battle, the last victory. Away with all hesitation, away with all doubts, away with all resignation! Only the complete dedication to the task at hand will lead to a full victory.[128]

July 13-22, 1944— The Soviet army encircles and decimates the combined German and Ukrainian forces in the Waffen-SS (including the Ukrainian SS-Galizien division) at the battle of Brody, a little town on the main highway between Równe and Lwów. After this defeat, some of the remaining SS-Galizien members are reintegrated into the reformed SS-Galizien along with fresh volunteers, while others join the UPA. This is confirmed by Wasyl Veryha, a former member and the historian of the SS-Galizien, now residing in Toronto: "While recalling the fairly well known facts that the personnel trained in the division had become the backbone of the UPA, it should be mentioned that the UPA command also sent groups of its people to the division to receive proper military training."[129]

With this revelation we now have a near complete picture of the military core of the UPA: the German-trained and equipped remnant of the Nachtigall and Roland units, the German-equipped members of Taras Borovets's Polesian Stronghold who were later forced to join OUN-B, the German-trained and equipped leaders and members of the OUN-M *pokhidni hrupy* who joined Borovets' partisans and were later "converted" to OUN-B forces, some members of the German-trained and equipped OUN-M Bukovinian Battalion of 1941, the 5,000 German-trained and equipped Ukrainian policemen who joined in March of 1943, the additional Ukrainian policemen who joined subsequently, and now these German-trained and equipped officers, instructors, and soldiers from the SS-Galizien. It seems, then, that the UPA can be best described as a German-organized, trained and equipped, deserter, military organization turned guerrilla.

In addition to these mostly OUN-B personnel, the UPA also housed volunteers, peasants mobilized by force, Ukrainian POWs from Soviet Ukraine who escaped German captivity, members of other nationalities who chanced into its ranks, and even some Jews in support capacities (doctors, dentists, nurses, etc.) who were freed from the ghettos in 1942 with the help of the Ukrainian police and kept in camps at Poryck and Kurdynki for the exclusive use of the UPA. (See entry for October 1944.)

July 27, 1944—Lwów is liberated by the Soviet army.

September 4, 1944—An Army Group North—Ukraine report states: "After the recent events at the front, the leadership of the UPA has recognized that it cannot wage the struggle against the Bolsheviks by itself and has repeatedly asked the Wehrmacht for support in the form of arms."[130] In exchange for diversionary activities in the rear of the Soviet front, the UPA—on Himmler's orders—was equipped with German arms, supplies, and radio equipment. These arms they turned against the Soviets, ambushing and killing officers and soldiers, including Marshal Nikolay Vatutin, commander of the First Ukrainian Front. They were also used against innocent civilians during the continuous ethnic-cleansing campaign.

September 15, 1944—The SS-Galizien is reformed and reinforced with new volunteers.

Fall of 1944—All Ukrainian-Nationalist leaders are released from German prisons to assist the rapidly deteriorating German war effort. Among them were: Taras Borovets in August, Stepan Bandera on September 25, and Andrii Melnyk on October 17.

October 1944—All of Eastern Poland now lies in Soviet hands. According to Wiktor Poliszczuk, before evacuating behind the German armed forces to its base of operation west of the so-called Curzon line, the UPA murdered its non-Ukrainian members (including 500 Jews) and the OUN-SB forces executed numerous Ukrainians on the mere suspicion of possible future collaboration with the Soviet forces.[131]

In this same month and year, the SS-Galizien is ordered to proceed to the occupied Slovak Republic and to participate in the suppression of an anti-Nazi partisan rebellion.

October-November, 1944—The pro-German Ukrainian National Committee (Ukrainskyi Natsionalnyi Komitet, or UNK) is formed in Berlin under General Pavlo Shandruk.

November 2, 1944—A German field report from the eastern territories to Gerhard von Mende, indicates that the UPA and the Wehrmacht had joined forces in August 1944. (See Appendix C: Excerpts from Documents, German, "Field Report from the Eastern Territories to Gerard von Mende, Director of the Department of Affairs in the Occupied Eastern Territories, Ministry of the Third Reich, November 2, 1944.")

November 14, 1944—General Andrei Vlasov issues his "Manifesto of Prague" calling into existence the Russian Liberation Army (Russkaya Osvoboditelnaya Armiia, or ROA).

On this same date, Volodymyr Kubiovych brings a delegation of Ukrainian-Nationalist peasants to Hans Frank to underscore his continued loyalty to the German authorities.[132]

November 18, 1944—In response to the "Manifesto of Prague," ten non-Russian nationalist groups address a "protest" (signed by Melnyk alone) to Hitler through Rosenberg. In that "protest" they remind him of Germany's great debt to the Ukrainian Nationalists in the following words:

> It is therefore not astounding that these (non-Russian) peoples greeted the outbreak of the German-Russian war with the greatest joy. They placed themselves at the side of the German army from the first day on, helped where they could, welcomed the troops with open arms and with cordial friendship. Standing shoulder to shoulder with the German soldiers in battle, they proved their loyalty to the national idea.[133]

1944-47—Massive population exchanges. Just before the end of the war, millions of Germans fled Poland in advance of the Red Army. The rest were expelled by the Communist authorities in the immediate postwar years in accordance with the decree of the Allied Powers at Potsdam. In all, Germany reclaimed about six million of its citizens and Volksdeutsche.

Between October 15, 1944 and August 2, 1946, about 482,000 Ukrainians were relocated from Poland to Soviet Ukraine.[134]

Poland, in turn, reclaimed over one-and-a-half million ethnic Poles—those who were deported from the lost territories in the east to the smaller, prewar German, western "recovered (*odzyskane*) territories" awarded it by the Allies in compensation for the loss of Eastern Poland. On the basis of the September 9 and 22, 1944, Polish-Soviet agreements, between September 1944 and January 1, 1947, some 784,000 Poles were repatriated from Soviet Ukraine, 272,000 from Soviet Belorussia, and 170,800 from Soviet Lithuania. On the basis of the July 1945 agreement, between 1945 and 1950 about 226,000 Poles were repatriated from the interior of the Soviet Union as well. During Phase II (1956 and 1957), more Polish people were repatriated from all these areas.[135]

Mid-January 1945—The SS-Galizien is transferred to Slovenia, where it fights Josip Broz Tito's anti-German partisans.

March 12, 1945—Alfred Rosenberg officially recognizes the UNK as the sole Ukrainian political representative body and, in the name of the German government, places all Ukrainian military formations in the German armed forces under it.

On this same date, the UNK forms the pro-German Ukrainian National Army (Ukrainska Natsionalna Armiia, or UNA) under Paulo Shandruk.[136] In the last months of the war, all the major Nationalist leaders are called to Berlin to assist the dying Third Reich through the UNK.

End of March 1945—The SS-Galizien is moved to the Austrian front near Gleichenberg and Feldbach.

April 21, 1945—Despite protests from the Polish government-in-exile, Communist-dominated Poland and the USSR sign a bilateral agreement which delineates their respective national boundaries. Southeastern Poland (Western Ukraine) now becomes a part of the Ukrainian SSR.

May 8, 1945—End of World War II. The SS-Galizien surrenders to the British near the town of Radstadt, Austria. Eventually, after a nominal screening process, its members gain entrance to England, and many of them emigrate to Canada and the United States. This is also true of a substantial number of OUN-UPA members and other nationalists.

October 1945—The Lemko Company of the UPA is formed. By spring of 1946, this military unit consisted of 260 men in six platoons. In the first 18 months of its existence, the Lemko Company was involved in over 200 military skirmishes with the Polish army and police units. The successful ambush on General Karol Świerczewski was its doing. (See the following entry.) During Operation "Wisła" (*Akcja "Wisła"*), the company sustained heavy losses and, on June 29, 1947, was forced to retreat to the east. It was demobilized on September 10, 1948.[137]

March 28, 1947—Polish vice-minister of defense, General Karol Świerczewski, is killed during a UPA ambush.

April 17, 1947—The Polish State Committee on Public Security issues orders for the implementation of Operation "Wisła."

April 28-July 31, 1947—Operation "Wisła," the code name for the concerted military action whose objective was to annihilate the UPA in the Polish regions of Podlasie, Chełm/Zamość, San Basin, and the Lemko area (collectively called Zakerzonnia in Ukrainian-Nationalist literature but having no corresponding Polish geographical designation). This operation was carried out by the Communist-controlled Polish armed forces with the active assistance of Soviet and Czech military units. In the judgment of the Communist authorities, the only effective way of accomplishing this mission and of preventing the resurgence of the UPA in these areas was to resettle the entire Ukrainian/Lemko population onto the territories "recovered" from Germany (primarily in the provinces of Olsztyn, Szczecin, Wrocław, and Gdańsk). To prevent the resurgence of the UPA in Poland, it was furthermore stipulated that in the area of resettlement, Ukrainians could not constitute more than ten percent of the local population. According to historians Szcześniak and Szota, the critical situation in these Polish borderlands forced the Polish government to "resettle the Ukrainian population, terrorized by the UPA, to the northern and western territories of Poland. Only by liquidating its social base could the destruction of the UPA be hastened."[138]

The UPA began to transfer its center of operations to these areas already in the fall of 1943 in the event of a Soviet counteroffensive and Allied victory. In full retreat behind the Wehrmacht in 1944, the UPA became entrenched in the mountainous and forested terrain of Zakerzonnia, where it depended on the sometimes willing, sometimes extorted, support of the local civilian population.

When the massive population exchanges began, the UPA intensified its ethnic-cleansing campaign in Eastern Galicia in order to ensure the departure of Poles from that area. In the month of February 1945 alone, more than 1,000 Poles were massacred and more than 50 villages burned to the ground in the Tarnopol region.[139] One Jewish Holocaust survivor recalls the state of affairs in the town of Rozdół near Stryj *after* the arrival of the Soviet troops:

> Although we were supposedly liberated, our troubles were not over. The Ukrainians took the opportunity to cause mischief of

their own. A band of them, called *Banderowtsi* [Banderowcy] roamed the streets at night. They tortured and killed Poles and hung them from lampposts. They would come during the night and knock on the window and tell you that you had twenty-four hours to get out, that this was their country now. All around us families were leaving, and taking with them what meager possessions they could.[140]

At the same time, the UPA actively opposed the transfers of Ukrainians from Poland to Soviet Ukraine, attacked Polish settlements, and defended Ukrainian villages against Polish retaliatory attacks. The UPA also attacked Polish military installations and units and engaged in a variety of sabotage activities (for example, in the destruction of bridges, railway lines, transportation centers, communication networks) and in the burning of the vacated Ukrainian villages in order to prevent them from falling into Polish hands.[141] In assuming the role of the defender of the Ukrainian/Lemko population in Zakerzonnia, the UPA also won their allegiance (but not the allegiance of the entire Ukrainian/Lemko population, to be sure, since in many instances that population was itself the object of UPA harassment).

Thus, when the Polish military units were dispatched to Zakerzonnia to "facilitate" the (initially voluntary) resettlement program and to protect the transports, they encountered heavy resistance on the part of the UPA. In the skirmishes that followed, 3,392 OUN-UPA-SKV members were killed by Polish military and security forces between June 1945 and March 1947 (i.e., before Operation "Wisła"). Of these, about 1,500 were UPA members. During this same period 2,199 Poles were killed by the Ukrainian Nationalists. Of these, 997 were members of the Polish armed forces, 603 were public officials and members of various political parties, the military and the security service, and 599 were civilians. Szcześniak and Szota provide a listing with dates of the major acts of terror and sabotage carried out by the UPA between July 1945 and March 1947.[142] It is important to note the reason why this particular group of Ukrainian Nationalists (members of OUN-UPA-SB-UNS-SKV) decided to occupy Zakerzonnia in the first place. If they wanted simply to save their lives, they could have fled to the West behind their leaders and most of the other OUN-UPA members; instead, they halted their retreat midstream. According to Polish sources, in 1947 there remained over 2,400 persons in the Ukrainian underground in Zakerzonnia. Of these, 1,770 were UPA soldiers and 720 were members of the supportive civilian OUN network. According to Col. Myroslav Onyshkevych ("Orest," the commander in chief of the UPA in Poland after the death of Iaroslav Starukh), the UPA of that day had fewer than 1,390 soldiers and an undisclosed number of civilians in the service of the OUN.[143] But according to Władysław Filar, in 1947 there were 6,000 Ukrainian Nationalists in *Zakerzonnia* divided into 2,500 "well-trained and well-armed" UPA members, about 3,000 members of the SKV who were "on call," and about 200 members of the infamous SB. Their organizational network embraced 325 villages, and they had ample stores of ammunition and supplies, a well-fortified complex of bunkers, and even hospitals.[144]

Without doubt, these Ukrainian Nationalists were among the most hardened, the most dedicated, the most fervent believers in the political platform of Ukrainian integral nationalism. (Most of them were also from Eastern Galicia.) They halted in Zakerzonnia because they were convinced that a Third World War would inevitably follow in which the West would be pitted against the Soviet Union. They were also convinced that, in the event of a western victory in that coming war, their military might in that region (in addition to their anti-Soviet efforts) would guarantee

Zakerzonnia's eventual "reunification" with "Greater Ukraine"—as prescribed by the articles of the proceedings of the 1929 conference in Vienna.

The plan, then, was the same as that enunciated by Osyp Dumyn in his 1926 report to the German Ministry of Foreign Affairs. It was the same as that proposed by the OUN Provid in its 1929 conference in Vienna, except that now the Ukrainian Nationalists had a well-trained, well-armed, experienced, and disciplined "Ukrainian army" at their disposal.

To assure the above-mentioned outcome (the separation of Zakerzonnia from Poland and its eventual reunification of with Ukraine), the Ukrainian Nationalists intended to continue their ethnic-cleansing campaign in these Ukrainian ethnolinguistic territories. If, thanks to their prodigious efforts, no Poles remained in Zakerzonnia, Wołyń, and Eastern Galicia at the conclusion of WW III, who would be there to resist the inclusion of these lands into independent Ukraine? Such was the thinking of the Ukrainian Nationalists in the postwar period—the same as it had been during the war in reference to Wołyń, Eastern Galicia, and the Lublin region. Such was the setting for Operation "Wisła" in 1947. General Ignacy Blum provides a handy, but only a partial, summary of the results of that military campaign:

> In all, following the action of the operational group Wisła, 1,509 [UPA] bandits were liquidated. This represents 75 percent of the total band members as of April 1947. At the same time, the entire civil network of the OUN was liquidated, thus destroying the social and material basis of the UPA. A total of 2,781 active Ukrainian fascists were sent to [Jaworzno].[145]

According to Eugeniusz Misiło, "Among the 3,873 persons interned in the camp [Jaworzno] were Uniate and Orthodox priests, almost the entire Ukrainian intelligentsia, and most of all, villagers suspected of aiding and abetting the UPA."[146] Of this number, according to the Main Commission for the Investigation of Crimes Against the Polish Nation, 161 prisoners died in Jaworzno from various causes (including typhus epidemics, and the lack of sanitation and food) and 114 were beaten and generally mistreated by the camp personnel. The Commission reports also maintain that the Ukrainians incarcerated in Jaworzno during Operation "Wisła" had the benefit of due process of law—such as it was under Communist rule—and that the conditions of life in that prison camp did not differ from the conditions obtaining in other Polish prison camps of the day.[147] It may be added that thousands of non-Ukrainian Polish citizens were also interned in Jaworzno at various times for various reasons.

The other result of Operation "Wisła," not mentioned in General Blum's quote above, was the tragic resettlement of about 140,000 Ukrainians, Lemkos, and even mixed (Polish-Ukrainian) families from Zakerzonnia. Although it has been said that in many respects their subsequent material well-being had improved considerably because of that action (i.e., they were generally resettled on larger and better farms and moved from poor cottages to brick homes left behind by the Germans), the manner in which it was carried out (often at gunpoint) was brutal and, more important, their culture was utterly destroyed. Many Ukrainian scholars have claimed, and continue to claim, that this in fact was the real intention of the Communist political authorities in the first place and that the "fight against the UPA" was merely a pretext. Others claim that this was a clear case of punishing the Ukrainian people on the basis of the principle of "collective responsibility." According to the *Encyclopedia of Ukraine*:

> The principle of collective responsibility was applied, and all Ukrainians in the affected territories, regardless of their political views

and affiliations, were deported. The deportation process was swift and brutal: deportees were often given only a few hours to prepare themselves, could take only limited belongings, and were transported to their destination in crowded box-cars. The food supply was irregular, sanitary conditions were poor, there were many delays en route, and the deportation process was accompanied by considerable violence. Some deportees died in transit; those who resisted deportation, or were suspected of aiding the UPA, were imprisoned in the Jaworzno prison camp in Silesia.[148]

This description of the deportation process during Operation "Wisła" has been verified time and again by personal testimonies of survivors.

Whether there was another way of liquidating the UPA — entrenched as it was in the Carpathian Mountains and labyrinthine forests of Zakerzonnia and living off the peasants — without this massive resettlement program is a matter of ongoing discussion. Lev Shankovskyi, a Ukrainian-Nationalist activist and scholar, has said:

> The armed resistance of the UPA and the OUN underground in Przemyśl as well as on all Ukrainian Zakerzonnia was halted not because of the military superiority of the enemy but because of the loss of the population base: the people who supported this battle and who in one way or another participated in it. When almost all the Ukrainians were resettled from Zakerzonnia — some to the USSR, some to the northern and western regions of Poland — the UPA units as well as the OUN underground could no longer exist. They were compelled to leave this territory.[149]

Militarily speaking, Operation "Wisła" was a total success inasmuch as it accomplished its mission of destroying the UPA and, by removing civilians from a zone of intensive fighting, saved many lives. In human terms, it was also a great tragedy inasmuch as it involved brutality, loss of life, and the destruction of an autochthonous culture. However, one thing is perfectly clear: Without the presence of the UPA on Polish soil, without its terror and sabotage, without its continuous efforts to tear this last remnant of Eastern Poland from the only nation in the anti-German coalition that sustained a net loss of territory after World War II, there would have been no need for Operation "Wisła" — as there had been no need for such a concerted *military* action in the case of the postwar resettlement of Germans, Poles, and Belorussians to their respective countries. These people also lost their autochthonous cultures in the territories from which they were removed, and had to leave their homes on short notice and under harsh conditions.

September 17, 1947 — Iaroslav Starukh, head of the Provid in Zakerzonnia and of the UPA forces in Poland, is killed in his bunker by Polish forces.

1947 — Dmytro Dontsov (neither a member of UVO nor OUN), a severe critic of all humanitarian virtues and democratic forms of government which he considered to be weak and unfit in the struggle for survival, emigrates to the United States, then to Canada in 1948.

September 3, 1949 — According to the *Encyclopedia of Ukraine*:

> Except for two units, they [UPA units] were demobilized at the end of the summer of 1948. On September 3, 1949, R. Shukhevych ordered the command structure and the remaining combat units to be deactivated, and their members to be transferred to the underground network. After Shukhevych's death (5 March 1950) the underground continued the armed struggle under V. Kuk's ("Koval's") leadership until 1954.[150]

According to Misiło, the UPA was dissolved by Onyshkevych, Starukh's successor, at the end of September or the beginning of October 1947.[151]

March 5, 1950 — Roman Shukhevych perishes in the village of Biłohorszcza near Lwów. Some authors maintain that he was killed by Soviet forces, others claim that he committed suicide, and still others, that he and other UPA leaders died in the bunker which they themselves blew up.

April 11, 1950 — The head of the OUN-SB, Petro Fedoriv, is executed by Polish authorities.[152]

July 6, 1950 — Myroslav Onyshkevych is executed by Polish authorities.[153]

1954 — A break occurs in the OUN-B. The OUN-z (OUN-abroad, also called "binary") is founded by Lev Rebet and Zenon Matla.

October 15, 1959 — Stepan Bandera is murdered by a Soviet agent in Munich.

1989 — Poland regains its independence.

June 22, 1990 — A lengthy "Proclamation of the OUN Home Provid" bearing this date circulates throughout the Polish community in 1992.[154] There is disagreement whether this document, which addresses the present-day strategic goals of the OUN, is genuine or a forgery.

August 3, 1990 — The Polish Senate condemns Operation "Wisła."

1991 — Ukraine becomes an independent nation.

March 28, 1993 — The Congress of Ukrainian Nationalists (Konhres Ukrainskykh Natsionalistiv, or KUN; an OUN-B organization) holds a conference in Kiev dedicated to the memory of Dmytro Dontsov on the anniversary of his death in Montreal on March 30, 1973. (Dontsov is buried in a Ukrainian cemetery in South Bound Brook, New Jersey, where many emigré Ukrainian Nationalists lie.)

July 2-4, 1993 — The Great Conference of the Congress of Ukrainian Nationalists convenes in Kiev.

August 29, 1993 — The Union of Ukrainian Youth and the Congress of Ukrainian Nationalists hold a conference in honor of the 110th anniversary of Dmytro Dontsov's birth (August 30, 1883).

Summer 1993 — The 50th anniversary of the founding of the SS-Galizien. SS-Galizien veterans hold a reunion in Lviv.

March 1, 1994 — After 54 years, a general meeting takes place in Kiev between the representatives of OUN-B and OUN-M.

May 1995 — At a conference on Poland, Germany, and Ukraine organized by the Institute of History of the Higher Pedagogical School in Rzeszów, Prof. Leonid Zashkilniak of the Lviv State University states that "the leadership of various nationalist factions [in Western Ukraine] lost their sense of political realism and at the same time draw with them to the edge of the abyss the masses of Western Ukrainian society. Only in such extreme circumstances could arise the antihumanitarian slogans of 'cleansing' the Ukrainian lands of Poles that led, in 1942-44, to the massive annihilation of the Polish population of Wołyń, Eastern Galicia, the Chełm region, Podlasie, and the Carpathian region."[155]

September 2-3, 1995 — The Second Great Conference of the Congress of Ukrainian Nationalists convenes in Kiev and proclaims its strategy for the new world order based on national states within their own ethnolinguistic borders.

Summer 1996—In response to a petition requesting combat status for former UPA members, the Ukrainian Parliament appoints a Parliamentary Commission to conduct a legal-political assessment of the OUN-UPA. Also in response to that petition, 95 members of that Parliament—among them leaders of the parliamentary constituencies of the Socialist Party of Ukraine, the Communist Party of Ukraine, the Agrarian Party of Ukraine, and the Peasants' Party of Ukraine—affix their signatures to an appeal entitled: "To the nations, parliaments and governments of Ukraine, Belarus, Israel, Poland, Russia, Slovakia, and Yugoslavia." In this appeal, the parliamentarians ask for a condemnation of the OUN and UPA by the countries mentioned.[156]

February 22, 1997—The Ukrainian Congressional Committee of America (Ukrainskyi Konhresovyi Komitet Ameryki, or UKKA) holds a meeting at its headquarters in New York, the object of which is to establish a Home Committee for the commemoration (in 1997) of the 55th anniversary of the founding of the UPA, the 50th anniversary of the departure of UPA units for the West, and the 50th anniversary of Operation "Wisła." The meeting, attended by 32 representatives of 25 Ukrainian organizations, was spearheaded by former veterans of the UPA and the SS-Galizien. The latter now refer to themselves as members of the 1st Ukrainian Division of the Ukrainian National Army (UNA).

April 5-6, 1997—The Congress of Ukrainians in Poland holds a conference in Warsaw. During this conference appeals are made to the Polish government to condemn Operation "Wisła," to make appropriate restitution to those resettled or to their legal heirs, to materially assist those wishing to return to their former domiciles in Zakerzonnia, to return the properties of Ukrainian corporate bodies to presently active Ukrainian organizations, to accord those imprisoned in Jaworzno the status of "victims of Stalinist repressions," and to impart a suitable burial and erect suitable monuments to the Ukrainian victims of World War II and the postwar period. The 300 delegates, representing 20 Ukrainian organizations, also expressed the hope for Polish-Ukrainian reconciliation, and offered forgiveness for the transgressions of the Polish people.

May 21, 1997—Presidents Aleksander Kwaśniewski and Leonid Kuchma sign a "Mutual Declaration of the Presidents of the Republic of Poland and Ukraine Regarding Understanding and Reconciliation." (See Appendix E)

1998—The 55th anniversary of the Ukrainian-Nationalist ethnic-cleansing campaign in Wołyń.

Appendix E: Mutual Declaration of the Presidents of the Republic of Poland and Ukraine Regarding Understanding and Reconciliation

The President of the Republic of Poland and the President of Ukraine, mindful of historical accountability to present and future generations of Ukrainians and Poles, as well as the role of Poland and Ukraine in the strengthening of security and stability in East Central Europe, and also appreciative of the importance of the strategic partnership of both nations, guided by the resolution of the Treaty of Good Neighborliness, Friendly Relations and Cooperation of May 18, 1992, certain that the future of Polish-Ukrainian relations should be constructed on truth and justice, as well as deep and sincere understanding and reconciliation, desiring mutually to overcome the complicated heritage of Polish-Ukrainian misfortunes, so that the shadows of the past may not fall on the present and future friendly and partnership ties between both nations and peoples, hereby declare:

In the centuries-old history of Polish-Ukrainian relations there are many moving examples of genuine friendship, mutual assistance and cooperation between both countries. In it are also threads of brotherly military ties, cultural influences enriching both nations, and neighborly good will.

We should not, however, omit the moments of tragedy, such as the ten-year wars in the seventeenth and eighteenth centuries, the manifestation of anti-Ukrainian policies during the twenties and thirties in the twentieth century, and the persecution of the Polish people in Soviet Ukraine during the time of Stalinist repressions. We cannot forget about the blood of Poles spilled in Volhynia particularly in 1942-43, or about the cruelty of the Ukrainian-Polish conflicts in the first years of the postwar era. A separate, dramatic page in the history of our relations was writ by Operation "Vistula," aimed at the Ukrainian community as a whole in Poland. To keep silent about all these facts or to present them from a single perspective does not mitigate the suffering of those wronged or their near ones, does not promote a deepening of understanding between our nations. The road to genuine friendship leads above all through truth and mutual understanding. We acknowledge that no end can constitute a justification for resorting to criminal behavior and the use of force, or the application of collective responsibility. At the same time, we must remember that sometimes the sources of these conflicts lay beyond Ukraine and Poland, that they were occasioned by circumstances unrelated to Poles and Ukrainians and imposed upon our nations against their will by undemocratic political systems. We pay homage to the innocent — those murdered, fallen and forcibly resettled Poles and Ukrainians. We condemn those responsible for their suffering. At the same time, we express our gratitude to all those who, in the course of these difficult years, acted in behalf of bringing our nations closer together.

At the present time, Poland and Ukraine are sovereign nations, good neighbors and strategic partners. For that reason, it is imperative to overcome the bitterness lingering in the memories of many Ukrainians and Poles. This is necessitated not only by our respect for democratic values, human rights, and the basic principles and norms of international law, but also by the desire to see Ukraine and Poland within a unified Europe.

The interpretation of our mutual past and its various periods is a task which should be taken up by specialists who, in an atmosphere of openness, will rigorously investigate the facts and prepare their objective assessments.

For the sake of a better mutual understanding between the Polish and Ukrainian nations, a dialogue should be stimulated within the media. Greater advantage should be taken of the capabilities of the Polish citizens of Ukrainian origin and of Ukrainian citizens of Polish origin who, through their work, make significant contributions to the cultural and economic development of our nations. They should be the animators of a close-knit cooperation between Poland and Ukraine. Both nations, for their part, should look after them and support the well-being of the Polish minority in Ukraine and the Ukrainian minority in Poland.

The Republic of Poland and Ukraine will do their part to make sure that the consciousness of young Ukrainians and Poles will not be burdened by the memory of the tragic pages of history. May future generations live in a common European home in which there will be no room for prejudice and mistrust.

With this conviction we, the Presidents of the Republic of Poland and Ukraine, intend mutually to assume guardianship over the preservation of the idea of Polish-Ukrainian understanding and reconciliation.

In former days, our predecessors poured water on swords as a sign of peace, alliance and brotherhood. And today, we Poles and Ukrainians wish to pour feelings of friendship and solidarity into our hearts.

On the threshold of the twenty-first century, let us remember the past but let us think of the future.

President of the Republic of Poland,
President of Ukraine,
Aleksander Kwaśniewski
Leonid Kuchma
Kiev, May 21, 1997.

Notes

Introduction

1. The official statistics in Tables 1 and 2 come from *Drugi powszechny spis ludności z dnia 9.XII.1931r. Statystyka Polski, seria C, zeszyt 70, województwo wołyńskie* (Warszawa: Główny Urząd Statystyczny Rzeczypospolitej Polskiej, 1938), p. 21. The adjusted figures in Table 3 come from Jerzy Tomaszewski, *Rzeczpospolita wielu narodów* (Warszawa: Czytelnik, 1985), p. 78. Tomaszewski's table is reproduced in Tadeusz Piotrowski, *Poland's Holocaust: Ethnic Strife, Collaboration with Occupying Forces and Genocide in the Second Republic, 1918-1947* (Jefferson, NC: McFarland, 1998), p. 353.

2. "Wołyń. Referat specjalny," February, 1936, CA KC PZPR, UWW, microfilm 1800/1, p. 70. The percentages for Ukrainians and Poles living in villages come from Władysław Filar, ed., *Przed akcją "Wisła" był Wołyń* (Warszawa: Światowy Związek Żołnierzy Armii Krajowej, Okręg Wołyń, 1997), p. 5.

3. The statistics following n. 2 have been compiled from the tables in Tomaszewski, p. 78.

4. In point of fact, Shevchenko is of the opinion that in the nineteenth century his people suffered more at the hands of their Ukrainian overlords than under the yoke of either the tsarist or the Polish ones. His poem "My Friendly Epistle" contains the telling stanza:

> Thus in her struggle, our Ukraine
> Reached the last climax of pure pain:
> Worse than the Poles, or any other,
> The children crucify their mother.

This passage can be found in C. H. Andrusyshen and Watson Kirkconnell, trans., *The Poetical Works of Taras Shevchenko: The Kobzar* (Toronto: University of Toronto Press, 1964), p. 255.

5. Myron B. Kuropas, *The Ukrainian Americans: Roots and Aspirations 1884-1954* (Toronto: University of Toronto, 1991), pp. 233-34. See also Tadeusz Piotrowski, *Vengeance of the Swallows: Memoir of a Polish Family's Ordeal Under Soviet Aggression, Ukrainian Ethnic Cleansing and Nazi Enslavement, and Their Emigration to America* (Jefferson, NC: McFarland, 1995), pp. 36-39, and Piotrowski, *Poland's Holocaust*, 179-87.

The distribution of (mostly Polish) land in Eastern Poland to the so-called military settlers from western Polish territories was especially resented by the local Ukrainian population; however, as Polish scholars point out, in all of the Second Republic of Poland, there were less than 8,000 such parcels of land. See the summary statement in Romuald Niedzielko, ed., *Polska—Ukraina: Trudne pytania. Materiały II międzynarodowego seminarium historycznego "Stosunki polsko-ukraińskie w latach 1918-1947," Warszawa, 22-24 maja 1997*, 2 vols. (Warszawa: Światowy Związek Żołnierzy Armii Krajowej—Związek Ukraińców w Polsce, 1998), p. 227.

6. See Alexander J. Motyl, "Ukrainian Nationalist Political Violence in Inter-War Poland, 1921-1939," *East European Quarterly* 19 (March 1985): 45-55. See also M. Feliński, "Acts of Sabotage Committed by the Ukrainian Military Organisation in Eastern Malopolska During the Second Half of 1930," in *The Ukrainians in Poland* (London: n.p., 1931), pp. 158-73.

7. Petro Mirchuk, *Narys istorii Orhanizatsii Ukrainskykh Natsionalistiv 1920-1939* (München: Ukrainske Vydavnytstvo, 1968), pp. 22-25, quoted in Wiktor Poliszczuk, *Integralny nacjonalizm ukraiński jako odmiana faszyzmu*, vol. 1 (Toronto: n.p., 1998), p. 105.

8. Antoni Szcześniak and Wiesław Szota, *Droga do nikąd: Działalność Organizacji Ukraińskich*

Nacjonalistów i jej likwidacja w Polsce (Warszawa: Ministerstwo Obrony Narodowej, 1973), p. 43.

9. Ryszard Torzecki, *Kwestia ukraińska w polityce III Rzeszy 1933-1945* (Warszawa: Książka i Wiedza, 1972), p. 136.

10. "The Report. A Minority in Poland — The Ukrainian Conflict," *Times* (London), December 12 and 18, 1930. This report is reprinted in the appendix of Piotrowski, *Poland's Holocaust*, Document 13, pp. 287-91.

11. "Permanentna revoliutsiia," *Surma* 37, no. 10 (October 1930), p. 7; quoted in Motyl, "Ukrainian Nationalist Political Violence," p. 53.

12. Osip Dumin [Osyp Dumyn], "Prawda o Ukraińskiej Organizacji," written in May 1926, received in Berlin on June 17, 1926, trans. from German, *Zeszyty Historyczne* (Paris) 30 (1974): 103-37. The two paragraphs can be found on p. 104.

13. Dmytro Dontsov, *Natsionalizm* (Lwów: n.p., 1926; London: The Ukrainian Publishers, 1966). See also Wiktor Poliszczuk, *Ideologia nacjonalizmu ukraińskiego według Dmytra Doncowa* (Warszawa: n.p., 1996).

14. See Appendix C: Excerpts from Documents, Ukrainian, "First Congress of Ukrainian Nationalists (Also Called the First Great Conference of Ukrainian Nationalists — Velykyi Zbir Ukrainskykh Natsionalistiv, or VZUN) in Vienna, January 28-February 3, 1929."

15. See Piotrowski, "Ukrainian Collaboration," chap. 7 in *Poland's Holocaust*.

16. Maksym Skorupskyi, "U nastupakh i vidstupakh," in Vasyl Mykhalchuk, ed., *Tudy, de bii za voliu: Zbirnyk viiskovo-politychnykh materialiv u pamiat Maksyma Skorupskoho-Maksa kurinnoho UPA* (London/Paris: Fundatsiia im. O. Olzhycha, 1989; Kyiv: "Kozaky," 1992), p. 174, quoted in Wiktor Poliszczuk, *Legal and Political Assessment of the OUN and UPA*, English trans. by Tadeusz Piotrowski (Toronto: n.p., 1997), p. 38.

See Appendix C: Excerpts from Documents, Ukrainian, "Blank Mobilization Card from Wołyń" and "OUN-B Mobilization Order, April 5, 1943." The first of these documents specifies that non-compliance would result in a referral of the individual to the "Revolutionary Court of the UPA." Needless to say, all Ukrainians were well aware that a referral to the "Revolutionary Court" was, in effect, a death sentence. The second, addressed to the Ukrainian police and civil servants who had been ordered to desert their posts and join the OUN, states that "the OUN will catch and shoot as deserters all those who will be wandering about the territory."

17. In addition to the main text, see Appendices A, B, and C for some of this evidence.

18. See account of Julian Grzesik, in Jerzy Dębski and Leon Popek, comps., *Okrutna przestroga* (Lublin: Towarzystwo Przyjaciół Krzemieńca i Ziemi Wołyńsko-Podolskiej, 1997), pp. 261-62. A part of that account is included in Appendix A: Ukrainian Victims by County, Sarny County, "Wiry."

19. Oleksandr Hrytsenko, "Armiia bez derzhavy," in Mykhalchuk, p. 405, quoted in Poliszczuk, *Legal and Political Assessment of the OUN and UPA*, p. 37.

20. See Appendix C: Excerpts from Documents, Ukrainian, "Taras 'Bulba'-Borovets's Open Letter, August 10, 1943."

21. See Appendix C: Excerpts from Documents, Ukrainian, "Taras 'Bulba'-Borovets's Statement."

22. See Appendix C: Excerpts from Documents, Polish, "Other Home Army Field Reports on the Ethnic-Cleansing Campaign" for April 20, 1944.

23. See Appendix C: Excerpts from Documents, Soviet, "Field Report of the Soviet Unit I. I. Shitov, March 30, 1943."

24. See Appendix C: Excerpts from Documents, German, "Abwehr (Counterintelligence) Report, July 13, 1943," and "Summaries of Other Field Reports and a German Leaflet," May 18, 1943.

25. See Appendix C: Excerpts from Documents, German, "Nehring's Report, May 19, 1944."

26. See Appendix C: Excerpts from Documents, German, "Report on a UPA Meeting with the Wehrmacht, March 13, 1944." Emphasis added.

27. See Appendix C: Excerpts from Documents, Ukrainian, "Secret Directive Issued and Signed by Roman Dmytro Klachkivskyi ('Klym Savur'), Commander of UPA 'Pivnych,' June 1943."

28. See Appendix C: Excerpts from Documents, Ukrainian, "Report of Iurii Stelmashchuk ('Rudyi,' 'Kaidash'), Commander of UPA 'Turiv' Region, to Mykola Lebed ('Maksym Ruban'), June 24, 1943," and also "Court Testimony of Iurii Stelmashchuk ('Rudyi,' 'Kaidash'), Commander of the UPA 'Turiv Region, February 20, 1945."

29. See Appendix C: Excerpts from Documents, Ukrainian, "Field Report of 'Lysyi,' September 1943."

30. Agnieszka Muzyka, "Relacja Świadka Agnieszki Muzyki," *Na Rubieży* (Wrocław) 2,

no. 3 (1993): 15. For a part of her account see Chapter 6, Luboml County, "Ostrówki," first account, penultimate paragraph.

31. See Appendix C: Excerpts from Documents, Ukrainian, "Orest Karat's Special Instructions, April 6, 1944."

32. See Appendix C: Excerpts from Documents, Ukrainian, "OUN Order to SKV Provid Leaders and Administrators, February 9, 1944."

33. See Chapter 10, Włodzimierz County, "Bubnów," the account of Zuzanna Sebestiańska and Halina Hilbrecht (née Sebestiańska) from Chrobów Colony (Łuck County).

34. See Chapter 7, Łuck County, "Andrzejówka Colony," the account of Aleksandra Ostrowska.

35. See Appendix C: Excerpts from Documents, Polish, "Letters (January 24, 1943-March 25, 1944) of Stanisław Czekanowski of Hrubieszów," entries for September 5, 1943 and February 24, 1944.

36. See Appendix C: Excerpts from Documents, Ukrainian, "Political Report of June 27, 1944, for the Period June 13-28, 1944."

37. See Appendix C: Excerpts from Documents, Ukrainian, "Chronicle of a UPA Unit."

38. See "Zbrodnie niemieckie w Zamojszczyźnie," *Biutelyn Głównej Komisji Badania Zbrodni Niemieckich w Polsce* 2 (1947): 45-120.

39. See "Do ludności ukraińskiej zamieszkałej na terenie pow. Hrubieszowskiego," in Wasyl Veryha, *Dorohamy Druhoi Svitovoi viiny: Legendy pro uchast ukraintsiv u zdushuvanni varshavskoho povstannia v 1944 r. ta pro Ukrainsku Dyviziiu "Halychyna"* (Toronto: Brotherhood of Veterans of the I.UD UNA, 1981), Document No. 2, pp. 214-15.

40. For implementation, see "Do ludności ukraińskiej" in Veryha, Document No. 5, pp. 224-26. Evhen Pasternak provides a listing of the Ukrainian villages in Hrubieszów County that were attacked. No attacks were listed in 1942. There were five in 1943: the first four took place on May 26, the fifth on October 27. Evhen Pasternak, *Narys istorii Kholmshchyny i Pidliashshia (Novishi chasy)* (Winnipeg: Research Institute of Volyn, 1968), Appendix 16, pp. 425-26. For a fuller treatment of this episode, see Piotrowski, *Poland's Holocaust*, pp. 248-50, and 383-84, notes 508-10.

41. Grzegorz Motyka, "Ukraińska orientacja." *Karta* (Warszawa) 23 (1997): 52.

42. According to Andrzej Żupański, although the AK had an "organizational presence" in Wołyń in 1943, there were no Polish partisan units there until the end of that summer. Andrzej Żupański, *Ujawnić prawdę: Wysiłki byłych mieszkańców i żołnierzy Wołynia, by prawda o rzeziach na Kresach została ujawniona* (Warszawa: Światowy Związek Żołnierzy Armii Krajowej, Okręg Wołyń, 1997), p. 12.

According to Henryk Piskunowicz, at the end of 1943, there were about 1,000 persons in nine Polish partisan units in Wołyń. Henryk Piskunowicz, "Polskie podziemie na Wołyniu i w Małopolsce Wschodniej w latach II wojny światowej," in Niedzielko, p. 163.

43. Mykola Lebed, *UPA: Ukrainska Povstanska Armiia: Ii heneza, rist i dii u vyzvolnii borotbi ukrainskoho narodu za Ukrainsku Samostiinu Sobornu Derzhavu* (n.p.: Presove Biuro UHVR, 1946), pp. 26, 79. The second quoted passage is Lebed's answer to the alleged Polish attack on Omelno, where, according to him, ten Ukrainians were killed. However, 40 pages earlier (p. 39), before any mention of the Omelno incident, he already explains how this "clearing" was being conducted by the UPA: "In the summer of 1943 Wołyń was completely under the control of the UPA. The Poles who received an injunction to leave the territory [*sic*], generally complied willingly with this order [*sic*]. Their fixed property passed into the possession of the Ukrainian people." (Incidentally, Turowski and Siemaszko mention that on June 5, 1943, a 200-man unit set out from the defense center in Przebraże to evacuate the Polish population from some of the villages in Polesie. On their way back, they also rescued, after a battle with the UPA, the Poles from the Ukrainian village of Omelno. Perhaps this is the incident to which Lebed refers. See Józef Turowski and Władysław Siemaszko, *Zbrodnie nacjonalistów ukraińskich dokonane na ludności polskiej na Wołyniu 1939-1945* (Warszawa: Główna Komisja Badania Zbrodni Hitlerowskich w Polsce — Instytut Pamięci Narodowej and Środowisko Żołnierzy 27 Wołyńskiej Dywizji Armii Krajowej w Warszawie, 1990), p. 65.)

In another passage Lebed states: "The Ukrainian Insurgent Army attempted to draw the Poles into mutual battle against the Germans and the Bolsheviks. When that proved unsuccessful, the UPA ordered the Polish people to leave the Ukrainian territories of Wołyń and Polesie." Lebed, *UPA* (Drohobych, 1993), p. 53.

Lebed fails to mention that the residents of Wołyń and Polesie had nowhere to go and so could not and, moreover, would not have "complied willingly" with such an order. As the result, they were simply slaughtered by the UPA.

In fact, many people were killed while trying desperately to flee — anywhere.

Lebed is also deliberately confusing the facts. With the possible exception of the counties of Dubno and Krzemieniec (this according to the unreferenced statement that appears in Grzegorz Motyka, "Od Wołynia do akcji 'Wisła,'" *Więź* 473, no. 3 (March 1998): 112), these injunctions, nailed to people's doors, which basically said "Get out, or die!" were not issued in Wołyń. In Wołyń, the slogan ran: "*Smert lakham, zhydam, i moskalam!*" (Death to the Poles, Jews and Russians). See Piotrowski, *Vengeance of the Swallows*, p. 61. At times, the injunctions mentioned by Lebed were issued in 1944 in Eastern Galicia, where there was a possibility of escape to the other parts of the General Government. See Appendix C: Excerpts from Documents, Ukrainian, "Evacuation Injunction," three entries; and "Order from the Main OUN Provid to County Provid Members, May 5, 1944." Such orders, in the form of leaflets, were also issued in the Lublin Province. According to Zygmunt Mańkowski: "Already in the second half of 1943 … in the districts of Hrubieszów, Chełm, Włodawa, leaflets were circulated calling on all Poles to leave by September 10, 1943, under penalty of death, the territories recognized as a part of 'Greater Ukraine.'" In Ryszard Torzecki, *Polacy i Ukraińcy: Sprawa ukraińska w czasie II wojny światowej na terenie II Rzeczypospolitej* (Warszawa: Wydawnictwo Naukowe PWN, 1993), 281, n. 66. See also Appendix C: Excerpts from Documents, Polish, "Other Home Army Field Reports on the Ethnic-Cleansing Campaign" for May 4-5, 1944 and May 24, 1944. These orders were enforced from the beginning of 1944 by Ukrainian units remaining in German service, including those in the SS-Galizien (in Beyersdorff's unit of 2,000 men) and other police units.

44. See Appendix C: Excerpts from Documents, Polish, "Letters (January 24, 1943-March 25, 1944) of Stanisław Czekanowski of Hrubieszów," entry for February 26, 1944.

45. See Appendix C: Excerpts from Documents, German, "Field Report from the Eastern Territories to Gerhard von Mende, Director of the Department of Affairs in the Occupied Eastern Territories, Ministry of the Third Reich, November 2, 1944."

46. Filar, *Przed akcją "Wisła" był Wołyń*, p. 31.

47. Filar, *Przed akcją "Wisła" był Wołyń*, p. 32.

48. See Turowski and Siemaszko, p. 85.

49. Roman Catholic churches (some ancient and magnificent) in the following locations were razed to the ground by the UPA (a partial listing): Dubno County — Drańcza Polska, Łysinia, Onyszkowce, Ptycza, Złoczówka; Horochów County — Drużkopol, Kisielin, Koniuchy; Kostopol County — Dermanka, Huta Stepańska, Kazimierka, Myszakówka, Potasznia; Kowel County — Karasin, Małe Hołoby; Krzemieniec County — Białozórka, Kąty (Kuty), Wyszogródek; Luboml County — Ostrówki, Przewały; Łuck County — Kołki, Sienkiewiczówka, Torczyn, Zofiówka; Sarny County — Bereźnica, Okopy, Wójtkiewicze; Włodzimierz County — Szwojczów. Photos of these churches appear in Dębski and Popek, p. 389ff. See also Leon Popek, *Świątynie Wołynia* (Lublin: Ośrodek Studiów Polonijnych i Społecznych PZKS and Towarzystwo Przyjaciół Krzemieńca i Ziemi Wołyńsko-Podolskiej, 1997).

50. According to Ihor Iliuszyn, a total of about 100 Polish self-defense centers existed in Wołyń and Eastern Galicia. See Ihor Iliuszyn, "Polskie podziemie na terytorium Ukrainy Zachodniej podczas II wojny światowej," in Niedzielko, p. 177. The self-defense centers in Wołyń embraced about 300 villages. See Piskunowicz, in Niedzielko, p. 163.

According to Władysław Siemaszko and Ewa Siemaszko, the 14 major centers in Wołyń that survived until the Soviet liberation were: in Dubno County — Pańska Dolina; in Horochów County — Zaturce; in Kostopol County — Huta Stara; in Kowel County — Zasmyki and Dąbrowa; in Krzemieniec County — Rybcza and Dederkały; in Luboml County — Jagodzin and Rymacze; in Łuck County — Antonówka Szepelska and Przebraże; in Włodzimierz County — Bielin; in Zdołbunów County — Witoldówka and the town of Ostróg on the Horyń River. Władysław Siemaszko and Ewa Siemaszko, *Terror ukraiński i zbrodnie przeciwko ludzkości dokonane przez OUN-UPA na ludności polskiej na Wołyniu w latach 1939-1945* (Warszawa: Stowarzyszenie Upamiętnienia Ofiar Zbrodni Nacjonalistów Ukraińskich w Warszawie, 1998), p. 19.

See also Adam Peretiatkowicz, "Samoobrona ludności polskiej na Wołyniu w latach 1943-1944," in Janina Snitko-Rzeszut, ed., *Armia Krajowa na Wołyniu* (Warszawa: Światowy Związek Żołnierzy Armii Krajowej, Okręg Wołyń, 1994), pp. 33-44.

51. See Appendix C: Excerpts from Documents, Ukrainian, "UPA Field Report — Group Zahrava." In turn, the Soviets returned the favor

by launching a host of special groups which pretended to be UPA units. In April-June 1945 there were 157 of such groups numbering 1,808 persons. See Motyka, "Od Wołynia do akcji 'Wisła,'" p. 120.

52. Turowski and Siemaszko, p. 158.
53. Siemaszko and Siemaszko, p. 15.
54. Torzecki, *Polacy i Ukraińcy*, p. 267.
55. Siemaszko and Siemaszko, p. 22.
56. Stanisław Kaniewski, "Informacja o stanie śledztw prowadzonych w Głównej Komisji Badania Zbrodni przeciwko Narodowi Polskiemu — Instytucie Pamięci Narodowej wygłoszona na XVII Zjeździe Okręgu Wołyń Światowego Związku Żołnierzy AK, 23 sierpnia 1997r.," *Biuletyn Informacyjny* (Światowy Związek Żołnierzy AK, Okręg Wołyń, Warszawa) 3, no. 55 (July-August 1997). This report can also be found in Siemaszko and Siemaszko, pp. 35-41. The passage is on p. 37.
57. Stanisław Kaniewski, quoted in Siemaszko and Siemaszko, p. 38.
58. Stanisław Kaniewski, quoted in Siemaszko and Siemaszko, pp. 38-39. Prosecutor Kaniewski confirmed all these statistics during my visit with him in October 1997.
59. See Appendix C: Excerpts from Documents, United Nations War Crimes Commission and source note.
60. From an article in *Samostiina Ukraina*, an OUN-B publication out of Stanisławów (July 10, 1941).
61. Wiktor Poliszczuk, *Ukraińskie ofiary OUN-UPA* (Warszawa: n.p., 1998). (Paper presented at a symposium in Wrocław, July 12, 1998, and subsequently published.) Poliszczuk estimates that in all there were about 40,000 Ukrainian victims: 4,000 died at the hands of the Poles in battles of the Home Army (AK) and the Peasant Battalions (BCh) with the UPA, as well as in retaliation actions; 36,000 died at the hands of the Ukrainian Nationalists. The latter were mainly civilians; their murderers were mainly the OUN-SB.
62. Wiktor Poliszczuk, *Gorzka prawda: Zbrodniczość OUN-UPA (spowiedź Ukraińca)* (Toronto: n.p., 1995), p. 79.
63. Danylo Shumuk, *Za skhidnym obriiem. Spomyny. Peredruk samvydavnoho tvoru z Ukrainy* (Paris: Persha Ukrainska Drukarnia u Frantsii, 1974), p. 193.
64. Poliszczuk, *Gorzka prawda*, pp. 188-89.
65. Shumuk, 1974, pp. 104-07.
66. See Jan Kurdybelski, "Wołyński rodowód parafii Minkowice Oławskie koło Wrocławia," *Semper Fidelis* (Wrocław) 5, no. 22 (1994): 22.

67. Szcześniak and Szota, p. 150, n. 29.
68. Mykhailo Senkiv, quoted in Poliszczuk, *Ukraińskie ofiary OUN-UPA*, pp. 15-16.
69. See Appendix C: Excerpts from Documents, Ukrainian, "UPA Field Reports Regarding the Liquidation of Ukrainians," no. I.
70. See Appendix C: Excerpts from Documents, Ukrainian, "UPA Field Reports Regarding the Liquidation of Ukrainians," no. III and no. VII.
71. Quoted in Wiktor Poliszczuk, *Fałszowanie historii najnowszej Ukrainy* (Warszawa-Toronto: n.p., 1996), p. 82.
72. See Appendix C: Excerpts from Documents, Ukrainian, "UPA Field Reports Regarding the Liquidation of Ukrainians," no. VI.
73. For an excerpt, see Appendix C: Excerpts from Documents, Ukrainian, "From the Register Containing the Names of 9,018 Ukrainians Murdered by the OUN-UPA in Wołyń [Volyn], Published by the Rivne [Równe] Archive in 1990-91."
74. Helena Piotrowiak, personal interview. Quoted in Piotrowski, *Vengeance of the Swallows*, p. 79. For additional information on the murder of Ukrainians by the OUN-UPA in Berezów Niżny, see Ivan Kuzych-Berezovskyi, *Berezivski boiarstvo na tli istorii Ukraiiny* (Detroit, 1962), pp. 284-85.
75. "Zbrodnie banderowskich bójówek OUN-UPA w powiecie Buczacz, województwo tarnopolskie," in *Na Rubieży* (Wrocław) 4, no. 14 (1995): 24. This article (pp. 4-25) provides information regarding 25 Ukrainians (mostly listed by name & location) killed by the UPA in the county of Buczacz, in Tarnopol Province. Some reasons are listed for the murders:

- "for open condemnation of the UPA" (p. 8);

- "for condemning the methods of the Banderowcy out loud" (p. 12);

- "for opposing the murders of Poles" (p. 12);

- "for being a *sołtys* [head of a village] during the Soviet occupation" (p. 12);

- "for refusing to cooperate with local Ukrainian chauvinists" (p. 14);

- "for refusing to participate in the murder of Poles" (p. 14);

- "probably by mistake, due to the fact that a Pole was to have been on duty at the time [at a train station in Korościatyn]" (pp. 14-15);

- "for calling the Banderowcy criminals" — this from three mothers whose sons perished in attacks on Polish villages — and for their "insolence" (all three of these elderly women were hanged by the UPA) (p. 23);

- "for refusing to assist in the murder of Poles" (p. 23);

- "for warning Poles of imminent [UPA] attacks and for saving Polish lives" (p. 23);

- "for refusing to participate in the murder of Poles" (p. 24);

- "for refusing to kill his Polish mother" (p. 25);

- and "for discovering the remains [of Bronisława Drozda's father] and reporting the finding of the remains ... to the authorities" (pp. 17-18). This case involved the death of Maryska Kurmylo, whose father was Ukrainian and whose mother was Polish. Maryska was in an advanced state of pregnancy at the time of her vicious murder. Her stomach was cut open, the unborn child was removed, and stones were placed inside her womb. She was then thrown into the same place by the dam in the river, where Bronisława's father's body was retrieved.

The article also lists the names of numerous Poles who were murdered by the UPA in Buczacz. Almost every issue of *Na Rubieży* provides information on both Polish and Ukrainian victims of the OUN-UPA, mostly in the three provinces of Eastern Galicia.

76. See Jędrzej Giertych, "O przeprowadzonej przez Ukraińców rzezi polskiej ludności," *Komunikaty Towarzystwa imiemia Romana Dmowskiego* (London) 2, no. 1 (1979/80): 341-42. For a register of the Ukrainians and Poles murdered in this village, see the Ukrainian newspaper from Ivano-Frankivsk (Stanisławów), *Prykarpatska pravda* (November 13, 1990). Another work containing the names of victims of the OUN-UPA in Tarnopol Province is Czesław Blicharski's, *Petruniu, ne ubywaj mene!* (Biskupice, 1998).

77. See Appendix C: Excerpts from Documents, Ukrainian, "UPA Field Reports Regarding the Liquidation of Ukrainians," no. II.

78. Relying on the National Archive of the Rivne Oblast (Derzhavnyi Arkhiv Rivnenskoi Oblasti, or DARO), inv. 35 (6446), Poliszczuk states in his *Ukraińskie ofiary OUN-UPA*, p. 6, that such "black lists" were kept by the SB.

79. See Appendix C: Excerpts from Documents, Ukrainian, "UPA Field Reports Regarding the Liquidation of Ukrainians," no. V.

80. Maksym Skorupskyi, *U nastupakh i vidstupakh: Spohady* (Chicago, 1961), p. 145.

81. Mykhailo Podvorniak, *Viter z Volyni: Spohady* (Winnipeg: T-vo: "Volyn," 1981), pp. 182, 187, 199. For other statements regarding OUN-B SB atrocities against Ukrainians see: Mykhalchuk, pp. 144-45, 158-59, 174-75, 192-95; Poliszczuk, *Gorzka prawda,* pp. 294-98; Shumuk, 1974; and Hryhorii Stetsiuk, *Nepostavlenyi pamiatnyk: Spohady* (Winnipeg: Instytut Doslidiv Volyni, 1988), pp. 82, 88, 91, 98, 105, 119.

For a short work dealing with one of the leaders of the SB, Dmytro Hryhorovych Kupiak, see Bronisław Szeremeta, *Watażka: Wspomnienie nierozstrzelanego i jego zbrodnie* (Wrocław: n.p., 1995). This work was written in response to Kupiak's sanitized memoir called *Spohady nerostrilanoho* (Toronto: n.p., 1991). A 1991 eyewitness court deposition (Sygn. akt Zh I Kpp 53/91, Warszawa — in my possession — obtained from the Polish Main Commission for the Investigation of Crimes against the Polish Nation) establishes Kupiak's guilt beyond any doubt. Here is but one passage from that lengthy testimony, a passage that follows a description of a whole array of other atrocities perpetrated both on Poles and Ukrainians by Kupiak ("Klei") and his gang of a dozen or so SB members. Unfortunately, I am not at liberty to disclose the name of this Ukrainian witness because, although Kupiak died in 1995 while "under investigation" for war crimes by the Canadian Department of Justice, the case is still under investigation in Poland in respect to the other members of his unit who are mentioned by name in the deposition.

> One day, they [Kupiak's unit] sent me a notice to come to the forest where the unit was stationed. When I got there, the members of the unit went to the road leading from Toporów to Busk. Shortly thereafter, they brought over a young Ukrainian girl that I knew, Janina [Ivanna] Palyga. She was a student in Lwów and was between 23 and 25 years of age at the time. They stopped her while she was on her way by wagon from her house to Lwów. Janina Palyga was taken down from the wagon and the driver was told to go on. The girl was left with me. The members of the unit went off to

the side. Palyga asked me what they wanted with her. I did not know how to answer her. She then said that it was probably [name withheld] who denounced her and that the members of Kupiak's unit believed him. I gathered that she must be talking about someone named [same name withheld] who suspected her of informing the Soviet authorities in Lwów regarding the whereabouts of the UPA units.

Janina Palyga was in my company for a very short time. The members of Kupiak's unit returned and took her with them. They led her into a thicket where some entrenchments (*szańce*) were located. In the group that took her away was Dmytro Kupiak. [Three others are named later in the testimony.] After a while, I heard a few rounds from a machine gun. Then the members of the unit returned to where I was standing. I gathered that they had shot her. I did not see her remains. In the course of the discussion among the members of the unit that followed, I heard that they had buried her in one of the entrenchments. After the war, I was taken to that thicket and all the entrenchments were dug up. In one of them, they found the remains of Janina Palyga. Her two false teeth were still in her skull. Janina Palyga had two false teeth and that is why I am convinced that it was her remains that were exhumed.

I would also like to mention the circumstances known to me surrounding a crime which Dmytro Kupiak committed personally. In September 1946 Bohdan Moroz came to my cousin [name withheld] in Lwów, where I and Kupiak were hiding. We all knew him. He came from [name of village withheld]. He lived on the same street as I. He was about my age. As soon as Bohdan Moroz entered the home, Kupiak said to him, "How nice that you came, but we can't talk here. Let's go out on the street to talk."

Until that time, Kupiak never went out on the street because he felt threatened. His going out surprised me. After about two hours, Kupiak returned home. He said to me, "He won't inform any more."

He admitted that he was in the Łyczakowski cemetery with Bohdan Moroz and that he had shot him there.

[From a previous section in this testimony, where this witness mentions testifying at an earlier hearing.] After the hearing,

I was informed that Kupiak was in a camp in Munich and that he later emigrated to Canada and now lives in Toronto, where he operates a hotel.

I cannot vouch for Kupiak's hotel, but I do know that he ran a restaurant in Etobicoke (metropolitan Toronto) called the Mayfair. A Soviet publication [Vladimir Molchanov, *There Shall Be Retribution: Nazi War Criminals and Their Protectors* (Moscow: Progress Publishers, 1981), p. 191] also addresses Kupiak's guilt:

In 1964, the Soviet Union demanded that the Canadian government extradite war criminal Dmitry Kupiak. Kupiak lives in Toronto and owns a restaurant. Several years ago he even tried running for a seat in Parliament. During the occupation of the Soviet Ukraine Kupiak, nicknamed "Klei" meaning "glue," was the ringleader of a band and took part in mass executions of civilians in a number of villages in Lvov Region. On March 25, 1944, the bandits burned down Mazarnia farm and killed 33 people, in April plundered Shmonzaki farm and killed two people, in June burned down all the 200 houses in Adamy village, destroyed Verbiany village and killed 50 people. On August 17 Klei's band plundered Vodai village and burned 10 people alive. On December 10 they burned down Pobuzhany village and killed 15 people. In Yablunivka village, 70 kilometers from Lvov, there is a communal grave. I visited the village and put down the names of Kupiak's victims and their age: Ivanna Palycha [called Janina Palyga in the account above], age 22, Stefania Babiychuk, age 15, Elena Vovk, age 12, Evgeny Balkovski, age 9, Ivan Balkovski, age 8, Bogdan Balkovski, age 5, Zinoviy Vuitskik, age 10 months, 16 days ... And Kupiak lives peacefully in Canada.

A series of Soviet documents regarding the Kupiak case appears in V. N. Denisov and G. I. Changuli, eds., *Nazi Crimes in Ukraine, 1941-1944: Documents and Materials*, comp. A. F. Vysotsky et al., trans. V. I. Biley et al. (Kiev: Naukova Dumka Publishers, 1987), pp. 331-45. The titles of these documents read as follows: "News Report on the Note of the USSR Ministry of Foreign Affairs on the Case of War Criminal D. G. Kupiak," (October 20, 1964), p. 331; "News Report on the Note of the USSR Ministry of Foreign Affairs on the Case of War Criminal D. G. Kupiak," (June 24, 1965), pp. 332-33; "Subpoena to War Criminal Kupiak D. G. for Summons to the Procurator's Office of Lvov Region," (September 15, 1967), pp. 333-34; "Judgment of Investigator to Institute Criminal Proceedings Against the Accused Kupiak D. G.," (December 10, 1968), pp. 334-43; "News Report on the Note of the USSR Ministry of Foreign Affairs on the Case of War Criminal Kupiak D. G.," (August 1970), pp. 344-45.

In these documents, the "News Reports" deal with the futile attempts of the USSR to extradite Kupiak from Canada to stand trial for his personal role in the "murder of almost 200 persons, including women, children and elderly citizens." The "Judgment" details the various atrocities — the "monstrous acts of butchery," including cruel tortures, executions, and senseless violence — in which Kupiak and his unit were involved during and after World War II. The following incidents come from this lengthy and macabre catalogue of the unthinkable: In 1941, as organizer of the Ukrainian police, Kupiak tortured two Jews, Grigory Karavan and Maier Gatsfraied. In 1944 he tortured Emilia Chuchman, Ivan Chuchman, and Chuchman's wife, Natalka, for sheltering Jews. In September of that year he ordered his gang to kill Ivan and Natalka Chuchman and "personally looted the victims' belongings." On November 28, 1944, Kupiak killed an elderly couple, Filimon and Anastasia Yaremkevich, because their son "who had been forced to join the gang, escaped from it." On January 30, 1945, Ganna Palyga (not the same as Ivanna) and her daughter Olga Bedryi who was in her final month of pregnancy, were killed because their relatives, Izidor Palyga and Ilaryi Bedryi, "had abandoned the OUNite band [which they had been forced to join], confessed their guilt and were mobilized into the Soviet Army." In the spring of 1945, Kupiak got hold of some poison and, anxious to try it out, had his henchmen "seize anyone they could and bring him to the Yablunivka Forest." There, the poor victim was first interrogated and tortured by Kupiak and then forced to swallow the poison that killed him.

When Kupiak left for Poland in October 1945, and then for Canada in May 1946, he "took with him gold and other valuables which he had obtained by robbery," states the "Judgment."

Despite repeated Soviet requests, Canada, having allowed yet another war criminal entry into its commonwealth, refused to extradite Kupiak because "there is no such law" in Canada that would allow for the extradition of war criminals. Therefore, the Soviet claim, said the Canadian government, had no "judicial basis."

The 1965 Soviet response to Canada's refusal reads as follows: "These assertions are unfounded. According to modern international law all countries are obliged to prosecute crimes committed against peace and humanity. The norms of the domestic laws of any state which do not conform to this norm of international law recede before it. Reference to domestic legislation cannot justify a state's refusal to fulfill its international obligations."

The 1970 Soviet response refers the Canadian government to "the Convention on the Non-Applicability of Statutory Limitations to War Crimes and Crimes Against Humanity adopted at the 23rd Session of the United Nations General Assembly and signed on November 26, 1968, which once again stressed the necessity of the extradition and punishment of all persons responsible for war crimes in abidance with international law."

Of course, once having found out about Kupiak's sordid past, Canada could have and should have prosecuted him under its own legal system at any time before 1995 (the year of Kupiak's death), but it did not, and now it is too late. Such is the story of the infamous Dmytro Hryhorovych Kupiak, born on November 6, 1919, OUN member since 1938, organizer of the Ukrainian police, member of the Ukrainian Committee, organizer and leader of an OUN-B SB unit, fascist "freedom fighter," Canadian restaurateur with political ambitions, and author of his own "heroic" memoirs.

82. Witold Biegański, Mieczysław Juchniewicz, and Stanisław Okęcki, *Polacy w ruchu oporu narodów Europy 1939-1945* (Warszawa: Polskie Wydawnictwo Naukowe, 1977), quoted in Czesław Piotrowski, *Krwawe żniwa za Styrem, Horyniem i Słuczą* (Warszawa: Światowy Związek Żołnierzy Armii Krajowej, Okręg Wołyń, 1995), p. 101.

83. Torzecki, *Kwestia ukraińska w polityce III Rzeszy 1933-1945*, pp. 192, 196.

84. Unfortunately, there were also instances where Soviet partisans attacked Polish settlements during their quest for requisitions; for example, in Naliboki, where in May 1943 a Soviet partisan unit attacked and burned a part of the town and executed over 120 men from the self-defense center. What is even more surprising (for example, in Eastern Galicia, in the regions of Złoczów and Stanisławów), there were reports of Soviet officers leading Ukrainian bands in attacks on Poles. See Komisja Historyczna Polskiego Sztabu Głównego w Londynie, *Polskie Siły Zbrojne w Drugiej wojnie światowej. Tom 3.*

Armia Krajowa (London: Instytut Historyczy im. Gen. Sikorskiego, 1950), p. 529. The source for the reference to Eastern Galicia is given as: Meldunek organizacyjny dowódcy A.K. Nr 240 z 29.II.1944 r. Ldz 6874/44.

85. See Appendix C: Excerpts from Documents, Jewish, "Deposition of M. V. (b. 1912 in Tomaszów Mazowiecki), Gathered by the Jewish Historical Commission of Poland, Recorded in Landsberg, Bavaria, on April 10, 1946."

86. See Appendix C: Excerpts from Documents, Polish, "Order of Kazimierz Damian Bąbiński ("Luboń"), Commander of the Union for Armed Struggle-Home Army, Wołyń (ZWZ-AK, "Hreczka"), to AK Partisan Units" for April 22, 1943, and February 16, 1944.

87. See Torzecki, *Polacy i Ukraińcy,* p. 289, n. 125.

88. Żupański, p. 4. For other cases of retaliation and organized reprisals, see Piotrowski, *Poland's Holocaust,* p. 252. For a Ukrainian listing of villages attacked in 1944-45 by Poles and for victim tolls, see Mikołaj Siwicki, comp., *Dzieje konfliktów polsko-ukraińskich,* vol. 3 (Warszawa: n.p., 1994), pp. 307-08. For a listing of the Ukrainian villages in Hrubieszów County which were attacked by Poles beginning in 1943, see Pasternak, pp. 425-26. For a Polish translation, see Siwicki, vol. 3, pp. 126-28.

89. See, for example, Appendix A: Ukrainian Victims by County, Sarny, "Olena Chorna from Budki Borowskie."

90. An interesting account of mutual assistance, but one with a sad ending, comes from the village of Skorodyńce in the province of Tarnopol. On March 7, 1945, a UPA unit halted in Skorodyńce on its westward march to the Carpathian Mountains. Unit members helped themselves to the meager resources of the village and headed out early the next morning. Just before noon on March 8, a Red Army unit in pursuit of the UPA also halted in the village. The narrator's (Tomasz Bandura's) mother was among those recruited by the Russians to drive them in pursuit of the UPA. Before she departed, she told her children not to spend the night at home but to seek shelter with one of the Ukrainian families.

Just as Tomasz, his 22-year-old sister, Frania, and her two-year-old daughter, Stefania, were about to leave their house, two Ukrainian sisters from Kaminciv, fearing deportation to Siberia by the Russians, knocked on their door and requested a night's lodging. One of them was Kateryna, and with her was her 11-year-old son. Tomasz and Frania knew that Kateryna's oldest son, Volodymyr, was a member of the Banderowcy. Nevertheless, states Tomasz Bandura, "We did not refuse to let them in." He continues the story:

> My sister made beds on the floor for the women, I slept with the Ukrainian boy in my bed, and my sister and her child slept in the other bed.
>
> In the middle of the night, a loud banging on the windows and shouts of "Open up!" awakened us. I thought it was the Russians. Frania lit a lamp and opened the door. In came a man dressed in a Russian uniform. On his hat was the trident [a symbol of Ukrainian independence and also an emblem of the UPA]. He looked us over and left. After a while, three other Ukrainians entered our house and one of them said, "Whoever does not belong to this family should get dressed and get out!" A second Ukrainian readied his automatic.
>
> Just then, one of the Ukrainian women [Kateryna] came up to me and said, "Ivasiu (my name is Tomasz), go get dressed and let's go home."
>
> Being 14 years of age, I understood perfectly what was going on and, although frozen with fear, I somehow managed to get myself dressed. My sister bid me farewell with her eyes. In the hall, I saw several Ukrainians of my own age; they were taking a course on how to commit murder.
>
> After we arrived in her home in Kaminciv, Kateryna told me to remove my boots and climb up on the stove. She herself sat down on the edge of the stove. In the next room, the Banderowcy launched a party and drank and sang until the morning hours. At night, Volodymyr came in with a flashlight and asked his mother, "Where's Tomek?" Kateryna swore up and down that I was not there, that I ran off to the village when they had gone out for a moment. He believed her.
>
> In the morning, on March 9, 1945, I returned to my house. My sister lay on the floor in a pool of blood. Her two-year-old daughter lay as if asleep, with her fist tucked under her head. I lifted her up and her blood spilled over my arms. I ran out of there yelling at the top of my lungs. Why did that child deserve to die?
>
> That previous night they also murdered our neighbor, Franciszek Domyk, an invalid, as well as the five-member family

of Franciszek Bandura, whose daughter married a Ukrainian. She was murdered along with her 18-month-old son. So was Anna (née Sitko) Szatkowska, who was pregnant, and her five-year-old son.

My mother returned before noon on March 9 in a state of half-consciousness. She took a loaf of bread and some flour and we set out along the Seret River for Czortków. We traveled with this thought in mind: if pursued, rather than allowing ourselves to be caught alive, we will jump into the river and drown ourselves. We left for the West [i.e., for central Poland] on May 30, 1945.

From the account of Tomasz Bandura (b. 1931 in Skorodyńce), in my possession. I received this narrative from Czesława (née Zarówny) Grygorczyk, now living in Montreal. It is one of several which she has collected from her relatives and her mother's [Antonina (née Sitko) Zarówny's] acquaintances in Poland that deal with her family history and the events in Skorodyńce.

Chapter 1

1. This and the following summary sections dealing with the counties in Wołyń are based on the chapter introductions in Dębski and Popek. The tables are derived from *Drugi powszechny spis ludności z dnia 9.XII.1931r.*, pp. 26-29.
2. *Na Rubieży* (Wrocław), no. 30 (1998): 30. In this and all subsequent entries, the locations following the narrators' and the rescuers' names in the headings are their former places of residence, not their current ones.
3. Stanisław Biskupski, comp., *Świadkowie mówią* (Warszawa: Światowy Związek Żołnierzy Armii Krajowej, Okręg Wołyń, 1996), pp. 9-11.
4. Dębski and Popek, p. 16.
5. Dębski and Popek, pp. 22-23.

3. Dębski and Popek, p. 37.
4. Biskupski, p. 135.
5. Henryk Cybulski, *Czerwone noce* (Warszawa: Ministerstwo Obrony Narodowej, 1969), p. 156.
6. Dębski and Popek, p. 38. See also Padlevskyi as well as Shkuropaka.
7. Dębski and Popek, p. 64. Urszula Sawicka's (Jolanta's sister's) account follows on p. 65. Urszula (b. 1937) refers to Jolanta's tragedy and adds, "My brother Antoś went to Markowski family and was murdered together with them. He was buried in a mound in front of their house. One Markowska daughter was severely wounded, but she was rescued by a decent Ukrainian."
8. Dębski and Popek, p. 38.
9. Dębski and Popek, p. 37. See also Parfeniuk as well as Shkuropatka.
10. Dębski and Popek, p. 63. An incomplete list of the names of 42 victims from Kupowalce, Lulówka, and Boroczyce appears on this page as well.
11. *Polityka* (February 10, 1990); Wiesław Myśliwski, comp., *Wschodnie losy Polaków*, vol. 3 (Łomża: Oficyna Wydawnicza "Stopka," 1991), pp. 315-22; and Poliszczuk, *Gorzka prawda*, pp. 205-08.
12. This account, obtained from Teresa Radziszewska, is in my possession.
13. This account, obtained from Władysław Dziemiańczuk, is in my possession.
14. Dębski and Popek, p. 46.
15. Turowski and Siemaszko, pp. 101, 140. Henryk Kitaszewski states that Ukrainian Baptists did not take part in the murder of Poles. See his account in Giertych, p. 304. For an account of the decapitation of two young Ukrainian Baptists by the UPA in the village of Wiry, county of Sarny, see Julian Grzesik, in Dębski and Popek, p. 261. An excerpt from that account is also contained in Appendix A: Ukrainian Victims by County, Sarny County, "Wiry."
16. Dębski and Popek, pp. 49-50.
17. Dębski and Popek, p. 43.

Chapter 2

1. Unless otherwise noted, all "see" and "see also" cross-references apply to the chapter in which they appear.
2. Dębski and Popek, p. 51. An incomplete listing containing 33 names of people who were murdered in Horochówka accompanies this entry.

Chapter 3

1. *Na Rubieży* (Wrocław) 1, no. 10 (1994): 16.
2. This account, obtained from Teresa Radziszewska, is in my possession.
3. Biskupski, pp. 113-14. For a Ukrainian report regarding the attack on Janowa Dolina,

see Appendix C: Excerpts from Documents, Ukrainian, "Litopys UPA on the Destruction of Janowa Dolina (April 23, 1943)."

4. Dębski and Popek, pp. 92-93.

5. Dębski and Popek, p. 93.

6. *Na Rubieży* (Wrocław) 1, no. 11 (1995): 6-7.

7. Biskupski, pp. 102-04, 109.

8. *Na Rubieży* (Wrocław) 1, no. 11 (1995): 5-6.

9. The quoted passage comes from Dębski and Popek, p. 75. See also Tadeusz Bagiński, *Lipniki Wołynia polskiego* (Elbląg: n.p., 1995); Henryk Słowiński and Bogusława Rudnicka-Kędzierska, eds., *Lipniki* (Wrocław, 1998).

10. Dębski and Popek, p. 95. Regarding the murder of the Horodecki family, see also Piotrowski, *Vengeance of the Swallows*, pp. 92-93. There, a similar account (based on my personal interview with Stanisław Domalewski) is presented regarding a Polish family called "Podhorodecki," consisting of the parents and five children who were murdered with axes on January 27-28, 1943, in the nearby village of Karaczun. That work also refers (p. 68) to a Ukrainian *sołtys* named Grzegorz Smułka (Hryhorii Smulka) from another nearby village, Kazimirka (Kazimierka), who was murdered for befriending the Poles and speaking out against the senseless fratricide. Undoubtedly, Domalewski's story concerns the same family and *sołtys* as the account of Kazimierz Boruta. Domalewski's story regarding Smulka is included in Appendix A: Ukrainian Victims by County, Kostopol County, "Hryhorii Smulka."

11. *Na Rubieży* (Wrocław) 1, no. 11 (1995): 7.

12. C. Piotrowski, p. 157.

13. Biskupski, pp. 67-68.

Chapter 4

1. Both letters, obtained from Teresa Radziszewska, are in my possession.

2. Turowski and Siemaszko, p. 104.

3. Jan Kurdybelski, "Wołyński rodowód," *Semper Fidelis* (Wrocław) 6, no. 23 (1994): 21. The reference to the gouging out of eyes appears in many accounts. It is not without reason, therefore, that long after the war was over, one Ukrainian woman in Chicago lamented over the fate of her son who was born blind. This fate she attributed to divine judgment for the sins of his father, who used to gouge out the eyes of the *Lakhy* (a derogatory term for "Poles") during the war. See Bronisław Terpin, *Na koszt wielkiej trójki: Saga rodziny kresowej* (Chicago: Jan Beyzym Sons, Inc., 1985), p. 63.

4. Turowski and Siemaszko, p. 118.

5. Dębski and Popek, pp. 131-32. An incomplete list of the family names of 140 victims murdered by the UPA in Stary and Nowy Gaj on August 30, 1943, can be found on p. 132. According to Turowski and Siemaszko, Gaj was attacked on July 13, 1943; there were about 600 victims.

6. Turowski and Siemaszko, p. 129.

7. Turowski and Siemaszko, p. 27.

8. Dębski and Popek, p. 121.

9. Dębski and Popek, p. 101.

10. Dębski and Popek, pp. 106-07. Teresa Radziszewska now lives in Zamość and is very active in keeping alive the memory of the victims of the OUN-UPA. Her various responsibilities as president of the Association for the Remembrance of Poles Murdered in Wołyń include the organization of annual trips to Wołyń for the survivors and the maintenance of the cell in the Zamość Rotunda which commemorates the UPA victims. I had the great pleasure of visiting with her and some of the members of her society in October 1997 during my three-week stay in Poland. It was at that time that she provided me with a large bundle of survivors' accounts collected by her organization. Some of these narratives had already appeared in the work by Dębski and Popek; others had not been published. Since then, she has graciously shared other such accounts with me through the mail.

11. Dębski and Popek, pp. 103-04.

12. Dębski and Popek, pp. 101-02. Józefa Brudzińska's account is followed by a list of 88 names of those murdered in Aleksandrówka.

13. Dębski and Popek, p. 111. Two lists of names of the victims in Adamówka, murdered on July 16, 1943, appear in the accounts on pp. 112-13. The first contains 24 names; the second, 38. (Note the discrepancy in the dates.) A third list, containing the names of 15 persons murdered in Adamówka on August 29, 1943, can be found on p. 114. Turowski and Siemaszko (pp. 92, 127) provide two dates of major attacks on Adamówka: July 13, 1943 — 48 victims; and August 1943 — several dozen victims.

14. Dębski and Popek, pp. 118-20.

15. Turowski and Siemaszko, p. 129.

16. Turowski and Siemaszko, p. 123.

17. The quoted passage comes from Dębski and Popek, p. 100. A list with 88 names of those killed in Aleksandrówka can be found on

pp. 102-03. The information regarding Teofil and Bronisława comes from Turowski and Siemaszko, p. 137.

18. Dębski and Popek, p. 12.

19. Dębski and Popek, p. 121. A list of 54 names of those murdered in Doszno on August 28, 1943, can be found on p. 123. In all, only 24 persons or 30 percent of the Polish residents of Doszno survived the attack.

20. Dębski and Popek, pp. 128-30. Regarding the blessing of the instruments of death by Ukrainian clergy (also mentioned in several other accounts that follow); Turowski and Siemaszko state (p. 121) that on August 28, 1943, in the Ukrainian village of Sztuń (Luboml Province), an Orthodox priest named Pokrovskyi blessed knives, scythes, axes, and other implements and distributed them to the faithful for the task of murdering the *Lakhy*. These instruments were then used in the attack on the local Polish settlements which occurred two days later.

Leon Żur writes: "Our friendly Ukrainians from Borowe [Sarny County] informed us that an Orthodox priest, Mykhailo Symonovych, blessed the Bulbowcy gathered in the church yard as well as their implements of future crimes. Our informant told us this with tears in his eyes. Among the implements which were to be used to murder the Poles in the neighboring villages were scythes, sickles, knives, axes, and ordinary sharpened oak stakes. Thus, the murder of the Polish people took place with the blessing of an Orthodox priest, which served to absolve the murderers as well as to eliminate all their scruples and humanitarian feelings." Leon Żur, *Mój wovński epos* (Suwałki: Hańcza, 1997), p. 58.

21. Biskupski, pp. 41-43.

22. Cyniak's account comes from Dębski and Popek, pp. 124, 126. A list of family names of the 96 victims murdered by the UPA on August 30, 1943, in Sucha Łoza appears on p. 126. Turowski and Siemaszko give the date of the attack as July 13, 1943 — 97 victims. The information on Mielnica comes from Turowski and Siemaszko, pp. 28, 44, 121.

23. Dębski and Popek, pp. 122-23.

24. Turowski and Siemaszko, p. 137.

Chapter 5

1. Dębski and Popek, pp. 191-92.

2. Dębski and Popek, pp. 184-87. Lists of names of murdered victims follow. Among the names is the family name of Świątkowski. There were two families by that name in Wiśniowiec Stary. One of them was saved by being hidden for several weeks in a crib in the stable belonging to a Ukrainian acquaintance. In all, about 350 people were killed in Wiśniowiec during the February 1943 UPA attacks. See Turowski and Siemaszko, p. 155.

3. Dębski and Popek, p. 176.

4. Biskupski, pp. 115-19.

5. Myśliwski, vol. 2, 301, pp. 311-12.

6. Poliszczuk, *Gorzka prawda*, pp. 188-89.

7. Dębski and Popek, p. 198.

Chapter 6

1. Biskupski, pp. 24-26.

2. Leon Popek, Tomasz Trusiuk, Paweł Wira, and Zenon Wira, comps., *Wołyński testament* (Lublin: Towarzystwo Przyjaciół Krzemieńca i Ziemi Wołyńsko-Podolskiej, 1997), p. 173.

3. Popek et al., pp. 132-33.

4. Janina Martosińska's account is in Popek et al., pp. 100-5; Aleksander Pradun's account is on pp. 122-30; Agnieszka Muzyka's account is on pp. 107-09, and also in *Na Rubieży* (Wrocław) 2, no. 3 (1993): 15-16.

5. In Popek et al., pp. 155-56. The names of the victims in Ostrówki, their ages, and other family-related information can be found in Annex 11 on pp. 200-10.

6. Aleksander Lubczyński's account is in Popek et al., pp. 95-96; Władysław Soroka's account is on pp. 136-37. The names of the victims in Wola Ostrowiecka, their ages, and other family-related information can be found in Annex 12 on pp. 211-26.

7. Popek, et al., pp. 115-16.

8. Popek et al., p. 134.

9. Popek et al., p. 155.

10. Popek et al., p. 97.

11. Popek et al., p. 111. Although the authors also refer to a Ukrainian *sołtys* from Sokół who rescued the Polish wife of Alosha Basiuk and her two "half-Polish" children (six months and three years old) from being murdered by their Ukrainian husband and father and then transported them to Luboml, I was not able to locate this particular incident in the accounts included in their work. The reference to this heroic rescue is on p. 39.

12. Popek et al., p. 109.

13. Dębski and Popek, p. 207.

14. Dębski and Popek, p. 208. A list of the

names of eight victims with a reference to ten other families consisting of 4-5 members each, murdered by the UPA in Zamostecze, can be found on pp. 211-12.

Chapter 7

1. Dębski and Popek, pp. 230-31. In this account, Sabina Królikowska refers to Olha's brothers as "bandits." In another account, that of Irena Justyna (see Ivan Sheremeta, below), we read that two Ukrainian brothers from Koszów by the name of Petro and Ivan Chervak were murdered by the UPA for refusing to reveal the hiding place of their brother's (Roman's) family. Roman was wed to a Polish girl.

I wondered whether these two brothers were in fact the same "bandits" to whom Sabina referred in her account. I therefore wrote to Sabina for clarification. In her letter to me of March 14, 1998, she responded:

> These were most certainly Olha's brothers, although I don't remember their names. One of them was married to Boguszewska's daughter, who was my father's cousin. I know for certain that Boguszewska and her daughter Aniela were murdered in November along with the other persons mentioned by Irena Justyna. However, I did not know that Petro and Ivan Chervak were also murdered. To learn more about this episode, I went to Jadwiga Biernacki, whose husband's parents perished in this last attack. Jadwiga did not know that the Chervak brothers were murdered either. But that they hung around with the bandits is certain, or so my mother always told me. How else would they have gotten my brother's watch? It was an unusual watch with a built-in alarm. And what about my brother's horse, which often stood behind their house? If they themselves did not participate in the atrocities, then at least they must have had some contact with the bandits; perhaps they were informers. I cannot, however, state this as an absolute fact since I was only a child at that time and know only that which my parents and the elders told me. The decision, as to whether to include them among the bandits or among those who helped the Poles, I leave up to you.

I have included Petro and Ivan Chervak among those who helped the Poles as well as among those Ukrainians who were murdered by the UPA.

Sabina Królikowska now lives with her ailing husband, her daughter, son-in-law, and two lovely grandchildren on an old-fashioned farm in Horyszów Polski near Zamość. Sabina's brother, Dominik Tarnawski, was my brother-in-law. He married my sister Aniela after the war. His tragic story, involving the brutal murder of his entire first family by the UPA is recounted in my *Vengeance of the Swallows*, pp. 86-87, as well as in the account of Irena Justyna below (see Ivan Sheremeta). My wife Terri and I had the privilege of staying at Sabina's country home in Horyszów Polski for a few days during our three-week trip to Poland in October 1997. I can assure the reader that this energetic woman, whose finely sculptured face was undimmed by a life of tragedy and continuing hard work, was a most gracious host, a true repository of all that is noble in the Polish tradition of survival, and a living inspiration to us both.

2. Zenobiusz Janicki, *W obronie Przebraża i w drodze do Berlina* (Lublin: Ardabliju S.C., 1997), pp. 52-53.
3. Biskupski, pp. 73, 75-77, 79, 90.
4. *Na Rubieży* (Wrocław), no. 30, (1998): 18. An account of Leokadia Grzybowska (née Zawilska, b. 1924) appears in Dębski and Popek, p. 215. A part of that account can be found in Appendix A: Ukrainian Victims by County, Łuck County, "Tsisar family from Dębowa Karczma Colony." Undoubtedly this is the same Leokadia as quoted herein.
5. Turowski and Siemaszko, p. 156.
6. *Na Rubieży* (Wrocław), no. 30 (1998): 20. Bukowce was a Ukrainian village wherein also lived three Polish families consisting of 12 persons. Bukowce Colony was settled exclusively by Czechs. See also Turowski and Siemaszko, p. 66.
7. Dębski and Popek, pp. 216-17.
8. Biskupski, pp. 120-24. As previously stated, Dominik Tarnawski was my brother-in-law. See also note to Olha Chervak, above.
9. *Na Rubieży* (Wrocław), no. 30 (1998): 19.
10. *Na Rubieży* (Wrocław), no. 30 (1998): 19-20.
11. Turowski and Siemaszko, p. 132.
12. Dębski and Popek, pp. 236-37.
13. Dębski and Popek, pp. 226-27. A list of 78 victims of the UPA murdered in Jeziorany Szlacheckie (June 19, 1943), Górka Połonka (June 22 and 23, 1943), and Jeziorany Czeskie (July 25, August 20, and September 10, 1943) follows this narrative.

14. *Na Rubieży* (Wrocław), no. 30 (1998): 24-25.
15. Z. Janicki, pp. 17, 49, 69, 77. The quoted passage appears on p. 71.
16. Dębski and Popek, pp. 234-35.
17. Turowski and Siemaszko, pp. 17-18; Piotrowski, *Vengeance of the Swallows*, pp. 65-66.
18. Z. Janicki, p. 35. See also Turowski and Siemaszko, p. 42.

Chapter 8

1. Turowski and Siemaszko, p. 39.
2. Piotrowski, *Vengeance of the Swallows*, pp. 82-85, 95-96, 103-07. Filip, his wife, and his youngest daughter, Ludwika, who was still at home, were murdered by the Ukrainian Nationalists shortly after we left Ryświanka. His three oldest daughters, Halina, Marysia, and Zosia, and his married son, Staszek, survived the war.

After the above-quoted passage was already in print, my brother Franciszek informed me that both he and my brother Jan had spent several nights with the Pasichnyk family before the attack on our house. Pasichnyk may have also transported some members of our family to Tuczyn and back for some reason. I therefore should not have been as surprised as I was, when Franciszek added that he had heard, possibly from one of Filip's oldest daughters who went back to our village for a visit sometime after the war, that Pasichnyk and his family were murdered by the Ukrainian Nationalists for befriending us and offering us assistance. At this time, I have no way of confirming the veracity of this hearsay information.
3. In Poliszczuk, *Gorzka prawda*, pp. 190-91. Poliszczuk adds that this respondent had also provided him with a photo copy of church records that listed the cause of death of the persons mentioned in the account as "murdered."
4. Dębski and Popek, p. 245.

Chapter 9

1. Bronisław Janik, *Było ich trzy* (Warszawa: Książka i Wiedza, 1970), quoted in Władysław Dziemiańczuk, comp., *Wybaczyć nie znaczy zapomnieć* (Toronto: Związek Ziem Wschodnich RP, 1996), pp. 325-26, 329.

2. Żur, p. 117. For a fuller account of the events, see Appendix A: Ukrainian Victims by County, Sarny, "Olena Chorna and her two children, Semen and Zhenia, from Budki Borowskie."
3. *Na Rubieży* (Wrocław), no. 33-34 (1999): 56-59. For accounts regarding Ukrainian-Nationalist attacks on Poroda, Prurwa, Stachówka, and Włodzimierzec, see pp. 60-65.
4. Dębski and Popek, pp. 258-59.
5. Turowski and Siemaszko, p. 38.

Chapter 10

1. Biskupski, pp. 94-95. The Orthodox priest mentioned in this account was undoubtedly Ukrainian. He most probably conducted his services in Old Church Slavonic, regarded by the peasants as a "Russian" language.
2. Dębski and Popek, p. 284.
3. Turowski and Siemaszko, p. 43.
4. Dębski and Popek, p. 324.
5. Dębski and Popek, p. 291; Turowski and Siemaszko, p. 19. In the latter work, the names of the three Ukrainians are spelled as follows: Michał Kardaszuk [Mykhailo Kardashuk], Mitka Bronicki [Mytka Bronytskyi], and Mikołaj Dębicki [Mykola Dembytskyi].
6. Dębski and Popek, pp. 324-25.
7. Turowski and Siemaszko, p. 122.
8. Dębski and Popek, p. 301.
9. Dębski and Popek, p. 323.
10. Turowski and Siemaszko, p. 80.
11. Dębski and Popek, p. 291.
12. Although I was familiar with Bronisław Terpin's lengthy and moving published account of his 1994 travels in Poland and Wołyń, I did not meet him until my March 27, 1998, presentation in London, Ontario. When, in the course of our informal conversation after my talk, I learned of the Kamila episode, I asked him to write it and send it to me — which he did on April 2, 1998. His quoted passage comes from the second part of that lengthy letter.

I then wrote to Kamila, Bronia, and Elżbieta to verify the information contained in Terpin's letter.

Kamila's account comes from her two letters to me dated April 28 and June 5, 1998, respectively. Kamila's first letter also contained a list of names of 18 persons who were murdered either in the church or in the vicinity of Poryck. They were all related to the Aleksander and Wiktoria (née Palinka) Cybuchowski family, as was Kamila. She was their granddaughter. Two persons on that list — Apolonia Bobrowska, a 90-year-old widow, and Bolesław Palinka — were married to Ukrainians. Apolonia had seven children. Her two youngest daughters (Helena and Aleksandra), in the words of Kamila, "became Polish," that is to say, they were baptized Roman Catholic. Nevertheless, they, too, married Ukrainians: Sroda and Romaniuk. They both survived in spite of the fact that their Ukrainian relatives refused to offer them any assistance whatsoever during or after the Poryck incident. The second person on the above-mentioned list, Bolesław Palinka, was killed in his house in the village. His Ukrainian wife, however, was spared.

In her reply (dated May 1998), Bronisława Ryś stated:

> I apologize that you had to wait for my response, but the translation of your text took longer than I anticipated. I have no reservations to what you have written. Everything that I conveyed to Mr. Terpin has been addressed. As far as my experiences during those days are concerned, I would like to add the following information as to what happened to my own family.
>
> My brother, Adam Ryś, worked in a mill in Poryck; he was 19 years of age. One day, while he was at work, his friends — Ukrainians who belonged to the band — came over and beat him up as well as another Pole: the director of the mill, who was from Włodzimierz. Then they took them to the forest. The remains of my brother were never found. Those of the Pole from Włodzimierz were discovered in the Zawidów Forest. My father, Andrzej Ryś, was murdered by the band in that forest while searching for my brother. The same fate befell the rest of my family as well: my mother, my aunt, and another brother of mine — they were all murdered.
>
> As far as I remember, the older generation of Ukrainians was more friendly toward the Poles than the younger, although there were exceptions among the younger generation as well. A young boy, Mitko Kulai, stands out in my mind. He warned many Poles of the impending slaughter in the church of Poryck and even helped the wounded. Among others, Dr. Secherchuk, who lived with her family in Poryck, also warned the Poles.
>
> I would write more about all of this, but my memory is beginning to fail and I assume that you would like to rely on concrete accounts which are backed up by detailed information.
>
> P.S. This letter is being written by my niece, since I am unable to write it myself.

I did not receive a response from Elżbieta, but in a separate letter dated June 5, 1998, Kamila's husband, Stefan Kamiński, assured me that Elżbieta had confirmed the events as presented by his wife and informed me that she apologized for not responding to my letter since she had nothing new to add to Kamila's account.

Regarding the two additional accounts provided by Terpin: for a segment from Tadeusz Wojewódka's account, see Poryck, first account. The account of Stanisław Filipowicz dealing with the tragedy in Poryck did not contain any references to Ukrainian rescue efforts and was therefore not included in this work.

13. Dębski and Popek: Konstancja's account is on pp. 320-21; Katarzyna's is on pp. 318-19; Eugeniusz's is on pp. 314-15; Maria's is on pp. 134-36. A list of 67 known family names and the number of persons killed in each family (a total of 168 victims) in Głęboczyce Colony can be found on p. 316. A note indicates that information is lacking on an additional ten families. In all, about 200 persons perished there on August 29, 1943.

14. Turowski and Siemaszko, pp. 82-83.

15. *Na Rubieży* (Wrocław), no. 30 (1998): 22-23.

16. Dębski and Popek, pp. 287-88. According to Turowski and Siemaszko (p. 125), in August 1943 the Ukrainian Nationalists murdered 17 persons in four Polish families from Bużanka near the Uściług-Włodzimierz road. Two Ukrainian families in Bużanka rendered assistance to several Poles.

17. Biskupski, p. 93.

18. Edward Rosa, *Wspomnienia lat przeżytych na Wołyniu* (Toronto: Alliance of the Polish Eastern Provinces, 1997), pp. 61-62.

19. Dębski and Popek, p. 303.

20. Letter of Bronisława Rosa to her nephew, Edward Rosa. Rosa, pp. 58-60.

21. Dębski and Popek, pp. 305-06, 308-09, 313. See Appendix C: Excerpts from Documents, Ukrainian, "UPA ('Lysyi's') Field Report on the destruction of Ziemlica."

22. Dębski and Popek, pp. 313-14.

23. Turowski and Siemaszko, p. 156.

24. Jacek Wilczur, "Nawroty do złej przeszłości," *Przegląd Tygodniowy*, no. 26 (1948), reprinted in Michał Fijałka, *27. Wołyńska*

Dywizja Piechoty AK (Warszawa: Instytut Wydawniczy Pax, 1986), pp. 11-12, n. 9. According to Turowski and Siemaszko (p. 83), Orzeszyn Colony was attacked on the same day as the church in Poryck, July 11, 1943. In all, 306 Poles were slaughtered in that colony.

25. Dębski and Popek, p. 273. Stanisława Dąbrowska-Brzozowska's sister's (Zofia Kowalska's) account, as transcribed by Zofia Szwal, follows on pp. 274-75.

26. Dębski and Popek, pp. 268-71.

27. Dębski and Popek, p. 272.

28. Dębski and Popek, p. 272. For the postwar court testimony of Ohorodnychuk regarding his role in the attack on the church in Poryck, see Appendix C: Excerpts from Documents, Ukrainian, "Court testimony of Ohorodnychuk, a.k.a. Mykola Kvitkovskyi."

29. Poliszczuk, *Gorzka prawda*, pp. 191-92.

30. This account, obtained from Teresa Radziszewska, is in my possession. For two other rescuers from Sielec, see Moisei Iadziuk.

31. Dębski and Popek, pp. 289-90. According to the account of Edward Kondracki from Bielin (p. 290), after being abducted, the pastor of the church in Stężarzyce, Fr. Józef Baran, "was tied to a wagon like a dog" and taken to the Strzelec Forest. There, "he died in great agony after being sawed in half."

32. Dębski and Popek, p. 296.

33. This detailed, typed, 31-page account, obtained from Teresa Radziszewska, is in my possession.

34. Dębski and Popek, pp. 291-92.

35. Dębski and Popek, pp. 296-98. A list of names of 43 victims murdered by the UPA in Fiodorpol, a village belonging to the Swojczów parish, follows this account.

36. Dębski and Popek, pp. 360-62.

37. Dębski and Popek, p. 41.

38. Rosa, pp. 51-52.

39. This account, obtained from Teresa Radziszewska, is in my possession.

Chapter 11

1. Romuald Wernik, *Tajkury — wioska która była miastem* (London: Caldra House, 1997), p. 71.

2. Dębski and Popek, pp. 333-37. An incomplete list of names of 41 victims of the Zielony Dąb massacre can be found on p. 337. Twenty-seven of them bear the name of Wereszczyński. Among the victims were 14 children under the age of 11, and 12 women.

Appendix A

1. Dębski and Popek, p. 22.
2. Dębski and Popek, p. 16.
3. Turowski and Siemaszko, p. 46.
4. Dębski and Popek, p. 17.
5. Dębski and Popek, p. 24.
6. *Na Rubieży* (Wrocław), no. 30 (1998): 26-27.
7. Turowski and Siemaszko, p. 59.
8. This account, obtained from Edward Prus, is in my possession. The names of the murdered Ukrainians in this account are not listed separately because Lubieszów was in Polesie, not Wołyń. This account is included herein because of Konoplanko, the Ukrainian priest who lived in Dubno and was murdered there. Part of the account of Zbigniew Małyszczycki appears in *Na Rubieży* (Wrocław), no. 30 (1998): 33-35. The reference to Konoplanko in that account is on p. 35.
9. Poliszczuk, *Gorzka prawda*, p. 188.
10. Dębski and Popek, p. 14.
11. See *Polityka* (February 10, 1990); Myśliwski, vol. 3, pp. 315-22; and Poliszczuk, *Gorzka prawda*, pp. 205-08.
12. Dębski and Popek, p. 231.
13. Shumuk, 1974, pp. 104-07.
14. Turowski and Siemaszko, p. 33.
15. Turowski and Siemaszko, pp. 103, 128.
16. *Na Rubieży* (Wrocław) 1, no. 11 (1995): 7.
17. *Na Rubieży* (Wrocław) 1, no. 11 (1995), 5.
18. Turowski and Siemaszko, p. 60.
19. Piotrowski, *Vengeance of the Swallows*, pp. 67-68. See also the entry "Małyńsk" and the accompanying note in Chapter 3 of the present work. A reference to the *sołtys* (unnamed) and the bells of Kazimirka also appears in Bagiński, p. 52, n. 8.
20. Biskupski, p. 109.
21. Turowski and Siemaszko, p. 128.
22. This letter, obtained from Teresa Radziszewska, is in my possession.
23. Turowski and Siemaszko, p. 92.
24. Biskupski, p. 43.
25. Turowski and Siemaszko, p. 121.
26. Dębski and Popek, pp. 128-29.
27. Turowski and Siemaszko, p. 26.
28. Turowski and Siemaszko, p. 29.
29. Turowski and Siemaszko, p. 51. See also Edmund Bosakowski, "Na mojej drodze. Wspomnienia z Wołynia," in Myśliwski, vol. 2, pp. 301, 308. In that work, Tetiana's last name is given as "Nykoluk." She was said to have been

the daughter of Iosyp and Horpyna. According to Władysław Wolski from Bielinówka (Dębski and Popek, p. 190), the Ukrainian Nationalists "also murdered Fania, the daughter of Horpyna and Iuzva [or Iosyp], because, being a Ukrainian, she had a child by a Pole." Undoubtedly, these three accounts refer to the same person.

30. Dębski and Popek, p. 175.
31. Debski and Popek, p. 167.
32. Turowski and Siemaszko, p. 51; Myśliwski, vol. 2, p. 301.
33. Poliszczuk, *Gorzka prawda*, p. 188.
34. Dębski and Popek, pp. 208-09. A list of family names of 141 victims, including 64 children, in Kąty appears on pp. 209-10. The information in the last paragraph comes from Turowski and Siemaszko, p. 124.
35. Turowski and Siemaszko, p. 123. A list of names of the victims appears in Dębski and Popek, pp. 210-11.
36. Biskupski, pp. 62-63.
37. Biskupski, p. 123. See Ivan Sheremeta as well as Olha Chervak and the accompanying note, both in Chapter 7, Łuck County.
38. Turowski and Siemaszko, p. 51.
39. Turowski an Siemaszko, p. 76.
40. Dębski and Popek, p. 220, from a list of 156 victims of the UPA.
41. Biskupski, p. 123.
42. Turowski and Siemaszko, pp. 36-37.
43. Turowski and Siemaszko, p. 56. See also the eyewitness account of Michał Dąbrowski from Klepaczów as summarized in Z. Janicki, p. 33. In this attack, Michał Dąbrowski's brother, Władysław, was stabbed 27 times. Another resident, Adam Markowski, sustained 52 stab wounds.
44. Dębski and Popek, p. 215. As an eyewitness to Ukrainian-Nationalist atrocities, Leokadia was asked to testify at the Provincial Prosecutor's office in Koszalin. The above is her summary of a part of that testimony.
45. *Na Rubieży* (Wrocław), no. 30 (1998): 20.
46. *Na Rubieży* (Wrocław), no. 30 (1998): 19.
47. Turowski and Siemaszko, p. 15.
48. Giertych, pp. 335-36.
49. Turowski and Siemaszko, p. 111.
50. Szcześniak and Szota, p. 150, n. 29.
51. Z. Janicki, pp. 72-73.
52. Dębski and Popek, p. 249. A list containing eight names of those murdered by the UPA in Piotrowice can be found on the same page.
53. Turowski and Siemaszko, p. 53.
54. Giertych, p. 332. There are many references in the accounts which I have perused to tragedies precipitated by mixed marriages. Murders by Ukrainians of Ukrainians married to Poles (recorded in the present work) occurred, for example, in Antolin, Czarna Łoża, Czartorysk, Hucisko Pikulskie, Huta Majdańska, Józefin, Klepaczów, Łyczki, Maria Wola, Piotrowice, Rokitnie Nowe, Stepań, Szubków, and Zielony Dąb.

In Dębowa Karczma, Maria Budiakivska, the Polish wife of a Ukrainian, was murdered by her husband on orders from the regional OUN Provid leader. *Na Rubieży* (Wrocław), no. 30 (1998): 23.

In Sawosze, there were two incidents of Ukrainian husbands killing their Catholic wives as well as two children. (See Luboml County, Volodymyr Krasovskyi.)

Józef Sobiesiak tells of Sachko, a Ukrainian who converted to Roman Catholicism in 1938 and became Saczkowski, the *wójt* of Kołki. In 1943 Sachko reverted back to the Orthodox faith in the presence of a UPA commander and was presented by the priest with a blessed knife for use against Poles and Russians. To redeem himself for his previous conversion and to prove his sincerity, Sachko then personally hanged his Polish wife from a pine tree in the presence of a large crowd. (Józef Sobiesiak, *Przebraże* [Lublin: Wydawnictwo Lubelskie, 1973], pp. 11-12). In another incident, when a son from a mixed Polish-Ukrainian family attempted to kill his Polish mother, his Ukrainian father killed him instead, As summarized by Czesław Madajczyk, *Polityka III Rzeszy w okupowanej Polsce*, vol. 1 (Warszawa: Państwowe Wydawnictwo Naukowe, 1970), p. 474. According to Henryk Kitaszewski:

> Polish wives in mixed-marriages were also murdered. As far as I know, this was left up to the Ukrainian husband. These women were not regarded as wives, and they were not given an opportunity to become Ukrainianized.... Many of the husbands not only did not protect their wives but also lent a hand in their murders. There were many instances when other Ukrainians would come by and order the husband to kill his Polish wife ... and often the children who were raised as Poles and Catholics would also me murdered.
>
> Many of the husbands who converted to Catholicism also fled just like the Poles. I believe that the only way for such a convert to become Ukrainian again was to murder his

own wife and children with his own hands. All Polish wives and Polish husbands in these mixed marriages succumbed to the same law: death. In Łuck, we met many former wives of Ukrainians who had run away from their husbands. Some of them said that their own husbands told them to flee because when their neighbors or relatives would come for them, no one would be able to save them. We know of one case, that of Władysław Mazurkiewicz, who married a Ukrainian girl. She as well as her relatives assured him that nothing would happen to him. He went into hiding with his relatives and was murdered, most probably by them.

Giertych, p. 304. Kitaszewski's account deals mainly with the attack on the church in Kisielin in Horochów County, but he addresses the general situation in Wołyń as well.

For a case involving the murder of a Polish husband by his Ukrainian wife in Antolin, see Kostopol County, Mykhailo Mishchaniuk.

In her tragic account, Teresa Borowska from Kostopol describes how the Poles had to sleep in a German-operated factory which was surrounded by a high wall in order not to fall into the hands of the Ukrainians. In the morning they would return to their homes and fields. She adds, "The [Polish] husbands of Ukrainian women also came there because death awaited them." From the account of Teresa Borowska (née Hudeczek, b. 1931), in Dębski and Popek, p. 247; this account, obtained from Teresa Radziszewska, is also in my possession. All the above examples come from Wołyń. The following incidents occurred in different provinces. According to Wanda Oswald[owa], who lived with her parents in Lwów:

> One night after curfew someone knocked. A bit frightened, my parents answered the door. It turned out to be our old acquaintances from a village near Lwów who provided us with dairy products. He was Ukrainian; she, Polish. They looked terrible. What had happened? Well, on the previous night, when the mother went out to milk the cows, her son — a Banderowiec — entered the room and told his father that during that night they planned to slaughter all the Poles in the village. The father said to him, "But your mother is Polish; will you kill her too?"
>
> The son replied, "I will not kill her, but there will come another who will."
>
> The father could stand it no longer; he grabbed an axe and killed his son. The wife, meanwhile, came in with the container of milk and tripping over her son's body in the dark said, "The dog must be lying here."
>
> The husband answered, "You're right — a dog is lying here." There was nothing else for them to do but to pack a bundle and flee.

Giertych, p. 333, as transcribed by Kazimierz Moszory. Another such incident transpired in Świrz, a small town in the province of Tarnopol. The source is Anna Lewandowska (née Matkowska) from Świrz:

> According to Mrs. Lewandowska, the son, a Banderowiec, confided in his Ukrainian father that he had received an order to kill his own mother that night. This act, he was told, would make him a trustworthy member of the organization. Supposedly, the father answered, "That's too bad, if you have such an order, do as you see fit." That night, after all were in bed, the father killed his son.

In the village of Chlebowice near Świrz, according to Jan Grzeszczyszyn (Jan Gres from Chlebowice, now living in New Jersey), a son of Polish-Ukrainian heritage was sawn in half because, the Nationalists said, he was "half-Polish." Both of these incidents were related to me by Helena Piotrowiak. See my *Vengeance of the Swallows*, pp. 95, 240-41, n. 63.

The setting for the following narrative is also the province of Tarnopol, the county of Czortków, the village of Biały Potok:

> Mr. Angielskyi [a Ukrainian mill owner in Biały Potok] was married to a Pole. Their family was numerous: three sons and four daughters. In accordance with the prevailing custom of the times [in Eastern Galicia] relating to mixed marriages, the daughters were raised as Latin-rite Roman Catholics. It is difficult to say how many of the men in this family had ties with the Nationalists, but the oldest son received an order from the Banderowcy to murder his mother and his sisters. This order went against his character and conscience. He carried out the order, but only on himself: he hung himself, wishing thereby to avoid the suffering and death to which he would have been otherwise subjected [by the UPA for not carrying out the given order].

The above account is accompanied by a photocopy of a photograph of the 1993 blessing of the mass grave in Biały Potok that contains the remains of the victims murdered by the UPA on December 23, 1944. A list of 24 names of victims murdered in December 1944 and June 1945 in that village by the Banderowcy is also attached. One of these, Franciszek Butra, had a Ukrainian wife; his children were raised as Latin-rite Catholics. One day, a group of Banderowcy, dressed in Soviet uniforms, came to his home and led him away. His family found out about his murder when their dog brought home one of his legs. After a thorough search, they found his body cut into pieces in the local quarry. His ten-year-old son died shortly thereafter. His daughter was taken to a Ukrainian (Uniate) church by her mother and re-christened. "From all that this daughter had lived through," stated the narrator, "she developed a case of epilepsy." From the account of Stanisława Kilimnik, as recorded by Jan Kilimnik, obtained from Czesława Grygorczyk, in my possession.

We also have the account of Petro Petrovych Vershyhora (Petr Petrovich Vershigora in Russian), a Ukrainian partisan from the Sidor Kovpak Soviet brigade who tells of his 1943 meeting with an OUN-B member who was ordered "to kill his Polish wife to prove to his UPA comrades that he was a good Ukrainian. After he had killed his wife, his UPA commander ordered him to slay his 12-year-old girl and five-year-old boy because they were of 'impure blood' and when he refused, the UPA men cut them down with axes before his eyes." This summary comes from Reuben Ainsztein, *Jewish Resistance in Nazi-Occupied Eastern Europe (With a Historical Survey of the Jew as Fighter and Soldier in the Diaspora)* (London: Paul Elek, 1974), p. 254. The title of Vershigora's work is *Lyudi s chistoy sovestyu* (Moskva: Sovetskiy pisatel, 1955.) The reference is on pp. 492-93.

55. Żur, pp. 66-72, 117.
56. Żur, pp. 148-50, 153-54.
57. Kurdybelski, "Wołyński rodowód," *Semper Fidelis* (Wrocław) 5 no. 22 (1994): 22.
58. Dębski and Popek, pp. 261-62.
59. Żur, p. 73.
60. Turowski and Siemaszko, p. 91.
61. First account: H. D. in Poliszczuk, *Gorzka prawda*, p. 191. Second account: Stanisława Jóźwiak (née Morelowska) from Sielec, obtained from Teresa Radziszewska, in my possession.
62. Turowski and Siemaszko, p. 80.
63. Dębski and Popek, p. 303.
64. Wilczur, as reprinted in Fijałka, p. 12, n. 9.
65. Dębski and Popek, pp. 285-86.
66. Dębski and Popek, pp. 178-80. The names of Pavlo Kirychuk, Lishchuk, and Samolei have not received separate entries in this appendix, which focuses on innocent Ukrainian victims. The one possible exception to this is the entry for the Chervak brothers. Feliks Jasiński's lengthy account also contains the following episode (p. 177):

Another Krasicki family, while fleeing to Mizocz, took with them two girls orphaned when the rest of their family, that of Jan Ostaszewski, was murdered. The small group was attacked along the way, and the Krasickis were murdered. Leokadia, one of the orphans, was wounded and left on an anthill, while the second orphan, a 15-year-old, jumped off the wagon, ran to the forest, and survived. On the following day, the wounded orphan, who was still alive, was picked up by a larger group that was passing by and nursed back to health.

A similar account comes from Teresa Borowska (b. 1931) from Kostopol (Równe County): "Then they caught one of the Poles in the forest. They plucked out his eyes, cut off his hands and feet, and threw him on an ant hill" (p. 247; this account, obtained from Teresa Radziszewska, is also in my possession).

A list of 160 family names comprising 947 persons belonging to the 19 villages and hamlets of the Kąty (Kuty) parish who were either displaced or killed appears on pp. 182-83. Zielony Dąb was attacked by the UPA in May 1943. In all, 55 Poles were killed or burned to death in their homes. Roman Krasicki was among these. He was hung from a tree and when the rope broke, he was clubbed to death. Roman Krasicki was one-hundred years old. See Turowski and Siemaszko, p. 63.

67. Dębski and Popek, p. 331.
68. Wernik, p. 71.

Appendix B

1. Helena's story: personal interview, April 24, 1998, Mont St-Hilaire, Quebec.

Rakowiec was another small village in the province of Lwów. On March 26, 1944, around 11:00 A.M., a contingent of the UPA surrounded the Roman Catholic church in Rakowiec just as

Fr. Błażej Jurasz was delivering his sermon to the faithful. The priest and the men were told to leave the church. Four Poles were then shot and the rest were herded toward the forest. Fortunately, the Ukrainians of this village—led by a Greek Catholic (Uniate) priest, Fr. Bereziuk from Polany, and the *wójt*—came to their assistance. They immediately set out after the intended victims and, after a lengthy negotiation, managed to redeem the Poles for 10,000 zloty and four pigs. Soon after that, almost all the Poles left Rakowiec. This story of rescue comes from Jerzy Węgierski, *Armia Krajowa na południowych i wschodnich przedpolach Lwowa* (Kraków: Platan, 1994), pp. 160, 162.

2. Emilia's story: personal interview, August 14, 1997, Toronto, Ontario.

3. Adela's story: personal interview, June 22, 1997, Upper Grandview, New York.

4. *Na Rubieży* (Wrocław) 4, no. 5 (1993): 15. According to Adela, the following information in that listing is either inaccurate or incomplete:

> Introductory paragraph: The unnamed parish priest is said to have been abducted by the UPA (Banderowcy) in October of 1943 and to have perished without a trace. In fact, Fr. Ludwik Chrabko survived the Boków attack and left the village thereafter.
>
> Entries 1-6: The family name is spelled Cywiński, not Cewiński.
>
> Entries 12-15: the family name is spelled Pilichowski, not Pielechowski. Two unnamed sons are listed as having perished (entries 14 and 15), whereas one of them, Aleksander (Oleś), survived in spite of the gash across his throat.
>
> Entry 24: The unnamed wife of Bronisław Szymkowicz was Sabina.
>
> Entry 25: This entry is erroneous. This Szymkowicz family did not include a son, only daughters.
>
> Entry 27: Karol Szymkowicz's wife was named Marcela.
>
> Entry 28-29: The daughters' names were Krystyna and Czesława.
>
> Entry 34: The name of Adela's mother should read Eugenia, not Genowefa, Zacharko.
>
> Entry 36: The first name of Adela's grandfather should read Pantelemon, not Telemon.
>
> Finally, another name should be added to that list, that of Karolina Kołaczkowska, who also perished in the attack on Boków.

An editorial heading on the previous page (p. 14) of *Na Rubieży* tells us that in 1939, 95,000 people lived in the county of Podhajce. Of these 30,000 were ethnic Poles. Between 1939 and 1945, at least 80 locations have been identified where Poles were the victims of the Ukrainian Nationalists. Based on eyewitness testimonies, they also affirm that in the 37 locations documented in that issue, 869 persons perished. They estimate that between 1,800 and 2,000 Poles perished in this county at the hands of the UPA and its collaborators.

5. Stanisław Jastrzębski, *Oko w oko z banderowcami: Wspomnienia małoletniego żołnierza Armii Krajowej*, exp. 2d ed. (Warszawa: Wydawnictwo Archidiecezji Warszawskiej, 1996), p. 116. The author of the quoted passage bases his account on the testimony of a resident of Boków, Józef Jastrzębski, who helped to bury the victims. He also provides some of their names and states that according to the respondent, there were 39 victims in all. The attack, according to this author, was led by a Uniate priest from Sławentyn. This same unit of Ukrainian Nationalists was also responsible for similar attacks on the Polish people in Marianów, Szumlany, Sławentyn, and Krasnolesie.

6. One of them, Maria Szkolnicka (probably an assumed name), now a physician living on Long Island, brought Sister Chmielewska to America for a visit after the war simply out of sheer gratitude.

7. Another account from Podhajce County tells of the heroic rescue of Poles by an Orthodox priest named Humnytskyi. In her letter to me from Warsaw, dated May 18, 1998, Janina (née Gandurska) Saran wrote:

> I was born in 1932 in the village of Sokołów in the county of Podhajce, the province of Tarnopol. I remember that in the middle of our village there stood a Catholic church on one side of the road and an Orthodox church on the other. I know that our priest and the Orthodox priest were of friendly terms because they used to visit each other and participate mutually in both Catholic and Orthodox holidays. The Poles and Ukrainians in our village also lived in peace, and genuine friendships among them were not rare. On my way to the Catholic church, I often listened to the beautiful melodies coming from the Orthodox church.
>
> During the German occupation, something got mixed up in people's heads.

The Ukrainians began to treat the Poles in a negative way and even to harass them. I remember how a Ukrainian lad, our neighbor, chased me over a meadow yelling, "*Za San lashe, bo tu nashe!*" [Beyond the San River, Pole, because this is our land!] I was terrified of him at the time. Ukrainian bands also prowled throughout the area, especially at night, robbing whatever they could. People whispered that they were murdering Poles in villages. But there were also those who said that they would not attack our village because the Orthodox priest Humnytskyi would not allow it. And so it was. At night, he would go out onto the bridge over the Strypa River and halt the bands coming from the forest.

From early spring until July 1944 our village was caught up in the Soviet-German front, which, wreaked havoc on both the Poles and Ukrainians. I believe that the destruction caused by these forces also deprived the Banderowcy of the desire for aggressive action.

Appendix D

1. Stanisław Skrzypek, *The Problem of Galicia* (London: Polish Association for the South-Eastern Provinces, 1948), p. 65.
2. Szcześniak and Szota, pp. 31-32.
3. Alexander Dallin, *German Rule in Russia, 1941-1945: A Study of Occupation Policies*, 2d ed. (London: Macmillan, 1981), p. 114.
4. Torzecki, *Kwestia ukraińska w polityce III Rzeszy 1933-1945*, p. 116.
5. Poliszczuk, *Gorzka prawda*, p. 132.
6. Volodymyr Kubijovyč, ed., *Encyclopedia of Ukraine*, vol. 2 (Toronto: University of Toronto Press, 1988), p. 381.
7. Dumin [Dumyn], in *Zeszyty Historyczne*, pp. 111-12 and n. 11.
8. Dontsov, *Natsionalizm*, 1966, p. 276.
9. Dontsov, *Natsionalizm*, 1966, pp. 220-21.
10. Dontsov, *Natsionalizm*, 1966, p. 244. Emphases in the original.
11. Dmytro Dontsov, *Masa i provid* (1939), reprinted in Dmytro Dontsov, *Khrestom i mechem* (Toronto, 1967), p. 139.
12. Dmytro Dontsov, *Dukh nashykh istorychnykh tradytsii* (1923), reprinted in Dmytro Dontsov, *Khrestom i mechem*, p. 58.
13. Dontsov, *Natsionalizm*, 1966, p. 228.

14. Dontsov, *Natsionalizm*, 1966, p. 270.
15. See Alexander, J. Motyl, *The Turn to the Right: The Ideological Origins and Development of Ukrainian Nationalism, 1919-1929* (Boulder, CO: East European Monographs, 1980), pp. 9, 113-14, 162-69, 174-75; Kuropas, pp. 231, 238-39; B. F. Sabrin et al., eds., *Alliance for Murder: The Nazi-Ukrainian Nationalist Partnership in Genocide* (New York: Sarpedon, 1991), p. 15; Kost Pankivskyi, *Roky nimetskoi okupatsii* (New York: Vydavnytstvo Kliuchi, 1965), p. 13; Orest Subtelny, *Ukraine: A History*, 2d ed. (Toronto: University of Toronto Press and Canadian Institute of Ukrainian Studies, 1994), p. 442; Mirchuk, *Narys istorii*, 93. John A. Armstrong attributes the following characteristics to integral nationalism:

(1) a belief in the nation as the supreme value to which all others must be subordinated, essentially a totalitarian concept; (2) an appeal to mystically conceived ideas of the solidarity of all individuals making up the nation, usually on the assumption that biological characteristics or the irreversible effects of common historical development had welded them into one organic whole; (3) a subordination of rational, analytic thought to the "intuitively correct" emotions; (4) expression of the "national will" through a charismatic leader and an elite of national enthusiasts organized in a single party; (5) glorification of action, war, and violence as an expression of the superior biological vitality of the nation.

About Ukrainian Nationalism, Armstrong says: "The theory and teachings of the Nationalists were very close to Fascism, and in some respects, such as the insistence on 'racial purity,' even went beyond the original Fascist doctrines." John A. Armstrong, *Ukrainian Nationalism*, 3d ed. (Englewood, CO: Ukrainian Academic Press, 1990), pp. 13, 212.

16. Poliszczuk, *Ideologia*, p. 15.
17. Motyl, "Ukrainian Nationalist Political Violence," p. 50. See also Feliński, pp. 158-73.
18. Mirchuk, *Narys istorii*, p. 130.
19. Danylo Husar Struk, ed., *Encyclopedia of Ukraine*, vol. 3 (Toronto: University of Toronto Press, 1993), p. 747.
20. Torzecki, *Polacy i Ukraińcy*, p. 325.
21. Torzecki, *Kwestia ukraińska w polityce III Rzeszy 1933-1945*, pp. 126-27.
22. Mykoła Kuczerepa, "Polityka narodowościowa Drugiej Rzeczypospolitej wobec

Ukraińców w latach 1919-1939," in Niedzielko, p. 42.

23. Struk, vol. 4, p. 680. A lengthy note penned by Ambassador Józef Lipski dealing with the assassination of Minister Pieracki and the arrest of Lebed on German soil (his passport was issued by the consulate general of the Reich in Danzig) appears in Wacław Jędrzejewicz, ed., *Diplomat in Berlin, 1933-1939: Papers and Memoirs of Józef Lipski, Ambassador of Poland* (New York: Columbia University Press, 1968): 135-42.

24. Stanisław Wroński, introduction to *Czerwone noce* by Cybulski, p. 13.

25. Janusz Kania, "Likwidacja cerkwi na Lubelszczyźnie w okresie międzywojennym," *Chrześcijanin w świecie* 14, no. 6 (1982): 50-89; Janusz Kania, "Rozbiórki cerkwi na Lubelszczyźnie w roku 1938 a stanowisko biskupa Fulmana," in Ryszard Łużny, ed., *Chrześcijański wschód a kultura polska* (Lublin: Katolicki Uniwersytet Lubelski, 1989), pp. 31-53. See also Bohdan Rostyslav Bociurkiw, *The Ukrainian Greek Catholic Church and the Soviet State, 1939-1950* (Edmonton: Canadian Institute of Ukrainian Studies Press, 1996), p. 10.

26. In a note on his conversation with Göring (October 21, 1938) Ambassador Lipski stated:

> In connection with the Hungarian claims to Slovakia and Carpathian Ruthenia, Nazi activities concentrated mainly on the Ukrainian question; Vienna, which was then the headquarters of the Ukrainian terrorists (under the auspices of Himmler), became the center of this agitation in which every form of subversive intrigue and seditious propaganda was fully utilized.

On November 12, 1938, in his letter to Poland's minister of foreign affairs, Józef Beck, Ambassador Lipski wrote:

> Upon the occupation of Vienna, the local Ukrainian headquarters were transferred to the Reich. They consisted in the majority of groups of the Konowalec type, whose active character pushed them to the front line. A number of local organizations are dealing with Ukrainian matters, for instance, Ribbentrop's office, Rosenberg's office, certain offices of the Propaganda Ministry, and, last but not least, the German Intelligence Service. All these elements, as far as can be observed, at present lack a precise directive from the top as to the line to follow in such a complicated affair. But they are bursting with dynamism, and the groups most harmful to us, such as Jaryj [Jary] and Melnyk type, are taking advantage of this atmosphere.

Jędrzejewicz, pp. 451, 464-65.

27. Torzecki, *Kwestia ukraińska w polityce III Rzeszy 1933-1945*, pp. 181-82.

28. Sol Littman, "The Ukrainian Halchyna Division: A Case Study of Historical Revisionism," in Saul Friedman, ed., *Holocaust Literature. A Handbook of Critical, Historical, and Literary Writings* (Westport, CT: Greenwood Press, 1993), p. 297.

29. Poliszczuk, *Gorzka prawda*, pp. 132, 140.

30. Czesław Łuczak, *Polska i Polacy w drugiej wojnie światowej* (Poznań: Wydawnictwo Naukowe Uniwersytetu imienia Adama Mickiewicza, 1993), pp. 349-50; Tadeusz Andrzej Olszański [Jan Łukaszów], *Historia Ukrainy XX w.* (Warszawa: Oficyna Wydawnicza Volumen, 1993), p. 165; Andrzej Szefer, "Dywersyjno-sabatażowa działalność wrocławskiej Abwehry na ziemiach polskich w przededniu agresji hitlerowskiej w 1939 r.," *Biuletyn Głównej Komisji Badania Zbrodni Hitlerowskich w Polsce* 32 (1987): 274.

31. Subtelny, p. 444.

32. The phrases in quotation marks come from "The [1930] Report. A Minority in Poland—The Ukrainian Conflict," as cited in the notes to the introduction above.

33. Szefer, p. 317.

34. Torzecki, *Polacy i Ukraińcy*, p. 29.

35. Stolze, affidavit, Document USSR-231, *Trial of the Major War Criminals Before the International Military Tribunal,* vol. 7 (published at Nuremberg in 1949), pp. 272-73, quoted in Dallin, pp. 116-17.

36. Madajczyk, *Polityka III Rzeszy w okupowanej Polsce*, p. 465, n. 6.

37. Madajczyk, *Polityka III Rzeszy w okupowanej Polsce*, p. 466.

38. Torzecki, *Polacy i Ukraińcy*, pp. 317-18.

39. Ryszard Torzecki, "Die Rolle der Zusammenarbeit mit der deutschen Besatzungsmacht in der Ukraine für deren Okkupationspolitik 1941 bis 1944," in Werner Röhr, ed., *Okkupation und Kollaboration (1938-1945): Beiträge zu Konzepten und Praxis der Kollaboration in der deutschen Okkupationspolitik* (Berlin: Hüthig Verlagsgemeinschaft, 1994), p. 245; Joe Conason, "To Catch a Nazi," *The Village Voice*, February 11, 1986, p. 19; Christopher Simpson, *Blowback: America's Recruitment of Nazis and Its*

Effects on the Cold War (New York: Weidenfeld and Nicolson, 1988), p. 161.

40. Łuczak 349; Madajczyk, *Polityka III Rzeszy w okupowanej Polsce*, p. 466.

41. Madajczyk, *Polityka III Rzeszy w okupowanej Polsce*, p. 465, n. 6.

42. Stanisław Piotrowski, *Dziennik Hansa Franka* (Warszawa: Wydawnictwo Prawnicze, 1956), p. 412.

43. Struk, vol. 3, pp. 740-41; Wolodymyr Kosyk, *The Third Reich and Ukraine* (New York: Peter Lang, 1993), pp. 82, 94, 108-09, 121. The phrase in quotation marks appears in Philip Friedman, "Ukrainian-Jewish Relations during the Nazi Occupation," in Michael R. Marrus, ed., *The Nazi Holocaust: Historical Articles on the Destruction of European Jews. Vol. 5, Public Opinion and Relations to the Jews in Nazi Europe*, vol. 1 (Westport, CT: Meckler, 1989), p. 365.

44. Armstrong, *Ukrainian Nationalism*, p. 52.

45. Torzecki, *Polacy i Ukraińcy*, pp. 55-56.

46. In Roman Drozd, *Ukraińska Powstańcza Armia. Dokumenty—Struktury* (Warszawa: Burchard Edition, 1998), p. 39. See also Poliszczuk, *Ideologia*, 90; Torzecki, *Polacy i Ukraińcy*, p. 177.

47. Dallin, p. 118.

48. Dallin, p. 118, n. 5.

49. Kosyk, *The Third Reich and Ukraine*, pp. 503-04.

50. Madajczyk, *Polityka III Rzeszy w okupowanej Polsce*, p. 469; Struk, vol. 5, pp. 404-05.

51. Torzecki, *Polacy i Ukraińcy*, pp. 63-64.

52. Hans-Joachim Torke and John-Paul Himka, eds., *German-Ukrainian Relations in Historical Perspective* (Edmonton: Canadian Institute of Ukrainian Studies Press, 1994), p. 140.

53. Szcześniak and Szota, p. 106; Dallin, p. 119, n. 4.

54. Torzecki, *Polacy i Ukraińcy*, p. 179.

55. Armstrong, *Ukrainian Nationalism*, p. 58.

56. Central State Archives of the October Revolution, Organs of State Government and State Management of the Ukrainian SSR, fund 4620, invt. 3, file 378, p. 58, quoted in Yu. Yu. Kondufor et al., eds., *History Teaches a Lesson*, trans. from Russian by Vadim Piatkovsky (Kiev: Politvidav Ukrainy, 1986), p. 217.

57. Torzecki, *Polacy i Ukraińcy*, pp. 124-25.

58. Dallin, p. 120.

59. Sabrin et al., p. 51.

60. Armstrong, *Ukrainian Nationalism*, p. 63; also in Dallin, p. 121, n. 3.

61. Torzecki, *Polacy i Ukraińcy*, pp. 127-28.

62. Kubijovyč, *Encyclopedia of Ukraine*, vol. 1, p. 321.

63. Filar, *Przed akcją "Wisła" był Wołyń*, pp. 20-21, n. 33.

64. Shmuel Spector, *The Holocaust of Volhynian Jews 1941-1944* (Jerusalem: Yad Vashem — The Federation of Volhynian Jews, 1990), p. 73.

65. Central State Archives of the October Revolution, Organs of State Government and State Management of the Ukrainian SSR, fund 4620 invt. 3, file 378, p. 53, quoted in Kondufor et al., p. 220.

66. Bandera's letter in German is reprinted in *Ukrainskyi Istoryk* 25, no. 1-4 (1988): 193.

67. Home Army (AK) field report dated November 11, 1941, quoted in Tadeusz Pełczyński et al., eds., *Armia Krajowa w dokumentach 1939-1945*, vol. 2 (London: Studium Polski Podziemnej, 1976), p. 143, quoted in Filar, *Przed akcją "Wisła" był Wołyń*, pp. 12-13.

68. Kosyk, *The Third Reich and Ukraine*, p. 526.

69. Bundesarchiv, Koblenz, R 58/216 f. 20; R 58/216 f. 71, quoted in Filar, *Przed akcją "Wisła" był Wołyń*, p. 12.

70. Sabrin et al., p. 50.

71. See Maria Wardzyńska, *Formacja Wachmannschaften des SS- und Polizeiführers im Distrikt Lublin* (Warszawa: Główna Komisja Badania Zbrodni przeciwko Narodowi Polskiemu, 1992), pp. 10-31.

72. Ukrainian State Museum of the History of the Great Patriotic War (1941-1945), entry book 11479, file 2064, pp. 28-30, quoted in Kondufor et al., pp. 221-22.

73. Bundesarchiv — Militararchiv, Freiburg, RH 20-11/333 Fernschreiben 29735, 18.9.1941, in Filar, *Przed akcją "Wisła" był Wołyń*, p. 12.

74. Torzecki, *Polacy i Ukraińcy*, p. 121.

75. S. Piotrowski, 470-71. For some of the privileges extended to Galician Ukrainians by the Germans, see Torzecki, *Polacy i Ukraińcy*, pp. 121, 131ff, and 158, n. 17; as well as Madajczyk, *Polityka III Rzeszy w okupowanej Polsce*, p. 471.

76. David Littlejohn, *The Patriotic Traitors: The History of Collaboration in German-Occupied Europe, 1940-45* (New York: Doubleday, 1972), p. 316. This was also true of the Ukrainians from the General Government. See Torzecki, *Polacy i Ukraińcy*, p. 121.

77. Hryhorii Mykolaiovych Stetsiuk, *"Chorni dni Volyni": Spohady kolyshnioho zviazkovoho okruzhnoho provodu OUN* (Lutsk, 1992), p. 40; Filar, *Przed akcją "Wisła" był Wołyń*, p. 12.

78. Kosyk, *The Third Reich and Ukraine*, p. 207.
79. Central State Archives of the October Revolution, Organs of State Government and State Management of the Ukrainian SSR, fund CMF-8, v. 454, roll 92, stills 715-17, quoted in Kondufor et al., pp. 223-24.
80. Turowski and Siemaszko, pp. 15, 17-20, 23-24, 27-28, 44, 94; Peretiatkowicz, in Snitko-Rzeszut, pp. 33-34.
81. Władysław Filar, "Rozwój ukraińskiego ruchu niepodległościowego na Wołyniu w latach 1939-1944. Powstanie UPA," in Niedzielko, p. 75.
82. Torzecki, *Polacy i Ukraińcy*, p. 181.
83. Szcześniak and Szota, p. 121.
84. Poliszczuk, *Gorzka prawda*, p. 220; Filar, *Przed akcją "Wisła" był Wołyń*, p. 28; Jerzy Markiewicz, *Nie dali ziemi skąd ich ród. Zamojszczyzna 27 XI 1942-31 XII 1943* (Lublin: Wydawnictwo Lubelskie, 1967), p. 203.
85. Władysław Filar, *"Burza" na Wołyniu: Z dziejów 27 Wołyńskiej Dywizji Piechoty Armii Krajowej* (Warszawa: Rada Ochrony Pamięci Walk i Męczeństwa, 1997), p. 30; and Filar, in Niedzielko, p. 75.
86. Spector, *The Holocaust of Volhynian Jews*, p. 186.
87. Filar, *Przed akcją "Wisła" był Wołyń*, p. 32.
88. Kosyk, *The Third Reich and Ukraine*, p. 261.
89. Otaman Taras Bulba-Borovets, *Armiia bez derzhavy: Slava i trahediia ukrainskoho povstanskoho rukhu. Spohady* (Lviv, 1993), pp. 137-41.
90. Filar, *Przed akcją "Wisła" był Wołyń*, p. 18.
91. Quoted in Szcześniak and Szota, p. 121.
92. Volodymyr, Kubiiovych, *Meni 85* (München: "Malode Zhyttia," 1985), pp. 113-14.
93. Bulba-Borovets, *Armiia bez derzhavy*, 1993, pp. 141-50.
94. Szcześniak and Szota, p. 121.
95. Quoted in Poliszczuk, *Fałszowanie historii*, p. 80.
96. Torzecki, *Polacy i Ukraińcy*, pp. 258-59.
97. Torzecki, *Polacy i Ukraińcy*, p. 225.
98. John A. Armstrong, introduction to *The Ukrainian Division "Galicia," 1943-45. A Memoir* by Wolf-Dietrich Heike (Toronto: The Shevchenko Scientific Society, 1988), p. xix.
99. Armstrong, *Ukrainian Nationalism*, pp. 127-28.
100. Heike, p. 25.
101. Armstrong, *Ukrainian Nationalism*, p. 128.
102. Michael O. Logusz, *Galicia Division: The Waffen-SS 14th Grenadier Division 1943-1945* (Atglen, PA: Schiffer Military History, 1997), p. 17.
103. See Piotrowski, *Poland's Holocaust*, pp. 229-31.
104. Central State Archives of the October Revolution, Organs of State Government and State Management of the Ukrainian SSR, fund 4620, invt. 3, file 378, p. 57, quoted in Kondufor et al., p. 226.
105. A photocopy of the letter of transfer can be found in Sabrin et al., p. 258.
106. Filar, *Przed akcją "Wisła" był Wołyń*, p. 21.
107. Filar, *Przed akcją "Wisła" był Wołyń*, p. 31.
108. Szcześniak and Szota, p. 121.
109. Bulba-Borovets, *Armiia bez derzhavy*, 1981, p. 272. Emphasis added.
110. Filar, *Przed akcją "Wisła" był Wołyń*, p. 32.
111. Józef Turowski, *Pożoga: Walki 27 Wołyńskiej Dywizji AK* (Warszawa: Polskie Wydawnictwo Naukowe, 1990), p. 58.
112. Bulba-Borovets, "Open letter," in *Ukrainskyi Istoryk*.
113. CA KC PZPR AM 1616/16, t. 202/II, k. 41. Department of Internal Affairs, quoted in Filar, *Przed akcją "Wisła" był Wołyń*, p. 54.
114. CA KC PZPR AM 1640/12, t. 202/III/132, k. 253. See Filar, *Przed akcją "Wisła" był Wołyń*, p. 54. The date of the appeal of the Ukrainian Committee of Wołyń is not given by Filar. The appeal can be found in Appendix C: Excerpts from Documents, Ukrainian, "Appeal of the Ukrainian Committee of Wołyń."
115. Filar, *Przed akcją "Wisła" był Wołyń*, pp. 23, 25.
116. See Popek et al., pp. 174-99.
117. Siwicki, p. 430.
118. Torzecki, *Polacy i Ukraińcy*, pp. 194, 220, and 228, n. 58.
119. Torke and Himka, p. 145.
120. *Ridna Zemlia* (Lwów), no. 52, December 26, 1943.
121. Iliuszyn, in Niedzielko, p. 184.
122. Torzecki, *Polacy i Ukraińcy*, p. 257.
123. Henryk Piskunowicz, "'Burza' na Wołyniu," in Snitko-Rzeszut.
124. Pełczyński et al., vol. 3, p. 443.
125. Torzecki, *Kwestia ukraińska w polityce III Rzeszy 1933-1945*, p. 326.
126. Central State Archives of the October

Revolution, Organs of State Government and State Management of the Ukrainian SSR, fund CMF-8, v. 454, roll 24, still 810, quoted in Kondufor et al., p. 236.

127. Shmuel Spector, "Ukrainska Povstanska Armyia," in Israel Gutman, ed., *Encyclopedia of the Holocaust*, 4 vols. (New York: Macmillan, 1990), p. 1531-32.

128. *Ridna Zemlia* (Lwów), no. 16, July 16, 1944.

129. Wasyl Veryha, *Visti Kombatanta* 5 (6), [36-37] (1968): 23.

130. Dallin, p. 622.

131. Poliszczuk, *Fałszowanie historii*, pp. 83-84.

132. Torzecki, *Kwestia ukraińska w polityce III Rzeszy 1933-1945*, p. 333.

133. Armstrong, *Ukrainian Nationalism*, p. 140.

134. Eugeniusz Misiło, ed., *Akcja "Wisła." Dokumenty* (Warszawa: Archiwum Ukraińskie, 1993), p. 17.

135. Hieronim Kubiak, "Polacy i Polonia w ZSRR: Kwestie terminologiczne, periodyzacja, rozmieszczenie przestrzenne, szacunki ilościowe," in Hieronim Kubiak et al., eds., *Mniejszości polskie i Polonia w ZSRR* (Wrocław, Kraków, Warszawa: Zakład Narodowy Imienia Ossolińskich — Wydawnictwo Polskiej Akademii Nauk, 1992), pp. 30-31.

136. Struk, vol. 5, pp. 403, 405.

137. Struk, vol. 3, p. 76.

138. Szcześniak and Szota, p. 427.

139. Jerzy Węgierski, *Armia Krajowa w okręgach Stanisławów i Tarnopol* (Kraków: Platan, 1996), pp. 270-75.

140. Anita E., quoted in Joachim Schoenfeld, ed., *Holocaust Memoirs: Jews in the Lwów Ghetto, the Janowski Concentration Camp, and as Deportees in Siberia* (Hoboken, NJ: KTAV Publishing House, 1985), p. 195.

141. See, for example, the September 1945 order of "Stal" in Drozd, pp. 237-38. An October 1945 leaflet issued by the OUN Provid in Poland states: "We burn and will continue to burn all our resettled villages." Drozd, p. 169.

142. Szcześniak and Szota, pp. 421-23, 530-36.

143. Misiło, *Akcja "Wisła." Dokumenty*, p. 27.

144. Filar, *Przed akcją "Wisła" był Wołyń*, p. 62.

145. In Poliszczuk, *Gorzka prawda*, p. 340. See also Szcześniak and Szota, p. 465.

146. Misiło, *Akcja "Wisła." Dokumenty*, p. 24.

147. Wanda Gałązka, "Notatka informacyjna w sprawie oświadczenia Pani Senator Marii Berny z 17.04.1997r." Warsaw, May 15, 1997. In my possession.

148. Struk, vol. 3, p. 700.

149. Lev Shankovskyi, "Dii UPA i ukrainskoho zbroinoho pidpillia na tereni Peremyshchyny 1944-1947," in B. Zahaikevych, ed., *Peremyshl — zakhidnyi bastion Ukrainy* (New York: Peremyskyi Vydavnychyi Komitet, 1961), p. 196.

150. Struk, vol. 5, p. 395.

151. Misiło, *Akcja "Wisła." Dokumenty*, 32. John A. Armstrong (*Ukrainian Nationalism*, p. 224) states:

> It is impossible to provide a complete analysis of the factors which made protracted resistance by the UPA possible [in Zakerzonnia and elsewhere]. In summary, however, they appear to have been the following: (1) favorable terrain — relatively impenetrable to large bodies of regular troops, yet close to sources of food; (2) nearly unanimous support of the rural population; (3) a fairly large nationality group (about 3,500,000, considering the Ukrainian Catholics alone) as a supporting base; (4) a very powerful — indeed — fanatic nationalist ideology; (5) a highly integrated, authoritarian organizational structure; (6) a considerable period of preparation under favorable conditions; and (7) a moderate degree of outside arms supply at the outset.

152. Misiło, *Akcja "Wisła." Dokumenty*, pp. 402-03, n. 1.

153. Misiło, *Akcja "Wisła." Dokumenty*, p. 461, n. 1.

154. For a fragment of that proclamation see Poliszczuk, *Gorzka prawda*, pp. 372-79, and Żupański, pp. 25-32.

155. In Włodzimierz Bonusiak, ed., *Polska — Niemcy — Ukraina w Europie: Uwarunkowania, założenia i przesłanki wzajemnej współpracy* (Rzeszów: Wydawnictwo Wyższej Szkoły Pedagogicznej, 1996), p. 199.

156. For the text of the appeal, see Piotrowski, *Poland's Holocaust*, pp. 255-56.

Bibliography

The designation "n.p." indicates that no publisher's imprint appears in the work, a fact confirmed by the author in compiling this bibliography. A listing with a city and date but neither a publisher's name nor an "n.p." designation indicates that information on the publisher's imprint was not available.

Ainsztein, Reuben. *Jewish Resistance in Nazi-Occupied Eastern Europe (With a Historical Survey of the Jew as Fighter and Soldier in the Diaspora)*. London: Elek, 1974; New York: Barnes and Noble Books, 1975.

Albert, Zygmunt, ed. *Kaźń profesorów lwowskich, lipiec 1941: Studia oraz relacje i dokumenty*. Wrocław: Wydawnictwo Uniwersytetu Wrocławskiego, 1989.

Alef-Bolkowiak, Gustaw. *Gorące dni: Pamiętnik partyzancki, wyróżniony przez Ministra Obrony Narodowej*. Warszawa, 1962.

Anczarski, Józef. *Kronikarskie zapisy z lat cierpień i grozy w Małopolsce Wschodniej, 1939-1946*. Kraków: n.p., 1996.

Andrusyshen, C. H., and Watson Kirkconnell, trans. *The Poetical Works of Taras Shevchenko: The Kobzar*. Toronto: University of Toronto Press, 1964.

Antybolshevytskyi Blok Narodiv: Zbirka dokumentiv 1941-1956 rr. n.p., 1956.

Arad, Yitzhak, et al., eds. *Einsatzgruppen Reports: Selections from the Dispatches of the Nazi Death Squads' Campaign Against the Jews, July 1941-January 1943*. New York: Holocaust Library, 1989.

Arlt, Fritz. *Polen, Ukrainer, Juden—Politik im Generalgouvernement*. Lindhorst: Wissenschaftlicher, Buchdienst, Herbert, Taege, 1995.

Armstrong, John A. *Ukrainian Nationalism*. 1955. 3d ed., Englewood, CO: Ukrainian Academic Press, 1990.

Bagiński, Tadeusz. *Lipniki Wołynia polskiego*. Elbląg: n.p., 1995.

Bandera, Stepan. (Letter in the German language.) *Ukrainskyi Istoryk* 25, no. 1-4, (1988): 193.

Berkhoff, Karel C. "Ukraine under Nazi Rule (1941-1944): Sources and Finding Aids." *Jahrbücher für Geschichte Osteuropas* (Stuttgart) 45, Part I, no. 1 (1997): 85-103; Part II, no. 2 (1997): 273-309.

Białowąs, Jan. *Zdawało się, że pomarli a oni wciąż żyją: Wspomnienia z życia Polaków i Ukraińców w Ihrowicy oraz tragicznej nocy wigilijnej 1944 roku*. n.p., 1995. Exp. and rev. 2d ed., *Wspomnienia z Ihrowicy na Podolu: Banderowska rzeź ludności polskiej w wigilię 1944 roku*. n.p., 1997.

Biegański, Witold, Mieczysław Juchniewicz, and Stanisław Okęcki. *Polacy w ruchu oporu narodów Europy 1939-1945*. Warszawa: Polskie Wydawnictwo Naukowe, 1977. English ed., *Polish Resistance Movement in Poland and Abroad, 1939-1945*. Warszawa: Polskie Wydawnictwo Naukowe, 1987.

Biskupski, Stanisław, comp. *Świadkowie mówią*. Warszawa: Światowy Związek Żołnierzy Armii Krajowej, Okręg Wołyń, 1996.

Biuletyn (Koło Lwowian) 3 (June, 1982): 8. [Photocopy of an original (May 11, 1944) Ukrainian-Nationalist notice in Cyrillic ordering the Polish people to leave Eastern Galicia or be killed.]

Bizuń, Stanisław. *Historia krzyżem znaczona:*

Wspomnienia z życia Kościoła katolickiego na Ziemi Lwowskiej 1939-1945. Lublin: Oddział Lubelski Stowarzyszenia "Wspólnota Polska," 1993.

Blicharski, Czesław E. *Petruniu, ne ubywaj mene!* Biskupice: n.p., 1998.

Bocheński, Aleksander, Stanisław Łoś, and Władysław Bączkowski. *Problem polsko-ukraiński w Ziemi Czerwieńskiej.* Warszawa: Polityka, 1938.

Bociurkiw, Bohdan Rostyslav. *The Ukrainian Greek Catholic Church and the Soviet State, 1939-1950.* Edmonton: Canadian Institute of Ukrainian Studies Press, 1996.

Bohachevskyi, Danylo. *Na vozi i pid vozom: Kartyny z zhyttia halytskoho voiaka i pravnyka.* Toronto, 1976.

Boiko, Maksym. *Bibliohrafichnyi ohliad zbroinoi borotby Volyni.* Pratsi Oseredka Bibliohrafii Volyni, no. 11. Toronto, 1976.

———. *Kulturna pratsia volynian u Pivnichnii Amerytsi.* Pratsi Oseredka Bibliohrafii Volyni, no. 13. Bloomington, IN, 1978.

———. *Volyniiana—Materiialy do bibliohrafii.* Pratsi Oseredka Bibliohrafii Volyni, no. 8. Bloomington, IN, 1973.

Bonusiak, Włodzimierz. *Kto zabił profesorów lwowskich?* Rzeszów: Krajowa Agencja Wydawnicza Rzeszów, 1989.

———, ed. *Polska—Niemcy—Ukraina w Europie: Uwarunkowania, założenia i przesłanki wzajemnej współpracy.* Rzeszów: Wydawnictwo Wyższej Szkoły Pedagogicznej, 1996.

Boshyk, Yury, et al. *A Guide to the Archival and Manuscript Collection of the Ukrainian Academy of Arts and Sciences in the U.S., New York City: A Detailed Inventory.* Canadian Institute of Ukrainian Studies Research Report, no. 30. Edmonton, 1988.

———, ed. *Ukraine During World War II: History and Its Aftermath, a Symposium.* Edmonton: Canadian Institute of Ukrainian Studies, 1986.

Bulba-Borovets, Otaman Taras. *Armiia bez derzhavy: Slava i trahediia ukrainskoho povstanskoho rukhu. Spohady.* Winnipeg: Tovarystvo "Volyn," 1981; Lviv, 1993 (with omissions of sections on Jews and OUN-B).

———. "Open letter [of August 10, 1943] to members of the Provid of the Organization of Ukrainian Nationalists of Stepan Bandera." *Ukrainskyi Istoryk* 27, no. 1-4 (1990): 114-19.

Butsko, Olexander M. *Never to be Forgotten...* Kiev: Ukraina Society, 1986.

Chartoryskyi, Mykola S. *Mizh molotom i kovadlom: Prychynky do istorii U.P.A. (Spomyny 1942-1945 rr.).* New York, 1970.

———. *Vid Sianu po Krym (Spomyny uchasnyka III Pokhidnoi Grupy-Pivden).* New York, 1951.

Cherednychenko, Vitalii. *Anatomiia predatelstva: Ukrainskii burzhuaznyi natsionalizm orudie antisovetskoi politiki imperializma.* Kiev: Izd-voapolit. literatury Ukrainy, 1983.

———. *Collaborationists.* Kiev: Politvidav Ukrainy, 1975.

———. *Kontrrevoliutsiia na eksport: Ukrainskii burzhuaznyi natsionalizm v arsenale sovremennogo antikommunizma.* Kiev: Izdvoapolit. literatury Ukrainy, 1985.

———. *Truth and Myths about UPA.* Lviv: Kamenyar, 1981.

———. *Ukrainskyi bruzhuaznyi natsionalizm: Zahetrennia ideino-orghanizatsiinoi kryzy, krah.* Kiev: Vyshcha Shkola, 1986.

Chirovsky, Nicholas. *Ukraine and the Second World War.* New York, 1985.

Chojnowska, Aldona. "Operacja 'Wisła': Przesiedlenie ludności ukraińskiej na ziemie zachodnie i północne w 1947 r." *Zeszyty Historyczne* (Paris) 102 (1992): 3-102.

Chojnowski, Andrzej. *Koncepcje polityki narodowościowej rządów polskich w latach 1921-1939.* Warszawa: Zakład Narodowy im Ossolińskich, 1979.

Chubai, Mstyslav Z. *Reid orhanizatoriv OUN vid Popradu po Chorne more.* München, 1952.

Cieślak, T. *Hitlerowski sojusz z nacjonalizmem ukraińskim w Polsce.* Warszawa, 1968.

Colvin, J. *Das Problem der Westukraine.* Berlin, 1939.

Cybulski, Henryk. *Czerwone noce.* 1969. Rev. 5th ed., Warszawa: Ministerstwo Obrony Narodowej, 1990.

Cyprian, Brat. (Letter from Krzemieniec, dated June 7, 1943.) *Karta* (Warszawa) 8 (1992): 65.

Czerwiński, Józef. *Z wołyńskich lasów na berliński trakt.* Warszawa: Ministerstwo Obrony Narodowej, 1985.

Dallin, Alexander. *German Rule in Russia, 1941-1945: A Study of Occupation Policies.* 1957. London: Macmillan, 1981.

Danyliuk, Mykhailo. *Povstanskyi zapysnyk.* New York: Dzherzi Syti, 1968; Kiev, 1993.

Darski, Józef. *Ukraina: Historia, współczesność, konflikty narodowe.* Warszawa: Instytut Polityczny, 1993.

Dębski, Jerzy, and Leon Popek, comps. *Okrutna przestroga.* Lublin: Towarzystwo Przyjaciół Krzemieńca i Ziemi Wołyńsko-Podolskiej, 1997.

Dębski, Włodzimierz Sławosz. *Antylitopys UPA*. Lublin: Motor, 1995.

———. *W kręgu kościoła kisielińskiego czyli Wołyniacy z parafii Kisielin*. Lublin: n.p., 1992.

Denisov, V. N., and G. I. Changuli, eds. *Nazi Crimes in Ukraine, 1941-1944: Documents and Materials*. Comp. A. F. Vysotsky et al. Trans. V. I. Biley et al. Kiev: Naukova Dumka Publishers, 1987.

"Die führenden ukrainischen Kreise Iehnen Bandera und Stecko ab, glaubten aber, dass Regierungsbildung im Einvernehmen mit dem Reich." Ereignismeldung UdSSR no. 23, July 15, 1941. U.S. National Archives microfilm T175, reel 233, frame 721518.

Dobrivlianskyi, P. *Ukraina v druhii svitovii viini: U svitli faktiv*. Philadelphia, 1963.

"Dokumenty z okresu mordowania Polaków w Małopolsce Wschodniej w czasie ostatniej wojny." *Biuletyn* (Koło Lwowian), no. 43 (June, 1982): 8-9.

Dontsov, Dmytro. *Khrestom i mechem*. Toronto: n.p., 1967.

———. *Natsionalizm*. Lwów: n.p., 1926; London: The Ukrainian Publishers, 1966.

Dmytryk, Ivan. *U lisakh Lemkivshchyny: Spomyny voiaka UPA*. München: Suchasnist, 1982.

Drozd, Roman. *Ukraińska Powstańcza Armia: Dokumenty — struktury*. Warszawa: Burchard Edition, 1998.

Dróżdż-Satanowska, Zofia, et al., eds. *Przez uroczyska Polesia i Wołynia: Wspomnienia Polaków uczestników radzieckiego ruchu partyzanckiego*. Warszawa: Ministerstwo Obrony Narodowej, 1962.

Drożdżyński, Aleksander, and Jan Zaborowski. *Oberländer: Przez Ostforschung, "wywiad i NSDAP do rządu" NRF*. Poznań: Wydawnictwo Zachodnie, 1960.

Drugi powszechny spis ludności z dnia 9.XII.1931r. Statystyka Polski, seria C, zeszyt 70, województwo wołyńskie. Warszawa: Główny Urząd Statystyczny Rzeczypospolitej Polskiej, 1938.

Druzhyny Ukrainskykh Natsionalistiv: Zbirka spohadiv uchasnykiv. n.p.: Ukrainskoho samostiinyka and Obiednannia Ukrainskykh Kombantantiv, 1953.

Druzhyny Ukrainskykh Natsionalistiv v 1941-42 rokakh. München: Nasha Knyhozbirnia, 1953.

Dumin, Osip [Osyp Dumyn]. "Prawda o Ukraińskiej Organizacji." Written in May 1926. Received in Berlin on June 17, 1926. Translated from German. *Zeszyty Historyczne* (Paris) 30 (1974): 103-37.

Dziemiańczuk, Władysław, comp. *Wybaczyć nie znaczy zapomnieć*. Toronto: Związek Ziem Wschodnich RP, 1996.

Evintov, V., V. Leonenko, and A. Shishko. *No Statute of Limitations for War Criminals*. Translated from Russian by Nina Brezhko and Valentin Markelov. Kiev: Politvidav Ukrainy Publishers, 1986.

Fajkowski, Józef, and Jan Religa. *Zbrodnie hitlerowskie na wsi polskiej 1939-1945*. Warszawa: Książka i Wiedza, 1981.

Fedorowski, G. *Leśne ognie*. 1965. Warszawa: Ministerstwo Obrony Narodowej, 1983.

Feliński, M. *The Ukrainians in Poland*. London: n.p., 1931.

Fiala, Jan. "Československá Armáda v boji protiv banderovcům v roce 1947." *Historie a vojenství* 3 (1960).

———. *Zpráva o Akci B*. Vyšehrad: n.p., 1994.

Fijałka, Michał. *27. Wołyńska Dywizja Piechoty AK*. Warszawa: Instytut Wydawniczy Pax, 1986.

Filar, Władysław. *"Burza" na Wołyniu: Z dziejów 27 Wołyńskiej Dywizji Piechoty Armii Krajowej*. Warszawa: Rada Ochrony Pamięci Walk i Męczeństwa, 1997.

———. *Eksterminacja ludności polskiej na Wołyniu w Drugiej Wojnie Swiatowej*. Warszawa: n.p., 1999.

———. "Zbrodnicza działalność OUN-UPA przeciwko ludności polskiej na Wołyniu w latach 1942-1944." *Semper Fidelis* (Wrocław) 5, no. 28 (September-October 1995): 3-5.

———, ed. *Przed akcją "Wisła" był Wołyń*. Warszawa: Światowy Związek Żołnierzy Armii Krajowej, Okręg Wołyń, 1997.

Filonenko, Petro. *Zbroina borotba na Volyni: Spomyn uchasnyka*. Winnipeg: Volynskyi Vydavnychyi Fond, 1958.

Friedman, Saul, ed. *Holocaust Literature. A Handbook of Critical, Historical, and Literary Writings*. Westport, CT: Greenwood Press, 1993.

Giertych, Jędrzej. "O przeprowadzonej przez Ukraińców rzezi polskiej ludności." *Komunikaty Towarzystwa imiemia Romana Dmowskiego* (London) 2, no. 1 (1979-80): 300-52.

Golczewski, Frank. "Ukraińska karta niemieckiej akcji przeciwko Polsce." *Niepodległość: Czasopismo Poświęcone Najnowszym Dziejom Polski* (New York, London, Wrocław) 46, no. 26 (1993): 231-38.

Gross, Edward. *Tragedia Podola*. Warszawa: PoliKart, 1995.

Gutman, Israel, ed. *Encyclopedia of the Holocaust.* 4 vols. New York: Macmillan, 1990.

Hai-Holovko, Oleksa. *Poedynok z dyiavolom: Filmy nashikh dniv.* 2 vols. Winnipeg: Ivan Tyktor, 1950. English ed., Oleksa Hay-Holowko. *Duel with the Devil.* Winnipeg: Communigraphics, 1986.

Halan, Iaroslav. *Ludy bez batkivshchyny.* Kiev, 1967.

Hanusiak, Michael. *Lest We Forget.* New York: Ukrainian-American League, 1973; Toronto: Progress Books, 1976.

Heike, Wolf-Dietrich. *Sie wollten die Freiheit: Die Geschichte der Ukrainischen Division 1943-1945.* Dornheim/H., 1973. Exp. Ukrainian ed., Volf-Ditrikh Haike. *Ukrainska Dyviziia "Halychyna": Istoriia formuvannia i boiovykh dii u 1943-45 rokakh.* Zapysky Naukovoho Tovarystva im. Shevchenka, vol. 188. Paris, Toronto, München, 1970. English ed., Wolf-Dietrich Heike. *The Ukrainian Division "Galicia," 1943-45: A Memoir.* Edited by Yury Boshyk. Translated by Andriy Wynnyckyj. Introduction by John A. Armstrong. Toronto: The Shevchenko Scientific Society, 1988.

Heiman, Leo, ed. "We Fought for Ukraine! The Story of Jews with the UPA." *Ukrainian Quarterly* 20, no. 1 (1964): 33-44.

Hermaszewski, Władysław. *Echa Wołynia.* Warszawa: Bellona, 1995.

Hillebrandt, B. "Działalność bojowa zgrupowania polskich oddziałów partyzanckich na Polesiu, Wołyniu i Lubelszczyźnie w latach 1942-1944." *Wojskowy Przegląd Historyczny* 3 (1961): 40-58.

Himka, John-Paul. "Western Ukraine Between the Wars." *Canadian Slavonic Papers* 34, no. 44 (December 1992): 391-412.

Himmelraikh, Kost [noms de guerre "Shelest," "Kyi"]. *Spohady komandyra viddilu osoblyvoho pryznachennia "UPA-Skhid."* Litopys, vol. 15. Toronto: Litopys UPA, 1987.

Hirniak, Kost. *Ukrainskyi Lehion Samooborony: Prychynky do istorii.* Toronto, 1977.

———, and Ostap Chuiko. *Front Ukrainskoi Revoliutsii: Prychynok do istorii zbroinoi borotby Volyni.* Toronto, 1979.

Hlid, Stepan. *Fragmenty zhyttia i muk: Spohady z chasiv nimetskoi okupatsii Ukrainy.* London, 1955.

Hofman, Jiří. *Češi na Volyni.* Praha: n.p., 1995.

Holzer, Jerzy. *Mozaika polityczna Drugiej Rzeczypospolitej.* Warszawa: Książka i Wiedza, 1974.

Hontar, Ivan. *Molochnyi shliakh: Spomyny — avtobiohrafiia.* 1955. Toronto: n.p., 1994.

Hordiienko, Mykola. *Z volynskykh i poliskykh reidiv: Iz dii UPA-Pivnich, 1943-44.* Toronto, 1959.

Hryniewiecki, Witold. *My z Zamojszczyzny.* 2d ed. Warszawa: Pax, 1988.

Huk, Bohdan, comp. *Zakerzonnia: Spohady voiakiv Ukrainskoi Povstanskoi Armii.* Vol. 1. Warszawa: Ukrainskyi Arkhiv, 1994.

Hunchak, Taras. *U mundyrakh voroha.* Kiev, 1993.

———, and Roman Solchanyk, comps. *Ukrainska suspilno-polytychna dumka v 20 stolitti: Dokumenty i materiialy,* vol. 3. München, 1983.

Ievdokymenko, Volodymyr. *Krytyka ideinykh osnov ukrainskoho burzhuaznoho natsionalizmu.* Kiev: Nauk. Duma, 1967.

Ilnytskyi, Roman. *Deutschland und die Ukraine, 1934-1945. Tatsachen europäischer Ostpolitik, ein Vorbericht.* 2 vols. München: Osteuropa Institut, 1958.

Istoriia ukrainskoho viiska. Winnipeg: Ivan Tyktor, 1953.

Janicki, Jerzy. *Towarzystwo Weteranów...: 2. Alfabet Lwowski.* Warszawa: Polska Oficyna Wydawnicza "BGW," 1994.

Janicki, Zenobiusz. *W obronie Przebraża i w drodze do Berlina.* Lublin: Ardablju S.C., 1997.

Janik, Bronisław. *Było ich trzy.* Warszawa: Książka i Wiedza, 1970.

Jastrzębski, Stanisław. *Oko w oko z banderowcami: Wspomnienia małoletniego żołnierza Armii Krajowej.* Katowice: n.p., 1994; Exp. 2d ed., Warszawa: Wydawnictwo Archidiecezji Warszawskiej, 1996.

Jędrzejewicz, Wacław, ed. *Diplomat in Berlin, 1933-1939: Papers and Memoirs of Józef Lipski, Ambassador of Poland.* New York: Columbia University Press, 1968.

Juchniewicz, Mieczysław. *Na wschód od Bugu.* Warszawa: Ministerstwo Obrony Narodowej, 1985.

Jurewicz, Lesław. *Niepotrzebny.* London: Polska Fundacja Kulturalna, 1977.

Juzwenko, Bernard. *Syn ziemi Podolskiej: Wspomnienia — relacje.* Wrocław, 1996.

Kalba, Myroslav. *"Nachtigal" (Kurin DUN): u svitli faktiv i dokumentiv.* Denver: Ukapress, 1984.

———. *Nachtigal. Ukraiński Batalion 1941r.* Detroit: Wydawnictwo Drużyny Ukraińskich Nacjonalistów, 1995.

———, comp. *U lavakh druzhynnykiv: Spohady uchasnykiv.* Denver: Vyd. Druzhyn Ukrainskykh Natsionalistiv, 1982.

Kamenetsky, Ihor. "Dokumenty pro ukrainskykh partyzaniv." *Ukrainskyi Istoryk* 25, no. 1-4 (1988): 188-96.
———. *Hitler's Occupation of Ukraine 1941-1944: A Study of Totalitarian Imperialism.* Milwaukee: Marquette University Press, 1956.
———. *Secret Nazi Plans for Europe: A Study of Lebensraum Policies.* New York: Bookman Associates, 1961.
———. "Some Aspects of Ukrainian Politics of National Self-Determination in View of Hitler's 'Drang nach Osten': Analysis of Prof. W. Kosyk's Documentation on the Third Reich and the Ukrainian Question." *Ukrainskyi Istoryk* 29, no. 1-4 (1990): 104-27.
Kania, Janusz. "Likwidacja cerkwi na Lubelszczyźnie w okresie międzywojennym." *Chrześcijanin w świecie* 14, no. 6 (1982): 50-89.
Kaniewski, Stanisław. "Informacja o stanie śledztw prowadzonych w Głównej Komisji Badania Zbrodni przeciwko Narodowi Polskiemu — Instytucie Pamięci Narodowej wygłoszona na XVII zjeździe Okręgu Wołyń Światowego Związku Żołnierzy AK, 23 sierpnia 1997r." *Biuletyn Informacyjny.* (Światowy Związek Żołnierzy AK, Okręg Wołyń, Warszawa) 3, no. 55 (July-August 1997).
Kasiian, Stepan. *Vohonrodytsia z iskry...: Rozpovid Stepana Kasiiana (Karpa), ioho spohady z pidpillia i partyzantky.* Toronto, 1967.
Kazanivskyi, Bohdan. *Shliakhom legendy: Spomyny.* London, 1975.
Kedryn-Rudnytskyi, Ivan. *Zhyttia — podii — liudy.* New York, 1976.
Klietmann, Kurt-Georg. *Die Waffen-SS: Eine Dokumentation.* Osnabrück: Verlag Der Freiwillige, 1965.
Klukowski, Zygmunt. *Diary from the Years of Occupation, 1939-44.* Ed. Andrew Klukowski and Helen Klukowski May. Trans. George Klukowski. Chicago: University of Illinois Press, 1993.
Klymyshyn, Mykola. *V pokhodi do voli: Spomyny.* Vol. 1. Toronto, 1975.
Knysh, Zynovii [Bohdan Mykhailiuk, pseud.]. *Bunt Bandery.* 3d ed. Toronto: n.p., 1950. (Published under the pseudonym.)
———. *Iaroslav Baranovskyi: Zhertva zloby i nenavysty.* Paris, 1990.
———. *Pered pokhodom na skhid: Spohady i materiialy do diiannia Orhanizatsii Ukrainskykh Natsionalistiv u 1939-1941 rokakh,* vols. 1-2. Toronto: n.p., n.d.
———. *Spohady i materiialy do diiannia OUN naperedodni nimetsko-moskovskoi viiny 1941 r.* Toronto: n.p., n.d.
———, ed. *Nepohasnyi ohon viry: Zbirnyk pa poshanu polkovnyka Andriia Melnyka, holovy Provodu Ukrainskykh Natsionalistiv.* Paris, 1974.
Kobylański, Władysław. *W szponach trzech wrogów.* Chicago: Wici, 1988.
Komański, Henryk. "Eksterminacja polskiej ludności: Powiat Radziechów." *Na Rubieży* (Wrocław) 4, no. 10 (1994): 4-14.
———. "Zagłada polskiej wsi Jeziorany Szlacheckie (19-23 czerwca 1943 roku)." *Semper Fidelis* (Wrocław) 2, no. 15 (1993): 21-27; and 3, no. 16 (1993): 16-22.
Komisja Historyczna Polskiego Sztabu Głównego w Londynie. *Polskie Siły Zbrojne w Drugiej wojnie światowej. Tom 3. Armia Krajowa.* London: Instytut Historyczy im. Gen. Sikorskiego, 1950.
Kondufor, Yu. Yu., I. F. Kuras, A. G. Mityukov, and V. I. Yurchuk, eds. *History Teaches a Lesson.* Translated from Russian by Vadim Piatkovsky. Kiev: Politvidav Ukrainy, 1986.
Konieczny, Zdzisław, ed. *Źródła do dziejów regionu przemyskiego w latach 1944-1949.* Przemyśl: Wojewódzkie Archiwum Państwowe w Przemyślu, 1979.
Konovalets, Ievhen. *Prychynky do istorii ukrainskoi revoliutsii.* 2d ed. n.p.: Provid Ukrainskykh Natsionalistiv, 1948.
Korman, Aleksander. *Nieukarane zbrodnie SS-Galizien z lat 1943-1945.* London: Koło Lwowian, 1990.
———. "Osobowe i materialne straty Polaków wynikłe z działalności terrorystów OUN-UPA." *Semper Fidelis* (Wrocław) 2, no. 15, (1993): 18-20.
———. *Piąte przykazanie Boskie: Nie zabijaj!* London: Koło Lwowian, 1989.
———. "W 50. rocznicę Operacji 'Wisła': UPA — formacja zbrodnicza." *Na Rubieży* (Wrocław) 2, no. 21 (1997): 1-10.
———. "Zbrodnia OUN-UPA w Połowcach." *Semper Fidelis* (Wrocław) 4, no. 5 (1990): 9-11.
———. *Z krwawych dni Lwowa 1941 roku.* London: Koło Lwowian, 1990.
Kosek, Karol. *Od wyzwolicieli zachowaj nas Panie: Wspomnienia z Wołynia, 1939-1944.* Wrocław, 1997.
Kosyk, Wolodymyr [Volodymyr Kosyk]. *The Third Reich and Ukraine.* New York: Peter Lang, 1993.

_____. *Ukraina i Nimechchyna u druhii svitovii viini.* New York: n.p., 1993.

_____. *Ukraina pid chas druhoi svitovoi viiny, 1938-1945.* Kyiv, Paris, Toronto, New York, 1992.

_____. "'Ukrainskyi Istoryk' pro OUN i UPA." *Ukrainskyi Istoryk* 31, no. 1-4 (1994): 82-89.

_____, ed. *The Third Reich and the Ukrainian Question: Documents 1934-1944.* London, 1991.

Koval, M. V. *My ukraintsi!* n.p., 1948.

_____. "OUN-UPA: mizh 'tretim reikhom' i stalinskym totalitaryzmom." *Ukrainskyi Istorychnyi Zhurnal,* no. 2-3 (1994): 94-101.

_____, et al., comps. "OUN i UPA u druhii svitovii viini." *Ukrainskyi Istorychnyi Zhurnal* (1994) no. 2-3: 102-29, no. 4: 89-107, no. 5: 98-115, no. 6: 98-114; (1995) no. 1: 87-108, no. 2: 93-122, no. 3: 101-23, no. 5: 100-08.

Krokhmaliuk, Roman. *Zahrava na skhodi: Spohady i dokumenty z pratsi u Viiskovoi upravi "Halychyna" v 1943-1945 rokakh.* Toronto: Bratstvo kol. Voiakiv 1-o Ukrainskoi Dyvizii UNA, 1978.

Krychevskyi, Roman. *Orhanizatsiia Ukrainskykh Natsionalistiv v Ukraini; Orhanizatsiia Ukrainskykh Natsionalistiv zakordonom i ZCh OUN: Prychynok do istorii Ukrainskoho natsionalistychnoho rukhu.* New York: Vydavnytstvo Politychnoi Rady Odnodumtsiv OUN v SSHA, 1962; Lviv: Memorial, 1991.

Kubiak, Hieronim, et al., eds. *Mniejszości polskie i Polonia w ZSRR.* Wrocław, Kraków, Warszawa: Zakład Narodowy Imienia Ossolińskich — Wydawnictwo Polskiej Akademii Nauk, 1992.

Kubiiovych, Volodymyr [Volodymyr Kubijovč]. *Meni 85.* München: "Malode Zhyttia," 1985.

_____. "Moi vizyty u Mytropolyta Andreia Sheptytskoho." *Ukrainskyi Istoryk* 26, no. 1-3 (1989): 121-23.

_____. *Ukraintsi v Heneralnii Hubernii: 1939-1941.* Chicago: Vydavnytstvo Mykoly Denysiuka, 1975.

_____, ed. *Encyclopedia of Ukraine,* vols. 1-2. Toronto: University of Toronto Press, vol. 1, 1984; vol. 2, 1988.

Kubów, Władysław. *Polacy i Ukraińcy w Berezowicy Małej koło Zbaraża: Wspomnienia.* 2d ed. Warszawa: Autorska Spółka Wydawnicza Alexander, 1994. 3d ed., *Polacy i Ukraińcy na Podolu: Tragedia Polaków w Berezowicy Małej koło Zbaraża.* Wrocław: n.p., 1997.

Kuczyński, Józef. *Między parafią a łagrem.* Paris: Éditions Spotkania, 1985.

Kunicki, Mikołaj. *Pamiętnik "Muchy."* 1959. 3d ed., Warszawa: Ministerstwo Obrony Narodowej, 1971.

Kupetskyi, Hrytsko. *Tam, de sontse skhodyt: Spohady boiovyka OUN na Dalekomu Skhodi.* Toronto: Vydavnytstvo Viktora Polishchuka, 1988.

Kupiak, Dmytro. *Spohady nerostrilanoho.* Toronto: n.p., 1991.

Kurdybelski, Jan. "Wołyński rodowód parafii Minkowice Oławskie koło Wrocławia." *Semper Fidelis* (Wrocław) 5, no. 22 (1994): 21-24; and 6, no. 23 (1994): 19-23.

Kuropas, Myron B. *The Ukrainian Americans: Roots and Aspirations, 1884-1954.* Toronto: University of Toronto Press, 1991.

Kuzych-Berezovskyi, Ivan. *Berezivski boiarstvo na tli istorii Ukraiiny.* Detroit, 1962.

Landwehr, Richard. *Fighting for Freedom: The Ukrainian Volunteer Division of the Waffen-SS.* Silver Springs, MD: Bibliophile Legion Books, 1985.

Lappo, Henryk, et al., eds. *Z Kresów Wschodnich Rzeczypospolitej: Wspomnienia z osad wojskowych, 1921-1940.* 1992. Exp. 2d ed., London: Ognisko Rodzin Osadników Kresowych, 1998.

Lapychak, Toma. *Ukrainskyi natsionalizm.* New York: n.p., 1962.

Lebed, Mykola. *UPA: Ukrainska Povstanska Armiia: Ii heneza, rist i dii u vyzvolnii borotbi ukrainskoho narodu za Ukrainsku Samostiinu Sobornu Derzhavu.* n.p.: Presove Biuro UHVR, 1946. Exp. 2d ed., *UPA: Ukrainska Povstanska Armiia. 1 chastyna: Nimetska okupatsia Ukrainy.* München: Suchasnist, 1987; Drohobych, 1993.

Littlejohn, David. *Foreign Legions of the Third Reich.* 4 vols. San Jose, CA: R. James Bender Publishing, 1985.

_____. *The Patriotic Traitors: The History of Collaboration in German-Occupied Europe, 1940-45.* New York: Doubleday, 1972.

Liubchenko, Arkadii. *Shchodennyk: Knyzhka persha.* Toronto, 1951.

Logusz, Michael O. *Galicia Division: The Waffen-SS 14th Grenadier Division 1943-1945.* Atglen, PA: Schiffer Military History, 1997.

Łoziński, E. "Obrona Przebraża 30 sierpnia 1943 roku." *Wojskowy Przegląd Historyczny* 2 (1964): 293-99.

Łuczak, Czesław. *Polska i Polacy w drugiej wojnie światowej.* Poznań: Wydawnictwo Naukowe Uniwersytetu imienia Adama Mickiewicza, 1993.

Łużny, Ryszard, ed. *Chrześcijański wschód a kultura polska.* Lublin: Katolicki Uniwersytet Lubelski, 1989.

Lyisak, Oleh. *Brody, Zbirnyk stattei i narysiv.* München, 1951.

―――, ed. *Bii pid Brodamy: Zbirnyk stattei u trydtsiatylittia.* New York: 1-oi Ukr. dyvizii Ukr. natsionalnoi armii, 1974.

Madajczyk, Czesław. *Polityka III Rzeszy w okupowanej Polsce.* 2 vols. Warszawa: Państwowe Wydawnictwo Naukowe, 1970.

―――, ed. *Zamojszczyzna—Sonderlaboratorium SS: Zbiór dokumentów polskich i niemieckich z okresu okupacji hitlerowskiej.* 2 vols. Warszawa: Ludowa Spółdzielnia Wydawnicza, 1977.

Magocsi, Paul Robert. *Galicia: A Historical Survey and Bibliographic Guide.* Toronto: University of Toronto Press in association with the Canadian Institute of Ukrainian Studies and the Harvard Ukrainian Research Institute, 1983.

―――. *A History of Ukraine.* Toronto: University of Toronto Press: Toronto, 1996.

Malashchuk, Roman. *Z knyhy moho zhyttia: Spomyny,* vol. 1: *Vyrostesh ty, synu, vyrushysh v dorohu.* Toronto, 1987.

Mańkowski, Zygmunt. *Między Wisłą a Bugiem 1939-1944: Studium o polityce okupanta i postawach społeczeństwa.* Lublin: Wydawnictwo Lubelskie, 1978.

Manuilskyi, Dmytro. *Ukrainsko-nimetski natsionalisty na sluzhbi u fashystskoi Nimechchyny: Dopovid 6-ho sichnia 1945 roku na naradi uchyteliv zakhadnykh oblastei Ukrainy.* Kiev: Ukrainske Derzhavne Vydavnytsvo, 1945.

Mariański, Antoni. *A w krzaku było mrowisko...* Opole: Wydawnictwo Św. Krzyża, 1993.

Markiewicz, Jerzy. *Nie dali ziemi skąd ich ród: Zamojszczyzna 27 XI 1942-31 XII 1943.* Lublin: Wydawnictwo Lubelskie, 1967.

―――. *Partyzancki kraj.* 2d ed. Lublin: Wydawnictwo Lubelskie, 1985.

Marrus, Michael R., ed. *The Nazi Holocaust: Historical Articles on the Destruction of European Jews. Vol. 5, Public Opinion and Relations to the Jews in Nazi Europe.* 2 vols. Westport, CT: Meckler, 1989.

Martynets, V. *Ukrainske pidpillia vid UVO do OUN: Spohadi i materialy do peredistorii ta istorii ukrainskoho orhanizovanoho natsionalizmu.* Winnipeg: n.p., 1949.

Marunchak, Mykhailo H., ed. *V borotbi za ukrainsku derzhavu: Esei, spohady, svidchennia, litopysannia, dokumenty Druhoi svitovoi viiny.* Winnipeg: Svitova Liga Ukrainskykh Politychnykh Viazniv, 1990.

Matla, Zynovii. *Pivdenna pokhidna hrupa.* München: Nasha Knyhozbirnia, 1952.

Medynskyi, Stepan. *Dyviziinymy stezhkamy: Spohady.* Toronto, 1991.

Micgiel, John. "Zapatrzeni w przeszłość. Stosunki polsko-ukraińskie według źródeł." *Suchasnist: literatura, mystetstvo, suspilne zhttia. Zeszyt w języku polskim,* no. 1-2 (1985): 145-57.

Mikhnovskyi, Mykola. *Samostiina Ukraina.* Lwów: E. Kosevych, 1900.

Mirchuk, Petro. *Akt vidnovlennia ukrainskoi derzhavnosty 30. chervnia 1941 roku: Ioho geneza ta polytychne i istorychne znachennia.* New York: Vyd. Holovnoi upravy Orhanizatsii Oborony Chotyrokh Svobid Ukrainy, 1952.

―――. *Ievhen Konovalets: U 20-richchia smerty.* Toronto: Liga Vyzvolennia Ukrainy, 1958.

―――. *Narys istorii Orhanizatsii Ukrainskykh Natsionalistiv 1920-1939.* München: Ukrainske Vydavnytstvo, 1968.

―――. *Revoliutsiinyi smah za USSD: Khto taki "banderivtsi," "melnykivtsi," "dviikari,"* vols. 1-2. New York, Toronto, London, 1985-1987.

―――. *Roman Shukhevych.* New York: T-vo Kolyshnikh Voiakiv UPA z ZSA, Kanadi i Evropi, 1970.

―――. *Stepan Bandera: symvol revoliutsiinoi bezkompromisovosty.* New York: Orhanizatsiia Oborony Chotyrokh Svobid Ukrainy, 1961.

―――. *Ukrainska povstanska armiia, 1941-1952.* München, 1953.

―――, and V. Davydenko, eds. *V riadakh UPA: Zbirka spomyniv buv. voiakiv Ukrainskoi Povstanskoi Armii.* New York, 1957.

Misiło, Eugeniusz. "Polskie 'bandy UPA.'" *Karta* (Warszawa) 2 (February 1991): 122-28.

―――, comp. "Kwestia ukraińska w polityce polskiego rządu i podziemia w latach 1939-1944. Dokumenty." *Zustriczi* (Warszawa), no. 3-4 (1990): 141-72.

―――, ed. *Akcja "Wisła." Dokumenty.* Warszawa: Archiwum Ukraińskie, 1993.

Molchanov, Vladimir. *There Shall Be Retribution: Nazi War Criminals and Their Protectors.* Moscow: Progress Publishers, 1981.

Motyka, Grzegorz. "Od Wołynia do akcji 'Wisła.'" *Więź* 473, no. 3 (March 1998): 109-31.

———. "Ukraińska orientacja." *Karta* (Warszawa) 23 (1997): 48-73.

Motyl, Alexander J. "The Rural Origins of the Communist and Nationalist Movements in Wołyń *Województwo*, 1921-1939." *Slavic Review* 37 (September 1978): 412-20.

———. *The Turn to the Right: The Ideological Origins and Development of Ukrainian Nationalism, 1919-1929*. Boulder, CO: East European Monographs, 1980.

———. "Ukrainian Nationalist Political Violence in Inter-War Poland, 1921-1939." *East European Quarterly* 19 (March 1985): 45-55.

Mroczkowski, Józef. "Kronika parafii w Oleszycach." *Karta* (Warszawa) 22 (1997): 42-71.

Muzyka, Agnieszka. "Relacja świadka Agnieszki Muzyki." *Na Rubieży* (Wrocław) 2, no. 3 (1993): 15-16.

Mykhalchuk, Vasyl, ed. *Tudy, de bii za voliu: Zbirnyk viiskovo-politychnykh materialiv u pamiat Maksyma Skorupskoho-Maksa Kurinnoho UPA*. London, Paris: Fundatsiia im. O. Olzhycha, 1989; Kyiv: "Kozaky," 1992.

Myśliwski, Wiesław, comp. *Wschodnie losy Polaków*. 4 vols. Łomża: "Stopka," 1991.

Nakonechnyi, Vladyslav. *Mertvi zaklikaiut zhyvykh*. Lutsk, 1994.

Na Rubieży. Wrocław: Stowarzyszenie Upamiętnienia Ofiar Zbrodni Ukraińskich Nacjonalistów. Series.

Nicieja, Stanisław Sławomir. "Mord na Zboczu Kadeckim we Lwowie." *Miesięcznik Społeczno-Kulturalny* (Opole) 4 (1983).

Niedzielko, Romuald, ed. *Polska—Ukraina: Trudne pytania. Materiały II międzynarodowego seminarium historycznego "Stosunki polsko-ukraińskie w latach 1918-1947," Warszawa, 22-24 maja 1997*. 2 vols. Warszawa: Światowy Związek Żołnierzy Armii Krajowej—Związek Ukraińców w Polsce, 1998.

Novosad, Petro. *Z Ukrainoiu v sertsi: Spohady*. Lviv, 1995.

Obviniaet zemlia. Organizatsiia Ukrainskikh Natsionalistov: Dokumenty i materialy. Moskva, 1991.

Oliwa, Apolinary. *Gdy poświęcano noże*. Opole: Polskie Towarzystwo Kulturalno-Oświatowe, 1973.

Olszański, Tadeusz Andrzej [Jan Łukaszów pseud.]. *Historia Ukrainy XX wieku*. Warszawa: Oficyna Wydawnicza Volumen, 1993.

———. "Konflikt polsko-ukraiński 1943-1947." *Więź* 34 (November-December, 1991): 214-32.

———. "Walki polsko-ukraińskie 1943-1947." *Zeszyty Historyczne* (Paris) 90 (1989): 159-99.

Orhanizatsiia Ukrainskykh Natsionalistiv, 1929-1954. Zbirnyk stattei u 25-littia OUN. Paris, 1955.

Otrębowicz, Janina. "Nasze losy." *Semper Fidelis* (Wrocław) 6 (1990): 25-29.

OUN u Kyievi 1941-1943. Buenos Aires, 1950.

OUN u viini, 1939-1945. n.p., 1946.

OUN v svitli postanov Velykykh Zboriv, Konferentsii ta inshykh dokumentiv z borotby 1929-1955. Biblioteka Ukrainskoho Pidpilnyka, vol. 1. München, 1955.

Ożarowski, Filip. *Gdy płonął Wołyń*. Chicago: Wici, 1995.

Pająk, Henryk. *Za samostijną Ukrainę*. Lublin: n.p., 1992.

Pankivskyi, Kost. *Roky nimetskoi okupatsii*. New York: Vydavnytstvo Kliuchi, 1965.

———. *Vid derzhavy do komitetu*. New York, Toronto, 1957.

Partacz, Czesław. "Stosunki polsko-ukraińskie w Galicji Wschodniej i na Wołyniu w 1943 r." *Rocznik Koszaliński* (Koszalin) 26 (1996): 85-101.

Pasternak, Evhen. *Narys istorii Kholmshchyny i Pidliashshia (Novishi chasy)*. Winnipeg: Research Institute of Volyn, 1968.

Pełczyński, Tadeusz, et al., eds. *Armia Krajowa w dokumentach 1939-1945*, vol. 3, April 1943-July 1944. London: Studium Polski Podziemnej, 1976.

Pelekh, Teodor. *Moi molodi lita u vyri borotbi*. München, Toronto, 1988.

Peretiatkowicz, Adam. *Polska samoobrona w okolicach Łucka*. Katowice: Ośrodek Badań Społeczno-Kulturowych Towarzystwa Zachęty Kultury, 1995.

Petryshyn, Roman W., and Natalia Chomiak. *Political Writings of Post-World War Two Ukrainian Émigrés: Annotated Bibliography and Guide to Research*. Canadian Institute of Ukrainian Studies Research Report, no. 4. Edmonton, 1984.

Piotrowski, Czesław. *Krwawe żniwa za Styrem, Horyniem i Słuczą*. Warszawa: Światowy Związek Żołnierzy Armii Krajowej, Okręg Wołyń, 1995.

Piotrowski, Stanisław. *Dziennik Hansa Franka*. Warszawa: Wydawnictwo Prawnicze, 1956.

Piotrowski, Tadeusz. "Akcja 'Wisła'—Operation 'Vistula,' 1947: Background and Assessment." *The Polish Review* 43, no. 2 (1998): 219-38.

———. *Poland's Holocaust: Ethnic Strife, Collaboration with Occupying Forces and Genocide in the Second Republic, 1918-1947.* Jefferson, NC: McFarland, 1998.

———. *Vengeance of the Swallows: Memoir of a Polish Family's Ordeal Under Soviet Aggression, Ukrainian Ethnic Cleansing and Nazi Enslavement, and Their Emigration to America.* Jefferson, NC: McFarland, 1995.

Pobihushchyi-Ren, Ievhen. *Mozaika moikh spomyniv.* München, London, 1982.

———, et al. *Druzhyny Ukrainskykh Natsionalistiv u 1941-1942 rokakh.* n.p., 1953.

Pobóg-Malinowski, Władysław. *Najnowsza historia polityczna Polski, 1864-1945.* 3 vols. London: n.p., 1983.

Podvorniak, Mykhailo. *Viter z Volyni: Spohady.* Winnipeg: T-vo: "Volyn," 1981.

Polikarpenko, Hryhorii. *Orhanizatsiia Ukrainskykh Natsionalistiv pidchas Druhoi svitovoi viiny.* [Winnipeg?]: n.p., 1951.

Poliszczuk, Wiktor. *Akcja Wisła: Próba oceny.* Toronto: n.p., 1997.

———. *Apokalipsa według Wiktora Ukraińca.* Warszawa, Toronto: n.p., 1996.

———. *Fałszowanie historii najnowszej Ukrainy.* Warszawa, Toronto: n.p., 1996.

———. *Gorzka prawda: Zbrodniczość OUN-UPA (spowiedź Ukraińca).* Toronto: n.p., 1995. Ukrainian ed., *Hirka pravda: Zlochynnist OUN-UPA (spovid ukraintsia).* Toronto: n.p., 1995. English ed., *Bitter Truth: The Criminality of the Organization of Ukrainian Nationalists and the Ukrainian Insurgent Army (The Testimony of a Ukrainian).* Translated by Christina Eljasz and Lester Korneluk. Toronto: n.p., 1999.

———. *Ideologia nacjonalizmu ukraińskiego według Dmytra Doncowa.* Warszawa: n.p., 1996.

———. *Integralny nacjonalizm ukraiński jako odmiana faszyzmu.* Vol. 1. Toronto: n.p., 1998.

———. *Legal and Political Assessment of the OUN and UPA.* English section translated by Tadeusz Piotrowski. Toronto: n.p., 1997. (A trilingual publication: English, Polish, Ukrainian.)

———. *Pojęcie Integralnego Nacjonalizmu Ukraińskiego.* Warszawa: n.p., 1997.

———. *Ukraińskie ofiary OUN-UPA.* Warszawa: n.p., 1998. (Paper presented at a symposium in Wrocław, July 12, 1998, and subsequently published.)

Popek, Leon, Tomasz Trusiuk, Paweł Wira, and Zenon Wira, comps. *Wołyński testament.* Lublin: Towarzystwo Przyjaciół Krzemieńca i Ziemi Wołyńsko-Podolskiej, 1997.

Postanovy II. Velykoho zboru Orhanizatsii Ukrainskykh Natsionalistiv. Stryj: Ukrainska Drukarnia im. Hen. Tarnavskoho, 1941.

Potichnyj, Peter. "'Akcja Wisła': The Forcible Relocation of the Ukrainian Population in Poland." *Ukrainian Quarterly* 44, no. 1-2 (spring-summer 1988): 72-90.

———, ed. *Poland and Ukraine: Past and Present.* Edmonton: The Canadian Institute of Ukrainian Studies, 1980.

———, and Yevhen Shtendera, comps. *Political Thought of the Ukrainian Underground 1943-1951.* Edmonton: Canadian Institute of Ukrainian Studies, 1986.

———, and Ievhen Shtendera, comps. *Volyn i Polissia: Nimetska okupatsiia.* Litopys, vols. 1-2. Toronto: Vydavnytstvo Litopys UPA, 1976-1977.

———, and Ievhen Shtendera, eds. *Litopys Ukrainskoi Povstanskoi Armii.* Toronto: Vydavnytstvo Litopys UPA. (Series beginning in 1976.)

Prus, Edward. *Atamania UPA. Tragedia Kresów.* 2d rev. ed. Wrocław: Nortom, 1996.

———. *Banderowcy—defekt historii,* Wrocław: Semper Fidelis, 1992.

———. *Bluff XX wieku.* London: Koło Lwowian, 1992.

———. *Herosi spod znaku tryzuba: Konowalec, Bandera, Szuchewycz.* Warszawa: Instytut Wydawniczy Związków Zawodowych, 1985.

———. *Holocaust po banderowsku.* Wrocław: Nortom, 1995.

———. *Kurhany: Dążenia galicyjskich nacjonalistów ukraińskich.* Warszawa: Polska Oficyna Wydawnicza "BGW," 1993.

———. *Legenda Kresów: Szare Szeregi w walce z UPA.* Wrocław: Nortom, 1995.

———. *Melnykowcy—kolaboracja czy opór?* Wrocław: Stowarzyszenie Upamiętnienia Ofiar Zbrodni Ukraińskich Nacjonalistów, 1994.

———. *Operacja "Wisła."* Wrocław: Nortom, 1994.

———. *Taras Czuprynka—hetman UPA i wielki inkwizytor OUN.* Wrocław: Nortom, 1998.

———. *UPA—Armia powstańcza czy kurenie rizunów?* Wrocław: Stowarzyszenie Upamiętnienia Ofiar Zbrodni Ukraińskich Nacjonalistów, 1994.

———. *Z dziejów współpracy nacjonalistów ukraińskich z Niemcami w okresie II wojny*

światowej i okupacji. Katowice: Akademia Ekonomiczna im. Karola Adamieckiego, 1985.
Pundyk, Iurii. *Ukrainskyi natsionalizm.* Paris: Natsionalistychne vyd-vo v Evropi, 1966.
Pysma-poslannia Mytropolyta Andreia Sheptytskoho, ChSVV: Z chasiv nimetskoi Okupatsii. Biblioteka Lohosu, vol. 30. Yorkton, 1969.
Rachwalski, Eugeniusz. *Wołyń i jego żołnierze.* Wrocław: Polskie Towarzystwo Turystyczno-Krajowe, Oddział Wrocławski—Komisja Krajoznawcza, 1991.
Rebet, Lev. *Svitla i tini OUN.* München: Ukrainskyi samostiinyk, 1964.
"Relacja policjanta." *Karta* 24 (1998): 129-40.
———. *Teoria natsii.* München: V-vo Suchasna Ukraina, 1955.
Reshetar, John S. "Ukrainian Nationalism and the Orthodox Church." *Annual Slavic and East European Review* 10 (February 1951): 38-49.
———. *The Ukrainian Revolution, 1917-1920: A Study in Nationalism.* New York: Arno Press, 1972.
Revyuk, Emil, comp. *Polish Atrocities in Ukraine.* New York: United Ukrainian Organizations of the United States, 1931.
Rezac, Tomas and Valentin Tsurkan. *Wanted...* Translated from Russian by Sergei Syrovatkin. Moscow: Progress Publishers, 1988.
Ripetsky, Modest. *UPA Medical Services.* Toronto: Litopys UPA, 1992.
Röhr, Werner, ed. *Okkupation und Kollaboration (1938-1945): Beiträge zu Konzepten und Praxis der Kollaboration in der deutschen Okkupationspolitik.* Berlin: Hüthig Verlagsgemeinschaft, 1994.
Rokicka, J., "Było sobie takie miasteczko na Pokuciu." *Semper Fidelis* (Wrocław) 5, no. 22 (September-October 1994): 29-32.
Roman, Vasyl. *Moia pratsia i borotba: Spohady chlena OUN.* München, 1983.
Romanowski, Wincenty. *Kainowe dni.* Warszawa: Instytut Wydawniczy Związków Zawodowych, 1990.
———. *ZWK-AK na Wołyniu 1939-1944.* Lublin: Katolicki Uniwersytet Lubelski, 1993.
Rosa, Edward. *Wspomnienia lat przeżytych na Wołyniu.* Toronto: Alliance of the Polish Eastern Provinces, 1997.
Sabrin, B. F., et al., eds. *Alliance for Murder: The Nazi-Ukrainian Nationalist Partnership in Genocide.* New York: Sarpedon, 1991.
Samchuk, Ulas. *Na bilomu koni: Spomyny i vrazhennia.* Winnipeg, 1972.
———. *Na koni voronomu: Spomyny i vrazhennia.* Winnipeg, 1975.
Savchuk, S. V. "'Akt proholoshennia Ukrainskoi Derzhavy' 30-ho chervnia 1941 roku." *Novyi Litopys* (Winnipeg) 1, no. 1 (1961): 3-25.
Schoenfeld, Joachim, ed. *Holocaust Memoirs: Jews in the Lwów Ghetto, the Janowski Concentration Camp, and as Deportees in Siberia.* Hoboken, NJ: KTAV Publishing House, 1985.
Schwarz, Leo W., ed. *The Root and the Bough: The Epic of an Enduring People.* New York: Rinehart, 1949.
Serczyk, Władysław. *Historia Ukrainy.* 1979. Wrocław: Zakład Narodowy im. Ossolińskich, 1990.
Serhiichuk, Volodymyr. *OUN-UPA v roky viiny: Novi dokumenty i materialy.* Kyiv: Vydavnytstvo Khudozhnoi Literatury "Dnipro," 1996.
Shankovskyi, Lev. *Initsiatyvnyi komitet dlia stvorennia Ukrainskoi Holovnoi Vyzvolnoi Rady: Dokumentalnyi spohad suchasnyka.* New York, 1985.
———. *Pokhidni hrupy OUN: Prychynky do istorii pokhidnykh hrup OUN na tsentralnykh i skhidnikh zemliakh Ukrainy v 1941-1943 rr.* München: Ukrainskyi samostiinyk, 1958.
———. "Soviet and Satellite Sources on the Ukrainian Insurgent Army." *The Annals of the Ukrainian Academy of Arts and Sciences in the U.S.* 9, no. 1-2 (27-28) (1961): 234-261. (Published under the Anglicized name of Lew Shankowsky.)
———. "'Spohady D. Shumuka' u svitli faktiv." *Vyzvolnyi Shliakh* 28, no. 1 (1975): 64-81, no. 2: 177-89, no. 3: 326-42, no. 4: 431-48.
Shtendera, Ewhen (Ievhen). "Badania nad dziejami UPA w PRL." *Suchasnist: literatura, mystetstvo, suspilne zyhttia. Zeszyt w języku polskim,* no. 1-2 (1985): 125-44.
———, ed. *Volyn i Polissia: Nimetska okupatsiia.* Litopys, vol. 5. Toronto: Vydavnytstvo Litopys UPA, 1984.
Shuliak, O. [Oleh Shtul-Zhdanovych]. *V imia pravdy: Diisnist pro Ukrainsku Povstanchu Armiiu.* n.p., 1948.
———. *V imia pravdy: Do istorii povstanchoho rukhu v Ukraini.* Rotterdam, 1947.
Shumuk, Danylo. *Za skhidnym obriiem. Spomyny. Peredruk samvydavnoho tvoru z Ukrainy.* Paris: Persha Ukrainska Drukarnia u Frantsii, 1974. Rev. ed., *Perezhyte i*

peredumane: Spohady i rozdumy ukrainsko-ho dysydenta-politviaznia z rokiv blukan i borotby pid trioma okupatsiiamy Ukrainy (1921-1981). Detroit, 1983. Eng. abbrev. ed., *Life Sentence: Memoirs of a Ukrainian Political Prisoner*. Edited by Ivan Jaworsky. Translated by Ivan Jaworsky and Halya Kowalska. Edmonton: Canadian Institute of Ukrainian Studies, University of Alberta, 1984.

Siemaszko, Władysław. "Stan badań nad terrorem ukraińskim na Wołyniu w latach 1939-1944." *Lwów i Kresy* (London), no. 3 (July-September 1992): 37-47.

―――, and Ewa Siemaszko. *Terror ukraiński i zbrodnie przeciwko ludzkości dokonane przez OUN-UPA na ludności polskiej na Wołyniu w latach 1939-1945*. Warszawa: Stowarzyszenie Upamiętnienia Ofiar Zbrodni Nacjonalistów Ukraińskich w Warszawie, 1998.

Sikorski, Feliks. *Kabewiacy w akcji "Wisła."* Warszawa: Ministerstwo Obrony Narodowej, 1989.

Simpson, Christopher. *Blowback: America's Recruitment of Nazis and Its Effects on the Cold War*. New York: Weidenfeld and Nicolson, 1988.

Sirč, Václav. *Minulost zavátá časem*. n.p., n.d.

Siwicki, Mikołaj, comp. *Dzieje konfliktów polsko-ukraińskich*. 3 vols. Warszawa: n.p., 1992 (vols. 1 and 2), 1994 (vol. 3).

Skorupskyi, Maksym. *U nastupakh i vidstupakh: Spohady*. Chicago, 1961.

Skrzypek, Stanisław. *The Problem of Galicia*. London: Polish Association for the South-Eastern Provinces, 1948.

―――. *Ukraiński program państwowy na tle rzeczywistości*. London: Koło Lwowian, 1967.

Śliwowska, Wiktoria, ed. *The Last Eyewitnesses: Children of the Holocaust Speak*. Translated from Polish by Julian and Fay Bussgang. Evanston: Northwestern University Press, 1998.

Słowiński, Henryk, and Bogusława Rudnicka-Kędzierska, eds. *Lipniki*. Wrocław, 1998.

Smovskyi, Kostiantyn. *Spohady uchasnyka banderivskoi UPA*. Mt. Dale, NY: Nasha Batkivshchyna, 1982.

Snitko-Rzeszut, Janina, ed. *Armia Krajowa na Wołyniu*. Warszawa: Światowy Związek Żołnierzy Armii Krajowej, Okręg Wołyń, 1994.

Sobiesiak, Józef. *Brygada Grunwald*. 1964. Warszawa, 1973.

―――. *Przebraże*. Lublin: Wydawnictwo Lubelskie, 1973.

―――, and Ryszard Jegorow. *Burzany: Wspomnienia*. 1964. Lublin: Ministerstwo Obrony Narodowej, l974.

―――, and Ryszard Jegorow. *Ziemia płonie*. Lublin: Wydawnictwo Lubelskie, 1974.

Sobotko, Mieczysław. *Między Turią a Bugiem*. Olsztyn, Białystok, 1980.

Sodol, Petro R. *Ukrainska Povstancha Armiia, 1943-49. Dovidnyk*. New York: Proloh, 1994.

―――. *Ukrainska Povstancha Armiia, 1943-49. Dovidnyk druhyi*. New York: Proloh, 1995.

―――. "UPA — The Ukrainian Insurgent Army: An Overview." *Ukrainian Quarterly* 51, no. 2-3 (summer-fall 1995): 139-75.

―――. *UPA. They Fought Hitler and Stalin: A Brief Overview of Military Aspects from the History of the Ukrainian Insurgent Army, 1942-1949*. New York: Committee for the World Convention and Reunion of Soldiers in the Ukrainian Insurgent Army, 1987.

Sosnovskyi, Mykhailo. *Dmytro Dontsov: Politychnyi portret. Z istorii rozvytku ideolohii Ukrainskoho natsionalizmu*. New York: Trident International, 1974.

Spector, Shmuel. *The Holocaust of Volhynian Jews 1941-1944*. Jerusalem: Yad Vashem — The Federation of Volhynian Jews, 1990.

Stakhiv, Ievhen. [E. Pavliuk, pseud.]. "Borotba ukrainskoho narodu na skhidno-ukrainskykh zemliakh, 1941-1944. Spomyny ochevydtsia i uchasnyka." *Kalendar Provydinnia Stovaryshennia Ukraintsiv Katolykiv v Amerytsi na zvychainyi rik 1947* (Philadelphia) (1947): 37-57. (Published under the pseudonym).

―――. *Kriz tiurmy, pidpillia i kordony: Povist moho zhyttia*. Kyiv: "Rada," 1995.

―――. "Kryvyi Rih v 1941-1943 rr." *Suchasna Ukraina* (München) (January 22, 1956): 10.

Stan i perspektywy badań historycznych lat wojny i okupacji 1939-1945. Warszawa: Instytut Pamięci Narodowej, 1988.

Stegner, Tadeusz, ed. *Polacy o Ukraińcach, Ukraińcy o Polakach: Materiały z sesji naukowej*. Gdańsk, 1993.

Sterzer, Abraham. "We Fought for Ukraine!" *Ukrainian Quarterly* 20, no. 1 (1964): 37-41.

Stetsiuk, Hryhorii Mykolaiovych. *"Chorni dni Volyni": Spohady kolyshnioho zviazkovoho okruzhnoho provodu OUN*. Lutsk, 1992.

―――. *Nepostavlenyi pamiatnyk: Spohady*. Winnipeg: Instytut Doslidiv Volyni, 1988.

Stetsko, Iaroslav S. *30 chervnia 1941: Proholoshennia vidnovlennia derzhavnosty Ukrainy*. Toronto: Liga Vyzvolennia Ukrainy, 1967.

_____. *Ukrainska vyzvolna kontseptsiia.* München: Vydannia Orhanizatsii Ukrainskykh Natsionalistiv, 1987.

Struk, Danylo Husar, ed. *Encyclopedia of Ukraine,* vols. 3-5. Toronto: University of Toronto Press, 1993.

Stsiborskyi, Mykola. *Natsiokratiia.* Paris: n.p., n.d.

Styrkul, Valery (Valerii). *The SS Werewolves.* Lviv: Kamenyar Publishers, 1982.

_____. *We Accuse: Documentary Sketch.* Translated from the Ukrainian by George Sklyar and Andriy Medvid. Kiev: Dnipro Publishers, 1984.

Subtelny, Orest. *Ukraine: A History.* 2d ed. Toronto: University of Toronto Press and Canadian Institute of Ukrainian Studies, 1994.

Sulewski, Wojciech. *Lasy w ogniu: Zamojszczyzna, 1939-1944.* Warszawa: Czytelnik, 1962.

Szawłowski, Ryszard (Karol Liszewski, pseud.). *Wojna polsko-sowiecka 1939.* London: Polska Fundacja Kulturalna, 1986; Exp. and rev. 3d ed. 2 vols. Warszawa: Neriton, 1998.

Szcześniak, Antoni, and Wiesław Szota. *Droga do nikąd: Działalność Organizacji Ukraińskich Nacjonalistów i jej likwidacja w Polsce.* Warszawa: Ministerstwo Obrony Narodowej, 1973.

Szefer, Andrzej. "Dywersyjno-sabatażowa działalność wrocławskiej Abwehry na ziemiach polskich w przededniu agresji hitlerowskiej w 1939 r." *Biuletyn Głównej Komisji Badania Zbrodni Hitlerowskich w Polsce* (Warszawa) 32 (1987): 271-372.

Szelągowski, Władysław. *Wzburzony San.* Warszawa: Książka i Wiedza, 1973.

Szeremeta, Bronisław. *Watażka: Wspomnienie nierozstrzelanego i jego zbrodnie.* Wrocław, 1995.

_____. "Zagłada wsi Adamy — rok 1943." *Semper Fidelis* (Wrocław) 1, no. 14 (1993): 19-20.

Szetelnicki, Wacław. *Trembowla: Kresowy bastion wiary i polskości.* Wrocław: Rubikon, 1992.

_____. *Zapomniany lwowski bohater ks. Stanisław Frankl 1903-1944.* Rome: P.U.G., 1983.

Szota, Wiesław. "Zarys rozwoju Organizacji Powstańczych Nacjonalistów i Ukraińskiej Powstańczej Armii." *Wojskowy Przegląd Historyczny* 1 (1963): 163-218.

Tereshchuk, Petro [Oleksandr Matla]. *Istorychni notatky.* Toronto: Homin Ukrainy, 1985.

Terleś, Mikołaj. *Ethnic Cleansing of Poles in Volhynia and Eastern Galicia 1942-1946.* Toronto: Alliance of the Polish Eastern Provinces, 1993.

Terpin, Bronisław. *Na koszt wielkiej trójki: Saga rodziny kresowej.* Chicago: Jan Beyzym Sons, 1985.

Tomaszewski, Jerzy. *Rzeczpospolita wielu narodów.* Warszawa: Czytelnik, 1985.

Torke, Hans-Joachim, and John-Paul Himka, eds. *German-Ukrainian Relations in Historical Perspective.* Edmonton: Canadian Institute of Ukrainian Studies Press, 1994.

Torzecki, Ryszard. "Kontakty polsko-ukraińskie na tle problemu ukraińskiego w polityce polskiego rządu emigracyjnego i podziemia (1939-1944)." *Dzieje Najnowsze* (Warszawa) 1, no. 2 (1981): 319-46.

_____. *Kwestia ukraińska w polityce III Rzeszy 1933-1945.* Warszawa: Książka i Wiedza, 1972.

_____. *Kwestia ukraińska w Polsce w latach 1923-1929.* Kraków: Wydawnictwo Literackie, 1989.

_____. *Polacy i Ukraińcy: Sprawa ukraińska w czasie II wojny światowej na terenie II Rzeczypospolitej.* Warszawa: Wydawnictwo Naukowe PWN, 1993.

_____. "Ukraińska Powstańcza Armia w świetle dokumentów niemieckich." *Dzieje Najnowsze* (Warszawa) 2 (1988), 191-95.

Trunk, Isaiah. *Jewish Responses to Nazi Persecution: Collective and Individual Behavior in Extremis.* New York: Stein and Day, 1979.

Turowski, Józef. *Pożoga: Walki 27 Wołyńskiej Dywizji AK.* Warszawa: Polskie Wydawnictwo Naukowe, 1990.

_____, and Władysław Siemaszko. *Zbrodnie nacjonalistów ukraińskich dokonane na ludności polskiej na Wołyniu 1939-1945.* Warszawa: Główna Komisja Badania Zbrodni Hitlerowskich w Polsce — Instytut Pamięci Narodowej and Środowisko Żołnierzy 27 Wołyńskiej Dywizji Armii Krajowej w Warszawie, 1990.

Tys-Krokhmaliuk, Yuriy. *UPA Warfare in Ukraine: Strategical, Tactical and Organizational Problems of Ukrainian Resistance in World War II.* New York: Society of Veterans of Ukrainian Insurgent Army of the United States and Canada and St. George the Victorious Association of Veterans of Ukrainian Insurgent Army in Europe, 1972.

"Ukraine in the Second World War." *Ukrainian Quarterly* 51, no. 2-3 (summer-fall 1995).

Ukrainska Holovna Vyzvolna Rada: Dokumenty, ofitsiini publikatsii, materiialy. Litopys, vol. 8. Toronto: Litopys UPA, 1980.

Ukrainska Povstanska Armiia: Zbirka dokumentiv za 1942-1950 rr. Part 1. Biblioteka

Ukrainskoho Pidpilnyka, vol. 6. n.p., 1957. Part 2, *Ukrainska Povstanska Armiia: Boiovi dii UPA za 1943-1950 rr.* Biblioteka Ukrainskoho Pidpilnyka, vol. 7. n.p., 1960.

UPA v svitli nimetskykh dokumentiv. Toronto: Litopys UPA, 1983.

Urban, Wincenty. *Droga krzyżowa Archidiecezji Lwowskiej w latach II wojny światowej 1939-1945.* Wrocław: n.p., 1983.

Velychkivskyi, Mykola. "Sumni chasy nimetskoi okupatsii, 1941-1944 roky." *Vyzvolnyi Shliakh* (London) 18 (1965), no. 1: 40-54, no. 2: 152-62, no. 3: 295-306, no. 4: 392-401, no. 5: 517-23, no. 7-8: 801-06, no. 10: 1073-81.

Vereta, L., and V. Chudovskyi, comps. *Rozplata: Dokumenty i materialy sudovoho protsesu nad hrupoiu bandytiv OUN.* Lviv, 1970. Abridged translation, *Day of Reckoning.* Kiev, 1972. (On the Soviet trial in 1969 of SB members.)

Vershigora, Petr Petrovich. *Lyudi s chistoy sovestyu.* 2 vols. Kiev: Ukr. derzh. vydvo, 1946-47; Moskva: Sovetskiy pisatel, 1955.

Veryha, Wasyl. *Dorohamy Druhoi Svitovoi viiny: Legendy pro uchast ukraintsiv u zdushuvanni varshavskoho povstannia v 1944 r. ta pro Ukrainsku Dyviziiu "Halychyna."* 1980. Toronto: Brotherhood of Veterans of the I.UD UNA, 1981.

―――. "The 'Galicia' Ukrainian Division in Polish and Soviet Literature." *Ukrainian Quarterly* 36, no. 3 (1980): 253-70.

―――. *Pid sontsem Italii.* Toronto: Vyd-vo Novyi Shliakh, 1984.

―――. *Vtraty OUN v chasi Druhoi svitovoi viiny abo "Zdobudesh ukrainsku derzhavu abo zhynesh u borotbi za nei."* Toronto, 1991.

Warchocki, Czesław. *Rzeczpospolita partyzancka.* Warszawa, 1972.

Wardzyńska, Maria. *Formacja Wachmannschaften des SS- und Polizeiführers im Distrikt Lublin.* Warszawa: Główna Komisja Badania Zbrodni przeciwko Narodowi Polskiemu, 1992.

Węgierski, Jerzy. *Armia Krajowa na południowych i wschodnich przedpolach Lwowa.* Kraków: Platan, 1994.

―――. *Armia Krajowa na zachód od Lwowa.* Kraków: Platan, 1994.

―――. *Armia Krajowa — Oddziały leśne 19. pułku piechoty.* Kraków: Platan, 1993.

―――. *Armia Krajowa w okręgach Stanisławów i Tarnopol.* Kraków: Platan, 1996.

―――. *Armia Krajowa w Zagłębiu Naftowym i na Samborszczyźnie.* Kraków: Platan, 1993.

―――. *W lwowskiej Armii Krajowej.* Warszawa: Pax, 1989.

Węgrzecki, Kazimierz. *Czarne plamy historii i kronikarskie odnotowania 1.9.1939-17.5.1989.* London: Veritas Foundation, 1990.

Wells, Leon Weliczker. *The Janowska Road.* New York: The Macmillan Company, 1963.

Wernik, Romuald. *Operacja San-Wisła.* Warszawa: n.p., 1965.

―――. *Tajkury — wioska która była miastem.* London: Caldra House, 1997.

Wiśniewski, Aleksander. *Możemy wszystko przebaczyć, nie wolno nam niczego zapomnieć.* Wołów, 1994.

Wołczański, Józef. "Korespondencja Arcybiskupa Bolesława Twardowskiego z Arcybiskupem Andrzejem Szeptyckim w latach 1943-1944." *Przegląd Wschodni* 2, no. 6 (1992-93): 465-84.

Wroński, Stanisław, and Maria Zwolakowa, eds. *Polacy Żydzi, 1939-1945.* Warszawa: Książka i Wiedza, 1971.

Zadeberny, Franciszek. "Wigilia 1943 w Kruhowie." *Semper Fidelis* (Wrocław) 6, no. 29 (1995): 25-27.

Zahaikevych, B., ed. *Peremyshl — zakhidnyi bastion Ukrainy.* New York: Peremyskyi Vydavnychyi Komitet, 1961.

"Zbrodnie banderowskich bójówek OUN-UPA w powiecie Buczacz, województwo tarnopolskie." *Na Rubieży* (Wrocław) 4, no. 14 (1995): 4-25.

"Zbrodnie niemieckie w Zamojszczyźnie." *Biutelyn Głównej Komisji Badania Zbrodni Niemieckich w Polsce* 2 (1947): 45-120.

Żeleński, Władysław. *Zabójstwo Ministra Pierackiego.* Warszawa: Iskry, 1995.

Żołnowski, Władysław. *Niebo i piekło mojej ziemi.* n.p., 1992.

Zovenko, Orest. *Bezimenni: Spohad uchasnyka novitnikh vyzvolnykh zmahan.* n.p., 1946.

Żupański, Andrzej. *Ujawnić prawdę: Wysiłki byłych mieszkańców i żołnierzy Wołynia, by prawda o rzeziach na Kresach została ujawniona.* Warszawa: Światowy Związek Żołnierzy Armii Krajowej, Okręg Wołyń, 1997.

Żur, Leon. *Mój woyński epos.* Suwałki: Hańcza, 1997.

Zvony. Rome and Detroit: n.p., 1978.

Index

Abwehr (German military intelligence) 206–07, 223, 227–30, 233, 236, 258
Abwehr II 229
"Act of June 30, 1941" 232
"Action on Peter and Paul" see "Peter and Paul action"
Adamarek, Julia 168
Adamowicz, Bronisława 69, 268
Adamowicz, Franciszek 63, 65
Adamowicz, Jan 62–63
Adamowicz, Stanisław 65, 68
Adamowicz, Stasia 62
Adamowicz, Teofil 69, 268
Adamowicz, Teresa see Radziszewska, Teresa
Adamówka 66, 267
Adamska, Władysława see Naklicka, Władysława
Adamy 263
Adwent, Tadeusz 138
Agrarian Party of Ukraine 254
Ainsztein, Reuben 275, 282
AK (Armia Krajowa, or Polish Home Army) 14, 25, 27, 100, 120, 150, 173 74, 184, 193, 195, 203–04, 242–46, 258–61, 265; see also Polish underground
AK Wołyń (the 27th Infantry Division of the AK) 27, 244–45
Akcja "Wisła" see Operation "Wisła"
Albert, Zygmunt 282
Alef-Bolkowiak, Gustaw 282
Aleksandria 107, 109, 115, 188
Aleksandrówka 59–66, 68–69, 97, 155, 267
Allies 199, 246, 248

America 122, 225, 276
"amnesty" (August 12, 1941) 228
Anatolia 101, 156
Anczarski, Józef 282
Anders, Władysław 228
Andrusyshen, C. H. 257, 282
Andrzejówka 16, 101–02, 156, 259
Andusikiewicz 220
Angielskyi 274
Antolin 150, 273–74
Antoniuk, Porfyrii ("Sosenko") 33, 56, 120, 180, 187
Antonowce Forest 73
Antonówka 116, 119, 153, 189
Antonówka Szepelska 260
Arad, Yitzhak 177, 282
"Arkadii" see Havryliuk, Mykola
Arlt, Fritz 282
Armia Krajowa see AK
Armstrong, John A. 233, 240, 277, 279–82, 285
Army Group North 14, 247
Arsenowicze 61, 66
Association for the Remembrance of Poles Murdered in Wołyń 4, 5, 267
Association for the Remembrance of the Victims of the Crimes of the Ukrainian Nationalists 4
Association of the Children of the Holocaust in Poland 218
Association of the 27th Wołynian Division of the [Polish] Home Army 4, 22
Association of Ukrainian Fascists 225

Association of Ukrainian Nationalists 225
Austria 10, 149, 227–28, 249

Babii, Ivan 226
Bąbiński, Kazimierz Damian ("Luboń") 27, 193–94, 203, 265
Babiychuk, Stefania 263
Baby (Otiniyshe) 184
Bach-Zelewski, Erich von dem 238
Bączkowski, Władysław 283
Bagińska, Halina 110
Bagińska, Marcelina see Piotrowska, Marcelina
Bagińska, Marynia see Piotrowska, Marynia
Bagińska, Michalina 50
Bagińska, Władysława (Władzia) 110, 113
Bagiński, Adolf 109
Bagiński, Gracjan 53
Bagiński, Ignacy 53
Bagiński, Jan 50, 110, 157
Bagiński, Tadeusz 53, 267, 272, 282
Bagiński, Władysław 110
Bahnschutz (railway security police) 194
Bakonów 129–30
Balada, Josef 98
Balkovski, Bogdan 263
Balkovski, Evgeny 263
Balkovski, Ivan 263
Balytskyi 122, 125
Bambylo, Petro 35, 99–100
Bamki 115
Banach, Kazimierz (Jan Linowski, pseud.) 71
Bandera, Stepan 12, 14–15, 69, 73, 95, 116, 177, 180,

186, 206, 208–10, 214,
218, 226–34, 236, 242, 247,
253, 279, 282; *see also* Consul II
Banderowcy (Ukr., Banderivtsi; OUN-B members) 24, 31, 35–36, 38–39, 41–42, 44, 50–52, 54, 60–61, 64, 66, 75–77, 79, 83, 96–97, 100–06, 114–15, 119, 123–25, 129–31, 134–38, 141, 143, 147, 150–56, 158, 161–66, 169–72, 190, 195, 199, 205, 214–17, 250, 261–62, 265, 274–77; *see also* OUN-B
Bandura, Franciszek 266
Bandura, Frania 265
Bandura, Stefania 265
Bandura, Tomasz 265–66
Baptist(s) 14, 43, 68, 102, 123, 128–29, 144, 162, 266
Barabash, Nataliia Mykhailivna 191
Baran, Józef 170, 272
Baran, Karol 20
Baranowicze 86
Baranowski, Jarosław (Iaroslav Baranovskyi) 219–21
Barański 90
Barbarówka 202
Bartoszewski, Piotr 68
Barwinski (Barvinskyi) 219, 221
Basilian Fathers 224
Basiuk, Alosha 268
Basowy Kąt 115
Baszkowce 73
Bataliony Chłopskie *see* BCh
"Batko" *see* Hrabets, Omelian
battle of Brody 246
Bavaria 214, 265
Bayer 239
Bazyluk, Petro 48
BBH (Bergbauernhilfe, or Mountain-Peasants' Help) 228
BCh (Bataliony Chłopskie, or Peasant Battalions) 261
Bdychaj, Władysława *see* Główka, Władysława
Bebel 148
Beck, Józef 278
Bednarz, Natasha 150
Bednarz, Paweł 150
Bednarz, Stanisław 150
Bedryi, Ilaryi 264
Bedryi, Olga 264
Belgorod 191

Belorussia 234, 238
Belozotsovka 207
Bełżec 235
Bełżów family 220
Bereść 184
Beresta 42
Beresteczko 33
Bereza Kartuska 228
Bereźce 73, 81
Bereziuk 276
Berezne 46, 53, 205, 216–17, 239
Bereźnica 260
Berezołupy 102
Berezów Niżny 23, 261
Berezówka 237
Bergbauernhilfe *see* BBH
Berkhoff, Karel C. 282
Berkut unit 189
Berlin 177, 208, 212–13, 223–26, 228, 236–37, 246–48, 258
Berling, Zygmunt 228
Berstowo 69
"Besket" 187
Bessarabia 234
Beyersdorff, Friedrich 260
"Bezridnyi" 46
Bezukhy 109, 115
Białokrynica 73
Białowąs, Jan 282
Białowola 63
Białozórka 73, 75, 79, 153, 260
Biały Lake 83
Biały Potok 274–75
Białystok 4
Biczal 178
Biegański, Witold 264, 282
"Biegun" *see* Tabaczyński, T.
Bielecki 170
Bielin 94, 122–23, 201, 260, 272
Bielinówka 273
Bielska Wola 116
Bieniów 196
Bierkamp 210–11, 245
Biernacki, Jadwiga 269
Biernacki, Kajetan 100
Biernacki, Marceli 100
Biernacki, Stanisław 96
Bijas (née Prończuk), Janina 153
Biley, V. I. 263, 284
Biłgoraj 197, 246
Biłgoraj County 16
Biłohorszcza 253
Biskupski, Stanisław, 266–73, 282

Bitkov 185
Bitner, Heinrich 109
Bitner, Helena 138
Bitner (née Prokopowiec), Pawlina 109, 111
Bizuń, Stanisław 282
"black lists" 24, 262
Blashchuk, Valerii 154–55
Blaszczyńska (née Łagodowska), Jadwiga 132
Blessed Mother of Swojczów 143; *see also* Our Lady of Swojczów
Blicharski, Czesław E. 262, 283
Blum, Ignacy 251
Bober, Józef 104
Bober, Marianna 104
Bober (village) 237
Boboshko 75
Bobrowska, Aleksandra 271
Bobrowska, Apolonia 271
Bobrowska, Helena 271
Bobruga 207
Bocheński, Aleksander 283
Bociurkiw, Bohdan Rostyslav 278, 283
Bodnarchuk, Hanna 191
Bogorodchik 184
Bogusława (village) 106
Bogusze 162
Boguszewska, Aniela 100, 269
Bohachevskyi, Danylo 283
"Bohdan" 188
"Bohun" 243
Boichuk, Kostiantyn 92, 101
Boichun, Omelian 58–59, 152
Boiko, Maksym 283
Bojanice 168
Boków 172–74, 276
Bolsheviks 11, 20, 177, 183–87, 197, 199–200, 209–10, 223, 239, 246–47, 259
Bonusiak, Włodzimierz 281, 283
Borek 48, 219–20
Boremel 29, 32, 69, 148, 150
Borki 81, 84
Borkniuk 59
Boroczyce 35, 38, 266
Borovets, Taras ("Bulba") 13–14, 26, 46, 73, 116, 118, 120, 180, 187, 194, 207, 209, 231, 235–36, 238–39, 241–44, 247, 258, 280, 283
Borowe 2, 84, 87, 118, 159–60, 162, 268

Borówka 48–49
Borowno 204
Borowska (née Hudeczek), Teresa 274–75
Bortnica 215
Boruta, Kazimierz 54, 267
Bosakowski, Edmund 79, 272
Boshyk, Yury 283, 285
Boża Wola 143
Bożek, Apolonia 220
Bozhevskyi, Arsenii 189
Brandenburg 33
Brandenburg regiment 232
Brany 33
Branytskyi, Myta (Mitka Bronicki [Mytka Bronytskyi]) 122–23, 270
Breslau 223
Brezhko, Nina 284
Brocik, Franciszek 49
Brody 26, 211, 241, 245–46
Brodyszcze 58, 152
Brodzki district 219
Bronicki, Mitka see Branytskyi, Myta
Bronne 54
Bronowicki, Hilary (author's paternal uncle by marriage) 113
Bronytskyi, Mytka see Branytskyi, Myta
Brown-shirt Storm Troopers see SA
Brozek family 148
Bruchlewski family 115
Brudzińska, Józefa 65, 267
Brychka, Fedosia 161–62
Brychka, Hanna 162
Brychka, Hordii 59
Brys, Oleksyi ("Ostap") 33
Brześć County 243
Brzezina 119, 237
Brzeżniakiewicz, Ferdynand 98
Bubnów 122, 129, 259
Buczacz 262
Buczacz County 24, 261
Buczakowa 220
Buczyn 149
Buczyńska, Jadwiga see Wilkowska, Jadwiga
Buczyński, Władysław 98
Buderaż 145
Budiakivska, Maria 273
Budki Borowskie 118, 158–59, 162, 265, 270
Budki Kudrańskie 49
Budkiewicz, Józef 96
Budy Ossowskie 58, 68, 152

Budzyński, J. 220
Bug River 16, 27–28, 60, 63, 81, 84, 90, 102, 130, 167, 195, 197, 200–01, 246
Bugai 122
Bukaczowce 217
Bukovina 230, 234, 243
Bukovinian Battalion 234, 247
Bukowce 97–98, 101, 269
"Bulba," Taras see Borovets, Taras
Bulbowcy (Ukr., Bulbivtsi; members of Taras Borovets's organization) 46, 49–50, 62, 95–96, 104, 118, 124, 130, 139, 157–60, 182, 194, 217, 268
Bunasiówka 189
Burawska, Jadwiga 50
Burawska, Maria 50
Burawska, Stanisława 50
Burawska, Stefania 50
Burawska, Zofia 50
Burawski, Bolesław 50
Burawski, Władysław 50
"Burlak" see Koval, Stepan
Bursztyn 168–71
"Burza" 244
Burzany 41–42, 150, 180
Busk 262
Bussgang, Fay 218, 292
Bussgang, Julian 218, 292
Butejki 48
Butra, Franciszek 275
Butsko, Olexander M. 283
Bużanka 130, 187, 271
Bydychaj, Stanisław 129
Bystrzyce 49–50, 53, 181
Byteń 61, 237
Bytom 174
Byzantine Catholic Church see Uniate Church

Canada 168, 171, 225, 249, 252, 263–64
Canadian Department of Justice 262
Canaris, Wilhelm 206, 223, 233
Carpathian Mountains 197, 228, 246, 252, 265
Cechy 205
Centkiewicz family 79
Central Committee of the Communist (Bolshevik) Party of Ukraine 206
Changuli, G. I. 263, 284
Chapayev, V. I. 159

Chartoryskyi, Mykola S. 283
Chełm 17, 26, 131, 154, 184, 197, 201, 204, 221, 229–31, 243, 249, 253, 260
Chełm County 197
Chełm Province 90
Cherednychenko, Vitalii 283
Cheremshyna 24, 190
Chernyk family 60, 72
Chervak, Ivan 95, 100–01, 155, 269
Chervak, Olha 42, 92, 94–95, 269, 273
Chervak, Petro 95, 100–01, 155, 269
Chervak, Roman 101, 155, 269
Chervak brothers 275
Chicago 267
Chiniewicz, Danuta 32, 148
Chinoczy 237
Chirovsky, Nicholas 283
Chlebowice 274
Chmielewska, Helena 173, 276
Chmielewski, Wacław 58–59, 152
Chmielówka 46
Chobut 237
Chodorowski, Bronisław 238
Chojnowska, Aldona 283
Chojnowski, Andrzej 283
Cholewa 72
Chołodecki, Jan 49
Chołoniewicze 19
Chomiak, Natalia 289
Chorna, Olena 158–59, 162, 265, 270
Chornomorets, Iaroslav 179
Chornyi (UPA commander) 190
Chornyi, Iukhym 35
Chornyi, Semen 158, 270
Chornyi, Stepan 158
Chornyi, Zhenia 158, 270
Choromce 119
Chorosznica 203
Chorów 33, 145
Chotiaczów 120
Chrabko, Ludwik 276
Chrobów 16, 129–30, 259
Chrynów 19, 120, 137
Chubai, Mstyslav Z. 283
Chuchman, Emilia 264
Chuchman, Ivan 264
Chuchman, Natalka 264
Chudovskyi, V. 294
Chuiko, Ostap 285
"Chuprynka, Taras" see Shukhevych, Roman

Chwoszczowata 182
Ciesielszuk, Jerzy 226
Cieślak, T. 283
Cieszyn 22
Ciołkowska, Leontyna 118
Ciołkowska, Stefania 118
Colvin, J. 283
Communist Party of Ukraine 254
Communist Party of Western Ukraine *see* KPZU
Conason, Joe 278
conference: VZOUN *see* VZOUN
conference: VZUN *see* VZUN
conference of the captive nations of Eastern Europe and Asia (November 1943) 244
conference of the Congress of Ukrainians in Poland (April 5–6, 1997 in Warsaw) 254
conference of the KUN: March 28, 1993 in Kiev 253; first great (July 2–4, 1993 in Kiev) 253; second great (September 2–3, 1995 in Kiev) 253
conference of the OUN and UVO: first (May 1930 in Lwów) 225; second (June 1930 in Prague) 225
conference of the OUN-B: June 22, 1941 in Kraków 232; first (September 1941) 236; second (April 1942) 12, 178, 238; third (February 17–21, 1943) 178, 240
conference of the OUN-M: third (May 24–25, 1942 in Poczajów) 238; Home Conference [August 14–15, 1942 in Kiev (?)] 238
conference of the UHVR (July 11–15, 1944 in the Carpathian Mountains, Sambor County) 246
conference of the Union of Ukrainian Youth and the KUN (August 29, 1993 in Kiev) 253
conference of Ukrainian Nationalists: first (November 3–7, 1927 in Berlin) 225; second (April 8–9, 1928 in Prague) 225
conference on Poland, Germany and Ukraine (May 1995 in Rzeszów) 253

Congregation of Franciscan Sisters of the Family of Mary 173
Congress of Ukrainian Nationalists *see* KUN
Congress of Ukrainians in Poland 254
"Consul I" (Andrii Melnyk) 229; *see also* Melnyk, Andrii
"Consul II" (Stepan Bandera) 229; *see also* Bandera, Stepan
Convention on the Non-Applicability of Statutory Limitations to War Crimes and Crimes Against Humanity 264
Council for Aid to Jews *see* Żegota
Council of Ambassadors 10, 223
Council of Trust of Wołyń 235–36
Cracow *see* Kraków
"creative coercion" 225
"Cult of Tombs of the Fallen" 226
Cumań 14, 102, 106, 205
Curran, Michael 5
Curzon line 247
Cwynar, Walerian 170
Cybuchowska, Kamila *see* Kamińska, Kamila
Cybuchowska, Stanisława 126
Cybuchowska (née Palinka), Wiktoria 270
Cybuchowski, Aleksander 270
Cybulski, Henryk 266, 278, 283
Cyniak, Józefa 71, 268
Cyprian, Brother (Jan Lasoń, secular name) 199, 283
Cywiński, Adam 172
Cywiński family 276
Czacki Forest 127
Czajkowo 205
Czajkowski, Tomasz 96
Czarna Łoża 148, 273
Czartorysk 155, 273
Czaruków 92
Czechoslovakia 225
Czechowska, Aniela 132–33
Czechowska, Urszula 132
Czechowska, Wacława 132
Czechowski, Emilian 226
Czechowski, Stanisław 132–33
Czekanowski, Stanisław 16, 17, 200, 259–60
Czepielowski, Leon 78
Czepielowski, Regina 78

Czernica 245
Czerniejów 60
Czerwiński, Józef 283
Czerwonogród 218
Czestny Krest 163
Czetwertnia 106
Czmykos 81
Czortków 266
Czortków County 274
Czudec 171
Czudła 118
Czudwy 49
Czuhale 73

Dąbrowa 73, 237, 260
Dąbrowica 116
Dąbrowska-Brzozowska, Stanisława 133, 272
Dąbrowski, Michał 273
Dąbrowski, Stanisław 49
Dąbrowski, Władysław 273
Dagońska, Katarzyna 101, 156
Dagoński, Zenon 101, 156
Dallin, Alexander 177, 206, 223, 233, 277–79, 281, 283
Dankevych 191
Danyliuk, Mykhailo 283
Danyliuk, Trokhym 60
Danzig *see* Gdańsk
Darski, Józef 283
Datsiuk, Nykon 36
Datyń 56, 67
Davydenko, V. 288
Dębica 204
Dębicki, Mikołaj *see* Dubytskyi, Mykola
Dębowa Karczma 155, 269, 273
Dębska, Veronika 148
Dębski, Jerzy 5, 128, 199, 201–02, 258, 260, 266–75, 283
Dębski, Sławosz 36
Dębski, Włodzimierz Sławosz 284
Decalogue (Dekaloh) 175–76, 225
Dederkały 73, 198, 260
Delegation for the Homeland 204, 242, 245
Dembytskyi, Mykola *see* Dubytskyi, Mykola
Demianenko, Irka 149
Demidówka 29
Denisov, V. N. 263, 284
Denys family 61
Derazhne *see* Deraźne
Deraźne 46, 49–51, 151–52, 178, 205, 207

Dermań 79, 165, 191
Dermańka 158–59, 260
Derżów 197
Diabuk, Nestor see Dziabak, Nestor
Diabuk, Zofia see Dziabak, Zofia
Diadkiewicze (Diatkowicze, Didowicze) 107, 191
Dionizy 94
Distrikt Galizien 239
Długowola 118
Dmytruk, Trofym 118–19
Dmytryk, Ivan 284
Dnieper 209, 237
Dniestr 217
Dobrawski 43
Dobrivlianskyi, P. 284
Dobroszklanka, Seweryn 216
Dobrowolski (from Jarosławicze) 32
Dobrowolski, Witold 70, 242
Dobrowoła family 48
Dobryłów 90
Dołhań 118, 158–59, 163
Dołhonosy 71
Dolina 196
Dołwiat 122
Domalewska (née Piotrowska), Stanisława (Stasia, author's sister) 112
Domalewski, Feliks (Felek, author's brother-in-law) 112
Domalewski, Stanisław 151, 267
Dominican monastery 245
Domyk, Franciszek 265
Donets, Kostiantyn 95, 105
Dontsov, Dmytro 12, 19, 176, 223–25, 252–53, 258, 277, 284
Dórak, Józefa see Pilch, Józefa
Durociński, Bolesław 136
Dorohusk 88, 202
Doszno 62, 66, 68–69, 72, 268
"Dovbeshka-Korobka" see Perehiiniak, Ivan
Dovbush 185
Dovhal, Mykhailo 160–61
Dragan family 132
Drańcza Polska 260
Drohobycz 197, 218
Drohomirecka, Wanda 51
Drohomirecki, Włodzimierz 50, 152
Drozd, Roman 177, 193, 279, 281, 284
Drozda, Bronisława 262

Dróżdż-Satanowska, Zofia 284
Drożdżyński, Aleksander 284
Druzhyny Ukrainskykh Natsionalistiv see DUN
Druzkopol 207, 260
Drzewiecka 95
Drzewiecki, Zygmunt 95
Dubenchuk, Iakiv 122, 142–43
Dubenchuk, Katia 122, 142–43
Dubenchuk family 140
Dubieńska Road 32
Dubieńska Street 115
Dubniki 131, 144
Dubno 29, 148–50, 178, 191, 215, 239, 272
Dubno County 18, 29, 145, 148, 215, 238, 242–43, 260
"Dubovyi" see Lytvynchuk, Ivan
Dubytskyi, Mykola (Mikołaj Dębicki [Mykola Dembytskyi]) 123, 270
Dudkowska (née Sawicka), Jolanta 37, 266
Dudkowski family 76–77
Dukla 230
Duliby 124
Dumyn, Osyp 11, 175, 224, 251, 258, 277, 284
DUN (Druzhyny Ukrainskykh Natsionalistiv, or Units of Ukrainian Nationalists) 230, 238–39
Dunaj 66
Dworzec 19
Dychka see Misiuk, Petro
Dykietyn 170
Dzhum 192
Dziabak (a.k.a. Diabuk), Nestor 157
Dziabak (a.k.a. Diabuk), Zofia 157
Dzidukh, Vladyslav 163
Dziekańska, Franciszka 54
Dziekańska, Jadwiga 54–55
Dziemba, Karol 159
Dziemiańczuk, Władysław 266, 270, 284
Dzięsław family 65–66
"Dzvin" see Shukhevych, Roman

E. Anita 281
"Easter Action" 73, 92
Eastern Europe 4
Eastern Galicia 1, 9–10, 17–19, 21, 25–26, 28, 167, 170, 185, 197, 201, 212, 222–23, 225–26, 234, 237, 240, 242–44, 246, 249–51, 253, 260, 262, 264–65, 274, 282; see also Małopolska Wschodnia
Eastern Little Poland see Eastern Galicia
Eastern Orthodox Church see Orthodox Church
Eastern Poland 1, 3, 9, 22, 27, 116, 167, 174, 195, 228–29, 231, 241, 247–48, 252, 257
Eastern-rite Catholic Church see Uniate Church
Edwardpole 139
Einsatzgruppen (mobile execution squads) 20, 177, 234
Ejsmont, Józef 119
Eljasz, Christina 290
"Eneia" see Oliinyk, Petro
"Eneia" group 189
"Eneia" region 29, 73, 92, 107, 145, 243
England 5, 221, 227, 249
Englot, Emilia see Krupka, Emilia
Englot, Filip 168, 171
Englot, Franciszek 168, 171
Englot (née Maćków), Franciszka 168
Englot, Władysław 168
Etobicoke 263
Eum family 72
Evintov, V. 284

Fajfer family 50
Fajkowski, Józef 284
Falkowska 156
Fedoriv, Petro 253
Fedorov, O. F. 205–06
Fedorovych, Anastasiia 163
Fedorowicz, Czesław 150
Fedorowicz, Stanisław 122
Fedorowski, G. 284
"Fedos" see Havryliuk, Mykola
Feldbach 248
Feldman, Borys 149
Feliński, M. 257, 277, 284
Ferenc, Dr. 173
Ferszt, Jan 69–70, 152
Fesiuk family 48
Fiala, Jan 284
Fiel 207
Fijałka, Michał 271, 275, 284
Fila, Antoni 60–61
Fila, Janina 60
Filar, Paweł 170

Filar, Władysław 5, 179–81, 188–89, 192, 194, 200, 205–06, 208, 250, 257, 260, 279–81, 284
Filip (author's neighbor in Ryświanka) 112–14, 270
Filip, Halina 270
Filip, Ludwika 270
Filip, Marysia 270
Filip, Staszek 270
Filip, Zosia 270
Filipkowski, Władysław ("Janka") 27
Filipowicz, Stanisław 127, 271
Filonenko, Petro 284
Fiodorpol 272
Firlejów 196
First Ukrainian Division 254
First Ukrainian Front 247
First World War 105; *see also* World War I
Fisch 216
Flajsz, Szyja 217
Florida 23
Fornal 60
Fotek, Janina 83
Fotek family 87
Fourth Panzer Army 209
France 244
Frank, Hans 26, 229–32, 237, 240, 248
Frankfurt am Main 144
Frankfurt on the Oder 233
Frederic, Dr. (a security service agent) 246
Freitag, Fritz 219
French Resistance 234
Friedman, Philip 177, 279
Friedman, Saul 278, 284
Fuks, Kalina 95–97
Fulman, Marian Leon 227

Gaj 61, 69–71, 129, 152, 267
Gałązka, Wanda 281
Galicja Colony 181
Galiński, Karol 218
Gandurska, Janina *see* Saran, Janina
Garczyńska, Leokadia *see* Jakubowska, Leokadia
Garczyńska, Władysława 36
Garczyński, Feliks 36
Garczyński, Jan 36
Gargała, Bronisława 170
Gargała, Franciszek 170
Gargała, Jan 170
Gargała, Wojciech 170
"Garkusha" 184
Garlicki, Stanisław 155

Gąsiorowski 80
Gatsfraied, Maier 264
Gdańsk (Danzig) 55, 224, 278
Gdańsk Province 249
Gdowski family 50, 151
Gębała, Jan 220
Genek, Anna 23–24
Genek, Antek 23
Genek, Vasyl 23–24
General Government (Generalgouvernement) 3, 26, 102, 198, 209–10, 229–30, 233–34, 237, 241, 260, 279
Generalplan Ost 16
Geneva 223
German-Soviet Boundary and Friendship Treaty (September 28, 1939) 229
German-Soviet line of demarcation 167; *see also* Ribbentrop-Molotov line of demarcation
Germany: Ministry of Foreign Affairs 11, 175, 224, 251; militia 194; occupation by 18, 96, 123, 192–93, 214, 276; police 26, 145, 178
Gerulis, Georg 233
Gestapo 24, 109, 171, 178, 208, 226, 229, 232, 244
Gewandter, Leon 217
Giebel 211
Giertych, Jędrzej 156, 262, 266, 273–74, 284
Gilewicz, Eugeniusz 38
Gilewicz, Filipina *see* Sawicka, Filipina
Gilewicz, Halina *see* Markowicz, Halina
Gilewicz, Irena *see* Łaszczewska, Irena
Gilewicz, Leokadia *see* Konopko, Leokadia
Giżycko 159
Głęboczyce 124, 127–28, 271
Gleczman, Kamil 199
Gleichenberg 248
Globocnik, Odilo 235
Głowińska, Aleksandra (Ola, Olesia) 38, 40, 42, 150
Głowińska-Krawiec, Alfreda 131, 164
Główka (née Bdychaj), Władysława 139
Głuboczanka 52–53, 151
Gniła Lipa River 169
Gnojo 139
Godomski 225
Goebbels, Paul Joseph 245

Golczewski, Frank 284
Golisz, Edward 35
Golisz, Helena *see* Włosowska, Helena
Gończybród 237
Gonta (from Werba) 148–49
Gonta, Ivan ("Haydamaks") 200
Gontar 122, 133
Göring, Hermann 223, 278
Górka Połonka 105
Górniki 56
Gorokhov 207
Górska, Maria *see* Piotrowska, Maria
Górski, Paweł (author's maternal uncle) 113
Goszczyńska, Danuta 38
Gozdów (Hwozdów) 158, 163
Grab 192
Grabina 124
Grabovets (Bogorodchany) 184; *see also* Grabowiec
Grabowiec 133; *see also* Grabovets
Great Conference of the Organization of Ukrainian Nationalists *see* VZOUN
Great Conference of Ukrainian Nationalists *see* VZUN
Great Commandments of the Revolutionary-Fighter 175, 225
"Greater Ukraine" 225, 251, 260
Greek Catholic Church 3, 240; *see also* Uniate Church
Greguła, Bolesław 61
Grenschutz (border patrol guard) 228
Gres, Jan *see* Grzeszczyszyn, Jan
Gródek 56, 157
Gronowicz 136, 138
Gross, Edward 284
"Grot" *see* Rowecki, Stefan
Group "L" 184
Gruntkowski 112, 114
Gruszka, Janina 136
Gruszka, Zofia 136
Gruszów 133
Grygorczyk (née Zarówny), Czesława 5, 266, 275
Grynowicz family 43
Grys, Zofia *see* Syloviak, Zofia
Grzesik, Julian 90, 123, 162, 258, 266
Grzeszczyszyn (Gres), Jan 274
Grzybowica 120, 131, 200

Grzybowska (née Zawilska), Leokadia 97, 155, 269, 273
Gucin 125, 164
Gulag 1, 17, 25
Gulak (née Paluszyńska), Maria 42
Gutenberg, Kuna 215
Gutman, Israel 281, 285
Guz (née Persona), Teresa 122
Guza, Wł. 220
Guzowska, Stanisława 157

Hai-Holovko (Hay-Holowko, Eng.), Oleksa 285
Hajki 123, 131
Halan, Iaroslav 182–83, 285
Halia family 75–79
Hały 116
Halytskyi 77
Hamernia 219–20
Hanusiak, Michael 285
Hanuszewicz, Franciszek 59
Harasym, Semen 61
Harasymovskyi see Hryniokh, Ivan
Hardzik family 131
Harkys, Artem 122, 135
Harmata, Agnieszka see Łysiak, Agnieszka
Harmata, Wiktoria 88
Harmazij, Jadwiga 170
Hasiak, Ryszard 142
Hasiak, Zofia 141–42
Hauke-Nowak, Aleksander 227
Havryliuk, Mykola ("Fedos," "Arkadii") 189
Havryliuk, Semen 122, 132
Haydamaks (Taras Shevchenko's poem) 9, 200
Heike, Wolf-Dietrich 240, 280, 285
Heiman, Leo 285
Hermaszewski, Władysław 285
Heuman, Karolina 217–18
Hilbrecht (née Sebestiańska), Halina 129–30, 259
Hillebrandt, B. 285
Himka, John-Paul 279–80, 285, 293
Himmelraikh, Kost ("Shelest," "Kyi") 285
Himmler, Heinrich 16, 220, 232, 240, 245, 247, 278
Hirniak, Kost 285
Hitler, Adolf 177, 192, 228, 231–35, 237, 239, 244, 248
Hlid, Stepan 285
Hnat, Volodymyr 152

Hnidawa 19, 103
Hofman (from Mołodawo-Ukraińskie) 191
Hofman, Jiří 285
Hojarska, Rozalia see Wasilewska, Rozalia
Holendernia 131
"Holobenko" 56, 180, 187
Hołoby 56, 71, 187–88
Holocaust 1, 4
Holod ("Sliusar") 56
Hołodnica 155
Hołówko, Tadeusz 226
Hołownica estate 109
Hołowno 15, 81, 181
"Holub" 33, 35
Holubytskyi 139
Holy Trinity parish 169
Holzer, Jerzy 285
Home Political Representation of the Polish People see KRP
"Honta" 56
Hontar, Ivan 285
Horbovyi, Volodymyr 229, 232, 234
Hordiienko, Mykola 285
Horochów 33, 35, 41, 99, 159
Horochów County 18–19, 21, 33, 38, 56, 92, 120, 129, 143, 150, 195, 242–43, 260, 274
Horochówka 35, 266
Horodecki (Podhorodecki) family 54, 267
Horodziec 116
Horoszówka 49
Horshchar, Ivan 149
Horshchar, Serhii 149
Horyń River 46, 49, 73, 107, 115–16, 145, 260
Horyszów Polski 269
Hoszcza 107
"Hrabenko" 46
Hrabets, Omelian ("Batko") 243
Hrady see Kalusów
"Hreczka" (code name for ZWZ-AK) see ZWZ-AK
Hrodskyi, Ivan 97, 101
"Hroznyi" 107
Hrubieszów 16, 133, 197, 200–01, 259–60
Hrubieszów County 16–17, 197, 204, 246, 259, 265
Hryniewiecki, Witold 285
Hryniokh, Ivan (Harasymovskyi, pseud.) 14–15, 210–11, 213

Hrytsaiuk 165
Hrytsenko, Oleksandr 14, 258
Hubetskyi, Leon 190
Hucisko Horodyńskie 77–78
Hucisko Kowalowe 77
Hucisko Pikulskie 153, 273
Hudeczek, Teresa see Borowska, Teresa
Huk (UPA commander) 181
Huk, Bohdan 285
Huk, Vasyl 165–66
Hul, Ievhen 132
Hulub, Slavko 24
Humań ("Haydamaks") 201
Humnytskyi 276–77
Hunchak, Taras 285
Hupał 89
Hurby 147, 165
Huszcza 81
Huta Antonowiecka 73
Huta Majdańska 20, 165–66, 273
Huta Pieniacka 219, 245
Huta Stara 260
Huta Stepańska 51, 116, 119, 188, 195, 260
Huzuvatyi, Petro 46
Hwozdów see Gozdów

Iadziuk, Moisei 122, 129, 272
Ianiv, Volodymyr 227
"Iarema" 118
"Iarlan" see Starukh, Iaroslav
"Iarmak" 46
Iashchuk, Volodymyr 119
Iatsiv, Dmytro 233
Iatsura, Semen 97, 101
Iavnyi, I. 233
Ievchuk 97
Ievdokymenko, Volodymyr 285
Ievhen Konovalets battalion 234
Ikwa River 73
Iliuszyn, Ihor 260, 280
Ilnytskyi, Roman 233, 285
Institute of History of the Higher Pedagogical School 253
"Iron Guard" 233
Ishchuk 153
Iskra 185
istrebitelnyye (destruction) battalions 27
Italy 225, 227
Iukhno 122, 136, 138, 163
"Iurko" 33, 35
Ivasyk see Sheremeta, Ivan
Ivko, Stanislav 154

Iwańcza 116
Iwańczyce 138
Iwanicze 122, 127, 188
Iwanie 191
Iwaniwka 59
Izbica 131

Jachemek, Stasia 31–32
Jachemek, Stefan 31
Jadowski family 53
Jagliński family 61
Jagodzin 84, 86–87, 90, 153, 203, 260
Jakubowska (née Garczyńska), Leokadia 36
Jakubowska, Mirka 66
Jakubowski, Walerek 66
Jakubowski, Zbigniew 66
Janicka, Hanna 132
Janicka, Helena 132
Janicka, Stanisława 132
Janicki, Antoni 132
Janicki, Gustaw 132
Janicki, Jerzy 185, 285
Janicki, Zenobiusz 95, 105–06, 156, 269–70, 273, 285
Janik, Bronisław 118, 270, 285
Janina, Sister 173
"Janka" see Filipkowski, Władysław
Jankowce 81, 154
Jankowski, Mieczysław 31
Jankowski, Mikołaj 31
Jankowski family 32
Janowa Dolina 24, 49, 159, 179, 194, 208, 266–67
Janówka 19, 58, 152
Januszkiewicz, Antoni 158
Januszkiewicz, Janina 158–59
Januszkiewicz, Władysław 158
Japan 227
Japołoć 48
Jarosław 197, 230, 246
Jarosław County 205
Jarosławicze 29, 31–32, 149
Jary, Richard ("Riko") 223–24, 226, 232–33, 278
Jasiniec 35
Jasińska (from Sucha Łoza) 71
Jasińska (from Zielony Dąb) 147
Jasiński, Feliks 77, 153, 165, 275
Jasionówka 131, 164
Jaskut, Karol 98
Jaskut, Kazia 98–99
Jastrzębski, Józef 276

Jastrzębski, Stanisław 172, 276, 285
Jaworsky, Ivan 292
Jaworzno 251–52, 254
Jazłowce 158
Jaźwiński, Wiktor 173
Jędrzejewicz, Wacław 278, 285
Jedynowicz, Karolina 67
Jedynowicz, Kazimierz 67
Jedynowicz, Maria 67
Jedynowicz, Tadeusz 67
Jegorow, Ryszard 292
Jehovah's Witness(es) 127–28
Jesionek, Bronek 89
Jesionek, Ewa see Palec, Ewa
Jesionek, Maria see Pendel, Maria
Jesionek family 88
Jesionkiewicz, J. 220
Jesionówka 36
Jeske 220
Jewish Committees in Poland 217
Jewish Historical Commission of Poland 214, 265
Jewish Historical Institute 217
Jews 9, 13, 17, 22, 109, 127, 135, 149, 156, 169, 177, 186, 191, 193, 206, 214–17, 228, 230, 232, 234–35, 238–39, 247, 260, 264
Jeż, Józef 87
Jezierce (Ozirce) 237
Jezierzany 170
Jeziorany Czeskie 103, 269
Jeziorany Polskie 103–05
Jeziorany Szlacheckie 95–96, 104, 129, 269
Jezioro 95, 105, 156
Jeżyny 188
Jodl, Alfred 229
Józefatka 134
Józefin 155, 273
Józefina 49
Józefówka 107
Józewski, Henryk 226–27
Jóźwiak (née Morelowska), Stanisława 137, 275
Juchniewicz, Mieczysław 264, 282, 285
Jurasz, Błażej 276
Jurewicz, Lesław 285
Justyna, Irena 99, 155, 269
Juzwenko, Bernard 285

K-Organisation 206, 228
Kachynskyi, Serhii ("Ostap") 116, 239

Kaczorowska, Aniela 124
"Kaidash" see Stelmashchuk, Iurii
Kaizer 234
Kalba, Myroslav 285
Kalina 195
Kalinin 1
Kaliszewski family 102
Kałusów (now called Hrady) 123, 125
Kamenetsky, Ihor 286
Kamianets-Podilskyi/Vynnytsia region 243
Kamień Koszyrski 81
Kamień Koszyrski County 33, 58, 243
Kamieniecki 66
Kaminciv 265
Kamińska (née Cybuchowska), Kamila 126–27, 270–71
Kamiński, Rev. 137–38
Kamiński, Stefan 127, 271
Kamionka 49–50, 150
Kamionka Strumiłowa 14, 197, 212–13
Kania, Janusz 278, 286
Kaniewski, Stanisław 21, 261, 286
Kański family 65
Kantor, Franciszek 32
Kantor, Weronika 32
Kapturkiewicz 136
Kapuscianski (Mykola Kapustianskyi) 219–21
Karaczun 151–52, 267
Karasin 260
Karat, Orest 15, 183, 259
Karavan, Grigory 264
Karbovych, Z. see Stetsko, Iaroslav
Karczunek 196
Kardashuk, Mykhailo see Kordashuk, Mykola
Kardaszuk, Michał see Kordashuk, Mykola
Karłowicz, Leon 69, 152
Karpiłówka 2, 159–162
Karpińska (née Łączyńska), Katarzyna 48
Karpińska, Lala 55
Karpiński, Kazimierz 55
Karpiuk, Roman 190
Karpo (UPA commander) 207
Karta Center—Eastern Archive 4
Kasiian, Stepan 286
Kaszuba, Kazimierz 144
Katerburg 73
Katerynówka 154–55

Kąty 81, 86, 153–54, 273
Kąty (Kuty) 73, 77, 81, 153, 165, 178, 198, 260, 275
Katyn 1
Kazakhstan 149
Kazanivskyi, Bohdan 286
Kazimirka (Kazimierka) 52, 151–52, 260, 267, 272
Kedryn-Rudnytskyi, Ivan 286
Keitel, Wilhelm 229
Kharkov 1
Kharyton 164
Khmelnytskyi, Bohdan 9, 201
Khmil 213
Khrapchynskyi, Stanislav 72
Khropot, Vasyl 190
Khrushchev, Nikita 206
Kieras, Ludwik 162
Kieraszewicz, Elramina 42
Kiesz, Wadiusz 69
Kiev 10, 53, 63, 207, 222–23, 235–39, 243, 253, 256
Kilimnik, Jan 275
Kilimnik, Stanisława 275
Kirkconnell, Watson 257, 282
Kirychuk, Pavlo 165, 275
Kirychuk, Stepanyda 165
Kirylozuk, Patia 219–20
Kisielin 19, 33, 35–38, 42–43, 62, 143, 207, 260, 274
Kisielówka 43
Kisorycze 116
Kitaszewski, Henryk 266, 273–74
Kiwerce 92, 155, 188
Kizilin *see* Kisielin
Klachkivskyi, Roman Dmytro ("Klym Savur," "Okhrym," "Klym," "Krymskyi," "Omelian") 15, 46, 180, 187–88, 243, 258
Klecka Wielka 109
"Klei" *see* Kupiak, Dmytro Hryhorovych
Klepaczów 155, 273
Klesów 116
Klewań 107, 203, 205
Klewieck 71
Klietmann, Kurt-Georg 286
Kłopoczyn 135
Kłosiński, Bogdan 220
Klukowski, Andrew 286
Klukowski, George 286
Klukowski, Zygmunt 204, 286
"Klym" *see* Klachkivskyi, Roman Dmytro
Klymushyn, Ivan ("Kruk") 29, 73, 145

Klymyshyn, Mykola 286
Kniahinin 29
"Kniaz" 56
Kniaz family 76–77
"Kniazhenko" 33, 35
Knysh, Zynovii (Bohdan Mykhailiuk, pseud.) 286
Koapernyk, Serhii 48
Kobryń County 243
Kobylański, Władysław 286
Kobyłecki, Mieczysław 48
Kobylnia (Kobylnica) 115
Kobylnica *see* Kobylnia
Koch, Erich 25–26, 236
Koch, Hans 236
Kochanówka 204
Kochman, Janina 170
Kochman, Józef 168, 170
Kociołek, Józefa 129
Kołaczkowska, Karolina 276
Kołaczkowski, Kazimierz 172
Kolada, Viktor 190
Kolba, Arsen 48–49
Kołbyń 105
Kolchak, Vasyl 61
Kołcowska (née Kułakowska), Genowefa 104–05
Kołcowski, Antoni 104
Kołki 92, 95, 157, 241, 260, 273
Kołodno 198
Kolodzynskyi unit 182
Kołomyja County 23
Kolonia Wielka 131, 144
Komański, Henryk 31, 95, 104, 286
Komar 185
Komarów 186
Komińska 32
Komunistyczna Partia Zachodniej Ukrainy *see* KPZU
Kondracki, Edward 123, 272
Kondufor, Yu. Yu. 177, 185, 207, 209, 211–12, 279–81, 286
Konhres Ukrainskykh Natsionalistiv *see* KUN
Konieczny, Zdzisław 205, 286
Koniuchy 19, 260
Konopacka, Antonina 48
Konopacka, Helena 48
Konopacka, Teodozja 48
Konopacka, Weronika 48
Konopacki (from Wiśniowiec) 80
Konopacki, Adam 48
Konopacki, Bolesław 48
Konopacki family (from Rużyn) 71

Konopko (née Gilewicz), Leokadia 38
Konoplanko, Halyna 149
Konoplanko, Rev. (Halyna's father) 148, 272
Konotopy 167–68
Konovalets, Ievhen 223, 225–28, 278, 286
Kopecký, Karol 103
Kopecký, Vladislav 103–04
Kopernyk, Serhii 49
Kopryian 35
Korbecki, Augustyn 170
Korchak 31, 143
Korchak, Ivan 190
Kordashuk, Mykola 122–23, 270
Korecka Huta 237
Korenchuk (née Kozińska), Michalina 118, 158–59
Korenchuk, Oleksandr 118, 158–59
Korenchuk, Volodymyr 118, 159
Korfes, Otto 206, 233
Korin, Mykola 61–64
Korman, Aleksander 203, 286
Korman, Mieczysław 217
Korneluk, Lester 290
Korościatyn 261
Korosten 209
Korostowice 170
Korszów 101, 156
Korytnica 2, 20, 27, 120
Korzec 107, 109, 115, 163
Kosakviskyi, Mykyta 228
Kościuszkowo 98, 189
Kosek, Karol 286
Kosiak 61
Kosińska, Franciszka 66
Kossak-Szczucka, Zofia 198
Kostiuk (from Kamionka) 49
Kostiuk, Andrii 159–61
Kostiuk, Petro 160
Kostopol 46, 50, 107, 151, 178, 194, 207, 237, 274–75
Kostopol battalion 46
Kostopol County 18, 46, 150, 179, 194, 200, 237, 242–43, 260, 267, 274
Kosyk, Wolodymyr 279–80, 286
Kosynska, Nastka 62
Kosynskyi, Nykanor 62
Koszalin 273
Koszewski, Count 189
Koszów 92, 95, 97–101, 150, 155, 269
Koszyszcze 156, 237

Kotarski, Tadeusz 70, 152
Kotów 156
Kots, Nestor S. 84
"Koval" see Kuk, V.
Koval, M. V. 287
Koval, Stepan ("Rubashenko," "Burlak") 51, 92, 116, 118, 188, 241
Kovalchuk 65, 166
Kovaluk (née Szostek), Antonina 123
Kovaluk, Vasyl 123, 125
Kovpak, Sidor 275
Kowalówka 58, 152
Kowalska, Halya 292
Kowalska, Regina see Śliwa, Regina
Kowalska, Zofia 133, 272
Kowalski, Dominik 106
Kowalski, Witold 43
Kowel 56, 61, 64–65, 68, 71, 180, 187, 189, 196, 242
Kowel County 18–19, 33, 35, 56, 58, 120, 129, 152, 163, 195, 237, 242–43, 260
Kozakowa Dolina 97
Kozar, Michał 185
Kozel 62, 68
Kozhushko family 48–49
Koziarniki 237
Kozidło, Jadwiga 164
Kozidło, Stefania 164
Kozidło, Tomasz 164
Kozińska, Michalina see Korenchuk, Michalina
Koziński, Franciszek 118
Kozłowska, Anna 202
Kozłowska, Irena 202–03
Kozłowski, Andrzej 202
Kozłowski, Jan 202
Kozłowski, Leon 203
KPZU (Komunistyczna Partia Zachodniej Ukrainy, or Communist Party of Western Ukraine) 148
Krajewska, Jadwiga 122
Krajowa Reprezentacja Polityczna Narodu Polskiego see KRP
Kraków 4, 12, 16, 126–27, 174, 177, 198, 210, 229–33, 245
Kraków Province 9
Krakowiak, Ania 128
Krakowiak, Katarzyna see Ograbek, Katarzyna
Krakowiak family 129
Krakus 155
Krashkevych 123, 126

Krasicki, Roman 275
Krasińska, Stanisława 72
Kraśnica 157
Krasnobrod 220
Krasnolesie 169, 276
Krasnystaw County 131
Krasovskyi, Volodymyr 153–54, 273
Kravchuk (from Szumsk) 153
Kravchuk, Paraska 109
Kravchuk, Ulian 98
Kravchuk, Valerian 97
Krel, M. 220
Kremasz 35
Kremenets see Krzemieniec
Krokhmaliuk, Roman 287
Królikowska (née Tarnawska), Sabina 92, 150, 269
Królikowski, Bolesław 76
Królikowski, Józef 76
Królikowski family 76–77
"Kropyva" see Lukashchuk, Volodymyr
Krosno 231
KRP (Krajowa Reprezentacja Polityczna Narodu Polskiego, or Home Political Representation of the Polish People) 199–200
Krüger, Walter 229
"Kruk" see Klymushyn, Ivan
Kruk (colony) 49
"Kruk" group 107
Krupka (née Englot), Emilia 5, 168–71, 276
Krupp foundries 151
Krychevskyi, Roman 287
"Krylatyi" 56
Krymno 19, 56
"Krymskyi" see Klachkivskyi, Roman Dmytro
Krynica 230
Krysiak, Bogusława see Nowicka, Bogusława
Krystynopol 230
Kryzhov, Serhii 159, 162
Krzemieniec 35, 73, 76–79, 178, 198, 207, 238
Krzemieniec County 29, 73, 75, 79, 81, 153, 198, 237, 243, 260
Krzeszów 152
Krzysztan, Jan 125
Krzysztyniak, Antoni 170
Kubiak, Hieronim 281, 287
Kubiiovych, Volodymyr 16, 219–20, 229–31, 239–41, 243, 248, 277, 279–80, 287
Kubów, Władysław 287

Kucewicz, Jan 78
Kucewicz, Olga 78–79
Kuchma, Leonid 254, 256
Kuców family 220
Kuczerepa, Mykoła 277
Kuczyńska, Franciszka 109
Kuczyński, Józef 287
Kudan, Julian 87
Kuk, V. ("Koval") 252
Kulai, Mitko 124, 271
Kulai, Volodymyr 124, 134
Kułakowska, Genowefa see Kołcowska, Genowefa
Kułakowska, Maria 104
Kułakowski (Genowefa's father) 105
Kulczycka, Helena 75
KUN (Konhres Ukrainskykh Natsionalistiv, or Congress of Ukrainian Nationalists) 253
Kunicki, Mikołaj 193, 239, 287
Kunysz, Anna see Szyjkowska, Anna
Kunysz, Bronisław 124
Kunysz, Ludwika 124
Kunysz, Maria 124
Kunysz, Zygmunt 124
Kupetskyi, Hrytsko 287
Kupiak, Dmytro Hryhorovych ("Klei") 262–64, 287
Kupiczów 56
Kupowalce 35, 38, 266
Kuras, I. F. 286
Kurdyban-Warkowiecki 215
Kurdybelski, Jan 59, 162, 261, 267, 275, 287
Kurdynki 247
Kurek 129
Kurhanowicz, Hela 149
Kuriata, Zygmunt 217
Kurmylo, Maryska 262
Kuropas, Myron B. 257, 277, 287
Kuropatniki 170
Kuryluk 166
Kuś family 198
Kushch Self-Defense units see SKV
Kushneruk, Aleksy 124
Kustycze 242
Kuts, Oleksandr 226
Kuty see Kąty (Kuty) and also Uhły
Kuwałek, Bolesław 83
Kuwałek, Czesław 83
Kuwałek, Janina see Martosińska, Janina

Kuwałek, Marianna 85
Kuwałek, Władysław 83
Kuźniar, Władysław 170
Kuzych-Berezovskyi, Ivan 261, 287
Kvitkovskyi, Mykola *see* Ohorodnychuk
Kwasiłów 109
Kwaśniewski, Aleksander 254, 256
Kwiatkowski family 31–32
"Kyi" *see* Himmelraikh, Kost
Kyslyi, Iukhym 124, 135
Kyts, Pavlo 61–62, 64, 66

Lachów 122, 125
Łączyńska, Katarzyna *see* Karpińska, Katarzyna
Łagodowska, Jadwiga *see* Blaszczyńska, Jadwiga
Łagodowska, Maria 132
Łagodowski, Mieczysław 132
Laidak 181–82
Lake Quenz, Austria 227
Łamane 19
Łańcut 168
Landsberg 214, 265
Landwehr, Richard 287
Łanowce 198
Lappo, Henryk 287
Lapychak, Toma 287
Las Ryświanecki 111, 114
Lashuk (Halushka's father) 124, 142–43
Lashuk, Halushka 124, 142–43
Łasków 184
Lasoń, Jan *see* Cyprian, Brother
Łaszczewska (née Gilewicz), Irena 38
Ławrów 98, 104
League of Nations 10, 222, 226
Lebed, Mykola ("Maksym Ruban," "Skyva") 12–14, 17, 46, 83, 180, 187, 226–27, 230, 234, 239, 242–43, 258–60, 278, 287
Lebensraum (living space) 16
Lemiecha, Jadwiga 131
Lemiecha, Jan 131
Lemiecha, Józef 131
Lemiecha, Konstancja 131
Lemiecha, Marysia 131
Lemiecha, Stanisław 131
Lemko Company 249
Lemko region/area 22, 229–31, 249

Lemkos 9
Leniewo 105
Lenkavskyi, Stepan 176, 225
Leonenko, V. 284
Leonówka (in Łuck County) 155
Leonówka (in Równe County) 2, 107, 109–12
Leśko, Władysław 134
Letishev 207
Levkovich 207
Levytskyi, Andrii 237
Lewandowska (née Matkowska), Anna 274
Liniów 35, 42, 92, 94, 99–100, 150
Linowski, Jan *see* Banach, Kazimierz
Lipczyńska 155
Lipian family 132
Lipniki 53
Lipski, Józef 278
Lishchuk 165, 275
Liski 131
Lisowska, Amelia 97
Listowski, Józef 78
Liszewski, Karol *see* Szawłowski, Ryszard
Litawski 219
Lithuania 225
Litogoszcz 153
Littlejohn, David 237, 279, 287
Littman, Sol 227, 278
Liubchenko, Arkadii 287
Łódź 4
Logusz, Michael O. 241, 280, 287
Lokachi *see* Łokacze
Łokacze 36, 45, 94–95, 150, 207
London: England 5, 221, 227; Ontario 270
Long Island, New York 276
Lopatin (a.k.a. Zubenko) 207
Łopuszyński, Jan 45
Los, Marko 159
Łoś, Stanisław 283
Lower Silesia 217
Łoziński, E. 287
"Lozovskyi, Roman" *see* Shukhevych, Roman
Lubaczów 205
Lubczyński, Aleksander 87, 268
Lubczyński, Czesław 90
Lubczyński, Jan 90
Lubczyński, Stanisław 87
Lubieszów 148–49, 272

Lubitów 56
Lublatyn 19
Lublin 1, 4, 21–22, 27, 76, 90, 123, 162, 197, 201, 227, 235, 244, 251
Lublin Province 9, 16–17, 26, 41, 81, 120, 150, 204, 227, 260
Lubliniec 71, 70
Luboml 15, 75, 81, 86–87, 154, 187–88, 203, 268
Luboml County 18–19, 33, 81, 83, 153–54, 242–43, 259–60, 268, 273
"Luboń" *see* Bąbiński, Kazimierz Damian
Łuck 16, 31, 43, 63, 92, 98–106, 130, 137–38, 149, 155–57, 178, 189, 194, 196, 201, 203, 207–08, 234, 239, 241, 274
Łuck County 16, 18–20, 33, 35, 42, 92, 105, 129, 154, 237, 242–43, 259–60, 269, 273
Łuczak, Czesław 278–79, 288
Łuczyce 61, 68
Ludvipol *see* Ludwipol
Ludwikówka 168–71, 191, 238
Ludwipol 46, 181, 207
Ługa River 122
Lukaichuk, Harasym 64–65
Lukash 36, 97
Lukashchuk, Volodymyr ("Kropyva") 107
Łukaszów, Jan *see* Olszański, Tadeusz Andrzej
Lulówka 35, 37–38, 41, 150, 266
Lutsk *see* Łuck
Łużny, Ryszard 278, 288
Lviv *see* Lwów
Lviv State University 253
Lvov *see* Lwów
Lwów (Lvov, Lviv) 9, 12, 27, 29, 35, 107, 126–27, 173–74, 195–97, 204, 210–11, 213–14, 217, 222, 224–27, 232–33, 235–37, 245–47, 253, 262–63, 274–75
Lwów Province 9, 18, 22, 24, 28, 137, 167, 217–18
Łyczakowski cemetery 263
Łyczki 155–56, 273
Łysiak (née Harmata), Agnieszka 89
Lyisak, Oleh 288

Łyisnia 260
"Lysyi" 15, 81, 83, 180–81, 187, 258, 271
Lytvynchuk, Ivan ("Dubovyi") 46, 243
Lytvyniuk, Anna *see* Stasik, Anna

Machiavelli, Niccolò 225
Maciejewska 102
Maciejów 56, 194
Maćków, Franciszka *see* Englot, Franciszka
Maćków, Józef 170
Maćkowiak family 94
Maczkowce 104
Madajczyk, Czesław 230, 273, 278–79, 288
Mądro, Roman 244
Magocsi, Paul Robert 288
Maidan *see* Majdan
Mailov, Aleksei 226
Main Commission for the Investigation of Crimes Against the Polish Nation 4, 21, 251, 262
Maisky, Ivan 234
Majdan 19, 73, 185
Majdan Wielki 196
Majer, Ryszard 115
Majków 107
Makar (from Hucisko Horodyńskie) 77–78
Makar (from Piotrowice) 157
Makar family (from Przekurka) 83–84
Makarov 209
Makhonko 89
"Maks" *see* Skorupynskyi, Maksym
Maksymchuk-Kardash, Mykola 238
Mała Iłowica 153
Malashchuk, Roman 288
Malashka 124
Małe Hołoby 260
Małecka, Adela 127
Małecka, Karola 127
Małecka, Konstancja *see* Szczepańska, Konstancja
Małecki, Eliasz 127
Małecki, Wacław 127
Malin 29
Malin Czeski 191
Maliniski 245
Malinowski, Ludwik 157
Małopolska Wschodnia (Eastern Little Poland) 1; *see also*

Eastern Galicia 21, 195–97, 246
Małyńsk 46, 52, 54, 216, 272
Małyszczycki, Zbigniew 149, 272
"Mamai" 191
Mandrivnyk 23, 182, 190
Manias, Anna *see* Świderska, Anna
Maniewicze 56, 60–61, 188
"Manifesto of Prague" 248
Maninkhvast 63
Mańkowski, Zygmunt 260, 288
Manuilskyi, Dmytro 288
marching, or expeditionary groups *see pokhidni hrupy*
Marchuk, Helena 65–66
Marchuk, Vasyl 65
Maria Wola 137–38, 163, 273
Marianów 276
Marianówka 129, 131–32, 188
Mariański, Antoni 288
Markelov, Valentin 284
Markiewicz, Krzysztof 70, 242, 280, 288
Markowicz (née Gilewicz), Halina 38
Markowska, Tekla (from Klepaczów) 155
Markowska, Wanda (from Klepaczów) 155
Markowski (from Lulówka) 37, 266
Markowski, Adam (from Klepaczów) 273
Marmucki, Jan 96–97
Marrus, Michael R. 177, 279, 288
Marszałówka 58, 152
Martosińska (née Kuwałek), Janina 84, 268
Martyn 219–21
Martynets, V. 288
Martynovskyi, Mykola ("Mukha") 189
Marunchak, Mykhailo H. 288
Marynki 77–78
Masliuk 84
Maszko 128
Matkowska, Anna *see* Lewandowska, Anna
Matla, Oleksandr *see* Tereshchuk, Petro
Matla, Zenon 253
Matla, Zynovii 288
Matseiko, Hryhorii 227
Matushevskyi 49

Maurras, Charles 225
Mavzelepa, Laktion 97–98
May, Helen Klukowski 286
Mayfair (restaurant) 263
Mazarnia farm 263
Maziarnia 197
Mazurkiewicz, Władysław 274
Mazurok, Fylyp 134
Medical Academy of Lublin 244
Medvedev, Dmitri 238
Medvid, Andriy 293
Medwedówka 54
Medweże 92
Medynskyi, Stepan 288
Medzarykha 77–78
Meleshko, M. ("Virlyk") 234
Melichevskyi 237
Melnychuk, Mykola 148–49
Melnyk, Andrii 12–13, 73, 120, 206, 208, 223, 227–28, 230–33, 237–39, 244, 247–48, 278; *see also* Consul I
Melnyk, Grzegorz (Hryhorii Melnyk) 219–21
Melnykowcy (Ukr., Melnykivtsi; OUN-M members) 21, 75; *see also* OUN-M
Mende, Gerhard von 18, 213, 236, 248, 260
Micgiel, John 288
Michałek, Jan 129
Michałkiewicz family 138
Michałowicz family 136
Michałówka 62
Michowska, Zofia 139
Międzyrzec 107
Mielnica 19, 60, 68, 71–72, 152, 237, 268
Mikhnovskyi, Mykola 288
Mikołajówka 109, 114
Mikulicze 120
Milewicz, Jan 54
Military Historical Institute (Warsaw) 4
military settlers 98, 133, 257
Miller family 50
Ministry of Propaganda (German) 245, 278
Ministry of State Administration in Warsaw 205
Mirchuk, Petro 176–77, 226, 257, 277, 288
Mishchaniuk (née Szyndrów), Genowefa 150
Mishchaniuk, Mykhailo 150, 274
Misiło, Eugeniusz 251–52, 281, 288

Misiuk, Petro (also known as Dychka) 132
"Mitla" 46
Mityukov, A.G. 286
Mizocz 145, 190, 275
Młynów 29, 32, 148, 150, 215
Młynowce 198
"Mochul" 33
Modrzejewska (née Sobczyńska), Genowefa 105
Mokwin 48, 239
Molchanov, Vladimir 263, 288
Mołodawo-Ukraińskie 191
Mołotków 75, 237
Monasterichy 185
Mont St-Hilaire, Quebec 168, 275
Montreal 168, 253, 266
Morelowska, Irena see Papowszek, Irena
Morelowska, Stanisława see Jóźwiak, Stanisława
Morelowski family 136–37
"Moroz" 188
Moroz, Bohdan 263
Mościska 196
Moscow 11, 63, 177, 186, 231
"Moskalenko" 33, 35
Mosty 73, 150
Mosty Wielke 218
Mosur 122, 132–33, 181
Moszory, Kazimierz 274
Motyka, Grzegorz 178, 182–86, 204, 210–13, 259–61, 289
Motyl, Alexander J. 175–76, 226, 257–58, 277, 289
Mountain-Peasants' Help see BBH
Mrochko, Petro 125
Mroczkowski, Józef 289
Mroz, Ivan 152
Mstyslav see Skrypnyk, Stepan
Mühlhausen 168
"Mukha" see Martynovskyi, Mykola
Müller, Heinrich 208, 212–13
Munich 223, 253, 263
Murawska, Basia 1, 52
Murawska-Żygadło, Bronisława 52
Murawski, Adam 1, 52
Murawski, Aleksander 2, 52
Murawski, Antoni 52
Murawski, Marian 52–53
Musionka family 135
Mussolini, Benito 224

Mutual Declaration of the Presidents of the Republic of Poland and Ukraine Regarding Understanding and Reconciliation 254–55
Muzyka (from Gucin Colony) 125, 164
Muzyka, Agnieszka 15, 86, 258, 268, 289
Muzyka, Bonifacy 90
Muzyka, Tomasz 90
Mykhailiuk, Bohdan see Knysh, Zynovii
Mykhalchuk, Vasyl 258, 262, 289
Mykoluk (Nykoluk), Horpyna 273
Mykoluk (Nykoluk), Iosyp 272
Mykoluk (Nykoluk), Tetiana 153, 272
Mykolus family 83–84
Mykytchuk, Karpo 233
Myron, Dmytro 239
Myśliwski, Wiesław 266, 268, 272–73, 289
Myszakówka 237, 260

Nachtigall 25, 230, 232–33, 238–39, 247
Nadorozhye 184
Nadvornaya 185
Naklicka, Irena 130
Naklicka (née Adamska), Władysława 130
Naklicki, Roman 130
Nakonechnyi, Vladyslav 289
Nalepka 160
Naliboki 264
Nastaszczyn 170
Natalka family 76, 78
"national dictatorship" 225
National Union of Ukrainian emigrés in Germany 237
Nationalist Military Detachments see VVN
"Nazar" 58
Nechai 185
Nedatypolskyi unit 182
Nedzelskyi 137
"Negus" 29, 73, 107, 145
Nehring 14, 212–13, 258
Netreba 23, 118–19, 158–59, 162
Neuhammer 233, 245
New Hampshire 174
New Jersey 274
New York 174, 254, 276
Nicieja, Stanisław Sławomir 289

Niebrzydów 122
Niedzieliska 217
Niedzielko, Romuald 257, 259–60, 278, 280, 289
Niedźwiedzie Jamy 37–38
Nielisz 220
Niemilia 50
Niemowicze 116
Niesuchojeże 56
Nieświcz 96–97, 102, 129
Nietzsche, Friedrich 225
Niezgoda, Jadwiga 77
NKVD (Soviet security police) 24, 77, 145, 183, 190, 227
Non-Aggression Pact (between Germany and the Soviet Union) 228
northwestern Ukraine 7
Novosad, Petro 289
Novovolyńsk 123
Nowa Huta 237
Nowa Moszczanica 190
Nowa Nosowica 32
Nowa Nowina 178
Nowa Wieś 220
Nowe Gniezno 35, 38
Nowicka (née Krysiak), Bogusława 44
Nowojanka 164
Nowomalin 145
Nowosiółki 59, 133
Nowy Gaj 60, 267
Nowy Jagodzin 89
Nowy Majdan 197
Nowy Sącz 217
Nuremberg 229
Nychypir family 50, 150
Nykoluk, Horpyna see Mykoluk, Horpyna
Nykoluk, Iosyp see Mykoluk, Iosyp
Nykoluk, Tetiana see Mykoluk, Tetiana
Nyzhynska, Fedora (Teodora) 158–59, 162

Obeniże 68
Obórki 106, 239
Ochotniki 237
Ochrona 113–14
Odessa 233
ODVU (Orhanizatsiia Derzhavnoho Vyzvolennia Ukrainy, or Organization for the Rebirth of Ukraine) 225
Ograbek (née Krakowiak), Katarzyna 128, 271
Ohorodnychuk (a.k.a. Mykola Kvitkovskyi) 188, 272

Okęcki, Stanisław 264, 282
"Okhrym" *see* Klachkivskyi, Roman Dmytro
Okopy 118, 158–59, 201, 260
Oksiutych, Ivan 71, 152
Oksiutych, Lonka 71, 152
Oksiutych, Serhii 71, 152
Oktawin 19
"Oleh" 187–88
Oleksiniec 73, 198
Olesk 120
Olgin 155
Oliinyk (teacher from Deraźne) 151
Oliinyk, Petro ("Eneia") 179, 243
Oliwa, Apolinary 289
Olshanskyi, Teofil 224
Olszańska 66
Olszański, Tadeusz Andrzej (Jan Łukaszów, pseud.) 278, 289
Olszowski, Wojciech 169
Olsztyn Province 249
Ołyka 19, 92, 191
Omelchenko, Tymish 237
"Omelian" *see* Klachkivskyi, Roman Dmytro
Omelianovych-Pavlenko 237
Omelno 259
Onufrii 157
Onyshkevych, Myroslav ("Orest") 250, 252–53
Onyszkowce 260
Operation "Wisła" (*Akcja "Wisła"*) 249–55
Opulsko 168
Orel (UPA commander) 183, 212
Orel (village) 191
"Orest" *see* Onyshkevych, Myroslav
Organization for the Rebirth of Ukraine *see* ODVU
Organization of Ukrainian Nationalists *see* OUN
Orhanizatsiia Derzhavnoho Vyzvolennia Ukrainy *see* ODVU
Orhanizatsiia Ukrainskykh Natsionalistiv *see* OUN
Orlenko 182
Orthodox Church 3–4, 7, 26, 236, 240
Orzeszyn 35, 125, 133, 164, 272
Ośmigowicze 63
"Ostap" *see* Brys, Oleksyi *and also* Kachynskyi, Serhii

Ostasz (née Ziółkowska), Kamila 62, 65
Ostaszewski, Jan 275
Ostaszewski, Leokadia 275
Ostróg 145, 260
Ostrówki 15, 19, 81, 83–87, 89–90, 181, 243–44, 259–60, 268
Ostrowska, Aleksandra 101, 156, 259
Ostrowski, Stanisław 155
Ostrowski, Wacław 155
"Ostryi" 46, 51, 107
Osuchowski, Witek 138
Oswald[owa], Wanda 274
Otiniyshe *see* Baby
Otrębowicz, Janina 289
OUN (Orhanizatsiia Ukrainskykh Natsionalistiv, or Organization of Ukrainian Nationalists) 4, 9, 11–12, 14–16, 18–19, 22–24, 26–27, 46, 95, 105, 133, 173, 176–80, 182, 185, 189, 191–92, 197, 206, 208–11, 213–14, 223, 225–28, 230–32, 234, 239–40, 244, 247, 249–54, 258–62, 264, 267, 273, 281
OUN-B (Organization of Ukrainian Nationalists, Bandera faction) 12–15, 17, 21, 23, 25, 29, 46, 73, 83, 95, 116, 120, 178–80, 186, 207–11, 213, 223, 230–47, 253, 258, 261, 264, 275; *see also* Banderowcy
OUN-M (Organization of Ukrainian Nationalists, Melnyk faction) 12, 22, 26, 120, 177, 230–32, 234, 236–37, 240–42, 246–47, 253; *see also* Melnykowcy
OUN-z (OUN-abroad, also called "binary") 253
Our Lady of Częstochowa 151
Our Lady of Kazimirka (Kazimierka) 151
Our Lady of Ostra Brama 151
Our Lady of Swojczów 140; *see also* Blessed Mother of Swojczów
Owadno 180
Ożarowski, Filip 289
Oździutycze 180
"Ozero" 24, 189, 190
Ozierany 65
Ozierany Polskie 189
Ozirce *see* Jezierce

Padlevskyi, Viktor 36, 266
Paduch (a farmer in Załawie) 31
Pająk, Henryk 289
Pakhoma family 65–66
Pakuła (née Ryl), Ewelda 90
Palcze 156
Palec (née Jesionek), Ewa 90
Palec, Jan 84
Palestine 149
Palikrowa *see* Palikrowy
Palikrowy 219–20, 245
Palinka, Bolesław 271
Paluszyńska, Maria *see* Gulak, Maria
Paluszyńska, Stanisława 42
Paluszyńska, Zofia 42
Paluszyński, Grzegorz 42
Palyga, Ganna 264
Palyga, Izidor 264
Palyga, Janina (Ivanna) 262–63
Pankivskyi, Kost 277, 289
Pankowski family 165–66
Pańska Dolina 215, 260
Papowszek, Apolonia 137–38
Papowszek (née Morelowska), Irena 137–38
Papowszek, Józef 137–38
Papowszek, Stanisław 137–38
Paraska 118
Parcheta, Aniela *see* Persona, Aniela 123
Parfeniuk 36–37, 266
Parośle 116, 119, 205, 240
Partacz, Czesław 289
partisans: Bolshevik 20, 24, 184, 187; Josip Broz Tito's 248; Polish 28, 94, 149, 159, 203, 259; Slovak 160; Soviet: 26–27, 31, 106, 139, 158, 160–61, 193–94, 212, 234–35, 238, 264; Taras Borovets's 231, 236, 247; Ukrainian 209
Pasechnaya 185
Pasichnyk family 3, 109, 114, 157, 270
Pasieca 147
Paśnieski, Gienek 110, 113
Pasternak, Evhen 259, 265, 289
Pasteruk, Kharyton 97–98, 101
Pavliuk, E. *see* Stakhiv, Ievhen
Pavliuk, Iurko 37
Pavliuk family 37
Pawlaczyk[ówna], Ela 149
Pawłów 204, 219–20

Pawłówka 124, 134, 188
Pawłowski, Stanisław 49
Peasant Battalions *see* BCh
Peasants' Party of Ukraine 254
Pełczyński, Tadeusz 195, 197, 204, 279–80, 289
Pelekh, Teodor 289
Pendel (née Jesionek), Maria 89
Pendyki 51
Pendyki Duże 50
Pendyki Małe 50
Perehiiniak, Ivan ("Dovbeshka-Korobka") 116, 239
Pererosl 184
Perespa 119
Peretiatkowicz, Adam 260, 280, 289
Perevysianka 159
Persona, Aleksander 123
Persona (née Parcheta), Aniela 123
Persona, Bogumiła 123
Persona, Kazimierz 123
Persona, Krystyna 123
Persona, Piotr 123
Persona, Teresa *see* Guz, Teresa
"Persona Field" 123
"Peter and Paul action" (or "Action on Peter and Paul") 19, 35, 58, 73, 188, 242
Petliura, Symon 10, 48, 208, 222
"Petliura Action" 232
Petriv, Volodymyr 232
Petruk (Prystupa), Piotr 84
Petryshyn, Roman W. 289
Piast, Maria 129, 271
Piatkovsky, Vadim 177, 185, 207, 209, 211–12, 279, 286
Pidhaietska company 29
"Pidkhmurnyi" 56
Pieczykolan, Bronisława 164
Pieczykolan, Józef 164
Pieczykolan (maiden name), Zofia 164
Piejak 102
Pienki 50–51
Pieracki, Bronisław 11–12, 226–27, 278
Pilch, Helena *see* Wysocka, Helena
Pilch (née Dórak), Józefa 167
Pilch, Wojciech 167–68
Pilichowski, Aleksander 173
Pilichowski family 276
Piłsudski, Józef 225
Piłsudski-Petliura offensive 10

Pińkowski 87
Pińsk 149
Pińsk County 243
Piotrowiak, Helena 23–24, 261, 274
Piotrowice 157, 273
Piotrowska, Ala (author's daughter) 5
Piotrowska, Aniela (author's sister) *see* Tarnawska, Aniela
Piotrowska, Anna (author's sister) 112, 114
Piotrowska, Franciszka 54
Piotrowska (née Bagińska), Marcelina (author's aunt by marriage to Władysław) 109–10, 112–13
Piotrowska (née Górska), Maria (author's mother) 112, 114
Piotrowska (née Bagińska), Marynia (author's aunt by marriage to Stanisław) 111
Piotrowska, Mirosława (authors first cousin) 109–11
Piotrowska, Renia (author's daughter) 5
Piotrowska, Romualda (author's first cousin) 109–10, 113
Piotrowska, Stanisława (Stasia, author's first cousin) *see* Plaza, Stanisława
Piotrowska, Stanisława (Stasia, author's sister) *see* Domalewska, Stanisława
Piotrowska, Teresa (Terri, author's wife) 5, 269
Piotrowska, Władysława (author's first cousin) 109–10, 113
Piotrowska, Zofia (author's first cousin) 109, 111
Piotrowski (from Watyniec) 43
Piotrowski, Andrzej (author's son) 5
Piotrowski, Antoni 119
Piotrowski, Czesław 264, 267, 289
Piotrowski, Fransiszek (Franek, author's brother) 2, 112–13, 157, 270
Piotrowski, Jan (Janek, author's brother) 2, 112, 270
Piotrowski, Roman 54
Piotrowski, Stanisław 279, 289

Piotrowski, Stanisław (author's uncle) 111
Piotrowski, Stefan (author's first cousin) 109–13
Piotrowski, Tadeusz (author) 178, 221, 257–61, 265, 267, 270, 272, 280–81, 289–90
Piotrowski, Waldemar (author's first cousin) 109–13
Piotrowski, Władysław (author's uncle) 109
Piskunowicz, Henryk 259–60, 280
"Pivnych" 180, 188, 258; *see also* UPA-North *and* UPA-Z
Piwkowski, Stanisław 130
Płaskociński 72
Platon 123, 125
Plaza (née Piotrowska), Stanisława (Stasia, author's first cousin) 109–11
Płock 220
Płoska 75
Płoteczno 48–49
Pniaki 131
Pobihushchyi-Ren, Ievhen 290
Pobóg-Malinowski, Władysław 290
Pobuzhany 263
Poczajów 73
Podberezie 33, 102
Poddębce 92
Podhajce 29, 172–74
Podhajce company 107
Podhajce County 276
Podhorodecki, Rev. 145, 166
Podhorodecki family *see* Horodecki family
Podkamień 197, 204, 210–11, 220, 245
Podłamia *see* Podkamień
Podlasie 249, 253
Podole 79, 151, 208
Podvorniak, Mychailo 24, 262, 290
Pogorzelec, Paulina 89
pokhidni hrupy (marching, or expeditionary groups) 25, 230, 234–36, 247
Pokorny, Antonín 98
Pokrovskyi 268
Pokydko 122, 125
Polany 276
Polesia *see* Polesie
Polesian Stronghold *see* Poliska Sich
Polesie (Polesia) 1, 13–14, 21, 33, 56, 79, 81, 116, 148–49,

151, 162, 193, 238–39, 243, 259, 272
Polesie Province 9
Polikarp (Sikorskyi) 208
Polikarpenko, Hryhorii 290
Polish government-in-exile 27, 248
Polish Home Army *see* AK
Polish Institute of National Memory 220
Polish Library in London (England) 5
Polish Main National Office for War Crimes 220
Polish Main Social Welfare Council 201
Polish People's Republic 135
Polish police 167, 226, 243, 249
Polish Red Cross 124
Polish-Russian war 10
Polish Senate 253
Polish Social Welfare Committee 201
Polish State Committee on Public Security 249
Polish TV 244
Polish-Ukrainian Association 59
Polish-Ukrainian treaty of alliance (April 21, 1920) 10
Polish-Ukrainian (Galician) war 10, 222
Polish underground 16–17, 27, 160, 204, 214, 238; *see also* AK
Poliska Sich (Polesian Stronghold) 26, 235–36, 238, 247
Poliszczuk, Wiktor 22–23, 79, 150, 153, 176, 178–79, 181–82, 186–87, 189–91, 208, 240, 247, 257–58, 261–62, 266, 268, 270, 272–73, 275, 277–81, 290
Połonka 92
Popek, Franciszka 61
Popek, Helena 60–61
Popek, Kazimiera 60
Popek, Leon 5, 75, 128, 188, 199, 201–03, 208, 214, 258, 260, 266–75, 280, 283, 290
Popek, Marianna 60
Popek, Mieczysław 60–61
Popek, Mikołaj 60
Popek, Stanisław 60
Popek, Zofia 60
Porada 119
Porębski, Władysław 169

Poroda 270
Porogy 184
Porsk Duży 237
Poryck 19, 35, 103, 120, 122–24, 126–27, 129, 131, 133–36, 144, 188, 247, 270–72
Potasznia 260
Poteriukha, Iaryna 145, 147
Poteriukha, Petro 145, 147, 166
Potichnyj, Peter 179, 208, 290
Potoczyska 24
Pototskyi 61, 66
Pots, Zakhar 98
Potsdam 248
Poznań 41, 186
Poźniary 237
Pradun, Aleksander 86, 268
Prague 10, 223, 225, 237
Preis (née Ziółkowska), Adela 36
Preußisch-Holland 223
Procajło, Piotr 43
"Proclamation of the OUN Home Provid" 253
Prokop family 63–66
Prokopiuk 125
Prokopowiec, Pawlina *see* Bitner, Pawlina
Prończuk, Anna 154
Prończuk, Franciszek 154
Prończuk, Helena 154
Prończuk, Jan (Janina's brother) 154
Prończuk, Jan (Janina's uncle) 153–54
Prończuk, Jan (Józef's and Maria's son) 154
Prończuk, Janina *see* Bijas, Janina
Prończuk, Józef 154
Prończuk, Józefa-Zofia 154
Prończuk, Karolina 154
Prończuk, Marcin 154
Prończuk, Maria 154
Prończuk, Paweł 154
Prończuk, Stanisława *see* Sawosz, Stanisława
Prończuk, Teresa 154
Proskurov 207
Protsiuk (the father) 76–77
Protsiuk, Myshko (the son) 77
Provid 12–15, 23, 27, 29, 177, 180, 182, 185, 187, 189–90, 194, 223, 238–39, 241, 243, 251–52, 259–60, 273, 281
Prurwa 270

Prus, Edward 272, 290
Prützmann 212
"Prymak" 118
Prymas, Anna 133
Prypeć River 56, 81
Prystupa family *see* Petruk family
Przebraże 95, 105–06, 156–57, 188, 259–60
Przekurka 83–84, 87–89
Przemyśl 169, 197, 232, 246, 252
Przemyślany 196
Przerwa 119
Przewały 125, 260
Przewłocka, Jadwiga 32
Przewłocka, Lucia 32
Przybylski family 131
Przybysz, Antoni 119
Przystupa, Helena *see* Twaróg, Helena
Ptycza 148, 260
Pulmieniec 81
Pundyk, Iurii 291
Putnowice 197
Pütz 208, 239
Puznia 20, 187
Pyndus 219–21
Pyrzek, Marcela 220

Rachwalski, Eugeniusz 291
Radom 133
Radomle 19, 58
Radomyshl *see* Radomyśl
Radomyśl 105, 209
Radowicze 136, 188
Radstadt 249
Radymno 230
Radziechów 219–20
Radziszewska (née Adamowicz), Teresa 5, 62, 266–67, 272, 274–75
Radziwiłłów 29
Rafailov 185
Rafałówka 54, 116, 163, 188, 205
Rajewski, Stefan 97
"Rakoń" *see* Rowecki, Stefan
Rakowiec 275–76
Ramza, Teresa 60
Ratniów 98
Ratno 56, 62, 68–69, 72
Ravlyk, Ivan 233
Rawa Ruska 196, 204
Rebet, Lev 227, 233, 253, 291
"recovered territories" 105, 248–49
Red Army 22, 48, 71, 145, 160, 165, 167–68, 182,

212, 214–16, 223, 231, 248, 265
Red Cross 63
Red Half-Moon 63
Red Ruthenia 9
Reichsarbeitsdienst (Reich work service) 230
Reichskommissariat Ukraine (RKU) 26, 33, 211, 233
Reichsministry for Occupied Eastern Territories 246
Reichswehr 223
Rejowiec 204, 219–20
Rejtanów 149
Religa, Jan 284
Remel 109
Reshetar, John S. 291
"revindication campaign" 227
Revolutionary Court 19–20, 23, 179, 190, 258
Revolutionary Directory 230
Revyuk, Emil 291
Rewuszki 58–59, 152
Rezac, Tomas 291
Ribbentrop, Joachim von 278
Ribbentrop-Molotov line of demarcation 228, 232; *see also* German-Soviet line of demarcation
Righteous Among the Nations 4
"Riko" *see* Jary, Richard
Ripetsky, Modest 291
RKU *see* Reichskommissariat Ukraine
ROA (Russkaya Osvoboditelnaya Armiia, or Russian Liberation Army) 248
Rodziewicz, Hipolit 97
Rodziewicz, Jan 97
Rodziewicz, Justyna 97
Rogowicz 35
Rohatyn 171, 196, 217
Rohatyn County 168, 217
Röhm, Ernst 223, 226
Rohovskyi, Iakiv 87
Röhr, Werner 278, 291
Rokicka, J. 291
Rokitnie Nowe 155, 273
Rokitno 59–60, 160
Rolak, Józef 124
Roland 25, 230, 232–33, 238–39, 247
Roman, Vasyl 291
Roman Catholic Church 230
Romaniewicz, Aniela 118
Romaniuk 271
Romaniuk, Antoni 49

Romaniuk family (from Orzeszyn) 125, 133
Romanko, Hrymuchyi 62, 66, 68
Romanówka 173
Romanowski, Wincenty 291
Rome 177, 223, 228
Rosa, Bronisława 131, 271
Rosa, Edward 131, 144, 271–72, 291
Rosa, Honorata 144
Rosenbaum, Wilhelm 230
Rosenberg, Alfred 223, 238, 248, 278
Rosenfeld, Alfred 245
Rosilnoye 184–85
Roslop 220
Rotunda (in Zamość) 267
Rovno *see* Równe
Rowecki, Stefan ("Grot," "Rakoń") 194, 233
Równe 23, 25, 53, 90, 107, 109, 115, 147, 156, 166, 188, 191, 196, 205, 207, 215, 237–39, 244, 246, 261
Równe County 18, 29, 83, 107, 155, 157, 242–43, 275
Równo 90
Rozalewicz, Wincentyna 38
Rozdół 249
Rozolovsky 207
"Rozvazhnyi" 56
Rożyszcze 70, 92, 182
"Ruban, Maksym" *see* Lebed, Mykola1
Rubashenko" *see* Koval, Stepan
Rubinowska, Antonia 68–69
Rubinowska, Ewa 67
Rubinowska, Józia 69
Rubinowska, Karolina 68
Rubinowska, Paulina 68–69
Rubinowska, Tanka 62
Rubinowski, Florian 67
Rubinowski, Jan 69
Rubinowski, Leon 68
Rubinowski, Piotr 67
Rubinowski, Władysław 69
Rudnia 35–36
Rudnia Łęczyńska 237
Rudnicka-Kędzierska, Bogusława 267, 292
Rudnicki, Kazimierz 96
Rudniki 106
Rudniki Wojtkowickie 237
"Rudyi" *see* Stelmashchuk, Iurii
Rudyk, Adam 207
Rumania 26, 230
Rumel, Zygmunt 70, 242

Rusiecka, Jadwiga 140
Rusiecka, Julia 140
Rusiecka, Karolina 140, 142–43
Rusiecka, Stanisława *see* Sobczuk, Stanisława
Rusiecki, Jędrych 142
Rusiecki, Józef 140
Rusiecki, Karol 139, 142–43
Rusiecki, Stanisław 143
Rusiecki family 139
Russian Liberation Army *see* ROA
Russkaya Osvoboditelnaya Armiia *see* ROA
Ruthenia 278
Rużyn 70–71, 152
"Rybak" 188
Rybcza 260
Rybga 202
Ryl, Ewelda *see* Pakuła, Ewelda
Ryl, Gustav 90
Ryl, Stanisław 90
Ryl, Zofia 91
Rymacze 260
Ryś, Adam 271
Ryś, Andrzej 271
Ryś, Bronisława (Bronia) 127, 270–71
Ryświanka 2, 3, 107, 109, 112, 114, 157, 270
Rzeszów 4, 21–22, 123, 169, 171, 253

SA (Sturmabteilung, or Brown-shirt Storm Troopers) 226
Sabrin, B. F. 277, 279–80, 291
Sachko (Saczkowski) 273
Sachkovskyi 106
Sachsenhausen 12, 233, 244
Saczkowski *see* Sachko
Sadovyi, O. S. 17
Sadów 33, 94, 188
Sadów Forest 241
Sahryń 184
St. George Uniate Cathedral 232
St. Peter and Paul (holiday) 19
Sambor County 246
Samchuk, Ulas 291
Samolei 165, 275
Samooboronnyi Kushchovi Viddily *see* SKV
samostiina Ukraina (independent Ukraine) 17, 32, 201
Samowola 133, 164

San Basin 249
San region 230, 244
San River 177, 185–86, 197, 209
Sandecka, Irena 79
Sanok 197, 230–31, 246
Sanuryk, Pelahiia 84
Sapieha, Adam 198
Sapozhnyk, Makar 98, 101
Sapozhnyk, Shura 101, 155
Saradko 68
Saran (née Gandurska), Janina 276
Sarnki Dolne 170
Sarnki Górne 170
Sarnki Średnie 170
Sarny 55, 116, 151, 162, 194, 205, 207, 239–40
Sarny County 12, 18, 116, 158, 162–63, 194, 239, 242–43, 258, 260, 265–66, 268, 270
Sarżyńska, Elżbieta *see* Zając, Elżbieta
Sarżyńska, Tekla 126–27
Sarżyński, Leon 126
Sarżyński, Ryszard 126
Saubersdorf 233
Savchuk, S. V. 291
Savluk 68
"Savur, Klym" *see* Klachkivskyi, Roman Dmytro
Sawicka, Alina 37
Sawicka (née Gilewicz), Filipina 38
Sawicka, Jolanta *see* Dudkowska, Jolanta
Sawicka, Krystyna 37
Sawicka, Urszula 266
Sawicki, Antoś 266
Sawicki, Józef 66
Sawosz, Jan 153
Sawosz (née Prończuk), Stanisława 153
Sawosze 153–54, 273
SB (Sluzhba Bezpeky, or Security Service) 13, 17, 20–24, 29, 35, 46, 56, 107, 148, 150, 181, 186–87, 189–91, 234, 242–43, 247, 250, 253, 261–62, 264
Schmitz 212
Schoenfeld, Joachim 281, 291
Schöne, Heinrich 208
Schopenhauer, Arthur 225
Schulenburg, Friedrich Werner von der 231
Schuschnigg, Kurt von 233

Schutzmannlandesdienst 194
Schutzmannschaft 21; (Ukrainian) battalion 149
Schutzmannschaften Bataillon *201*, 238–39
Schutzmannschaftsbataillon *202*, 203–04
Schutzmannschafts-Ersatz-Bataillo *203*, 235
Schwarz, Leo W. 291
SD (Sicherheitsdienst, or Security Service) 208, 210, 212, 228, 236, 244
Sebestiańska, Halina *see* Hilbrecht, Halina
Sebestiańska, Zuzanna 129, 259
Secherchuk, Dr. 126, 271
Sechów 60
Second Republic of Poland 4, 7, 10–12, 193, 222–23, 226, 257
Second World War 22; *see also* World War II
Security Service *see* SD
Senechko 68
Senkevych family 68, 72, 152
Senkiv, Mykhailo 23, 261
Serchuk, Litman 149
Serczyk, Władysław 291
Seret River 266
Serhiichuk, Volodymyr 291
Servytniuk, Ievhen 98
Sevrukov 50, 53
Shabatura, Fedor 56
Shaburevsky 207
Shandruk, Pavlo 247–48
Shankovskyi, Lev 252, 281, 291
Sharpshooter Association 155
Sharpshooters' Council 223
"Shavul" 51
"Shelest" *see* Sydor, Vasyl *and also* Himmelraikh, Kost
Sheptytskyi, Andrei 180, 232, 235, 237–39, 241, 243, 246
Sheremeta, Adam 159, 162
Sheremeta, Ivan (also known as Ivasyk) 35, 92, 95, 97–99, 269, 273
Sheremeta, Mykola 118–19
Shevchenko, Taras 9, 200–01, 257
Shishko, A. 284
Shitov, I. I. 14, 205, 258
Shkuropatka 37–38, 266
Shmatkovskyi family 165–66
Shmonzaki 263
Shostachuk, Ivan 136, 138

Shostachuk, Vladyslav 126, 136, 138
Shpak (member of Borovets's UPA) 207
Shpak, Nina 154
Shtendera, Ievhen 179, 208, 290–91
Shtukalko 134
Shtul-Zhdanovych, Oleh (O. Shuliak, pseud.) 291
Shukhevych, Roman ("Taras Chuprynka," "Dzvin," "Roman Lozovskyi," "Tur") 25, 226–27, 230, 234, 241–44, 246, 252–53
Shulhyn 101
Shuliak, O. *see* Shtul-Zhdanovych, Oleh
Shumuk, Danylo 261–62, 272, 291
Shumylo, Dorofei 191
Shumylo, Hanna 191
Shvorobey 207
Siatecki family 100
Siberia 98, 147, 265
Sich Sharpshooter Organization (*striltsi*) 223
"Sich Svynarynska" (Świnarzyn Stronghold) 56, 120
Sicherheitsdienst *see* SD
Siedlicka (née Świderska), Teresa 36–38
Siedliszcze 56, 188
Sieklucki, M. 220
Sielce 154
Sielec 122, 126, 129, 136–38, 163, 272, 275
Siemaszko, Ewa 21, 260–61, 292
Siemaszko, Władysław 21, 259–61, 266–73, 275, 280, 292
Sienkiewicz, Henryk 198
Sienkiewiczówka 97, 260
Sigda, Tomasz 109
Sigda, Zofia 109
Sijańce 145
Sikorski, Feliks 292
Sikorski, Władysław 234
Sikorskyi *see* Polikarp
Silesia 233, 252
Silno 92, 106
Sima, Horia 233
Simpson, Christopher 278, 292
Siokh, Adam 126–27
Siokh, Anysia 123–24, 126–27
Siokh, Vasyl 123–24, 126–27

Sirč, Václav 292
Sisters of Charity 218
Sitko, Anna *see* Szatkowska, Anna
Sitko, Antonina *see* Zarówny, Antonina
Siunia, Tymish 127, 129
Siwicki, Mikołaj 179, 244, 265, 280, 292
Siwki 237
Sixth (German) Army 239
Skakalska 78–79
Sklyar, George 293
Skobełka 33
Skobelska, Kamila 158
Skobelski, Bronisław 158
Skobelski family 159
Skorodyńce 5, 265–66
Skorupskyi, Maksym 13, 24, 258, 262, 292
Skorupynskyi, Maksym ("Maks") 29
Skosalas 142
Skowron, Stefan 71
Skowrońska (from Chrobów) 129
Skowrońska, Leokadia 64
Skrypnyk, Stepan (Mstyslav) 235–36
Skrzypek, Stanisław 277, 292
Skuba 207
Skurcze 99–100, 102, 105, 129–30
Skurzyński, Franciszek 163
SKV (Samooboronnyi Kushchovi Viddily, or Kushch Self-Defense units) 4, 13, 15, 19, 21, 23, 25, 35, 83, 107, 150, 182, 190, 238, 242, 250, 259
"Skyva" *see* Lebed, Mykola
"Slavko" 33
Sławentyn 276
Sławotycze 106
Sławski 128
"Sliusar" *see* Holod
Śliwa (née Kowalska), Regina 143
Śliwowska, Wiktoria 218, 292
Słojewska, Helena 48
Słojewska, Marcelina 48
Słojewski, Edward 48
Słojewski, Mieczysław 48
Slovak Republic 247
Slovakia 278
Slovenia 248
Słowiński, Henryk 267, 292
Słucz River 46, 50, 116
Sluzhba Bezpeky *see* SB

Śmidyń 72
Smołowa 164
Smovskyi, Kostiantyn 292
Smulka, Hryhorii 52, 151–52, 267
Smyk, Anna 220
Snitko-Rzeszut, Janina 260, 280, 292
Sobczuk (née Rusiecka), Stanisława 140
Sobczyńska, Emilia 105
Sobczyńska, Genowefa *see* Modrzejewska, Genowefa
Sobczyński, Paweł 105
Sobibór 202, 235
Sobieraj, Eugeniusz 128, 271
Sobiesiak, Józef 273, 292
Sobiński, Stanisław 226, 227
Sobotko, Mieczysław 292
Socha (village) 219–20
Socha (née Zacharko), Adela Katarzyna 5, 172–74, 276
Socialist Party of Ukraine 254
Society of the Friends of Krzemieniec and the Wołyń-Podole Territory 4–5
Sodol, Petro R. 292
Soiuz Ukrainskoi Natsionalistychnoi Molodi *see* SUNM
Sokal 133, 135, 167–68, 183–84, 186, 196–97
Sokół 15, 83–87, 89–90, 268
Sokolov, Mariia 137–38
Sokolov, Slavek 137–38
Sokołów 276
Sokołowski, Julek 100
Sokul 19
Solchanyk, Roman 285
"Solomianyi" 56
Solotvino 184–85
Solovei (from Gozdów) 158, 163
Solovei family (from Dziadkiewicze) 191
sołtys (village administrator) 17, 54, 72, 77, 94, 96, 123, 132–33, 141, 143, 149, 151–52, 261, 267–68, 272
Sorel, Georges 225
Soroczyń 124
Soroka, Edward 84
Soroka, Franciszek 89
Soroka, Józefa 88
Soroka, Julia 144
Soroka, Vasyl 144
Soroka, Władysław 88, 268
Soroka family 76, 79
"Sosenko" *see* Antoniuk, Porfyrii

Sosnovskyi, Mykhailo 292
Soszniki 116
South Bound Brook, New Jersey 253
southeastern Poland 1, 12–13, 18, 22, 28, 249
Soviet Belorussia 248
Soviet Bloc 151
Soviet liberation 27, 156, 260
Soviet Lithuania 248
Soviet occupation 17–18, 96, 101, 168, 214, 261
Soviet Ukraine 10, 22, 26, 46, 73, 107, 116, 145, 197, 199, 223, 230–31, 237, 243, 246–48, 250, 255, 263
Sozański family 50
Spain 227
Spałek family 32
Spector, Shmuel 216, 279, 280–81, 292
Spyrydon 109, 114–15
Sroda 271
SS-Galizien 22, 26, 196–97, 204, 209, 212–13, 219–21, 240–41, 244–49, 253–54, 260; police regiments 236, 240–41, 245
Stachów, Genowefa 133
Stachówka 119, 270
Stakhiv, Ievhen (E. Pavliuk, pseud.) 233, 236, 292
Stakhiv, Volodymyr 233
"Stal" 281
Stalingrad 178, 239–40
Stanisławów 261–62, 264
Stanisławów Province 9, 18, 22–24, 28, 137, 168, 217
Stanisławski, Edward 137
Stanisłówka 218
Stankiewicz, Stanisław 169
Stankiewicz family 31
Stanko 127–28
Stański 79
Stański, Zygmunt 131
Stara Dąbrowa 58
Stara Huta 165, 238
Starak, Teodozyi 59
Stare Koszary 56
Starukh, Iaroslav ("Iarlan," "Stiakh") 250, 252
Stary Gaj 60, 267
Stary Jagodzin 89
Stary Poryck 134
Staryki 59
Stasik (née Lytvyniuk), Anna 171
Stasik, Wojciech 171
Stasiowa Wola 170

Stasiuk 90
Stegner, Tadeusz 292
Steiger, Stanisław 224
Steiner, Felix 240
Stelmashchuk, Iurii ("Rudyi, " "Kaidash") 15, 33, 68, 83, 180, 243
Stemplowska, Helena 76
Stemplowska, Jadwiga 76
Stemplowska-Niezgoda, Maria 75–77
Stemplowski, Dominik 76–77
Stemplowski, Józef 76
Stemplowski, Piotr 76
Stepań 46, 48, 51, 53, 151–52, 205, 273
Sterzer, Abraham 292
Stetsiuk, Hryhorii Mykolaiovych 262, 279, 292
Stetsko, Iaroslav (Z. Karbovych, pseud.) 227, 230, 233–34, 236, 292
Stężarzyce 125, 138–39, 272
"Stiakh" see Starukh, Iaroslav
Stobnitsky 207
Stochód River 56, 60, 70
Stolariuk, Kyrylo 127, 129
Stolin 186, 193
Stolin County 243
Stolze 278
Strażyc, Aleksander 88
Struga 119
Struk, Danylo Husar 277–79, 281, 293
Strutńyski family 41
Stryj 196–97, 249
Stryłki 203
Strypa River 277
Strzelec Forest 272
Strzelecka 125
Stsiborskyi, Mykola 293
Studenny, Jorko 215
Studułł, Zbigniew G. 158
Studyń 46, 207
Studyń Wielki 46, 51
Stundites see Baptist(s)
Stupnytskyi 48, 107
Sturmabteilung see SA
Styczyński family 137–38, 163
Stydin see Studyń
Styr River 31, 92, 116, 156–57
Styrkul, Valery (Valerii) 293
Subtelny, Orest 228, 277–78, 293
Sucha Łoza 19, 71, 129, 152, 268
Suchodoły 164
Suchowola 220

Sudobicze 29
Sudrak, Mykola 119
Suk family 32
Sulejówek 233
Sulewski, Wojciech 293
Sulima 184
SUNM (Soiuz Ukrainskoi Natsionalistychnoi Molodi, or Union of Ukrainian Nationalist Youth) 176, 224
Supreme Council of the Four Powers 10, 222
Supreme Liberation Council see UHVR
Surmacz, Gustaw 132
Surmacz, Maria 132
Surmacz, Władysław 133
Sushko, Roman 223, 228, 230
Suszek 87
Suszka (Sushko) 219–21
Svynarynskyi (Świnarzyn, a.k.a. Włodzimierz) battalion 33, 120
Świątkowski family 268
Świderska (née Manias), Anna 131, 164
Świderski, Janina 36, 38
Świderski, Szymon 36, 38
Świderska, Teresa see Siedlicka, Teresa
Świerczewski, Karol 249
Świerz 217
Świerże 201
Święte Jezioro 125
Świnarzyn battalion see Svynarynskyi battalion
Świnarzyn Stronghold see "Sich Svynarynska"
Świniuchy 33
Świrz 274
Swojczów 19, 122, 124, 139, 141–43, 272
Sydor, Uliana 64
Sydor, Vasyl ("Shelest," "Vyshytyi") 13, 238, 243
Syloviak, Pavlo 155
Syloviak (née Grys), Zofia 155
Symonovych, Mykhailo 268
Synich, Julian 94
Syrotiuk, Mykola 37
Syrotiuk family 36–38
Syrovatkin, Sergei 291
Szack 81
Szałacka, Agnieszka 220
Szatkowska (née Sitko), Anna 266
Szawłowski, Bolesław 103, 126, 134, 136

Szawłowski, Ryszard (Karol Liszewski, pseud.) 293
Szczecin 131
Szczecin Province 249
Szczepańska (née Małecka), Konstancja 127, 271
Szczepański, Władysław 127
Szcześniak, Antoni 179, 182, 186, 206, 223, 249–50, 257, 261, 273, 277, 279–81, 293
Szczurzyn 92
Szefer, Andrzej 206, 278, 293
Szelągowski, Władysław 293
Szeletowski, Adam 44
Szepel 23, 156
Szeremeta, Bronisław 262, 293
Szeroka 38
Szerokie 35
Szetelnicki, Wacław 293
Szklarczyk, Wiktor 170
Szklarz 149
Szkolnicka, Maria 276
Szopy 237
Szostek, Antonina see Kovaluk, Antonina
Szota, Wiesław 179, 183, 186, 206, 223, 249–50, 257, 261, 273, 277, 279–81, 293
Sztuń 268
Sztyk, Michał 94
Szubków 158, 273
Szumlany 276
Szumsk 73, 153, 165, 178, 198
Szurkowski, Włodzimierz 140
Szuryński, Jan 155
Szuryński, Józef 156
Szuryński, Mieczysław 155
Szwal, Zofia 272
Szwojców 260
Szyjkowska (née Kunysz), Anna 124
Szymbowicz, Antonina 174
Szymkowicz, Adela 173
Szymkowicz, Anna 173
Szymkowicz, Bronisław 276
Szymkowicz, Czesława 276
Szymkowicz, Karol 172, 276
Szymkowicz, Krystyna 276
Szymkowicz, Marcela 276
Szymkowicz, Marcelina 172
Szymkowicz, Sabina 276
Szymonisko 116
Szymonowicz, Leonka 62
Szyndlar, Władysław 170
Szyndrów, Genowefa see Mishchaniuk, Genowefa

Tabaczyński, T. ("Biegun") 27
Tajkury 145, 147, 166, 191
Tappanzee Bridge 174
Tarakanów 150
Tarasiewicz, Maria 43
Taraż 95
Tarnawska (née Piotrowska), Aniela (author's sister) 269
Tarnawska, Gienia 94
Tarnawska, Helena 94, 100
Tarnawska, Sabina see Królikowska, Sabina 92
Tarnawska, Władzia 94
Tarnawski, Dominik (author's brother-in-law) 94, 100-01, 269
Tarnawski, Edzio 94
Tarnawski, Marian 95, 150
Tarnopol 196
Tarnopol Province 5, 9, 18, 22, 24, 28, 172, 204, 206, 233, 249, 261-62, 265, 274, 276
Tarnovka Lesnaya 184
Tarnów 231
Tartak estate 148
Tchórzewski, Bolesław 96
Teklówka 119
Tereshchuk, Petro (Oleksandr Matla) 293
Teresin 129
Terles, Mikołaj 293
Terlikowski 79
Terpin, Bronisław 126-27, 267, 270-71, 293
Tesłuchów 29
Tetylkowce 78
Third Polish Republic 135
Third Reich 151, 206, 229-31, 234-35, 240, 248; Ministry of the 18, 213, 260
Third World War 250; see also World War III
Thüringen 168
Tito, Josip Broz 248
"Tiutiunyk" 243
Tkachuk family 38
Tkaczyk, A. 220
Tomaszewski, Jerzy 7, 257, 293
Tomaszów County 16, 197, 246
Tomaszów Mazowiecki 196, 214, 265
Toporów 262
Torczyn 92, 94, 101, 260
Torgoń 217
Torke, Hans-Joachim 279-80, 293

Toronto 171, 246, 263, 276
Torzecki, Ryszard 21, 177, 203, 208-10, 238, 240, 258, 260-61, 264-65, 277-81, 293
Tovmach 184
Tovmachina see Zelenovka
Trąb 168
Traczykiewicz, Apolonia 125, 164
Transcarpathia 223, 228, 243
Trawniki 232, 235
treaty of alliance (between Poland and Ukraine) 222
Treaty of Good Neighborliness, Friendly Relations and Cooperation 255
Treaty of Riga 10, 223
Treaty of Versailles on the Protection of Minorities 222
Treblinka 235
Trefka 207
Trofymchuk, Petro 155
"Troian" 185
Trojniar, Jan 170
Trościaniec 92, 196, 207
Trostyanets see Trościaniec
Trunk, Isaiah 216, 293
Trusiewicz, Stanisława 106
Trusiuk, Bolesław 83, 87
Trusiuk, Tomasz 5, 188, 203, 208, 214, 268, 290
Truskawiec 217
Truskoty 71
Tryputnia 205
tsarist rule 227
Tsaruk, Mykola 162-63
Tsebula 141, 143
Tsentkevych 148-49
Tsipiukh family 38
Tsisar family 155, 269
Tsurkan, Valentin 291
"Tsygan" 46
Tsykhosh, Irina 128
Tsykhosh, Petro 128
Tuczyn 107, 109, 112, 114, 157-58, 270
Tuliczów 191
Tuńska 129
Tur (region) 187-88
"Tur" see Shukhevych, Roman
Tur Colony 54
Turia River 56, 127
"Turiv" 33, 58, 83, 92, 180, 187, 258, 243
Turka 202
Turowski, Józef 21, 259-61, 266-73, 275, 280, 293
Turzyce 66

Turzysk 56, 58, 180
Tverdokhlib, Sydor 226
Twaróg (née Przystupa), Helena 89
Tykhon 52-53
Tymoshchuk 158
Tyndorf, Richard 5
Tynne 162
Tys-Krokhmaliuk, Yuriy 293

UHA (Ukrainska Halytska Armiia, or Ukrainian Galician Army) 223
Uhły (Kuty) 60
Uhorsk 73, 79, 153, 202
UHVR (Ukrainska Holovna Vyzvolna Rada, or Ukrainian Supreme Liberation Council) 192, 246
Ujście River 145
UKKA (Ukrainskyi Konhresovyi Komitet Ameryki, or Ukrainian Congressional Committee of America) 254
"Ukraine for Ukrainians" 177, 225
Ukrainian auxiliary police 20, 25, 29, 56, 234, 238
Ukrainian Central Committee see UTsK
Ukrainian Central Council 222
Ukrainian Committee 229-30, 264
Ukrainian Committee of Wołyń 191-92, 243, 280
Ukrainian Congressional Committee of America see UKKA
Ukrainian Galician Army see UHA
Ukrainian guards 235
Ukrainian integral (or "active") nationalism 10, 225, 250
Ukrainian Legion (Roman Sushko's) 228, 230
Ukrainian Military Organization see UVO
Ukrainian militia 17
Ukrainian militiamen 127
Ukrainian National Army see UNA
Ukrainian National Committee 232
Ukrainian National Committee (UNK) see UNK
Ukrainian National Council 236

Ukrainian National Federation see UNO
Ukrainian National Rada 222
Ukrainian National Republic see UNR
Ukrainian National Revolutionary Army see UNRA
Ukrainian National Self-Defense units see UNS
Ukrainian Parliament 254
Ukrainian police 17, 21, 61, 72, 92, 104, 106, 156, 171, 195, 212–13, 228, 236–37, 239, 241, 247, 258, 264
Ukrainian Soviet Socialist Republic 151
Ukrainian Supreme Liberation Council see UHVR
Ukrainian underground 214
Ukrainska Halytska Armiia see UHA
Ukrainska Holovna Vyzvolna Rada see UHVR
Ukrainska Narodna Respublika see UNR
Ukrainska Narodna Revoliutsiina Armiia see UNRA
Ukrainska Natsionalna Armiia see UNA
Ukrainska Natsionalna Samooborona see UNS
Ukrainska Viiskova Orhanizatsiia see UVO
Ukrainske Natsionalne Obiednannie see UNO
Ukraiński, Bronisław 97
Ukrainskyi Konhresovyi Komitet Ameryky see UKKA
Ukrainskyi Natsionalnyi Komitet see UNK
Ukrainskyi Tsentralnyi Komitet see UTsK
Ulewicz, Antoni 87
UNA (Ukrainska Natsionalna Armiia, or Ukrainian National Army) 248, 254
Uniate Church 3–4, 9; see also Greek Catholic Church
Union of Breść 10
Union of Ukrainian Nationalist Youth see SUNM
Union of Ukrainian Youth 253
United Nations General Assembly 264
United Nations War Crimes Commission 219, 221, 241, 261

United States 10, 223, 225, 249, 252
Units of Ukrainian Nationalists see DUN
University of New Hampshire 5
UNK (Ukrainskyi Natsionalnyi Komitet, or Ukrainian National Committee) 247–48
UNO (Ukrainske Natsionalne Obiednannie, or Ukrainian National Federation) 225
UNR (Ukrainska Narodna Respublika, or Ukrainian National Republic) 208, 222
UNRA (Ukrainska Narodna Revoliutsiina Armiia, or Ukrainian National Revolutionary Army) 242–43
UNS (Ukrainska Natsionalna Samooborona, or Ukrainian National Self-Defense units) 242, 250
Unyshchuk, Myshko 52
UPA (Ukrainska Povstanska Armiia, or Ukrainian Insurgent Army) cadet school 83
UPA-East 243; see also UPA-S
UPA-Middle 209
UPA-North 46, 209, 243; see also "Pivnych" and UPA-Z
UPA-S (UPA-East) 184; see also UPA-East
UPA-South 209, 243
UPA-West 243
UPA-Z (UPA-North) 184; see also "Pivnych" and UPA-North
Upper Grandview, New York 174, 276
Upper Silesia 174
Urban, Wincenty 294
Uście Zielone 24
Uściług 16, 125, 130, 201, 271
Usicze 97
USSR 137, 149, 177, 231, 249, 252, 264; Ministry of Foreign Affairs 263
Uszejec family 220
UTsK (Ukrainskyi Tsentralnyi Komitet, or Ukrainian Central Committee) 16, 209, 222, 229–31, 239, 243
UVO (Ukrainska Viiskova Orhanizatsiia, or Ukrainian Military Organization) 10–12, 175, 222–26, 252

Uzbek Legion 56
Użyński, Michał 125

Vakoluk family 129, 135
Valuch-Ianenko, Norbert 227
Vashchenko, Ostap 241
Vasiuk, Ivan 190
Vatutin, Nikolay 247
Velychkivskyi, Mykola 236, 294
Velykyi Zbir Orhanizatsii Ukrainskykh Natsionalistiv see VZOUN
Velykyi Zbir Ukrainskykh Natsionalistiv see VZUN
Verbiany 263
Veremiichuk, Mitia 149
"Vereshchak" see Vorobei, Fedor
Vereta, L. 294
Vershigora, Petr Petrovich see Vershyhora, Petro Petrovych
Vershyhora, Petro Petrovych (Petr Petrovich Vershigora) 275, 294
Veryha, Wasyl 246, 259, 281, 294
Vidynskyi family 68, 72
Vienna 9, 11–12, 176, 225, 233, 251, 278
Viiskovi Viddily Natsionalistiv see VVN
Viknyany 185
"Virlyk" see Meleshko, M.
"Viun" 191
Vlasiuk, Petro 35, 56
Vlasov, Andrei 248
Vloshchynska, Anna 51–52, 152
Vloshchynskyi 53, 152
Vodai 263
Voitovych, Nastusia 40–42
Voitovych family 38, 41–42, 150
Voitsekhivskyi 42, 95, 150
Volksdeutsche 184, 186, 192, 235, 248
Voloshin 207
Voloson see Zhebrach
Vorobei, Fedor ("Vereshchak") 243
"Vorona" 56
"Voronyi" 46
Vovk, Elena 263
Vovk (from Antolin) 150
"Vovk" (UPA commander) 29
Vozhniak 168
Vuitskik, Zinoviy 263

VVN (Viiskovi Viddily Natsionalistiv, or Nationalist Military Detachments) 228
Vychyniuk 98, 101
Vynnytsia 233
"Vyshytyi" *see* Sydor, Vasyl
Vysotsky, A. F. 263, 284
VZOUN (Velykyi Zbir Orhanizatsii Ukrainskykh Natsionalistiv, or Great Conference of the Organization of Ukrainian Nationalists): second (April 1941 in Kraków) 177, 231; third (August 21–25, 1943 in "Western Ukraine") 83, 208, 234, 243, 246
VZUN (Velykyi Zbir Ukrainskykh Natsionalistiv, or Great Conference of Ukrainian Nationalists): first (January 28–February 3, 1929 in Vienna) 9, 12, 176, 225, 251, 258; second (August 26–27, 1939 in Rome) 177, 228

Wachmannschaften (guard units): des SS- und Polizeiführers im Distrikt Lublin 232; SS-ukrainische 235–36
Wächter, Otto 209, 239–40, 244–45
Waffen-SS 244–46
Waławka 167
Wannsee conference 9
Warchocki, Czesław 294
Wardach, Hieronim 154
Wardzyńska, Maria 279, 294
Warkowicze 29
Warsaw 4, 12, 15, 192, 203, 205, 210, 220, 223, 227, 233, 244, 254, 276, 281
Warsaw ghetto 235
Warsaw Uprising 192
Warszawska 35
Wąsek, Bolesław 31
Wąsek, Jan 31
Wąsek, Kazimierz 31
Wasilewska (née Hojarska), Rozalia 125
Watyniec 43
Wawel Castle 230
Wawryszuk, Władysław 132
Wawrzyk 90
Wazów 168
Węgierski, Jerzy 276, 281, 294

Węgrzecki, Kazimierz 294
Wehrmacht 14, 21, 24, 49, 197, 206, 210–14, 231–33, 235, 238, 244–49, 258
Weissberg, Moshe 216
Wells, Leon Weliczker 214, 294
Werba 29, 120, 148–49, 178
Wereszczyński, Ambroży 147
Wereszczyński, Cezary 165
Wereszczyński, Jan 147
Wereszczyński family 272
Werner family 69
Wernik, Romuald 272, 275, 294
Werpczna 54–55
Western Belorussia 229
Western Ukraine 3, 9–10, 13, 17–18, 22, 173, 176, 197, 208–09, 222–23, 229, 231, 240, 249, 253
Western Ukrainian National Republic *see* ZUNR
Więcek, A. 220
Wielick 56, 72, 237
Wielimcze 66, 68–69, 72
Wielka Lubasza 48
Wiener-Neustadt region 227
Wierchówka 149
Wierzbowska-Robaszko, Danuta 103
Wiezinski, Antek 215
Wiktorówka 124
Wiktowska, Stefania 136
Wiktowski, Józef 136
Wilczur, Jacek 271, 275
Wilczy Przewóz 83, 90
Wilia River 73
Wilkowska (née Buczyńska), Jadwiga 98
Wira, Paweł 5, 188, 203, 208, 214, 268, 290
Wira, Zenon 5, 188, 203, 208, 214, 268, 290
Wiry 158, 162, 258, 266
Wisłok River 197
Wiśniewski, Aleksander 294
Wiśniowiec 73, 75–80, 198–99, 268
Wiśniowiec Stary 75, 77, 268
Witkowska (Marcin's wife) 153
Witkowska, Anastazja 150
Witkowska, Stefania 138
Witkowski, Antoni 150
Witkowski, Józef 138
Witkowski, Marcin 153
Witkowski, Roman 38
Witoldówka 260

Witwicki 36
Władyga-Rusiecka, Petronela 139
Władysława, Sister 218
Włodawa 260
Włodzimierz 94, 102, 120, 123, 128, 131–32, 136–39, 141, 143–44, 163–64, 200, 205, 271
Włodzimierz battalion *see* Svynarynskyi battalion
Włodzimierz County 18–21, 27, 33, 56, 103, 120, 123, 131, 163, 195, 200–01, 242–43, 259–60
Włodzimierz Wołyński 61, 122, 130, 133, 136–37, 141
Włodzimierzec 116, 119, 163, 270
Włodzimierzówka 129
Włosowska (née Golisz), Helena 35
Wojciechowska (from Tajkury) 147, 166
Wojciechowski, Stanisław 224–25
Wojcieszak, Zbigniew 32, 148, 150
wojewoda (provincial administrator) 227
Wojewódka, Bronisław 135
Wojewódka, Czesław 135
Wojewódka, Jadwiga 135
Wojewódka, Janina 135
Wojewódka, Tadeusz 127, 134, 271
wójt (headman) 155, 173, 273, 276
Wójtkiewicze 260
Wojtków family 217
Wola Ostrowiecka 15, 19, 81, 83–90, 181, 202–03, 243–44, 268
Wołczański, Józef 294
Wolica 126, 191
Wólka Kotowska 188
Wólka Lubitowska 19
Wólka Markowiecka 35
Wólka Profecka 235
Wólka Sadowska 35
Wólka Swojczowska 127, 129
Wolski, Władysław 75, 273
World Association of the Home Army, Wołyńian Branch 5
World War I 7, 10, 13; *see also* First World War
World War II 1, 4, 7, 12, 16, 18, 228, 249, 252, 254,

264; see also Second World War
World War III 251; see also Third World War
Woronczyn 19, 35, 65
Woronówka 217
Wrocław 4, 53, 189, 203, 261
Wrocław Province 249
Wrodarczyk, Franciszek 162
Wrodarczyk, Ludwik 159–62
Wroński, Stanisław 217, 278, 294
Wybult 71
Wybulta, Józef 152
Wyka 129
Wynnyckyj, Andriy 285
Wyrka 54–55
Wyrobisz, Bruno 162
Wyrobki 116
Wysock 193, 205, 239
Wysocka (née Pilch), Helena 5, 167–68, 275
Wysocki, Antoni 168
Wyszogródek 73, 260

Yablonka 184
Yablunivka 263
Yablunivka Forest 264
Yalta 151
Yaremkevich, Anastasia 264
Yaremkevich, Filimon 264
Yurchuk, V. I. 286

Zababa 161
Zabara 73
Żabecznik 155
Zaborowski, Jan 284
Zacharko, Adela Katarzyna see Socha, Adela Katarzyna
Zacharko, Eugenia 172, 276
Zacharko, Marcelina 173
Zacharko, Pantelemon 276
Zacharko, Wiktor 172
Zadeberny, Franciszek 294
Zagaje 35
Zagładów family 115
Zahaikevych, B. 281, 294
"Zahrava" 20, 46, 73, 92, 107, 118, 186, 188, 260
Zając (née Sarżyńska), Elżbieta 126–27, 270–71
Zakerzonnia 249–50, 252, 254, 281
Zakharuk, Oleksandr 122, 129
Zakhidno-Ukrainska Narodna Respublika see ZUNR
Zakopane 24, 231, 229
Żalanka 109–11

Załawie 31
Zalewski, Ludwik 125
Zalewski family 65
Zalizniak, Maksym ("Haydamaks") 200
Zamlicze 23, 44–45, 150
Zamojszczyzna (Zamość region) 16
Zamość 4, 22, 63, 219–21, 231, 236, 249, 267, 269
Zamość County 16, 197, 246
Zamostecze 90–91, 269
Zaporozec, Michał (Mykhailo Zaporozets) 219–20
Zapust 36–38, 143
Żarczyński, Władysław 118–19
Zarębska, Helena 133
Zarębska, Honorata 133, 164
Zarębski, Antoni 133
Zarówny (née Sitko), Antonina 266
Zarówny, Czesława see Grygorczyk, Czesława
Zarudzie 191
Zarzycki, Antoni 62
Zashkilniak, Leonid 253
Zasmyki 61, 66, 260
Żaszkiewice 134, 144
Zaturce 36–38, 42–43, 260
Zavydivskyi battalion 33, 120
Zawadzki 156
Zawidów Forest 35, 271
Zawilska, Adela 97
Zawilska, Anna 97
Zawilska, Helena 97
Zawilska, Julia 97
Zawilska, Leokadia see Grzybowska, Leokadia
Zawilski, Apolinary 97
Zawilski, Ignacy 97
Zawilski, Marian 97
Zawilski, Mieczysław 97
Zawilski, Paweł 97
Zawiśnie 168
Zawuń 197
Zbaraż 76
Zbereże 202
Zborów County 196
Zbrucz River 10, 222–23
Zdołbica 145
Zdolbunov see Zdołbunów
Zdołbunów 107, 145, 208
Zdołbunów County 18, 20, 29, 145, 165–66, 242–43, 260

Żegota 3
Żelazko, Maria 118
Zelenaya 185
Zelenovka (Tovmachina) 184
Żeleński, Władysław 294
Zellenbau 12, 233, 244
Zembroń, Antoni 170
Zembroń, Florian 169
Zembroń, Franciszek 170
Zembroń, Katarzyna 169–70
Zemówka (Zeniowka) 216
Zeniowka see Zemówka
Zgorany 81, 203
Zhebrach (Volosov) 184
Zheleznyak 184–85
Zherdytska, Mariia 149
Zherdytska, Nadia 149
Zherdytskyi, Andrii 149
Zherdytskyi, Seriozha 149
Zhitomir 23, 208–09, 243
Zhuk family 68, 72
Zhuraky 185
Zielińska, Feliksa 132
Zielony Dąb 147, 165, 272–73, 275
Ziemlica 132, 181, 271
Zienkiewicz 36
Ziółkowska, Adela see Preis, Adela
Ziółkowska, Kamila see Ostasz, Kamila
Ziółkowska, Leokadia 65
Ziółkowska, Maria 65
Ziółkowski, Bogusław 65
Ziółkowski, Feliks 65
Ziółkowski, Witek 65
Złoczów 196, 206, 233, 264
Złoczów County 196
Złoczówka 32, 148–49, 260
Złotolin 48
Żmudzki family 144
Zofiówka 122, 188, 260
Żołnowski, Władysław 294
Zonka 149
Zovenko, Orest 294
Zubenko see Lopatin
Zubkiewicz, Władysław 60
Zukh 181
Żukowska, Anna 31
Żukowski, Aleksander 157
Żukowski, Feliks 31
Żukowski, Kazimierz 31
Żukowski family 32
ZUNR (Zakhidno-Ukrainska Narodna Respublika, or Western Ukrainian National Republic) 222

Żupański, Andrzej 27, 259, 265, 281, 294
Żur, Leon 118, 158–63, 268, 270, 275, 294
Żurawiec 37, 45
Żużlin 204
Zvenyachy 185
Zwierów 156
Zwolakowa, Maria 217, 294
ZWZ-AK (Związek Walki Zbrojnej-AK, or Union for Armed Struggle-Home Army; code name: "Hreczka") 27, 193, 203, 265
Żydaczów 196
Żylibory 170
Żytomierz *see* Zhitomir
Żywer, Genowefa 170
Żywer, Stanisława 170

www.ingramcontent.com/pod-product-compliance
Ingram Content Group UK Ltd.
Pitfield, Milton Keynes, MK11 3LW, UK
UKHW050542150426
5217IPUK00026B/2045